The
AMERICAN HERITAGE
Picture History of
WORLD WAR II

The
AMERICAN HERITAGE
Picture History of

WORLD
WAR II

By
C. L. SULZBERGER
And the Editors of
AMERICAN HERITAGE
The Magazine of History

Editor in Charge
David G. McCullough

Pictorial Commentary
Ralph K. Andrist

AMERICAN HERITAGE/BONANZA BOOKS
New York

Staff for this Book

EDITOR
David G. McCullough

ART DIRECTOR
Kenneth Munowitz

ASSISTANT EDITORS
Ralph K. Andrist, Judith Harkison,
Nancy Lindemeyer

COPY EDITOR
Barbara Ackerman

EDITORIAL ASSISTANTS
Susan J. Lewis, Lynne Vietor

EUROPEAN BUREAU
Gertrudis Feliu, *Chief*

TITLE PAGE: Hitler and top Nazis at a Party Rally in September, 1934; European Picture Service.
BELOW: A near miss on the Murmansk Run, September, 1942; Imperial War Museum, London.

This edition is published by Bonanza Books,
distributed by Outlet Book Company, Inc., a Random House Company, 225 Park Avenue South, New York, New York 10003,
by arrangement with American Heritage, a division of Forbes Inc.

25 24 23 22 21 20 19 18

Table of Contents

Introduction 7

The March to the Abyss 17

Blitzkrieg 57

England Alone 97

Arsenal of Democracy 129

Japan Strikes 145

War at Sea 181

The Desert War 217

The War in Russia 249

The Politics of World War 305

Counterattack in the Pacific 327

Italy 369

Over Here 397

The Air War 417

The Home Fronts 449

Assault on Fortress Europe 481

Closing In on Japan 529

Smashing the Third Reich 553

The End of the Rising Sun 587

The Legacy 623

Acknowledgments and Index 630

Introduction

It began after years of screaming threats and menacing troop movements and desperate grasping for peace at almost any price. It began at a time when most Europeans had resigned themselves to its coming and most Americans seemed to agree that the best thing their country could do would be to stay out of it. "Let Europe stew in its own juices," many people were saying. But this world war was not to be primarily a European conflict, like the one before it. This time virtually the whole world would be at war. Once started, it would quickly become the worst war in history.

It lasted only six years, which is not long as history goes, but it produced the biggest armies, the longest battle lines, the most devastating weapons of any war; it inflicted more suffering, it destroyed more and cost more than any other war. It put some seventy million people in uniform and killed perhaps as many as thirty-five million, including many millions who were never in uniform; for it was also a war that slaughtered a great deal more indiscriminately than any war before it.

Like other wars, it summoned up the best and the worst in men. It put immense power in the hands of a few and made their names immortal. And like other wars, it conferred immortality on a number of places —places such as those on the next eight pages, seen years after the guns were stilled: a stretch of beach, a remote island, a forest, a city that few people in London or Chicago had ever heard of before 1945. And, as in every war before it, the fighting was done largely by men who knew little about why it had started, who was to blame, or exactly what sort of world it would leave when it was all over.

There was never much doubt about what we were fighting for or whether victory was worth the price. Few wars have had such a clear-cut purpose or conclusion. We fought to win and win we did. We fought to destroy a monstrous evil that threatened all civilization, and in that we most definitely succeeded. But when peace came, the world was very different than it had been before, and it would never be the same again. The atomic age was upon us. The world was perplexed and divided, full of fear and uncertainty. What was not so clear then, as it is now, is that the Second World War was a vast, earth-convulsing revolution, the effects of which are still going on.

This book is by no means the whole story of the war. No one book could contain the complete history. Our aim here is to cover, in words and pictures, the essential history of this greatest of human tragedies, and to re-create a feeling of what it meant in terms of the people who were swept up by it.

—THE EDITORS

Arlington National Cemetery, Arlington, Virginia

Dunkirk Beach

The hulk of an American tank off Saipan, in the Marianas

*A cemetery near the
Hürtgen Forest, Germany*

A playground in the center of Hiroshima

The March to the Abyss

Triumph in battle offers twin trophies to the victors. Their writers can impose on history their version of the war they won, while their statesmen can impose the terms of peace. In each case the opportunity was missed after the 1914–18 conflict. Ernest Hemingway later called it "the most colossal, murderous, mismanaged butchery that has ever taken place on earth," and the treaty-making assumptions of Allied leaders almost all proved falsely based. Those leaders, gathered around Paris in 1919 to draft the security they had pledged the world, found themselves trapped by secret promises they had made one another and by slogans they had uttered to hearten their mud-bound troops. When the machine guns subsided in November, 1918, there was actually less chance of a safe and democratic earth than when the slaughter started, more than four years earlier.

The series of treaties signed in Paris's agreeable suburbs—Versailles, St. Germain-en-Laye, Neuilly-sur-Seine, Trianon, and Sèvres—spoke of dreams and ignored realities. For better or worse, they imprisoned Germany, isolated Austria, fragmented Turkey, chopped up Hungary and Bulgaria, and overlooked murmurous Russia. Their harsh decisions might have provided a stable order, had they not been based on numerous miscalculations: that the United States would help police international justice; that Britain and France would enhance their strength and maintain the will to use it; that Russia would stay weak and Germany supine.

No one realized that Woodrow Wilson's idea of self-determination, leading toward "complete independence of various small nationalities now forming part of various Empires," would inflame Asia and Africa and sap the colonial vigor on which the European victors relied to keep the peace. Colonial markets for goods manufactured in Manchester and Lille faded as hitherto enfeoffed peoples began asserting their industrial freedom; and slowly, over subsequent decades, the general staffs of Britain and France became aware that soon they would be deprived of their famous regiments of Sikhs, Marathas, Tonkinese, and Goumiers.

Among the diplomats who gathered in Paris to blueprint a happy future were a few outstanding figures: Wilson, the tigerish Georges Clemenceau, David Lloyd George, and Eleutherios Venizelos, the scrappy Greek who captivated everyone and led them to another war. Ah, how soon again the troops began to march: Rumanian, Polish, Greek, French, British, and Turkish, and German and Italian freebooters. And all but Rumania's moved east. Germany set off on a secret search for power, and Russia began its devious negotiations.

Since those days we have raced from pit to pit. Wilson discovered that to make a world truly "safe for democracy" requires knowledge of democratic processes at home. Misjudging the strength and temper of his political opposition, he saw the United States Senate spurn the Versailles Treaty and the League of Nations. Vladimir Ulyanov, a conspirator who took the name Lenin after his brother was hanged by Czar Alexander III, con-

A German Army recruit receives his first lesson in how to goose-step.

solidated the revolutionary control he had seized in Russia and set out to convulse the globe. France relaxed, on the assumption that its wounded Army, despite a wracking mutiny in 1917, was Europe's finest. Britain's "balance of power" policy dwindled as Britain's decreased vitality became manifest. Slowly, accompanied by economic disaster, political apathy, and the rise of revolutionary dynamists, pleasant auguries dissolved.

The empires of eastern Europe had been destroyed, and the empires of western Europe were ailing. But burning ambitions had not left Europe's heart. There remained that dreadful verity discerned by Julius Fröbel, a leader of the 1848 revolution: "The German nation is sick of principles and doctrines, literary existence and theoretical greatness. What it wants is Power, Power, Power: And whoever gives it Power, to him will it give honor, more honor than he can ever imagine."

The German General Staff was not destroyed by the treaty of Versailles. It merely changed its name, becoming the *Truppenamt* of the *Heeresleitung* office. The *Truppenamt* saw that World War I's most signal creation had been a renascent Russia, and it was there the German generals sought sustenance. They were the first to realize that the principal event of World War I was the rise of Russia, just as the principal event of World War II was to be the rise of China.

In 1920, Enver Pasha, a romantic Turkish revolutionary, wrote from Moscow to Hans von Seeckt, head of the *Heeresleitung*, who had resolved to build an army far exceeding anything envisioned at Versailles and also to explore the possibility of partitioning the new Polish state with Russia. Enver told Seeckt that Trotsky, Lenin's War Commissar, would welcome German instructors and arms collaboration. Seeckt wanted a remote hinterland in which to experiment beyond Allied supervision. He created "Special Group R" to negotiate with the Kremlin and signed an agreement without even confiding in his Government. Once again the world would learn, as Mirabeau had written in the eighteenth century, that Germany was "an army in search of a country."

By 1922, when the Berlin Government arranged the Treaty of Rapallo with Moscow, German officers had already made dispositions to manufacture tanks, shells, aircraft, and even poison gas in the Soviet towns of Lipetsk, Saratov, Kazan, and Tula. At Lipetsk, the famous Stuka dive bombers and all-metal aircraft were developed, ten years before they appeared on Allied drawing boards. Picked Soviet commanders, selected by the brilliant Marshal Mikhail Tukhachevski, were trained in German military academies and eventually made mass experiments with armored and air-borne forces. The ar-

rangement suited both Versailles pariahs. Seeckt told Lenin's secret envoy, the journalist Karl Radek: "You missed your chance in 1919 and 1920. It is possible that Germany, allied with your Red Army, may fight a war against France, but not," Seeckt added as a warning, "with a German Red Army."

The victors found that the pernicious anemia produced by bloodletting, imperial dissolution, and political misjudgment also had horrid economic symptoms. The new century's early economic expansion was totally disrupted. European investments in Russia became worthless; England, the world's banker, was supplanted by the United States; competitive industries arose in Asia.

The European Allies, with little economic logic, hoped to make the losers foot an impossible bill. Initially they sought $56,500,000,000 in German reparations. This claim was pared down, then postponed by a moratorium during which France occupied the Ruhr. Charles G. Dawes, an American financier who later became Vice-President, negotiated a formula whereby Germany would settle its debt through a series of escalating annual payments, but even his compromise vanished in 1932 in the midst of world depression.

Germany was engulfed by the most dismal inflation. At the end of the war, the mark was worth about twenty-five cents; by November, 1923, the value of the mark had shrunk a billion times. Workers in Essen took their pay home in barrels, and three hundred paper factories and one hundred and fifty printing establishments were unable to turn out notes fast enough to keep the economy off a barter basis. Eventually, Hjalmar Schacht, later Hitler's Minister of Economy, introduced a device called the *Rentenmark*, based, theoretically, on a mortgage of all Germany. This device created a new currency but did not salvage the ruined and embittered middle class.

Preceded by an atmosphere of uncertainty abroad and fostered by overconfidence at home, Wall Street's abysmal collapse hit at the end of 1929. For a decade, America had been entranced by the idea of being a leading economic power. American soldiers returned home believing they had made a new world. Optimism was the prevailing theme of American life. Absorbed in becoming ever more prosperous, the American people built a never-never land on Wall Street that lasted until shortly after Labor Day, 1929. All through a hot Indian summer there was an uncertain scramble for securities. Then, on Thursday, October 24, panic began. Almost thirteen million shares were unloaded. Tuesday, October 29, was, in the words of Professor John Kenneth Galbraith, the most devastating day in our financial history. Within weeks, investors lost thirty billion dollars—almost what the nation had spent on World War I. And prices kept on dropping until June, 1932. By 1933 there were some twelve million unemployed. Men retired wealthy and awoke paupers. Banks failed; mortgages were foreclosed, farm families evicted. Mines and factories ground to a halt. Shantytowns, known as Hoovervilles, grew like fungus around the edges of cities, and incredible as it may now seem, *Business Week* reported that some one hundred thousand Americans were seeking jobs in Russia.

The effect of the Wall Street disaster was felt throughout Europe. On May 11, 1931, Vienna's powerful Credit-Anstalt bank collapsed. On September 21, England abandoned the gold standard. World trade dwindled. Wages shrank fantastically, and Europe's growing numbers of unemployed workers joined the ruined bourgeoisie in following the Fascist, National Socialist, and Communist movements, which thrived on despair.

In 1933, the pattern of leadership among the world's three most powerful nations was set for the next dozen years with the arrival in office of Roosevelt in Washington and Hitler in Berlin and the consolidation of Joseph Stalin's Moscow despotism.

Roosevelt came in on promises of immediate relief, recovery, and improvement. His makeshift New Deal grew in a curiously effective way, revitalizing the economy. He lowered tariffs, repealed prohibition, relieved pressure on the farmers, revalued gold. Vast public works were launched to take up the employment slack. Exuding self-confidence and galvanizing national faith, Roosevelt brought a number of competent, imaginative men into office and almost haphazardly, in his famous first Hundred Days, concocted a new style and direction in Federal Government that would do more to change life in America than any administration since Wilson's. By the time Hitler succeeded in detonating another world war, the United States, though still not fully cured of its economic illness, was again on its feet.

Roosevelt was a great man. Hitler was not; but he was a genius, an evil genius. With infallible acumen he was able to discern and use powerful traits in the Germanic soul. Hitler had had a respectable corporal's career in World War I, during which he won the Iron Cross. After the 1918 armistice, he became involved in the furious plots that fermented inside Germany and joined the disgruntled World War I general Erich Ludendorff in an abortive 1923 *Putsch* in Munich. Robert Murphy, who was the American vice-consul, consulted the papal legate, Monsignor Pacelli, about the incident's significance. The legate assured him Hitler would never again be heard from. Murphy remembered this in 1944 when, as adviser to General Mark Clark, he called on Pacelli, then Pope

Pius XII, in newly liberated Rome. "Bob," said His Holiness, patting Murphy on the knee, "that was before I was infallible."

Tried and convicted for his part in the *Putsch*, Hitler spent nine months in Landsberg prison, during which time he wrote his brutally frank testament, *Mein Kampf*, a book that too few foreigners read with any care, and too many Germans both read and believed.

Germany, using Schacht's *Rentenmark* and the essential fact that, while it had lost the war, its territory had remained unravaged, had recaptured much of its industrial and trading position. However, it harbored bitter psychological complexes of defeat and thirsted for revenge. By playing on middle-class resentments, the ambitions of the industrialists, and a fear of communism that was fanned by monarchists, officers, and the Church, Hitler and his hodgepodge National Socialist (Nazi) party seized power. Not much more than one German out of three voted for the party in 1933, yet Hitler gained control of the Reichstag, which he subsequently burned.

During the astonishing six years between his accession in 1933 and the outbreak of World War II, Hitler made himself dictator and made Germany Europe's strongest military power, while the victors of World War I looked on in confusion. He brought into the open the remilitarization program that Seeckt had started secretly in 1921, putting the unemployed and discontented into uniforms. He smashed democracy, dispossessed (and ultimately liquidated) Germany's cultivated Jewish population, and crushed party dissidents through terror or sometimes outright murder. He silenced the General Staff, seized the economy, and assumed direction of foreign policy. The rich Saarland, temporarily removed by the Allies from German administration, voted in 1935 to rejoin the Reich. On March 7, 1936, Hitler sent his troops into the demilitarized Rhineland and began to fortify it. The Allies did nothing but mumble. Next he sent agents to subvert Austria, and in March of 1938, with the help of armed Austrian Nazis, he added that mountain land and more than 6,500,000 people to the German Reich. Again the Allies did nothing; and Hitler announced he wanted no more territory.

Hitler reckoned that France and Britain would leave Germany alone so long as their interests were not directly threatened. Initially, he was more concerned with Italy and Russia. In 1921, Benito Mussolini, a renegade Socialist, had developed an antidemocratic party from restless elements and, dressing them in black shirts, had used them to take over Rome from a flabby parliamentary regime. Mussolini was personally more attractive than Hitler. He was flamboyant, cultivated, with a literary flare and a way with women; and, like Hitler, he dreamed of empire. However, the huge army he created was backed neither by economic sinews nor by national will.

There was no formal military alliance between Berlin and Rome when Hitler seized Austria on Italy's frontier. He forced an Austrian showdown despite Mussolini's vaunted "8,000,000 bayonets," which failed to protect a country whose independence was vitally important to Rome. After that, Hitler knew he could bind Italy to the German juggernaut. On March 11, 1938, he explained to Mussolini why he had grabbed Austria, and on September 29, they signed the Munich Agreement, which gave Hitler a free hand in eastern Europe, gave Mussolini nothing, and gave the world war.

Stalin, meanwhile, was consolidating his power by purging Russia's peasants, Army officers, and intellectual elite. A rocklike personality, devoid of humanity or fear, he was sustained by the same icy faith as the Spanish inquisitor Torquemada, who could do horrible things and then sleep like a child. Stalin's small frame, his withered left arm and pocked face, concealed a mixture of strength, vision, and ruse. He wrote dismally and spoke dully in heavy Georgian accents. Yet Mustapha Kemal said that "when the fame of all other dictators will have vanished," history would single out Stalin as the century's most important international statesman. Stalin was a brutal realist. After he had liquidated or starved millions of peasants, he remarked: "It is ridiculous to expatiate today on the expropriation of the kulaks. We do not lament the loss of the hair of one who has been beheaded."

While Stalin murdered and repressed, he also molded the apparatus for eventual war. He feared Germany, but even more, he feared a German alliance with the West. He permitted the Comintern to proclaim: "The conquest of power by Hitler does not signify a defeat for the Communist Party." It is possible this assertion contained the first hint that Stalin wished to renew the old Seeckt-Lenin tie and make a deal with Hitler. There is evidence that Stalin sent Radek (who had dealt with Seeckt) in 1936 to discuss Polish partition with one of Hitler's secret-service colonels. Marshal Tukhachevski, the erstwhile collaborator with Seeckt, had prepared contingency plans for preventive war against the Nazis. Stalin's agents framed Tukhachevski and then executed him to betoken Moscow's desire for accommodation with Berlin.

While these murky events were taking place, the League of Nations was in the process of dissolution. Sixteen of its sixty-four members quit before World War II. And, starting with Greece's invasion of Turkey in 1920, wars again became commonplace. In 1931, a newly industrialized, bellicose Japan took advantage of a trumped-up "incident" on the South Manchuria Railroad to conquer that wealthy portion of North China. A courageous United States Secretary of State, Henry Stimson, unsuccessfully sought international intervention. The Japanese created a puppet state called Manchukuo in the conquered province, and then, in 1937, invaded China proper, capturing its principal cities. In the summer of 1938 Japan's headstrong Army even clashed with Russia on the Manchukuo frontier. These Asiatic incursions saw the most brutal fighting and the most vicious savagery experienced by the world since 1918. They also exposed the frailty of international peace machinery and, while particularly horrifying the American people, reinforced the shelter of America's isolationist cocoon.

Mussolini, anxious to prove his new Fascist troops and to expand his new Roman Empire in Africa, provoked a border skirmish at Walwal, near the border of Ethiopia, in December, 1934. Although Emperor Haile Selassie appealed for help to the League of Nations, the League could do nothing because the Great Powers refused to intervene. On October 3, 1935, the attack came. Mussolini's own son-in-law, Count Galeazzo Ciano, led a bombing raid on Aduwa, and a carefully prepared expeditionary force then marched inland from Eritrea and Somaliland, strafing, gassing, and shelling Haile Selassie's ill-equipped tribal warriors. Britain left the Suez Canal open to Italian troop ships. Fascist forces, helped by a remarkable engineering corps, marched across mosquitoed swamps and craggy mountains to Addis Ababa; and Haile Selassie fled the country. The war lasted only six months and was marked by terrible atrocities. Vittorio Mussolini, the conqueror's son, wrote enthusiastically of an air attack: "One group of horsemen gave me the impression of a budding rose unfolding as the bomb fell in their midst and blew them up."

The wildest, bloodiest, and most heart-rending of these lesser conflicts was the civil war in Spain, where Germany, Italy, and Russia tested weapons, tactics, and commanders. On July 18, 1936, a handful of well-financed right-wing generals, headed by forty-four-year-old Francisco Franco, led a military revolt against the weak Republic. Communists and liberal groups throughout the world joined to support the Republican militia, while Fascists and conservatives backed Franco. The Germans sent him tanks, planes, and 10,000 men; the Italians, another 75,000. The Russians sent planes, tanks, and ammunition to the Republican forces, plus some of their best officers, operating under aliases.

Spain aroused infinite passions and came to represent, in some weird prevision, the ideological fanaticism of World War II, so soon to explode. Before their own bodies and souls were torn on far greater battlefields, millions of people were caught in the emotional and symbolic Spanish vortex. Picasso painted his greatest picture, "Guernica," after Hitler's *Luftwaffe* first practiced mass bombing on that city. Hemingway wrote his finest novel about Republican guerrillas. Miguel de Uṇamuno, Spain's famous author, died of a broken heart, and the poet García Lorca was murdered. Georgi Dimitrov, later head of the Comintern, and Josip Broz, now called Marshal Tito, gained conspiratorial experience working for the Republican cause. André Malraux led an air squadron against Franco. Yet what the Spanish War lacked was another Goya. Only a Goya could describe the horrors committed by both sides: burned churches, raped nuns, massacred labor leaders, tortured intellectuals; the slaughter in a bull ring, the shooting of prisoners on the cold Castilian killing ground of Cuenca; the savagery of Spaniards against Spaniards, in the name of ideologies that were foreign to Spain.

While German tanks, bombers, and tacticians were being tested, Hitler turned his attention to the great Slavic plains that the Teutons long had coveted as living space, or *Lebensraum*. By seizing Austria, he managed to outflank a ring of fortifications that conglomerate Czechoslovakia had erected around its curved western frontier. Then, using the large German minority in the Czech Sudetenland, the *Führer* applied massive new pressures. A schoolteacher named Konrad Henlein, who much admired Hitler, succeeded brilliantly in Nazifying the Sudeten German minority, or *Volksdeutsch*. When Eduard Beneš, the solemn little soccer-playing Czechoslovak President, turned for help to his French allies and British friends, they cynically ignored him.

Initially, Beneš was resolute. I was in Prague as a newspaperman much of that fateful summer of 1938, and I remember how, on one hot afternoon in his baroque palace, he unrolled a large map and with pointer showed me which German cities he intended to bomb if Hitler invaded. He recited impressive military production figures from his famous Skoda and Tatra ordnance works. But Paris and London were more impressed by Hitler. Unctuous French statesmen, cautious generals who hoped to gain strength with time, and pro-German pressure groups in the British establishment persuaded Premier Daladier and the umbrella-toting Chamberlain to appease the Germans at Munich, sell out the Czechs, and proclaim that they had preserved peace. An argument still is heard that the twelve months purchased had value, but I agree with Churchill, who then commented: "You have gained shame and you will get war."

Axis dynamism thrust eastward. Mussolini invaded impoverished Albania on Good Friday, 1939, and King Zog, a tribal chieftain, fled into Greece with his family and all available gold, leaving behind a tiny rear guard.

That March, Hitler had already blandly violated pledges to make no further claims on the Czechs. He partitioned the rest of the country, installing his own satraps. Too late, the French and British issued territorial guarantees to Poland and Rumania and started negotiations with Russia. But Stalin was not interested.

Thanks to his purges, the Soviet Army was in a state of confusion. The Red Air Force was no match for the *Luftwaffe*, which had developed so impressively from its Russian incubator. Furthermore, Stalin had lost all respect for the will power of the West. He suspected that the inner intention of Daladier and Chamberlain was to encourage Hitler's embroilment with Russia by urging his attentions eastward across Czechoslovakia. He decided to reverse that political strategy and urge Hitler westward, hoping to see his capitalistic enemies destroy themselves against each other.

Hitler also was attracted by the thought of another German-Soviet deal, in the tradition of the Seeckt arrangements and Rapallo. He could eliminate potential threats from eastern Europe by partitioning it with Stalin, and then invade the West. On August 23, 1939, Molotov and Joachim von Ribbentrop, Hitler's Foreign Minister, signed a nonaggression pact in Moscow that arranged to divide Poland, granted Russia eventual sovereignty over the Baltic states, conceded a potential Soviet sphere in Finland, and gave Moscow a free hand to take Bessarabia from Rumania when it wished. Under a further secret protocol, Russia promised to supply Germany with raw materials and to join in suppressing Polish "agitation" after that country had been occupied.

World War II, already inevitable, was thus made imminent. A Polish boy born Armistice Day, 1918, when Poland was re-created, was now old enough to be killed fighting the German or Russian armies that would soon roll once again across his country.

August spun swiftly to September. There was tense anticipation in Berlin and stunned astonishment in Moscow. The French people marched wearily to their comfortable Maginot fortifications. Gloom and disappointment swept London. But in the United States, the cynosure for most eyes was the New York World's Fair, with its trylon and perisphere, its "Town of Tomorrow," its General Motors show, and a Japanese Shinto shrine enclosing a replica of our Liberty Bell, made of diamonds and pearls. The news from Europe was indeed dark, but Europe was, after all, a distant continent from which the United States had sensibly withdrawn.

"The Lamps Are Going Out"

Foreign Secretary Sir Edward Grey gave the epitaph for an entire era the day his country went to war in 1914. Looking from a window across a twilit London, he said sadly, "The lamps are going out all over Europe; we shall not see them lit again in our time." He was an accurate prophet. The hysterical joy of the 1918 armistice was soon blunted by unemployment, hunger, and inflation. The promises of self-determination often were ignored in fixing postwar boundaries, leaving disgruntled minorities as seedbeds for future trouble. War-bred epidemics of influenza and typhus killed millions. Nor did nations abandon war: Turks fought Greeks, Poles fought Lithuanians, Greeks clashed with Italians, Russians killed Russians—and this is only part of the catalogue. Hindsight, always so crystal clear, shows that in the first few years after the war, men and nations had already started to move blindly on the courses that would lead to another and greater world conflict. The lamps would not be lit again.

The victors at Versailles (from left): Lloyd George, Orlando of Italy, Clemenceau, and Wilson.

The happy released Austrian war prisoners (top right), like most returning soldiers, were soon disillusioned by mass unemployment at home. In Germany, fuel-starved by disrupted transportation, women and children (right) glean bits of coal in the dump heap of a mine in 1922.

WIDE WORLD

Nikolai Lenin, who led the Russian Communists to power, harangues a crowd (upper left) in Moscow's Red Square on May Day, 1918. On Lenin's death in 1924, Stalin (right) entered a several-sided power struggle to succeed him. Slightly behind him in the picture walks Aleksei Rykov, one of those he deposed to become absolute dictator by 1927. At lower left, Mussolini parades with Fascist leaders soon after the infamous October 28, 1922, "March on Rome" that brought him to top power.

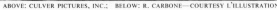

ABOVE: CULVER PICTURES, INC.;   BELOW: R. CARBONE—COURTESY L'ILLUSTRATION

New Breed of Tyrants

"The world must be made safe for democracy," President Wilson told Congress in his war message. But war-prostrated Europe proved sterile ground for the growth of democracy and produced instead the new tyranny of totalitarianism. In Russia, in October, 1917, the Communists had already seized power, not from the ancient despotism of the Czars but from the constitutional Kerensky Government. Strutting Benito Mussolini formed the first cell of his Fascist party in 1919; by 1922, his black-shirted bullyboys had so cowed the Government that he was able to make himself dictator. The German Nazi party was also formed in 1919, but Hitler's rise to supreme power was to be slower than that of Mussolini.

Totalitarianism was antithetical to everything democracy stood for, with its police state controlling the economic, political, and cultural lives of its citizens. But until well into the 1930's, most Americans worried only about communism. Many openly expressed admiration for Mussolini, who had "made the trains run on time," while Hitler was a man with a comical mustache who headed only a minority party and held no position of political power.

Calvin Coolidge (above), more impassive here than his Sioux friends, pleased the business community by doing nothing to "rock the boat" while he was President. And in Geneva the increasingly impotent League of Nations droned on, and a bored journalist yawned (right) during a delegate's endless speech. The Alabama (below), bombed in 1921, was one of four obsolete battleships sunk from the air in Gen. Billy Mitchell's futile campaign to convince an economy-minded Government and conservative military men that the nation needed a strong air force.

Back to Normalcy

The war had been a stirring experience, but the country had had enough of world affairs. The Senate rejected Wilson's League of Nations, and the people happily elected Warren Harding for his handsome face and his promise to "return to normalcy." But, except for the glad return to isolationism, there was no going back to prewar moods and tempos. Old verities had been questioned and old patterns broken during the war, and nothing could ever be the same again.

The twenties are remembered for prohibition, the speakeasy, and home brew. It was the decade of jazz and the Charleston, when the collegian's coonskin coat and the flapper's rolled stockings symbolized a flaming youth that took advantage of relaxing moral standards and the multiplying automobile to discover Sex. It was the heyday of Al Capone and rival gangster mobs who machine-gunned each other over the lucrative bootleg business, and it was the time of million-dollar boxing gates, home-run kings, and general sports mania. It was a period of prosperity, when thin-nosed Cal Coolidge could say, "The business of America is business," and adman Bruce Barton could write a long-lasting best seller, *The Man Nobody Knows*, a book about Jesus made up of such statements as, "He would be a national advertiser today."

But fact and legend about the twenties are becoming blurred. The decade was not universally prosperous—farmers were one conspicuous exception. Millions did not make bathtub gin and continued to support prohibition, else it would not have remained the law of the land. And the frantic speculation on the stock market and in Florida real estate involved only a minority of the people. There was, too, a glimmer of concern with the world outside. The United States took the lead in calling the Washington Conference of 1921–22, which put some limits to the big-ship tonnage of the leading naval powers. And Brig. Gen. William Mitchell, who sank obsolete battleships with bombs (left) in 1921 and 1923, cried so hard the importance of building air power that he was court-martialed as a troublemaker. But in the main the decade was as it is pictured, an era of frenetic—and often dogged—seeking after gaiety and thrills. It ended in October, 1929, with the Wall Street crash, and the country awoke to reality again.

While the United States tried to forget wars and armies, General Hans von Seeckt, head of the German Army after 1920, was quietly and skillfully violating the clause of the treaty of Versailles that forbade an army of more than 100,000. By secret agreement, the Soviet Union permitted German forces to train and develop equipment on Russian soil, and in return Germans trained Russian officers and built armament factories for their Russian hosts.

The army General von Seeckt built in Germany was virtually an independent state within a state, opposed to the Republic and follow-

ing the old Prussian traditions. But it was a compact, efficient machine, ready by the 1930's to be a dictator's instrument of power.

The Roots of a Tyranny

Adolf Hitler's rise to power was not meteoric. In September of 1919, he joined the minuscule German Workers party after some soul searching—"I finally came to the conviction that I had to take this step." The party later prefixed "National Socialist" to its name, becoming, in German, *Nationalsozialistische Deutsche Arbeiterpartei*, or Nazi for short. Hitler brought to it a fanatical belief in his own mission and a genius for rabble-rousing oratory and was soon its leader. The party appealed to those embittered by Germany's defeat, but Hitler misread public sentiment when he attempted to seize Munich in the Beer Hall *Putsch* of 1923; the police opened fire instead of joining the marchers, and sixteen Nazis were killed. Hitler was sentenced to prison for five years but was out after nine months of being treated like an honored guest. In prison he wrote most of *Mein Kampf*, the turgid presentation of his political and social beliefs. On his release, he set himself to rebuild the party and to achieve power by constitutional means. In 1928, the Nazi party received only 810,000 votes out of 31,000,000 in the national elections, and Hitler was a joking matter. But the turning point came fast. In 1930, the Nazis got six and a half million votes and were the second party in Germany; in 1932, they became the largest.

ULLSTEIN-BIRNBACK

Hitler spent the three years after his release from prison in the Bavarian Alps, usually in native garb (above); he later spoke of these as his happy years. At right, he hobnobs with young Nazis in the Munich Brown House, which became the national headquarters of the party during the last years of the Republic.

NATIONAL ARCHIVES

After the 1930 German elections, the jokes about Hitler ceased, and when he came from a meeting in the Brown House (right), correspondents were on hand to record what he had to say.

Growth of an Ism

The Nazi party grew very slowly during its early years. Hitler appealed to the German people by constantly reminding them of the humiliation of their defeat in the war. He repeated the popular myth that the German armies had been "stabbed in the back" by collapse of the home front. He railed at the wrongs done Germany by the treaty of Versailles. And he damned democracy. With these subjects for his tirades went a virulent anti-Semitism in which he blamed the Jews for all ills of Germany and of the world, past and present. But despite Hitler's ability as a rabble rouser, the Nazi party remained small until the slump of 1929. Then, as unemployment rose, the Nazis exploited the growing despair skillfully. They had received less than a million votes in the elections of 1928, but in 1930 they got over six million, and by 1932, almost fourteen million. The German Communist party had also grown with hard times, but Hitler was more adept at intrigue. He made political alliances with the industrialists, with nationalist politicians, and with the Army generals, and got himself named Chancellor by Hindenburg in January, 1933. The next month, the Nazis used the Reichstag fire as an excuse to jail, beat, and torture the Communists wholesale. Other political parties were also gagged. Hitler was *Führer*; his ambition was achieved.

A storm trooper makes a street collection for Nazi party funds in 1932. By that time, though, the lean days of the party were past.

A campaign leaflet tells workers and farmers that electing their old party means Jewish domination, but that the Nazis will free them.

This unbearably handsome Nordic youth with his flag brightens a recruiting poster for Hitler's National Student Organization.

Spectacle at Nuremberg

Just as devout Muslims made a pilgrimage to Mecca, so faithful Nazis attended the annual Party Rally at Nuremberg. There, in a delirious round of music, parades, speeches, and pagan pageantry, all party members, from Hitler down to the shabbiest little village block leader, regenerated their enthusiasm and faith. The rallies were held in early September and lasted a week; the first was in 1933, after Hitler became chancellor, and thereafter they remained the high point of the Nazi calendar until the war, when Nuremberg became a popular Allied bombing target. Nothing was spared to make a rally a memorable experience. Torchlight parades and other night spectacles were frequent, for Hitler believed that "in the evening the people's will power more easily succumbs to the dominating force of a stronger will." The climactic finale of each rally was a speech by Hitler that sent both speaker and his hundreds of thousands of listeners into emotional frenzies. The world listened too, for here Hitler often gave the first hints of what he planned for the future.

CAPTURED GERMAN PAINTING, U.S. ARMY

Hitler strides down the center aisle of Luitpold Arena (left) with storm-trooper chief Ernst Röhm at the first Nuremberg Party Rally in 1933. The next June, Hitler had Röhm and other brown-shirt leaders killed after the Army had demanded, as the price of its support, the suppression of the semiautonomous storm-troop army. At right, Hitler is portrayed as a white knight by a German artist. Millions of Germans saw nothing ridiculous in such idolatry, and certainly it was not discouraged by Hitler, who had ranked himself with Alexander, Caesar, and Napoleon as a man of destiny. The picture was captured during the war, and in the process, the head and the face were slashed by a G.I. who obviously was left unawed by the entire Hitler mystique.

"They looked up at him as if he were a Messiah"

CBS NEWS

William L. Shirer

A number of American journalists reporting on what was going on inside Germany had badly underestimated Adolf Hitler and the hold he had on the German people; but not William L. Shirer, correspondent for the Columbia Broadcasting System in Berlin during the 1930's and later author of the massive history of Nazi Germany, The Rise and Fall of the Third Reich. *The following is taken from Shirer's earlier book,* Berlin Diary. *It describes what he saw and heard at Nuremberg as the Nazis gathered there for a week of parades, speeches, and frenzied adulation for Hitler, who, then only forty-five, was just getting rolling. Hitler's proclamation for the rally stated: "The German form of life is definitely determined for the next thousand years."*

NUREMBERG, SEPTEMBER 4, 1934

Like a Roman emperor Hitler rode into this mediæval town at sundown today past solid phalanxes of wildly cheering Nazis who packed the narrow streets that once saw Hans Sachs and the *Meistersinger.* Tens of thousands of Swastika flags blot out the Gothic beauties of the place, the facades of the old houses, the gabled roofs. The streets, hardly wider than alleys, are a sea of brown and black uniforms. I got my first glimpse of Hitler as he drove by our hotel, the Würtemberger Hof, to his headquarters down the street at the Deutscher Hof, a favourite old hotel of his, which has been re-modelled for him. He fumbled his cap with his left hand as he stood in his car acknowledging the delirious welcome with somewhat feeble Nazi salutes from his right arm. He was clad in a rather worn gaberdine trench-coat, his face had no particular expression at all—I expected it to be stronger—and for the life of me I could not quite comprehend what hidden springs he undoubtedly unloosed in the hysterical mob which was greeting him so wildly. He does not stand before the crowd with that theatrical imperiousness which I have seen Mussolini use. I was glad to see that he did not poke out his chin and throw his head back as does the Duce nor make his eyes glassy—though there *is* something glassy in his eyes, the strongest thing in his face. He almost seemed to be affecting a modesty in his bearing. I doubt if it's genuine. . . .

About ten o'clock tonight I got caught in a mob of ten thousand hysterics who jammed the moat in front of Hitler's hotel, shouting: "We want our Führer." I was a little shocked at the faces, especially those of the women, when Hitler finally appeared on the balcony for a moment. They reminded me of the crazed expressions I saw once in the back country of Louisiana on the faces of some Holy Rollers who were about to hit the trail. They looked up at him as if he were a Messiah, their faces transformed into something positively inhuman. If he had remained in sight for more than a few moments, I think many of the women would have swooned from excitement. . . .

SEPTEMBER 5

I'm beginning to comprehend, I think, some of the reasons for Hitler's astounding success. Borrowing a chapter from the Roman church, he is restoring pageantry and colour and mysticism to the drab lives of twentieth-century Germans. This morning's opening meeting in the Luitpold Hall on the outskirts of Nuremberg was more than a gorgeous show; it also had something of the mysticism and religious fervour of an Easter or Christmas Mass in a great Gothic cathedral.

The hall was a sea of brightly coloured flags. Even Hitler's arrival was made dramatic. The band stopped playing. There was a hush over the thirty thousand people packed in the hall. Then the band struck up the *Badenweiler March*, a very catchy tune, and used only, I'm told, when Hitler makes his big entries. Hitler appeared in the back of the auditorium, and followed by his aides, Göring, Goebbels, Hess, Himmler, and the others, he strode slowly down the long centre aisle while thirty thousand hands were raised in salute. It is a ritual, the old-timers say, which is always followed. Then an immense symphony orchestra played Beethoven's *Egmont* Overture. Great Klieg lights played on the stage, where Hitler sat surrounded by a hundred party officials and officers of the army and navy. Behind them the "blood flag," the one carried down the streets of Munich in the ill-fated putsch. Behind this, four or five hundred S.A. standards. When the music was over, Rudolf Hess, Hitler's closest confidant, rose and slowly read the names of the Nazi "martyrs"— brown-shirts who had been killed in the struggle for power—a roll-call of the dead, and the thirty thousand seemed very moved.

In such an atmosphere no wonder, then, that every word dropped by Hitler seemed like an inspired Word from on high. Man's—or at least the German's—critical faculty is swept away at such moments, and every lie pronounced is accepted as high truth itself. . . .

SEPTEMBER 6

Hitler sprang his *Arbeitsdienst*, his Labour Service Corps, on the public for the first time today and it turned out to be a highly trained, semi-military group of fanatical Nazi youths. Standing there in the early morning sunlight which sparkled on their shiny spades, fifty thousand of them, with the first thousand bared above the waist, suddenly made the German spectators go mad with joy when, without warning, they broke into a perfect goose-step. Now, the goose-step has always seemed to me to be an outlandish exhibition of the human being in his most undignified and stupid state, but I felt for the first time this morning what an inner chord it strikes in the strange soul of the German people. Spontaneously they jumped up and shouted their applause. There was a ritual even for the Labour Service boys. They formed an immense *Sprechchor*—a chanting chorus—and with one voice intoned such words as these: "We want one Leader! Nothing for us! Everything for Germany! *Heil Hitler!*". . .

SEPTEMBER 7

Another great pageant tonight. Two hundred thousand party officials packed in the Zeppelin Wiese with their twenty-one thousand flags unfurled in the searchlights like a forest of weird trees. "We are strong and will get stronger," Hitler shouted at them through the microphone, his words echoing across the hushed field from the loud-speakers. And there, in the flood-lit night, jammed together like sardines, in one mass formation, the little men of Germany who have made Nazism possible achieved the highest state of being the Germanic man knows: the shedding of their individual souls and minds—with the personal responsibilities and doubts and problems—until under the mystic lights and at the sound of the magic words of the Austrian they were merged completely in the Germanic herd. Later they recovered enough —fifteen thousand of them—to stage a torchlight parade through Nuremberg's ancient streets, Hitler taking the salute in front of the station across from our hotel. . . .

SEPTEMBER 10

Today the army had its day, fighting a very realistic sham battle in the Zeppelin Meadow. It is difficult to exaggerate the frenzy of the three hundred thousand German spectators when they saw their soldiers go into action, heard the thunder of the guns, and smelt the powder. I feel that all those Americans and English (among others) who thought that German militarism was merely a product of the Hohenzollerns— from Frederick the Great to Kaiser Wilhelm II—made a mistake. It is rather something deeply ingrained in all Germans. They acted today like children playing with tin soldiers. The Reichswehr "fought" today only with the "defensive" weapons allowed them by Versailles, but everybody knows they've got the rest—tanks, heavy artillery, and probably airplanes.

LATER.—After seven days of almost ceaseless goose-stepping, speech-making, and pageantry, the party rally came to an end tonight. And though dead tired and rapidly developing a bad case of crowd-phobia, I'm glad I came. You have to go through one of these to understand Hitler's hold on the people, to feel the dynamic in the movement he's unleashed and the sheer, disciplined strength the Germans possess. And now—as Hitler told the correspondents yesterday in explaining his technique—the half-million men who've been here during the week will go back to their towns and villages and preach the new gospel with new fanaticism. Shall sleep late tomorrow and take the night train back to Berlin.

ABOVE AND BELOW: BLACK STAR

Twentieth-Century Caesar

Benito Mussolini talked grandiosely about building Fascist Italy into a modern Roman Empire. "We have a right to empire," he said, "as a fertile nation which has the pride and will to propagate its race over the face of the earth, a virile people in the strict sense of the word." Besides, depression and unemployment were creating problems, and a foreign adventure would help take people's minds off their troubles. On October 3, 1935, the new Caesar sent his legions into Ethiopia, attacking the primitive nation with an army of a quarter of a million plus a great force of native auxiliaries, and using all the machines of modern warfare, including mustard gas when the barefoot tribesmen resisted unduly. The League of Nations voted to deny credits and materials to Italy, but it went only part way, for it did not ban the sale of coal, iron, steel, or oil, all basic to waging war. And so the conquest of Ethiopia went ahead, and in little more than half a year, at a very modest cost in Italian lives, Mussolini had his shabby empire. Soon after, in October, 1936, he and Adolph Hitler reached the agreement that created the Rome-Berlin Axis.

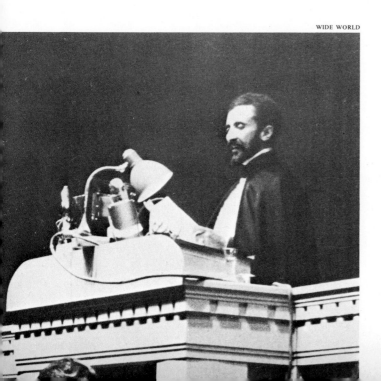

Mussolini, in a 1927 photograph, sits on the terrace of his villa (upper left). And at lower left, he poses bare-chested as a fieldworker while speaking at the opening of the 1938 harvest. Also in 1938, he leads a parade of goose-stepping militiamen (above). After taking over the German goose step, Mussolini renamed it the "Roman step." Italian planes attack Ethiopian tribesmen (center); the warriors had no weapons better than rifles with which to fight back. At left, Emperor Haile Selassie appeals to the League of Nations for help in 1936, after his country had become an Italian colony. The Italian newsmen in the gallery hissed and booed to drown the speech; the League heard him out but gave him no help.

39

In his picture of a Loyalist soldier caught at the instant of death (above), photographer Robert Capa achieved one of the great portrayals of the ultimate meaning of battle. Francisco Franco (near right) was expansive in the days following final victory. Pablo Picasso began work on his "Guernica" (far right) in 1937, only two days after German planes had bombed the Basque city of Guernica, with casualties of over 2,500.

40

Murder, Spanish Style

It was a civil war, but a good part of its fighting men did not even speak Spanish. Before it ended, an estimated 40 per cent of Franco's armed forces were German or Italian, and there were Russian advisers and international brigades with the Loyalists. The war, basically, was the Army's reaction to the young Spanish Republic's attempts to remove some of the medieval control by Church, Army, and aristocracy over the nation's life. On the pretext that the Government was communistic, the Army revolted in July, 1936. Hitler and Mussolini sent troops and weapons to aid the Fascist-led rebels; Russia sent weapons and technicians to the Loyalists, and also secret agents to help Spanish Communists seize control of the Government by terror and intrigue. And again the democracies stood supinely aside while the savage conflict went on. Britain, France, and the United States maintained a strict neutrality that hurt only the hard-pressed Loyalists with whom they really sympathized. Not surprisingly, Franco was victorious and promptly joined the Rome-Berlin Axis.

Our Own Concerns

President and Mrs. Roosevelt and their son James arrive at the White House after the 1933 inauguration to begin an eventful administration.

During the early 1930's, most Americans could not have cared less about what happened in the rest of the world. They had enough troubles of their own. The euphoria of the twenties had died in October of 1929 with the stock market crash, and the thirties dawned with the bleak reality of the Great Depression. The jobless became an army, wages sagged, farm prices went so low that farmers often found it just as profitable to use grain for fuel as to market it. In the general climate of despair, Franklin D. Roosevelt easily defeated President Hoover after reiterating during his campaign his belief that the Government had a responsibility for the welfare of every citizen.

But Roosevelt, though later to become known as an internationalist, was at first almost indifferent to the rest of the world. It was not just that domestic worries were so many and so pressing that they left no time for other concerns. It was also that the President, like his compatriots, was steeped in the old isolationist tradition that the only proper business of the United States lay right at home. During this decade, isolationism reached what was probably an all-time peak. It was a time for being cynical about war and patriotism; it was commonly accepted that we had become involved in the First World War only because we had been the naïve dupes of shrewd British and French propaganda. In the search for scapegoats for war guilt, the investigations of munitions makers by the Nye committee in the Senate offered one of the most popular; it was believed that these "merchants of death" deliberately fomented wars to increase the market for their wares. As soon as the sound of aggression from across the seas—in Manchuria, Ethiopia, Spain—began to be disturbing, we insulated ourselves with neutrality laws that forbade trade with either side in a conflict. It made no difference that our neutrality always seemed to harm the victim more than the aggressor. We were safe—so we thought—and that was what mattered.

Charles A. Lindbergh, the great hero of 1927, was being reviled ten years later for his views on Germany. He visited Hitler's Reich in 1936 and after, and, convinced that the German Luftwaffe was invincible, said so, to the outrage of America. At left, he inspects a sword with Göring, one of the Nazi bigwigs who became a close friend. Below, the XB-15 experimental bomber makes one of its few test flights in 1937. Although its engines proved too small and only one was built, the same development program produced the great wartime B-17.

The Army was called in 1932 to evict bonus-demanding veterans from their shantytowns in Washington. General Douglas MacArthur, here at the scene with his aide, Major D. D. Eisenhower, commanded the operation, in which bayonets, tanks, and tear gas were used. At right is a scene from the movie All Quiet on the Western Front, whose antiwar theme reflected popular feeling.

The New Samurai

It was not too surprising that the first open aggression of the 1930's should have been by Japan. The folklore of the island was heavy with tales of the warrior samurai, whose code of *Bushido*, or honor, had dominated the nation for centuries. It was not hard, under such circumstances, for the military to seize control and embark on aggression. During the 1920's the political parties and commercial interests tried to assert themselves, but with the coming of hard times after 1929, the military offered the tempting panacea of conquest abroad. In September, 1931, a minor incident was used as a pretext for seizing Manchuria; five months later, the huge province was proclaimed the puppet nation of Manchukuo, while divided China stood helplessly by and the League of Nations debated. More of North China was occupied in 1933, and in Japan, by terror and political pressure, the military took complete control of the government.

The samurai warriors above were painted at the time of Perry's visit to Japan. The samurai, who were intensely brave and utterly loyal, disappeared as Japan was modernized, but the officers at right, in bulletproof armor during a 1932 Shanghai incident, seem to symbolize the resurgence of the samurai spirit.

A Giant Stirs

For Japan to attack China appeared like a pygmy assaulting a giant, but China was a giant in size only. It was flabby, broken into warring segments, and defenseless. The hand of the central Government extended weakly, or not at all, into many parts of the country. During the 1920's, when Chiang Kai-shek was emerging as the strong man of the Nationalist Government, the Communists were also growing powerful, while many local war lords each reigned supreme in his own region, levying tribute on the peasants and fighting wars with neighboring war lords.

Chiang adopted a policy of civil war against the Communists after 1927, even though he had once been chosen for training in Moscow, and he did not waver from that policy even after the Japanese began their aggressions in Manchuria in 1931. So, in the tangled situation, he appeased the Japanese and fought Communists, while the Communists fought the Japanese. Then, in December of 1936, Chiang was kidnapped and apparently given the choice of joining the Communists in a united front against the Japanese or of being killed. Chiang took the prudent choice, and from that time the two armies joined in fighting the common enemy. As resistance grew, the Japanese blows became more widespread. The invading armies took the coastal cities and territories first, then moved up the rivers and spread inland. But the giant was too big to swallow. The Chinese armies always slipped away, and though they won virtually no victories, they continued to tie down a large number of Japanese troops throughout the war.

The above picture of Chiang Kai-shek was made in November, 1936, only a month before he was forced to join with the Communists against the Japanese. Mao Tse-tung (near right) is shown in 1938, when, as top Communist leader, he was active against the Japanese. Below, a Chinese student speaker exhorts his audience at a street-corner rally to rise to greater efforts to defeat the Japanese invaders.

Japanese soldiers use bayonets (upper right) to prod captured guerrillas in Manchuria in 1932. And at lower right, in a scene typifying the brutality of war, Japanese tanks move through Shaka in southern China during 1938.

ABOVE: CAPTURED GERMAN PAINTING, U.S. ARMY; BELOW: NATIONALBIBLIOTHEK, VIENNA

Study in Aggression

No one should have been surprised at the course Adolf Hitler followed, for he had sketched it all out in *Mein Kampf.* But few paid much attention. The world was so full of men who wanted peace at any price that he was able to do exactly as he had planned. Once he had made himself absolute dictator, he set about rearming Germany openly. In October, 1933, he took his country out of the League of Nations and the Geneva Disarmament Conference, claiming that Germany was not given equality with other nations. His act meant Germany was to rearm in defiance of the treaty of Versailles, and the small German Army braced itself for possible Allied action. But Hitler had judged well the mettle of his adversaries. The Allies did nothing. In March of 1935, Hitler revealed that a German Air Force already existed, and he provided for a peacetime army of thirty-six divisions. The Allies protested, but nothing more. A year later German troops marched into the demilitarized Rhineland. The generals had advised against the move, certain it would bring French reaction, but again Hitler had been right about the timidity of the democracies. Neither France nor Britain moved, and the last chance to stop Hitler without risking a major war was lost.

With his border secured and with an efficient war machine, the Nazi *Führer* turned to expanding the borders of the Third Reich. The first victim was Austria, whose people were ethnic Germans and so close to Hitler's heart. Austrian Chancellor von Schuschnigg was summoned to see Hitler on February 12, 1938, and presented with a set of demands that would have made his country's independence a mockery. Although forced to give in, he tried for a while to preserve some shreds of Austrian freedom. But it was an impossible task, and on March 11, he resigned. Two days later, *Anschluss,* the union of Germany and Austria, was announced by Hitler. A few weeks later the dictator's attention began to turn to Czechoslovakia, now surrounded on three sides by German territory. The pattern was becoming familiar.

Hitler delivered one of the most frenzied speeches of his career at the Nazi Party Rally at Nuremberg in September, 1938, when he took up the matter of Czechoslovakia.

Austrian-born Adolf Hitler came to Vienna when he was nineteen. There he spent four years as an impoverished vagrant, sleeping in flophouses, doing odd jobs, often eating in charity soup kitchens, and turning out hundreds of mediocre water colors (upper left), which was as close as he got to achieving his dream of becoming an artist. He left Vienna in 1913. When he returned in 1938 (lower left), it was as a conqueror.

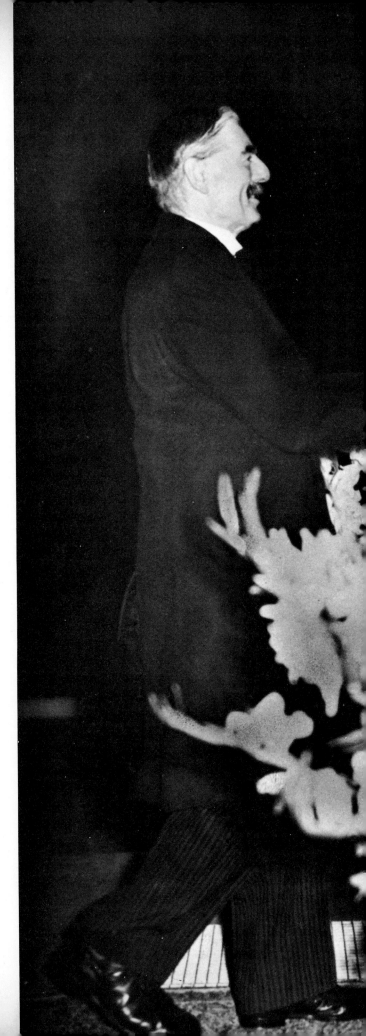

Peace with Dishonor

In March of 1938, only two weeks after *Anschluss* with Austria, Hitler was already planning his strategy against Czechoslovakia. Thereafter, Europe moved from crisis to crisis as his pretense of wishing only to protect the rights of Czechoslovakia's Sudeten German minority turned by September into open demands for annexation of the Sudetenland. Even the German General Staff was certain the Allies would fight this time if pressed and warned Hitler his Army was not ready—but there was no fight in Britain or France. The Czechs were resolute but were bluntly told that unless they assented to any agreements made by their timid allies, they might have to fight alone. Soviet offers of alliance were discouraged. And while Hitler threw Europe into a succession of war scares, Prime Minister Chamberlain (above) made three humiliating trips to appease the Nazi dictator. On September 30, he and French Premier Daladier signed away the remnants of their countries' honor at Munich. Hitler gained all he had asked for, and Chamberlain went home deluded into believing he had purchased peace.

We, the German **Führer** and Chancellor and the British **Prime Minister**, have had a further meeting today and are agreed in recognising that the question of Anglo-German relations is of the first importance for the two countries and for Europe.

We regard the agreement signed last night and the Anglo-German Naval Agreement as symbolic of the desire of our two peoples never to go to war with one another again.

We are resolved that the method of consultation shall be the method adopted to deal with any other questions that may concern our two countries, and we are determined to continue our efforts to remove possible sources of difference and thus to contribute to assure the peace of Europe.

Neville Chamberlain

September 30. 1938

Chamberlain (above) signs the Munich Agreement. The document above is a meaningless statement he got Hitler to sign; it says only that their two nations would settle problems peacefully. Chamberlain brandished this on returning home as meaning "peace in our time." At left, he greets Hitler at Godesberg, where their second meeting was held.

Chamberlain after Munich: "I believe it is peace in our time."

Requiem for a Republic

Darkness soon fell on post-Munich Czechoslovakia. Shorn of the Sudetenland, she was both defenseless and bankrupt, for the region had contained her fortifications and most of her mines and industry. Hitler ignored his pledge to guarantee the new Czech borders and began a campaign of intrigue and intimidation that ended in March, 1939, when German troops occupied the harassed land. Czechoslovakia was annexed to Germany and was wiped out as an independent nation. France and Britain, meanwhile, did nothing to honor their Munich pledge to protect Czech integrity. And Hitler's next conquest was already planned.

WIDE WORLD

MANSELL COLLECTION

Hitler had often spoken his contempt for the non-German Czechs and had brutally destroyed their country, yet there were Czech Nazis to guard his route and fawn on him, and crowds to cheer him (left), when he entered Prague, March 15, 1939, the day of annexation to Germany. Happy faces like those in the picture, however, were a small minority that day. Above, Nazi airmen use a training device to sharpen their bombing marksmanship during the same period in which Hitler was talking about peace.

A French political cartoonist of the period made his cynical comment (right) on the German-Soviet treaty. Hitler and a buxom Göring, depicted as strumpets, snuggle up against Stalin as Hitler coaxes, "Now, then, you are going to pay us, eh?" At below right, Stalin beams as Ribbentrop signs the nonaggression pact.

— alors, tu nous les donne, tes roubles, dis ?

Time Is Running Out

Chamberlain refused even to censure Hitler in the House of Commons for the rape of Czechoslovakia, but the national outcry was so loud that the astonished Prime Minister quickly reversed himself. And so, after having spinelessly yielded every position where Hitler might have been turned back, Great Britain, with France concurring, announced at last a firm position: they would defend the integrity of Poland against any threat from outside. For it was obvious that Poland was next on Hitler's list. The two Allies asked Russia to join in stopping Germany, but Stalin was still angered at the way he had been ignored during the Munich crisis; moreover, he had little faith in the Allies after their record of appeasement. He chose Germany. The Nazi-Soviet nonaggression pact was signed August 23, 1939; its secret clauses divided eastern Europe into zones of influence that cut Poland in two. Time was running out for the peace of Europe. That same summer, Americans were enjoying the New York World's Fair (left). It was called "The World of Tomorrow." Some of those attending had begun to worry about the possibility of war in the world of their tomorrow.

Blitzkrieg

By 1939 both Hitler and Stalin wanted war—although for different reasons. Until then, Hitler had judged correctly that he could attain his goals without fighting. He believed that France and Britain no longer had the will to risk another generation on the battlefield and that they would cede what he wished. "Why should I demoralize him (the enemy) by military means," he asked, "if I can do so better and more cheaply in other ways?"

Nevertheless, the *Führer* became giddy with success and determined to shed the "corrupting" influence of peace. Prior to Munich, the German General Staff had warned that an attack on Czechoslovakia would mean war with the West, and that defeat in such a war would be a certainty. But when Western resolve collapsed at Munich, Hitler interpreted the Munich pact as permission by Paris and London for him to drive eastward with a free hand. The Anglo-French guarantee of Poland seemed a deception. Therefore he resolved to smash the West—with Russia's tacit help.

Stalin, for his part, was resolved to do nothing to help the inept Paris and London Governments. He proclaimed that Moscow would not be drawn into "conflicts by the warmongers who are accustomed to have other countries pull the chestnuts out of the fire for them." On March 10, 1939, when the likelihood of war was mounting, he told his Eighteenth Party Congress that he intended "to allow the belligerents to sink deeply into the mire of war . . . to allow them to exhaust and weaken one another; and then, when they have become weak enough, to appear on the scene with fresh strength, to appear, of course, in the interest of peace and to dictate conditions to the enfeebled belligerents." He was therefore ready to accept Hitler's bribe of eastern Poland, the Baltic States, and Bessarabia in exchange for pledging the security of the German rear in any confrontation with the West. The fact that hundreds of thousands of anti-Nazis from these bartered territories were eventually sent by Moscow to German concentration camps, while hundreds of thousands of anti-Stalinists were sent by Berlin to Soviet concentration camps, disturbed neither dictator.

All spring and summer of 1939, while his agents were feeling out Russian intentions, Hitler made plans for a lightning assault on Poland. By April 3, he had already issued his directive for the attack, known as Case White. There was no longer much effort to obscure extensive military preparations. Arms and Nazi thugs disguised as tourists were dispatched to the Germanic free city of Danzig, on the Baltic.

Poland was a particularly desirable target. About a third of its population was of non-Polish stock. Its leaders too often showed excessive ambition and limited talent. Its flat, fertile fields, protected by antiquated matériel, offered optimum conditions for the Germans to experiment with their new blitzkrieg—lightning war.

Huge German armies were concentrated on two sides of the chosen victim, in Pomerania, East Prussia, Silesia, and subdued Czechoslovakia, and a series of armed incidents and provocations was carefully orchestrated to in-

A German soldier heaves a "potato masher" grenade at resisting Poles.

flame the border. Although the Pope, President Roosevelt, and the King of Belgium appealed for peace, the Germans merely prepared a sixteen-point ultimatum that they knew to be unacceptable and published it before allowing the Poles to turn it down. At 4:45 A.M., September 1, they attacked. Two days later France and Britain declared war on Germany, and Ribbentrop invited the Soviet Government to move into Poland from the east.

Fifty-six German divisions, nine of them armored, rumbled toward Warsaw, Bialystok, Cracow, and Lvov, under a galaxy of generals whose clumsy Teuton names, like mortar crumps, were soon to be feared from the Caspian to the Channel: Von Küchler, Guderian, Von Kluge, Von Reichenau, List, Von Bock. The brave but antiquated forces of Marshal Edward Smigly-Rydz, the Polish commander, were squeezed to death in one gigantic pincer. Fifteen hundred *Luftwaffe* planes, including Stuka dive bombers with their terrifying whistles, smashed gravely baroque Polish towns and wooden villages festooned with harvest symbols. The Poles fought bravely, but their old-fashioned infantry, lancers, and armor proved useless. The Polish Government fled Warsaw to Lublin on September 6. On the seventeenth, surrounded by thousands of refugees riding everything from barrows to fire engines, the Government crossed the Rumanian border near Cernăuţi (now incorporated in the Soviet Union). Eventually it established itself in Paris and then London, the first of those pitiful exile cabinets to become so commonplace in World War II.

Poland was squashed like an egg. Britain and France, although they proclaimed belligerency, did nothing helpful. On September 17, the day the German pincer snapped shut south of Warsaw, the Polish ambassador in Moscow was handed a note announcing that the Soviet-Polish nonaggression pact was void. The explanation was curt. "A Polish state no longer exists," and the Red Army was moving in "to protect White Russian and Ukranian minorities in Poland."

Isolated Warsaw fought with exemplary fortitude. There was no bread; the bakers had been mobilized. A few barrage balloons were hoisted above the smoking city, and trenches were dug in the outskirts. Surrounding roads were encumbered by peasant carts and by corpses. Day after day the radio broadcast Chopin's "Military Polonaise" and appeals for "the quickest aid" from France and Britain.

Walter Schellenberg, chief of Hitler's espionage service, described Warsaw after its surrender on September 27: "I was shocked at what had become of the beautiful city I had known—ruined and burnt-out houses, starving and grieving people. The nights were already unpleasantly chilly and a pall of dust and smoke hung over the city, and everywhere there was the sweetish smell of burnt flesh. . . . Warsaw was a dead city."

The end came on September 28, when Warsaw, Modlin, and a few scattered military units in the hinterland gave up. That same day, in Moscow, Ribbentrop and Molotov signed a treaty, completing Poland's fourth partition. Germany took some 71,000 square miles; Russia, about 75,000. The Germans admitted to having lost 10,572 killed and claimed 450,000 prisoners. The Russians suffered almost no losses. They rounded up a huge Polish force, whose officers were incarcerated. Most of them were later murdered in the Katyn forest. Temporarily freed from preoccupation with the East, the *Wehrmacht* turned its attentions westward. Britain and France found themselves faced at last with war.

Then, a sudden new explosion burst on the distant Baltic. Russia, intent on securing every advantage offered by its cynical pact with Hitler, decided to subdue Finland. Provocation was nonexistent, and the formula was blunt. The Soviets invited Helsinki to send a negotiator to the Kremlin, October 5, 1939, to discuss Moscow's demand for cession of territory on the Karelian Isthmus, exchange of woodlands in the north, and the right to establish a Russian naval base in the Finnish gulf. The suggestions were not acceptable to the Finns, and on November 30, after denouncing another nonaggression pact, Soviet planes bombed Helsinki and Viipuri. The Red Army rumbled across Finland's border at five different points. The vapid League of Nations responded by expelling the Soviet Union.

It was evident from the start that Stalin's myrmidons must win this patently unequal conquest. But the Finns proved to be hardy warriors, while the enormous Soviet Army showed itself badly trained, ill equipped, and above all, poorly led. Purges in the Red Army officer corps had upset the command structure. Furthermore, the Russians, deceived by their own propaganda, had expected to be hailed as liberators by an enthusiastic proletariat. Instead, they were slaughtered by careful artillery barrages and expert rifle marksmanship. Their loosely organized supply lines were easily severed by Finnish ski patrols. White-uniformed Finnish infantry knifed Soviet patrols in the long nights and blocked off entire battalions on the edges of frozen lakes. There the Russian troops congealed into awkward agonies of death. One eyewitness wrote: "For four miles the road and forest were strewn with the bodies of men and horses. . . . The corpses were frozen as hard as petrified wood."

Despite their valor, the Finns could expect but limited aid from the slow-moving Allies and the wary Scandinavian neutrals. The Swedes transgressed their neutral affirmations by sending eager but limited numbers of volunteers; the British and French permitted a few adventurous handfuls to participate; the Americans cheered lustily; and the Russians won. The sheer weight of their matériel, of their massive if clumsy gunnery and their aerial onslaught, plus the bravery of their bewildered infantry, managed an ultimate penetration. Helsinki capitulated. It granted Moscow even greater concessions than those originally asked.

The Russians both lost and gained by this dismal experience. They lost in the sense that Finland was thrust uncomfortably into German arms, but they won in that they were forced to realize their own defects. Old-fashioned officer ranks were restored, after years of experimentation with less formalized discipline. Attention was paid to the need for modernizing equipment and training and, above all, for revising fundamental concepts of strategy. The costly and humiliating Finnish campaign in a sense could be said to have saved Russia from absolute disaster when the final Nazi onslaught came in 1941.

The Finland episode shifted the attention of the main adversaries to Scandinavia. The Norwegian port of Narvik, which was linked by a railroad over the mountains to Sweden's iron mines, had been used in a small way to supply the Finnish armies. With British strategic interest beginning to focus on Germany's industrial dependence on Swedish iron, the Admiralty studied means of blockading this route, unaware that Hitler had been tentatively planning the occupation of Norwegian bases as early as October of 1939. By April 8, when London and Paris proclaimed they had mined the area south of Narvik, a Nazi invasion was already secretly under way. The very next night, Hitler's forces landed in Norway while the *Wehrmacht* rolled unopposed across Denmark.

Although the German fleet was no match for the Royal Navy, by stealth and efficiency it succeeded in landing sufficient troops in Norway, and the *Luftwaffe* achieved prompt superiority, enabling it to offset British naval power. The Norwegians showed an intense will to resist, fighting vigorously and sinking several Nazi vessels. But the Allies came late with little. Vidkun Quisling, a local Nazi, arose to help the insidious aggression, thereby adding his name to history's leaden roll of traitors.

The notable but miniature campaigns fought by British and French expeditionary forces at Namsos, Andalsnes, and Trondheim are today, outside Norway itself, remembered primarily on regimental rosters. The Royal Navy managed to land a considerable army around Narvik, but the R.A.F. was based too far away to provide the desperately needed cover. Resolute German defenses suc-

ceeded in first discouraging and then repulsing inexperienced Allied troops, who were pinned against the sea and eventually routed when Hitler overwhelmed France.

The Danish King Christian X yielded with dispatch and locked himself in his castle. The King of Norway, Haakon VII, fled with his Government to London. And the few French and British, aided by disorganized Norwegian bands, found themselves doomed along the northern fiords. Winston Churchill concluded: "We, who had the command of the sea and could pounce anywhere on an undefended coast, were outpaced by the enemy moving by land across very large distances in the face of every obstacle." Hitler's ruthless audacity succeeded in sealing off Europe's northern flank, insuring access to Sweden's invaluable iron, and closing off the Baltic.

From late summer, 1939, until late spring, 1940, the British and French gave the appearance of being removed from the conflict they had accepted. Britain, with all its sea power, mustered only small overseas land expeditions, for which it was able to grant only marginal air support. The French, comfortable in their casemates, sent a gallant group to Norway, talked of their audacious Army, and waited for the inevitable showdown. President Roosevelt sought to intervene, but he found no peace.

On May 10, the so-called Phony War, eight months of watching and waiting along the principal Western front, came to a sudden end. Hitler attacked Holland, Belgium, and Luxembourg. On the same day, Winston Churchill became Britain's Prime Minister. "I was sure I should not fail," he wrote later. "I slept soundly and had no need for cheering dreams."

Case Yellow, as the Germans named their carefully devised plan for the swift defeat of France, called for an armored thrust through the Ardennes, past Sedan to the Channel coast at Abbeville, in which tanks, followed by motorized infantry and protected by Stuka dive bombers, would thrust forward to join paratroops landed behind the Allied lines. For this purpose, a gigantic force of about one hundred and seventeen divisions was disposed, seventy-five of which took part in the initial attack under Generals Fedor von Bock and Gerd von Rundstedt. The offensive depended on lancing north of the Maginot Line through nonbelligerent Luxembourg, Belgium, and Holland. Hermann Göring's air-borne forces were assigned the task of reducing the Dutch, while armored wedges pierced Luxembourg, swung across Belgium, and entered France. The fortresses around Liege were captured with surprising ease by Nazi engineers and paratroopers who had trained for the assault against full-scale replicas of the Belgian defenses. At Fort Eben Emael, the most vital of these strongholds, some twelve hundred

Belgian defenders capitulated to only eighty Germans.

The German juggernaut rolled through thirty-six British, French, and Belgian divisions while its sapper units constructed pontoon bridges across waterways. By May 19, the panzers, led by newly rising commanders such as Von Kleist and Rommel, had smashed a great gap in the northwestern Maginot Line and joined a vast army grunting southward from Belgium.

On May 28, the Belgians surrendered unconditionally. King Leopold, refusing the appeals of his ministers to flee and carry on the fight, chose to capitulate and sought solitude in a quiet castle near Brussels, where he later married a beautiful Flemish girl. The Belgian surrender exposed the entire left flank of the Anglo-French defenses, and France itself was crumbling fast.

The *Wehrmacht* had accomplished a shattering triumph. Within a few weeks it had disintegrated a French army that considered itself Europe's finest; and this was done by superior quality of command, weapons, techniques, and soldiery, not by an advantage in quantity. Indeed, Hitler's armies actually were inferior in numbers and had fewer tanks. The combined Anglo-French forces alone disposed four thousand armored vehicles, against twenty-eight hundred for Germany. The French tanks were superior in both armor and gun caliber, although slower and more difficult to control. Only in the air and in the skill of handling troops were Hitler's forces superior. What a harvest they reaped from this advantage!

The battle of Dunkirk, which reached its peak May 30, was one of the remarkable moments of British history. By a miracle of improvisation an Allied army of 338,226, which appeared to be hopelessly cut off on the French Channel coast, was taken away by more than a thousand hastily mustered boats. Virtually every ship afloat had been pressed into service by the Admiralty to save the men at Dunkirk. There were French fishing boats, coasters, paddle steamers, colliers, yachts, lifeboats from sunken ships. And these were manned by Royal Navy veterans and merchant seamen, by dentists, stevedores, taxi drivers, farmers, civil servants, and downy-faced Sea Scouts. Swung by tides, stranded in shallows beside the burning beach, harried by airplanes that hunted them by night with parachute flares and riddled them by day with tracers, this extraordinary flotilla headed across the cluttered channel waters for a shore that was black with men —and took them off.

Dunkirk was typical of a British strategy that specializes in losing battles and winning wars. It was a dreadful affair, but the survivors—and their number was astonishing—became the heart of a new army that would one day march through London in the Victory Parade.

The total number of British troops either killed, wounded, or taken prisoner at Dunkirk came to 68,111. Field Marshal von Rundstedt, whose Army Group A held the British in its grasp, later said: "If I had had my way the English would not have got off so lightly at Dunkirk. But my hands were tied by direct orders from Hitler himself. While the English were clambering into the ships off the beaches, I was kept uselessly outside the port unable to move. I recommended to the Supreme Command that my five Panzer divisions be immediately sent into the town and thereby completely destroy the retreating English. But I received definite orders from the Führer that under no circumstances was I to attack. . . ."

Hitler had consigned the Dunkirk annihilation task to Göring's *Luftwaffe*, for several reasons. He feared the cost to his straining tanks of direct ground assault over difficult terrain while the French armies to the south had not yet been destroyed. He overrated the destructive power of air bombardment. And finally, he seems to have had vague thoughts that perhaps, once France had fallen, he could force a swift peace upon the British.

Of all Hitler's misjudgments, those concerning Britain were the most profound. He didn't think they would fight in 1939; he didn't think they would persevere in 1940; and until late 1942, it never occurred to him that the British might actually win.

Meanwhile France dissolved, militarily and morally. General Maxime Weygand, then seventy-three years old, replaced General Maurice Gamelin as supreme commander. Weygand, a fine fighting man, came too late. He attempted to stand on the Somme and Aisne rivers, but on June 5, the Germans hit this feeble line like a pile driver and drove through to the Seine. Nazi propaganda encouraged tales of terror and a mass flight of civilians, who blocked important roads to both the retreating French and the pursuing German armies. On June 12, Paris was declared an open city. Two days later the German forces entered, clattering down empty avenues. Only one cafe was open on the broad Champs-Élysées. Within hours, the swastika flew from public buildings.

Hitler thus obliterated the army he supposed to be his greatest enemy, at a cost of only 27,074 German dead. And in Rome, on June 10, on a balcony above the Piazza Venezia, protruding his jaw to obscure the fatness of his chops, Mussolini announced to the cheers of a huge crowd carefully assembled below that Italy had joined the fray. Ciano, his son-in-law and Minister of Foreign Affairs, whom Mussolini later ordered shot, confided to his diary: "I am sad, very sad. The adventure begins. May God help Italy." President Roosevelt said in a speech at the University of Virginia: "The hand that held the dagger has struck it into the back of its neighbor." A huge new army and a sizable navy and air force thus entered the war.

Once the Germans took Paris, it was evident that the conflict in western Europe was over. Even the silly old Kaiser, exiled in Holland, wired Hitler congratulating his former corporal on "the mighty victory granted by God." Premier Paul Reynaud and his Government fled south to Bordeaux and sent a junior cabinet official, Brigadier General Charles de Gaulle, to London to discuss ways of transporting forces to North Africa. De Gaulle was much impressed by the vigor of British resolve and even brought back to France an offer from Churchill for a Franco-British union with a joint defense program, joint economy, and joint citizenship for all Englishmen and Frenchmen. But the rot of despair had gone too far.

The offer was ignored. The Reynaud cabinet resigned on June 16, and Marshal Philippe Pétain, an august symbol of French glory whose body but not whose mind had survived World War I, took power. He was backed by the fleet commander, Admiral Jean Louis Darlan, and by Pierre Laval, a brilliant but unscrupulously ambitious politician who saw a future for France only as triumphant Germany's mistress. Pétain asked for an armistice, later claiming that he had thus "performed an act of salvation."

On June 22, 1940, the French surrender was formally signed at the same clearing in Compiègne forest, north of Paris, where Marshal Ferdinand Foch had dictated terms to Germany in November, 1918. The identical railway car, hitherto kept as a museum piece, was wheeled out of its shed to serve as the parlor for France's funeral. It was a lovely, warm day. Hitler stood with Göring and other gloating chieftains while General Wilhelm Keitel, Chief of his Supreme Command, began reading out the conditions to the French delegation. Hitler didn't wait. Followed by Göring, Hess, Ribbentrop, and a strut of officers, he walked out of the rickety Pullman toward a French monument honoring Alsace and Lorraine. The band played "Deutschland über Alles" and the "Horst Wessel Lied," a Nazi party song commemorating an ignominious street-fighting thug.

The armistice provided that German troops would occupy more than half of France, including the entire Atlantic coastline. The French Army was demobilized and its fleet rendered immobile. France yielded its German prisoners and any German refugees Berlin wanted. French prisoners were left in the Reich. Hitler had three objectives: to establish a French Government in the unoccupied zone that would help him extract what he needed materially from France; to prevent Darlan's fleet from joining Britain; and to frustrate any support for

Britain. He clearly hoped to turn the French slowly against the British if the latter refused to transact with him, a possibility he had been sounding out through an intermediary in Sweden.

The British, however, were resolute. Churchill expressed to the House of Commons "brotherly sentiment for the French people" but promised to fight on without mercy. And he was determined to keep alive the embers of resistance in smoking Europe. Here he was to find aid from a virtually unheard-of leader.

Charles de Gaulle, at forty-nine the youngest general officer in France, was little known except by military theorists. But Churchill appreciated his pugnacity and took the initiative in allowing him to broadcast an appeal to the French people. On June 18, a text of less than three hundred words was read aloud by "Moi, le général de Gaulle," summoning Frenchmen and Frenchwomen throughout the world to carry on the fight. There were only a few of them in Britain: veterans from the Norway campaign, refugees from Dunkirk, pilots, seamen, diplomats, and a purchasing mission headed by Jean Monnet. Inside dazed France, de Gaulle's words were heard by only a small number of people; among them were Pierre Mendès-France, a future premier, and Maurice Schumann, later a minister, who was in a railway station that was being bombed at that very instant. At Locminé, a small Breton town through which a German motorized unit was rumbling, a youth ran into the central square to shout: "A general has just spoken on the radio and said that we must continue to fight. His name was de Gaulle." An old woman, hanging to the arm of a priest, murmured, "It is my son." Twelve days later she died.

And so the preposterous first phase concluded. Stalin swiftly and brutally carried out the remaining privileges allotted him by his pact with Hitler. He sent an ambassador to Pétain's Vichy and ordered his troops into Latvia, Lithuania, and Estonia. In the wake of a hasty ultimatum, he took Rumania's Bessarabia and north Bucovina provinces. From the Black Sea across Poland to Finland and the Arctic, a huge band of territory, once czarist, was returned to Russian control. Although Moscow had arguable legal claims to the area, the method of expressing them was appalling.

Strangely enough, it was also in a grim sense the final payment for that deal with Seeckt that initially had permitted German militarism to revive, long before it waxed amid Allied lassitude. But the Kremlin's calculation that in revenge for inept Western diplomacy it could sit back while Europe tore itself to pieces and then move in as arbiter, proved wrong. The price that Russia eventually paid in blood was terrible and huge.

Twentieth-Century Conqueror

By the eve of his Russian adventure, Adolf Hitler had already achieved domination over an incredible amount of territory in a short period of time. By threats, subterfuge, broken pledges, and open warfare, he had overrun lands and peoples so extensive and so numerous as to rank him with Napoleon, Caesar, and history's other great conquerors. However, his real genius did not lie on the battlefield but in his ability to gauge his adversaries and to manipulate them. He was certain, for instance, that France and England would do nothing if he annexed Austria, although his own generals thought otherwise. He blackmailed the Allies at Munich because he knew they would appease him to keep the peace. Up to the moment the German Army crossed the Polish border, he had won everything without firing a shot. Even after war began, his conquests were made with remarkable ease by the superbly trained *Wehrmacht* with its new and devastating blitzkrieg tactics. France, supposed possessor of the world's best army, fell almost as easily as Poland. Only the English Channel finally stopped the wide-ranging panzer columns. Then Hitler made the great mistake of assuming, after the French campaign, that he was a military as well as a political genius. It was a bit of egotism that would soon cost the *Wehrmacht* and Germany dearly.

Close Your Hearts to Pity

Hitler called his generals together just before the invasion of Poland to brief them on the political situation and to fire them up for the job ahead. Be harsh and remorseless, he told them. They were to act with brutality, close their hearts to pity. It was, he said, the stronger man who was always right. On September 1, 1939, these gentle maxims were put into action as the *Wehrmacht* swept without warning into Poland. It was as brutal and harsh an assault as the *Führer* could have wished. The Polish Army and Air Force were antiquated; those of Germany were the most modern in the world, and the German command was putting into effect, for the first time, the devastating methods of blitzkrieg—lightning war. The Poles were brave, but their valor was largely futile, as on one occasion when a brigade of horse cavalry armed with lances attacked a Nazi tank column. Within a week the far-ranging German ground forces and the *Luftwaffe* had wrecked the Polish Army.

Polish cavalry—here shown during maneuvers—tried to stop Nazi panzers and were slaughtered.

German Stuka dive bombers (top right) first won fame in the Polish invasion, when they panicked and demoralized the defense far behind battle lines. Germany used some 2,000 planes in all during the campaign. German troops at center right break down a border barricade at the start of the invasion on September 1. And at bottom right, an infantry column marches somewhere in Poland. While the plane-panzer combination, ranging deep into enemy areas to split and encircle the defenses, was the heart of the blitzkrieg, infantry remained as necessary as ever to mop up and to occupy territory.

The Reluctant Allies

France and Great Britain, though pledged by treaty to aid Poland, still hesitated after the Nazi onslaught and inanely talked of negotiating for a return to peace. Not until September 3, two days after the attack, did the Chamberlain Government declare war, and then it had been prodded by an angry House of Commons. The French Government was even more reluctant. Having her allies in the war did nothing to help anguished Poland. By treaty, France had promised to launch a major offensive against Germany within days of an attack on Poland. Hitler's Siegfried Line facing France was largely a fraud, constructed of a minimum of concrete and a maximum of propaganda. Its garrison was fighting in Poland, and only 23 second-class divisions faced the Maginot Line, where there were 110 Allied divisions, mainly French. But the French, grown timid with memories of their losses in the First World War, did not attack. And so the Poles fought on heroically and hopelessly, and were doubly betrayed when the Russians moved in behind them to grab the eastern half of their country. The conquered nation disappeared from the map and sank into a night of Nazi barbarism, where the people, contemptuously called "subhumans," were systematically enslaved, brutalized, and often exterminated. No other occupied country suffered so much.

General Walther von Brauchitsch, at left front (above), confers a few miles from Warsaw with members of his staff. Brauchitsch, who was the Army Commander in Chief, carried out the Austrian and Czechoslovakian occupations and the Polish conquest but was forced to resign when the Russian war bogged down. London headlines (below) reflected national sentiment: no martial fervor, but a let's-get-on-with-the-job attitude. At right, a Pole is executed by the Nazis. Countless such murders only increased the resolve of the underground forces.

SUN, LONDON

Daily Herald

No. 7349   MONDAY, SEPTEMBER 4, 1939   ONE PENNY

WAR DECLARED BY BRITAIN AND FRANCE

We Have Resolved To Finish It—PRIME MINISTER

GREAT BRITAIN DECLARED WAR ON GERMANY AT 11 O'CLOCK YESTERDAY MORNING.

Six hours later, at 5 p.m., France declared war.

Britain's resolution to defend Poland against Nazi aggression was described by the newly-formed Ministry of Information in one of its first announcements, as follows:—

"At 11.15 this morning (Sunday) Mr. R. Dunbar, Head of the Treaty Department of the Foreign Office, went to the German Embassy, where he was received by Dr. Kordt, the Charge d'Affaires.

"Mr. Dunbar handed to Dr. Kordt a notification that a state of war existed between Great Britain and Germany as from 11 o'clock B.S.T. this morning. This notification constituted the formal declaration of war."

Unthinkable We Should Refuse The Challenge

—THE KING

Broadcasting last evening from his study at Buckingham Palace, the King said:—

IN this grave hour, perhaps the most fateful in our history, I send to every household of my people, both at home and overseas, this message, spoken with the same depth of feeling for each one of you as if I were able to cross your threshold and speak to you myself.

For the second time in the lives of most of us we are at war.

Over and over again we have tried to find a peaceful way out of the differences between ourselves and those

WAR CABINET OF

POLES SMASH WAY INTO E. PRUSSIA

OFFICIALS in Warsaw stated late last night that the Polish army has smashed a way across the Northern border into East Prussia, after driving the Germans from several Polish towns in bitter fighting.

London Hears Its First Raid Warning

LONDON was calm yesterday when it heard its first air raid warning.

This is the official statement issued by the Air Ministry:—

At 11.30 a.m. yesterday an aircraft was observed approaching the South Coast.

As its identity could not be readily determined an air-raid warning was given.

On the Northern Front the Poles are reported to have defeated the German effort to drive a barrier across the upper part of the Corridor. The Germans fell back behind their frontiers.

The Poles say they have broken through the German fortifications as far as the railway terminus of Deutsch Eylau.

One of the most important towns recaptured is stated to be Zbaszyn. Dispatches from the front state that furious fighting is going on at Czestochowa and Katowice. German reports that they have captured Czestochowa are denied. Warsaw was again raided yesterday by German aircraft.

(Continued on Page 2; Earlier fighting details on Page 10)

BLACK-OUT TIME TO-NIGHT—7.40

"Hitler wanted to know what had proved particularly satisfactory about our tanks"

General Heinz Guderian

The German war machine that crashed into Poland on September 1 was far from what would later be turned against France and the Low Countries. It looked very effective against the Poles, to be sure, and carefully controlled Nazi propaganda made the most of its swift successes; but there were, nonetheless, a good many bugs to be worked out before a war in the West could be waged. Not the least important was a lack of any real enthusiasm for war. William Shirer in his Berlin Diary *described the prevailing mood of gloom in Berlin when the news of the Polish invasion was announced. Here, in an excerpt from his excellent book on the war,* Panzer Leader, *General Heinz Guderian describes a similar attitude among the military, as well as other aspects of the Polish campaign. It was Guderian who had organized Hitler's tank units, who officially received the Russians when the German-Soviet pincer on Poland closed at Brest Litovsk, and who later led the great German tank assaults against the Russians.*

The attack was to take place early on the 26th of August.

By means of a secret agreement with the Russians during these days Hitler had ensured the protection of his rear in the event of war. Owing to Ribbentrop's disastrous influence, illusions were still being cherished concerning the probable reactions of the Western Powers; it was considered unlikely that they would declare war.

In any case it is not with the knowledge of hindsight that I can declare that the attitude of the Army was very grave indeed and that, had it not been for the Russian pact, there is no telling what the Army's reactions might not have been. We did not go light-heartedly to war, and there was not one general who would not have advocated peace. The older officers, and many thousands of men, had been through the First World War. They knew what war would mean if it were not simply confined to a campaign against the Poles. There was every reason to fear that this would not be the case, since after the creation of the Bohemian Protectorate, the British had guaranteed Poland's integrity. Each of us thought of the mothers and wives of our German soldiers and of the heavy sacrifices that they must be called upon to bear even if the outcome of the war were a successful one. Our own sons were on active service. My elder boy, Heinz Günter, was regimental adjutant of Panzer Regiment 35; my younger son, Kurt, had been commissioned Second Lieutenant in the 3rd Armored Reconnaissance Battalion of the 3rd Panzer Division and so was in my Army Corps.

During the night of 25–26th August the attack was cancelled. Certain troops had already begun to move forward and had to be recalled. It was plain that diplomatic manœuvres were in progress. There was a last flicker of hope that peace might yet be preserved. But nothing positive reached the troops at the front. On the 31st of August there was a new alert. This time it was serious. . . .

On the 1st of September at 0445 hrs. the whole corps moved simultaneously over the frontier. There was a thick ground mist at first which prevented the air force from giving us any support. I accompanied the 3rd Panzer Brigade, in the first wave, as far as the area north of Zempelburg where the preliminary fighting took place. Unfortunately the heavy artillery of the 3rd Panzer Division felt itself compelled to fire into the mist, despite having received precise orders not to do so.

The first shell landed 50 yards ahead of my command vehicle, the second 50 yards behind it. I reckoned that the next one was bound to be a direct hit and ordered my driver to turn about and drive off. The unaccustomed noise had made him nervous, however, and he drove straight into a ditch at full speed. The front axle of the half-track vehicle was bent so that the steering mechanism was put out of action. This marked the end of my drive. I made my way to my corps command post, procured myself a fresh vehicle and had a word with the over-eager artillerymen. . . .

On the 4th of September the noose was tightened about the encircled enemy. The battle for the Corridor was approaching its end. . . . The troops had fought brilliantly and were in good spirits. The casualties among our other ranks were small, but our losses of officers had been disproportionately heavy, for they had thrown themselves into battle with the greatest devotion to duty. General Adam, State Secretary von Weizsäcker, and Colonel Freiherr von Funk had each lost a son. . . .

On the 5th of September our corps had a surprise visit from Adolf Hitler. I met him near Plevno on the Tuchel-Schwetz road, got into his car, and drove with him along the line of our previous advance. We passed the destroyed Polish artillery, went through Schwetz, and then, following closely behind our encircling troops, drove to Graudenz where he stopped and gazed for some time at the blown bridges over the Vistula. At the sight of the smashed artillery regiment, Hitler had asked me: 'Our dive bombers did that?' When I replied, 'No, our panzers!' he was plainly astonished. . . . We drove back through parts of the 23rd and 2nd (Motorized) Infantry Divisions. During the drive we discussed at

first the course of events in corps area. Hitler asked about casualties. I gave him the latest figures that I had received, some 150 dead and 700 wounded for all the four divisions under my command during the Battle of the Corridor. He was amazed at the smallness of these figures, and contrasted them with the casualties of his own regiment, the *List* Regiment, during the First World War: on the first day of battle that one regiment alone had lost more than 2,000 dead and wounded. I was able to show him that the smallness of our casualties in this battle against a tough and courageous enemy was primarily due to the effectiveness of our tanks. Tanks are a life-saving weapon. The men's belief in the superiority of their armored equipment had been greatly strengthened by their successes in the Corridor. The enemy had suffered the total destruction of between two and three infantry divisions and one cavalry brigade. Thousands of prisoners and hundreds of guns had fallen into our hands. . . .

Our conversation turned on technical matters. Hitler wanted to know what had proved particularly satisfactory about our tanks and what was still in need of improvement. I told him that the most important thing now was to hasten the delivery of Panzers III and IV to the fighting troops and to increase the production of these tanks. For their further development their present speed was sufficient, but they needed to be more heavily armored, particularly in front; the range and power of penetration of their guns also needed to be increased, which would mean longer barrels and a shell with a heavier charge. This applied equally to our anti-tank guns.

With a word of recognition for the troops' achievements Hitler left

us as dusk was falling and returned to his headquarters.

It was noteworthy that the civilian population, which was re-emerging from its hiding-places now that the fighting was over, cheered as Hitler drove past and brought him flowers. The town of Schwetz was decorated with our national colors. The impression made by his visit on the troops was a very good one. . . .

Meanwhile the Fourth Army under Colonel-General von Kluge had caught up with us, and we were once again placed under its command. . . . Fourth Army now ordered that XIX Army Corps move forward, one division to go south, one to go east toward Bialystok. Such a move would have split the corps and would have made all attempts at command impossible. The appearance of the Russians rendered these orders obsolete before they could be carried out.

As a forerunner of the Russians there appeared a young officer in an armored reconnaissance car, who informed us that a Russian Tank Brigade was on its way. Then we received information concerning the demarcation line which the Foreign Ministry had agreed; this surrendered Brest to the Russians, since the Bug was to be the boundary. We did not regard this as a very advantageous decision; and finally we were informed that we only had until 22nd of September in which to evacuate the territory east of the line of demarcation. This was so little time that we could not even move all our wounded or recover our damaged tanks. It seems unlikely that any soldier was present when the agreement about the demarcation line and the cease fire was drawn up.

The Winter
the War Stood Still

The French Army showed no desire to attack Hitler's Siegfried Line defenses, nor did the Germans act at all aggressive, and so the fall and winter of 1939–40 produced one of the strangest interludes of the war. An American senator dubbed it the phony war; to the Germans it was the *Sitzkrieg*. Opposing troops often worked and rested in plain sight of each other, like the French poilus at right; outposts were reduced to tokens; German supplies moved up the Rhine-side railroad undisturbed by French big guns just across the river. But while Hitler was only pausing to repair the wear and tear of the Polish campaign, the French and British seemed to think that somehow they might still find a way out without actual fighting. Field Marshal (then General) Montgomery told how Chamberlain came to France in December and asked Montgomery hopefully if he did not agree that the Germans really had no intention of attacking. And back in England, the prevailing mood of unbelligerency was expressed in a less-than-immortal ditty of the day:

Mother dear I'm writing you from
*   somewhere in France*
Hoping this finds you well—
Sergeant says I'm doing fine "A soldier
*   and a half"*
Here's the song that we'll all sing
*   it'll make you laugh.*
CHORUS:
WE'RE GONNA HANG OUT THE
*   WASHING ON THE SIEGFRIED LINE*
Have you any dirty washing mother dear?
WE'RE GONNA HANG OUT THE
*   WASHING ON THE SIEGFRIED LINE*
'Cos the washing day is here—
Whether the weather may be wet or fine
We'll just rub along without a care—
WE'RE GONNA HANG OUT THE
*   WASHING ON THE SIEGFRIED LINE*
If the Siegfried Line's still there.

70

WILMINGTON NEWS

Soviet soldiers (right) wave in triumph after having captured a strongpoint of the battered Mannerheim Line. Although strongly and expertly built, the line, which defended the Karelian Isthmus, could not possibly stand up against the terrible artillery fire to which it was subjected at the last, and which was said to total 300,000 shells in one single 24-hour period.

Cartoonist Herblock neatly satirized (above) the dictator's standard practice of claiming self-defense as his excuse for attacking a smaller nation. At right, a Finnish ski patrol returns from a mission. The white-clad soldiers, hard to see as they moved swiftly over the snow, were known as Bielaja Smert ("the White Death"). Marshal Mannerheim of Finland, later analyzing the Russian failures, said that the most serious weakness of Soviet troops was their lack of any training in the use of skis.

NOVOSTI PRESS AGENCY

Finland: Aggression in the North

Stalin's winter war against Finland was in the classic pattern of totalitarian aggression: first, unreasonable demands on a small nation; then trumped-up incidents and screams about being attacked; and finally, a crushing armed assault. But after Russian armies attacked on November 30, 1939, the formula went wrong. The Finns refused to be overwhelmed. Although outnumbered almost 500,000 to 130,000 and at a tremendous disadvantage in planes, guns, and tanks, their superior tactics, leadership, and adaptability to conditions enabled them to fight their ponderous foe to a standstill and inflict dreadful losses on him. World opinion backed Finland. Foreign volunteers came, and in early March, Great Britain and France were ready to send a large expeditionary force. But there were difficulties about transit across neutral Norway and Sweden—and besides, the Finns were skeptical about two countries that would not fight in France but wanted to fight in the north. So, with their defenses at last giving way under the sheer weight of the Russian assault, the Finnish Government sued for peace, bowing to all of Stalin's demands.

Scandinavian Nightfall

Germany's admirals had argued for the seizure of Norway, with its long, indented coastline; it would let them circumvent a British blockade like that which had choked Germany in World War I. Hitler, though, was fairly content to have the country neutral—as long as it was neutral in his favor. Ships with the iron ore he needed so much could sail from Narvik most of the way to Germany through Norwegian territorial waters, which was better than the German Navy and Air Force having to escort them. But he changed his mind when a British destroyer entered a fiord in February, 1940, to rescue 299 British seamen imprisoned on the German ship *Altmark*. The Nazi dictator ordered invasion, which came on April 9. Denmark, which had been included as a victim, fell almost without resistance; the Norwegians fought where confusion did not rob them of all organization. The Germans did, however, suffer heavy naval losses, which were later to handicap them. British and French forces sent to Norway were poorly equipped and ill supported, brave men sacrificed to incompetence in high places.

NORSK TELEGRAMBYRA

Although his name became a synonym for traitor, Vidkun Quisling himself (left) was never much of a success as a turncoat. He proclaimed himself Prime Minister on behalf of the Nazis when they took over Norway, but six days later they threw him out. They gave him back the office in 1942, but in spite of all his efforts to be a good lackey, he had no power. The Norwegians loathed him, and after the war he was tried and executed for treason. At right, Germans search a Norwegian soldier. Most Norwegian troops were taken by surprise.

Assault on the Low Countries

Despite what had happened to Denmark and Norway, the Low Countries went on hoping Hitler might respect their neutrality. But about three hours after midnight on May 10, 1940, the Nazi blitzkrieg swept across the borders of Belgium, the Netherlands, and Luxembourg. The Germans announced that they were coming to protect the three victims from an invasion planned by Great Britain and France and gave an ultimatum that any resistance would be ruthlessly crushed. The attack was well under way before the ultimatums were delivered.

In the Netherlands, the assault came mainly from the sky, by glider and parachute troops. They at once seized bridges intact, enabling panzer units to penetrate deep into the country, unhindered by the water defenses on which the Dutch had depended so heavily. But the defenders rallied surprisingly well. At The Hague they threw back a Nazi force that had landed on the airfields expressly to capture the Queen and the Government. And they resisted so stoutly before Rotterdam that Hitler ordered a mass bombing of the city, an act of pure brutality and spite, for negotiations for its surrender were under way when the planes appeared. Rotterdam's heart was wiped out, some eight hundred were killed, several thousand injured. That same evening, May 14, all Dutch troops were ordered to stop fighting, and the next day the surrender was officially signed. But Queen Wilhelmina had escaped to England, and her government-in-exile remained in the war.

German infantrymen cross the Maas River from Holland into Belgium (near right) during the early hours of the lowlands invasion. At far right, Nazi paratroops leap into Holland. Although most of the sky-borne invaders came by parachute or in gliders, one company landed on the river at Rotterdam in old seaplanes.

Nazi Heel on Holland

After defeat came oppression in the Netherlands—as it did for all Nazi victims. On May 18, Artur von Seyss-Inquart became Reichs Commissioner for Holland. His name was not one to calm fears. He was the Viennese quisling who had helped Hitler take over Austria and later had been deputy to the unspeakably brutal Hans Frank, Governor General of beaten Poland. He began with false moderation, promising the Dutch he would not try to make Nazis of them, but gradually the grip tightened as he forced the nation toward complete subjection. In response, the backs of the Dutch stiffened, their traditional stubbornness asserted itself, and a resistance movement developed and grew strong among them.

Opposition came into the open when the Nazis first moved against the Jews in February, 1941 (at left is the roundup of victims in Amsterdam's Jewish quarters at that time). Four hundred Jews were sent to concentration camps, and two days later the Dutch people went on strike. Their protest was ruthlessly suppressed, but they became only more careful instead of cowed. All through the war they hid and protected Jews as much as possible; it was in Amsterdam that teen-age Anne Frank hid with her family for two years and wrote her diary before she was discovered and sent to die in a concentration camp. The hand of Seyss-Inquart became more harsh, and the Dutch became more skillful at sabotage, spying, and the midnight murder of Nazis. But they paid heavily: some 200,000 were sent to concentration camps, and many were summarily executed.

Rotterdam was destroyed not for military reasons but for Schrecklichkeit *("frightfulness"), the doctrine that the deliberate use of*

terror tactics will break a people's will to resist. Its use was to boomerang as badly for Hitler as it once had for the Kaiser.

Disaster in Belgium

Nazi paratroopers relax after taking "impregnable" Fort Eben Emael in only thirty hours.

Nazi forces had swept into Belgium at the same moment they had struck Holland, and with equally devastating effect. Blitzkrieg tactics confused the defenders. Glider troops seized bridges before they could be destroyed, and by the second day, Fort Eben Emael, considered impregnable, had fallen, taken by only eighty men led by a sergeant; their principal secret weapon was that they had rehearsed the operation endlessly on a replica of the fort. Britain and France responded to pleas for help by sending powerful forces that joined the Belgian Army on a strong defense line between Antwerp and Namur. Over most of this front they outnumbered the Germans; but that was exactly what the German high command had planned on. Nazi columns forced crossings of the difficult Meuse River, and a mighty army of tanks broke through the Ardennes Forest, which was lightly guarded because it was believed impassable by armor. Then, as the Allies struggled desperately to plug the gap, King Leopold III surrendered the Belgian Army on May 28 with virtually no warning to his allies, leaving their flank almost fatally exposed. The German panzers pushed onward to the Channel, and the Allied forces in the north, now cut off, retreated toward the one remaining port of Dunkirk.

WIDE WORLD

King Leopold III (above) ignored his cabinet's plea not to surrender, nor would he exile himself. The Nazis kept him a prisoner during the war, but afterward the Belgians did not want him back. At left, a dazed mother and children wander through the aftermath of a German air raid.

83

The Riddle of Dunkirk

The story of Dunkirk is already half legend; the episode has even come to be called "The Miracle of Dunkirk." But tremendous as this rescue of a third of a million trapped men was, it succeeded not for miraculous but for entirely explainable reasons. One was bad weather that grounded the *Luftwaffe* part of the time. Another was the supreme effort by which the Royal Air Force won superiority in the sky over the evacuation area. But strangest of all was Hitler's May 24 order that stopped his panzers short of Dunkirk, leaving the trapped army to be handled by the *Luftwaffe*. No one knows for certain what influenced the *Führer's* decision. In the meantime, the Allies were making their escape across the channel, rescued by one of the most oddly assorted flotillas in history. By the time Hitler realized what was happening and started his tanks moving again on May 26, the British had organized a strong defense ring of heavy artillery. By June 4, when resistance ended, the last of the English and most of the French were gone; only 40,000 French still held out.

Field Marshal (then General) von Rundstedt (left) commanded the Army group attacking Dunkirk. Afterward, he blamed Hitler's ignorance of the situation for the order stopping his tanks outside Dunkirk. However, there are those who claim that Rundstedt himself argued for the halt at the time. At top right, British soldiers on the beach fire at Nazi planes with their rifles. And at right, the long lines of men, still maintaining perfect discipline under enemy attack, wind out toward the water to meet the rescuing boats.

"By the time we had fifty on deck, I could feel her getting distinctly tender..."

Commander C. H. Lightoller, R.N.R.

The fantastic armada that crossed the Channel to rescue the men trapped at Dunkirk was made up of more than a thousand ships of every shape and size, manned by every variety of British seaman. Fishermen, yachtsmen, taxicab drivers, retired Navy men, they plowed back and forth for nine days under a storm of German bombs and shells. When it was all over, they were heroes, and full of stories. The following is an account given by one of the most distinguished gentlemen of their number. It is from Dunkirk, *the book on the battle and rescue by A. D. Divine.*

Half an hour after they had left Ramsgate the yacht *Sundowner* began her crossing. *Sundowner* belonged to Commander C. H. Lightoller, D.S.C., R.N.R. (Retd.), who, as senior surviving officer of the *Titanic*, had been the principal witness at the inquiry into that disaster. She was a biggish craft, approximately 60 feet with a speed of 10 knots, and with the assistance of his son and a Sea Scout, Commander Lightoller had taken her out of Cubitt's Yacht Basin at Chiswick on May 31st and had dropped down the river to Southend as part of a big convoy of forty boats which had mustered at Westminster. At dawn on June 1st he left Southend with five others and, reaching Ramsgate, was instructed in the casual manner of those days to 'proceed to Dunkirk for further orders'. . . . At 10 o'clock he left by the route laid down. His account of the voyage is clear and detailed.

'Half-way across we avoided a floating mine by a narrow margin, but having no firearms of any description—not even a tin hat—we had to leave its destruction to someone better equipped. A few minutes later we had our first introduction to enemy aircraft, three fighters flying high. Before they could be offensive, a British destroyer—*Worcester*, I think—overhauled us and drove them off. At 2.25 p.m. we sighted and closed the 25-foot motorcruiser *Westerly*; broken down and badly on fire. As the crew of two (plus three naval ratings she had picked up in Dunkirk) wished to abandon ship—and quickly—I went alongside and took them aboard, giving them the additional pleasure of again facing the hell they had only just left.

'We made the fairway buoy to the Roads shortly after the sinking of a French transport with severe loss of life. Steaming slowly through the wreckage we entered the Roads. For some time now we had been subject to sporadic bombing and machine-gun fire but as the *Sundowner* is exceptionally and extremely quick on the helm, by waiting till the last moment and putting the helm hard over—my son at the wheel—we easily avoided every attack. . . .

'It had been my intention to go right on to the beaches, where my second son, Second Lieutenant R. T. Lightoller, had been evacuated some forty-eight hours previously; but those of the *Westerly* informed me that the troops were all away, so I headed up for Dunkirk piers. By now dive-bombers seemed to be eternally dropping out of the cloud of enemy aircraft overhead. Within half a mile of the pierheads a two-funnelled grey painted transport had overhauled and was just passing us to port when two salvoes were dropped in quick succession right along her port side. For a few moments she was hid in smoke and I certainly thought they had got her. Then she reappeared still gaily heading for the piers and entered just ahead of us.

'The difficulty of taking troops on

board from the quay high above us was obvious, so I went alongside a destroyer (*Worcester* again, I think) where they were already embarking. I got hold of her captain and told him I could take about a hundred (though the most I had ever had on board was twenty-one). He, after consultation with the military C.O., told me to carry on and get the troops aboard. I may say here that before leaving Cubitt's Yacht Basin, we had worked all night stripping her down of everything movable, masts included, that would tend to lighten her and make for more room.

'My son, as previously arranged, was to pack the men in and use every available inch of space—which I'll say he carried out to some purpose. On deck I detailed a naval rating to tally the troops aboard. At fifty I called below, "How are you getting on?" getting the cheery reply, "Oh, plenty of room yet." At seventy-five my son admitted they were getting pretty tight—all equipment and arms being left on deck.

'I now started to pack them on deck, having passed word below for every man to lie down and keep down; the same applied on deck. By the time we had fifty on deck, I could feel her getting distinctly tender, so took no more. Actually we had exactly 130 on board. . . .

'During the whole embarkation we had quite a lot of attention from enemy planes, but derived an amazing degree of comfort from the fact that the *Worcester*'s A.A. guns kept up an everlasting bark overhead.

'Casting off and backing out we entered the Roads again, there it was continuous and unmitigated hell. The troops were just splendid and of their own initiative detailed look-outs ahead, astern, and abeam for inquisitive planes as my attention was pretty wholly occupied watching the steering and passing

orders to Roger at the wheel. Any time an aircraft seemed inclined to try its hand on us, one of the look-outs would just call quietly, "Look out for this bloke, skipper," at the same time pointing. One bomber that had been particularly offensive, itself came under the notice of one of our fighters and suddenly plunged vertically into the sea just about fifty yards astern of us. It was the only time any man ever raised his voice above a conversational tone, but as that big black bomber hit the water they raised an echoing cheer.

'My youngest son, Pilot Officer H. B. Lightoller (lost at the outbreak of war in the first raid on Wilhelmshaven) flew a Blenheim and had at different times given me a whole lot of useful information about attack, defence and evasive tactics (at which he was apparently particularly good) and I attribute, in a great measure, our success in getting across without a single casualty to his unwitting help.

'On one occasion an enemy machine came up astern at about 100 feet with the obvious intention of raking our decks. He was coming down in a gliding dive and I knew that he must elevate some 10 to 15 degrees before his guns would bear. Telling my son "Stand by", I waited till as near as I could judge, he was just on the point of pulling up and then "Hard a-port". (She turns 180 degrees in exactly her own length.) This threw his aim completely off. He banked and tried again. Then "Hard a-starboard", with the same result. After a third attempt he gave it up in disgust. Had I had a machine-gun of any sort, he was a sitter—in fact there were at least three that I am confident we could have accounted for during the trip.

'Not the least of our difficulties was contending with the wash of fast craft, such as destroyers and

transports. In every instance I had to stop completely, take the way off the ship and head the heavy wash. The M.C. being where it was, to have taken one of these seas on either the quarter or beam would have at once put paid to our otherwise successful cruise. The effect of the consequent plunging on the troops below, in a stinking atmosphere with all ports and skylights closed, can well be imagined. They were literally packed like the proverbial sardines, even one in the bath and another on the W.C., so that all the poor devils could do was sit and be sick. Added were the remnants of bully beef and biscuits. So that after discharging our cargo in Ramsgate at 10 p.m., there lay before the three of us a nice clearing-up job.

'Arriving off the harbour I was at first told to "lie off". But when I informed them that I had 130 on board, permission was at once given to "come in" (I don't think the authorities believed for a minute that I had 130), and I put her alongside a trawler lying at the quay. Whilst entering, the men started to get to their feet and she promptly went over to a terrific angle. I got them down again in time and told those below to remain below and lying down till I gave the word. The impression ashore was that the fifty-odd lying on deck plus the mass of equipment was my full load.

'After I had got rid of those on deck I gave the order "Come up from below", and the look on the official face was amusing to behold as troops vomited up through the forward companionway, the after companionway, and the doors either side of the wheelhouse. As a stoker P.O., helping them over the bulwarks, said, "God's truth, mate! Where did you put them?" He might well ask. . . .'

General Weygand (standing at the left) inspects the trenches of his Somme-Aisne defense system. It delayed the Germans only briefly.

The Battle and Debacle of France

Even while the Battle of Dunkirk was being fought, German forces were regrouping for the final Battle of France to shatter the rest of the French Army. But the French were doomed even before the assault began. Their best divisions had been lost in Belgium; those that remained were mainly second-rate. The French Air Force had been almost wiped out, and the R.A.F. could give little help because its bases were too far away. General Maxime Weygand, then 72 years old, had been appointed to supreme Army command in this desperate situation, to replace the fired General Gamelin. With 66 divisions available to him, he established a line on the Somme and Aisne rivers, but against these hastily prepared defenses the Germans struck like a sledge hammer on June 5 with 120 divisions, and another 23 in reserve. The Weygand Line was quickly pierced, then crumbled. The collapse was hastened by the inert fighting spirit of the defeatist, politics-ridden French Army. General Weygand and old Marshal Henri Philippe Pétain, now vice-premier, had both been with France's Army in the days of its greatness but no longer had much stomach for fighting. On June 14, Paris, declared an open city, was occupied. Although some French units continued to fight tenaciously, in most cases the battle had become a rout. At last, on June 17, Pétain, who had become premier the day before, asked for an armistice.

A study in expressions: the weary face of this captured French soldier (at right) reflects all of the bitterness and the humiliation of defeat. His German guard shows the strain of hard campaigning, but he is plainly much happier about the entire situation.

"One fact the enemy grasped and exploited— that men fill small space in the earth's immensity"

PHOTO E.C.A.

Antoine de Saint-Exupéry

As the French Army fell back in full retreat during the last weeks of May, Antoine de Saint-Exupéry, the celebrated French writer and pilot, was flying reconnaissance missions over the rapidly advancing German lines. There were only fifty reconnaissance crews left in the entire French Army; and in three weeks time, of the twenty-three crews in Exupéry's own unit, seventeen were knocked out of the sky. Still, he wrote later in Flight to Arras, *none of them gave much thought to the risk or danger. It was a time when everything seemed an absurdity to them, including death.*

. . . Burning is a great word when you look down from thirty-three thousand feet; for over the villages and the forests there is nothing to be seen but a pall of motionless smoke, a sort of ghastly whitish jelly. Below it the fires are at work like a secret digestion. At thirty-three thousand feet time slows down, for there is no movement here. There are no crackling flames, no crashing beams, no spirals of black smoke. There is only that grayish milk curdled in the amber air. Will that forest recover? Will that village recover? Seen from this height, France is being undermined by the secret gnawing of bacteria.

About this, too, there is much to be said. "We shall not hesitate to sacrifice our villages." I have heard these words spoken. And it was necessary to speak them. When a war is on, a village ceases to be a cluster of traditions. The enemy who hold it have turned it into a nest of rats. Things no longer mean the same. Here are trees three hundred years old that shade the home of your family. But they obstruct the field of fire of a twenty-two-year-old lieutenant. Wherefore he sends up a squad of fifteen men to annihilate the work of time. In ten minutes he destroys three hundred years of patience and sunlight, three hundred years of the religion of the home and of betrothals in the shadows round the grounds. You say to him, "My trees!" but he does not hear you. He is right. He is fighting a war.

But how many villages have we seen burnt down only that war may be made to look like war? Burnt down exactly as trees are cut down, crews flung into the holocaust, infantry sent against tanks, merely to make war look like war. Small wonder that an unutterable disquiet hangs over the land. For nothing does any good.

One fact the enemy grasped and exploited—that men fill small space in the earth's immensity. A continuous wall of men along our front would require a hundred million soldiers. Necessarily, there were always gaps between the French units. In theory, these gaps are cancelled by the mobility of the units. Not, however, in the theory of the armored division, for which an almost unmotorized army is as good as unmanœuvrable. The gaps are real gaps. Whence this simple tactical rule: "An armored division should move against the enemy like water. It should bear lightly against the enemy's wall of defence and advance only at the point where it meets with no resistance." The tanks operate by this rule, bear against the wall, and never fail to break through. They move as they please for want of French tanks to set against them; and though the damage they do is superficial,—capture of unit Staffs, cutting of telephone cables, burning of villages,—the consequences of their raids are irreparable. In every region through which they make their lightning sweep, a French army, even though it seems to be virtually intact, has ceased to be an army. It has been transformed into clotted segments. It has, so to say, coagulated. . . .

The highways too were part of our experience. We were pilots, and there were days when in a single morning our sortie took us over Alsace, Belgium, Holland, and the sea itself. But our problems were most often of the north of France, and our horizon was very often limited to the dimensions of a traffic tangle at a crossroads. Thus, only three days earlier, I had seen the village in which we were billeted go to pieces. I do not expect ever to be free of that clinging, viscous memory.

It was six in the morning, and Dutertre and I, coming out of our billet, found ourselves in the midst of chaos. All the stables, all the sheds, all the barns and garages had vomited into the narrow streets a most extraordinary collection of contrivances. There were new motorcars, and there were ancient farm carts that for half a century had stood untouched under layers of dust. There were hay wains and lorries, carryalls and tumbrils. Had we seen a mail-coach in this maze it would not have astonished us. Every box on wheels had been dug up and was now laden with the treasures of the home. From door to vehicle, wrapped in bedsheets sagging with hernias, the treasures were being piled in.

Together, these treasures had made up that greater treasure—a home. By itself, each was valueless; yet they were the objects of a private religion, a family's worship. Each filling its place, they had been made indispensable by habit and beautiful by memory, had been lent price by the sort of fatherland which, together, they constituted. But those who owned them thought each precious in itself and for itself. These treasures had been wrenched from their fireside, their table, their wall; and now that they were heaped up in disorder, they showed themselves to be the worn and torn stock of a junk-shop that they were. Fling sacred relics into a heap, and they can turn your stomach.

"What's going on here? Are you mad?"

The café owner's wife shrugged her shoulders.

"We're evacuating."

"But why, in God's name!"

"Nobody knows. Mayor's orders."

She was too busy to talk, and vanished up her staircase. Dutertre and I stood in the doorway and looked on. Every motorcar, every lorry, every cart and charabanc was piled high with children, mattresses, kitchen utensils.

Of all these objects the most pitiful were the old motorcars. A horse standing upright in the shafts of a farm-cart gives off a sensation of solidity. A horse does not call for spare parts. A farm-cart can be put into shape with three nails. But all these vestiges of the mechanical age! This assemblage of pistons, valves, magnetos, and gear-wheels! How long would it run before it broke down?

"Please, Captain. Could you give me a hand?"

"Of course. What is it?"

"I want to get my car out of the garage."

I looked at the woman in amazement.

"Are you sure you know how to drive?"

"Oh, it will be all right. The road is so jammed, it won't be hard."

There was herself, and her sister-in-law, and their children—seven children in all.

That road easy to drive? A road over which you made two or ten miles a day, stopping dead every two hundred yards? Braking, stopping, shifting gears, changing from low to second and back again every fifty yards in the confusion of an inextricable jam. Easy driving? The woman would break down before she had gone half a mile! And gas! And oil! And water, which she was sure to forget! . . .

"Why don't you stay home?"

"God knows, we'd rather stay."

"Then why do you leave?"

"They said we had to."

"Who said so?"

"The mayor."

Always the mayor.

"Of course we'd all rather stay home.". . .

"Look here, why don't you unload and put that stuff back into your house. At least you'll have your pump-water to drink."

"Of course that would be the best thing."

"But you are free to do it. Why don't you?"

Dutertre and I are winning. A cluster of villagers has collected round us. They listen to us. They nod their heads approvingly.

"He's right, he is, the captain."

Others come to our support. A roadmender, converted, is hotter about it than I am.

"Always said so. Get out on that road and there's nothing but asphalt to eat."

They argue. They agree. They will stay. Some go off to preach to others. And they come back discouraged.

"Won't do. Have to go."

"Why?"

"Baker's already left. Who will bake our bread?"

The village has already broken down. At one point or another it has burst; and through that hole its contents are running out. Hopeless. . . .

Very few photographs were made of the French Army during the Battle of France showing it in any attitudes other than defeat and retreat. This picture is one of the exceptions: it is of some long-forgotten counter-attack by a small unit of poilus. It was found on the body of a German soldier killed in battle in 1944; without much doubt he was one of those who had stopped the French attack, and he had carried the picture throughout the four years since.

Coup de Grâce to France

France was disintegrating by the time Marshal Pétain asked for an armistice on June 17. The Government had fled from Paris to Tours to Bordeaux; Paris had been occupied on June 14. The French Army was falling apart. Throngs of refugees, heading south in panic to escape the onrushing Germans, were harassed by Nazi flyers who wantonly strafed and bombed the crowded roads. Winston Churchill had become Prime Minister the day the blitzkrieg hit the Low Countries and had dealt with nothing but disaster since; on June 14 he decided that the jig was up for France and gave orders to begin removing the remaining British troops. In this atmosphere of disaster, Hitler gave his harsh terms on June 21 at his malevolently staged meeting at Compiègne, precisely where Germany had surrendered in 1918. On June 24 a Franco-Italian armistice was signed, and the next day the scattered fighting ended, with German forces in most of France. Mussolini gained little from his jackal's role. He had waited until June 10, when France was already reeling, to declare war, but even with thirty-six divisions he could make no headway against six defending French divisions. Hitler would let him occupy only the few hundred yards his troops had overrun. Germany, on the other hand, occupied more than half the country. In the other half, with its capital at Vichy, Marshal Pétain assumed dictatorial powers in July; the aged Marshal and the collaborationist crew around him governed always in a manner calculated to satisfy the Germans. France was beaten and spiritless. But some Frenchmen still had the heart to fight on, and these General Charles de Gaulle began rallying under his Free French banner.

ABOVE: EUROPEAN PICTURE SERVICE; BELOW: UPI

BELOW: CAPTURED GERMAN RECORDS, U.S. ARMY

Nazi troops occupying Paris (left) pass the Arc de Triomphe. At top right, Hitler stamps his foot in exultation at his headquarters at Brûly-de-Pesche in Belgium on being told that Marshal Pétain had asked for an armistice. By clever splicing of the film of the event, Hitler was made to repeat his stamp several times in rapid succession so that it appeared to be a jerky dance. Millions of Americans saw the synthetic "jig," which was included in a Why We Fight *series shown across the nation. At middle right is one of the classic photos of the fall of France. The man is in Marseilles; the cause of his emotion is a parade of historic French battle flags being taken across the Mediterranean to forestall capture. At bottom right, Hitler and Pétain meet in late October, 1940. The picture was found in Ribbentrop's personal photograph album. Ribbentrop, Hitler's Foreign Minister, stands in the center.*

England Alone

Remember him, for he saved all of you: pudgy and not very large but somehow massive and indomitable; baby-faced, with snub nose, square chin, rheumy eyes on occasion given to tears; a thwarted actor's taste for clothes that would have looked ridiculous on a less splendid man. He wore the quaintest hats of anyone: tinted square bowlers; great flat sombreros squashed down on his head; naval officer's caps rendered just slightly comic by the huge cigar protruding beneath the peak. On grave and critical occasions he sported highly practical Teddy-bear suits few grown men would dare to wear in public. He fancied oil painting, at which he was good, writing, at which he was excellent, and oratory, at which he was magnificent. His habits were somewhat owlish (a bird he faintly resembled), and he stayed up late at night, often working mornings in bed with a lap tray for his desk. (Once, after the war, when I called on him at 11:00 A.M., he inquired whether I wished a drink, ordered me a whiskey and soda, then, reaching for the empty glass beside him, told his manservant: "And bring me another.")

This was the man, blooded at Omdurman and Cuba, among the Pathans and the Boers, long before most of those he led were even born, who guided Britain to victory in World War II—and, one might add, who was the guiding spirit for the whole Free World. For had Britain succumbed, as it had every logical reason to do in 1940, probably no successful coalition could have formed.

Winston Churchill once complained that democracy is the worst system of government—except for all the others. And it was democracy, with its curious and lethargic workings, that, allied with its Russian antithesis, produced Hitler's defeat. One may argue that the *Führer's* strategic errors caused his ultimate downfall: that he allowed Britain's Army to escape him at Dunkirk; that he misjudged Germany's strength in attacking Russia; that he overextended himself both at El Alamein and Stalingrad. But it was not in the end the negative factor of Nazi miscalculation but the positive factor of democratic vigor that brought the German Götterdämmerung. This democratic vigor, freely voiced in a moment of bleak despair, produced Churchill as Prime Minister and a government resolved to win the war.

Even before France collapsed, an irate House of Commons had summoned the irresolute and gullible Neville Chamberlain to defend the conduct of the Norwegian debacle. It was no longer a party matter; the nation's life was evidently at stake. Clement Attlee, the Labor leader, said: "We cannot afford to leave our destinies in the hands of failures." Arthur Greenwood added: "Wars are not won by masterly withdrawals." The retired Fleet Admiral, Sir Roger Keyes, appearing in full uniform, thundered that the Norwegian disaster was "a shocking story of ineptitude which I assure the House ought never to have happened." And spry little Leopold Amery, a staunch Conservative, told the Government, in Cromwell's famous words: "You have sat too long here for any good you have been doing. Depart, I say, and let us have done with you. In the name of God, go!"

R.A.F. pilots sprint to man their Hurricanes to repel enemy aircraft.

Churchill had loyally served Chamberlain as First Lord of the Admiralty and accepted ministerial responsibility for his share of the Norway mess. But even old Lloyd George, arising as it were from the grave of an earlier Great War, urged that "Mr. Churchill will not allow himself to be converted into an air-raid shelter to keep the splinters from hitting his colleagues." Chamberlain won an initial vote of confidence, but two days later, on May 10, as the Nazis launched their attack on the Low Countries, he resigned and designated Churchill to succeed him. Churchill named a national coalition government of all three parties and set his jaw in the bulldog expression that was to become so famous.

Although Hitler did not know it at the time, this political event was the single greatest disaster he would experience. Without Churchill's skill and determination, it is doubtful that Britain could or would have carried on the fight long enough for the German invasion of the Soviet Union and the Japanese bombing of Pearl Harbor to take effect. When Russia and the United States went to war, there was still a fortified island position bristling off the shores of occupied Europe and the remnants of a global empire bounded by the pulsing power of the sea.

This was a power with which Britain's new leader was entirely familiar. In his correspondence with Roosevelt he called himself "Former Naval Person." He had headed the Admiralty in World War I and in the early days of World War II. In a long life of adventuring, he had seen how ships, properly deployed, could nourish beleaguered peoples, outflank armies, and frustrate the plans of even the most brilliant and successful generals. With a Royal Navy virtually intact; with a friendly United States led by another naval enthusiast; with the wealth and geographical facilities of empire; with the knowledge that the British people were thoroughly behind him; and with the suspicion that sulking Europe might eventually gnaw at its conqueror's vitals, Churchill took over, never doubting that he would succeed.

Britain's military preparedness at the war's start was sadly lacking, but the quantitative deficiency was made up for, in part, by a qualitative genius. A committee at the Air Ministry, under the scientist-educator Sir Henry Tizard, acted as broker to float new scientific issues, accelerating research and development. Relying on studies by the brilliant inventor Sir Robert Watson-Watt, Tizard rushed through a radar system far superior to similar German devices. The Nazis soon found their U-boats being bombed at night when they surfaced to recharge batteries, and their bombers being attacked in the darkness long before they had approached their targets. While building up the protection of the home islands and strengthening their ties with bastions around the world, Churchill bottled up the French fleet and then began to nibble at boastful Italy. He refused to heed his admirals who counseled that Britain should abandon the east Mediterranean to Mussolini and instead slowly took the offensive there. He pushed convoys through to embattled Malta and across the hostile narrows on to Egypt.

At home, the British imagination had been busy picturing the horrors of aerial assault. *Ordeal*, a novel by Nevil Shute, published in 1939, depicted nerve-wracking days and nights of steady bombing, when civilians would be forced to live in back-yard dugouts, with a shortage of food, polluted water, flooded sewers, and curtailed electricity and gas. Britain made ready for such a nightmare. A million and a half women and children were evacuated from the cities; blackouts were enforced; most people carried gas masks; hospitals were made ready for hundreds of anticipated victims.

After the fall of France there was a threat of immediate invasion. On July 16, the *Führer* ordered secret preparations for Operation Sea Lion, a landing on England's southern coast. Three days later, in an effort to avoid an amphibious campaign, which his generals warned against, Hitler publicly offered Churchill peace in exchange for recognition of Nazi domination of western Europe and a return of Germany's former colonies. The offer was ignored. After a heavy *Luftwaffe* raid on Channel convoys and southern British ports, it became clear that a new kind of battle, a purely aerial assault, had been launched against the resolute British.

The numerical odds were most adverse. Churchill's R.A.F. had but 704 serviceable aircraft, 620 of which were taut little Hurricane and Spitfire fighters. The Germans possessed 1,392 bombers and 1,290 fighters deployed for immediate action. All through July and August they intensified their attacks on airfields and radar stations along the vulnerable south and east coasts. On August 15, a thousand German planes took part in various actions. Nine days later, Göring decided that 50 per cent of British Fighter Command had been destroyed, and he began to throw the *Luftwaffe* against London itself. With squadrons of up to forty bombers each, escorted by more than one hundred fighters, he hoped to smash the huge imperial center. And indeed, he nearly succeeded. When the *Luftwaffe* shifted to night bombing tactics on September 7, almost one fourth of the R.A.F.'s pilots had been lost.

This was a brave and extraordinary period in English history. All along the coast, metallic loudspeakers hollered: "Squadron. Red Section. Scramble"; and the little eagles climbed into the sky, aimed by the radar beams of

Tizard and Watson-Watt. "This wicked man," said Churchill, ". . . this monstrous product of former wrongs and shame, has now resolved to break our famous island race by a process of indiscriminate slaughter and destruction." But the British responded to the challenge, and the *Luftwaffe* paid heavily. The R.A.F. lost 915 fighters during the 1940 Battle of Britain, but they claimed to have shot down 2,698 *Luftwaffe* planes.

By September 17, Hitler acknowledged the indefinite postponement of Sea Lion. Never, as Churchill was to say, had so many owed so much to so few—youngsters like Richard Hillary: "Then I was pulling out, so hard that I could feel my eyes dropping through my neck. Coming around in a slow climbing turn, I saw that we had broken them up"; or like Johnnie Johnson: ". . . the wicked tracer sparkles and flashes over the top of your own cockpit and you break into a tight turn. . . . You black out! And you ease the turn to recover in a grey, unreal world of spinning horizons. . . . You have lost too much height and your opponent has gone—disappeared."

When Hitler's aerial campaign failed to crush R.A.F. defenses, he changed it into a punitive assault on London, designed to break the spirit of the British people. The British turned from the Battle of Britain to what they dubbed "the Blitz," a terrifying, thunderous, brutal assault primarily on civilians. On August 24, 1940, the first German bombs struck London, and Churchill promptly ordered a retaliation raid on Berlin. Hitler furiously announced: "If they attack our cities, we will simply rub out theirs." And he tried. There was vast destruction along the blazing Thames, but neither the British Government nor the economic machinery of London was paralyzed. The population managed courageously to continue its daily functions while in its spare time beating out flames and minimizing destruction. "Disposal Squads" marked off and defused delayed-action bombs. Air raid wardens sanded or hosed incendiary blazes among toppling buildings from Coventry to Bristol.

The summer of 1940 was a historic moment for Europe. The abandonment of Operation Sea Lion, leaving an undefeated German Army stranded on the Channel beaches, marked the beginning of Hitler's defeat. The example and the success of Churchill served as a glowing reminder to occupied European peoples that, as in the days of Napoleon, a dictatorial land power need not succeed in ultimately triumphing over an intact sea power. And in secret, underground fashion, a susurrous continental resistance to the Nazis started.

To help this, the British in 1940 established an organization known as the Special Operations Executive. It began to organize subversion and sabotage in German-occupied lands, aided by skillful propaganda broadcast by the B.B.C. with its clever Morse code signal, V—for Victory. Slowly but remorselessly, in Poland, France, Belgium, Holland, and Norway, a collection of agents and adventurers, mostly amateur, threw back into the teeth of the German General Staff the cautionary words of the great Prussian military theorist, General Karl von Clausewitz: "Armed civilians cannot and should not be employed against the main force of the enemy, or even against sizable units. They should not try to crack the core, but only nibble along the surface and on the edges." And as another reminder of Napoleonic days, the first of Lord Louis Mountbatten's famous Combined Operations and Commando units began to experiment with the tactics and mechanics of small amphibious assaults.

During this summer of Hitler's first frustration, Stalin decided to collect what was left on the bill for his German pact. In June he successively completed the occupation of the three little Baltic states, Lithuania, Latvia, and Estonia, and five days after notifying Germany of his intention, he seized Bessarabia from Rumania. Sir Stafford Cripps, Churchill's new ambassador to Moscow, sought to convince the master of the Kremlin that Hitler was a danger "to the Soviet Union as well as England." He urged that the two countries should "agree on a common policy of self-protection," and he secretly offered a bribe—the promise to recognize Russia's claims in the Dardanelles and to give her a leading role in the Balkans. But Stalin turned a deaf ear.

It soon became evident that Germany was also looking to that part of eastern Europe it had not already conquered, where Russia was inching forward and where Italy, having entered the war without Hitler's permission and somewhat to his dismay, had staked its own claim. On August 30, 1940, Ribbentrop and Ciano signed an agreement in Vienna awarding 40 per cent of Rumania's Transylvania province to Hungary and the southern part of Rumanian Dobruja to Bulgaria. I accompanied the ragtag Hungarian army into Rumania as far as Cluj, where Admiral Miklós Horthy, Hungary's chief of state, balanced uneasily on a white circus horse at the head of a victory parade. I then joined the noisy Bulgarian troops as they poured into Rumania from the south, winding up in the hot streets of Balchik, where gypsy children begged the conquerors for handouts. King Carol, the dissolute Rumanian monarch, loaded a train with his mistress, his closest friends and courtiers, and all the valuables he could pack, and fled.

On October 28, again without asking Hitler's advice, Mussolini attacked Greece from Albania, expecting a swift and easy victory. But the courageous Greeks forgot their political differences and astonished the world by beating back the Italians and invading Albania themselves. I was also with that army, whose gallantry and conceit were formidable. Rickety trucks bounced to the front over impossible roads, bearing Hellenic fishermen and farmers. They rode to death and glory with garlands over their ears and their rifle muzzles stuffed with flowers, shouting "On to Rome." Antiquated mountain artillery was trundled along ridge combs to shell the Fascists in the valleys. Evzone guard patrols attacked with their knives and teeth, biting the scared little Italian infantrymen. I visited a forward prisoner's cage that included dozens of frightened Fascists with tooth wounds in their shabbily bandaged necks. The *Duce's* highly touted air force, furthermore, proved inaccurate and timid and was soon largely offset by a handful of British planes rushed to Greece from the Middle East. Churchill sent Sir Anthony Eden and General Sir John Dill to Athens to investigate the possibility of opening a land front against the Axis in Europe. He cautioned them: "Do not consider yourselves obligated to a Greek enterprise if in your hearts you feel it will only be another Norwegian fiasco. If no good plan can be made please say so." I talked with Eden at length; he was sufficiently impressed by the chances to take the gamble. Early in 1941, Britain began to move troops from Egypt into Greece.

In the long run, this decision was to have a profound and helpful strategic effect on the war, even though the British expeditionary force was smashed successively in Greece and Crete. Hitler had already reached the basic conclusion that since he could not use his Army directly against England, he would strike at Russia. As an initial step, he had begun moving divisions eastward from France into Poland and had signed a "transit agreement" allowing him to send troops into Finland, although that country had been cynically allotted to the Soviet sphere. The *Führer* then sent Rumania what was called a military mission. I pointed out in dispatches that this "mission" was headed by the same general who had led the Nazi military "mission" that had destroyed Rotterdam earlier that year, and that it comprised many regiments. Those days in Bucharest, it was hard to shove one's way to the bar and order a drink among all those fat-necked, stodgy Nazis talking openly about the coming war with Russia.

The Rumanian "mission" was followed by an accord permitting Germany to send troops into Bulgaria. This surrounding pressure understandably frightened the Yugoslavs. Their cultivated and gentlemanly regent, Prince Paul, sought to stave off trouble by permitting his Government to sign an accord with Hitler. But the example of Greece and exaggerated rumors of British

strength there, rumors ably guided by British intelligence agents, encouraged the Yugoslav Royal Guard and Air Force to revolt. On March 27, 1941, they ousted Paul and his regime. General Dušan Simović was installed as dictator, and Guards officers forged the boy King Peter's name to a declaration assuming power. This was read on the radio amidst wide rejoicing by the warlike Serbs. When Yugoslavia collapsed a month later, the Air Force general who arranged the coup escaped to Cairo, where he was given two-star rank in the British forces, although he did not speak English.

Hitler was infuriated at this insult to his prestige. He ordered a swift assault on Yugoslavia and embattled Greece. The invasion began early in the morning of April 6, 1941. Throughout the preceding night, under a full moon, I had watched peasant boys march into the old fortress at the tip of Belgrade, where the Danube and Sava rivers meet, pick up their uniforms and guns, and trundle out behind oxcarts, singing: "Oh my love, the German is again at our frontiers and there again he will meet the Serbian bayonet." Within hours the capital was shattered by the *Luftwaffe*. German tanks and motorized infantry rolled in, aided by the Hungarians and Bulgarians, who had been bought by the Vienna award; and the Italians launched their own offensive from Albania.

Yugoslavia was riddled with fifth-column movements among its Croatian, Albanian, and German *Volksdeutsch* minorities. Defections among the non-Serbs were manifold, and the Yugoslav armies were torn apart before they had even been deployed. The Germans captured Skoplje two hours after its commander assured me it was safe and poured across the undefended Monastir Gap into Greece. From Bulgaria they hammered southward against Greek pillbox positions in Thrace. The colonel commanding one of these, Fort Rupel, summoned his garrison and told them: "We will hold them with our teeth." When the Germans finally broke in, they found, written with chalk on a wall above the dead: "At Thermopylae, the three hundred were killed. Here the eighty will fall defending their country."

Greece, in an agony of despair and bitter confusion, collapsed. The Government fled to Cairo. The British defended themselves stubbornly, especially—and appropriately—in the area of Thermopylae, and managed to salvage a considerable part of their expeditionary force. But on April 17, Yugoslavia capitulated, and six days later, Greece did the same.

Initially, this seemed but another dreadful Nazi victory. The British lost 15,000 casualties against 5,300 for Germany. The Germans captured 200,000 Greek and 300,000 Yugoslav prisoners. They partitioned Yugoslavia, taking some bits and giving pieces to Hungary, Italy, and Bulgaria, while establishing puppet states in Croatia and Serbia. They allowed Mussolini, in theory, to take over Greece, after awarding a portion to the Bulgars.

And on May 20, 1941, history's first fully air-borne invasion was launched against Crete with remarkable efficiency. The combined British, Commonwealth, and Greek forces on Crete made the Germans pay a heavy price; yet by the end of the month, the legendary island was in German hands. All the Mediterranean's northern shore and central bastions were under Axis control, save for Gibraltar and beleaguered Malta, which at one time was defended principally by three old Gladiator biplanes called "Faith," "Hope" and "Charity." The Balkans had been lost; Turkey was trembling; and there were rumors of an impending invasion of Cyprus and the Middle Eastern Arab states.

Nevertheless, Hitler paid dearly for this improvised and impressive Balkan victory. It has been argued by his own generals that the time lost in conquering Greece and Yugoslavia delayed by two or three critical weeks the eventual assault on Russia. As a consequence, despite the mauling they suffered in June and early July, the Russians were able to check the *Wehrmacht* at Smolensk, to hold them at Moscow, and then to drive them backward into the most awful winter Russia had known for years. Had Hitler not run up a swastika on the Acropolis, he might have succeeded in draping it upon the Kremlin.

At approximately this point, a curious incident occurred. Forty-seven-year-old Rudolph Hess, the number three man in the Nazi hierarchy, flew secretly to England in an unarmed plane that he had persuaded the aircraft designer Willi Messerschmitt to lend him. Hess was seeking out the Duke of Hamilton, whom he had met at the Berlin Olympic Games in 1936. He hoped the Duke would help him get in touch with British leaders so that he could propose conclusion of a peace that would guarantee the integrity of Britain's Empire and leave Hitler free to attack Russia, thereby bringing about the end of bolshevism. Hess broke his ankle while parachuting to Scotland, was captured by a farmer with a pitchfork, and then was locked up as a prisoner of war. Hitler was baffled and furious. He denounced Hess as being in "a state of halucination," which was perhaps not wholly inaccurate. Hess was known to have been ill and psychologically disturbed. British propaganda made the most of this unexpected opportunity to create the impression of confusion in the highest Nazi ranks. The arrival of this haunted-looking enemy at a moment of bleak despair was a heaven-sent gift to England.

None of these dramatic events, including a new Axis offensive in North Africa and the failure of German efforts to hold Syria with Vichy French collaboration and to seize Iraq in a conspiracy, served to deflect Hitler from his main preoccupation, the forthcoming Russian campaign. Once he realized that his enormous Army, perched on the Channel, was doomed to an indefinite period of idleness, he decided to march it eastward against Stalin.

This, after Dunkirk and the failure to invade Britain immediately, was Hitler's second major strategic error. The Stalingrad campaign and the failure to bolster Rommel in North Africa came later.

But Hitler's decision to invade Russia was prompted by more than military stalemate in the west. Not only did he hate both bolshevism and the Slavs; in July, 1940, he summed up his credo: "Russia is the factor by which England sets the greatest store. . . . If Russia is beaten, England's last hope is gone. Germany is then master of Europe and the Balkans. . . . Decision: As a result of this argument, Russia must be dealt with. Spring 1941."

On July 29, 1940, General (later Field Marshal) Alfred Gustav Jodl, Chief of Staff of the Armed Forces High Command, informed a select group of *Wehrmacht* planners of the *Führer's* "expressed wishes" for an attack on Russia. On August 9, the first directive for an offensive was issued. Sunday morning, June 22, was set for the massive Soviet invasion—far later than Hitler's customarily prudent generals wished.

Because of the very immensity of the project—the building of the German Army to three hundred divisions, the concentration of vast forces from Finland across Poland to Rumania on the Black Sea—and because of inevitable indiscretions coming from such preparations, it was hardly a secret that a new assault was coming. Both London and Washington advised Stalin of the impending attack, but he refused to credit such warnings from the West, and he remained persuaded of the rocklike firmness of the Red Army.

On June 22, 1941, the greatest campaign of World War II began, and with it came the final and thunderous denouement of all those devious Russo-German dealings, started after World War I by Seeckt and Trotsky and continued well into World War II. Sir Stafford Cripps, a cold vegetarian teetotaller with the face of a seventeenth-century Puritan, was in London at the moment, believing his mission to Moscow had failed. Churchill called in his ambassador to help prepare a speech to the Russian people. The old Tory strode up and down, chewing a cigar. Cripps told me later he was startled to see that as the Prime Minister, who for so many years had berated the Soviets, began to dictate melodious phrases about suffering Russia, tears rolled down his cheeks.

Before the Storm

After the fall of France, Britain prepared for what would likely be a fight for survival. Beaches were manned against invasion; elderly men joined the home guards (below) and prepared to repel hostile intruders; many London children were sent to the country (left), beyond reach of the bombings that were certain to come. Great Britain was entirely alone that summer of 1940; even her dominions could not get help to her in time to do much good. And the army that would have to defend her shores had left its armor and artillery on the Dunkirk beaches. Hitler could not conceive that England would be foolish enough to go on fighting and waited into July for the British to sue for peace. At last he took the initiative in a Reichstag speech on July 19, saying he could see no reason why the war must go on. Within an hour a reply was coming back by radio from London. The British were not interested. However desperate their situation might appear, they did not want Hitler's kind of peace.

The Odds for England

The ominous shadow of Hermann Göring and his *Luftwaffe* hung over England while it awaited the attack. But though the situation of the British was grim, it was far from hopeless. England was still an island, and the Royal Navy, strong and battle-ready, controlled the surrounding waters. Hitler could not be sure that even his air power could protect an invasion attempt from a fate as melancholy as that of Spain's Great Armada. The battered British Army was recovering from Dunkirk and becoming less vulnerable each day; the United States had sent half a million rifles and quantities of machine guns and field artillery.

The big and immediate fear was the *Luftwaffe*. It outnumbered the Royal Air Force about three to one and was manned by veterans of the conquest of Europe, while the R.A.F. suffered a shortage of pilots. Yet in the fighting over France, British flyers had inflicted losses of two or more to one, and during Dunkirk they had successfully fought against odds as great as four or five to one. The outstanding advantage of the R.A.F. lay in its greater spirit and resolve, for the fighting qualities of the opposing aircraft were about equal; while R.A.F. planes were better armed and more maneuverable, those of the *Luftwaffe* were speedier and climbed faster. So, although Britain faced a bitter fight and cruel punishment, her foe would not escape unhurt.

A barrage balloon floats above London's Tower Bridge (left) in 1940. The balloons rode at about 7,500 feet and were anchored by steel cables that discouraged low-flying enemy planes. At right, Marshal Göring discusses plans with Lt. Gen. Ernst Udet during the air campaign against Britain. Udet, a leading ace of World War I, shot himself in 1941, when Hitler began blaming his generals for collapse of the Russian blitzkrieg.

Radar—Silent Skywatch

The respite granted Britain was brief. Just as soon as the *Luftwaffe* had shifted its squadrons to airfields in occupied France and Belgium nearer England, it began its attack; the first raids came on July 10, and the Battle of Britain was on. For a month the German Air Force probed and tested, attempting to draw out and destroy the defending R.A.F. fighters. Fighter Command refused to be lured into squandering its strength so early in the battle, but aggressive British pilots nevertheless shot down two German planes for every one of their own they lost. This R.A.F. advantage was achieved in no small part by the development of radar, the electronic watchdog that could detect enemy aircraft (or ships) at a distance—even through darkness, clouds, and fog—and determine their number, direction, and speed. By 1939, eighteen radar stations covered the island's east and southeast coasts. The Germans did not realize the importance of the radar detection system; after an August 12 strike destroyed one station and damaged five, Göring halted the attacks as wasted effort. It was the first of the tactical errors he was to make during the Battle of Britain.

A Messerschmitt flies above the Dover cliffs (above). Britain's radar stations (left), although primitive by modern standards, were effective. The inscribed bombs (below) were ostensibly for use by squadrons sent by Mussolini, which were returned to Italy after brief and inglorious service.

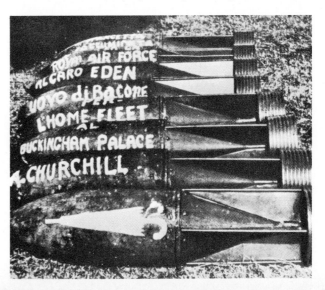

107

ABOVE: IMPERIAL WAR MUSEUM, LONDON; BELOW: AIR MINISTRY, LONDON

Operation Sea Lion

Hitler had no clear idea how to go about invading England, nor did the high commands of the armed services, although they ordinarily had plans ready for every possible contingency. Not until July 16 did Hitler issue orders for the preparation of an invasion, to be known as Operation Sea Lion; the date eventually was set for September 15, and the generals and admirals began making ready without enthusiasm. In fact, some officers claimed after the war that they had never really planned to invade because of the odds against them. Said Field Marshal von Rundstedt: "We looked upon the whole thing as a sort of game...." Only Göring was confident, certain his *Luftwaffe* could wreck the English fighter defenses in four days. On August 15 a huge air strike opened his Operation Eagle to drive the R.A.F. from the sky. The day was costly to the *Luftwaffe*; it lost seventy-five planes, the R.A.F. only thirty-four.

ERICH ANDRES, HAMBURG

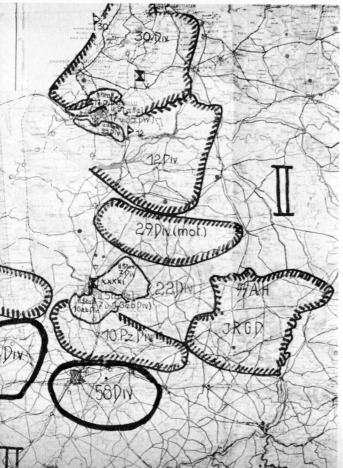

At left above, Göring (third from right, in profile) and his staff look across the Channel to England on July 1, 1940. The German map depicts the planned beachhead in England and the staging area with the units that were to comprise the three invasion waves. Above, German soldiers practice landing procedures; it was with such makeshift landing craft that the high command considered invasion.

Nazi fighter, photographed by motion picture camera in attacking British plane, is hit in tail; then pieces fly as flames spread.

New Breed of Warrior

The R.A.F. pilot was a new kind of fighting man, born of a new type of warfare. His appearance was studiedly unmilitary; the cloth crown of his officer's cap flopped loosely, and he often wore a neck scarf to thumb his nose at military conventions. He was little more than a boy but was doing more than a man's work, for R.A.F. pilots were in short supply, and he was often called on to go up and fight three, four, or even five times a day. He lived close to death and could never be sure the friend he chatted with at breakfast would be back to share experiences with over dinner. He was the man of whom Winston Churchill said, "Never in the field of human conflict was so much owed by so many to so few." R.A.F. pilots themselves pointedly ignored "Winnie" and his rolling oratory.

Reich Marshal Göring knew from the start that he would have to smash R.A.F. fighter defenses to conquer Britain, but it proved more difficult than he had foreseen. Then, as the battle went on, *Luftwaffe* pilots, overhearing the constant radio talk between R.A.F. pilots and the ground, came to realize that the British flyers were receiving some sort of guidance. So, beginning August 24, an average of a thousand planes a day were thrown against Fighter Command, damaging airfields and disrupting the intricate ground control communications network. Fighter pilots, bone weary, were sent up again and again after landing only long enough to refuel and replenish ammunition. For the first time, R.A.F. losses were greater than German, and in just two weeks a quarter of the carefree young men with the scarves became casualties. Then Göring blundered again. Infuriated by an R.A.F. bombing of Berlin, he abandoned his assault with victory in sight and on September 7 began the night bombing of London.

This is the weary and cynical face of an R.A.F. pilot just returned from once again staking his life against his skill in aerial combat. The record on the side of his plane shows that he is an expert at his trade; he has shot down nine German and one Italian aircraft.

"This...is London"

The deep, portentous voice of correspondent Edward R. Murrow, opening his radio broadcasts from England with "This . . . is London," brought Americans an eyewitness description of the British capital under air attack, but even he could convey only a limited idea of what such an ordeal meant. The first assaults on the city came on the afternoon of September 7 and continued throughout the night; in all, over 600 fighters and 600 bombers were in the enemy air fleets. High explosives and incendiaries did great damage to docks, gas works, rail terminals, and other nerve centers of the city, but homes were hit just as badly. Hundreds of fires burned, some of them great conflagrations. The night left more than 400 dead, four times that many badly injured. Thereafter the raids continued night after night—and by day until it became too costly to the *Luftwaffe*—in what came to be called the London Blitz. "Our outlook at this time," Winston Churchill later admitted, "was that London, except for its strong modern buildings, would be gradually and soon reduced to a rubble heap." But London and its people had more staying power than the German Air Force; though battered, the city was alive and vital when all *Luftwaffe* raids ceased in June, 1941.

Though German bombing missions arriving over London under conditions of good visibility usually aimed first for the dock areas, airdromes, and other strategic targets, all pretense of military justification was soon dropped, and the bombings became an instrument of terror to destroy the city and break civilian morale. Scenes of London during the Blitz, right, are (clockwise, beginning at upper left): the city aflame, seen through a window in the dome of St. Paul's Cathedral during the great fire-bomb raid of the night of December 29–30, 1940, London's worst conflagration since the Great Fire of 1666; next, a section of the subway system, whose deep tunnels were air-raid shelters for hundreds of thousands; third, firemen fighting a Victoria Street blaze; lastly, St. Paul's (which survived the Blitz intact) looming up against the burning city.

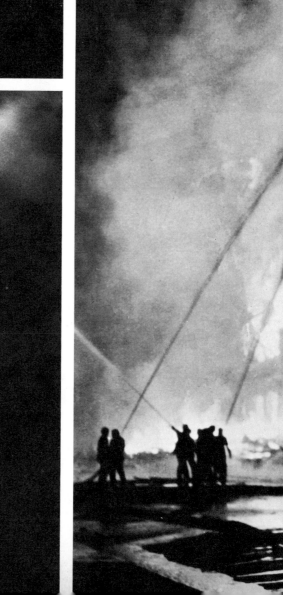

"...what a puny effort is this to burn a great city"

CBS

Edward R. Murrow

Edward R. Murrow was among the best of a new generation of radio newsmen, and one of the most courageous. Before the war ended, he would fly as an observer on twenty-five combat missions over Germany. Murrow was thirty-two years old in 1940, when his CBS broadcasts from London made him famous and brought home the war in Europe to millions of Americans. The following are taken from two of his broadcasts during the height of the Blitz.

SEPTEMBER 10, 1940

... We are told today that the Germans believe Londoners, after a while, will rise up and demand a new government, one that will make peace with Germany. It's more probable that they'll rise up and murder a few German pilots who come down by parachute. The life of a parachutist would not be worth much in the East End of London tonight.

The politicians who called this a "people's war" were right, probably more right than they knew at the time. I've seen some horrible sights in this city during these days and nights, but not once have I heard man, woman, or child suggest that Britain should throw in her hand. These people are angry. How much they can stand, I don't know. The strain is very great. The prospect for the winter, when some way must be found to keep water out of the shelters and a little heat inside, is not pleasant. Nor will it be any more pleasant in Germany, where winters are generally more severe than on this green island. After four days and nights of this air *Blitzkrieg*, I think the people here are rapidly becoming veterans, even as their Army was hardened in the fire of Dunkerque.

Many people have already got over the panicky feeling that hit everyone in the nerve centers when they realized they were being bombed. Those people I talked to in long queues in front of the big public shelters tonight were cheerful and somewhat resigned. They'd been waiting in line for an hour or more, waiting for the shelters to open at the first wail of the sirens. They had no private shelters of their own, but they carried blankets to throw over the chairs in this public underground refuge. Their sleep tonight will be as fitful as you could expect in such quarters without beds. Of course, they don't like the situation, but most of them feel that even this underground existence is preferable to what they'd get under German domination.

All the while strong efforts are being made to remind the British subjects who live underground that RAF bombers are flying in the other direction and that the Germans are having rather a rough time of it, too. For instance, tonight's British news broadcast led off with a long and detailed statement about last night's RAF air raids against Germany—the docks at Wilhelmshaven, Hamburg, Bremen, and Kiel were bombed again, a power station in Brussels wrecked, and a gasworks on the outskirts of Lorraine set afire. Docks and shipping at Calais, Ostend, Flushing, and Boulogne were also bombed.

OCTOBER 10, 1940

This is London, ten minutes before five in the morning. Tonight's raid has been widespread. London is again the main target. Bombs have been reported from more than fifty districts. Raiders have been over Wales in the west, the Midlands, Liverpool, the southwest, and northeast. So far as London is concerned, the outskirts appear to have suffered the heaviest pounding. The attack has decreased in intensity since the moon faded from the sky.

All the fires were quickly brought under control. That's a common phrase in the morning communiqués. I've seen how it's done; spent a night with the London fire brigade. For three hours after the night attack got going, I shivered in a sandbag crow's-nest atop a tall building near the Thames. It was one of the many fire-observation posts. There was an old gun barrel mounted above a round table marked off like a compass. A stick of incendiaries bounced off rooftops about three miles away. The observer took a sight on a point where the first one fell, swung his gun sight along the line of bombs, and took another reading at the end of the line of fire. Then he picked up his telephone and shouted above the half gale that was blowing up there, "Stick of incendiaries—between 190 and 220—about three miles away." Five minutes later a German bomber came boring down the river. We could see his exhaust trail like a pale ribbon stretched straight across the sky. Half a mile downstream there were two eruptions and then a third, close together. The first two looked like some giant had thrown a huge basket of flaming golden oranges high in the air. The third was just a balloon of fire enclosed in black smoke above the housetops. The observer didn't bother with his gun sight and indicator for that one. Just reached for his night glasses, took one quick look, picked up his telephone, and said, "Two high explosives and one oil bomb," and named the street where they had fallen.

There was a small fire going off to our left. Suddenly sparks showered up from it as though someone had punched the middle of a huge campfire with a tree trunk. Again the gun sight swung around, the bearing was read, and the report went down the telephone lines, "There is something in high explosives on that fire at 59."

There was peace and quiet inside for twenty minutes. Then a shower of incendiaries came down far in the distance. They didn't fall in a line. It looked like flashes from an electric train on a wet night, only the engineer was drunk and driving his train in circles through the streets. One sight at the middle of the flashes and our observer reported laconically, "Breadbasket at 90—covers a couple of miles." Half an hour later a string of fire bombs fell right beside the Thames. Their white glare was reflected in the black, lazy water near the banks and faded out in midstream where the moon cut a golden swathe broken only by the arches of famous bridges.

We could see little men shoveling those fire bombs into the river. One burned for a few minutes like a beacon right in the middle of a bridge. Finally those white flames all went out. No one bothers about the white light, it's only when it turns yellow that a real fire has started.

I must have seen well over a hundred fire bombs come down and only three small fires were started. The incendiaries aren't so bad if there is someone there to deal with them, but those oil bombs present more difficulties.

As I watched those white fires flame up and die down, watched the yellow blazes grow dull and disappear, I thought, what a puny effort is this to burn a great city. Finally, we went below to a big room underground. It was quiet. Women spoke softly into telephones. There was a big map of London on the wall. Little colored pins were being moved from one point to another and every time a pin was moved it meant that fire pumps were on their way through the black streets of London to a fire. One district had asked for reinforcements from another, just as an army reinforces its front lines in the sector bearing the brunt of the attack. On another map all the observation posts, like the one I just left, were marked. . . .

We picked a fire from the map and drove to it. And the map was right. It was a small fire in a warehouse near the river. Not much of a fire; only ten pumps working on it, but still big enough to be seen from the air. The searchlights were bunched overhead and as we approached we could hear the drone of a German plane and see the burst of antiaircraft fire directly overhead. Two pieces of shrapnel slapped down in the water and then everything was drowned in the hum of the pumps and the sound of hissing water. Those firemen in their oilskins and tin hats appeared oblivious to everything but the fire. We went to another blaze—just a small two-story house down on the East End. An incendiary had gone through the roof and the place was being gutted. A woman stood on a corner, clutching a rather dirty pillow. A policeman was trying to comfort her. And a fireman said, "You'd be surprised what strange things people pick up when they run out of a burning house."

And back at headquarters I saw a man laboriously and carefully copying names in a big ledger—the list of firemen killed in action during the last month. There were about a hundred names. . . .

The Scourging of Coventry

Historic Coventry, made famous by Lady Godiva, was pounded all through the night of November 14–15, 1940, until much of it was no more than a smoking waste. Hermann Göring, grown pessimistic about the possibility of doing to death so sprawling a city as London, decided to send some of his planes against the great Midlands industrial centers that produced much of Britain's war materials. Coventry, which had aircraft and machine-tool factories, was the first victim of these new tactics. The Germans bombed indiscriminately; operation of the factories was not even halted, but 70,000 homes were laid waste, and most of the city's ancient churches were destroyed or damaged. Other cities were hit in their turn, and London suffered again and again, but the effort cost the *Luftwaffe* dearly. The long British ordeal at last ended in June, 1941, when the German air strength was transferred to the Russian front.

Coventry Cathedral was completely bomb-gutted (left). Above, a time bomb is defused, an everyday chore for London's steel-nerved Bomb Disposal Unit. And below, a housewife is rescued after being trapped thirteen hours beneath rubble.

The Prime Minister makes one of his frequent walking tours of London streets, inspecting bomb damage and giving a boost to morale.

NEW YORK
Herald Tribune

LATE CITY EDITION

THE WEATHER

Today: Occasional rain, cloudy in afternoon, little change in temperature

Tomorrow: Partly cloudy and continued cold

Temperatures Yesterday: Max., 47; Min., 40

Detailed Report on Page 9, Sec. III

VOL. C No. 34,475

Copyright, 1941, New York Tribune Inc.

SUNDAY, APRIL 6, 1941

Section One

TEN CENTS
New York City and Vicinity

Germans March on Yugoslavia and Greece; Two Nations Defiant as Balkan War Begins; Moscow and Belgrade Sign Friendship Pact

Roosevelt Acts To Bar Strike At U. S. Steel

Calls Murray to Capital as C. I. O. Orders Men Out Tuesday Midnight

Mediator Assigned By Miss Perkins

Union Asks $52,000,000 Rise and Closed Shop; 261,000 Are Affected

By The United Press

PITTSBURGH, April 5.—President Roosevelt personally has intervened in the threatened work stoppage of the mills of the United States Steel Corporation and has summoned Philip Murray, C. I. O. president, to Washington for a conference, it was reported tonight.

It was learned authoritatively that the President had summoned Mr. Murray because he feared a strike in United States Steel mills would threaten the success of the nation's defense program.

Stoppage Tuesday Ordered

By The Associated Press

PITTSBURGH, April 5.—Philip Murray, president of the Congress of Industrial Organizations and the Steel Workers' Organizing Committee, announced today that work

Peace in Ford Strike Tomorrow Or Tuesday Seen by Conciliator

By Geoffrey Parsons Jr.
A Staff Correspondent

DETROIT, April 5.—The strike that has kept 85,000 men idle at the River Rouge plant of the Ford Motor Company since last Wednesday may be settled Monday or Tuesday, Governor Murray D. Van Wagoner of Michigan and Federal Conciliator James F. Dewey announced here tonight.

After a day of conferences, alternately with officials of the company and representatives of the United Automobile Workers, an affiliate of the Congress of Industrial Organizations, the Governor and the conciliator issued a statement which projected a joint conference Monday or Tuesday, adding:

"We hope to reach a settlement at that time, so that work can be resumed. Minor differences are rapidly disappearing, so that now it will be possible to discuss issues of settlement."

Meanwhile, whether the settlement comes fast or slow, Governor Van Wagoner pushed plans for the resumption of work early next week on the $21,000,000 Pratt & Whitney aircraft engine plant at River Rouge. Because there is a shortage of building trades workers in the Detroit area, many of the 600 workers employed at the nearly completed *(Continued on page 32, column 2)*

200,000 See Army Day Parade, With New Guns, Draftees, Rain

'They've Got Everything,' Sodden Spectator Says as Mechanized Might Rolls Down Fifth Ave.; Downpour Thins Ranks of 2½-Hour March

The thirteenth annual Army Day parade, the mightiest military display the city has seen since the World War, which the United States entered twenty-four years ago today, moved down upper Fifth Avenue yesterday afternoon. It was cheered by some 200,000 citizens, who with Governor Herbert H. Lehman, Mayor F. H. LaGuardia, Lieut. Gen. Hugh A. Drum, commander of the 1st Army, and other notables, braved a cold downpour for two and one-half hours to see the men and machines go by.

As far as marchers went, it was

Coal Settlement Reached, Mines To Open Soon

Assault Finds Yugoslavs Set To Resist Foe

Borders Closed a Day in Advance, Ships Called Back, Planes on Watch

Cabinet Is Ready To Flee Belgrade

American Envoy Plans to Stay; Few U. S. Citizens Remain, British Depart

By Russell Hill
By Telephone to the Herald Tribune
Copyright, 1941, New York Tribune, Inc.

BELGRADE, April 5.—With the zero hour at hand, Yugoslavia waited calmly tonight for the German army to move. Military preparations were being completed. Diplomatic activity had virtually ceased.

Yugoslavia is assuming more and more the aspect of an armed camp. All frontiers, with the exception of the Greek one, were closed today.

Private cars have requisitioned by the military authorities, and a censorship over mail has been imposed.

(Yugoslavia on Saturday night called all her ships into port, while Italy mined the international bridge at the Fiume border, The Associated Press reported.)

The Cabinet has met in long sessions in the last few days, and a

Herald Tribune map—Rickert

NEW THEATER OF WAR IN BALKANS—Area where Germany is at war with Yugoslavia and Greece

British Block Axis Columns East of Bengasi

Hitler Tells Balkan Army Hour Is Come

Berlin Radio Announces Troops Have Crossed Border in New Drive

Fuehrer Puts Blame On British Intrigue

Calls U. S. a Provocateur, Promises Salonica Will Be Another Dunkerque

By The Associated Press

BERLIN, April 6 (Sunday).—The German radio broadcast early today an order by Fuehrer Adolf Hitler to the German army to march into Yugoslavia and Greece.

Dr. Paul Joseph Goebbels, Nazi Propaganda Minister, who announced that German troops had begun to march, said the move was not an attack upon the "Greek people," but was directed solely by the policy of striking Great Britain wherever its forces appeared. He also accused Yugoslavia of mistreating Germans in that country.

Hitler's order said that the greatest patience had been exercised by Germany respecting Yugoslavia and Greece, but that now the moment for action had arrived.

Soldiers of the southeast front

Soviet Neutrality Pledge Aids Yugoslav Defense

Five-Year Non-Aggression Pact Signed at Moscow

Hitler's Personal Revenge

The Nazi blitzkrieg struck with a special harshness in Yugoslavia, which had had the ill fortune to incur the violent and personal wrath of Adolf Hitler. The Nazi dictator had concluded a German-Yugoslav treaty of "alliance" in the spring of 1941 to help secure his Balkan flank in preparation for his coming Russian adventure. But the Yugoslavs, irate at the prospect of their nation becoming a Nazi satellite, overthrew their Government and repudiated the treaty. Hitler took the action as a personal insult and reacted by going into a wild rage. He refused to listen to the new Yugoslav Government's offer of a nonaggression pact and sent a blitzkrieg attack against the unfortunate country, directing his commanders to act with special ruthlessness. In only eleven days the conquest of the rugged mountain country was complete, even before most of the Yugoslav Army had been able to mobilize. Hitler, exacting savage revenge for his affront, ordered the merciless bombing of Belgrade in what he called "Operation Punishment." The city had no antiaircraft guns, so planes roared over, unhindered, at low level; for three days and nights they pounded the capital to rubble, killing 17,000 civilians and injuring thousands more. Yugoslavia was dismembered; portions of its territory went to Germany, Italy, Hungary, Bulgaria, and to a newly created puppet state. But the victims had grim vengeance of a sort. Hitler had postponed his assault on Russia by some four weeks in order to punish Yugoslavia. It was by less than that margin of time that the *Wehrmacht*, several months later, was kept from capturing Moscow by the onset of winter. And if Moscow had been taken, Russia very probably would have been defeated. Hitler's revenge may well have cost him the war.

The body of a civilian, guilty of some offense against the Nazi occupation and summarily executed as a warning to the populace, hangs from a lamppost. Extreme Nazi ruthlessness gave rise to a bitter guerrilla campaign that soon cost the occupation forces very heavily in human lives and in matériel.

At upper left is a typical episode in the lightning conquest of Yugoslavia: a convoy of vehicles of the defending army, caught by the air-ground onslaught, burns on one side of a village street while a German armored column moves down the other. The speed of the conquest amazed military experts in other countries because Yugoslavia's precipitous mountain terrain had been considered to be completely unsuitable for blitzkrieg operations.

Greece and the New Barbarians

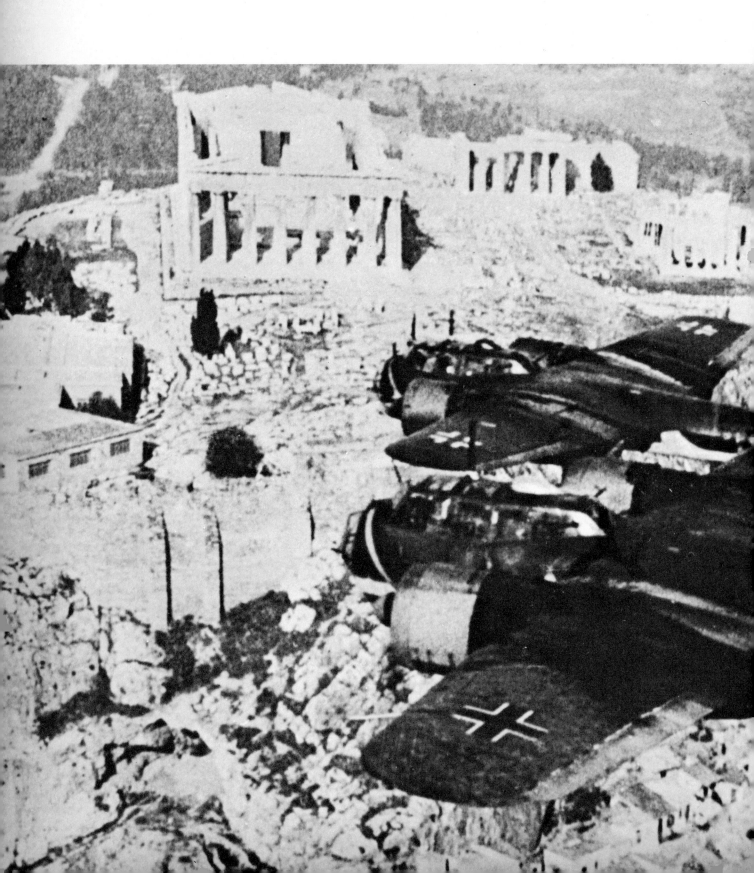

The *Luftwaffe* over Athens (below) and the Nazi flag flying from the Acropolis symbolized the modern barbarian invasion of Greece. The assault began on the same day, April 6, as the blitzkrieg on Yugoslavia. Hitler moved into Greece to rescue his Axis partner, Mussolini, whose own dreams of empire had turned sour when the Greeks, instead of being vanquished, had chased the Italian Army back into Albania, whence it had come. When the German threat arose, some 55,000 British Empire troops were sent to aid the Greeks, but they could only conduct a gallant delaying action against an army of half a million and then attempt a Dunkirk-like escape—doubly difficult this time, for they had no air cover. About 43,000 escaped.

Parachutes over Crete

The dismal retreat from Greece had hardly ended before the Nazi attack turned against Crete, defended by 28,500 British and Empire troops (most of them just escaped from Greece) and about 10,000 Greeks. There were no planes, few anti-aircraft guns, few tanks, even a scarcity of digging tools. The Nazis struck on the morning of May 20, first bombing the defenders, then loosing troop-carrying gliders and clouds of parachutists over Crete's three airfields. The attack was pressed with reckless indifference to losses. The defenders slew hundreds of paratroops; many others drifted into the sea and drowned. Gliders were blasted by artillery on landing, or missed the airfields to crash in the brush. The Royal Navy drowned some 4,000 Nazis who tried to land at night in small boats. But the air-borne troops came endlessly and gained lodgments by sheer numbers. By May 26, the decision to evacuate had to be made. Admiral Sir Andrew Cunningham took his ships in (below), and despite heavy losses, rescued 16,500 men by the time the battle ended June 1. British morale was down to its lowest point since Dunkirk.

German parachutists: at least 5,000 air-borne troops died in Crete.

Anthony Gross's "The Garrett Landing" depicts a party that escaped from Crete by drifting to North Africa in a motorless boat.

The Strange Mission of Rudolf Hess

A bizarre episode of the war was the flight of Rudolph Hess to Scotland on May 10, 1941. It was no small-fry Nazi who dropped on the astonished British, for only Hitler and Göring ranked ahead of Hess. He was under the delusion that he could bring peace between Britain and Germany, and he had selected as his go-between the Duke of Hamilton, whom he had once met, and whom he believed to be pro-Nazi. The Nazi leader was sure Great Britain would be defeated, and he explained that he wanted to save the British from the terrible consequences of that defeat. They could have peace and retain their Empire if they agreed to give Germany a free hand in Europe, returned Germany's former colonies, made peace with Italy, and got rid of Churchill. The flight shocked and infuriated Hitler, for Hess had been one of his most fanatically devoted followers. For days he pondered how to tell Germans about the embarrassing event. It was finally reported that Hess had become deranged due to World War I injuries. Not long after, the Hess incident was submerged in bigger happenings. On June 22, German armies invaded Russia.

LEFT AND RIGHT: WIDE WORLD

Rudolph Hess had been an old and trusted friend of Hitler, with whom he stands (above left) in a 1938 photograph. It was Hess to whom the future Führer *dictated most of* Mein Kampf *after they were both sent to prison in 1924. Above is the wreckage of the airplane from which Hess parachuted. His navigation was good enough to bring him within twelve miles of his destination. At right, Dr. Joseph Goebbels broadcasts Hitler's declaration that Germany is at war with Russia.*

Arsenal of Democracy

There are often confusing gaps in United States foreign policy between what we say we are going to do and what we actually do. As Gertrude Stein observed, Americans are brought up "to believe in boundlessness." This is manifest with respect to the behavior of our Government in matters outside its jurisdiction and therefore outside its control. In foreign policy we sometimes make laws in one way and apply them in another.

Our obsession for avoiding entanglements with the countries from which our forefathers escaped to a new society derived from both history and philosophy. In 1794, we passed our first Neutrality Act to escape involvement in a continental war between England and France. Two years later, George Washington warned in his Farewell Address against "interweaving our destiny with that of any part of Europe." Americans considered ours a noble and moral experiment, removed from the corruption and decay of other lands; and they wished to preserve it untarnished. But the consequent desire for total isolation did not become a real problem until early this century, when we became a world power.

During World War I, most Americans supported the Allies. There were, to be sure, many who did not, especially among those of German, Irish, and Jewish ancestry who cherished anti-British or anti-Russian sentiments. Thousands of such Americans actually left the United States to fight for the Kaiser. Nevertheless, the nation as a whole fervently hoped to stay out of the conflict, even though many leaders clearly saw that should the

Allies lose, the United States might become an island of democracy in a militaristic world.

Soon, however, reports of the brutal behavior of German troops in Belgium and France, exaggerated by Allied propaganda, began to stir American anger. At the same time, we rather arrogantly expected the Germans to accept our own special definition of neutrality: we committed ourselves to protect United States citizens on the high seas even when they traveled on belligerent ships. Thus when Berlin proclaimed unrestricted submarine warfare, it became inevitable that we would soon be involved in the war Woodrow Wilson had sworn to shun.

After peace came, isolationism still ran strong in the national bloodstream. In 1935, Congress enacted a law authorizing the President to stop arms shipments and prohibit United States citizens from traveling on foreign ships except at their own risk. Then, in 1936, Congress declared all loans to belligerent nations illegal. When civil war broke out in Spain, the 1936 legislation was extended to prevent American aid of any kind to either side.

But another Neutrality Act in 1939 repealed the arms embargo contained in previous measures and authorized a so-called "cash-and-carry" system designed to help our allied friends while keeping us out of the conflict. Once again, as in 1916, we were determined to have our cake and to eat it. We began selling arms to Britain and France, despite protests from the leonine Senator William E. Borah, Midwestern isolationists, and right-wing followers of the reactionary radio priest, Father Charles

E. Coughlin. Again we set out to maintain a neutral position that could continue only if one belligerent side, the Axis, accepted its paradoxical terms.

Even President Roosevelt admitted, when Hitler started World War II, that neutrality of thought was a different matter from neutrality of policy. After the Nazis overran nearly all of western Europe, he counseled: "Let us have done with both fears and illusions." When France fell, the United States Government was faced with the bleak reality that only Britain stood between America and the *Führer*'s European fortress. Within a year after the Nazis struck the lowlands, Congress appropriated $37,000,000,000 for rearmament and aid to the Allies, a sum larger than the total cost of World War I. But we had started very late. It was reckoned by military experts that the United States would not have an adequate air force until 1943, and it would be another two years before we possessed a two-ocean navy.

Furthermore, the nation was still riven by vigorous debate between outright interventionists and outright isolationists. William Allen White, the renowned editor of the Emporia, Kansas, *Gazette*, organized the Committee to Defend America by Aiding the Allies. He wrote Roosevelt urging that we become Britain's nonbelligerent ally and warned the President: "As an old friend, let me tell you that you may not be able to lead the American people unless you catch up with them." Robert Sherwood, a brilliant and ardently Anglophile playwright, took the lead by running a newspaper advertisement headed "Stop Hitler Now!" Nevertheless, various groups fought the current. The America First Committee preached a mixture of isolationism, pacifism, Anglophobia, and anti-Semitism and gained the support of many distinguished citizens, including Charles A. Lindbergh, Senator Burton K. Wheeler, and the Chicago *Tribune*'s powerful publisher, Colonel Robert McCormick. This was still the era of the Hitler-Stalin pact; pro-Fascist and pro-Communist groups joined in urging that we mind our own business.

President Roosevelt, who had begun a personal correspondence with Winston Churchill when Churchill was still First Lord of the Admiralty, began to prepare the country for a more active anti-Axis role. In his famous June 10 speech at Charlottesville, Virginia, he warned in his flat, reedy voice that we could not afford to become "a lone island in a world dominated by the philosophy of force." What is more, he promised to "extend to the opponents of force the material resources of this nation." Later, on July 29, he announced our protection over all Latin America and thus blocked the Nazis from assuming control of French or Dutch colonies. The United States then pooled defenses with Canada, a nation already at

war, and in September inaugurated the draft with a call-up of eight hundred thousand men. In July Churchill had cabled Roosevelt that the British had lost eleven destroyers in ten days and urgently requested help. The President responded by transferring fifty United States destroyers to hard-pressed Britain. All but three of them were antiquated four-stackers that had been in mothballs for eighteen years. Roosevelt called this "an epochal and far-reaching act of preparation for continental defense in the face of danger," since in return we had received ninety-nine-year leases on seven British bases from Guiana to Newfoundland. The United States was fast becoming a boundlessly unneutral neutral.

The problem of preparing the country for war itself was, however, appallingly difficult. Our regular Army, prior to the draft, had been legally limited to 375,000 men. Our factories needed to be retooled, and many of our workers required retraining before the nation could turn from civilian to military production. But by August of 1940, the Battle of Britain was on, shocking the United States out of its lassitude. On September 8, Roosevelt declared a state of emergency. An Office of Production Management was created to coordinate defense output and speed aid to Britain in every way "short of war." At the same time, a National Defense Research Committee, established the previous year under Dr. Vannevar Bush, was taking steps that would ultimately lead the United States—and the world—into the atomic age.

War was the major issue of the Presidential election that November. Roosevelt took the unprecedented step of running for a third term on the grounds that there was a world crisis. Like Wilson before him, he ran on a platform pledging that while we would help those fighting against aggression, we would not participate in foreign conflicts or send military forces outside America except in case of attack. The Republicans, despite the many influential and vocal isolationists in their party, finally nominated a liberal, pro-British Wall Street businessman, Wendell L. Willkie. His program promised "Americanism, preparedness, and peace." Willkie had a hard time campaigning. It was evident that he agreed on fundamentals with the man he wished to defeat, and he pledged himself to "outdistance Hitler in any contest he chooses." Republican propagandists depicted Roosevelt as a "war candidate." The Democrats called their rivals isolationists and appeasers, which Willkie, for one, was certainly not. The contest was uneven. Roosevelt received 449 electoral votes and Willkie only 82.

By the time 1940 drew to a close, our self-confidence, our growing sense of self-interest, our admiration for British courage, and our increasing detestation of the

Nazis had combined to produce a new national mood. In early December, Roosevelt went off on a two-week fishing trip in the Caribbean and returned with the ingenious —indeed revolutionary—idea that we keep Britain going with what he called a Lend-Lease program. There was no time to be lost. Britain was going broke and could ill afford our cash-and-carry terms for arms. She had begun the war with about $4,500,000,000 in gold, dollars, and United States investments; the money was almost gone. A week after the President returned from the Caribbean, he introduced his novel concept at a White House press conference. "Now, what I am trying to do," he said, "is eliminate the dollar sign. That is something new in the thoughts of everybody in this room, I think—get rid of the silly, foolish old dollar sign. Well, let me give you an illustration. Suppose my neighbor's home catches fire, and I have a length of garden hose. . . ."

On January 6, 1941, Roosevelt went before Congress and made the position of the United States entirely clear. "Today, thinking of our children and their children," he said, "we oppose enforced isolation for ourselves or for any part of the Americas." He called for a world that would be founded upon "four essential freedoms": freedom of speech, freedom of worship, freedom from want, and freedom from fear. It took no seer to recognize that this was a world in which Adolf Hitler had no place.

In the same speech, the President asked Congress to legislate Lend-Lease. The bill was cleverly presented. Its proponents argued that there was historical precedent, an 1892 statute enabling the Secretary of War to lease Army property "when in his discretion it will be for the public good." The bill went up to Congress under the happily patriotic designation of HR-1776 and was vigorously supported by the War Department. Its terms authorized the President to sell or lease military material to any anti-Axis country in return for any kind of direct or indirect payment "which the President deems satisfactory." The bill was savagely debated for two months. Isolationists, quite rightly, said its enactment would destroy what was left of our 1939 neutrality position. Robert M. Hutchins, the outspoken and respected president of the University of Chicago, regarded the entire concept as national suicide. But Churchill's strong voice pleaded from burning London: "Give us the tools and we will finish the job." In March, HR-1776 became law.

Never before had an American President received such immense discretionary authority. Within two weeks an initial appropriation of $7,000,000,000 was authorized by Congress. By the close of the war the total exceeded $50,000,000,000. Military goods started to flow across the Atlantic with maximum speed and minimum red tape,

and Churchill at last felt able to make what he called "long-term plans of vast extent." United States military leaders began to discuss joint preparations with the British and exchanged scientific, military, and intelligence information, from which we benefited greatly. R.A.F. pilots came to America to train. American warships helped shepherd lend-lease convoys and were soon tangling with U-boats in an undeclared shooting war. All but the figment of neutrality was gone.

This deliberate intrusion into the European conflict was mirrored in our relationships with Japan. Since 1931, when Secretary Stimson had sought unsuccessfully to muster international opposition to the Japanese invasion of Manchuria, the United States had found itself increasingly at odds with the dynamic Pacific nation that had so brilliantly imitated and improved on Western industrial ideas. Japan's assault on inchoate China and its subsequent accord with Hitler had brought it increasingly into the ranks of those we considered our enemies. After Germany's triumphs in Europe, it was clear that the only potentially effective opposition to Japanese expansion in Asia was that of the United States.

Pressure to curb Japan in the East more or less paralleled pressure inside the United States to bolster Britain in the West. In the summer of 1940, Washington initiated its first ban on sales of strategic materials to Tokyo. The embargo was rapidly extended, hurting the Japanese and producing an increasingly militant reaction among their military and political leaders. On September 27, 1940, Japan joined Germany and Italy in a Tripartite Pact that obliged the signatories to support each other should the United States enter the war. And the following April, Tokyo sought to insure itself against such a contingency by negotiating a neutrality pact with Russia, at that time still Germany's passive partner.

It is possible that the tightening American blockade accelerated the evident Japanese intention to expand. At any rate, fifty thousand Japanese troops seized Indochina from the Vichy French regime on July 2, 1941. Roosevelt promptly warned Tokyo to keep out of the Dutch East Indies, and the United States and Britain froze all Japanese funds under their control. By October the few remaining voices of moderation inside the Tokyo regime grew still. On the seventeenth the bellicose General Hideki Tojo was named Prime Minister, and it became more and more obvious that Tokyo, suffering especially from a freeze on petroleum imports from America, source of 90 per cent of its supplies in 1940, was preparing for imminent war before its stockpiles diminished. Indeed, we now know that the Japanese high command had started planning the attack on Pearl Harbor the preceding January—more than ten months before the event. That same October, a war council, in the presence of the Emperor, fixed the date for opening hostilities.

As the United States became more and more directly involved in the menacing problems of both the Atlantic and the Pacific, American diplomacy became increasingly active. Harry Hopkins, a lean, sickly social worker who enjoyed Roosevelt's particular confidence, served him as personal envoy on extraordinary missions. In July of 1941, Hopkins flew to England and talked to Churchill about a proposed conference with Roosevelt. At the end of his stay in London, on the night of July 25, Hopkins cabled Roosevelt: "I am wondering whether you think it important and useful for me to go to Moscow. Air transportation good and can reach there in twenty-four hours. I have a feeling that everything possible should be done to make certain the Russians maintain a permanent front even though they be defeated in this immediate battle. If Stalin could in any way be influenced at a critical time I think it would be worth doing by direct communication from you through a personal envoy." Roosevelt agreed.

The following Monday, wearing a grey Homburg Churchill had lent him after he had lost his own battered fedora, Hopkins climbed aboard a PBY Catalina that took him on a hasty and highly secret mission to Moscow. He bore a letter from Roosevelt to Stalin that said: "Mr. Hopkins is in Moscow at my request for discussion with you personally and with such other officials as you may designate on the vitally important question of how we can most expeditiously and effectively make available the assistance which the United States can render to your country in its magnificent resistance to the treacherous aggression by Hitlerite Germany. . . ."

The shift in attitude toward Russia, Hitler's colleague in the partition and plundering of Poland, was as dramatic and significant as the shift away from our originally proclaimed neutrality. Stalin bluntly suggested to Hopkins that the United States enter the war. Instead, Roosevelt sent Averell Harriman to Moscow together with Churchill's special agent, Lord Beaverbrook. On October 1, 1941, they signed a protocol with Molotov listing the supplies America and Britain would send to the Soviet Union. Roosevelt later authorized a Soviet lend-lease credit of up to $1,000,000,000.

And so, gradually but immutably, with a growing national awareness of what lay at the end of this unfamiliar road, the United States became ever more deeply committed to protect its friends and those who were at least the enemies of its enemies.

As we drew nearer and nearer to the edge of war, Roosevelt decided the time had come to meet Churchill per-

sonally. From August 9 to 12, 1941, the two leaders conferred with their staffs at Argentia Bay, Newfoundland, exchanging visits aboard their battle-camouflaged warships, *Prince of Wales* and *Augusta*. Thus began a personal and official relationship between the gallant cripple and the tough old artist-adventurer. No past President had ever been on such terms with the head of another Government. As Robert Sherwood later wrote, "It would be an exaggeration to say that Roosevelt and Churchill became chums at this conference. . . . They established an easy intimacy, a joking informality and moratorium on pomposity and cant—and also a degree of frankness in intercourse which, if not quite complete, was remarkably close to it." Each clearly respected the other not only for what he represented but as an individual. Roosevelt cabled Churchill shortly afterward: "It is fun to

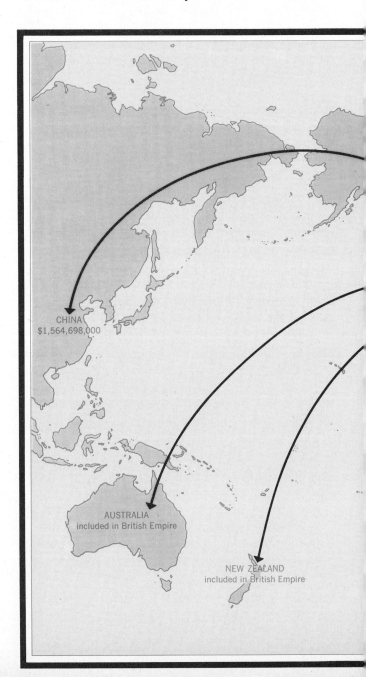

CHINA
$1,564,698,000

AUSTRALIA
included in British Empire

NEW ZEALAND
included in British Empire

be in the same decade with you." And Churchill recalled in his memoirs: "I felt I was in contact with a very great man who was also a warm-hearted friend and the foremost champion of the high causes which we served."

The Newfoundland conference was remarkable in that it produced a joint statement by the leader of a belligerent state and the leader of a nonbelligerent state, outlining the principles for which World War II was being fought—even before the war's greatest power had actually entered the fight. This statement, known to history as the Atlantic Charter, postulated certain basic tenets for the postwar world. It was drafted by Churchill and modified by the two statesmen together. On Janaury 1, 1942, after Churchill visited Washington, it was incorporated in a Declaration of the United Nations.

And so, in a most extraordinarily curious way, primarily through the will power and political genius of one man, Franklin Roosevelt, often inadvertently and sometimes only by executive order, the United States became deeply involved in history's greatest conflict without actually joining the war. In the East we helped China and squeezed and threatened Japan, more or less pushing her to do what she had planned to do anyway. In the West we armed first Britain, then Russia. We dispatched envoys to see what material was needed, and warships to insure that it was safely delivered. There is no doubt that we deliberately violated any internationally accepted concept of neutrality for eighteen months before we became belligerents. There is also no doubt that had we not done so, first Britain and then Russia would have lost the war. The isolation so many Americans craved would then have become both total and disastrous.

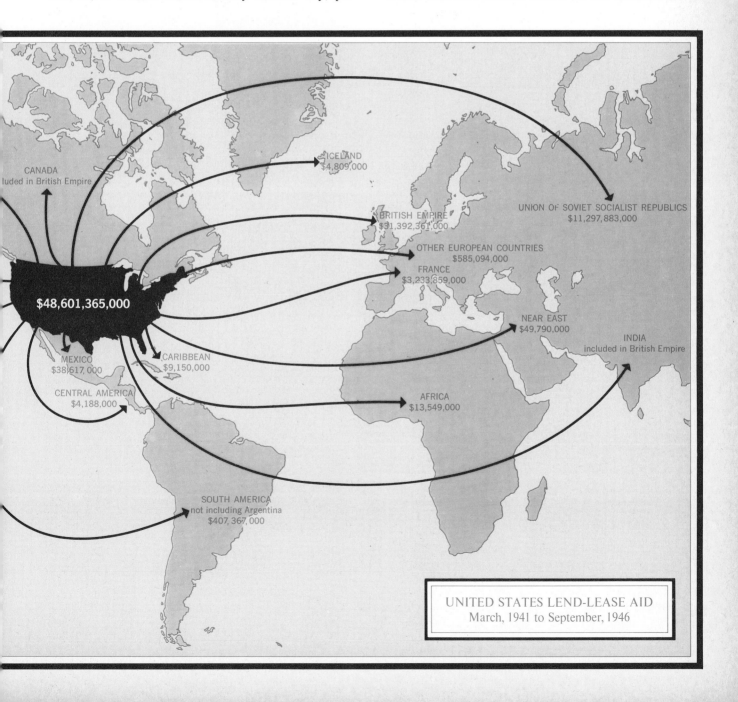

CANADA
Iuded in British Empire

ICELAND
$4,809,000

UNION OF SOVIET SOCIALIST REPUBLICS
$11,297,883,000

BRITISH EMPIRE
$31,392,361,000

OTHER EUROPEAN COUNTRIES
$585,094,000

FRANCE
$3,233,859,000

NEAR EAST
$49,790,000

INDIA
included in British Empire

$48,601,365,000

MEXICO
$38,617,000

CARIBBEAN
$9,150,000

CENTRAL AMERICA
$4,188,000

AFRICA
$13,549,000

SOUTH AMERICA
not including Argentina
$407,367,000

UNITED STATES LEND-LEASE AID
March, 1941 to September, 1946

Neutral in Name Only

Isolationism flowed strong in America during the early days of the European war, and there were loud cries that we mind our own business. But prevailing sentiment was that the Allies' cause was somehow also ours. President Roosevelt summed it up the day Great Britain and France declared war: "This nation will remain a neutral nation, but I cannot ask that every American remain neutral in thought as well." From then on, the Administration proceeded, as rapidly as the temper of the people permitted, to arm the nation and to aid its friends. The 1937 Neutrality Act, which embargoed arms to belligerents, was repealed in November, 1939; arms exports were put on a "cash and carry" basis, to the advantage of the Allies, who controlled the seas. In May, 1940, the President asked for large supplements to his January defense budget, including a program for 50,000 planes a year. In June the War Department released surplus arms to England, to replace some of those lost at Dunkirk. More help went to the hard-pressed British on September 3, when fifty overage destroyers were transferred to England, in return for American rights to build bases in British possessions in the Caribbean and the western Atlantic. In mid-September the first peacetime military draft in American history was passed by Congress. And on September 26 the first step to hamper Japanese aggression was made by placing an embargo on scrap iron and steel to all non-American countries except Britain. The Japanese at once protested it as an "unfriendly act." In deed as well as in thought, the United States was edging further and further away from the neutrality of which the President had spoken.

ABOVE: FRED MASTERS, © TIME, INC.; BELOW LEFT: U.S. ARMY; BELOW RIGHT: WIDE WORLD

The fifty destroyers traded to Britain for bases were old World War I types (upper right) but still able to fight Nazi U-boats. Churchill later admitted that the deal would have justified Hitler's declaring war on the United States. Blindfolded Secretary of War Henry L. Stimson (near right) on October 29, 1940, draws the first of the numbers to determine the order in which men will be called under the new Selective Service law. President Roosevelt is at far left in photo. At far right, on November 18, three of Chicago's first draftees receive their physical examinations.

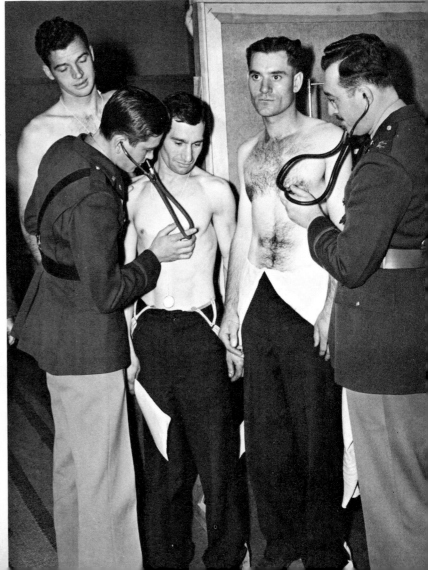

Voice of the People

When the American people elected a President in 1940, the Battle of Britain was being fought, and relations with Japan were growing increasingly strained. As a result, the campaign reflected the doubts, prejudices, and fears that confused and perplexed the nation as it considered its course in a perilous world. The Republican nominee that year was Wendell Willkie, corporation lawyer and utilities executive, a Democrat until 1938, and an amateur at politics. For the Democrats, President Roosevelt was nominated for an unprecedented third term, and justified his acceptance by saying that the international crisis made it his duty to continue in office. Willkie had defeated a strong isolationist wing of his party to get nominated; the Democrats also had a strong isolationist segment. Both parties had to mollify that element in writing the foreign-policy planks of their platforms. Both planks came out much the same: continue to aid England, but strengthen the defenses of the United States, and keep America out of war.

The war issue was the paramount one. There the differences in the positions of the two parties were reduced almost to nothing by Willkie in his acceptance speech, in which he completely rejected isolationism and put himself basically in agreement with the President. But as the campaign progressed, it degenerated into brawling and distortions. Roosevelt was attacked as a man hell-bent on getting the United States into war. The Republicans, in return, were castigated as isolationists and appeasers. Willkie found himself burdened with the unwanted backing of such groups as English-hating Irish Americans and pro-Nazi German Americans. He received support from an unexpected quarter when union leader John L. Lewis in late October charged that Roosevelt had betrayed labor and was taking the nation into war and dictatorship. But Lewis's move had little effect on the election. Roosevelt received about 55 per cent of the popular vote.

As their campaign buttons indicate, the Republicans bore down on the third-term issue. Many people felt strongly about the two-term tradition, and it undoubtedly had some effect on the vote.

Wendell Willkie, here in Elwood, Indiana, conducted a vigorous campaign in which he traveled 30,000 miles and made 540 speeches. Roosevelt, on the other hand, played the role of the statesman too busy guiding the nation to spend time on politics. He took to the stump only in the closing stages of the campaign. At Boston he made his now-famous pledge to parents: ". . . I shall say it again and again and again: Your boys are not going to be sent into any foreign wars."

"Roosevelt really enjoyed working on this speech"

Robert E. Sherwood

Few people were closer to the workings of the Roosevelt administration or to the President himself than Robert E. Sherwood, the well-known playwright. Sherwood had joined the White House staff in the summer of 1940 as one of F.D.R.'s speech writers and idea men. The following is from his Roosevelt and Hopkins, *one of the very best books ever written on Roosevelt or, for that matter, on World War II.*

. . . On December 2, the President left Washington as carefree as you please for a Caribbean cruise on *U.S.S. Tuscaloosa,* taking with him only his immediate staff—Pa Watson, Dr. McIntire and Captain Callaghan—with Harry Hopkins as the only guest, and it was noted that the party included no one qualified to advise or even consult on the grievous problems of Europe and the Far East. The White House announced that the main purpose of the cruise would be to inspect some of the new base sites recently acquired in the West Indies, but those most familiar with Roosevelt's vacation habits suspected that such inspections might be somewhat desultory and superficial and that the main business of each day would be fishing, basking in the sun and spoofing with cronies. This impression was borne out by the scraps of news sent back by the three press association representatives on the trip. . . .

At Guantanamo Bay, a large stock of Cuban cigars was purchased. At Jamaica, St. Lucia and Antigua, the President entertained British colonial officials and their ladies at lunch. Off Eleuthera Island he was visited by the Duke of Windsor, Governor General of the Bahamas. . . . There was one serious meeting when the *Tuscaloosa* lay to just outside the territorial waters of

Martinique and the U.S. Naval Observer there and the Consul came aboard to give the President a first-hand report on conditions on that potentially dangerous French island. During this brief conference many on board the *Tuscaloosa* were focusing their binoculars on the aircraft carrier *Béarn,* lying in the harbor of Fort-de-France, an ominous symbol of the French "fleet in being" which was still under the flimsy control of the Vichy Government.

According to custom, evenings on board ship were devoted either to poker games or to movies, the latter including "Northwest Mounted Police," starring Gary Cooper, Paulette Goddard and Madeleine Carroll; "I Love You Again," with William Powell and Myrna Loy; "They Knew What They Wanted," with Carole Lombard and Charles Laughton; "Arizona," with Jean Arthur and William Holden; and "Tin Pan Alley," with Alice Faye and Betty Grable—the last quite naturally being the favorite with the crew. . . .

At stated points along the route Navy seaplanes landed alongside the *Tuscaloosa* and delivered the White House mail. . . . One of these deliveries, on the morning of December 9, brought a long letter from Winston Churchill.

In upwards of 4,000 words, Churchill covered the broad picture and most minute details of the war situation from the North Sea to Gibraltar to Suez to Singapore. He dealt at great length with the critical problems of production and shipping and explained the dangers to both from the persistent attacks by bombers and U-boats. He stated Britain's present financial position in a few, blunt words. He asked for more destroyers either by a process of gift or loan. He concluded this memorable document with an expression of confidence that the American nation would support Britain's cause and meet her urgent needs, but he offered no suggestions as to how the President was to go about accomplishing all this with the Congress and the people.

This message from the Prime Minister had a profound effect on Roosevelt, and it filled Hopkins with a desire to get to know Churchill and to find out how much of him was mere grandiloquence and how much of him was hard fact.

. . . when homeward bound, Roosevelt held a press conference with the three correspondents, and talked affably about some of the advantages and disadvantages that he had noted in the various base sites visited, but he gave them nothing in the way of news calculated to cause the slightest excitement in their home offices. It still seemed that he had spent two weeks in a state of total relaxation and utter indifference toward the prospects of world calamity.

That, however, was only as it seemed. . . .

On December 16, he returned to Washington, tanned and exuberant and jaunty. The next day, he held a press conference, starting off with his usual statement that, "I don't think there is any particular news. . . ." Having thus paved the way, he said, "There is absolutely no doubt in the mind of a very overwhelming number of Americans that the best immediate defense of the United States is the success of Britain in defending itself." Then he jumped back to the outbreak of the First World War and told an anecdote at the expense of bankers on the Bar Harbor Express. "In all history," he said, "no major war has ever been lost through lack of money." He went on to say that

some people thought we should lend money to Britain for the purchase of American matériel, while other people thought we should deliver it as an outright gift. Roosevelt described this kind of thinking as "banal." (Actually, there were very few people who seriously made such ridiculous suggestions, neither one of which would have stood a chance in Congress; but Roosevelt brought them into his introduction to show what a reasonable middle-of-the-roader he really was.) He said,

Now, what I am trying to do is eliminate the dollar sign. That is something brand new in the thoughts of everybody in this room, I think—get rid of the silly, foolish, old dollar sign.

Well, let me give you an illustration. Suppose my neighbor's home catches fire, and I have a length of garden hose . . .

I believe it may accurately be said that with that neighborly analogy, Roosevelt won the fight for Lend Lease. There were to be two months of some of the bitterest debates in American history, but through it all the American people as a whole maintained the conviction that there couldn't be anything very radical or very dangerous in the President's proposal to lend our garden hose to the British who were fighting so heroically against such fearful odds. There were probably very few who had any expectation that we would ever get the hose back; there was indeed a devout popular hope that this new measure would eliminate the possibility of another twenty years of fruitless bickering and niggling over war debts.

Following the press conference, Roosevelt determined to go on the air with a Fireside Chat to explain the seriousness of the war situation. He could not give much attention

to the speech until after Christmas, which was always a real, old-fashioned family festival in the White House, with aunts and uncles, children and grandchildren, stockings and packages galore, and invariably a highly dramatic reading by the President of *A Christmas Carol.* . . .

In the preparation of the Fireside Chat (delivered December 29) Hopkins provided the key phrase which had already been used in some newspaper editorial: "We must be the great arsenal of democracy." I have been told that the phrase was originated by William S. Knudsen and also by Jean Monnet, but whoever originated it, Roosevelt was the one who proclaimed it. There was some debate at first over its use by the President, since it might seem to preclude the eventual extension of aid to the Soviet Union or to certain Latin American "republics," but the phrase was too good to be stopped by any quibbles. Roosevelt really enjoyed working on this speech for, with the political campaign over, it was the first chance he had had in months and even years to speak his mind with comparative freedom. He had indulged himself once, six months previously, in the "stab in the back" reference, but the political consequences of that were so awkward that he had felt compelled subsequently to confine himself to the most namby-pamby euphemisms in all references to the international situation. Now, for the first time, he could mention the Nazis by name. He could lash out against the apostles of appeasement. He could say, "We cannot escape danger, or the fear of danger, by crawling into bed and pulling the covers over our heads." He could speak plainly on the subject which was always in his mind—the disastrous folly of any attempt at a negotiated peace.

John L. Lewis, president of the CIO

Norman Thomas, 1940 Socialist candidate for President

Father Charles E. Coughlin

Fritz Kuhn (speaking),

The Great Debate

Concern over the European war and how best to avoid being caught in it led in 1940–41 to what was called "the Great Debate," an extended period of discussion, argument, recrimination, and soul-searching such as the nation has seldom seen. Roosevelt's foreign policy had split American opinion. On one hand, the traditional isolationists loudly accused the President of leading the country to war. On the other side, the so-called interventionists were just as eager to avoid war, but they argued that the best way to do so was to send all possible aid to Hitler's enemies and let them take care of defeating Germany. The debate cut through all levels of American life, and the arguments went on in Congress, on the radio, at public forums, in bars, wherever people gathered. Some seven hundred organizations became involved, most of them pro-isolationist. There was a good sprinkling of various hate groups, Fascist organizations of differing degrees of rabidness, and Communist groups. The leading isolationist body was the America First Committee: isolationist, pacifist, Anglophobic, tainted with anti-Semitism, limited chiefly to the Midwest. On the other side was the Committee to Defend America by Aiding the Allies, which was founded in May, 1940, and was the first organization to fight isolationism on a national scale. The Great Debate ended abruptly and completely with Pearl Harbor.

LEFT AND RIGHT: WIDE WORLD; ALL OTHERS: UPI

Colonel Charles A. Lindbergh

with American Nazi guards

Sen. Gerald P. Nye (Republican–North Dakota)

Kathleen Norris, authoress

As the gallery of pictures above suggests, the isolationist camp embraced very diverse personalities. Many, like authoress Kathleen Norris, wanted only to avoid war at any cost. Charles Lindbergh was among those who admired the technological efficiency of the Nazi war machine and were sure it was invincible. There were rabble rousers like Charles Coughlin, the anti-Semitic priest who called Roosevelt "a scab President," and there were the Fascist groups, such as Fritz Kuhn and his Nazi-aping German-American Bund. Representing the other camp was William Allen White (left), founder of the Committee to Defend America by Aiding the Allies, the most effective among the anti-isolationist groups.

141

The Atlantic Charter

By the summer of 1941, arguments about American neutrality had become academic. Though still non-belligerent, the nation was far from neutral. Since the previous March, it had been arming Great Britain under Lend-Lease and was about to do the same for Russia. American destroyers were convoying British ships halfway across the Atlantic. British pilots were training in the United States. And in the Pacific, economic sanctions were being taken against Japan. Against this backdrop, Roosevelt and Churchill met aboard ship in Argentia Bay, Newfoundland, and drew up the Atlantic Charter, a statement of principles for a postwar world living in peace and justice.

MARGARET BOURKE-WHITE, © TIME, INC.

Stalin poses with Harry Hopkins (above), who went to Moscow in July, 1941, to discuss Russia's Lend-Lease needs with the dictator. At right, Roosevelt and Churchill join in shipboard church services on August 10, 1941, during the meetings that produced the Atlantic Charter.

F L A S H

WASHINGTON--WHITE HOUSE SAYS JAPS ATTACK PEARL HARBOR.

222PES

B U L L E T I N

WASHINGTON, DEC. 7 (AP)-PRESIDENT ROOSEVELT SAID IN A
STATEMENT TODAY THAT THE JAPANESE HAD ATTACKED PEARL HARBOR, HAWAII,
FROM THE AIR.

THE ATTACK OF THE JAPANESE ALSO WAS MADE ON ALL NAVAL AND MILITARY
"ACTIVITIES" ON THE ISLAND OF OAHU.

THE PRESIDENT'S BRIEF STATEMENT WAS READ TO REPORTERS BY STEPHEN
EARLY, PRESIDENTIAL SECRETARY. NO FURTHER DETAILS WERE GIVEN
IMMEDIATELY.

AT THE TIME OF THE WHITE HOUSE ANNOUNCEMENT, THE JAPANESE AMBASSADORS
KIURISABORO NOMURA AND SABURO KURUSU, WERE AT THE STATE DEPARTMENT.

F L A S H

WASHINGTON--SECOND AIR ATTACK REPORTED ON ARMY AND NAVY BASES
IN MANILA.

Japan Strikes

During the last half of the nineteenth century, after Commodore Matthew Perry's "black ships" opened the self-isolated feudal nation of Japan to American trade, a group of militant and nationalist young samurai inspired an industrial and political revolution that by the early part of the twentieth century had placed a new kind of Japan squarely in competition with the West. Big business, a big army, and a big navy combined with native Japanese energy to produce a dynamism that eventually gave rise to massive expansion, first in Manchuria in 1931, then across the Pacific and deep into China.

The thrust into China began in the summer of 1937, when the so-called War Lords of Japan provoked several "incidents" and then invaded. They were censured by the League and received strong protests from the United States—all of which seemed only to reaffirm the Tokyo militarists' argument that war with the West was inevitable, and that the next step should be to pre-empt the oil and minerals of southern Asia. The principles of such bold expansion had been outlined ten years earlier in a secret memorandum called the Tanaka Memorial, a blueprint for military conquest that even included the conquering of Europe. But after Hitler overran Europe in the spring of 1940, Japan signed a Tripartite Pact with Germany and Italy to secure a free hand in the Orient.

Friction between Japan and the United States increased rapidly. In July, 1940, President Roosevelt froze all Japanese assets in the United States, and later a commercial blockade of Japan was put into effect. A moderate Prime Minister, Prince Fumimaro Konoye, urged restraint and tried to find some basis for a bargain with the United States. But his cabinet was dominated by General Hideki Tojo, known as "Razor Brain." Not long after, Konoye was almost murdered for his views, and on October 17, 1940, Tojo became Prime Minister. A United States Navy Department memorandum concluded that the "jingoistic military clique" was now supreme. Tojo resolved on war, arguing that "rather than await extinction it were better to face death by breaking through the encircling ring to find a way for existence."

From these impulses had already grown "the Greater East Asia Co-Prosperity Sphere," an economic and political program for a Japanese empire that would extend all the way from Manchuria and China to Thailand and New Guinea. In theory the program endorsed the anticolonial aspirations of Asian nationalists, but in practice it merely substituted one form of imperialism for another.

Unlike the Germans, the Japanese had a finite and audacious scheme, whose first postulate was the crippling of the United States Pacific fleet—and specifically the battleships—at Pearl Harbor. Thereafter, in concurrent moves, it envisioned the rapid seizure of Thailand, Burma, Malaya, and Singapore, and also the Philippines and Dutch East Indies archipelagoes. The idea was to achieve an impregnable position before America was ready to hit back. The program was endorsed at a Supreme War Council on September 6, 1941.

Five months earlier, British and American staff repre-

At left is the first public report of the news that stunned America.

145

sentatives had met in Washington and agreed on a defensive plan in the event of an Asian war. Known as ABC-1, it called for a concentrated effort against Germany and a holding operation in the East. The United States expected to hang on to the Philippines, especially after General Douglas MacArthur was named Far East commander that July. The possibility of an assault on Pearl Harbor was not considered. This was strange, since Joseph Clark Grew, our ambassador in Tokyo, had reported in January, 1941, that the Japanese might "attempt a surprise attack on Pearl Harbor using all their military facilities."

Even at the end of November, when we had managed to break the Japanese secret codes, nobody suspected that Honolulu might be in danger. Aircraft on Hawaiian bases were parked wing-to-wing to protect them from local sabotage; and it was only mere chance that three carriers were absent from Pearl Harbor when the attack came. Analysis in Washington was unimaginative; intelligence was faulty; communications were slack and mixed up.

Undoubtedly part of this muddleheadedness came from overconfidence. Ernest Hemingway later wrote: "All through the Pacific and the Far East in 1941 I heard about the general incapacity and worthlessness of, 'those Little Monkeys.' Everywhere I heard what we would do to those little monkeys when the day of the great pushover came. One cruiser division and a couple of carriers would destroy Tokyo; another ditto Yokohama. No one ever specified what the little monkeys would be doing while all this was going on. I imagine they were supposed to be consulting oculists trying to remedy those famous defects in vision which kept them from being able to fly properly. Or else trying to right all those battleships and cruisers which would capsize in a beam sea."

Specific plans for the Pearl Harbor attack were put together by a staff working under Admiral Isoroku Yamamoto, Commander in Chief of the Japanese Navy, an excellent officer and by no means an extreme jingo. Six carriers, protected by a heavy screen of surface vessels and submarines, were assigned to the task. The idea of surprise raised no moral problem, as such surprise is even recommended in *Bushido*, feudal Japan's code of honor.

By November the project was proven ready. Yamamoto assembled his commanders on the *Nagato* and told them that without a triumph at Honolulu, Japan could neither make war nor aspire to great-power rank. But he warned his subordinates: "The Americans are adversaries worthy of you." On December 2, the fleet received the coded message ("Climb Mount Niitaka") that irrevocably ordered the attack. Officers and pilots listened to their instructions, then bowed in prayer before the Shinto shrines aboard their carriers. On December 7, they struck.

That December, I was in Kuibyshev, temporary capital of war-torn Russia. Two days before Pearl Harbor, the confused provincial Soviet cable service delivered to me by mistake an enormously long cable in what was patently Russian code. It had been sent from Tokyo and was addressed to the Foreign Commissariat. I struggled through the snow to deliver the message to an embarrassed official. I have long since wondered what forebodings that ambassadorial message contained. In any case, it was clear that the news of Pearl Harbor was welcomed by Stalin; at last, as Lenin had predicted, Japan and the United States had "turned their knives against each other," and the Soviets could relax along their edgy eastern frontier. Three Japanese correspondents shared a room across the corridor from me in Kuibyshev's modest Grand Hotel. Affable fellows, they knocked on my door and told me, with happy smiles, how sorry they were that the United States Fleet had been destroyed. To my horror, I found that what they said was true.

World War II became truly global only in December, 1941; the majority of Latin America joined the United States in declaring war on the Axis, and the number of belligerents rose to thirty-eight, of whom only ten were on the Axis side. The sphere of operations extended from Ethiopia to the Aleutians and Papua, and from the Arctic Circle to the Tropic of Capricorn.

The abrupt change from unneutral neutrality to full belligerency came with shocking surprise to the incautious American high command. Since mid-November, Tojo's special envoy, Saburo Kurusu, had been in Washington to assist Ambassador Kichisaburo Nomura in seeking—or pretending to seek—a negotiated settlement. Kurusu and Nomura began negotiations with Secretary of State Cordell Hull on the seventeenth, almost two weeks after the Japanese fleet had received secret Operational Order No. 1, which led to Pearl Harbor. At 2:05 P.M., December 7, Kurusu and Nomura again called upon Secretary Hull —twenty minutes late for their appointment. They arrived just after Roosevelt had telephoned Hull to tell him of the attack on Honolulu. The handsome, tight-lipped Secretary coldly accepted the document presented by his visitors, which outlined the Japanese formula for a Pacific settlement. When he had finished reading it, he said: "In all my fifty years of public service I have never seen a document that was more crowded with infamous falsehoods and distortions—infamous falsehoods and distortions on a scale so huge that I never imagined that any government on this planet was capable of uttering them."

At that moment, early in the morning by Pearl Harbor time, the American fleet was smoking in disaster. Three hundred and fifty-three Japanese bombers, torpedo bombers, and fighters had within a few moments knocked out half of the entire United States Navy.

The surprise was total. Soldiers were taking their Sunday ease outside their billets; sailors were sauntering along the decks of their moored vessels. When the first enemy aircraft swept out of the morning haze above Diamond Head, few people paid attention. Passengers on an incoming American liner were pleased to be able to witness what they thought to be remarkably realistic preparatory exercises. Then the intruders leveled off. The torpedo planes, armed with special shallow-running devices, headed for the moored battleships, their prime targets. High-flying bombers blasted crowded Hickam Field. A group of unarmed United States planes coming in from the mainland found itself caught in the melee.

Six great battleships—*West Virginia, Tennessee, Arizona, Nevada, Oklahoma,* and *California*—were sunk or seriously damaged. Our Air Corps was left with only sixteen serviceable bombers. American striking power in the Pacific was virtually paralyzed. Tokyo newspapers proclaimed that the United States had been reduced to a third-class power. The American people were stunned. The next day, President Roosevelt told a joint session of Congress that December 7 was "a date which will live in infamy," and the Senate voted unanimously for war. There was one dissent in the House—from Montana's Jeannette Rankin, a pacifist who said she wanted to show that a "good democracy" does not always vote unanimously for war. Three days later, Germany and Italy declared war, and Congress passed a joint resolution accepting the state of war "which has been thrust upon the United States."

The Japanese onslaught continued with simultaneous attacks against Hong Kong, Malaya, and the Philippines, where the American Far East Air Corps was crippled in a catastrophe almost as bad as that of Pearl Harbor and one for which there was even less excuse, for there had been sufficient and accurate advance notice. General MacArthur had reason to expect an assault on at least Luzon. Nevertheless, Japanese planes succeeded in destroying eighteen of the thirty-five Flying Fortresses at Clark Field, as well as fifty-six fighters and twenty-five other planes. They lost only seven aircraft in the process. Within three weeks, strong amphibious forces under Lieutenant General Masaharu Homma had landed on the northern and southern shores of Luzon and were driving on Manila. The United States Asiatic Fleet withdrew with large convoys of merchant shipping to safer and more southerly waters. By January 2, 1942, Manila had fallen, and American and Philippine troops were retreating to the Bataan Peninsula.

While the United States reeled from these savage blows, the Japanese unleashed a multiple offensive on the Asian mainland. The Indochinese colonies of defeated France had already been occupied; now it was Britain's turn. Native populations under the Empire were restive, if not actually hostile, and as the hitherto dominant white tuans faltered, the Asiatic peoples proved willingly subject to Japanese propaganda. The Royal Navy adhered to obsolete tactics. Hong Kong was entirely isolated and fell on Christmas Day. Singapore, vaunted island citadel of the Orient, had all its guns and fortifications facing seaward and lay open to the Malayan land side, from which the attack developed. Wearing sneakers, carrying small sacks of rice, venerating their Emperor and believing implicitly in their commanders, some two hundred thousand Japanese soldiers rushed like lizards through the Malayan jungle. The British kept falling back, only to find their enemy already installed behind them. "It's like trying to build a wall out of quicksand," said one despairing officer. Within six weeks the Japanese had taken the peninsula. The British withdrew into Singapore, swarming with refugees, but Sir Arthur Percival, the commanding general, found himself outnumbered and outmaneuvered. With more than seventy thousand men, he surrendered on February 15, 1942. It was the worst military disaster ever suffered by any European nation in the Orient.

Even before that great island city fell, Britain suffered an unmitigated naval disaster. A flotilla of six ships, including the heavy cruiser *Repulse* and the powerful new battleship *Prince of Wales*, was cruising openly in Malayan waters, hoping to deter Japan. There was no aircraft carrier in the flotilla, and its commander, Sir Tom Phillips, an old-fashioned "battlewagon admiral," easily reconciled himself to the lack of support from land-based planes. When the Royal Air Force notified him, "Regret fighter protection impossible," Phillips merely remarked to an officer on the bridge, "Well, we must get on without it." Soon he found himself being shadowed by Japanese observation planes. By the time he turned back, it was too late. On December 11, the *Prince of Wales* and the *Repulse* were both sunk by Japanese bombers and low-flying torpedo planes. Phillips went down with his ships. Churchill told Parliament: "In my whole experience I do not remember any naval blow so heavy or so painful. . . ."

Already established in French Indochina with the helpless permission of Vichy's Governor General, the Japanese swarmed southward across Malaya toward the Dutch East Indies and far-off Australia, and westward over Thailand to Burma and the edge of India. In Burma the British were aided by a Chinese force under Chiang Kai-shek's chief of staff, the redoubtable American general

"Vinegar Joe" Stilwell. But his troops were soon cut off and had to make a difficult forced march out of Burma to northeast India. Stilwell confessed in his usual unabashed fashion: "The Japs ran us out of Burma. We took a hell of a beating!" The Burmese, like many other Asians, were pleased to see the Western overlords defeated. A Tokyo newspaper, commenting on the extent of collaboration in Mandalay, observed: "We do not have to reward our friends with posts in the government. They had taken them before we arrived."

The Japanese fleet meanwhile penetrated the Indian Ocean and hammered Ceylon. Admiral Jisaburo Ozawa captured the Andaman Islands in the Bay of Bengal, sank 112,000 tons of merchant shipping, and cruised menacingly along the coast. It seemed as if India, threatened by sea and by land from Burma, was about to disintegrate. Subhas Chandra Bose, a popular Bengali nationalist, began organizing an Indian army to fight the British. Radio Tokyo lauded the historic culture of Hindustan and called for rebellion against the alien masters. In March, 1942, Churchill sent Cripps, his Socialist ambassador to Moscow, on a special mission to Delhi to promise the Indians postwar independence. Mahatma Gandhi remarked, "They are offering us a postdated check on a bank that is obviously crashing"—and was put in jail.

But then, to the astonishment of the Allies, the Japanese high command, considering the Indian Ocean of but secondary importance, ordered its triumphant admirals eastward back to Singapore. Neither Ceylon nor India was ever again seriously threatened. The extreme danger that the Germans might come from Russia and Iran and the Japanese from Burma and India to join in a monstrous victory embrace was gone.

One of the principal objectives of the Japanese strategic plan was that wealthy colonial prize, the Dutch East Indies (now Indonesia). Japan desperately needed petroleum, and after Holland's occupation by the Nazis, Tokyo had applied increasing pressure on the Dutch colonial administration in Java. Even before the fall of Singapore, the Japanese landed troops near the Borneo oil fields, and shortly afterward, a massive invasion of Java began. To oppose this, the Allies assembled a small flotilla of American, Australian, and Dutch ships, which met the Japanese on February 27, 1942, in the three-day Battle of the Java Sea. The Allied force was entirely destroyed. By March 9, the whole archipelago was gone, and nearly one hundred thousand prisoners were marching off to Japanese concentration camps. In four weeks the Dutch lost an empire that they had owned for nearly four centuries.

One consequence of this sensational advance was to expose the entire continent of Australia to invasion. The Japanese pushed across the mountains of neighboring New Guinea and bombed Darwin, the northern Australian port. A landing seemed imminent. A member of parliament at Canberra warned: "We are facing the vile abomination of a Jap invasion." The country was placed on a total-war footing, but there was a dangerous shortage of troops because of the units sent to North Africa.

Australia looked to the United States for help, but we were hard put to shoulder any added responsibilities. Pearl Harbor was paralyzed, and Wake Island, deep in the Pacific, had been lost to amphibious assault two days before Christmas. In the Philippines, a tough, efficiently commanded Japanese force had bottled up MacArthur's defenders on the peninsula of Bataan. His first line of defense was crushed by a redoubtable infantry thrust in which Japanese hurled themselves on barbed-wire entanglements, permitting their comrades to cross upon their writhing bodies. Then, as MacArthur fell back on a second line, a Japanese battalion landed behind him.

On February 22, 1942, following Churchill's advice, Roosevelt ordered MacArthur to abandon his force and go to Australia. On March 11, the handsome general and his family and staff quit Corregidor by PT boats. At Mindanao they transferred to two Flying Fortresses that flew them to Darwin, Australia, where MacArthur issued his famous statement: "The President of the United States ordered me to break through the Japanese lines and proceed from Corregidor to Australia for the purpose, as I understand, of organizing the American offensive against Japan, a primary purpose of which is the relief of the Philippines. I came through and I shall return."

Meanwhile, under MacArthur's successor, General Jonathan Wainwright, the defenders of Bataan fought on with great courage but small hope. Their rations had been halved in early January. Now they were foraging for any kind of flesh: dogs, pack mules, monkeys, iguanas, snakes. Ill fed, ravaged by tropical diseases, totally isolated, the troops composed their own war song:

> We're the battling bastards of Bataan;
> No mama, no papa, no Uncle Sam;
> No aunts, no uncles, no nephews, no nieces;
> No pills, no planes, no artillery pieces.
> . . . and nobody gives a damn!

On April 8, Wainwright ordered the abandonment of Bataan. After destroying its ammunition dumps, the General and a few defenders retreated to the island fort of Corregidor; the rest surrendered. General Homma, the Japanese commander, then concentrated his artillery and bombers on the tunneled fortress, silencing its big guns one by one. On May 6, it too yielded.

The Japanese displayed particular callousness toward the American and Filipino soldiers they captured at Bataan, marching them sixty-five miles to a railway junction from which they were to entrain for an internment camp. Dazed and weak from thirst and starvation, the prisoners were formed into columns of fours, then driven forward under a blinding sun. Thousands of them died from disease or exhaustion or from Japanese brutality in what became known as "the Death March."

Despite the immense emotional pressures engendered by successive blows to American prestige in the Pacific, President Roosevelt and his Chiefs of Staff held to the strategy that had been fixed with Churchill well before Pearl Harbor. The first objective was still the defeat of Nazi Germany. In the Pacific, American planners emphasized the strategic triangle embracing Alaska, Hawaii, and Panama, thus implicitly accepting the loss of Wake, Guam, and the Philippines.

Both by his military strategists and by the officials chosen to mobilize the nation's industrial potential, Roosevelt was excellently served. Under their supervision, young men were drafted into the armed forces; women enlisted for noncombat duties; labor's work week was lengthened; a War Production Board took charge of America's immense factory potential. Between July 1, 1940, and July 31, 1945, the United States produced 296,601 aircraft, 71,060 ships, and 86,388 tanks. By the time peace came, over 15,000,000 Americans had served in the country's forces, 10,000,000 in the Army alone.

All the internal dissension occasioned by the lingering debate between isolationists and interventionists vanished after Pearl Harbor. Even Senator Wheeler said: "The only thing now to do is to lick the hell out of them." Colonel Lindbergh asked to be reinstated in the Air Corps; and since Hitler had attacked Russia, the Communists and other left-wing pacifists were now enthusiastic warriors. The Government saw to it that the pro-Nazi German-American Bund Organization was dissolved, but a wholly unjust penalty was paid by the nisei, Americans of Japanese ancestry, who were forcibly relocated from the West Coast because of exaggerated spy fears. Those Japanese Americans who later fought in the United States Army compiled a superb record for courage and endurance. I remember when at Cassino, as a nisei battalion was moving into a particularly difficult position where it suffered heavy losses, some German prisoners simultaneously marched to our rear. One of the puzzled and astonished Germans asked an American lieutenant: "But aren't those Japanese?" "Yes," said the lieutenant. "Didn't you know they were on our side? Or do you believe all that stuff Goebbels tells you?"

If there had been any doubts about the fighting spirit of the American people, they were quickly dissolved. But for all the national energy and purpose, the Red Cross volunteers, the Irving Berlin songs, the speeches, and the hurry, hurry, hurry, the fact was that the first part of 1942 was a very dark time indeed. The news was nearly all bad. U-boats were sinking American ships with terrible regularity. The Japanese, hitherto held in contempt, had smashed our best fleet in Hawaii, defeated our best general in Luzon, destroyed Britain's finest warships, captured her most impregnable fortress, and seized a huge empire in one incredibly swift campaign. It was clearly necessary for Americans to prove to themselves that they were capable of hitting back, and to prove to the Japanese that they would suffer for their impudence. Out of this determination was born the bombing raid on Tokyo led by Colonel James Doolittle.

The idea originated with a submarine staff officer, Captain Francis S. Low, who submitted a plan for using Army bombers from aircraft carriers. General "Hap" Arnold, head of the Army Air Corps, asked Doolittle to study the project. Doolittle ascertained that, properly modified, B-25 medium bombers could carry one-ton bomb loads and still manage the risky, short take-off. Sixteen planes with specially selected five-man crews were prepared for the dangerous mission and loaded aboard the carrier *Hornet*. On April 18, 1942, some 670 miles from Tokyo, they flew off one by one, in a strong wind that helped lift them from the short deck. Their orders were to strike the enemy capital and head for a small airfield deep inside unoccupied China. The resolute bombers swung in over Japan, spending some six minutes over the target, where, ironically, a practice air raid drill was going on. All but one of the planes later crashed or were abandoned in China or off the coast of China; one landed at Vladivostok, and its crew were interned by the Russians; two came down inside enemy territory, and three of their crewmen were later shot in reprisal for American bombing of Japanese residential areas. Of the eighty flyers on the mission, seventy-one eventually returned to the United States.

Tokyo had a hard time figuring out where Doolittle's planes had come from. President Roosevelt facetiously announced that they had taken off from Shangri-La, the Himalayan retreat of James Hilton's novel, *Lost Horizon*.

Doolittle's feat was audacious and psychologically important, even if, having inflicted minimal damage, it had little effect upon the course of the war itself. All that spring, the Japanese war machine continued to grind out victories. It was only later, near the little island of Midway, in June, 1942, that the tide began to turn.

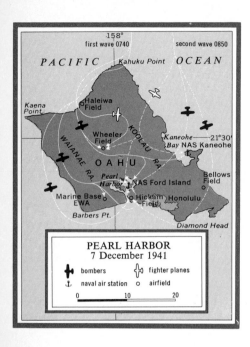

PEARL HARBOR
7 December 1941

bombers   fighter planes
naval air station o airfield

0   10   20

Pacific Blueprint

Japanese strategy for the Pacific was simple in concept but exceedingly ambitious in its scope. First, the American fleet was to be crippled by a surprise blow at Pearl Harbor. Then, while the United States was unable to resist, Japanese forces would swiftly overrun southeast Asia and then build an impregnable defense perimeter around their conquests. And finally, Japan would exploit southeast Asia at her leisure. The plan was overwhelmingly successful at first, as America and her allies suffered an appalling series of defeats. Japan was triumphant in all the Dutch East Indies and in the western Pacific from the Aleutians south. Not until the Battle of Midway, almost exactly half a year after Pearl Harbor, did the balance begin to change. And not until August 7, 1942, at Guadalcanal, was the first step taken on the long road back.

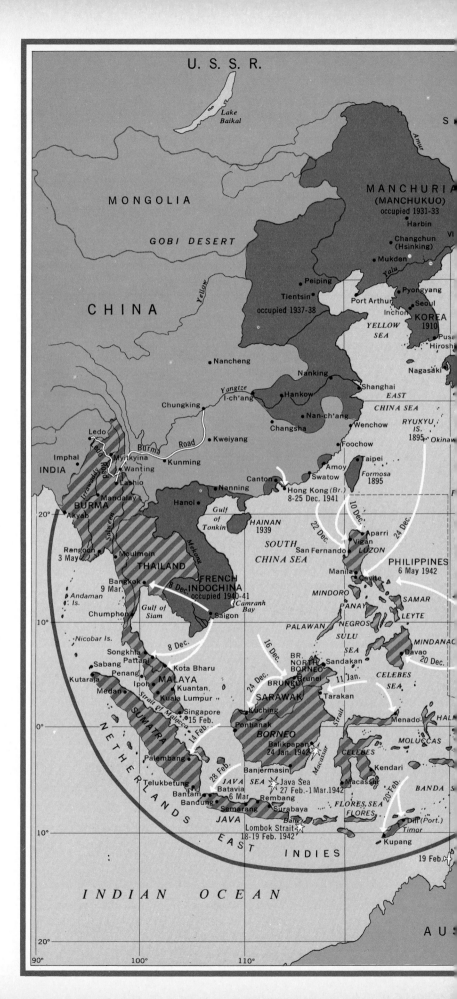

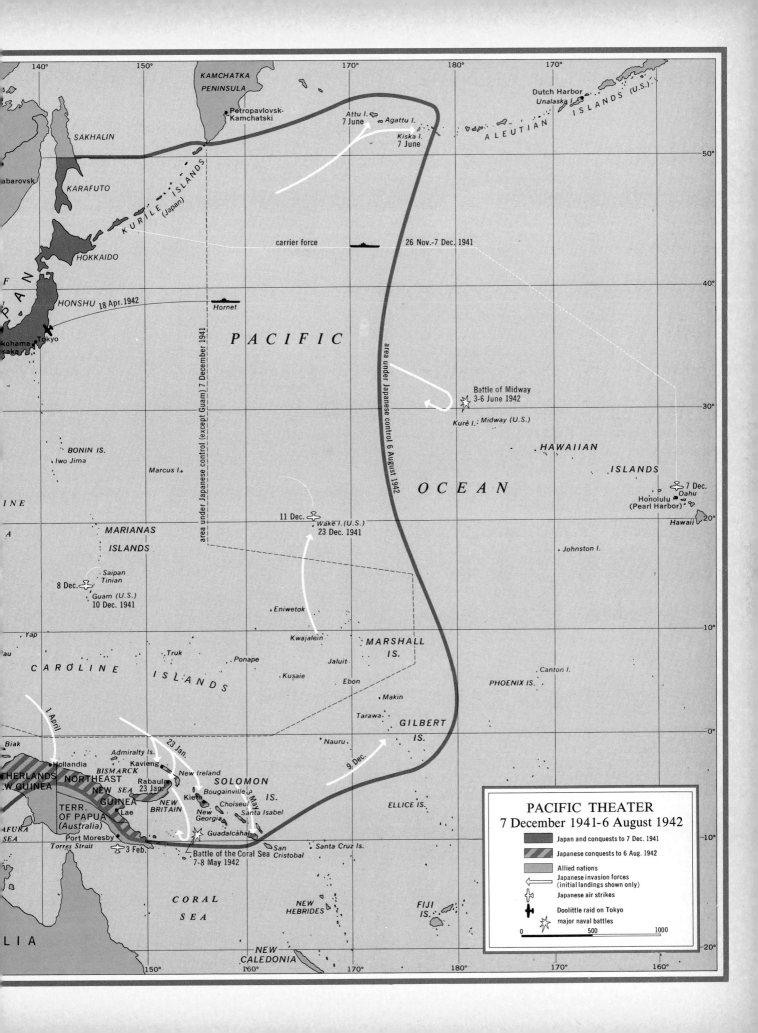

140°   150°   170°   180°   170°

KAMCHATKA
PENINSULA

Dutch Harbor
Unalaska I.   ISLANDS (U.S.)

Petropavlovsk-
Kamchatski   Attu I.   Agattu I.   ALEUTIAN
SAKHALIN   7 June   50°

Kiska I.
KARAFUTO   7 June

KURILE ISLANDS
(Japan)

carrier force   26 Nov.-7 Dec. 1941
HOKKAIDO   40°

Hornet

HONSHU 18 Apr. 1942

PACIFIC   30°

ohama   Battle of Midway
saka   Tokyo   3-6 June 1942

Kurē I.   Midway (U.S.)

BONIN IS.   HAWAIIAN
Iwo Jima

Marcus I.   ISLANDS

O C E A N   7 Dec.
Oahu
Honolulu
(Pearl Harbor)   20°

11 Dec.   Wake I. (U.S.)
MARIANAS   23 Dec. 1941
ISLANDS   Hawaii

Johnston I.

Saipan
Tinian
8 Dec.   10°
Guam (U.S.)
10 Dec. 1941   Eniwetok

Yap
Kwajalein   MARSHALL
CAROLINE   Truk   IS.
Ponape   Jaluit
Kusaie
ISLANDS   Ebon
Makin   Canton I.

Tarawa   PHOENIX IS.
GILBERT   0°
Nauru   IS.
1 April
9 Dec.
Admiralty Is.   23 Jan.
Hollandia   Kavieng
THERLANDS NORTHEAST BISMARCK
W GUINEA   NEW Rabaul New Ireland SOLOMON
SEA   23 Jan.   IS.
NEW   Kieta Bougainville 3 May
TERR. GUINEA NEW New Choiseul ELLICE IS.
OF PAPUA Lae BRITAIN Georgia Santa Isabel
(Australia)   10°
Port Moresby   Guadalcanal
FURA Torres Strait 3 Feb.   San   Santa Cruz Is.
SEA   Battle of the Coral Sea Cristobal
7-8 May 1942

CORAL   FIJI
SEA   NEW   IS.
HEBRIDES

┌───┐
│   PACIFIC THEATER   │
│   7 December 1941-6 August 1942   │
│   │
│ ▬▬▬ Japan and conquests to 7 Dec. 1941 │
│   │
│ ▨▨▨ Japanese conquests to 6 Aug. 1942 │
│   │
│ ▨▨▨ Allied nations   │
│ ⇐   Japanese invasion forces   │
│   (initial landings shown only)   │
│ ✈   Japanese air strikes   │
│   │
│ ✈   Doolittle raid on Tokyo   │
│ ✦   major naval battles   │
│   │
│ 0   500   1000   │
└───┘

NEW
CALEDONIA
150°   160°   170°   180°   170°   160°

The Road Whose End
Was Pearl Harbor

Japan's militarists had been involved in their "China incident" for eight years when the war in Europe began. Then wider vistas opened before them as the colonial powers gave way before Hitler and the treasures of all Asia appeared within reach. Only the United States remained a major obstacle. In September, 1940, despite an American warning, Japan forced Vichy France to grant military bases in Indochina; President Roosevelt countered with an embargo on Japan-bound scrap iron and steel. On September 27, Japan, Germany, and Italy signed a military alliance. Soon after, the Japanese military created a totalitarian state.

By the spring of 1941, American embargoes had cut to almost nothing Japanese imports of gasoline, copper, scrap iron, and other strategic commodities. In July, Japan occupied Indochina, claiming her desperate need for raw materials as justification. The United States at once retaliated by freezing Japanese credits in America. By fall impatient Japanese generals and admirals were determined to go to war if final attempts at diplomacy failed. But the positions of the two nations were irreconcilable. The Japanese, for instance, demanded a free hand to deal with China; the United States insisted that they get out of China entirely. In Washington two ambassadors, Nomura and Kurusu, continued to negotiate with Secretary of State Hull, but neither side had any room for give and take. The Japanese militarists had set November 25 as a deadline beyond which they would wait no longer for diplomatic progress. On that date a Japanese carrier force left the Kurile Islands. Its target was Pearl Harbor.

General Hideki Tojo was War Minister when this picture was taken August 1, 1941. Just six weeks later, as Japan's anti-American position grew firmer and war drew close, he became Premier, with a cabinet top-heavy with military men.

Tokyo's Ginza was decorated with flags of Japan, Italy, and Germany (left) when the three nations joined in an anti-Communist pact in 1937; the arrangement became a full-fledged military alliance of the three totalitarian states late in 1940.

ABOVE AND BELOW: CAPTURED JAPANESE RECORDS, U.S. NAVY

Sunday, December 7, 1941

It is never called simply the attack on Pearl Harbor, but always the "infamous" or the "sneak" attack. However, it succeeded so well not only because of its stealth, but because no one in authority seems to have imagined that the Japanese might hit at that spot. Ambassador Joseph Grew in Tokyo reported as early as January, 1941, that several sources had said Japan planned to bomb Pearl Harbor in the event of trouble, but Naval Intelligence deprecated his warnings. As tension grew, official speculation about possible Japanese targets never included Pearl Harbor. And when warnings that war might be imminent were sent on November 27 to Admiral Kimmel and General Short at Hawaii, it was accepted that any actual blow would come elsewhere. Consequently, the two commanders did little to alert their defenses, and when planes from six Japanese carriers came winging over Oahu just before eight o'clock on December 7, they found the fleet and the Army, Navy, and Marine airfields in typical peacetime Sunday-morning relaxation. The ships in the harbor had only watch sections aboard because it was Navy custom to spend the weekend ashore. Antiaircraft ammunition ready boxes were locked, and officers on watch had the keys. A brave and spirited defense was put up, considering the situation, but it was hopeless. By ten o'clock the fleet as a striking force was wrecked. Six of the eight battleships present were sunk or badly damaged; three destroyers in dry dock were torn by bombs; three cruisers were damaged; four other ships were sunk or damaged. Half the aircraft on the island were wrecked. Some 2,400 men had died; almost half as many were wounded. Japan had lost twenty-nine planes and four midget submarines. There was one bright spot: the Navy's three aircraft carriers were elsewhere that day.

Pilots are briefed while en route to Hawaii (top); deck crews hold bombers until engines have been revved up to take-off speed (middle); a Zeke fighter plane roars off (bottom).

All pictures on these pages are from captured film and show the Japanese side of the Pearl Harbor attack. At top right, pilots on a carrier are highly amused by a broadcast from a station in totally unsuspecting Honolulu. At bottom right, a torpedo plane pulls up (to right of water geyser in top center of picture) after hitting the Oklahoma. *The battleship capsized after taking two more torpedoes, all before the attack was five minutes old. The* Oklahoma *and the* Arizona *were the only battleships that did not eventually rejoin the fleet.*

ABOVE: MOVIETONE NEWS; BELOW: CAPTURED JAPANESE RECORDS, U.S. NAVY

Disaster on Battleship Row (from left): West Virginia, *resting on the bottom;* Tennessee, *badly damaged, but able three weeks later t*

il to the West Coast for repairs; Arizona, *mortally wounded—she still lies today, with most of her men, beneath Pearl Harbor.*

At left, Secretary of State Cordell Hull walks between Ambassador Nomura (left) and special envoy Kurusu as they arrive at the White House on November 17 to confer with President Roosevelt. The two Japanese apparently never knew that an attack was to be made on Pearl Harbor. At right, the President addresses Congress, asking for a declaration of war against Japan. It was at this time that he referred to December 7 as "a date which will live in infamy." The drawing below of American ships torn asunder by Japanese bombs was found in one of the enemy planes shot down at Pearl Harbor. The characters at the left margin translate to "Hear! The voice of the moment of death. Wake up, you fools." The artist also added some anti-American sentiments in not quite grammatical but completely understandable and emphatic English.

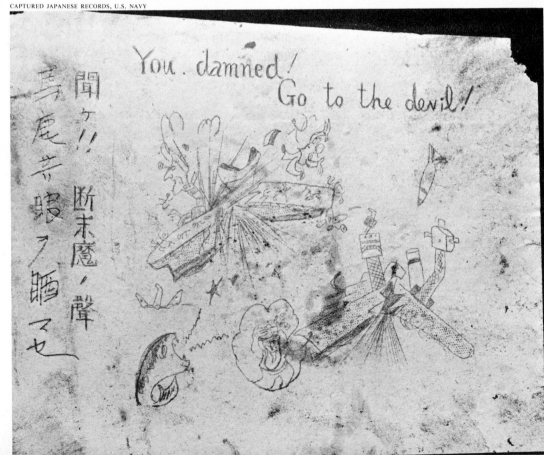

Japanese Blunder

With the Pearl Harbor attack, the war became a world war. The United States declared war on Japan on December 8. Churchill had pledged that if America went to war with Japan, Britain would at once join her, a promise kept so promptly that England's declaration actually came before America's. Germany and Italy declared war on the United States on December 11; before the week was out, nations representing half the world's population were in the conflict. The attack was a Japanese blunder, for it killed isolationism and replaced it with a single-minded determination to win the war. Even its military value was doubtful. The purpose of the attack had been to cripple the American Navy while the Japanese moved southward and then fortified their conquests. But the Pacific Fleet even before the attack would have been too vulnerable to land-based aircraft to prevent Japanese aggression, and American plans, in case of war, called for only a cautious advance into the western Pacific.

ABOVE: UPI; BELOW: MAINICHI GRAPHIC—BIRNBACK

Wrong-Way Bastion

Singapore will be remembered as the fortress where the cannon pointed the wrong way. British strategists for decades had grown complacent on visions of Singapore smashing and sinking any enemy fleet that dared attack it—but the Japanese chose to do it another way. They came in from the rear, first destroying British air bases and planes and then moving down the Malay Peninsula, with British troops making a heartbreaking, 400-mile rear-guard action. When the Japanese advance reached Singapore, the defenders could turn only a few of the guns of the fortress against them; most of the cannon were emplaced to fire only out to sea. A resolution to fight to the death was dropped, and surrender came February 15, 1942, when food, water, ammunition, and gasoline were nearly gone and civilian suffering had become unbearable.

After carrying out the whirlwind Malay-Singapore campaign, General Tomoyuki Yamashita (above) took command of the lagging Philippines operations and captured Bataan and Corregidor. He was executed after the war. At top left is a Singapore street scene (which was repeated, however, in countless variations across the world during the war): women weep for a child slain by enemy bombs. The Japanese nurses at left talk with surrendered soldiers at Singapore. The picture was made by the Japanese, but it was censored and not published, presumably because a portrayal of such friendliness by Japanese women toward an enemy was not in accord with the war spirit. And at right, a British officer resolutely strides ahead to the unhappy business of surrendering "impregnable" Singapore. Some 70,000 Empire troops, including General Sir Arthur Percival, were taken prisoner in this, the most catastrophic defeat ever suffered by Great Britain in the Far East.

Assault on the Islands

Artist Sato Kai painted the enemy version (right) of the air raid on Clark Field. Postwar attempts to fix the blame for lack of American defense measures have always led to conflicting charges. In a painting primitive but full of detail (below), Kohei Ezaki gave a Japanese-eye view of the landings on Guam.

CAPTURED JAPANESE PAINTING, U.S. AIR FORCE

CAPTURED JAPANESE PAINTING, U.S. ARMY

The Japanese advance, seemingly irresistible, swept down at once on the three American outposts west of Midway Island. Unfortified Guam, defended by perhaps 700 marines and Guamanians with no arms larger than .30-caliber machine guns, was hit by a landing force of 6,000 on December 10 and taken on the twelfth. On tiny Wake Island, 400 marines resisted heroically for fifteen days, sinking two destroyers and killing 700 of the foe before being overwhelmed on December 23. But the prime objective of the enemy was the Philippines; there the major air base, Clark Field, was struck only about ten hours after the Pearl Harbor attack. Despite ample warning that air raids could be expected, most of the B-17's were destroyed on the ground. Attacks on other fields virtually wiped out American air power. On December 10, Japanese troops began to land.

Crude signs saying "OPEN CITY" and "NO SHOOTING" greeted the Japanese Army, which observed the open-city convention, unlike the Air Force, which left widespread destruction.

Fall of a City

The day after Christmas, when his forces had cleared Manila on their withdrawal to Bataan and Corregidor, MacArthur declared it an open city. The blacked-out lights went on again, and the night clubs filled with frantically gay crowds. That same day, the huge oil dumps of Manila had been fired to keep the oil from the enemy; now heavy clouds of thick, sooty smoke rolled over the city, and orange flames glowed over the burning tanks. In the distance, demolitions explosions sounded from Cavite Naval Base, Fort McKinley, and Nielson Field. The open-city declaration had been broadcast and acknowledged by Tokyo, but the bombers soon appeared again, and merciless attacks continued until the city was taken.

As the Japanese neared the capital, many panicky people fled into the country. Others just waited. General Homma halted his columns, now unopposed, about fifteen miles from Manila and had his men clean themselves and tighten their formations. Dirty, battle-stained troops, he knew, do not parade with pride and are more likely to loot and rape. On January 2, late in the afternoon, Japanese units entered the city simultaneously from north and south and, while smoke from the still-burning oil tanks rose in the sky, raised the Japanese flag.

General Homma treated not only Manila with relative softness, but was soon after criticized by his inspecting superior for his leniency toward all Filipinos. He had ordered his troops to respect the customs of the people and to treat them as friends, not enemies. On one occasion he had even refused to distribute a propaganda pamphlet saying the Americans had exploited the Filipinos. It was just not true, said Homma, for the Americans had governed very well, and it was up to the Japanese to do even better. He was warned to be tougher but could not change and was soon removed from command. After the war he was tried as a war criminal on MacArthur's orders and shot.

CAPTURED JAPANESE RECORDS, U.S. ARMY

ABOVE AND BELOW: CAPTURED JAPANESE RECORDS, U.S. NAVY

Lt. Gen. Homma (above) was removed from command and virtually disgraced for his softness in the Philippines. Many Americans thought it unjust that after the war he should be brought to trial for war crimes by an old adversary, MacArthur, who also appointed prosecution and defense and reviewed the death sentence. At right, Japanese tanks roll through Manila. The below picture of happily fraternizing Japanese soldiers and Filipino girls, published in Japan, has signs of having been posed.

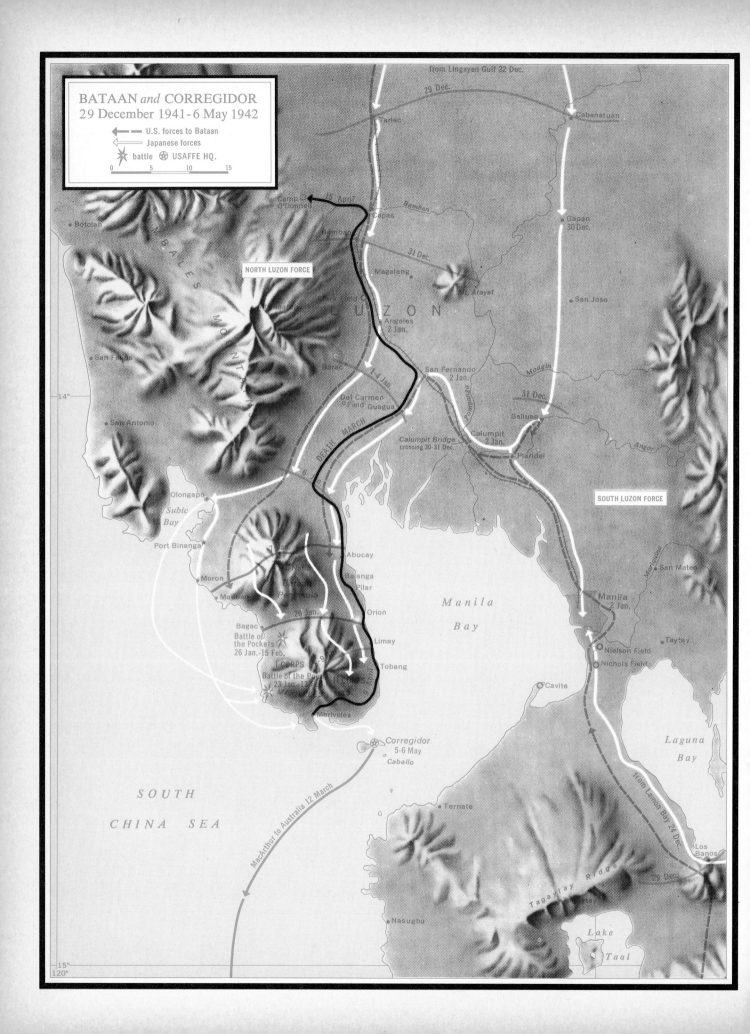

BATAAN *and* CORREGIDOR
29 December 1941 – 6 May 1942

U.S. forces to Bataan
Japanese forces
battle   USAFFE HQ.

0   5   10   15

from Lingayen Gulf 22 Dec.

29 Dec.

Cabanatuan

Tarlac

15 April

Camp O'Donnell

Bamban

Capas

Gapan
30 Dec.

Bamban

31 Dec.

NORTH LUZON FORCE

Magalang

Mt. Arayat

San Jose

L U Z O N

Angeles
2 Jan.

Clark Field

Botolan

San Felipe

Z A M B A L E S   M O U N T A I N S

14°

San Antonio

Bataan

Del Carmen
Field

San Fernando
2 Jan.

Moagin

31 Dec.

Baliuag

Guagua

Calumpit
2 Jan.

Angat

Calumpit Bridge
crossing 30-31 Dec.

Plaridel

SOUTH LUZON FORCE

Olongapo

Subic
Bay

Port Binanga

Moron

Mauban

Bataan
Peninsula

26 Jan.

Bagac
Battle of
the Pockets
26 Jan.-15 Feb.

I CORPS
Battle of the Points
23 Jan.-13

Abucay

Balanga

Pilar

Orion

Limay

Tobang

M a n i l a
B a y

Manila
2 Jan.

Taytay

Nielson Field

Nichols Field

Cavite

Mariveles

Corregidor
5-6 May
Caballo

MacArthur to Australia 12 March

S O U T H

C H I N A   S E A

Ternate

Laguna
Bay

San Mateo

Marikina

from Lamon Bay 24 Dec.

Los
Banos

29 Dec.

Nasugbu

Tagaytay Ridge

Lake
Taal

15°
120°

"If Food Fails You Will... Attack"

The defense of Bataan was heroic and inspiring, but it was nevertheless another in the long series of defeats. Japanese strategy was simple: to push the American-Philippine forces back into Manila and there destroy them. General MacArthur evaded the trap by retreating instead into Bataan Peninsula, whose mountains, jungles, and swamps made ideal defenses. Even so, there was a limit to what the embattled force could do in the face of hunger, sickness, and a scarcity of everything. General MacArthur, under orders, escaped from Corregidor but insisted on exercising command from Australia: "If food fails you will prepare and execute an attack upon the enemy." On April 4, General Jonathan Wainwright ordered an attack as the Japanese began to break through, but the weakened men could hardly respond. The Bataan forces surrendered on the ninth to prevent a slaughter, but Corregidor still held out.

To preserve the considerable talents of General Douglas MacArthur (at right, in his Corregidor headquarters) for future campaigns, President Roosevelt sent him direct orders to leave his Philippines command and proceed to Australia. The defending forces not only made the best possible use of Bataan's terrain but added a few tricks of their own, like the field of bamboo spears below. However, not any kind of ingenuity could compensate for food and equipment shortages.

The Bitter Road from Bataan

Surrender brought no rest or relief to the sick, starving defenders of Bataan. They were started at once on the nightmare trip—some sixty miles—that has ever since been known as the Death March. About 75,000 men, 12,000 of them American, began the march, but only 54,000 reached its end. Many escaped along the way, but 7,000 to 10,000 perished. The ordeal was not ended for those who survived the brutal trek; 40 per cent died of disease, hunger, or maltreatment during imprisonment at Camp O'Donnell during the next three months.

Stories told by participants in the march merge into a horror of heat, thirst, hunger, and savageries by sadistic guards. Yet the episode was not a deliberate carnival of cruelty. General Homma, the commanding officer, had laid down general procedures: transportation, field hospitals along the route to care for the sick, food for the prisoners. But arrangements began to collapse almost at once. There were more than twice as many prisoners as Homma had expected, and their physical condition was much worse. There were few officers, and many of the enlisted guards seemed not to grasp the difference between a fighting foe and one who had surrendered. But many of the marchers were treated decently and saw almost no brutalities on the route; they were given water and at least occasional food. At the same time, another group of men a mile or two behind them might be suffering inhuman tortures: clubbed, prodded with bayonets, forced to stagger past flowing wells though half crazed with thirst. Strangest of the anomalies of this tragic movement was that about half those on the Death March did not even walk but rode in trucks and suffered little. Although such instances were little publicized, the catalogue of atrocities was long enough to justify a dozen times over the name Death March. The story shocked and enraged America and hardened its resolution to defeat Japan.

"The hours dragged by and...the drop-outs began"

U.S. AIR FORCE

Colonel William E. Dyess

News of exactly what had happened in the Pacific did not hit the American people all at once. Stories of the Bataan surrender, of the suffering endured by American prisoners, came in scattered bits and pieces and were wholly inconclusive. It was not until the war was two years old that a full eye-witness account of the atrocities of the Death March was published. The Dyess Story was written by William E. Dyess, a young Air Corps pilot who had been captured on Bataan and had later escaped. It had been held back by the Government in case its publication might jeopardize others still being held in Japanese prison camps. The story appeared early in January, 1944, first in newspapers, then as a book; the month before, Colonel Dyess had been killed in a plane crash in California. The following is an excerpt.

. . . It was midnight when we recrossed Bataan field and kept going. We were within a short distance of Cabcaben field when the Japs diverted the line into a tiny rice paddy. There was no room to lie down. Some of us tried to rest in a half squat. Others drew up their knees and laid their heads on the legs of the men next to them. Jap guards stood around the edges of the little field, their feet almost touching the outer fringe of men.

I heard a cry, followed by thudding blows at one side of the paddy. An American soldier so tortured by thirst that he could not sleep had asked a Jap guard for water. The Jap fell on him with his fists, then slugged him into insensibility with a rifle butt.

The thirst of all had become almost unbearable, but remembering what had happened to the colonel earlier in the day we asked for nothing. . . .

At dawn of the second day the impatient Japs stepped among and upon us, kicking us into wakefulness. We were hollow-eyed and as exhausted as we had been when we went to sleep. As we stumbled into the road we passed a Jap noncommissioned officer who was eating meat and rice.

"Pretty soon you eat," he told us.

The rising sun cast its blinding light into our eyes as we marched. The temperature rose by the minute. Noon came and went. The midday heat was searing. At 1 P.M. the column was halted and Jap noncoms told American and Filipino soldiers they might fill their canteens from a dirty puddle beside the road. There was no food.

During the afternoon traffic picked up again. Troop-laden trucks sped past us. A grimacing Jap leaned far out, holding his rifle by the barrel. As the truck roared by he knocked an American soldier senseless with the gun's stock. Other Japs saw this and yelled. From now on we kept out of reach if we could. . . .

At 2 P.M. we were told it would be necessary to segregate the prisoners as to rank; colonels together, majors together, and so on. This separated all units from their officers and afforded opportunity for another hour of sun treatment. There was no mention of food.

The line of march was almost due north now. We reached Balanga, about twenty miles from Cabcaben field, at sundown. We were marched into the courtyard of a large prison-like structure, dating to the Spanish days, and told we would eat, then spend the night there.

At one side of the yard food was bubbling in great caldrons. Rice and soy sauce were boiling together. Jap kitchen corpsmen were opening dozens of cans and dumping vienna sausage into the savory mess. The aromatic steam that drifted over from those pots had us almost crazy. While we waited we were given a little water.

We imagined the rice and sausages were for us, though we saw hundreds of ragged and sick Filipinos behind a barbed wire barricade near-by who had only filthy, fly-covered rice to eat. After drinking we were ordered into the line for what appeared to be a routine search. When it was finished an officer shouted something and the attitude of our guards swiftly changed.

They ordered us out of the patio and lined us up in a field across the road. As we left, grinning Japs held up steaming ladles of sausages and rice. The officer followed us to the field, then began stamping up and down, spouting denunciations and abuse. When he calmed enough to be understood, we heard this:

"When you came here you were told you would eat and be let to sleep. Now that is changed. We have found pistols concealed among three American officers. In punishment for these offenses you will not be given food. You will march to Orani (five miles to the north) before you sleep."

The accusation was a lie. If a pistol had been found, the owner would have been shot, beaten to death, or beheaded on the spot. Besides, we knew that the searchers hadn't overlooked even a toothbrush, to say nothing of a pistol. The Japs simply were adding mental torture to the physical. The Jap officer saw he wasn't believed. He did just what a Jap might be expected to do. Shortly after we resumed the march a staff car pulled up beside us.

Three American officers were dragged out of line and thrown into it. This in the words of Gilbert and Sullivan's Pooh Bah was "corroborative detail, intended to lend artistic verisimilitude to an otherwise bald and unconvincing narrative." We never saw the three officers again, though it is not hard to guess their fate. Men who had stood near two of them during the search said no guns had been found.

Our guards had been increased for the night march, and rigid discipline was imposed. We were formed into columns of fours. A new set of guards came up on bicycles and we were forced to walk practically at double quick to keep up. After two hours these guards were replaced by a group on foot who walked slowly with short mincing steps. The change of gait so cramped our leg muscles that walking was agony.

We had learned by rough experience that efforts to assist our failing comrades served usually to hasten their deaths and add to our own misery and peril. So we tried the next best thing—encouraging them with words. . . .

It was during a period of slow marching that an old friend, a captain in the medical corps, began dropping back through the ranks. Presently he was beside me. It was plain he was just about done in. I said:

"Hello, Doc. Taking a walk?"

"Ed," he said slowly, "I can't go another kilometer. A little farther and I'm finished."

"Well, Doc, I'm about in the same fix," I told him. Nothing more was said until we had covered two or three kilometers. Every now and then Doc would begin to lag a little. When this happened, the fellow on the other side of Doc would join me in slipping back some and giving him a little shove with our shoulders. He always took the hint and stepped up. At length he spoke again.

"I'm done, Ed. You fellows forget me and go on. I can't make another kilometer."

"I don't think I can either, Doc. I feel just about as you do."

That was the way we passed the night. Kilometer after kilometer crawled by, but Doc didn't fall out. If he had, his bones would be bleaching now somewhere along that road of death that led out of Bataan.

The hours dragged by and, as we knew they must, the drop-outs began. It seemed that a great many of the prisoners reached the end of their endurance at about the same time. They went down by twos and threes. Usually, they made an effort to rise. I never can forget their groans and strangled breathing as they tried to get up. Some succeeded. Others lay lifelessly where they had fallen.

I observed that the Jap guards paid no attention to these. I wondered why. The explanation wasn't long in coming. There was a sharp crackle of pistol and rifle fire behind us.

Skulking along, a hundred yards behind our contingent, came a "clean-up squad" of murdering Jap buzzards. Their helpless victims, sprawled darkly against the white of the road, were easy targets.

As members of the murder squad stooped over each huddled form, there would be an orange flash in the darkness and a sharp report. The bodies were left where they lay, that other prisoners coming behind us might see them.

Our Japanese guards enjoyed the spectacle in silence for a time. Eventually, one of them who spoke English felt he should add a little spice to the entertainment.

"Sleepee?" he asked. "You want sleep? Just lie down on road. You get good, long sleep!"

On through the night we were followed by orange flashes and thudding shots.

ABOVE: U.S. ARMY; BELOW: CAPTURED JAPANESE PAINTING, U.S. ARMY

Last Days of the Rock

After the fall of Bataan, the Japanese assault turned on Corregidor, where some 13,000 defenders braced themselves. The island fortress, like all American outposts in the Pacific, suffered from misguided economy, but it was still a formidable work. Called The Rock, there had been driven through its central height, Malinta Hill, a long tunnel whose many laterals provided living quarters, storage, hospitals, and other necessities of life under siege. Barracks and other outside quarters were abandoned as everyone moved underground. Only those who manned artillery positions or other defense posts went into the open to face the enemy bombardment. Dust and dirt constantly sifted down into the tunnels as the earth shook from shell explosions. The air was bad; hunger was constant because rations had long since been cut in half; quarrels flared over trifles in the tense atmosphere. Some men were so terrified of the dangers outside that they refused to take their tours of duty there; they became known as tunnel rats and were bitterly resented by those who did go out.

By May 4, enemy shells were falling at the rate of one every five seconds, 16,000 in twenty-four hours. Corregidor's big guns were wrecked; little more than the beach defenses remained. Japanese landing forces came ashore on the night of the fifth, and after terrible losses, moved toward the tunnel. General Wainwright, fearful the enemy might advance with guns firing into the tunnels among the nurses and wounded, had his men lay down their arms. But he had previously released other commanders in the Philippines from further compliance with his orders, and General Homma refused to accept surrender under these conditions. Wainwright, almost distraught and with visions of the Japanese reopening hostilities against his now disarmed troops, took to the radio to plead with commanders elsewhere to lay down their arms. After weeks of uncertainty, all surrendered, although many of their men took to the hills to continue the war as guerrilla fighters.

General Wainwright broadcast to American commanders still resisting with the implied warning that if they did not surrender, the Japanese would probably massacre the prisoners on Corregidor. The attentive gentleman with him is Lt. Kano, schooled in New York and New Jersey and ready to cut off the broadcast if Wainwright left his prepared text.

Corregidor's tunnels (top) were almost impervious to shellfire, but as the picture indicates, they were short on space and comfort. At bottom is a Japanese artist's portrayal of surrender discussions in a small, battle-damaged house on Bataan. General Homma, the bulletheaded officer in profile, faces General Wainwright, second from left, across the table.

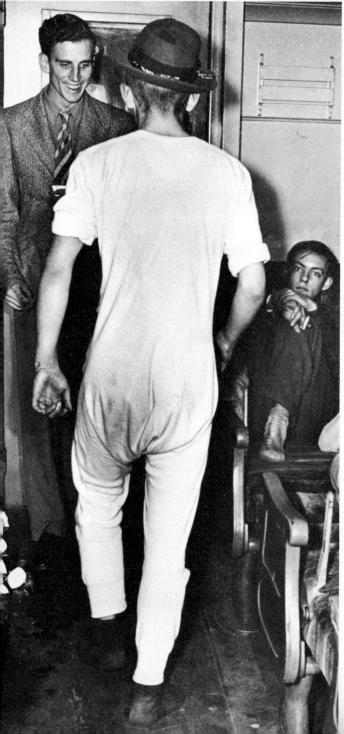

ABOVE: LIBRARY OF CONGRESS; BELOW: VICTOR BARRON

And Back Home...

Isolationism died when the first bomb fell on Pearl Harbor, and from that time the country was united in purpose. "Remember Pearl Harbor" was the national battle cry, and eager citizens everywhere volunteered to do whatever bit they could to help win the war. For young men there was no problem; the armed services were happy to see them. For others—and especially for women, who came into their own during the war—there were scores of jobs to fill: as air-raid wardens, in Red Cross corps, as messengers, making first aid supplies, and many others. There was a sense of great urgency to some of this volunteer work, for it was thought very likely that there would be Japanese air raids on the Pacific Coast, so that the first aid and other training would be put to grim practical use in the very near future.

FRANKLIN D. ROOSEVELT LIBRARY

Brooklyn Navy Yard workers (far left) assemble for farewell ceremonies before leaving for Hawaii in January of 1942. Several hundred of them had volunteered to work at Pearl Harbor. Women at top center volunteer for Red Cross work in San Francisco in December, 1941. And at near left, the young man in "long johns" was one of 188 Navy recruits on a special train on the way from Florida and Georgia to Norfolk for training. All volunteered shortly after Pearl Harbor. The poster above exhorted civilian workers to produce the supplies and the equipment needed by fighting men.

The Land of the Free

It is difficult to avoid all inequities in the democratic process in time of war, but the United States had little excuse for its treatment of citizens of Japanese ancestry. There were 126,000 of these people on the mainland when war began, 93,000 of them in California. About two thirds, being American-born (nisei), were citizens, but the foreign-born (issei) were not eligible for naturalization. The feeling against Japanese was partly the same unreasoning, rabid hysteria that in 1917 caused German to be banned in schools and sauerkraut to be renamed liberty cabbage. But race prejudice was also involved, and resentment from well before the war because of economic competition by industrious Japanese. President Roosevelt, on the urging of the War Department, which cried the dangers of sabotage, authorized moving 112,000 Japanese Americans to relocation centers that were, in fact, prison camps, complete with barbed wire and armed guards, although no one sent there had been charged with any crime. The first internees were not freed until 1944, and none were permitted to return home until after the war. Many had nothing to return to, for homes and occupations were gone. Justice Frank Murphy called it "one of the most sweeping and complete deprivations of constitutional rights in the history of this nation in the absence of martial law."

Earl Warren, then California Attorney General, was one who insisted on moving the Japanese inland. In this he was influenced by protectionist groups, of whom some were probably much more interested in eliminating the Japanese American as a business competitor than as a possible spy or saboteur.

The sign at left appeared in the window of a small Oakland, California, store on December 8, but the owner, though a University of California graduate and a citizen, was later moved with other Japanese Americans to a relocation camp. At top right, internees sign in upon their arrival at the Santa Anita, California, registration center; and at bottom right is the Salinas, California, camp, with a newly arrived contingent and their baggage in the foreground.

Bold First Blow at Japan

On the morning of April 18, 1942, as an air-raid drill was taking place in Tokyo, sixteen American B-25's swooped over the Japanese homeland at treetop level. At Tokyo and four other cities, the planes climbed to 1,500 feet and let go of their 500-pound bombs. Then they dropped back down again and headed for China. The raid, which was commanded by Lieutenant Colonel James Doolittle, was a total surprise. It caused considerable panic in Tokyo and left the world wondering where the land-based bombers had come from. President Roosevelt jokingly said the answer was "Shangri-La." The facts were these: the aircraft carrier *Hornet*, with a heavy escort, had brought the B-25's to within 700 miles of Tokyo. But early on the eighteenth, they were spotted by an enemy patrol boat; the boat was promptly sunk and the attack launched ten hours sooner than planned, and from about 150 miles farther out. As a result, most of the planes had to crash-land in China. One came down in Russia and two in Japanese territory, where three crewmen were later executed. The raid had little military importance, but it had an electrifying effect on American morale, and that alone, in early 1942, was quite important.

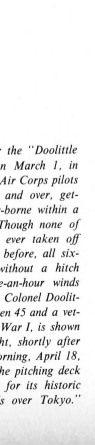

Preparation for the "Doolittle Raid" began on March 1, in Florida, where Air Corps pilots practiced, over and over, getting B-25's air-borne within a 750-foot run. Though none of the pilots had ever taken off from a carrier before, all sixteen got off without a hitch despite 45-mile-an-hour winds and rough seas. Colonel Doolittle, who was then 45 and a veteran of World War I, is shown at left. At right, shortly after eight in the morning, April 18, a B-25 leaves the pitching deck of the Hornet *for its historic "thirty seconds over Tokyo."*

War at Sea

When Hitler began his onslaught in 1939, he reckoned that sea power was not a crucial military matter. Unlike the favored *Luftwaffe*, the German Navy was ill prepared. Not even Germany's redoubtable U-boat fleet was ready for a long campaign. But it was the sea—the narrow English Channel—that inevitably thwarted Hitler's ambitions for total domination of Europe and led him to turn his armies eastward into the disastrous Russian snows. In North Africa, where Rommel almost broke the British on the verges of the Nile, failure to control the Mediterranean narrows cost the Germans still another important triumph. And ultimately, from across the seas, came a huge American armada. As time passed, even the U-boats began to lose their efficacy.

Japan made no such basic miscalculation. As a sea people, the Japanese were instinctively aware of the maritime key to victory, and they boasted a massive fleet that included the world's two largest battleships, the 72,908 ton *Yamato*, and the *Musashi*. The flaw in Tokyo's thinking was the belief that an initial advantage attained at Pearl Harbor would gain sufficient time to insure an impregnable economic and military position, and that this in turn could ward off eventual counterattack. As General Marshall reported in 1945, such assumptions proved erroneous because "the Japanese had reckoned without the shipyards of America and the fighting tradition of the United States Navy."

In 1939, when the conflict started, the world was accustomed to regarding Britain as the great maritime power, but the Royal Navy was no longer that Queen of the Seas that had dominated the nineteenth century. Its command had gradually succumbed to a hierarchy of class and was more preoccupied with tradition than with technology, despite admirable equipment made available by British scientists. Its tactics often were outdated, as shown when an admiral sailed off without air support in 1941 and lost two of the King's mightiest vessels. And the Royal Navy was not sufficiently strong for the immense combination of duties it had to face. Despite fifty destroyers that the United States had made available at Churchill's request, and despite a concentrated building program, the entire British Battle Fleet by the end of World War II was no larger than the single U.S. Task Force 77 in the Pacific.

Had the Germans produced a thoroughly rational and consistent strategy, they might have capitalized upon British weakness; but Hitler began full-scale naval preparations only in 1939. Admiral Erich Raeder, Commander in Chief of Hitler's Navy, had hoped there would be no conflict before 1942, by which date he planned to have ready a prodigious fleet that would include two hundred and fifty U-boats, thirteen battleships, and four aircraft carriers. When the *Führer* precipitated war, Raeder was forced to abandon this program and concentrate on the immediate construction of submarines.

Because the British were spread so thin and because the German fleet was inadequate, the naval potential of Italy and France assumed heightened importance. The

British seamen battle ice and high seas in the North Atlantic, 1943.

Italians had fast ships but showed more dash in maneuvers than in battle. They were never able to control the eastern Mediterranean, even when British power was at its ebb. Had the Axis gained the use of the French Navy, however, the balance might have been dangerously turned. After France's capitulation, those of its vessels to join Britain had little importance. Other units, seized in Alexandria harbor, were interned according to their wish. The main strength lay in Toulon, with substantial forces also anchored at the Mers-el-Kebir base of Oran in Algeria. On July 3, 1940, unwilling to risk the possibility that these might help the Axis, the British sent an ultimatum to the Oran flotilla. When the French commander failed to respond within six hours, the British then attacked and seriously damaged three battleships, a seaplane carrier, and two destroyers.

The Oran battle between the vessels of two allies was a difficult and heart-rending affair (more than a thousand French sailors were killed); but it was made necessary by British determination to retain the upper hand at sea. Inflammatory Nazi propaganda stressed this tragic engagement and sought to persuade the French to join the campaign against Britain. Nevertheless, as Churchill later and generously recalled in his history of the war: "The genius of France enabled her people to comprehend the whole significance of Oran, and in her agony to draw new hope and strength from this additional bitter pang. General de Gaulle, whom I did not consult beforehand, was magnificent in his demeanour, and France liberated and restored has ratified his conduct."

The first dramatic confrontations of the war at sea were between conventional surface vessels. The earliest of these was the hunting down of the *Graf Spee*, third and last of those German pocket battleships so neatly designed to get around the regulations of the Versailles Treaty: fast, light, heavily gunned and armored. When hostilities started, it dashed for the southern Atlantic to prey on Allied shipping and soon sank nine cargo vessels off the coast of Latin America.

On December 13, 1939, the *Graf Spee* appeared near Uruguay, where it was surprised by three British cruisers, *Exeter*, *Achilles*, and *Ajax*. For fourteen hours the ships pounded away at one another. Then the *Graf Spee* turned away through the phosphorescent offshore seas and sought haven in Montevideo. It was summarily ordered out by the neutral Uruguayans. On December 17, the *Graf Spee* blew itself up in the broad River Plate while three hundred thousand spectators lined the shore to watch. Captain Hans Langsdorff, a veteran of the famous World War I encounter at Jutland, was interned in Argentina with his crew. Three days later, he draped around

him the old German Imperial Naval flag, ignoring Hitler's swastika, and shot himself dead.

For the British people, the end of the *Graf Spee* was a comforting victory that their propaganda services were able to dramatize with some effect. The Germans, somewhat puzzled, sought to play down its importance. At the time, I was in Slovakia, the Nazi puppet state carved from the murdered Czechoslovak Republic, traveling with Edward Kennedy, an Associated Press reporter. We were arrested by the Gestapo and, despite United States neutrality, accused of espionage—a charge we easily refuted. The scuttling of the *Graf Spee* coincided with our release, and all the local press covered its front pages with accounts of the presence of two "English spies," Kennedy and myself. News of the River Plate battle occupied only a few brief inside paragraphs.

A second great sea encounter came in the spring of 1941, when the German dreadnought *Bismarck*, accompanied by the cruiser *Prinz Eugen*, sailed from occupied Poland through the British blockade, intent on sinking as much tonnage as possible on the cold, gray North Atlantic. Six U-boats were assigned to help the mighty surface raider. The British first spotted the *Bismarck* when it was refueling at Bergen, Norway, on May 21 and began to mark its passage through fog and clouds. Three days later, in clear weather, the powerful *Hood* and *Prince of Wales* found their enemy and opened fire. The *Hood* was destroyed by a formidable salvo; the *Prince of Wales*, badly damaged, limped away. But the *Bismarck*, also seriously wounded and leaving a steady oil trail, turned back, at reduced speed, to seek haven at Saint-Nazaire in occupied France.

On the morning of May 26, a Royal Air Force flying boat once again spotted the great ship, still seven hundred miles from the French coast, and the British sent torpedo planes to delay its escape. *Bismarck* was struck twice, once in the rudder. Its captain knew now that the end was not far off. His antiaircraft crews were out of ammunition, so he dropped them alongside on rafts and made ready for the inevitable. The next morning a squadron of British ships encircled their victim like yapping hounds and opened concentrated fire. They were unable to pierce the *Bismarck's* armored deck or destroy its engines, but one by one they smashed the machinery of its turrets. Finally, unable to proceed, the German captain scuttled. In a strategic sense this was a British naval triumph because Hitler lost his greatest and irreplaceable battleship. But in the process Britain also lost its most powerful vessel, the *Hood*, and suffered damage to two other battleships, a destroyer, and many planes. Furthermore, much of its fleet had been diverted from important

Mediterranean assignments in order to encompass the elusive *Bismarck*'s end, and this weakened the defense of Crete at the moment of its invasion on June 1. The victory proved to be an expensive one.

Second only in naval importance to the Home Fleet's task of supplying and guarding the United Kingdom itself was Britain's Mediterranean role. The lovely inland sea served as a lifeline to British possessions in the Middle East, to Suez and the route to India, and to the Army of the Nile, which had been concentrated in Egypt in 1939. From the start, the British depended heavily on France to police the western Mediterranean, and they weakened their own forces in the east by withdrawing ships to protect Atlantic convoys when Mussolini initially failed to declare war. However, the combined effect of Italian belligerency and French collapse suddenly altered the relative balance. With fewer vessels at their disposal, the British suddenly had to face the Italians in the eastern Mediterranean and assume in the west a burden hitherto left to the French. From Gibraltar to Malta and on to Alexandria, their bases were now directly menaced. The result was the War Cabinet order to attack France's Oran naval base and carry out a series of aggressive actions against Mussolini's speedy but inept fleet.

Admiral Sir Andrew Cunningham, a tough, hell-for-leather sea dog, first struck a large force of Italian warships off the Calabrian coast. He drove another Italian flotilla from the region of Cape Spatha, northwest of Crete. His hard-pressed units managed to convoy badly needed supplies to isolated Malta, and then, on November 11, 1940, he thrust a carrier raid at Taranto, on Italy's heel, while all Mussolini's battleships were in port. Heavy damage was inflicted by obsolete Swordfish aircraft. When the smoke cleared, the *Duce* found his battle force had been halved. Of his six mightiest ships, one never sailed again, and two others were out of action for months. Taranto was abandoned as a fleet base when the surviving vessels scurried for Naples. News of this famous victory was broadcast through embattled Greece, and the vivacious Greeks went mad with joy.

Until Sicily was successfully invaded by the Allies in 1943, the Mediterranean was constantly ripped apart by sea and naval-air battles. To gain the upper hand, Hitler's high command conceived a plan called Operation Felix, designed to bring Spain into the war and block the Gibraltar straits. However, Franco demurred, and ultimately the idea was dropped. Instead, the Germans first sent a mechanized Afrika Korps to help the Italians in the Libyan Desert and then rescued Mussolini's bogged-down Army in Albania by crushing Yugoslavia, Greece, and Crete. Malta, as a result, was more cut off and threat-

ened than ever before. *Luftwaffe* squadrons were moved into the Mediterranean, and Alexandria and the Suez Canal came under immediate danger. To supply its Middle East forces, Britain was now forced to send convoys by the long and costly route around the Cape of Good Hope. The Navy was further weakened during the Battle of Crete and the consequent need to evacuate British and Greek troops when that island fell. The Admiralty grimly notified the War Office that if it were to lose Cyprus after Crete, it could expect no further succor.

The next and immensely difficult naval task was to hold on to Malta and from that rocky base hamper the flow of Axis supplies from southern Italy to North Africa, where Rommel had begun to threaten the Nile Valley. British losses en route to Malta were enormous. In April, 1942, Churchill urged Roosevelt to make the carrier *Wasp* available to fly in help. The request was granted, and some sixty Spitfires were dispatched. Within a few days, all were destroyed. Nevertheless, the tough little island held out and kept Rommel pinched for supplies. Once again the *Führer* paid dearly for Italy's weakness.

The Mediterranean naval war was a desperate and hemmed-in affair in which land-based aircraft played an increasingly prominent role. But at least it had the advantage of being fought in an agreeable arena. When men jumped from their sinking ships, they stood a good chance of surviving. The war in the Atlantic was another story. There a dreary, lengthy, and far more strategically vital battle was fought to decide whether Britain would survive and become the marshaling point and base for the ultimate European assault. Britain was the node between triumph and disaster; and its safety, as it had for centuries past, relied on its ships.

The Battle of the Atlantic endured through two stages. In the first, before Pearl Harbor, Britain—with increasing United States support—fought to keep its supply channels open against the savage and expert U-boat hunters and to track down any German surface vessels that ventured out to open water. During the latter part of this stage, American warships, violating all technical definitions of neutrality, helped to escort convoys across the northern arc from Newfoundland to the Irish Sea. On the last day of October, 1941, more than a month before Pearl Harbor, the first United States warship was sunk: the *Reuben James*. A trim but obsolete American destroyer, "the Rube" was helping out the shorthanded British in the protection of a convoy west of Ireland when its direction finder locked on U-boat signals. Moments later, it was hit by a torpedo. The magazine exploded, and the ship was blown in two. More than one hundred men, including the captain and all of its officers, were lost.

After Pearl Harbor, Hitler launched a submarine offensive against the North American seaboard. Eastern ports such as New York, Boston, and Norfolk had to be protected with mines, nets, and booms. Coastal convoys were established, blackouts ordered, and ship radios restricted after U-boat packs, operating initially in northern waters off Newfoundland and then moving south to warmer bases in the Caribbean, achieved astonishing initial successes.

In the first seven months of 1942, German submarines sank an appalling total of six hundred and eighty-one Allied ships, at small cost. Nevertheless, as American radar and American planes came increasingly into play, the ratio changed to Germany's disadvantage. Long-range aircraft operating from Newfoundland, Northern Ireland, and Iceland hunted down enemy raiders and blasted them into the depths. As the Nazis lost their best submarine commanders, replacements proved less expert and less resolute. By late spring, 1943, Admiral Doenitz was forced to conclude: "Losses, even heavy losses, must be borne when they are accompanied by corresponding sinkings. But in May in the Atlantic the destruction of every 10,000 tons was paid for by the loss of one U-boat. . . . The losses have therefore reached an unbearable height." And Churchill proudly reported to the House of Commons that at sea, June "was the best month from every point of view we have ever known in the whole forty-six months of the war." Moreover, Roosevelt and Churchill, honoring their promises to Stalin, managed to start convoying vast amounts of material along the so-called Murmansk Run, a dangerous route from Scotland, north of Nazi-occupied Norway, and on to the northern Russian ports of Murmansk and Archangel.

The Atlantic battle was a dirty, cold, grueling business. Nerves were constantly on edge, whether in the quivering, claustrophobic submarines, dodging among depth bombs, or aboard the destroyers zigzagging overhead, always on the alert for telltale sonar signals. Vessels were generally sunk by submarine shellfire if they had not been finished off by the first torpedo salvos, and at times, during the early part of the Atlantic battle, before the Allies had perfected their defenses, U-boats even attacked from the surface. In those days, when crews escaped in lifeboats, they were sometimes overhauled, questioned on their destinations and cargoes, offered provisions and cigarettes, and told with bluff bonhomie to send the bill for damages to Roosevelt or Churchill. But such hearty comradeliness soon was to disappear. More and more frequently, survivors were machine-gunned as they tried to swim through viscous oil slicks, ducking to escape the searing flames, or as they floundered about, clinging to

rafts or life preservers. The Battle of the Atlantic became brutal and merciless.

It was apparent quite early that the United States was unprepared for the combined responsibilities of a naval war in two oceans, and this disadvantage was dreadfully emphasized by the disaster at Pearl Harbor, which crippled our Pacific striking power. In July, 1940, Congress had passed a "Two-Ocean Navy" bill, designed to make our fleets all-powerful by 1944. We were far from such a condition in early 1942, yet our productive capacity was able to keep well ahead of our initial losses. Shipyards began turning out a destroyer in five months instead of twelve. Big carriers were launched within fifteen months instead of three years. By the end of World War II, despite heavy casualties, the United States had six more battleships, twenty-one more aircraft carriers, seventy more escort carriers, and one hundred and twenty-seven more submarines than in 1941. United States industrial know-how and production wholly upset the calculations of both Japan and Germany, which reckoned respectively on surprise massacre and steady U-boat attrition to restrict America's capacity to fight overseas.

At Mare Island shipyard in California, the longest assembly line in the United States was established. Over twelve hundred miles inland, in Denver, Colorado, vessels were constructed in sections and sent by rail to the sea. Prefabricated landing craft were shipped in pieces and assembled abroad for attacks on distant shores. Andrew Higgins developed an amphibious assault boat that was used on almost every invasion beach from Guadalcanal to Normandy. Donald Roebling invented a tracked landing vehicle that could crawl from the water like a turtle. And both the Navy and the Marine Corps perfected ingenious encircling strategies and the tactics of envelopment by land, sea, and air that ultimately enabled them to bypass the tremendous range of Japanese positions on the long route to Tokyo.

But the greatest innovation in naval fighting during World War II was the aircraft carrier. This then relatively novel weapon was given its first major test in the Pacific during the Coral Sea battle of May, 1942. General MacArthur, heeding Roosevelt's orders to protect Australia, decided to base his defense north of that helpless continent. He chose the little town of Port Moresby on New Guinea as the hub for his strategic maneuver. The Japanese had been trying to take Port Moresby by land, but New Guinea's treacherous mountains seemed impassable. Therefore they decided to attack by water and sent a huge invasion fleet down past the Solomon Islands and into the Coral Sea. To insure success, they ordered in a carrier force commanded by Vice-Admiral Shigeyoshi

Inouye, who was met by Australian and American warships under Rear Admiral Frank Fletcher. Fletcher had at his disposal the two big flattops *Yorktown* and *Lexington*. The result was the first of those famous sea-air confrontations that became a phenomenon peculiar to the Pacific between 1942 and 1945.

Almost as if blindfolded, the two admirals groped toward each other, each dependent upon his pilots to tell him what was happening. Conventional naval artillery was silent during the engagement because the ships never came close enough to exchange fire. But antiaircraft guns blazed, and bombs and torpedoes came flashing out of the tropical sky. The unprecedented battle continued for two days. Consequent losses were rather evenly balanced, with both the great Japanese carrier *Shoho* and the *Lexington* sunk. But the Japanese assault force was turned back; Australia remained inviolate; and Port Moresby soon became the starting point for the long, island-hopping campaign that took MacArthur back to the Philippines and onward to Japan.

At this point the Japanese high command decided that it was time for a dramatic move. Admiral Yamamoto had convinced his colleagues at Imperial Headquarters that a single major naval engagement would prove decisive for the course of the rest of the war. The little-known island of Midway, situated some one thousand miles northwest of Honolulu, was selected as the focal point for the attack, and an armada of over one hundred warships plus transport and supply vessels was marshaled to deal the knockout blow. Yamamoto reasoned that the capture of Midway would mean Japanese penetration of Hawaiian waters, giving Japan a base in the eastern Pacific from which to harry and shake the American people. He ordered a diversionary attack against the Aleutian Islands of Alaska and fixed an operational date of June 7. Then he dispatched a coded order: "Commander in Chief Combined Fleet, in cooperation with the Army, will invade and occupy strategic points in the Western Aleutians and Midway Island."

The force assigned to this task was the most powerful in Japan's naval history. It included eight carriers and eleven battleships. Yamamoto himself took command of this Combined Fleet. Vice-Admiral Chuichi Nagumo was given the vital Carrier Striking Force. Yamamoto was relying once again on secrecy and surprise, but he was still unaware that the United States had broken the Japanese codes. This time the advantage was properly interpreted. Admiral Chester Nimitz in Honolulu knew of Yamamoto's intentions and began his countermeasures. Later he admitted: "Had we lacked early information of the Japanese movements, and had we been caught with

carrier forces dispersed . . . the Battle of Midway would have ended differently."

Vice-Admiral Jinichi Kusaka, a staff officer in the operation, thought it was merely a matter of bad luck that an American seaplane spotted the enormous fleet as it gathered up a convoy of assault troops from Saipan, some twenty-six hundred miles west of Midway. But Nimitz had ordered that sweeping searches be made, and two task forces under Admirals Spruance and Fletcher were deployed to meet the armada. Their strength, even in carriers, was not equal to the Japanese; but they relied on the support of land-based planes from Midway itself and ultimately from Honolulu.

The fighting started June 4, 1942. Japanese planes swept off from their carriers to hit the little island target, and American planes retaliated by seeking out the invasion force. During four entire days, furious fighting raged. Again, as in the Coral Sea, aircraft battered ships that were always too distant from each other to fire their customary broadsides. One group of fifteen American torpedo bombers continued to press home their attack until all had been shot down by a curtain of antiaircraft fire thrown up around the huge Japanese carriers. Only one man survived to tell the tale. But four of Yamamoto's carriers were so heavily hit that they became blazing hulks. The captain of the *Akagi* ruefully noted: "We were unable to avoid the dive bombers because we were so occupied in avoiding the torpedoes." As one by one the Japanese flattops were crippled, their planes flew off helplessly and dropped into the warm Pacific.

Yamamoto finally decided to turn homeward before his entire force vanished. As it was, he had suffered a smashing defeat, losing four carriers and a heavy cruiser plus many damaged vessels. The Americans lost one carrier, the *Yorktown*, one destroyer, and more than one hundred planes. But this was a small price to pay. The Japanese Navy had forced a showdown with superior strength, and it was decisively beaten. Instead of threatening Hawaii and the West Coast, Japan suddenly found itself upon the defensive for the first time.

From that historic instant, the American counteroffensive began to gather force and to move relentlessly toward the home islands of Japan. Midway was one of World War II's critical battles, ranking in importance with Dunkirk, El Alamein, and Stalingrad. The tiny atoll group was, indeed, properly named, for the contest marked a dividing line in strategy if not in time. Everything before Midway was an immense Japanese success, and everything afterward, a failure. At Midway the Rising Sun that had shone so suddenly and so ferociously over all Asia slowly began to set.

Fight for the Lifeline

The North Atlantic was the scene of the longest, most crucial battle of the war. All hopes for an Allied victory over Nazi Germany depended on Britain: the air offensive would be mounted from there; so would the second front. But Britain depended on supply from the sea. The 3,000-mile-long shipping lanes from North America were her lifeline. Cut that lifeline, Hitler said, and Britain soon would be starved into surrendering.

There was no question about which side had the advantage in a naval war. Britain's strength at sea was nine times that of Germany. But again, as in World War I, the German U-boat was a terrifyingly effective weapon. One convoy, SC-42, was hit by U-boats off Cape Farewell, Greenland, and lost twenty-two out of its sixty-three ships before fog set in and saved the rest from annihilation.

For a long time it looked as though Hitler might succeed in his mission. It was not until well into 1943 that the crisis passed. But by then, millions of tons of vital goods, thousands of ships, and many thousands of brave men had vanished into the icy depths of the Atlantic. The map at right shows the general pattern of those sinkings. What it does not show, of course, is the way men died at sea, or the hours upon hours of terrible boredom, the strain and cold and unbelievable fatigue they endured—on both sides.

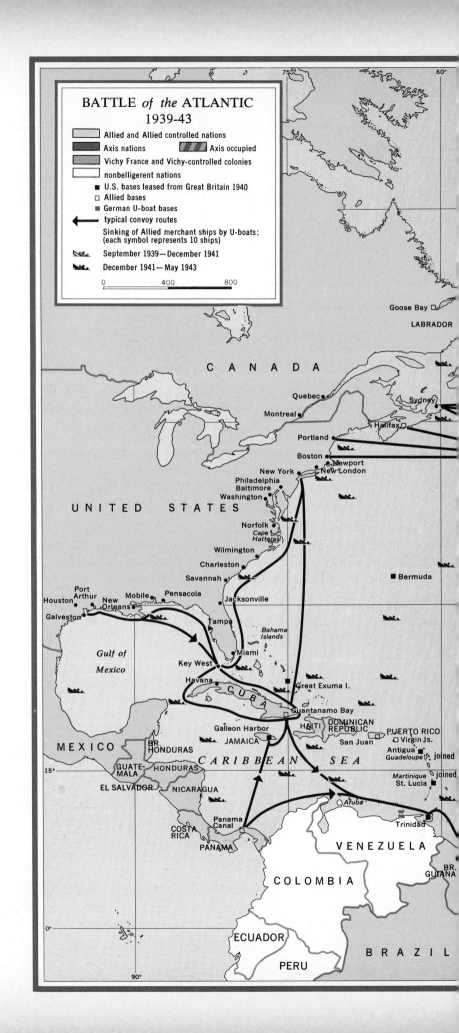

BATTLE *of the* ATLANTIC
1939-43

Allied and Allied controlled nations
Axis nations   Axis occupied
Vichy France and Vichy-controlled colonies
nonbelligerent nations
■ U.S. bases leased from Great Britain 1940
□ Allied bases
■ German U-boat bases
← typical convoy routes
Sinking of Allied merchant ships by U-boats:
(each symbol represents 10 ships)
September 1939—December 1941
December 1941—May 1943

0   400   800

Opening Guns

There never was a *Sitzkrieg* at sea. That war began an hour after Hitler's dawn attack on Poland, when the old German battleship *Schleswig-Holstein* opened fire on Danzig. Two days later, even before Great Britain had officially declared war, a German U-boat took aim at what the captain would afterward say he thought was an armed merchantman. The ship, the *Athenia*, was an ocean liner bound for Montreal. When she went to the bottom west of the Hebrides, 112 lives were lost, including 28 Americans. Then, on October 13–14, *U-47* slipped into the great British naval base at Scapa Flow, north of Scotland, and sank the battleship *Royal Oak* in one of the most daring submarine missions on record.

But the Royal Navy still ruled the waves and had the German Navy bottled up within days after war began. The only exceptions were two of Hitler's much publicized pocket battleships, *Deutschland* and *Graf Spee*, which had been at sea since August. The size of a heavy cruiser, they had enormous firepower and speed. One of them, the *Graf Spee*, was at large in the South Atlantic and by December had sunk nine British cargo ships. The British set out to hunt her down, and on December 13, three cruisers, *Exeter*, *Ajax*, and *Achilles*, sighted her. A running fight followed in which the *Exeter* was knocked out of action and the *Graf Spee* was hurt badly enough to head for neutral Uruguay, where she put in at Montevideo for repairs. When the Uruguayan Government informed the German commander, Hans Langsdorff, that he had 72 hours to get out, the whole world waited to see what would happen. On December 17, shortly after 6:00 P.M., the *Graf Spee* put to sea. The British cruisers were waiting, and more help was on the way. But at 7:56 P.M., the *Graf Spee* exploded and sank. Langsdorff had scuttled her. Three days later he put a bullet through his head.

A survivor of the Athenia *is helped ashore from rescue ship.*

When war began in Poland, the Schleswig-Holstein *opened up at point-blank range on Danzig (right above) and the big supply depot on the island of Westerplatte, where the Poles, much to the amazement of the Germans, held out for five days. At right, the* Graf Spee *explodes off Montevideo, where she had been trapped by British cruisers. Armed with six 11-inch guns, eight 5.9-inch guns, and eight torpedo tubes, she was one of Hitler's deadliest weapons. Captain Langsdorff, her commander, scuttled her rather than risk having her fall into British hands. Later, after he had seen that his crew was safely interned in Argentina, he felt honor-bound to follow the fate of his ship. Much to his credit, not one British seaman was killed through the* Graf Spee's *attacks on defenseless merchant ships.*

ABOVE: PARAMOUNT PICTURES; BELOW: IMPERIAL WAR MUSEUM, LONDON

"The Happy Time"

At left, the deadly looking prow of a U-boat on the ways at Bremen, Germany. Above, U-158 returns after a successful raid in the Atlantic. In command of the whole Nazi U-boat offensive was tough, brilliant Admiral Karl Doenitz (below), who would one day succeed Hitler as head of the Third Reich.

With the fall of France in June, 1940, Germany became a power in the Atlantic. Suddenly, Hitler had a 2,500-mile coastline to launch his U-boats from, and his reach into the Atlantic had been extended some 450 miles. Now even his smallest 250-ton subs could prowl the Atlantic shipping lanes. All that summer and fall, while Britain fought for its life against the *Luftwaffe*, the U-boats had their best hunting season of the whole war. The threat of invasion kept British destroyer forces close to home; convoys went out virtually without escort. As a result, between July and October, 1940, the U-boats sank 217 ships. On the average, each U-boat sank eight ships per month. German submariners would later call this "the Happy Time." But the number of U-boats in operation was relatively small, and despite the urging of his top naval commander, Erich Raeder, Hitler had refused to step up submarine production. The subs he had were doing very well, and besides, there was still hope that Britain might come to her senses and make peace. It was one of Hitler's crucial mistakes. In July of 1940, he lifted all restrictions on submarine production, but it was not until the following summer that the building program was really under way. By then, the British had worked out more effective defenses, and at long last they were getting help from the other side of the Atlantic.

191

ABOVE: *U.S. Destroyer Operations in World War II*, © NAVAL INSTITUTE; BELOW: UPI

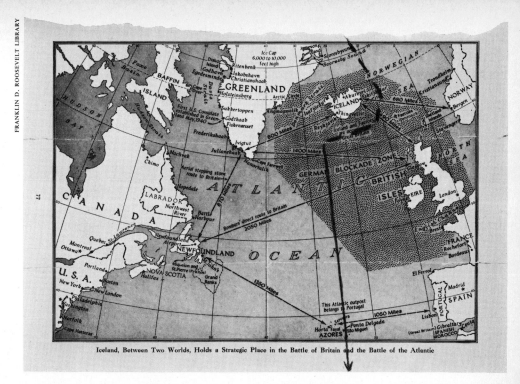

Iceland, Between Two Worlds, Holds a Strategic Place in the Battle of Britain and the Battle of the Atlantic

Roosevelt tore a map from the National Geographic *and drew a line to show how Britain and the United States should divide Atlantic defense. Harry Hopkins carried the map to Churchill.*

What Were Their Names?

Folk singer Woody Guthrie once wrote a ballad whose refrain went: "Tell me, what were their names;/ Tell me, what were their names;/ Did you have a friend on the good *Reuben James*?" Guthrie's lament was for some of the men who served and died almost unsung during America's undeclared war against Germany in the Atlantic in 1941. For it was war in all but the legalistic sense of the word. Ships of the United States Navy escorted convoys through cold northern seas; American vessels were torpedoed, American lives lost. The situation had come about by degrees as Roosevelt moved carefully to aid Britain without arousing the nation's isolationist sentiment. There had been the destroyers-for-bases agreement, and then Lend-Lease, and in July of 1941 the sending of American troops to Iceland to relieve British forces already there to defend that strategic island against possible Nazi seizure.

Then, in a step barely short of war, American naval units went on convoy duty. Roosevelt and Churchill had divided the Atlantic between them. The ocean west of the dividing line (above) was declared part of the American defense zone. and through its waters the American Navy shepherded the convoys; east of the line the Royal Navy was responsible. There could have been war any time Hitler wanted it, but he actually tried to avoid it. Even so, on September 4, the destroyer *Greer* exchanged torpedoes for depth charges with a submarine; both vessels were unharmed, but Roosevelt ordered the Navy to shoot German warships in the west Atlantic on sight. In mid-October, the *Kearny* was torpedoed with eleven killed but did not sink, and just after dawn on October 31, the *Reuben James* was hit and sank at once; 115 men, more than two thirds of all aboard, perished. Robert E. Sherwood, a Roosevelt adviser, observed that the public seemed more interested in the Army–Notre Dame football game.

The destroyer Kearny *(above left) survived a torpedo hit, thanks to modern construction with watertight compartmentation. She made it to Iceland, where a repair ship patched her well enough to proceed to the United States for permanent repairs. At lower left, American infantrymen prepare to land in Iceland on their arrival in 1941, after they had begun taking over defense of the island from British troops.*

193

NATIONAL MARITIME MUSEUM, GREENWICH

Death of the Bismarck

The *Bismarck* was the most nearly unsinkable ship of the entire war; a British fleet with its planes, pouring ton after ton of shells and torpedoes into her, could not send her down. English artist Norman Wilkinson here shows the German ship being spotted by a Catalina bomber on May 26, 1941, after she had evaded pursuers for 31 hours after sinking the battle cruiser *Hood.* She was never again free from harassment. Soon after, planes attacked her, one torpedo exploded harmlessly against her massive side armor, but another hit and jammed her vulnerable rudder beyond all possibility of repair. Impossible to steer, the big ship could do nothing more than wait to fight and die. When British warships arrived on the scene, accurate German fire at first kept them at a respectful distance, but before long the weight of the attack began to tell. Hits on the bridge killed the admiral and the captain, the upper works were blasted into twisted steel, and the gun turrets were knocked out of action. Unable to retaliate, the burning ship became a helpless target for every ship, large and small, until their ammunition was exhausted. Then the only destroyer with torpedoes left was sent in to finish her off. After three of the weapons exploded against her side, she slowly turned over and sank. However, one of her officers, one of the few survivors, claimed that she had sunk only because her commanding officer had ordered the crew to scuttle her to prevent the possible ignominy of a British crew boarding her. Until then, he said, her armored deck had remained unpierced by shells, her hull was still buoyant, and her engines were entirely intact.

Wolf Packs at Our Shores

The convoy system had beaten the U-boats in the First World War and had done very well in the Atlantic until the middle of 1941. Then, in the unending battle of wits between hunter and hunted, the Germans devised their wolf-pack tactics. A number of submarines lay in wait across the shipping lanes; the first to locate a convoy gave the signal, and all closed in for the kill. Beset from all sides, its protecting escort ships unable to fend off so many simultaneous attacks, a convoy usually suffered heavy losses.

It was, however, much worse to be a ship without a convoy. After the United States was in the war, German submarines moved into American waters, where they leisurely picked off ships that passed along the coast, alone and unprotected. Submarine captains became so choosy they let high-riding empty ships go by and sank only the laden ones. In the first four months of 1942, 87 ships were sunk off the Atlantic coast; then, when convoying was begun, most of the U-boats were moved to the Gulf of Mexico, where they destroyed 41 ships in May. Such easy hunting soon ended, though.

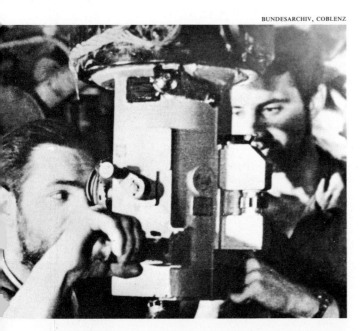

A Britain-bound convoy (left) steams quietly along, free for the moment, at least, from submarine attack; the nearest ship carries a deckload of planes. Above, a German submarine commander looks through the periscope of his ship. And at right are pictures of some of the victims of the Nazi U-boat warfare off the Atlantic coast in early 1942. From the top, they are: the tanker Dixie Arrow; *the merchant ship* Tiger; *the merchant ship* Bensen; *the tanker* Republic, *torpedoed with five lives lost; and the tanker* R. P. Resor, *still burning a day after having been hit some fifteen miles off the coast of New Jersey.*

The Unsung Service

"Give us the tools and we will finish the job," Winston Churchill had said to Roosevelt in a radio talk early in 1941, and the stream of supplies never stopped flowing to Britain. But while the tactics of fighting submarines to keep the convoys moving were always changing and improving, one element in the battle remained constant: men had always to suffer hardships and risk their lives to get the tools across. The North Atlantic, one of the stormiest, dreariest seas on earth, was the most dangerous, but there were no sinecures anywhere. The amazing thing was that seamen could always be found to man ships with cargoes of explosives that would blow them to glory if torpedoed, or to serve on tankers where they were likely to be incinerated if hit. Not all the heroes of the war got medals.

The American public was told to avoid loose talk that could give information to the enemy; this poster warned that careless gossip about ship sailings could lead to ship sinkings.

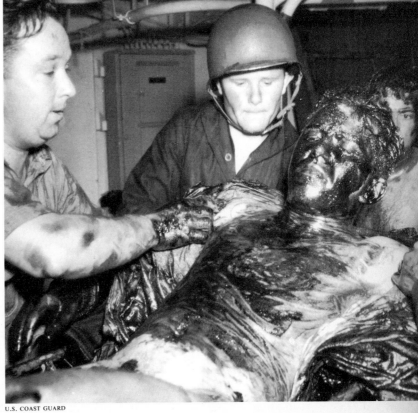

At top center, the cruiser H.M.S. Sheffield *drives through Atlantic waves more than fifty feet high; such towering seas did make it almost impossible for the U-boats to attack. A signalman operates an iced-up signal blinker (left); winter duty in the North Atlantic, where convoy routes reached almost to the Arctic Circle, was always arduous. At top above, a British seaman catnaps between constant submarine alerts. And at bottom above, American Coastguardsmen scrape oil from a Navy seaman rescued after his ship had been sunk by German planes off the coast of North Africa.*

Despite losses that were often appalling, the convoys continued to reach Britain. Brave men brought them there, but valor was no

monopoly of any side, for the German—not always Nazi—crewman served valiantly in a service that became increasingly suicidal.

"Now they came from all directions"

J. SCHERER

Alexander Werth

One of the epic achievements of the war at sea was the Murmansk Run, a fifteen-hundred-mile convoy route from England to Russia by way of the Arctic Ocean above Norway. Freezing weather and U-boats were constant companions to Allied freighters and their escorts. But the deadliest enemy of all was the Norway-based German bomber. The cost of getting help to Russia was terribly high. One convoy, PQ-17, lost twenty-two out of thirty-three ships. Here, Alexander Werth, a noted English journalist, describes an air attack along the Murmansk Run.

. . . Life on the *Empire Baffin* seemed to have returned to normal. Pushkov was again giving his Russian lesson to the R.A.F. boys in the smoke-room, and, after yesterday's feeble attempts, the Luftwaffe was clearly not as terrifying as people were apt to imagine. But then, at 10:30 the alarm bell went. From the gun-turret somebody shouted: "Here they come!" Again people rushed on deck—counting: three—three more, that's six—ten—twelve—fifteen. Now they came from all directions. Gun flashes and clouds of smoke came from the destroyers; then the barrage of the flak ship and the convoy ships went up; like a vulture pouncing on its prey, a dive-bomber swept down on to the submarine, right down to the water level, but she crash-dived, and the three pillars of water went high up in the air. For forty long minutes they attacked, usually in twos and threes, usually coming straight out of the sun, some diving low, others dropping their bombs from two hundred feet. From their yellow shark-like bellies, one could see the obscene yellow eggs dropping, and after a moment of suspense, one saw with relief the pillars of water

leaping up. They were concentrating in that first attack on the forward part of the convoy, and we were, apparently, reserved for later. And then we saw the first casualty. The pale-blue and pale-green destroyer was smoking furiously, and signalling, signalling, signalling. What were those flashes saying? Was it the destroyer that had picked up those Huns on Monday? Somebody on board said: "They are all right. They are not going to abandon her." That didn't seem so bad. She was still smoking, but they seemed to have got the fire under control. Soon they put it out. The planes disappeared; the attack was over. That wasn't so bad, people said; and then we realised that it *was* bad. Not very far away from us was a Russian ship—I had realised for the first time that we had two or three Russian ships in the convoy—and her foredeck was enveloped in clouds of smoke, and flames were bursting out of the hold. "They're going to abandon her," somebody said. Were they? Yes, they were lowering their life-boats. But no. She was still keeping up steam, still keeping up with the other ships, but the clouds of smoke rising from her were growing larger and larger, her whole fo'c'sle was in a cloud of black smoke—but she still went on, and through the cloud of smoke, one saw dim shapes of people running and doing something. I saw Alfred Adolphus rushing past me; he was steaming with sweat, and there was a look of panic in his yellowish eyes. "Hullo, Alfred Adolphus!" I said. "I think I'll go mad! I think I'll go mad!" he cried.

So the destroyer had been hit, and the Russian ship had been hit, and both were fighting with the flames. And somebody said two more ships had been hit.

They came again in less than an

hour. This was a short, sharp attack. They concentrated on the other end of the convoy. They dropped their bombs and disappeared. As we sailed on, I saw a ship that had stayed behind, with a corvette by her side, blazing furiously. We were already a mile or two away from her. And somebody said that another ship had received a direct hit and had blown up.

Then there was a lull. Dinner was served punctually at noon; Cook wasn't a minute late. Everybody was there, as usual, the lanky first mate, and the young second mate, and the long skinny engineer's mate with the fuzzy hair and the Hapsburg jaw, and our Flight-Lieutenant and the R.A.F. boys. Everybody gulped tea, but appetites were at a low level, and few words were exchanged. In their frames, the King and Queen were very calm. Like most of them, I drank a lot of tea, but the food seemed to stick to the palate. Pushkov, with a wan smile, said the lesson could, he hoped, be resumed to-morrow. I went out on deck. The Russian ship was still enveloped in smoke, though perhaps a little less than before. They had not abandoned ship. I saw Alfred Adolphus sauntering along the deck, now wearing his bright-blue suit with the red stripes and a new light-grey felt hat. "I'm through with it," he said defiantly. "I have refused to go down to the engine-room." "Why did you dress up like this?" "I want to save my clothes if we are torpedoed," he said. He was much calmer than in the morning. "It wouldn't matter," he suddenly cried, "but it's the *cargo*, the *cargo*!" With this remark, he slunk away. So that's what it is, I said to myself—T.N.T.? I had already heard somebody refer to it, but had taken no notice. The burning ship in the distance had now disappeared.

Then the alarm bell went again. I forget what exactly happened at the beginning of that third attack, but this time they concentrated on our end of the convoy. The obscene yellow bellies were over us, and they dropped their eggs all round us. The bearded bank clerk with the Oxford accent was on one of the Oerlikons, and the man with the beret and the Soviet badge on another, and Steward was working a machine-gun, and the Flight-Lieutenant, his hair waving in the wind, was, I think, on an Oerlikon, and aft, the little R.A.F. sergeant was on one of the two Lewis guns. And then something happened which I shall never forget. I was standing amidships with the R.A.F. boys and Pushkov and several others, and we realised that something had happened to our sister ship, the *Empire Lawrence*, now without her Hurricane on board. She was no longer steering a straight course. Her bows were pointing towards us—was she moving at all? She was showing a slight list. And we realised that she was being abandoned. Already two of her lifeboats were bobbing on the water, and beside her was a little corvette, taking more men off. As we watched her, we heard all our guns fire like mad. Then one of the yellow bellies swept over us, but, perhaps unnerved by our fire, it dropped the bombs into the water some distance away, but immediately after, two more of the yellow bellies swept over us with roaring engines, almost touching our topmast, and . . . they made a dead set at the helpless, dying ship. And suddenly from the yellow belly the five bombs detached themselves and went right into her. I don't think there was even a moment of suspense; there was an explosion that did not sound very loud, and a flash which, in the sun, was not

very bright, and like a vomiting volcano a huge pillar of fire, smoke and wreckage shot two hundred feet into the air—and then, slowly, terribly slowly, it went down to the sea. The *Empire Lawrence* was gone. The surface of the water was littered with wreckage—planks, pieces of wood, and then, perhaps five seconds later, the black triangle of the bows, detached from the rest of the ship, came to the surface for a second, and sank for ever again. The little white corvette was still there, seemingly intact, and perhaps looking for improbable survivors. What happened to the two lifeboats that had been near the *Empire Lawrence* only a few minutes before, I don't know. Nobody on board said anything at first. Faces were pale. I felt the blood pressing hard on my eardrums; it was horrible—and fascinating. Poor *Empire Lawrence*, our sister ship! It was strange to think of it. They had that Hurricane pilot on board, they also had their Captain, and their steward, and perhaps another Geordie, and another Jumbo McGhee, and another Alfred Adolphus, and a smoke-room like ours, and cigarettes, and bottles of rum, and pictures of the King and Queen, and tea-cups and saucers, and lavatories, and a great big deep engine-room like ours, and a refrigerator with a lot of cheese and ham. And now it was all smashed, at the bottom of the sea, or some of it still floating about—and it was horrible to think of parts of human bodies floating about the ocean in life-jackets.

Shipbuilder to the World

The demand for new ships became insistent—not only for naval craft, but for cargo vessels to replace the hundreds sunk by submarines, for any interruption of the flow of supplies moving overseas could be disastrous. Prodigies of shipbuilding were performed. Liberty ships were made in sections, which were then brought together, assembly-line fashion; construction time for one of the vessels was reduced to only six weeks. From January 1, 1942, through the end of the war, American shipyards produced 6,500 naval vessels, 64,500 landing craft, and 5,400 cargo ships, a total of 28,-000,000 gross tons, compared to 21,000,000 tons lost to all enemy action. It was a stupendous effort that made the United States by far the world's leading shipbuilder.

HANSEL MIETH, FORTUNE

WIDE WORLD

Above, workers put the deck on a freighter hull, which will then be launched and completed in the water while a new hull is started.

Henry J. Kaiser was a genius at ship production. By 1944, among other accomplishments, he had his Vancouver yard launching an escort aircraft carrier each week.

And in the Pacific...
Demise of
the Dreadnoughts

His Majesty's Ships the *Prince of Wales* and the *Repulse* were sunk on December 10, 1941, and with them died the venerable and time-tested doctrine that control of the seas rode on the surface with the biggest, largest-gunned, thickest-armored capital ships. Admiral Sir Tom Phillips took his two great vessels, with four escorting destroyers, north out of Singapore to attack and halt Japanese transports coming down from the north. His ship dispositions were faultless according to the book—but the book was out of date. Admiral Phillips had no planes to protect him from attack from the sky and did not appear to realize how vulnerable he was to assault from the air. Kenichi Nakamura, a Japanese artist, painted his version of what happened as the land-based 22nd Air Flotilla struck the two ships in the Gulf of Siam. Waves of bombing and torpedo attacks sent the 32,000-ton *Repulse* to the bottom in about an hour and a half; the new 35,000-ton *Prince of Wales*, which had exchanged shellfire with the *Bismarck* six months earlier, endured not quite an hour longer. Some one thousand of the three thousand men on the two ships were lost. The battle had cost the victors just three planes. Singapore was laid open to the advancing Japanese, and the strategic situation in the Pacific was affected for the entire war. And of historical note, the old rule of the sea by ships of the line had been forever shattered in just a few hours.

Carriers on the Coral Sea

The Battle of the Coral Sea ended in an American victory, even though not quite a resounding one. Historians cherish it for another reason: it was one of those milestones they like so well; it was the start of a new era. For here was the first action between carrier fleets. And here, for the first time since naval warfare began, two fleets fought an engagement without surface ships exchanging a single shot.

The battle came about when the Japanese moved to capture Port Moresby on southern New Guinea with an invasion convoy protected by a carrier force. It was intercepted in the Coral Sea by an Allied force built around the aircraft carriers *Lexington* and *Yorktown*, and on May 7 and 8, 1942, the planes of each force flew through fog and mist seeking out their enemy's ships. American planes sank the light carrier *Shoho* in minutes ("Scratch one flattop!" the flight commander radioed back to the *Lexington*) and an enemy destroyer. American losses were a destroyer, an oiler, and most grievous of all, the *Lexington*, which had to be sunk after the battle. The fight was an important strategic victory for the Allies, for the invasion force turned back. For what comfort it might bring them, the Japanese could claim a tactical victory, for their losses in tonnage were much the smaller. At the time, they could not even do that, for they did not know the *Lexington* had sunk.

Converted from a battle cruiser, the Lexington *was a tough ship, and it appeared for a time that she would survive her torpedo damage. Then internal explosions rent her, and she had to be abandoned and sunk by an American destroyer. She is shown with men going down her sides, while below is a boatful of her survivors.*

BOTH: U.S. NAVY

Japanese morale was riding high in the spring of 1942, despite any minor setbacks in the Coral Sea. Everyone knew that the Emperor

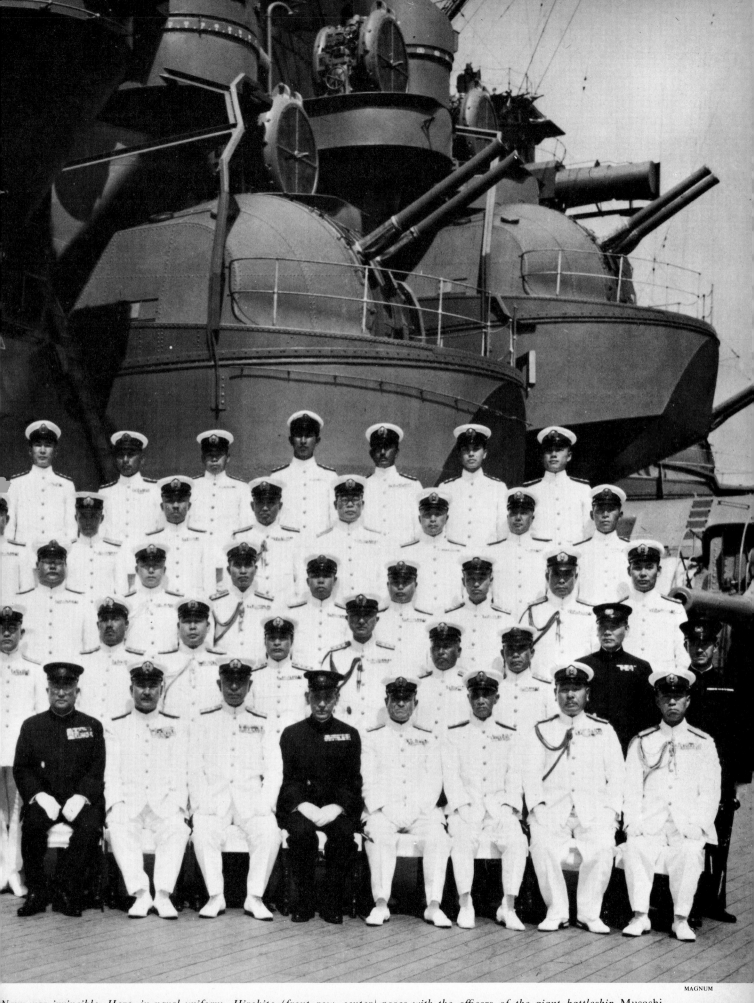

Navy was invincible. Here, in naval uniform, Hirohito *(front row, center) poses with the officers of the giant battleship* Musashi.

Turning Point at Midway

ROGER PINEAU

At the end of May, 1942, the Japanese sent a gigantic armada steaming eastward across some 2,000 miles of ocean to take the island of Midway and to draw out and destroy the much smaller American Pacific fleet. In command was Admiral Isoroku Yamamoto, architect of the Pearl Harbor attack. Again his scheme depended on surprise. But American naval intelligence had decoded enough of his messages to know fairly accurately when he would strike and where. This time it would be Yamamoto and the commander of his fast carrier force, Admiral Chuichi Nagumo, another Pearl Harbor veteran, who were in for a surprise.

When the battle began on June 3, with an attack on the Aleutians designed to decoy American ships to the north, Admiral Nimitz, who had over-all command, refused to take the bait. When Nagumo sent his bombers against Midway early on the morning of June 4, he discovered soon after that there were unidentified American ships not far to the northeast, where, according to Japanese plans, they had no business being. The ships were the carriers *Yorktown*, *Enterprise*, and *Hornet*; at approximately 9:30, their planes began attacking the enemy flattops. Forty-one torpedo bombers came in first. All but a few were shot down, and for a very brief time, it looked as though the Japanese had triumphed. Then, from 14,000 feet up, American dive bombers roared down on their targets and changed the course of the war. In a matter of minutes, three Japanese carriers (*Soryu, Kaga,* and *Akagi*) were knocked out. The next morning, a fourth (*Hiryu*) was sunk. Again, as at the Coral Sea, planes did all the fighting (Yamamoto's dozen battleships, held in reserve, never did much of anything); and again the United States lost a great carrier, *Yorktown*, which was badly damaged by enemy bombers, then sunk by a submarine. But this time there was no doubt about who came out on top. The Japanese had suffered their first naval defeat in history. Their long, impressive sea offensive had ended.

To stop the assault force under Nagumo (above), Nimitz sent out three carriers and their attending cruisers and destroyers, under Admirals Raymond Spruance (right) and Frank Fletcher (below). Spruance had taken over for Halsey, who was ill; he was calm and calculating, and made the crucial decision of launching an all-out attack at a time when Nagumo would be caught frantically attempting to refuel and rearm his own planes.

RIGHT: WIDE WORLD; BELOW: UPI

Yamamoto (left) was an aggressive and inspiring officer, but he made the error of dividing his huge force five ways and of thinking that his foe would behave in a predictable way. After his crushing defeat at Midway, he ordered a general retreat and then took ill in his cabin. In April, 1943, he was killed when his plane was shot down by P-38's. U.S. naval intelligence again was his undoing. When he took off on an inspection tour from Rabaul, American fighter planes were up and waiting for him.

One of the last victims of the Midway battle was the Japanese cruiser Mikuma, *shown dead in the water, her bow and stern swarming with survivors. Before dawn on June 5, the* Mikuma *and another ship,* Mogami, *had collided trying to avoid an American submarine. Later that day, Marine Corps planes from Midway attacked. There were no hits, but one pilot, Captain Richard Fleming, crashed into the* Mikuma's *turret. The next morning,* Enterprise *and* Hornet *planes made a last attack on the cruisers, during which this picture was taken. The* Mogami, *hit hard, managed to limp away. The* Mikuma *was less fortunate. That afternoon she rolled over and sank in about 2,000 fathoms.*

The Desert War

Shepheard's Hotel in Cairo was World War II's most singular hostelry. There, amid unaccustomed luxury, red-tabbed British colonels back from the fighting in Libya vied for a place at the bar. Brigadiers were allotted beds at the favor of a Swiss concierge, who cured one such officer of incipient alcoholism by rooming him with a subaltern who kept a crocodile in the bathtub. From the terrace, one could see passing on the street below a cinematic panorama of war: tough Australian sergeants advising enraged majors, "We ain't saluting today"; Free French subalterns; Greek commandos; Poles and Yugoslavs; vociferous English cockneys; huge South Africans from the veld and bearded Indian Sikhs.

The view from Shepheard's was romantic—and deceptive. It was easy to forget that the power implied by soldiers of so many nations had in fact been driven out of Europe, back to Stalingrad and to the very borders of the Nile. And yet, from the Egyptian capital, for all its tenuous neutrality, its good food and its belly dancers, its ancient monuments and its golf courses, a vast and patient strategy evolved.

Working according to the best of British imperial and naval traditions, this strategy slowly squeezed off victories in salients as far removed as Madagascar, Tripolitania, and the Dodecanese. From Cairo headquarters stemmed Colonel Orde Wingate's remarkable Ethiopian foray, against bravely commanded Italians, that succeeded in restoring Haile Selassie to his throne. Cairo pried a small corps out of the Western Desert and dis-

patched it on a hopeless mission to Greece. Cairo arranged the seizure of Italian Somaliland and of vital Eritrea, on the Red Sea. With armies that were little more than paper organizational tables, Cairo headquarters ran German sympathizers out of Iran, Iraq, Syria, and Lebanon and coordinated Balkan guerrillas. Cairo was the base for two daring British raiding officers who jumped into Crete and kidnapped the commanding German general. And Cairo was the base for a good-natured bunch of thugs assembled under a Belgian guerrilla who called his gang Popski's Private Army and led it from Alexandria to the Alps. Using a maximum of panache and a minimum of effectives, the sprawling, overstaffed Cairo command regained control of more square miles of hostile territory than it had soldiers to deploy.

When the war began, Britain had assembled in Egypt a force vaingloriously named the Army of the Nile, under the over-all command of Sir Archibald Wavell, a one-eyed general who boasted diplomatic skill and strategic talents more lavishly admired by his contemporaries than by history. It was Wavell who planned the first success in the famous Western Desert campaign.

In September, 1940, Marshal Rodolfo Graziani had penetrated Egypt at Sidi Barrani, but the Western Desert campaign really began that December, when the vastly outnumbered British attacked the Italian Army and drove it into Libya. The December, 1940, campaign was an unqualified British victory. While the Greeks were making mockery of Mussolini's invasion from Albania, Wavell

A disabled panzer sits where Montgomery passed en route to Tripoli.

took a series of Libyan citadels from the *Duce*'s badly commanded African army, penetrating deep into Cyrenaica and capturing enormous quantities of matériel and some one hundred and thirty thousand prisoners, including a red-bearded little general named Bergonzoli, who had been nicknamed "Electric Whiskers" by his troops and who had become something of a legend for his prowess at losing battles but always escaping.

As a result of Italy's humiliations in Albania and Libya, Hitler was forced to spread his forces by dispatching aid. General Marshall later concluded that this overextension "subsequently became one of the principal factor's in Germany's defeat." The *Führer* sent his *Fliegerkorps* X to stiffen the Italian Air Force. Then, along with a German armored corps, he sent in Rommel.

Erwin Rommel, who had once, if briefly, been a Nazi bullyboy, soon became Hitler's favorite general, a place he held until, suspected of helping plot the *Führer*'s downfall, he was ordered to commit suicide and so save his family from Gestapo torture. A keen, brave man, he became a master of armored warfare, leading his units into combat from the turret of his tank, exploiting the slightest opening presented. His men idolized him, and even Churchill said, "His ardor and daring inflicted grievous disasters upon us. . . . [He was] a great general."

Rommel opened his first offensive March 24, 1941, a few weeks before Hitler overran the Balkans. He drove into Egypt, leaving an isolated British garrison sealed off in the Libyan port of Tobruk. From bases in Tripolitania and Sicily, the *Luftwaffe* started to raid Alexandria, Port Said, and Suez and intensively mined the canal, thus cutting off the main route to India and hampering Wavell's normal supply lines. But the improvised fortress of Tobruk held out on Rommel's flank. It was reinforced by General Sir Alan Cunningham of the newly named Eighth Army. (The over-all commander for the Middle East was now General Sir Claude Auchinleck. In June, Churchill had decided that Wavell needed a rest from desert campaigning and had sent him to India.) All through the summer and autumn of 1941, coastal ships from Alexandria scurried along the dangerous North African shore to strengthen the besieged port.

During the fourteen months following Rommel's arrival in Libya, the Desert War was a seesaw affair. There were lengthy advances and retreats but no crucial victory in what the Tommies called "miles and miles and bloody miles of absolutely damn all." Soldiers learned to navigate like sailors, reckoning the featureless spaces by map, compass, speedometer, and stars. At night, formations of each side would encamp, unsure just where the other's hull-down tanks lay. Acres of flatness were marked by countless tracks left by the treads and tires of past battles, littered with piles of jerry-cans and discarded tins of food, swarming with insects. Drivers sought to steer to the windward of each other and thus escape the dust. From desert shoes to goggles, they were generally covered by a beige coating compounded of sand, dust, and sweat. Supply services were hard pressed to provide enough water for the thirsty vehicles and men.

From the start of this extraordinary campaign, the naval-minded British realized the critical importance of Malta to the desert fighting. They kept the island bastion alive, losing vast shipping tonnage in the process. But the price was not too heavy; Rommel's need for supplies and reinforcements could not be satisfied so long as Axis convoys were being smashed from Malta. Hitler and Mussolini therefore agreed on a full-scale amphibious and air-borne assault on the island, called Operation Herkules. But when Tobruk was finally taken from the besieged British in spring, 1942, the Malta attack was called off and the assault forces were allotted directly to Rommel instead. This was a capital strategic error. Despite the heavy cost to reinforcement convoys from Gibraltar and Alexandria, Spitfires, submarines, and destroyers from Malta kept on hammering Axis supply lines. Rommel's eventual defeat owed as much to these pilots and naval crews as to Montgomery's Desert Rats.

In August, 1942, Churchill flew to Cairo in order to weigh the military prospects before meeting Stalin for the first time. Rommel by then had established a new forward position deep inside Egypt. The British Prime Minister, in one of his most significant military decisions, reorganized his command. He named General Sir Harold Alexander to replace Auchinleck as head of all Middle Eastern forces. Then, to take over the Eighth Army after the officer slated for that post, W. H. E. ("Strafer") Gott, had been killed in an airplane crash, he picked Lieutenant General Bernard L. Montgomery.

Monty, as he became known to his soldiers, was a highly debatable figure, detested by many officers. At that moment he was fifty-five years old, lean, tough, conceited, insolent, and as yet relatively unknown. His tastes were plain; he was a stern disciplinarian who forced his staff to keep strenuously fit, frowned on smoking and drinking, fired many of the commanders he had inherited, and injected into his dispirited army a sudden surge of confidence. His troops began to cherish the label Desert Rats, first accorded with contempt, and stole for their own the Afrika Korps' favorite song, "Lili Marlene." Because his soldiers soon came to know their new leader, who wisely displayed his double-badged beret on visits to every unit, they came also to have personal faith in his craft and wisdom. He insisted on refraining from the offensive until he had overwhelming weapons superiority. And with such superiority, his army soon presented him with a massive string of victories.

Monty was a lonely man and in some respects a priggish puritan, a latter-day Cromwell. He was fascinated by his own homilies and had a habit of repeating them at least twice for the sake of stress. "There are only two rules of war," I have heard him say, "only two rules of war. Never invade Russia. Never invade China. Never invade Russia or China." Eisenhower believed that Montgomery was an inadequate strategist. At a French golf club he demonstrated his point, drawing maps on paper cloths and marking divisions with salt and pepper cellars to show how Monty should have fought at El Alamein and later at the Falaise Gap in France. Hans Speidel, at one time Rommel's chief of staff, insists that Montgomery understood only two maneuvers, a left hook and a thrust through the center, and that because he always telegraphed his punches, the Germans knew in advance what he planned to do. This may be, but he gave heart to a disheartened army at a critical moment. He combined the stern talents of Cromwell with the persistence of Wellington. If he is not accepted as Britain's greatest ground commander since the Iron Duke, at any rate, he never lost a battle. Let that be his epitaph.

Montgomery was aware that Rommel was then preparing his final push toward Alexandria and the Nile, but he was not dismayed. He propped Rommel's photograph in his headquarters and, with characteristic immodesty, remarked: "Give me a fortnight and I can resist the German attack. Give me three weeks, and I can defeat the Boche. Give me a month and I can chase him out of Africa." As it was, Monty spent two months just getting ready for the chase.

Fate threw these two great captains against each other sixty miles west of Alexandria, in an ugly, arid patch called El Alamein. To the north lay the Mediterranean flank, covered by the Royal Navy, and to the south gaped an impassable rock canyon named the Qattara Depression. Thus the battlefield was a narrow passage that restricted the customary wide, high-speed flanking movements of desert warfare. The passage itself was strewn with mines and packed densely with guns and tanks. It was impossible for infantry to dig in on the rock-studded terrain. Rommel was intent on punching through this gap before his opponent could thicken his own defenses. In August he said: "We hold the gateway to Egypt with full intention to act. We did not go there with the intention of being flung back sooner or later."

And indeed, his power seemed inexorable. Were he to penetrate, the entire Nile Valley would be exposed to the fanning out of his tanks and self-propelled guns. The British moved masses of stores from the neighborhood of Cairo, flew out dependents, and established distant contingency headquarters. Hitler ordered medals struck to honor the expected triumph of his Afrika Korps; Mussolini sent his favorite white charger to Libya so he could ride through Cairo in a victory parade. But the British lines held. In September, Rommel flew to Germany to report to Hitler, complaining at the *Führer*'s East Prussian headquarters that R.A.F. bombers were destroying his panzers with American 40-mm. shells. "Quite impossible," Göring observed, "Nothing but latrine rumors. All the Americans can make are razor blades and refrigerators." Rommel replied: "I only wish *Herr Reichsmarschall*, that we were issued similar razor blades!"

Rommel was resting at a German sanatorium when in late October, 1942, Montgomery at last felt strong enough to launch his own offensive. On October 23, Montgomery announced to his troops: "When I assumed command of the Eighth Army I said that the mandate was to destroy Rommel and his Army, and that it would be done as soon as we were ready. We are ready NOW!"

Thunderous artillery pieces, to the clattering counterpoint of mortars and machine guns, suddenly smothered the advance German positions with their blast, and that night, under a shining moon, the famous foot soldiers—Britons, Australians, New Zealanders, Indians, South Africans, Highlanders probing forward beside their kilted pipers—began to move into the mine fields. When these were partly cleared, the British tanks rumbled through. The Germans were outnumbered, outweaponed, and overwhelmed. General Georg von Stumme, Rommel's replacement, fell dead of a heart attack, and two days after the assault started, Hitler's youngest field marshal was back, surveying the wreckage of his burned-out panzers. Hitler sent him a desperate message: "In the situation in which you now find yourself, there can be no other consideration than to hold fast, never retreat, hurl every gun and every man into the fray. . . . You can show your troops no other way than that which leads to victory or death." This was the same counsel the *Führer* would give to Friedrich Paulus, his Stalingrad commander. Rommel was smarter. At last, later than he would have wished, he started a massive retreat. General Ritter von Thoma, when captured in full uniform by the British, expressed the feeling of the entire Afrika Korps command by assailing Hitler's order as "unsurpassed madness."

In the long rout from the Nile borders and westward across the Libyan frontier, Rommel helped protect his disciplined German troops by posting Italian rear guards and using their transport for evacuation. He lost approximately sixty thousand men as well as most of his guns and tanks before, under cover of a rain storm, he managed to establish a temporary holding position. And then, on November 8, came word of an Allied landing in French North Africa. Not only was Egypt irrevocably lost; now an enormous pincer started to close in.

The Afrika Korps and its Italian allies were trapped just as it became clear that another huge Nazi army was caught in the snowy wastes of the Volga bend at Stalingrad, and that the Americans were striking back against Japan in far-off Guadalcanal. Autumn of 1942 was the turning point of the war. As Churchill said, "Up to Alamein we survived. After Alamein we conquered."

The serious planning for Operation Torch, the Anglo-American landing in Morocco and Algeria, did not begin until early August, 1942. A still-obscure American lieutenant general, Dwight D. Eisenhower, had been sent to England by Marshall and was given over-all command of the expedition. A formal directive to proceed was sent to him only on August 13, after full consideration had been made of the strain the operation would place on Allied resources. Endorsement of Torch meant that in the Pacific the United States would be confined to holding a Hawaii-Midway line and preserving communications to Australia. In Europe it meant cancellation of Operation Sledgehammer, a diversionary attack across the Channel into France that Marshall had hoped to launch that same year. But it also put period to Hitler's dream of joining in the Middle East the Egyptian and Russian salients of his astonishingly advanced armies.

The Torch invasion was made up of three separate forces: thirty-five thousand Americans embarked from the United States for French Morocco; thirty-nine thousand Americans embarked from England to take Oran in western Algeria; and a third force of ten thousand Americans and twenty-three thousand British also sailed from Britain to seize Algiers. All were transported and protected by the U.S. and Royal navies. Eisenhower wrote of this extraordinary undertaking: "The venture was new —it was almost new in conception. Up to that moment no government had ever attempted to carry out an overseas expedition involving a journey of thousands of miles from its bases and terminating in a major attack."

The operation was further complicated by the confused situation of France itself, part occupied, part under Pétain's Vichy regime, part in a colonial limbo. Some French officers in North Africa were loyal to General de Gaulle's movement in England; others were conspiring to back General Henri Honoré Giraud, who had just escaped to France from a German prison camp; still others

were pledged to their Pétainist commanders; and there were those who were merely waiting to see how the war would go. In October, 1942, Eisenhower sent his deputy, Major General Mark W. Clark, with a handful of specialists, to visit Algeria secretly by submarine and confer with the State Department's Robert Murphy, who had spread an intelligence network throughout North Africa on direct orders from Roosevelt. De Gaulle, who was disliked in Washington and suspected in London of indiscretion by incautious talk, was excluded from all planning, an insult he never forgave.

Just eleven months after Pearl Harbor, at 3 A.M. on November 8, 1942, a series of convoys numbering more than eight hundred war vessels and transports began to assemble along the African coast between Morocco to the south and Algeria to the west, disembarking troops on the Atlantic and Mediterranean shores. The Axis was taken wholly by surprise, not knowing, when the convoys were first spotted, whether they were bound for Malta, for Egypt, or for where. Spain did not interfere by attempting to pinch off the Mediterranean straits, and the venture succeeded with relatively few casualties. The only serious fighting was at Oran and at Casablanca, where French naval units shelled the attackers until put out of action by bombing.

Eisenhower rapidly built up his armies and a huge stockpile of equipment. Pétain, senile and embittered, ordered French North African forces to resist and severed diplomatic relations with Washington. For a brief time the position of the fourteen French divisions remained uncertain. In the hope of finding a figure to whom the French would rally, the Allies had smuggled General Giraud out of France to Gibraltar, where he agreed to take part in the operation but at the same time arrogantly demanded command of the entire expeditionary force. Instead he was flown to Algiers, where, to everyone's surprise, the archcollaborationist Admiral Darlan had arrived to visit his sick son and was caught by the invasion. On November 10, after negotiations with Robert Murphy, Darlan ordered all French commanders to cease resistance. Eisenhower, seeking to establish some kind of order, made Darlan the French political chief for all North Africa and Giraud the military chief. This anomaly soon resolved itself. On Christmas Eve, Darlan was assassinated by a young French royalist. Giraud, a brave, vain, but somewhat inept and politically inexperienced officer, was soon outmaneuvered by the cunning and furious de Gaulle and found himself gradually stripped of all but the costume of authority. De Gaulle assumed real power over the gathering elements of Free France.

Despite their astonishment, the Germans reacted swiftly

and effectively to the landings. Long before Eisenhower managed to get his inexperienced forces moving, the Germans and Italians occupied Tunisia and, benefiting from its proximity to Sicily, built up impressive strength, especially in aircraft. Winter rains turned the roads into quagmires, bogging down the Allied eastward advance, and for the first time, the Americans were pounded by Stuka dive bombers and the remarkable German 88 artillery piece, which astonished the Allies by its deadly effect against troops, tanks, and even planes. On November 23, Eisenhower transferred his headquarters to Algiers, and that white, hilly city, surrounded by orchards, slowly assumed the role hitherto played by Cairo.

In February, 1943, the Germans made a sudden thrust at the uncoordinated Allied advance and hurled the Americans back through the Kasserine Pass. Major General George S. Patton, Jr., a formidable United States commander whose name, genius, and eccentricities were soon to become renowned, was blocked further to the south near El Guettar, where his troops met unexpectedly stubborn resistance from Italian infantry. At this point Eisenhower summoned an old West Point classmate, Brigadier General Omar Bradley, to serve as his "eyes and ears" and stimulate the faltering United States Army.

The American fighting man soon proved, however, that he was competent, crafty, and courageous. He learned the arts of camouflage, the value of digging, and the need for coordinated patrolling. Professional officers, national guard divisions, and drafted replacements were rapidly welded into an efficient, weather-beaten force. On Eisenhower's orders, Patton began to look forward to a new invasion, this time against Sicily, and before the North African campaign ended in the summer of 1943, General Clark had been assigned to develop and train a new Fifth Army in Morocco for the eventual assault on Italy itself.

By March it was apparent even in Berlin and Rome that the Allied pincer arms extending toward each other from Cairo and Casablanca could not be kept apart. Rommel was recalled by Hitler. The British, under Montgomery, moved on Tunisia from the east, aided by Jean Leclerc's tiny, glamorous French force that had fought its way up from the Chad Territory, and the British and Americans closed in on Tunisia from the west. On April 23, the final attack began. Montgomery had already pierced the Mareth Line between Libya and Tunisia and now swept up toward Tunis as the United States II Corps overran Hill 609, blocking the road to Bizerte, and the British First Army, under Eisenhower's command, took bloody Longstop Hill, the last great natural barrier. On May 7, Tunis and Bizerte fell, and the final line of Axis retreat on the Cape Bon Peninsula was severed.

The North African campaign, which succeeded beyond any original hope, was the largest pincers movement ever successfully applied in war, joining forces from the Nile Valley to the Atlantic. Its timing was superb. The coincidence between Montgomery's El Alamein breakthrough and the Moroccan-Algerian landings was carefully foreseen, but that impact, already immense, was enhanced by the simultaneity of triumphs at Stalingrad and Guadalcanal, the latter being of special political and morale importance to the United States.

All told, North Africa cost the Germans and Italians 349,206 in dead and prisoners. Apart from extensive losses at sea, they were deprived of nearly two hundred thousand tons of material. Italy's Field Marshal Alessandro Messe and Germany's General Jürgen von Arnim were among those taken. When it was suggested to Eisenhower that he receive the latter, Eisenhower refused, believing himself engaged in a "crusade" against "a completely evil conspiracy." (It was a policy he would stick to for the rest of the war.) Mussolini's vision of a new Roman Empire dissolved in blood where Rome had once obliterated its Carthaginian enemy; soon the *Duce* would lose Italy itself. And for Hitler it was a catastrophe. Montgomery analyzed the *Führer's* strategic error accordingly: "From a purely military point of view, the holding out in North Africa once the Mareth Line had been broken through could never be justified. I suppose Hitler ordered it for political reasons; it may sometimes be necessary, but they will generally end in disaster."

Rommel commented on the crucial El Alamein battle with justifiable acerbity: "The fact is that there were men in high places who, though not without the capacity to grasp the facts of the situation, simply did not have the courage to look them in the face and draw the proper conclusions. They preferred to put their heads in the sand, live in a sort of military pipedream and look for scapegoats whom they usually found in the troops or field commanders. Looking back, I am conscious of only one mistake—that I did not circumvent the 'Victory or Death' order twenty-four hours earlier."

The African victory gave resurgent confidence to the weary British. The experience proved the effectiveness of a new team of United States commanders and broke in an American army. It forged an alliance that, at Eisenhower's insistence, was led by an integrated, international staff. And, finally, it prepared the foundation for a liberated, Gaullist France. For de Gaulle, ignored in planning the invasion, then thrust aside in favor of Darlan and Giraud, forced his way by will power and artful maneuver to the leadership of French North Africa. From there he moved into France, carrying all his bitter memories.

Seesaw War Across a Continent

There were three phases to the war in North Africa. The first began in September, 1940, when a huge Italian army under Marshal Rodolfo Graziani invaded Egypt from Libya. There was not much fighting until December; then, in two months' time, the British Army of the Nile, commanded by General Archibald Wavell, ran the Italians back 500 miles into Libya. Phase two began in the spring of 1941. Hitler sent in his Afrika Korps and General Erwin Rommel, who fought the British back and forth over the Libyan Desert, winning and losing and winning again until he was within 70 miles of Alexandria. By then it was summer of 1942. The British had been hitting back hard, and Rommel was short on supplies, but Hitler and Mussolini still expected news any day that the Nile Valley was in the bag. Phase three began that fall, when the British and Americans invaded Morocco and Algeria, and the British Eighth Army, now commanded by General Bernard Montgomery, struck at El Alamein and sent the Axis armies reeling back on one of the longest retreats in history. In 80 days Rommel traveled 1,750 miles, or about as far as from Paris to Moscow. Behind him he left a desert strewn with burnt-out tanks and thousands of dead and wounded. At the end of his retreat, he ran into the British First Army and the Americans coming in from the west. The map below covers this third phase. At right is the battle at Kasserine Pass, where Rommel, reinforced with new armor, drove a "bulge" into the Allied lines and gave the American Army its first real taste of German fire. The weight of the attack had caught the Allies by surprise, and some 2,400 green GI's surrendered. But the Americans learned fast and after that fought hard and well.

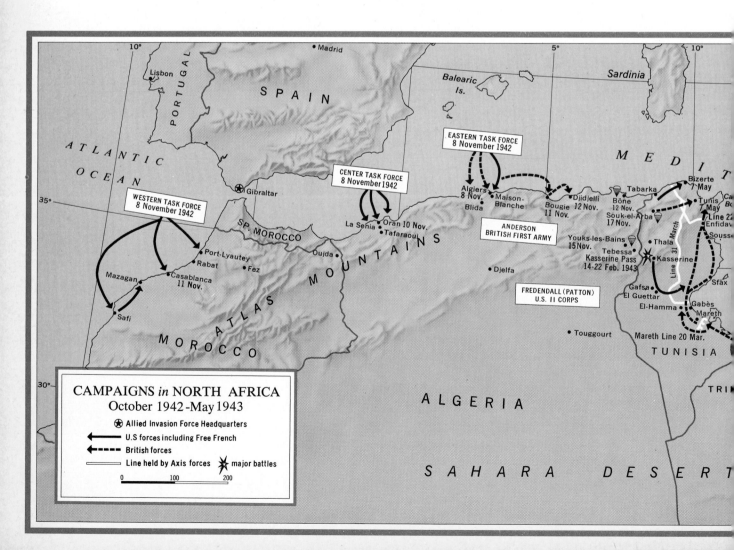

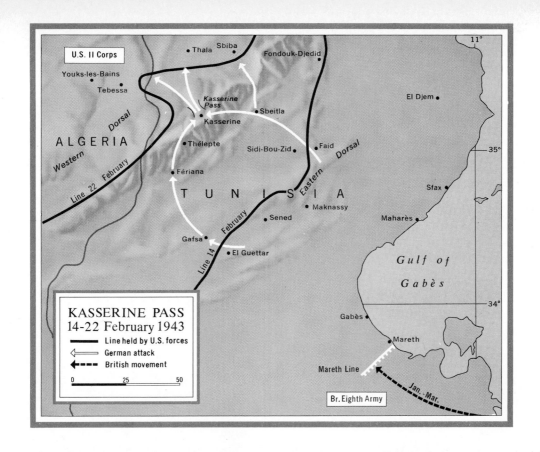

KASSERINE PASS
14-22 February 1943

- ▬▬ Line held by U.S. forces
- ⬅ German attack
- ◀╌╌ British movement

0   25   50

U.S. II Corps

Youks-les-Bains
Tebessa
Thala • Sbiba
Fondouk-Djedid
El Djem

Kasserine Pass
Kasserine
Sbeitla

ALGERIA
Thélepte
Sidi-Bou-Zid
Faid

Western Dorsal
Fériana
Eastern Dorsal

Line 22 February

T U N I S I A

Sfax

Sened
Maknassy

Maharès

Gafsa
El Guettar

Line 14 February

Gulf of Gabès

Gabès

Mareth

Mareth Line

Jan.-Mar.

Br. Eighth Army

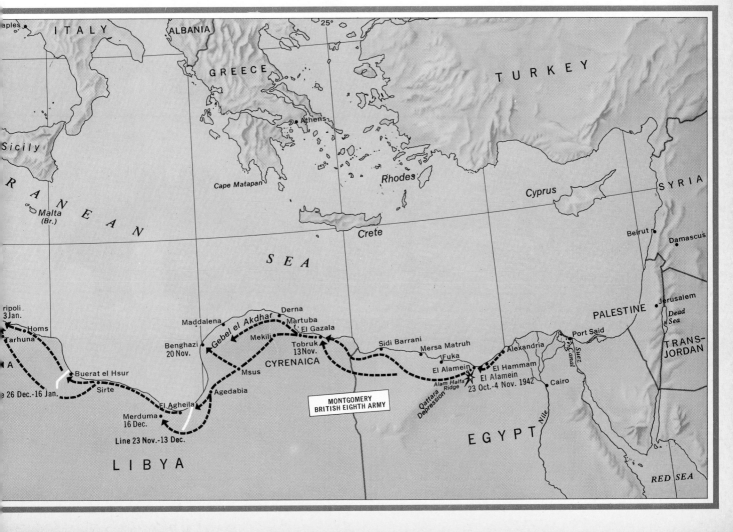

ITALY
ALBANIA
GREECE
TURKEY

Naples

Athens

Cape Matapan
Rhodes
Cyprus
SYRIA

Sicily

MEDITERRANEAN

Malta (Br.)

Crete
Beirut
Damascus

S E A

Tripoli
3 Jan.
Homs
Tarhuna

Derna
Maddalena
Martuba
El Gazala
Gebel el Akdhar
Benghazi
20 Nov.
Mekili
Tobruk
13 Nov.
Sidi Barrani
Mersa Matruh

Jerusalem
Dead Sea

PALESTINE

Buerat el Hsur
Sirte
26 Dec.-16 Jan.

Msus
CYRENAICA
Fuka
Alexandria
El Hammam
El Alamein

Port Said
Suez Canal

TRANS-JORDAN

Agedabia
El Agheila

MONTGOMERY
BRITISH EIGHTH ARMY

Alam Halfa Ridge
El Alamein
23 Oct.-4 Nov. 1942

Cairo

Nile

Merduma
16 Dec.
Line 23 Nov.-13 Dec.

Qattara Depression

E G Y P T

L I B Y A

RED SEA

A First, Fast Success

On September 13, 1940, the Italians sent five divisions against Egypt, fully expecting a quick victory. But at Sidi Barrani they dug in and then did nothing for three months. The British used the time to build their strength. When they struck, they had two divisions. But there seemed no stopping them. War on the rock-hard desert, where there was no cover and few landmarks to take bearings on, was more like a sea fight than anything else, which may have been one reason why the British were so good at it. But they also had better equipment than the Italians, and far better generals. They took one coastal stronghold after another, all the way to Benghazi, and captured 130,000 prisoners. Mussolini's new Roman Empire was vanishing like sugar in a fire.

Commanding the British were Gen. Wavell (at right in the picture above) and Lt. Gen. Richard O'Connor (left), a brilliant desert strategist who was later captured by the Germans. At right above, Wavell's guns pound Derna, a key seaport along the route to Tripolitania. At right are several thousand of Graziani's troops who surrendered during the first weeks of the two-month-long British offensive in Libya.

A Little Help from Hitler

When it looked as though Mussolini was about to lose everything in North Africa, Hitler reluctantly decided to send him two divisions and a first-rate general, Erwin Rommel. An early offensive campaign was not called for. Hitler had no heart for a desert war. He simply wanted Rommel to take charge in Libya, stop the British, and come up with a plan by mid-April. Rommel got to Tripoli in February, 1941. On March 24, he launched his attack. The British hardly knew what hit them. Their lines had been thinned down to about half strength, in order to send aid to Greece. In a matter of days they were outflanked, outfought, and chased clear back to Egypt. By April 12, the whole Libyan coast was Rommel's—except for Tobruk. Try as they would, the Axis armies seemed unable to crack that fortress. It was a crucial failure.

EUROPEAN PICTURE SERVICE

At left, Erwin Rommel (on the right) arrives in Tripoli on February 12. Beside him is General Italo Gariboldi, the over-all Italian commander. Above is another German contribution to the desert war, their 88-mm. gun, which was able to cut through British armor like butter.

General Rommel, at left above, rides to the front in Libya.

The Desert Fox Photographs His War

Rommel's first offensive was a heady time for his army. Most of them were Italians, as is often forgotten, and they were winning again. Their new leader was a hard, businesslike tactician who took to desert fighting with gusto. His troops said there was never a bullet made with his name on it. The pictures at right give some of the flavor of that time, from his viewpoint: Rommel was also an ardent amateur photographer.

But the fortunes of desert war were to change drastically, several times. Instead of pushing on into Egypt in 1941, Rommel used up months hammering away at Tobruk. It was like a knife pointed at his left flank, and he intended to do away with it. But the British garrison there held. Meanwhile, the British were regrouping in Egypt under a new commander, General Claude Auchinleck, and Rommel's supply line across the Mediterranean was being badly mauled by the R.A.F. and the Royal Navy. Auchinleck struck in November. Back again over the Libyan Desert rolled the British, now known as the Eighth Army. In two months, after desperate fighting, they had relieved Tobruk and raced to El Agheila. But by the start of 1942, Rommel was himself making ready for still another counterattack. And this time he intended to keep on going right up to Suez.

ALL: CAPTURED GERMAN RECORDS, NATIONAL ARCHIVES

Rommel took this photograph from atop an armored car.

British prisoners stream back from the front.

Photographer Rommel obviously took special care in focusing and composing this close-up of a dead British soldier.

Four of Rommel's comrades-in-arms smile for their commanding officer.

Two panzer warriors take a break from the business at hand.

"There will be no Dunkirk here"

General Leslie Morshead

General Wavell made the decision to hold Tobruk once Rommel had by-passed it, and Churchill backed him up, recognizing the immense strategic importance of the old Libyan seaport. From March until November, 1941, some 23,000 of Wavell's men—English, Australians, New Zealanders, Indians—withstood a murderous pounding from Rommel's ground forces and dive bombers. Their refusal to surrender infuriated Rommel; for the first time, the supposedly invincible Nazis had run up against a foe who did not either run or cave in. Tobruk had been heavily fortified by the Italians, and the Royal Navy kept the defenders supplied through the back door, but as one officer later wrote, "It was the spirit of the men within the fortress that won the 'Battle of Tobruk.'" The following is a selection of comments by a variety of people who were very much involved in that battle.

. . . On the ground of pure strategy Winston was therefore arguing passionately . . . for the retention of Tobruk. When Winston asked for my opinion, I supported his desire to hold on, not because it was his idea but because it seemed to me to offer absolutely the only hope of stopping the rot. . . .

Winston greeted this support for his own ideas with unfeigned delight. And at once he found the right phrase for Tobruk: "A sally port," he said, pronouncing this with his slight lisp between the "s" and the "a." He rolled the phrase round his mouth and repeated it. "Yes, a sally port, a sally port; that is what we want, that is the thing to do with them. The farther he advances the more you threaten, the more he has to fear. That is the answer, a sally port. . . ."

—Air Vice-Marshal Arthur Harris

There'll be no Dunkirk here. If we should have to get out, we shall fight our way out. There is to be no surrender and no retreat.

—General L. J. Morshead, *Commanding Officer at Tobruk*

The General Officer Commanding the German Forces in Libya requests that the British troops occupying Tobruk surrender their arms. Single soldiers waving white handkerchiefs are not fired on. Strong German forces have already surrounded Tobruk and it is useless to try to escape. . . .

—*A Leaflet Dropped on Tobruk*

Things are very warm in front of Tobruk. I shan't be sorry to see more troops arrive, for we're still very thin on the long fortress front. I've seldom had such worries—militarily speaking—as in the last few days. . . .

—General Rommel

When the fog lifted we saw about thirty tanks lined up near R2—half a mile to the west of us. The tanks dispersed, four or five going to each of the posts near by. Infantry followed, in parties of about sixty. As they got within range we opened up and they went to the ground, but four tanks came on. Their machine-guns kept our heads down and their cannon blasted away our sandbag parapets . . . but we sniped at the infantry whenever we got a chance. Our anti-tank rifle put one light tank out of action, but it couldn't check the heavier one, which came right up to the post. We threw hand grenades at them but these bounced off, and the best we could do was to keep the infantry from getting closer than a hundred yards.

After about an hour of this fighting the tanks withdrew, but about ten o'clock more came back. They drove through the wire and one even cruised up and down over our communication trench dropping stick bombs into it. We held their infantry off most of the morning, but eventually under cover of this attack they got into one end of the post, where the Bren crew had all been wounded. Then the Germans worked along the trench while the rest of us were still firing from the other pits. By this time more than half our chaps—we'd only had fifteen—had been killed or wounded, and the Germans got command of the post before we survivors realized what happened. Just then our artillery began shelling it heavily and the German tanks must have been driven off. So there we were, Germans and Aussies stuck in the post together with shells falling outside. A Jerry sergeant said, "I don't know who'll be the prisoners—you or us. We'd better wait awhile until the shelling stops." When the shelling stopped more Germans came in and the sergeant said, "You're the prisoners." And we were.

—Corporal R. McLeish

The Australians, who are the men our troops have had opposite them so far, are extraordinarily tough fighters. The German is more active in the attack, but the enemy stakes his life in the defence and fights to the last with extreme cunning. Our men, usually easy-going and unsuspecting, fall easily into his traps. . . .

—Lieutenant Schorm, *From a Diary*

. . . Rommel was deeply troubled by the attitude of the Italians. Rommel's nominal superior, General Bastico, the Italian commander in chief in North Africa, was convinced that the British were planning an offensive, and he said that "the enemy attack will not be merely diversion-

ary but a heavy offensive aimed at forcing a final decision." Bastico believed that it would be simultaneous with our assault on Tobruk, and accordingly he was very anxious for Rommel to cancel his plans for attacking the Fortress. Rommel would not hear of it. . . .

To ally the fears of the Italians and to prevent interference with his plans, Rommel instructed his staff to adopt a confident tone in all discussions with Italian officers. . . .

—General F. W. von Mellenthin

Nothing new. The heat's frightful, night time as well as day time. Liquidated four bugs. My bed is now standing in tins filled with water and I hope the nights will be a little more restful from now on. Some of the others are having a bad time with fleas. They've left me alone so far.

—General Rommel

Almost worse than the bombs as a tribulation to the flesh and the spirit were the fleas. The desert fleas are famous, and ours are obviously in the pay of the enemy. How we cursed them on the nights when the moon was late up and we hoped to catch a couple of hours' sleep before the inevitable procession of night bombers started. The fleas marched and counter-marched up and down our twitching bodies until we thought we would go crazy. . . . And we needed those hours of sleep, for when the moon was up we would get mighty little rest. Twenty-one alarms in one night was our record; and it was nothing to have half-a-dozen night after night. . . .

—A British Gunnery Sergeant

It's my turn down to the beach tomorrow, so I'll have a good scrub and do some washing. I'm black, or at least grey. This sand gets every-

where, and my clothes stand up by themselves when I get undressed. Sweat and sand make good concrete. I won't have much washing to do, only pants and socks. I don't wear anything else. Furthermore, I'll have to walk around in my boots until my clothes dry. It's nothing here for the boys to walk around stark naked for half a day as most of them have nothing else to wear while their clothes are drying, so at meal-times they line up with nothing on but their boots and hats. . . .

The sea was like a mill-pond when we got there, the day glorious, so things couldn't have been better. At night, another chap and I lit a fire and cooked some tinned food, and then lay in bed and had a good feed. . . . I remarked to my mate that I wouldn't swop beds with anyone in the world, and he agreed. It was beautiful lying there on the sand about five yards from the Med., a lovely still night with every star visible. We were wonderfully warm and comfortable and hadn't a care in the world. . . .

You women back home sit and worry about us. You don't realize the good times we have, days that we have at the beach or days when Jerry is quiet and we have a euchre party at threepence a game. . . .

I'm extremely happy here; I don't know why! There ain't no bird to sing, no flowers or lawns or trees or rivers to look at, but I'm just happy. . . .

I suppose I enjoy company and I enjoy the wonderful feeling of comradeship in Tobruk. We are more or less cut off from the world, and we have one job and one job only, that is, to hold this place. This is an experience I shall always relish. It will be a privilege later to say "I was there. . . ."

—A Young Australian Gunner, *In a Letter to His Mother*

The Battle of Malta

Time and again in the desert, victory went to the side with the most gasoline. The war ran on gasoline, and like nearly everything else, it had to be brought from a long way off and at great cost. The main British supply route to North Africa ran 3,000 miles around the Cape of Good Hope, while the Axis only had to cross 300 miles of Mediterranean. This should have given Rommel a big advantage; but the British held Malta, and Malta was the key to the whole issue of who would win on the desert. Set in the narrows between Sicily and Tunisia, the little island was in exactly the right place to batter enemy convoys. Hitler and Mussolini agreed that the British air and naval bases there had to be destroyed and the island taken before Rommel made another and, they hoped, final drive on Egypt. Churchill and his high command agreed that Malta had to be held at all cost. The *Luftwaffe* gave the island a merciless pounding. In December, 1941, the Germans flew 169 bombing raids on Malta; the next month, there were 262 raids. The British did everything possible to keep Malta supplied, at a terrible cost in men and ships. The situation grew desperate. Axis convoys began getting through, and as a result, Rommel set off on a new offensive toward the end of January, 1942, driving the Eighth Army back to the Gazala-Bir Hacheim line. Churchill urged a strong counteroffensive to stop Rommel and to relieve pressure on Malta; but Auchinleck did not think his army was ready yet. Then, in May, Rommel struck again. By the nineteenth of June, he was outside Tobruk. Two days later, Tobruk fell. Rommel was made a field marshal, and his army took possession of huge dumps of ammunition, food, and, best of all, gasoline. His supply problems, it appeared, were suddenly solved. Why stop now for an invasion of Malta, he argued. Hitler agreed. The invasion was canceled, and Rommel pushed on toward Egypt. But Auchinleck was fighting back with terrific determination now, and by July, near El Alamein, Rommel called a halt "for the time being."

Four precious gallons of gasoline go into a British tank.

At top left, on route from Alexandria to Malta, a British convoy escort fires a broadside at attacking Italian ships while a cruiser in the distance puts up a protective smoke screen. The photograph at left center was taken on Malta during one of the heavy raids in April, 1942. But Nazi air power in the Mediterranean was dwindling fast, the R.A.F. growing stronger by the day. By the fall of 1942, the Luftwaffe *was about finished in North Africa. At bottom left are the remains of some of Rommel's air support on a bombed field at Derna, Libya.*

"Rommel, Rommel, Rommel!" Churchill had cried, as he paced up and down his room in the Cairo Embassy. "What else matters but beating him!" The Rommel magic had become legend even among British troops. A shake-up might help break the spell, Churchill reasoned. General Sir Claude Auchinleck (above) was a much admired soldier, but his command seemed poorly coordinated and his troops lacking in confidence in their leaders. "To take or destroy" Rommel was now the assigned task of the two men shown at right, the very able General Sir Harold Alexander (on the left), and the then little known General Bernard Montgomery.

Command Decision

On the morning of August 4, 1942, the Prime Minister of Great Britain looked out of the window of a Liberator bomber and saw "in the pale, glimmering dawn the endless winding silver ribbon of the Nile stretched joyously before us." Winston Churchill had come to Cairo to see what was going wrong with the war against Rommel. Shaded by the same sort of pith helmet he had worn 44 years before on the march to Omdurman, he drove to the front to look things over for himself (above) and went striding about in the intense heat, talking to the troops and sizing up their leaders. When he left seven days later, General Auchinleck was out. Now in over-all command was General Alexander; under him, in charge of the Eighth Army, was General Montgomery. Firing Auchinleck was like killing a magnificent stag, Churchill said. But the decision proved to be one of his best.

The situation at the front remained a stalemate through the rest of the summer. Suez was only 200 miles to the rear; but British strength was building fast. New tanks were on the way from the United States. And, more important, the new command had injected a new spirit into the Eighth Army.

235

El Alamein

The battle began under a bright moon, when the silence of the desert night was broken by a thousand-gun artillery barrage that went on for five hours, blasting big passageways through the elaborate German mine fields that Rommel called "Devil's Gardens." It was October 23, 1942. Rommel, for the first time in his career, was on sick leave in Germany. His army since early September had done little else but dig in. Fuel and ammunition were in short supply (Malta was back in business). Montgomery meanwhile had been quietly building vast supply dumps along his northern front and staging a major sham build-up to the south. The deception worked. When he drove against the northern line, the surprise was total and his strength twice that of the enemy. He also had Rommel's army hemmed into a forty-mile corridor between the sea and the impassable Qattara Depression. Rommel, who was back at the front by the twenty-fifth, had no choice but to go forward or backward. Nine days later, he knew it would have to be backward. He had been bombed night and day. He had been hit by swarms of fast new tanks, by infantry and artillery that seemed inexhaustible. And he had been outfoxed by Montgomery. Hitler told him to stand firm; and he did, briefly. But the war, and history, had already reached one of its decisive moments.

The battle line at El Alamein was flat, stony desert with scattered patches of sand and ugly little clumps of camel's-thorn bushes. The photograph above shows a night artillery barrage seen from the vantage point of the Eighth Army lines. At right, German artillery scores a near miss on one of Montgomery's rapidly advancing heavy tanks.

In London on October 29, Churchill was in a terrible temper: Why was there no news from Egypt? What was Montgomery doing

Had he no fighting spirit? But at El Alamein, as this picture taken on the same day so dramatically suggests, the tide had already turned.

Rommel on the Run

Three members of a British Matilda medium tank crew (left) show elation over good hunting: sixteen Nazi tanks destroyed. Above, Crusader tanks follow the retreating Germans. This British machine was proved especially effective during the long chase because of its high speed.

Rommel was bitter afterward about Hitler's "victory or death" order, which, he said, kept him fighting at El Alamein twenty-four hours longer than he should have. As a result, a large part of Rommel's infantry and motorized troops were lost. After Axis forces began withdrawing on November 2, Montgomery sent armor sweeping around behind them, and two days later Rommel's escape road was blocked; yet somehow he slipped his forces through the barrier. Sudden, heavy rains that bogged down vehicles in mud were all, according to Montgomery, that saved his foe from annihilation. The R.A.F. constantly bombed Rommel; Montgomery's armor slashed at his columns. Rommel abandoned every non-essential, including his Italian infantry. His route was littered with burned-out vehicles and other debris of war. The Nazi leader had no choice but to try to continue his retreat some one thousand miles until he could link up with German forces in Tunisia and with them turn on Montgomery—and on the Americans newly landed in North Africa.

LEFT: ARCHIVES DOCUMENTATION FRANÇAISE; RIGHT: IMPERIAL WAR MUSEUM, LONDON

The Operation Called Torch

On November 8, 1942, American and British forces landed in French Morocco and Algeria in the campaign called Operation Torch. The invasion put the Allies in a position to strike Rommel's Afrika Korps from the rear; it was the best they could do at the time to answer the demands of the hard-pressed Soviet Union for a second front. A very involved political situation complicated the operation. For one thing, it was necessary to give the British a subordinate role because of French bitterness toward them, stemming, among other things, from the destruction of a French squadron at Oran by the Royal Navy in 1940. And because General de Gaulle and his Free French were considered traitors by Vichy French officers, they were left out of the operation completely. General Eisenhower, commanding the operation, felt it a necessary expedient to work through Vichy French officials, including the collaborationist Admiral Darlan, and was much criticized for doing so. But despite attempts to obtain cooperation, the French resisted most landings—although they did not resist Hitler's invasion of unoccupied France at this same time. However, the fighting lasted only a short time, and the North African French then joined the fight against Hitler.

Three days after the landings in Africa, Hitler moved into unoccupied France in violation of the armistice agreement. Later, on November 27, he sent troops to the Toulon navy base to seize the fleet there. But French sailors resisted long enough to permit crews to scuttle some seventy ships (above left). Admiral Darlan (left) had earlier ordered the admiral in command to escape with the fleet, but the latter had refused. Darlan was also far less effective than the Allies had hoped he would be in reducing French resistance to the African landings. Above, American troops head inland after coming ashore at Surcouf, near Algiers. The man kneeling behind the sandbank carries a flag, for it was hoped that the French would be less likely to kill Americans.

243

The Race for Tunisia

Only three days after the Torch landings, Eisenhower sent the British First Army—with American elements—racing for Tunisia, into which Hitler had begun pouring men on November 9. If its port cities of Tunis and Bizerte could be taken, the second arm of a great Allied pincers could be brought to bear on the Axis armies then retreating before Montgomery far to the southeast. But Hitler's air-lifted forces won the race and stopped the British in the mountains. Eisenhower ended the campaign in late December and brought up heavy American reinforcements to fight a holding action until Montgomery came up. But in mid-February, Marshal Rommel suddenly drove some fifty miles through American positions at Kasserine Pass. The victory had no lasting results, but it was the beginning of the education of the American forces.

Eisenhower (right) confers with Maj. Gen. Patton, whom he named to command a corps in Tunisia.

American medium bombers (top right) fly above the desert in Tunisia. Such planes habitually bombed from a 200-foot height despite antiaircraft fire. At lower right, American soldiers maneuver over typical North African terrain.

ABOVE: WIDE WORLD; BELOW: U.S. ARMY

These young Nazis (above), captured during the final days of the fighting in Tunisia, give every evidence of being cheerful about their fate. The German troops in Africa ignored Hitler's demand that they fight to the death, and most seemed happy to get out of the war. At right, the populace of Tunis cheers entering British forces who have broken through the German defenses.

Clean Sweep in Africa

Before he could accomplish much else in the Tunisian campaign, General Eisenhower had the basic problem of creating an efficient fighting force. There was the fundamental matter of welding British, American, and French units into a functioning army, for there were problems not only of communications but also of national pride and prestige—some serious, such as the bitterness of French toward British. As for the American forces, they were green, their training was not always all it might have been, and coordination between service branches was faulty, as when fighter planes sent to hit the enemy badly mauled an American tank destroyer unit instead. The winter's fighting in Tunisia, most of it on a small scale, did much to forge the American troops into a unified fighting force, although it was at Kasserine Pass that the real test came. The American troops had been tested and weak leaders weeded out by the time General Montgomery pursued the Afrika Korps into Tunisia in late March (and thereby came under Eisenhower's command). Eisenhower now began hitting the Axis forces from both west and south, gradually forcing them into the northeast corner of Tunisia. On May 7, both Tunis and Bizerte fell, and on May 13, the last enemy surrendered. Rommel and perhaps 700 others escaped, but some 275,000 prisoners were taken. It was a grievous loss for the Axis.

The War in Russia

The cynical military collaboration between Nazi Germany and Communist Russia came to a bloody end June 22, 1941, when Hitler hurled against Stalin the most powerful army ever seen. Between the Arctic Ocean and the Black Sea, more than two hundred and fifty divisions rumbled across the long Soviet frontier and headed for Moscow, Leningrad, and Kiev. Not quite four years later, their journey ended in the ruins of Berlin.

On July 29, 1940, Colonel General Alfred Jodl, chief of German operations, had told a conference of staff officers that the *Führer* had decided "to attack the U.S.S.R. in the spring of 1941." Two days later, Hitler himself revealed this plan to his leading generals. Colonel General Franz Halder took down Hitler's words at the briefing: "Wiping out the very power to exist of Russia! That is the goal!" That November, Stalin sent Molotov to Berlin to demand further extension of Soviet influence in eastern Europe. The request only reaffirmed Hitler's decision to double-cross his partner. On December 18, he issued military Directive No. 21, headed "Operation Barbarossa," in honor of the medieval German emperor who had won great victories in the East.

The object of Barbarossa was not merely to occupy Russian territory but to destroy the Red Army in huge battles of annihilation along a fantastically large front. Assuming his panzers would advance as rapidly as in France, the *Führer* reckoned that within eight weeks they could capture Leningrad, Moscow, and the Ukraine, putting an end to organized resistance. He decided the campaign could not be "conducted in a knightly fashion" and authorized Gestapo chief Heinrich Himmler to use his secret police independently of the Army in conquered territories. On March 21, 1941, he drafted his infamous Commissar Order: all Soviet commissars who were captured would be shot.

In the original timetable, Barbarossa was to begin in May to insure the conquest of Moscow and Leningrad before the first Russian snows set in. But Mussolini's misfortunes in Greece and the Belgrade coup d'état caused Hitler to postpone the date. The postponement deeply distressed Field Marshal Walther von Brauchitsch, supreme commander of the Eastern Front. Brauchitsch was right. When Nazi divisions began pounding Moscow and Leningrad, the first snows were falling.

German soldiering genius accomplished miracles in preparing this unprecedented offensive. The *Wehrmacht* deployed two hundred and seven divisions, twenty-five of them armored, fleshing out gaps with more than fifty satellite divisions, largely Finnish, Rumanian, and Hungarian. The two-thousand-mile front was divided into three main thrusts under Field Marshal Wilhelm von Leeb, aiming at Leningrad, Field Marshal Fedor von Bock, aiming at Moscow, and Field Marshal Gerd von Rundstedt, aiming across the Ukraine.

At 6 A.M., June 22, after initial bombings and barrages had begun, Count Werner von der Schulenburg, Hitler's rather pro-Russian ambassador in Moscow, handed Molotov a note officially declaring war. Pale, tense, silent,

Deeper into Russia: Nazi tanks advance over the first snows of 1941.

the Commissar for Foreign Affairs took the document, spat on it, tore it up, and then rang for Poskrebishev, his secretary. "Show this gentleman out through the back door," he said.

Despite numerous indications of Hitler's decision, Stalin had made no plans to meet an attack. The Soviet regime simply disbelieved all warnings. As a result, the onslaught came with terrible surprise, smashing an incompetently led Red Army that was still engaged in routine border exercises.

The speed of the Nazi advance was impressive on all fronts. Hundreds of Soviet aircraft were destroyed on the ground. Siege guns were trundled up to demolish fortresses of the so-called Stalin Line as they were successively isolated by German panzers. Three Red Army marshals, Kliment Efremovich· Voroshilov in the north, Semën Mikhailovich Budënny in the south, and Semën Konstantinovich Timoshenko in the center, faced Leeb, Rundstedt, and Bock. Of the three, only Timoshenko showed any competence.

On the very first day, Brest-Litovsk, key to Soviet central defenses, fell. Confused, cut-off Russian units radioed each other: "We are being fired on. What shall we do?" and received such answers as: "You must be insane. Why is your signal not in code?" On June 27, Minsk fell, and Bock crossed the Berezina, heading for Smolensk. Leeb raced along the Baltic toward Leningrad; Rundstedt paraded into the Ukraine against Budënny's inept cavalry.

When I reached Moscow early in July, after an eleven-day train trip from Ankara, the capital was in a curious daze. Stalin, greatly moved, addressed the nation July 3, calling his startled audience "brothers and sisters" and "friends" instead of "comrades." Radio sets were commandeered so that only public loudspeakers could announce carefully filtered bulletins. An iron censorship prevented foreign correspondents from transmitting news not culled from the official press.

Moscow itself, basking in the summer sun, had been draped in camouflage. The Bolshoi theater and other buildings easily identified from the air were hung with huge scenic curtains depicting woodland villages. Principal squares were painted to give the wholly unsuccessful impression of rural countryside. When the *Luftwaffe* came over the capital, it was met by thunderous antiaircraft barrages, whose fragments clattered down upon the streets. A few bombs struck the Kremlin compound, and one knocked a corner off the Bolshoi, leaving its pitiful camouflage curtain flapping like a torn dress.

It was not until mid-July that the Nazis met their first serious opposition. At Smolensk heavy fighting developed as Timoshenko threw in trained reserves, and by the time that city fell, three weeks later, a Russian defense line had been established to its east. In late summer, I visited the rolling fields around Yelnya with a Siberian division that had been rushed out of Asia to help pinch off a German sector and stage a brief counterattack. It was comforting to regard this first ground to be retaken from the Germans since September 1, 1939, all cluttered with the wreckage of panzer units, and to hear officers boast: "Now the war will end because the Siberians are here."

But Hitler's plan to encircle and destroy the Red Army had achieved considerable success. There were huge losses all along the front. At Kiev the Germans claimed to capture 600,000 Russians. (Even Soviet historians admit to 200,000.) At Smolensk the Germans claimed 348,000 prisoners. By the end of September Stalin had lost 2,500,000 men, 22,000 guns, 18,000 tanks, and 14,000 planes.

Nevertheless, the German advance was slowing down. Russian resistance hardened. Nazi brutality, the ravaging of towns and hamlets, the torture and execution had combined to turn against the invaders a population that in many areas had been inclined at first to accept the enemy as a relief from Stalinist terror. Stalin ordered a scorched-earth policy. Partisan bands were formed from encircled units far to the German rear. And in occupied Europe itself, Communists responded to a Moscow summons to sabotage Brauchitsch's bases and supply lines.

When the Nazi offensive started in June, the U.S.S.R. was incompletely mobilized, with but one hundred and fifty understrength divisions deployed. The Soviets possessed some twenty-one thousand tanks—more than four times the number opposing them—but few were of recent manufacture. The new medium model, T-34, was not thrown against the Germans until Smolensk.

Yet, despite initial disadvantages, the traditional soldiering qualities of the Russian and the traditional Russian strategy of trading space for time slowly rectified the balance. Moreover, man power was ever plentiful. The Germans began to realize that the Russians could afford to trade lives at a rate of five to one, making up their losses from a population that was three times the size of Germany's—and the Russians were fighting for their homeland. Slowly Soviet Slavs forgot resentments against dictatorship and rallied to Stalin's standard of Patriotic War. A new role was accorded to religion. Privileges and honors that had not existed since the Revolution were returned to officers. Guderian, the German panzer general, recalls meeting a former Czarist general at Orel who said: "If only you had come twenty years ago we should have welcomed you with open arms. But now it's too late. We were just beginning to get on our feet and now you arrive and throw us back twenty years so that we will have to start from the beginning all over again. Now we are fighting for Russia and in that cause we are all united."

German losses were both heavy and hard to replace. Halder estimated that by the end of November, 1941, Hitler had forfeited 743,112 men—or 23 per cent of the total originally thrown into the Russian campaign. And as the German advance lost momentum, the Russians managed to assemble quantities of artillery. Since 1936, a new series had been under mass production: guns of 76, 122, and 152 millimeters; tremendous 280, 305, and even 406 millimeter howitzers; the famous Katyusha rockets, which rolled up to the line on trucks for the first time on September 12, 1941, at Khandrov, outside Leningrad, and harassed the Germans with their multiple, whistling explosions. The infantry was re-equipped with Degtyarev and Goriunov machine guns and Shpagin machine pistols. And the Russians maintained a cavalry force of six hundred thousand men, which, though it took terrible losses, disheartened the Germans by filtering through snowbound forests or suddenly sweeping out of dawn fogs. To support this complex apparatus, on August 25, 1941, Stalin created a "Command of the Rear of the Red Army" to assure logistical support, and an "Army of the Interior" to maintain absolute internal security.

Nevertheless, by October 20, Bock was within forty miles of Moscow. A week earlier, Stalin had decided to evacuate his main ministries and the diplomatic corps to Kuibyshev, a ramshackle provincial town five hundred and fifty miles to the southeast on the Volga, although he himself, with his chief lieutenants, remained in the Kremlin. The evacuees drove to the Kazan railway station through a city consumed by panic. The usual police units had been taken from the streets and rushed into line to plug a gap on the main highway from Vyazma. Families with bundles were hurrying to rail depots. Trucks loaded down with old men, women, children, and deserting bureaucrats were heading eastward. Crowds were looting bakeries and food stores as the usual stern order crumbled into chaos. At the Kazan station, I joined diplomats in seeking to storm the buffet; every inch of the platform and track sidings was littered with huddled families and their pitiful belongings.

Fortunately, the first heavy snow was feathering down, obscuring our evacuation from the *Luftwaffe*. The train was jammed with distinguished passengers: Sir Stafford Cripps, the British ambassador, with his puzzled airedale; Laurence Steinhardt, the American envoy, who joined reporters in a steady poker game; all the diplomatic corps except for a few junior officials left behind as embassy caretakers; famous writers like Ilya Ehrenburg, Aleksei Tolstoi, and Mikhail Sholokhov; Comintern leaders such

as Dolores Ibarruri, "La Pasionaria" of the Spanish Civil War. Panayotis Pipinellis, the Greek ambassador, had reached Moscow just in time to join the unhappy voyagers. He dressed himself neatly in frock coat and with impeccable courtesy strode from compartment to compartment, paying his first formal calls.

Box cars and flat cars moved westward with silent troops and eastward with rusty machinery from Ukrainian and Russian factories, which, with astonishing success, were being reassembled in distant Soviet Asia. Steel production shifted from Mariupol to Magnitogorsk, small arms from Tula to Sverdlovsk, tanks from Kharkov to Chelyabinsk—all east of the Urals. And by November, some two million people had either been shifted from the capital or had somehow managed to flee. Later many were to be ashamed of their desertion.

This was Russia's moment of truth. A Red Army communiqué admitted: "During the night of October 14–15, the position of the Western Front became worse. The German-Fascist troops hurled against our troops large quantities of tanks and motorized infantry, and in one sector broke through our defenses." Actually, Nazi patrols came close enough to see Moscow's Khimke water tower, and the official Soviet history of the war later said: "It was the lowest point reached throughout the war."

From the Kremlin itself, Stalin personally conducted the battle on his doorstep. He dispatched the dogged Timoshenko to take over from Budënny on the southern front, where Rundstedt was now hammering at the gateway to the Caucasus, and replaced him with General Georgi Zhukov, who painstakingly built up his reserves and waited for his ally, "General Winter." Snow alternated with rain, ice with mud, and gradually the Germans bogged down to the west, southeast, and north of Moscow. Hitler's generals pleaded with him to establish a winter line, but he refused, ordering them to press on.

On December 6, Zhukov went over to the offensive. He threw one hundred divisions into a sudden counterassault, and the Nazi lines faltered and dissolved. As Halder was to write: "The myth of the invincibility of the German Army was broken." Droves of Nazi soldiers were taken prisoner and displayed in newspaper photographs wearing women's furs and silk underclothing to supplement their inadequate uniforms against the cold.

In those heroic days outside Moscow, one of the first publicized Soviet war heroes was the gigantic General Andrei Andreyevitch Vlasov, a dramatic and inspiring figure and one of Zhukov's most successful field commanders. Vlasov was later seized by the Germans and promptly switched sides, to become the highest-ranking traitor of World War II. He recruited an army of Russian prisoners and led them for Hitler until May, 1945. General Patton captured him in Czechoslovakia, handed him over to Stalin, and he was hanged.

Snow lay all along the Moscow front, even under birch copses and pine groves. The cold was savage. Everything froze totally and suddenly. Dead horses balanced stiffly on the edge of drifts as ravens pecked their eyes. The silent Russian infantry trudged forward, accompanied by sleighs; guns lumbered up from the rear, and small-arms fire rattled through the woods.

While Moscow was being relieved, Leningrad withstood an extraordinary siege, protected by no less than five thousand gun emplacements. Leeb's soldiers from the southwest and the Finnish Marshal Mannerheim's from the northwest had swiftly approached its suburbs. But although they invested this northern Venice until 1943 and smothered it with shells and bombs, they never managed to penetrate. The suffering of the Leningraders was immense, but they fought and worked with extraordinary grit. When the city was first encircled, it had only a few days' reserve in food. By the middle of that dreadful 1941–42 winter, 3,500 to 4,000 people were dying of starvation every day. By official Russian figures, 632,000 men, women, and children died during the blockade.

Meanwhile, in the Ukraine, Rundstedt was speeding across the Dnieper and isolating huge Soviet formations. Stalin ordered the destruction of his enormous Dnieper dam and, with the same obstinacy so often shown by Hitler, commanded Budënny to hold Kiev. It was too late. German panzers forged a ring of steel around the Ukrainian capital. In a radio appeal, the Soviet dictator exhorted the besieged garrison to hold on. The defenders died in charred clusters around jumbled heaps of gutted tanks, guns, and trucks. When the Kiev area was finally quiet, the Germans claimed they had rounded up some six hundred thousand prisoners. Hitler replaced Rundstedt with Field Marshal Walther von Reichenau, and the latter swiftly overran all the Ukraine. In the Crimea, only Sevastopol remained. After a nine-month siege, Sevastopol finally collapsed the following July, hammered to pieces by air attack, conventional artillery, and a giant siege gun that was called Dora.

Kharkov, the "Soviet Pittsburgh" on the Donets, was outflanked. Nikita Khrushchev, a Ukrainian commissar at the time, telephoned the Kremlin and protested that the endangered Russian Army should be extricated. Stalin did not personally accept the call, but through Georgi Malenkov he passed on the abrupt message: "Let everything remain as it is." The Nazis proceeded to smother the writhing pocket, and to the south, they thrust into Rostov and the gateway to the Caucasus.

The Germans were able to re-establish a fighting line out of the chaos that resulted from Zhukov's victorious Moscow counteroffensive and the stalwart defense that prevented them from making Leningrad a winter base. Timoshenko recaptured Rostov in the south, and for the duration of the winter, an uneasy stalemate persisted on the lengthy front as both sides regrouped. By this time, it was evident that Hitler would never again be able to muster an offensive along the entire fighting line. A Soviet general assured me the General Staff was preparing for one more German drive—in search of oil for its thirsty war machine. When I was in Washington during April, 1942, a group of intelligence officers, including former United States military attachés in Berlin, Moscow, and Bucharest, asked me for a forecast of the 1942 campaign. I predicted that the Germans would launch one single desperate offensive—in the south; that they would reach Stalingrad and the high Caucasus; that they would then be forced to retreat. The Americans thought I was crazy. They insisted that the Soviet Air Force and Army were already destroyed and without capacity to resist.

Hitler, in Directive No. 45, designated Stalingrad and the Caucasus as the objectives of his 1942 offensive. Halder, his Chief of the General Staff, grumbled that Germany no longer had the power to achieve such ambitious aims and complained that these decisions "were the product of a violent nature following its momentary impulses, which recognized no limits to possibility and which made its wish-dreams the father of its acts." Once, Halder said, when a report was read to the *Führer* of Stalin's reserve strength, "Hitler flew at the man who was reading with clenched fists and foam in the corners of his mouth and forbade him to read any more of such idiotic twaddle."

General Friedrich Paulus, commander of the Sixth Army, was assigned the conquest of Stalingrad. The summer offensive started in July, and Paulus advanced rapidly upon the Volga stronghold. In September Stalin again called upon Zhukov, his ace, and gave him command of the whole Stalingrad front. The city itself was confided to General Vasili Chuikov, commander of the Sixty-second Army, who had once advised Chiang Kai-shek and who was later to accept Berlin's surrender.

On September 13, a Nazi division broke deep into Stalingrad and, progressing through the bomb-shattered city block by block, room by room, almost reached Chuikov's command post. But Chuikov mined each building on the invader's path and set up zones of enfilading sniper nests. An unhappy Nazi lieutenant wrote: "The street is no longer measured by metres but by corpses. . . . Stalingrad is no longer a town. By day it is an enormous cloud of burning, blinding smoke; it is a vast furnace lit by the reflection of the flames. And when night arrives, one of those scorching, howling, bleeding nights, the dogs plunge into the Volga and swim desperately to gain the other bank. The nights of Stalingrad are a terror for them. Animals flee this hell; the hardest stones cannot bear it for long; only men endure."

While Chuikov held on, Zhukov brought up massive reinforcements and, on November 19, launched still another counterattack. He hurled six armies into an encircling movement so successful and so shattering that within four days, the enormous Paulus army was trapped. Hitler's generals urged him to order a break-out while there was still a chance. The *Führer* refused. Instead he told Paulus to fight on and promoted him to field marshal, thus adding savor to Paulus's eventual capture by the Russians. The denouement was dreadful and fantastic.

Later, when de Gaulle visited the devastated battlefield on his way to Moscow, he said quietly: "All the same, a formidable people, a very great people. I don't speak of the Russians, I speak of the Germans . . . to have pushed this far." On January 31, 1943, Paulus surrendered with ninety-one thousand emaciated, ragged survivors, all that were left of the three hundred thousand men of his Sixth Army who had first marched confidently into Stalingrad. Only about five thousand ever returned to Germany. The disaster, coming so unbelievably upon the heels of El Alamein, rocked the German people, and an overriding caution set in among the Nazi generals. Field Marshal von Manstein urged widespread withdrawal in the hope of enticing the Russians into traps. But Hitler, fearing the political consequences in an eastern Europe now crawling with guerrillas, spurned such strategy. He summoned his *Wehrmacht* to one final battle of annihilation. Choosing the Kursk salient, north of Kharkov, he built up a new force of five hundred thousand men, including seventeen Panzer divisions equipped with the new Tiger tank. On July 4, 1943, this last initiative, what was to be the greatest of all tank battles, began.

The guileful Zhukov, forewarned by Soviet intelligence and familiarity with German strategy, had begun preparing for a Kursk battle as early as April. He laid thick mine fields along stretches suitable to Nazi tank advances and built up an immense artillery force of nearly twenty thousand guns and a thousand Katyusha rockets. A Czech deserter tipped off the Russians on the exact date of the German assault, and "Operation Citadel" was shattered by crunching barrages. Then, deliberately choosing his time, Zhukov attacked. He launched the Red Army's first massive summer offensive and put an end, once and for all, to the shibboleth that the Russian soldier was good only when he was on the defensive.

The entire German front began to crumble. Orel, Kharkov, Smolensk, and Kiev were retaken before autumn ended. The first freeze caught the Nazis on the Ukrainian steppe, where infantry units, unable to dig trenches, made lean-tos of corpses roofed with canvas tenting to shelter themselves against the wind. A third Russian winter settled in, grim and hopeless. Hitler, in his East Prussian "Wolf's Lair," cut himself off from his generals and henceforth heeded only the counsel of party fanatics, his physician, and his astrologer. All illusions gone, the *Wehrmacht* began its creaking, tortured withdrawal.

The Russian Army that now headed toward the *Führer's* Fortress Europe was a vastly different army from that which had fallen apart in 1941. It was a strange mixture: an army of quantity, slogging along with antiquated guns behind horse-drawn transport; and an army of quality, spearheaded by magnificent tanks. Huge amounts of matériel had been brought around the Arctic capes by British convoys and out of Iran by the American Persian Gulf Service Command. But useful as these tremendous numbers of trucks, planes, tanks, munitions, and shipments of food proved to be, they were nevertheless still fractional in importance. The U.S.S.R. itself had developed a huge ordnance industry, both around Moscow and in the Siberian reaches, where evacuated machinery was reassembled. From 1942 to 1944, Soviet factories manufactured three hundred and sixty thousand artillery pieces alone. The heavy Stalin-JS tank replaced the old KV-2 and was supplemented by self-propelled guns and howitzers. Four aeronautic designers, Sergei Ilyushin, Alexander Yakovlev, Vladimir Petlyakov, and Semyon Lavochkin, were responsible for the production of improved series of fighters and bombers.

Although in the great encirclement of 1941 and 1942 the Red Army had lost 3,500,000 men in prisoners alone, by the time of the Kursk counteroffensive, Stalin had built a fresh force of 409 divisions.

To direct this ponderous array Stalin created hundreds of generals and, ultimately, twenty-nine marshals. Promising officers like Konstantin Rokossovski, who had been purged in 1937 and was in a concentration camp when the invasion came, were forgiven trumped-up offenses and awarded high commands. Even the professionally minded Germans conceded the prowess of the Red Army soldier and the talent of his top commanders. They gave high marks to Konev, who first bloodied their noses at Yelnya, but they reserved their fullest admiration for the short, barrel-chested Zhukov, who came to symbolize Russian military power, which had been held in contempt when World War II began and would be contesting global paramountcy when it ended.

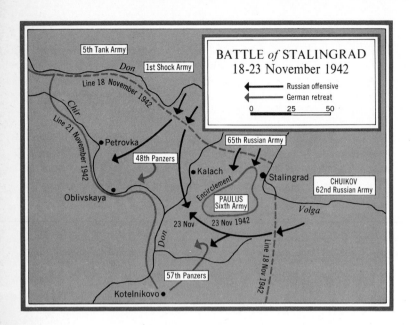

Battle of Stalingrad map:

BATTLE of STALINGRAD
18-23 November 1942

Russian offensive
German retreat

0   25   50

5th Tank Army
1st Shock Army
Don
Line 18 November 1942
Chir
Line 21 November 1942
Petrovka
48th Panzers
Oblivskaya
Don
Kalach
Encirclement
23 Nov
23 Nov 1942
57th Panzers
Kotelnikovo
65th Russian Army
Stalingrad
CHUIKOV 62nd Russian Army
PAULUS Sixth Army
Volga
Line 18 Nov 1942

The Operation Called Barbarossa

The basic strategy of Hitler's Operation Barbarossa for the conquest of Russia was simple: destroy the bulk of the Soviet Army in western Russia by first cutting it up with deep thrusts by far-ranging panzer forces, then following with infantry and artillery to force surrender of the isolated pockets of Russians. To accomplish this, the Nazi high command prepared the most devastating assault ever made by an army. Some three million men and all the machines and matériel of blitzkrieg were massed along a huge front stretching across Poland and East Prussia. To the south were allied Rumanian and Hungarian forces, stiffened by a German army, and far to the north, the Finns were joining the assault to recover the land Russia had taken in the Winter War of 1939–40.

German Army Group North, commanded by Field Marshal Wilhelm von Leeb, drove in the direction of Leningrad, Army Group Center, under Field Marshal Fedor von Bock, toward Moscow, and Field Marshal Gerd von Rundstedt and his Army Group South toward the Ukraine and the Caucasus. The map shows how near the *Wehrmacht* came to realizing these objectives before winter saved the shattered Soviet forces and almost brought catastrophe to the Germans. By the next summer, 1942, Nazi strength, though still tremendous, had been enough eroded to limit the German offensive to the south, as shown on the map, instead of having it extend along the vast front of the previous year. Even so, the offensive had Soviet forces reeling until Hitler uselessly sacrificed an entire army at Stalingrad (map above). From that point on, the fortunes of the *Wehrmacht* were always to tend downward.

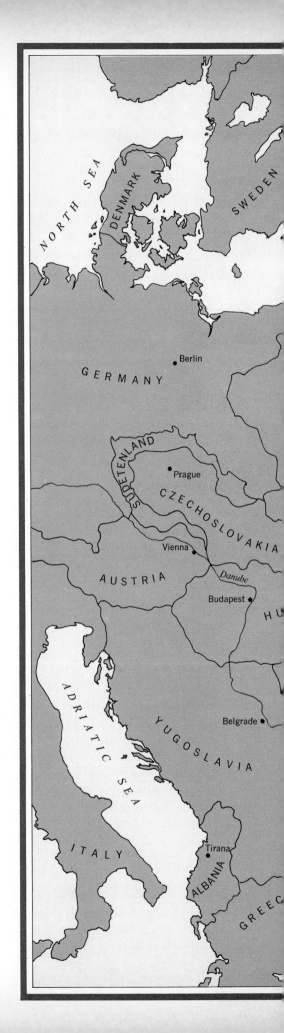

Map showing: NORTH SEA, SWEDEN, DENMARK, GERMANY (Berlin), SUDETENLAND, CZECHOSLOVAKIA (Prague), AUSTRIA (Vienna), Danube, Budapest, HU[NGARY], YUGOSLAVIA (Belgrade), ADRIATIC SEA, ITALY, ALBANIA (Tirana), GREECE

GERMAN OFFENSIVE
22 June 1941 – Nov., 1942

← German advance
- - - - Northern Line 5 Dec 1941

0   100   200

Stockholm

FINLAND
Helsinki

LAKE ONEGA

LAKE LADOGA

Tallinn
ESTONIA

Leningrad   Tikhvin

Line 9 July 1941

Riga
LATVIA

LITHUANIA

Volga

Line December 1941

Kalinin

Gorki

Moscow

EAST PRUSSIA

Vilna

Grodno

Minsk

Smolensk

Dnieper

Bialystok

Warsaw

Line 22 June 1941

Brest-Litovsk   Pinsk

Line November 1942

Orel

Pripet

Gomel

POLAND

Kursk

Saratov

Lvov

Kiev

Kharkov

Dnieper

Uman

Bug

Line November 1942

Don

Donets

Stalingrad

Leninsk

ANTONESCU
Rumanian Army

Dniester

Odessa

Melitopol

Rostov

Volga

RUMANIA

Bucharest

Danube

SEA OF AZOV

Sevastopol

Novorossisk

Ordzhonikidze

BULGARIA

BLACK   SEA

Istanbul

TURKEY

Hitler Turns on Russia

The Nazi-Soviet Pact had served both parties well. Hitler had fought his wars in Poland and the west without fear of Russian intervention, and he and Stalin had been able to swallow all or parts of eight East European nations with only a moderate amount of mutual double-crossing. But for Hitler, the pact's usefulness had ended. The invasion of England was bogged down, while Russia, with its *Lebensraum*, remained an unalterable Nazi objective, as Hitler had made clear in *Mein Kampf*. Oddly, Stalin, usually the most suspicious of men, refused to see this or heed warnings. In July of 1940, Hitler had his generals begin planning a Russian invasion, code-named Barbarossa, for the next spring. The *Führer* grew increasingly excited as the time neared. "When Barbarossa commences, the world will hold its breath and make no comment," he told his staff. Barbarossa began at 3:15 A.M. on June 22, 1941, a shattering assault against the unprepared and unsuspecting Soviet Union.

Citizens of Moscow (above) listen to a public broadcast of news that German forces have invaded Russia. At right, the jubilant crew of a German antitank gun cheers after destroying a Soviet tank during the July, 1941, fighting.

Nazi soldiers anticipate a meal of Russian duck and chicken.

Ukrainians treat the first Germans as liberators.

A panzer unit passes through a village in the summer of 1941. Panzer forces were made up of supporting forces as well as tanks. At from

Ukrainians give food to a Nazi warrior.

A pause during the blitzkrieg—picture found on a dead Nazi.

right is a Mark II tank, behind it, a half-track cargo and personnel carrier, and on the left are trucks followed by motorcycle troops.

Oppression and Partisans

Many Russians greeted the Nazi invaders as friends come to free them from Stalinist oppression. Had the Germans fostered this initial good will, they might have won Russian support against the Communist regime; but in Nazi philosophy, with its fantasy of a master race, the Russians were *Untermenschen*—subhumans—fit only for slave labor. Hitler had ordered a completely ruthless campaign—and he was not disobeyed. Russian good will turned to hate. The people retaliated by wrecking troop trains, poisoning wells, murdering soldiers. At first these acts were scattered and spontaneous, but as Nazi repressive measures grew more savage, the resistance gradually took on organization and discipline. Very soon the partisans behind the lines were playing an important part in the war.

BIRNBACK

WIDE WORLD

Erich Koch (left) governed the Ukraine with a rough hand as Reich Commissar. A loud proponent of the master race theory, he proclaimed that the lowliest German worker was "a thousand times more valuable than the population here." Above is Stalin's son after he had been taken prisoner. The Germans tried unsuccessfully to use him for antiSoviet propaganda. The two young Russians at the right died at Minsk in October, 1941, after they had been accused of having shot at German soldiers.

260

NOVOSTI PRESS AGENCY

Villagers search for their own dead among civilians slain by the Nazis. In carrying out Hitler's deliberate policy of enslavement

Soviet Life FROM SOVFOTO

or annihilation, the Germans killed Russian noncombatants not only on the slightest of pretexts, but very often for no reason at all.

Defeat and Retreat

The first weeks of the Russian war were ideal for blitzkrieg. The Nazi legions were in top condition; the Russian land was dry and hard; the unprepared enemy was demoralized. The *Wehrmacht* rolled into Russia with its usual brutal arrogance, leaving a trail of burning villages, smashed farms, innocent dead, and all the other wreckage of war. The German forces appeared unstoppable. Field Marshal Wilhelm von Leeb, striking with his army group for Leningrad, had driven his panzer spearheads fifty miles the first day of the campaign and within three weeks was halfway to that city. On the southern front, Von Rundstedt made even more spectacular progress against the armies of the inept Marshal Semën Budënny; no one knows how many hundreds of thousands of brave men in Budënny's command died needlessly or were taken prisoner because of his bumbling. But even on the central front, where the Russian troops were most competently led, their losses were appalling as Marshal von Bock raced toward Moscow.

Here was panzer warfare in the grand style. Armored columns raced forward along parallel roads, then converged, trapping great masses of Russian troops, sometimes even entire armies. The war appeared so clearly won only three weeks after the opening attack that on July 14, Hitler issued a directive to prepare for reducing the size of the Army in the near future. But the Nazi generals, in all the flush of victory, began to feel the cold chill of doubt. Instead of the Russians' losing heart in defeat, their resistance was actually increasing. Moreover, if Nazy military intelligence evaluations at the beginning of the war of the size of the Red Army were correct, there should have been no Red Army left after the losses it had taken. And yet fresh Soviet divisions that Nazi intelligence had never heard of kept appearing in battle. An even bigger shock came with the appearance of the Russian T-34 tank, which no one had had a hint of, and which proved to be better than anything the Germans possessed.

For the Russians, the shining moment of that first summer was the stand they made on the Smolensk front before Moscow. They showed that Germans could be stopped; in doing so, they electrified all of Russia.

The pictures at right, taken by a German, find no glory in warfare. From top to bottom: the body of a Russian pilot burns in the wreckage of his plane; a home goes up in flames; peasants abandon their village after Nazis have put it to the torch. At left, the brief mud left by a summer shower was a laughing matter to this Nazi, but the joking would end after the fall rains came.

NOVOSTI PRESS AGENCY

Marshal Semën Budënny, seated, with moustache (right), visits an army field headquarters. He was replaced by Marshal Timoshenko during October. At left, Marshals Semën Timoshenko and Georgi Zhukov (at the right) appear together at prewar Red Army exercises. Zhukov, Army Chief of Staff, took command of various threatened fronts from time to time. Below, Marshal Kliment Voroshilov reviews his troops. He was removed from operational command in 1942, and from that time on held nothing but strictly ceremonial posts.

WIDE WORLD

A Matter of Leadership

Joseph Stalin had played too well the game of cutting off every head that appeared above the crowd. The military had been a breeding ground for mediocrity, for ever since the purge of 1937, few generals had been brave enough to show any initiative, and the virus of fear and inaction had spread through all levels of command. Of the three top commanders who met the German attack, only one, Marshal Timoshenko on the central front, possessed any real ability. In the south, the grossly incompetent Marshal Budënny could do little with his enormous army but let it be captured and killed. His only qualification was that Stalin found him politically reliable. Marshal Voroshilov in the north was another party faithful of meager military talents; he was replaced by the able Marshal Zhukov when the Germans reached Leningrad. Stalin quickly realized that politically dependable incompetents would not win the war, and steps were taken to encourage initiative. The old prestige and privileges of officers were restored, and much of the power was taken from commissars attached to military units.

Advance on Moscow

The Germans might well have taken Moscow in 1941 if Hitler had not decided to play the military genius. Ignoring his generals' advice, he transferred forces from the Moscow front for use against Leningrad and the Ukraine. By the time the Moscow offensive could be resumed, it was October, and a great deal of valuable fall weather had been lost. But even so, the Nazi offensive, named "Typhoon," took a terrible toll. In the first two weeks of October, two entire Soviet armies were encircled at Vyazma and Bryansk, with a loss of 650,000 prisoners, according to Nazi claims (Soviet figures are much lower). Panzers caught Orel so by surprise that trolleys were still running.

As the German columns swept nearer Moscow, Stalin decided on October 12 to move most government offices east to Kuibyshev on the Volga. Stalin was one of those who would remain in Moscow. The most important armament plants were also to be moved to safety east of the Ural Mountains. Panic broke out in the capital on October 16 with the issuing of a gloomy communiqué. There were rumors that the Germans were about to arrive, and even that their tanks had appeared in the suburbs. There was a rush to leave the city; officials dropped their duties and fled without permission. But many stayed, and factory workers, most of them women, went out after working a full shift to spend hours in the mud digging trenches for last-ditch stands against the enemy. Before October was over, the German drive had pretty well ground to a mud-mired halt. The danger was far from over, but Moscow had won a brief respite.

The pleasures of being a Nazi superman were wearing thin when the above picture was taken in Russia. The German Eastern armies by November 26, 1941, had total casualties of 743,000, not including sick—with the end nowhere in sight.

Moscow factory workers (top left) turn out after hours to dig antitank ditches. The people of the capital were required to build four defense lines: one well beyond the city limits, a second on the city border, and two on the inner and outer boulevard rings within Moscow. At bottom left is a tank assembly plant in the Urals, producing the T-34 tank that was superior to German armor and caught the Nazis completely by surprise when it first showed up against them on the battlefield in 1941.

High Tide
for the *Wehrmacht*

The offensive against Moscow had worn itself out by the first of November, stopped by exhaustion, Russian resistance, and mud. During the lull, Stalin spoke to the nation on November 7, the anniversary of the Bolshevik Revolution. He evoked the picture of Mother Russia, ancient land of heroes who had routed many barbarian invaders. It was a skillful move, for it put the war in patriotic terms rather than as a defense of communism. The Germans resumed their offensive on November 16. Marshal Zhukov had taken over the defense from Timoshenko, who then replaced Budënny in the Ukraine. Zhukov carried on a flexible defense, retreating to avoid encirclement, then striking back. The Nazi armor became active again as the ground froze, and at one point, German forces got within fifteen miles of Moscow, the nearest they reached in strength. But temperatures continued to drop, Nazi equipment was immobilized by bitter cold, and the danger to Moscow was past.

Antiaircraft fire silhouettes the Kremlin (above) during an air raid. At right, women and children take shelter in a Moscow subway station from an air attack. Below is Stalin delivering his "Holy Russia" speech of November 7; and at left are troops parading in Red Square on the occasion of the speech.

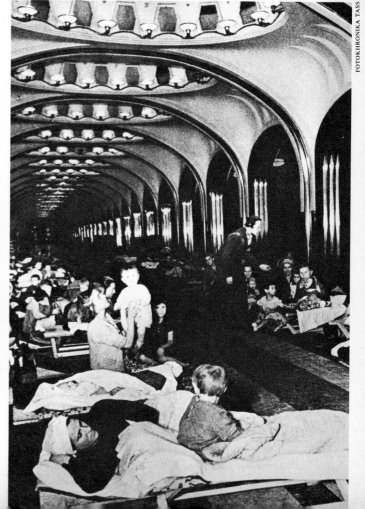

"Then the weather suddenly broke"

SOVFOTO

One of the German prisoners the Russians liked to call "Winter Fritz."

The comparison between Hitler and Napoleon was made often during the German drive on Moscow—in Russia, in the West, and in Germany. But there were important differences between the two campaigns. Napoleon marched to Moscow and then marched back again. Hitler was moving against the whole of Russia across one incredibly vast front, and when he was stopped, he stayed and fought on. But there was one part of both men's experience that turned out to be the same. Churchill put it this way. "There is a winter, you know, in Russia. For a good many months the temperature is apt to fall very low. There is snow, there is frost, and all that. Hitler forgot about this Russian winter. He must have been very loosely educated. We all heard about it at school; but he forgot it. I have never made such a bad mistake as that." The following are from some who lived through that winter of 1941–42 in front of Moscow.

Then the weather suddenly broke and almost overnight the full fury of the Russian winter was upon us. The thermometer suddenly dropped to thirty degrees of frost. This was accompanied by heavy falls of snow. Within a few days the countryside presented the traditional picture of a Russian winter. With steadily decreasing momentum and increasing difficulty the two Panzer groups continued to battle their way towards Moscow.

—General Günther Blumentritt

. . . General Winter did not belong to the Red army. If he did, he should have been shot for treason, because he opposed the Russians just as much as he did the Germans. He was fighting for no one but himself.

We heard in Moscow, during that first winter of the war, that a vague idea had gone abroad that winter was all on the Russians' side; that all the Germans' woes were due entirely to the weather, and not at all to the Red army. It would have been very hard to sell that idea to the men who fought the Germans to a standstill before Moscow, and then hunched their way through the snow and bitter cold to drive back the enemy. They, too, suffered and died at the hands of General Winter.

But two factors did favor the Russians in that first winter campaign. The weather was less severe on the defender than on the attacker, and since the Germans were on the offensive at the crucial point of the campaign, since the great issue was whether they would take or fail to take Moscow, they were at a disadvantage. Then the Russians were fully prepared for winter with their felt boots, padded jackets, fur hats, and white capes, their skis, sleds, and sleighs, while the Germans were completely unprepared—a ghastly, almost inconceivable error on the part of so supposedly brilliant a high command.

—Henry C. Cassidy,
An American Journalist

On 13 November we awoke and shivered. An icy blast from the northeast knifed across the snowy countryside. The sky was cloudless and dark blue, but the sun seemed to have lost its strength and instead of becoming warmer towards noon as on previous days, the thermometer kept falling and by sundown had reached minus twelve degrees Centigrade.

The soldiers, who up to now had not regarded the light frosts too seriously, began to take notice. One man who had been walking outside for only a short distance without his woollen *Kopfschutzer* or 'head-saver' came into the sick bay. Both ears were white and frozen stiff.

It was our first case of frost-bite.

We gently massaged the man's ears, taking care not to break the skin, and they thawed out. We powdered them and covered them with cotton-wool and made a suitable head-dressing. Perhaps we had managed to save the whole of the ears; we should have to wait and see.

This minor case of frost-bite was a serious warning. The icy winds from Siberia—the breath of death—were blowing across the steppes; winds from where all life froze, from the Arctic ice-cap itself. Things would be serious if we could not house ourselves in prepared positions and buildings, and I stopped to think of the armies marching on Moscow across open country at this very moment. All that those men had received so far were their woollen *Kopfschutzers*; the winter clothing had still not arrived. What was happening to the men's feet, for the ordinary army boot retained very little warmth?

Then, too, the thermometer showed only twelve degrees below zero. Temperatures would drop to minus twenty-four degrees—minus thirty-six degrees—minus forty-eight degrees—perhaps even lower. It was beyond comprehension—a temperature four times colder than a deep freezer. To attempt any movement without warm clothing in those conditions would be sheer suicide. Surely the older generals had been right when, after the battle of Vyasma and Bryansk, they had counselled: 'Dig in for the winter.' Some of them were men with experience of Russia during the 1914–1918 War. At the most they had said, continue the war through the winter only with a few thoroughly-equipped and well-provisioned divisions. Make the big push in the spring.

If only the battle for Moscow had

started fourteen days earlier, the city would now have been in our hands. Or even if the rains had held off for fourteen days. If—if—if. If Hitler had started 'Barbarossa' six weeks earlier as originally planned; if he had left Mussolini on his own in the Balkans and had attacked Russia in May; if we had continued our sweeping advance instead of stopping at the Schutsche Lake; if Hitler had sent us winter clothing. Yes, if, if, if—but now it was too late.

Those Arctic blasts that had taken us by surprise in our protected positions had scythed through our attacking troops. In a couple of days there were one hundred thousand casualties from frost-bite alone; one hundred thousand first-class, experienced soldiers fell out because the cold had surprised them.

A couple of days later our winter clothing arrived. There was just enough for each company to be issued with four heavy fur-lined greatcoats and four pairs of felt-lined boots. Four sets of winter clothing for each company! Sixteen greatcoats and sixteen pairs of winter boots to be shared among a battalion of eight hundred men! And the meagre issue coincided with a sudden drop in the temperature to minus twenty-two degrees.

Reports reached us that the issue of winter clothing to the troops actually advancing on Moscow had been on no more generous scale. More and more reports were being sent to Corps and Army Headquarters recommending that the attack on Moscow by a summer-clad army be abandoned and that winter positions be prepared. Some of these reports were forwarded by Central Army Group to the Führer's Headquarters, but no reply or acknowledgment ever came. The order persisted: 'Attack!' And our soldiers attacked. . . .

In this unearthly cold, in which the breath froze and icicles hung from nostrils and eyelashes all day long, where thinking became an effort, the German soldiers fought—no longer for an ideal or an ideology, no longer for the Fatherland. They fought blindly without asking questions, without wanting to know what lay ahead of them. Habit and discipline kept them going; that and the flicker of an instinct to stay alive. And when the soldier's mind had become numb, when his strength, his discipline and his will had been used up, he sank into the snow. If he was noticed, he was kicked and slapped into a vague awareness that his business in the world was not finished and he staggered to his feet and groped on. But if he lay where he had collapsed until it was too late, as if forgotten he was left lying at the side of the road and the wind blew over him and everything was levelled indistinguishably. . . .

—Heinrich Haape,
A German Medical Officer

West of Moscow and in the Tula area, miles and miles of roads were littered with abandoned guns, lorries and tanks, deeply embedded in the snow. The comic "Winter Fritz", wrapped up in women's shawls and feather boas stolen from the local population, and with icicles hanging from his red nose, made his first appearance in Russian folklore.

—Alexander Werth

Moscow Counteroffensive

Temperatures far below zero halted Nazi attacks almost completely. Oil congealed in motors, automatic weapons froze, artillery refused to function. Nazi soldiers, still clad only in summer uniforms, were maimed and frequently frozen to death by the intense cold. As the German offensive came to a halt (in one place a Nazi unit had come near enough to see the spires of the Kremlin), Zhukov struck back on December 6, 1941, on a 200-mile front before Moscow, with 100 new divisions the German high command did not even know existed. The Nazi front crumbled, but Hitler adamantly refused to permit the slightest retreat. Men died miserably and hopelessly. Field commanders forced to pull back were relieved and publicly disgraced. And on December 19, Hitler took over personal control of the Army by making himself the Commander in Chief.

ARTHUR GRIMM, ULLSTEIN-BIRNBACK

ABOVE: IMPERIAL WAR MUSEUM, LONDON; BELOW: *Soviet Life*, FROM SOVFOTO

The dark uniforms of Nazi soldiers on the Moscow winter front (above) contrast with those of the Russians crawling through the snow (top right) and attacking past a burned-out building (right). The white Russian uniforms not only camouflaged the wearer in the snow but were warmly quilted. The German soldiers tried to stay warm by stuffing denim overalls with paper.

274

Winter of No Decision

Hitler's commanders were bitter about his fanatical demand that they die rather than retreat; withdrawal to better positions, they said, could have saved tens of thousands of men. But some argued later that the dictator's adamant stand had saved the army, because a retreat, once begun, would have become a rout like the one that wrecked Napoleon's army. In any event, the German forces, although badly mauled, did not collapse; though the morale of the German soldier was often low, he was not yet beaten. The extreme cold hampered the Soviet armies, too; attempts to encircle large German forces failed. But by the time a late March, 1942, thaw with its mud ended the Russian offensive, total Nazi casualties on the Eastern Front had passed well over a million.

Winter war had many seemingly tranquil moments; the postcard-like scene above was actually photographed Christmas Day. However, the Russian sled drivers are being forced to work for the Nazis, and they are hauling German Army supplies. At right is a German winter "burial." With the earth frozen rock-hard, the Nazis simply laid out their blanket-wrapped dead under wood crosses until spring.

BOTH: DR. ALFRED OTT

The Red Army's Siberian troops—hard fighters, well trained, and inured to cold—turned the tide of the battle for Moscow. Stalin

delayed in bringing them west for fear Japan might then attack Siberia. Those pictured here were among the few the Nazis took alive.

ZEITGESCHICHTLICHES BILDARCHIV

Field Marshal Wilhelm von Leeb (above) commanded on the Leningrad front until sacked by Hitler in January, 1942. At right, dead sprawl on Leningrad's Nevsky Prospect after a trolley has been hit by a Nazi shell.

To Destroy a City

Leningrad, Russia's second city, was a main German objective. Field Marshal von Leeb drove his northern Army Group with such speed that on August 30, 1941, he cut the city's last rail connection with the rest of Russia, and a few days later his troops were in the suburbs and shelling the city. But Nazi expectations of taking Leningrad by storm faded as Marshal Zhukov took over the defense and turned the city into a maze of strongpoints. As the invaders settled down to a siege, Hitler told his commanders they were not to accept the surrender of the city. The city was to be razed to the ground by shelling and bombing, his monstrous directive said, and its people were to perish with it. Even though Hitler's plans would not be accomplished, a terrible ordeal was ahead for Leningrad.

Soviet Life, FROM SOVFOTO

Leningrad—the Great Siege

UPI

Even the old cruiser Aurora, *tied up in a Leningrad canal and preserved because of her part in the 1917 revolution, played a role in the defense of the city. Her guns were moved onto the city's fortifications and did very good work there.*

By early September, Leningrad's last land link with the rest of Russia had been cut. The city's plight was desperate: it had food to feed its three million people for little more than a month. A trickle of foodstuffs was flown in, but the defenders put their hopes on circumventing the German blockade by crossing broad Lake Ladoga to a point on the railroad east of where the Nazis had cut it. But organizing the route took time, and for a multitude there was not enough time. They dropped of hunger and died even as they walked along the streets or worked at their factory jobs. They ate their dogs and cats; they swallowed hair oil and vaseline; they made soup of dried glue from furniture joints and wallpaper. The "Ladoga Lifeline" across the frozen lake slowly began to catch up with food needs by January, 1942, but the effects of the famine were felt for months afterward. It is believed, official figures notwithstanding, that close to a million may have died as a result of the siege. In January, 1943, the Russians at last opened a railroad link to the rest of the country, but not until January, 1944, were the Nazis routed and the siege and shelling of the city finally ended.

SOVFOTO

The face of hunger (left) is a grim one. The worst sufferers from malnutrition, like this man, were given an extra bread ration as soon as supplies permitted. At upper right, women take water flowing from a broken main. Leningrad had no electricity, almost no heat, and no safe water supply because mains had burst from freezing. To prevent disease, some one-and-a-half-million persons were given antityphoid shots. At right, trucks cross frozen Lake Ladoga; this route, used by boats in summer and by vehicles in the winter, was Leningrad's only supply route. It was under frequent German attack, and losses were heavy: one truck in every four.

With the coming of spring, Leningraders all joined in cleaning up the accumulated filth of the winter in order to prevent an epidemic

macabre part of the task was the discovery of the bodies of thousands of starvation victims, which had been hidden by the deep snow.

SOVFOTO

German Summer Offensive, 1942

The *Wehrmacht* had lost some of the cream of its fighting men—one and a third million casualties in twelve months—and could not again mount an offensive like its 1941 all-fronts invasion of Russia. Even so, Hitler's plans for his 1942 summer offensive were ambitious enough: hold fast on the central front, capture Leningrad in the north, and make the main assault in the south, where Stalingrad would be captured or bombed into ruins, after which the German forces would move on to seize the Caucasus, with its rich oil fields. To flesh out its depleted forces, the Nazi high command went to its allies and associates and obtained fifty-two divisions: Hungarian, Rumanian, Italian, Slovakian, and even one Spanish. The German offensive opened in early June, and at first it looked like the old story of blitzkrieg advances through bewildered Russian defenders. But Hitler, with his vaulting ambition, now decided to capture both Stalingrad *and* the Caucasus at the same time, although his commanders warned him that the *Wehrmacht* did not have the strength for two such ambitious projects. Hitler was about to blunder the German Army into a catastrophe.

Even though German successes in the first months of the summer offensive caused something close to despair among the Russians, there was not the chaos of 1941 on the fighting front. Improved organization, leadership, and weapons all helped to make the Soviet Army a better fighting machine. Above are T-34 tanks attacking; this medium tank was superior to anything the Nazis had. At right, a Russian crew fires a 152-mm. howitzer. Stalin called artillery "the queen of battle," and the Russians massed large numbers of guns on a battlefront.

To the Gates of Stalingrad

As the 1942 German offensive swept on toward its objectives, the Russians could only fight desperate delaying battles. On August 21, Nazis troops set their flag on Mount Elbrus, highest peak of the Caucasus Mountains, while two days later, troops of General Paulus's Sixth Army to the north reached the Volga not far above Stalingrad. Hitler's unenthusiastic Rumanian, Hungarian (below), and Italian allies gave flank protection during the advance toward Stalingrad. But Hitler, playing the military expert again, bungled badly. When Stalingrad lay open for the taking in late July, he diverted to the south the panzer force that could have seized it. When he called the same force back two weeks later, the gates had closed. There would be a fight for Stalingrad.

DR. ALFRED OTT

IMPERIAL WAR MUSEUM, LONDON

Stalingrad—
First Phase

The German Sixth Army advanced rapidly toward Stalingrad during July and August, 1942, while Soviet morale sank and the Russian front threatened to collapse. Stalingrad was heavily hit by air attack; one raid of 600 planes started vast fires and killed 40,000 civilians. Hitler ordered that the city be taken by August 25; but although Nazi forces reached the Volga just above the city two days before that date, Russian resistance had been stiffening, and Stalingrad did not fall. But in spite of instances of supreme heroism—soldiers, for instance, sometimes bound grenades to their bodies and threw themselves under Nazi tanks—German superiority in weapons gradually told, and the Russian 62nd Army was pushed back into the city, surrounded on all sides but the Volga waterfront. (Stalingrad, a great industrial city, stretched for thirty miles along the Volga.) By mid-September the fighting had become a block-by-block, house-by-house affair (the Nazi infantrymen at left are listening to a briefing during the street fighting), and by the end of the month the Germans were in control of all the southern and most of the central parts of the city and were hammering at the industrial section in the north. Stalingrad was little more than rubble.

Stalingrad—Death in the Rubble

The fighting within Stalingrad was a fantastic kind of warfare, fought in cellars, in sewers, in blasted factories, behind the walls of blasted buildings. Every bit of the city was contested building by building, floor by floor, room by room, often in hand-to-hand fighting. Quarter was seldom asked or given, and in this savage battle it was common for surrounded units to fight on until annihilated. In spite of a heroic defense, the Russians continued slowly to lose ground before the superior German weight of weapons, especially aircraft. On October 14, a Nazi assault was launched against the tractor works in the northern part of the city; it was an offensive of unbelievable ferocity, but though the defenders were pushed back, they managed to hold. Soviet reinforcements and supplies had to come across the mile-wide Volga, under German bombing and shelling, and for a time the bridgehead became so small that only a single crossing remained, and it was under machine-gun fire. Russian reinforcements were fed into the inferno as they became available, sometimes a division, sometimes a couple of dozen men—many of whom were killed before reaching the front. Not until the Red Army opened its great offensive on the entire Stalingrad front in late November was the imminent danger to the city removed, and not until January did the last street fighting end.

NOVOSTI PRESS AGENCY

After the Soviet 62nd Army had retreated into Stalingrad, General (later Marshal) Vasili Chuikov took over the command from his demoralized predecessor and conducted the heroic defense of the city. Chuikov would later become a conqueror of Berlin, during the closing days of the war.

The fighting in Stalingrad presented few panoramic scenes of large bodies of men in action; it was made up of many savage struggles waged by men almost hidden in the smouldering ruins of wrecked buildings. At the left are Soviet troops during some typical moments in the fighting for the city. At top, a squad of soldiers attacks. In center, troops take cover in house-to-house fighting. At bottom, soldiers edge forward through the rubble of demolished buildings. At the right, a soldier drags off the hind quarters of a horse killed during the fighting. The hungry men of both sides quickly disposed of all such fresh meat.

ARCHIVES DOCUMENTATION FRANÇAISE

293

Russian cavalry, sweeping over the steppes, had an important part in the encirclement of the Nazi Sixth Army at Stalingrad. The Red Army had a number of divisions of horse cavalry; the Wehrmacht had none. Though mounted troops were an anachronism in a blitzkrieg age and often suffered ghastly casualties, they could travel over bad terrain and were expert at both concealment and dispersal. Mounted on hardy Siberian ponies that could withstand temperatures far below zero, the cavalry was at its best when cold weather had all but immobilized Nazi panzers.

Stalingrad—Agony of an Army

On the morning of November 19, 1942, a tremendous Soviet offensive surprised and overwhelmed the Rumanian Third Army, which held the Axis flank northwest of Stalingrad. The next day, south of the city, another massive assault sent German and Rumanian armies on that flank reeling back. The two offensives, more than a hundred miles apart, drove ahead so irresistibly that they joined up west of Stalingrad in four days (map, page 254). General Paulus's Sixth Army was cut off and isolated in Stalingrad. The Nazi command urged Hitler to let Paulus break out while the Russian cordon was still relatively weak, but the *Führer* refused. "I won't go back from the Volga," he shouted. He did create a special army corps to rescue the Sixth Army and put the exceptionally gifted Field Marshal von Manstein in command, but he refused to let Paulus fight his way to a junction with Manstein. The latter battled ahead through December blizzards for a week but was stopped thirty miles from Stalingrad. Then began the real agony of the Sixth Army. The bitter Russian winter set in with all its miseries for men without winter clothing. Medical supplies gave out, food ran short. As the Germans were forced into an ever-constricting area, their airstrip went, and it became impossible to send out wounded, who thereafter lay unattended. And all the while, Hitler sent messages exhorting the doomed men to fight on to their death. Meanwhile, fighting went on as deadly as ever between Russians and Germans among the ruins until January 31. Then, his forces exhausted and almost out of food and ammunition, Paulus surrendered his battered, sick survivors.

SOVFOTO

Stalingrad was completely destroyed in the months of fighting (left). Even the strongest buildings had been battered and gutted by fire, while not one dwelling remained, only debris with a few walls and chimneys still standing here and there. At the right is Field Marshal Friedrich Paulus shortly after his surrender. Hitler made him a field marshal the day before he capitulated, then ranted because Paulus and other generals at Stalingrad had not fought to the end and then shot themselves with their last bullets.

"So this is what the end looks like"

The last Nazi plane to fly out of Sta-lingrad in January, 1943, carried seven bags of soldiers' letters. None was ever delivered; the mail was seized by the Army and the letters read and classified to determine "troop mo-rale." The high command had looked for approval by the men doing the fighting; but well over half had a "negative attitude" toward the leader-ship, a third were indifferent, and only 2 per cent approved. A planned report was canceled, and the letters went into Army archives (with names of senders and addresses excised), where they were found in 1954.

. . . My life has changed in nothing; it is now as it was ten years ago, blessed by the stars, avoided by men. I had no friends, and you know why they wanted to have nothing to do with me. I was happy when I could sit at the telescope and look at the sky and the world of stars, happy as a child that is allowed to play with the stars.

You were my best friend, Monica. Yes, you read correctly, you were. The time is too serious for jokes. This letter will take two weeks to reach you. By then you will already have read in the papers what has taken place here. Don't think too much about it, for in reality every-thing will have ended differently: let other people worry about setting the record straight. What are they to you or me? I always thought in light-years, but I felt in seconds. Here, too, I have much to do with the weather. There are four of us and, if things were to continue the way they are now, we would be content. What we do is very simple. Our job is to measure temperatures and humidity, to report on cloud ceilings and visibility. If some bureaucrat read what I write here, he would have a fit . . . violation of military security. Monica, what is our life compared to the many million years of the starry sky! On this beautiful night, Andromeda and Pegasus are right above my head. I have looked at them for a long time; I shall be very close to them soon. My peace and contentment I owe to the stars, of which you are the most beautiful to me. The stars are eternal, but the life of man is like a speck of dust in the Universe.

Around me everything is collaps-ing, a whole army is dying, day and night are on fire, and four men busy themselves with daily reports on temperature and cloud ceilings. I don't know much about war. No human being has died by my hand. I haven't even fired live ammunition from my pistol. But I know this much: the other side would never show such a lack of understanding for its men. I should have liked to count stars for another few decades, but nothing will ever come of it now, I suppose.

. . . I might have been killed three times by now, but it would always have been suddenly, without my be-ing prepared. Now things are differ-ent; since this morning I know how things stand; and since I feel freer this way, I want you also to be free from apprehension and uncertainty.

I was shocked when I saw the map. We are entirely alone, without help from outside. Hitler has left us in the lurch. If the airfield is still in our possession, this letter may still get out. Our position is to the north of the city. The men of my battery have some inkling of it, too, but they don't know it as clearly as I do. So this is what the end looks like. Hannes and I will not surrender; yesterday, after our infantry had retaken a position, I saw four men who had been taken prisoner by the Russians. No, we shall not go into captivity. When Stalingrad has fallen, you'll hear and read it. And then you'll know that I shall not come back.

. . . You are the wife of a German officer; so you will take what I have to tell you, upright and unflinching, as upright as you stood on the station platform the day I left for the East. I am no letter-writer and my letters have never been longer than a page. Today there would be a great deal to say, but I will save it for later, i.e., six weeks if all goes well and a hundred years if it doesn't. You will have to reckon with the latter possibility. If all goes well, we shall be able to talk about it for a long time, so why should I attempt to write much now, since it comes hard to me. If things turn out badly, words won't do much good anyhow.

You know how I feel about you, Augusta. We have never talked much about our feelings. I love you very much and you love me, so you shall know the truth. It is in this letter. The truth is the knowledge that this is the grimmest of struggles in a hopeless situation. Misery, hunger, cold, renunciation, doubt, despair and horrible death. I will say no more about it. I did not talk about it during my leave either, and there's nothing more about it in my letters. When we were together (and I mean through our letters as well), we were man and wife, and the war, however necessary, was an ugly accompaniment to our lives. But the truth is also the knowledge that what I wrote above is no complaint or lament but a statement of objective fact.

I cannot deny my share of personal guilt in all this. But it is in a ratio of 1 to 70 millions. The ratio is small; still, it is there. I wouldn't think of evading my responsibility; I tell myself that, by giving my life,

I have paid my debt. One cannot argue about questions of honor.

Augusta, in the hour in which you must be strong, you will feel this also. Don't be bitter and do not suffer too much from my absence. I am not cowardly, only sad that I cannot give greater proof of my courage than to die for this useless, not to say criminal, cause. You know the family motto of the von H——'s: "Guilt recognized is guilt expiated."

Don't forget me too quickly.

. . . The Führer made a firm promise to bail us out of here; they read it to us and we believed in it firmly. Even now I still believe it, because I have to believe in something. If it is not true, what else could I believe in? I would no longer need spring, summer, or anything that gives pleasure. So leave me my faith, dear Greta; all my life, at least eight years of it, I believed in the Führer and his word. It is terrible how they doubt here, and shameful to listen to what they say without being able to reply, because they have the facts on their side. . . .

. . . In January you will be twenty-eight. That is still very young for such a good-looking woman, and I am glad that I could pay you this compliment again and again. You will miss me very much, but even so, don't withdraw from other people. Let a few months pass, but no more. Gertrud and Claus need a father. Don't forget that you must live for the children, and don't make too much fuss about their father. Children forget quickly, especially at that age. Take a good look at the man of your choice, take note of his eyes and the pressure of his handshake, as was the case with us, and you won't go wrong. But above all, raise the children to be upright human beings who can

carry their heads high and look everybody straight in the eye. I am writing these lines with a heavy heart. You wouldn't believe me if I said that it was easy, but don't be worried, I am not afraid of what is coming. Keep telling yourself and the children also when they have grown older, that their father never was a coward, and that they must never be cowards either.

. . . Today I talked to Hermann. He is south of the front, a few hundred yards from me. Not much is left of his regiment. But the son of baker B—— is still with him. Hermann still had the letter in which you told us of Father's and Mother's death. I talked to him once more, for I am the elder brother, and I tried to console him, though I too am at the end of my rope. It is good that Father and Mother will not know that Hermann and I will never come home again. It is terribly hard that you will have to carry the burden of four dead people through your future life.

I wanted to be a theologian, Father wanted to have a house, and Hermann wanted to build fountains. Nothing worked out that way. You know yourself what the outlook is at home, and we know only too well what it is here. No, those things we planned certainly did not turn out the way we imagined. Our parents are buried under the ruins of their house, and we, though it may sound harsh, are buried with a few hundred or so men in a ravine in the southern part of the pocket. Soon these ravines will be full of snow.

The *Wehrmacht* in Retreat

The *Wehrmacht* would not recover from the double disaster of El Alamein in Africa and Stalingrad on the Volga. Although there were many battles left in it, the turning point of the war had been reached. Even before the Stalingrad catastrophe, there had been over one and a half million German casualties on the Eastern Front. Now, added to that, Paulus's army of 300,000 had been squandered at Stalingrad; hundreds of thousands more had been lost in the winter fighting and in Africa. Such losses could no longer be made up.

But Hitler still hoped for a dramatic victory in the summer of 1943. West of the town of Kursk, between Orel and Belgorod, the front projected westward in a large bulge, or salient. If Nazi forces struck the base of this Kursk salient at both sides, pinching it off and trapping large numbers of Russians, the whole complexion of the war would be changed—or so Hitler thought. He brushed aside predictions that the Russians would probably be prepared, since the salient was the most logical place for an offensive. And the Russians were completely prepared. Marshal Zhukov, in command, had heavily mined the salient front. Men and tanks were massed for the defense and great numbers of cannon and rocket launchers put into position. The German offensive, which began July 5, never really got going. The panzers, equipped with new Tiger and Panther tanks, on which the Germans had placed high hopes, were blown apart. After a week of fruitless fighting, Hitler himself called off the offensive. Then the Russians counterattacked, taking Orel and Belgorod and continuing to push forward. Hitler refused to permit his generals to retreat to the east to establish a shorter and straighter line. His hope was to set up a "winter line," but morale sagged at thoughts of a third winter. As 1943 ended, the *Wehrmacht* outlook was bleak.

"Fighting Near Mozdok in 1943" by Russian artist F. Usipenko depicts a moment of battle in the vicinity of Mozdok in the Caucasus. Its accuracy is doubtful; for one thing, the artist has equipped a T-34 tank with an 85-mm. gun, which it did not use until 1944. At lower left, "Rest After Battle" by U. M. Neprintsev shows a popular wartime fictional character, Vasili Tyorkin, telling stories to soldiers. Tyorkin, the creation of a Soviet author, was the hero of a folk-type poem; he was a brave and shrewd soldier, cracking jokes as he worked his way out of difficult situations. The poem was long, and new verses kept appearing. It made heavy use of wartime slang.

This vignette of the Russian front, "German Soldiers Entrenched," the work of Franz Eichorst, was captured by the United States Army. The contrast between Nazi arrogance in the early days of the war and the self-pity evident in this picture of homesick, wounded, ragged soldiers tells the story of what defeat and retreat had done to morale.

Where the Goose-Stepping Ended

The Red Army's advance was never to be seriously checked after the breakthrough at the Kursk salient, and as its progress continued, its bag of prisoners increased. The growing inclination of Nazi troops to surrender rather than make forlorn last-ditch stands was another measure of sagging morale, although the *Wehrmacht* continued to fight well from old habits of discipline. The prisoners above, some 57,000 strong, are being led through the streets of Moscow to be entrained for prison camps.

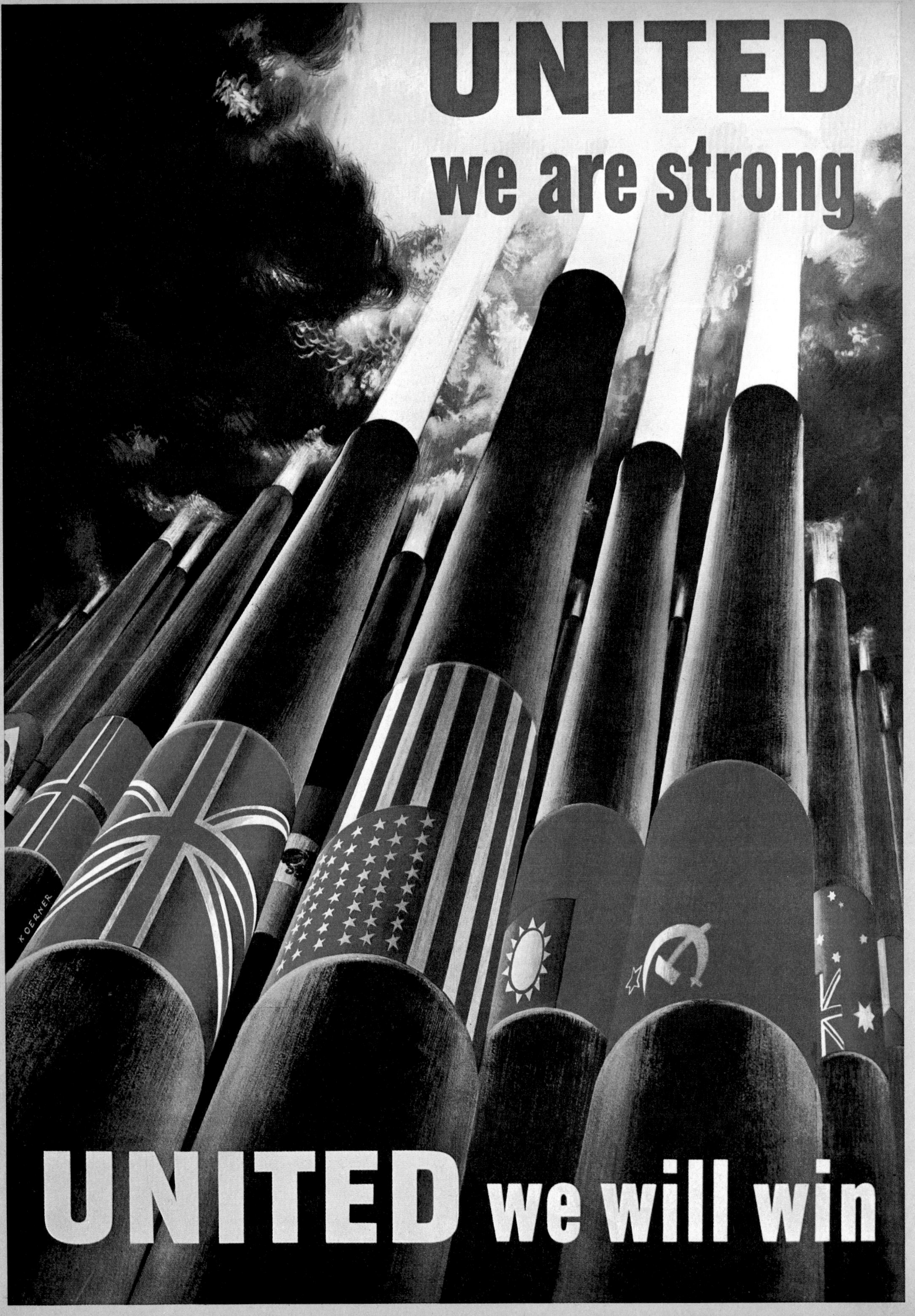
UNITED
we are strong
KOERNER
UNITED we will win

The Politics of World War

The politics of World War II were as dazzling and confusing as a pinball game. The West first tended to equate the evil of Stalin's communism with that of Nazism and then discerned in communism sudden Jeffersonian qualities. Hitler worshipped at the altar of the blond baboon; but his closest allies were the dark Italians, and he accorded the Japanese the dubious accolade of "honorary" Aryans. Before Pearl Harbor the United States joined Britain in planning grand military strategy and fought the Germans at sea, all under the banner of neutrality. Russia was first Germany's partner and then its most deadly enemy. Italy changed sides. Roosevelt violated custom to win a third and fourth Presidential term; Churchill, having led Britain through its toughest struggle, was voted out of office before its end.

Military convenience took precedence over ideology. Washington successively coddled France's General Giraud and the Vichy Admiral Darlan before begrudgingly accepting de Gaulle. London went to war to preserve Poland's integrity and then, when the conflict ended, agreed to Soviet demands to change Poland's borders. International communism endorsed Hitler until he invaded the U.S.S.R.; then it played the major part in guerrilla resistance to the Nazis. Until 1942, Stalin supported Tito's opponents in Yugoslavia; he consistently favored Chiang Kai-shek over Mao Tse-tung. Britain backed an *émigré* king for Greece and opposed an *émigré* king for Yugoslavia. Japan allied itself to Germany but told Berlin nothing about its plans for attacking Pearl Harbor and

honored its nonaggression pact with Stalin even while fighting Hitler's other enemies.

Allied generals squabbled with one another and yet joined in an unprecedented international command. Mussolini's and Hitler's generals squabbled less; but they quit the former and tried to murder the latter. The final showdown in Europe was run on one side from an East Prussian bunker by a madman listening to osteopaths and astrologers, and on the other side by a Combined Chiefs of Staff whose strategy evolved from a series of conferences among chiefs of government.

"It is not so difficult to keep unity in time of war," Stalin acknowledged, "since there is a joint aim to defeat the common enemy, which is clear to everyone. The difficult time will come after the war when diverse interests tend to divide the Allies." But such interests, though always evident, were deliberately repressed. The principal arguments were about the time and place of a second front: British planners wanted to invade the Balkans and keep Russia out of eastern Europe, while American planners were more interested in simply squashing Hitler swiftly and moving on to the defeat of Japan. The British and Free French were fighting to retain empires that Roosevelt hoped to end. Roosevelt initially foresaw a peace guaranteed by the United States, the U.S.S.R., Britain, and China, although he finally switched to the concept of a global United Nations; Churchill wanted a European balance of power that would include both France and Germany. Roosevelt preferred a direct offensive on the Continent; Churchill favored a flank assault through the Mediterranean. Roosevelt trusted Stalin almost to the end and romanticized Chiang Kai-shek's rotting China. Yet despite all the contradictions and underlying mistrust, the Allied coalition held together.

The reason it held together, General Lord Ismay, Churchill's military shadow, later observed, was perhaps partly because the Axis nations never coordinated their own actions. He wrote: "As we look back on that period we can never be sufficiently thankful that the three Axis powers had from the start pursued their own narrow, selfish ends, and that they had no integrated Plan." There, indeed, lay the crucial difference.

The Allies, on the other hand, hammered out their over-all strategy at dramatic meetings between Roosevelt and Churchill, Churchill and Stalin, the three together, and, on one occasion, Roosevelt, Churchill, and Chiang. They agreed that Germany must be defeated before Japan, and Stalin promised to help the Western powers in Asia within three months after Hitler's destruction.

Churchill, who was less naïve than Roosevelt, showed much patience in dealing with Stalin. As he later wrote: "I tried my best to build up by frequent personal telegrams the same kind of happy relations which I had developed with President Roosevelt. In this long Moscow series I received many rebuffs and only rarely a kind word. In many cases the telegrams were left unanswered altogether or for many days. The Soviet Government had the impression that they were conferring a great favour on us by fighting in their own country for their own lives. The more they fought, the heavier our debt became. This was not a balanced view."

Twice he flew to Moscow for private Kremlin talks, in August, 1942, and again in October, 1944. The first time he explained why an Allied landing in France was being delayed in favor of the North African invasion. He was rewarded with a series of insults, including a Stalin retort that the British were cowards. The second time, Churchill and Stalin divided the Balkans into spheres of influence—theoretically for the war period only. Churchill also acknowledged realities in Poland by persuading some leading Polish *émigrés* to accept the Curzon Line. This deal was kept quiet until after the United States elections in November, 1944, in order not to embarrass Roosevelt with Polish-American and other Catholic voters.

Roosevelt often deliberately played up to Stalin and sought to conciliate the Soviet dictator. At the Teheran Conference in 1943 and again at Yalta in 1945, the President strongly opposed the old-fashioned colonial system on which the British Empire was founded, even once suggesting that Britain should abandon Hong Kong. Church-

ill was sometimes hurt and angered, but Stalin remained unmoved. He coldly pushed Soviet interests and ignored, both in Russia and eastern Europe, all promises of political liberty to which he had agreed.

The first effort to bring together Roosevelt, Churchill, and Stalin was made in early December, 1942, when the time had come to discuss what moves should follow the conquest of North Africa. Roosevelt and Churchill invited Stalin to meet them at Casablanca, on Morocco's Atlantic coast; but the Soviet Premier, although he professed to welcome the idea, said he could not leave Russia "even for a day, as it is just now that important military operations of our military campaign are developing." He also reminded the Western leaders of their "promise" to establish a "second front in Western Europe in the spring of 1943."

Nonetheless, Roosevelt and Churchill went to Casablanca along with their top military planners. There they reluctantly concluded that a cross-Channel assault, then code-named "Roundup," was out of the question in 1943, but they also agreed that victory in Africa should be succeeded as quickly as possible by a drive into what Churchill called "the soft under-belly" of Hitler's Europe. Sicily was to be the target and July the date.

Although France as an immediate operational theater was relegated to the background at the Casablanca discussions, politically it was a central and disagreeable theme. On January 22, General de Gaulle was flown to Morocco. His disgruntled mood did not improve when he found himself guarded by American soldiers on what he considered French soil. General Henri Honoré Giraud, who had escaped from a Nazi prison and was at that time de Gaulle's principal rival, was already at Casablanca. Roosevelt later insisted: "My job was to produce the bride in the person of General Giraud while Churchill was to bring in General de Gaulle to play the role of bridegroom in a shotgun wedding." Roosevelt heartily disliked de Gaulle, who, the President thought, saw himself as a new Joan of Arc, "with whom it is said one of his ancestors served as a faithful adherent." "Yes," Churchill is said to have replied, "but my bishops won't let me burn him!" Churchill admonished the General: "You claim to be France! I do not recognize you as France. . . ." "Then why," de Gaulle interrupted, "and with what rights are you dealing with me concerning her worldwide interests?"

De Gaulle wrote of this tense encounter: "I was starting from scratch. In France, no following and no reputation. Abroad, neither credit nor standing. But this very destitution showed me my line of conduct. It was by adopting without compromise the cause of the national recovery that I could acquire authority. At this moment, the worst in her history, it was for me to assume the burden of France."

At the close of the Casablanca meeting, Roosevelt and Churchill mischievously contrived to have de Gaulle and Giraud sit with them at a press conference at noon on Sunday, January 24. Churchill later confessed: "We forced them to shake hands in public before all the reporters and photographers. They did so, and the pictures of this event cannot be viewed even in the setting of these tragic times without a laugh." When pondering de Gaulle's subsequent actions, one wonders who laughed last.

After their handshake, which they repeated for the benefit of photographers, the two French generals retired while the President and the Prime Minister talked to the press. Roosevelt, discussing the conference, said: "Peace can come to the world only by the total elimination of German and Japanese war power. . . . The elimination of German, Japanese, and Italian war power means the *unconditional surrender* [my italics] of Germany, Italy and Japan. . . ." The British, particularly Churchill and his R.A.F. commanders, disliked the phrase. Churchill said afterward: "I would not myself have used these words." He felt that the absolute and categorical expression could only stiffen enemy resolve.

In late 1943, a second series of conferences was held. From November 22 to 26, Roosevelt and Churchill met with Chiang Kai-shek in Cairo, where a chain of villas near the pyramids and Mena House Hotel was requisitioned for them and isolated behind barbed wire. The talk centered on Far Eastern problems, and it was agreed to strip Japan of all her twentieth-century conquests, starting with Korea, Formosa, and Manchuria. The atmosphere was not happy. General "Vinegar Joe" Stilwell used the occasion to lobby savagely against Chiang. Chiang himself fought back, extracting concessions from Roosevelt, while his beautiful Wellesley-educated wife occupied herself with shopping tours and with casting poisonous conversational darts while attending the meeting's numerous social gatherings.

The upshot of the Cairo Conference was that Japan was doomed to lose even its oldest colonies, and flabby China was to have Great Power status in the postwar world. The negotiations were held with maximum secrecy, and little was made public.

Roosevelt first met Stalin at the subsequent Teheran meeting, the first Big Three conference, which lasted from November 28 to December 1, 1943, and at which the American President unexpectedly became the Soviet dictator's house guest. Concerned that enemy agents might be active in the city, Stalin invited Roosevelt to live in the Soviet embassy compound, which, the American Secret Service agreed, was more easily protected than that of the United States. Special precautions also were taken at the nearby British compound where Churchill and his party were staying.

Roosevelt, who had looked forward to meeting the Communist boss, reported afterward to Congress that he "got along fine" with his host. Ismay rather less exuberantly recollected: "It is doubtful that many of those who listened to the discussion grasped the significance of Stalin's determination to keep Anglo-American forces as far as possible away from the Balkans. It was not until later that we realized that his ambitions were just as imperialistic as those of the Czars, whose power and property he now enjoyed, but that he was capable of looking much further ahead than they had ever been."

That was an extraordinary confrontation, held in the capital of an ancient empire whose Shah was a pawn in the hands of three guests whose armies occupied the country. There were the tall, almost gigantic American in a wheelchair, with his beautiful, strong features, graven by pain and humor, and his easy-going, affable manner; the lumpy, infinitely polite, but obstinate Englishman who reflected his compound lineage of dukes, millionaires, and generals as he fought to preserve a crumbling empire; and the short, almost frail Russian from Georgia, who had been a religious seminarian and a bank robber and who was the toughest of the three. Stalin spoke mildly and displayed unexpected charm. He listened to Roosevelt's sallies at Churchill's expense with little perceptible humor, accepted much, and gave little.

The two most important decisions at Teheran were that the Anglo-American invasion across the Channel (now known as Overlord) would be launched in June of 1944, supported by a landing from Italy on the south coast of France and a stepped-up Russian offensive in the east; and that once Germany was destroyed, Russia would enter the war against Japan. Further discussions centered on eastern Europe. The three agreed henceforth to support Tito's Communist partisans and decided that parts of eastern Poland would be ceded to Moscow. Stalin opposed suggestions that Turkey be brought into the war and Churchill's wish to invade the Balkans.

France featured at Teheran as a disagreeable footnote. On his way to the conference, Roosevelt told his Joint Chiefs of Staff that "France would certainly not again become a first class power for at least 25 years," and that Britain was supporting the French in order to use their future strength. Roosevelt also adduced the strange theory that no Frenchman over forty should be allowed to hold office in postwar France. He agreed with Stalin that "the

French must pay for their criminal collaboration with Germany." All this, needless to say, helped complicate Franco-American relations a generation afterward.

While the Great Power leaders were meeting in Casablanca, Cairo, and Teheran, a contest was taking place for influence in the enormously rich Middle Eastern petroleum fields. Stalin was not a prominent figure in the intra-allied oil competition. He had made an unsuccessful effort to move into that area back in the days when he was courting Hitler. On November 26, 1940, he had virtually offered to join the Axis in exchange for dominance of the Persian Gulf region, but Hitler had by then resolved on Barbarossa. Less than a year later, on August 25, 1941, Soviet and British troops moved into Iran to end German intrigues with the Shah. However, the southern oil fields fell within the British occupation zone. And at that time, the Russians were more preoccupied with German efforts to capture Soviet oil wells located around Grozny and the Apsheron Peninsula.

The British possessed extensive petroleum fields in the Arab provinces of the former Ottoman Empire, but in Saudi Arabia, a potentially huge development had been started by a United States company, California Arabian Standard Oil Company (later Aramco), which had been granted a concession in 1933 by King Ibn Saud. Although Washington had opened diplomatic relations with Ibn Saud to insure adequate reserves for our Navy and Air Corps, Aramco rejected a proposal by Interior Secretary Harold Ickes that the United States Government become a shareholder in the operation. As a result, Washington was put in the invidious position of protecting private companies without governmental profit. Nevertheless, rapid extension of American petroleum holdings for the first time engendered an active State Department involvement in the Middle East.

Oil was but one aspect of wartime economic competition. Hitler shaped his 1942 Russian strategy around his petroleum needs, but his agents were also continually engaged in a search for other raw materials that were required for new weapons systems: hard metals needed for jet engines and missiles; rare minerals available only in neutral lands such as Sweden, Portugal, and Turkey. The income of those countries zoomed as Axis purchasers competed with Allied pre-emptive buying missions for chromium, wolfram, and cinnabar.

There was global competition, too, for what may have been as important as oil, even in mechanized modern warfare: public opinion. Radio by this time had become a major weapon. Stalin, Roosevelt, and Churchill, Hitler and Mussolini, were all using it with powerful effect. The Axis found a pitiful chorus of traitors ready to echo its

cause on the airwaves: Axis Sally, Lord Haw Haw, Jane Anderson, Fred Kaltenbach, and Otto Koischwitz. Broadcasts were supplemented by leaflets, fired by artillery or dropped from bombers, that counseled soldiers to desert. The Russians added a grim note by trussing up the corpses of frozen Germans and dropping them from aircraft behind the Nazi lines. Nazi brochures asked GIs in Italy: "Who is cashing in on the huge war profits at home while Americans shed their blood over here?" Tokyo Rose broadcast to United States troops in the Pacific: "The girl back home is drinking with some 4-F who's rolling in easy money." The Americans distributed photographs of well-clad Axis prisoners eating enormous meals, captioned: "Better Free than a Prisoner of War: Better a Prisoner of War than Dead."

The British Political Warfare Executive (PWE) and the American Office of War Information (OWI) pooled their efforts to "reduce the cost of the physical battle" and undermine enemy morale. As the tide of conflict turned, the two organizations laid increasing stress on the terror that continued war would bring to Germany and Japan, and they dropped pictures of bomb-shattered cities on front-line troops. Code messages directed to guerrilla organizations and sabotage groups were mixed with skillfully camouflaged propaganda broadcasts that seemed to originate inside occupied territory.

At the same time, the classical wartime use of spies and saboteurs was rendered far more effective by employing aircraft and submarines to deliver them. Both sides produced audacious special agents, trained in silent killing and equipped with gold coins, counterfeit notes, booby-trap devices, portable communications systems, and light weapons. Yugoslavia, Greece, Albania, North Italy, and most of France gradually filled up with teams of Englishmen and Americans who fought beside local partisans and transmitted detailed information on enemy dispositions to air strike forces and commando assault groups abroad. Patrick Leigh Fermor, a young British officer, kidnapped the German commander in Crete and brought him off safely to Cairo. The American OSS (Office of Strategic Services) had nearly thirty thousand persons on its roster around the world by the time peace came. One OSS agent planted a microphone in the *Luftwaffe's* Paris headquarters. Allen Dulles, in charge of OSS operations from Switzerland and later head of the CIA, managed to penetrate the *Abwehr* (the German Intelligence Bureau) of Admiral Wilhelm Canaris, an anti-Hitler officer garroted after the 1944 attempt on the *Führer's* life.

On the German side, Nazi killers spread terror from Teheran to the Ardennes. And German spies were dropped in England, shipped by yacht to South Africa, landed by submarine in the United States. The FBI rounded up thirty-one Nazi agents on August 1, 1941. The following year, eight German saboteurs brought by U-boat to Long Island and the Florida coast were arrested and six of them executed.

Perhaps the most fascinating espionage tale of World War II was that of Elyesa Bazna, an Albanian citizen of Turkey and valet to the British ambassador in Ankara, Sir Hughe Knatchbull-Hugessen. He regularly opened Hugessen's safe and photographed top-secret papers, selling them for sterling to the German embassy. His activities, inspired primarily by avarice, were so successful that he was given the code name Cicero by Berlin and offered enormous sums as encouragement. However, the Nazis could not believe their own good fortune and not only mistrusted much of Cicero's information but paid him in counterfeit money. The Royal Navy commander in charge of British intelligence in Turkey later told me that the incident demonstrated criminal negligence. Hugessen was made envoy to Belgium after the war.

Although immensely valuable information on operational plans was supplied by agents like Cicero, the richest target for espionage was in the realm of secret weapons. A combination of spy reports and expert interpretation of aerial photographs provided the Allies with critically important data about German V-weapons, missiles, and robot aircraft, and enabled them to bomb the experimental rocket center at Peenemünde. Allied and Axis scientists, who had shared a common fund of atomic knowledge before the war, kept watch on each other's subsequent efforts through intelligence reports.

Never were new weapons of such vital importance as during World War II. Had Hitler been able to wed a nuclear warhead to his missiles, he could have achieved at least a stalemate. Had the United States not possessed atomic bombs, hundreds of thousands of American lives might have been lost in the assault on Japan's home islands. The scientists on both sides knew that they probably held the key to success or failure, and this was particularly true of nuclear physicists.

In January, 1939, the German Otto Hahn and his associates had achieved the first stage of nuclear fission, and French and American physicists were seeking to emulate his experiment as the war clouds gathered. Albert Einstein, fearful that the Nazis might develop a nuclear warhead, wrote to President Roosevelt on August 2, 1939, to warn him: "A single bomb of this type, carried by boat and exploded in a port, might very well destroy the whole port, together with some of the surrounding territory." Roosevelt was sufficiently impressed to appoint an Advisory Committee on Uranium that October. The com-

mittee reported that the kind of bomb mentioned by Einstein was "a possibility," and Western scientists began to censor their reports.

The Nazi victories of 1940 disrupted Allied scientific endeavors. French physicists, under Frédéric Joliot-Curie, had been conducting atomic experiments with heavy water that was manufactured in quantity only at Rjukan, Norway. While the Battle of France was still being fought, Joliot-Curie sent one of his principal aides, Hans von Halban, to England with the French stock of heavy water. Anglo-French scientists at Cambridge then managed to achieve a chain reaction. Their work was later coordinated with that of American colleagues.

In May of 1941, the United States Government created an Office of Scientific Research and Development under Dr. Vannevar Bush, and thirteen months later, President Roosevelt made the decision to try to manufacture an atomic bomb. Two months afterward, an organization called the Manhattan Engineer District was established under General Leslie R. Groves. On December 2, 1942, Enrico Fermi achieved a controlled chain reaction in an atomic pile at Chicago that prompted the famous message from Nobel-prize-winning physicist Arthur Compton to James B. Conant: "The Italian Navigator has just landed in the New World. The Natives are friendly."

Allied intelligence had, however, learned disquieting news. The Nazis, after occupying Norway, had ordered the factory at Rjukan to produce three thousand pounds of heavy water a year, and in 1942, this target was raised to ten thousand pounds. Norwegian underground agents reported that the heavy water was being shipped to the Kaiser Wilhelm Institute for nuclear research. For this reason, Rjukan was repeatedly attacked by Allied bombers, commandos, and saboteurs until its output came to a standstill. The Nazis decided to move the entire store of heavy water to Germany, but the transport was sunk by a Norwegian saboteur's time bomb.

Nevertheless, German physicists, led by Werner Heisenberg, came startlingly close to developing an atomic weapon. They might well have succeeded had Hitler not cut back nuclear research in order to accelerate his V-weapon program. As a result, German scientists, including Wernher von Braun, did manage to achieve brilliant success in rocket projectiles, manufacturing the V-1's and V-2's that caused much damage to London and Antwerp in 1944 and 1945. But they lacked the totally destructive warhead that might have staved off defeat. The conflict in Europe ended before any nuclear device had been successfully exploded. Roosevelt was dead, Churchill was out of office, Mussolini had been shot, and Hitler had committed suicide before the Atomic Age began.

The Commander in Chief

There had been little in his background to prepare him for running a war. He had never worn a uniform or received any military education. True, he had served with much enthusiasm in the Navy Department during the first war; but his profession had always been strictly politics. It was a line of work few men were better at, and perhaps because of that, he recognized from the first that victory would depend on unity among the Allies. "The United Nations" was his phrase, and he used it often with great effect. But he also knew that real unity would take some tall doing. Stalin wanted a second front right away; Churchill did not, and there was strong feeling at home for punishing the Japanese first. Roosevelt decided that Stalin would get something close to what he wanted in 1942. It was a second front in Africa instead of Europe, but American soldiers were fighting Germans in less than a year after Pearl Harbor, and there was going to be no American straying from the beat-Germany-first strategy. Furthermore, Franklin Roosevelt seemed to know how to judge men. Whatever he may have lacked for the job of Commander in Chief was more than made up for by the group of men he called on to help him.

Like nearly every Vice-President before him, Henry A. Wallace had very little to do. F.D.R. was not about to be upstaged by his number two man, and when he needed advice or a job done, there were others he preferred to turn to. He had picked Wallace for his running mate in 1940, much to the annoyance of most Democrats at the Chicago convention, and he kept him always at hand. But for four years, the former publisher and New Deal Secretary of Agriculture played virtually no role at all, except to be there—just in case.

The strain of the war had not begun to show when this portrait of the President was made in 1942. At right he is shown during an inspection tour at Camp Shelby, Mississippi, that same year. But three years later, he would look very different indeed.

311

Cordell Hull, a Tennessee senator, was Secretary of State from 1933 until 1944.

Sumner Welles, Undersecretary of State, was a Harvard-trained career diplomat.

Edward R. Stettinius, a steel executive, ran Lend Lease and later succeeded Hull.

Henry L. Stimson, Secretary of War, was one of the strong men of F.D.R.'s Cabinet.

Frank Knox, Secretary of the Navy, was a prominent Republican, like Stimson.

James V. Forrestal, Undersecretary of the Navy, had been a Wall Street banker.

General George C. Marshall, Army Chief of Staff, was F.D.R.'s ablest strategist.

Admiral Ernest J. King was the exacting, hard-driving Chief of Naval Operations.

General Henry H. Arnold headed the Air Corps, which was then part of the Army.

Joseph C. Grew, former U.S. ambassador to Japan, was Hull's top Asian expert.

Robert P. Patterson, Undersecretary of War, had been a lawyer and federal judge.

Admiral William D. Leahy, briefly ambassador to France, was Chief of Staff.

Harry Hopkins, an original New Dealer, was Roosevelt's controversial assistant.

The Washington High Command

The men Roosevelt picked for his high command were cut from much the same cloth. Of the eight civilians at left, for example, all were from the eastern half of the country; four had attended F.D.R.'s own Harvard, and four were from his home state, New York. With few exceptions, they were Democrats from the worlds of finance, diplomacy, and the law. (Stettinius had been head of U.S. Steel; Hull had been a practicing politician; Stimson and Knox were Republicans.) But while the over-all pattern was predictable, the level of competence was unpredictably high. All of them, the military men included, were remarkably able. Some were among the best leaders the country ever produced: the quiet, patient Marshall, King, and the forceful Stimson. Through all the war, a cabinet shake-up was never necessary. Every man but three stuck to his job. (Welles resigned in September, 1943, after a rift with Hull; Knox died in March, 1944; and Hull resigned that year because of illness.)

But the Roosevelt lieutenant who did the most to give the war regime its zest and direction, and who stirred up more controversy than all the rest combined, was the son of an Iowa harness maker, Harry Hopkins (above), Roosevelt's brash, brilliant, sometimes devious, always resourceful trouble shooter, hatchet man, and alter ego. But more than anything else, he was the prime mover behind F.D.R.'s every maneuver to bring about a solid working relationship first with Churchill, and then with the man the White House circle called "Uncle Joe."

The Ideal Ally

COURIER MAGAZINE, LONDON

Just perfect harmony.

The Anglo-American partnership was as spirited as the British cartoon above suggests, thanks in large part to the groundwork carried on by F.D.R.'s man in London, Averell Harriman (center below) and Churchill's Foreign Secretary Anthony Eden (right below). At left is Russia's ambassador to England, Ivan Maisky.

For a gentleman getting on toward seventy, the plucky "P.M." was a marvel. He seemed to be everywhere at once—about London, at the front in Africa, stopping over at the White House for Christmas, or, with his John Bull face on (right), giving Congress a speech it would long remember. He was immeasurably inspiring, the ideal Ally. He and F.D.R. had their differences (over timing for the France assault, primarily), but they were nothing in contrast with the way things were going with Stalin. When Churchill had flown to Moscow in August of 1942 to tell Stalin there would be no European invasion that year, the Russian had given him a dressing down. "When are you going to start fighting?" Stalin asked. "Are you going to let us do all the work?" Relations grew dangerously strained, and Churchill and F.D.R. agreed that the Big Three had better get together face-to-face. Roosevelt sent Stalin two urgent invitations but was turned down twice. So in January, 1943, Churchill and F.D.R. flew to Morocco to decide the next move.

WIDE WORLD

Casablanca

At the Hotel Anfa, four miles outside of Casablanca, on Saturday, January 23, 1943, after eleven days of deliberation, the Combined Chiefs of Staff came to an agreement on how the war should be run. The Atlantic, they said, was still the number one battlefield; aid to Russia should be pushed forward, and so should the build-up for a cross-Channel attack. But again that year, there would be no assault on France. Instead, Sicily would be next. The following afternoon, Roosevelt and Churchill sat down in the sunshine and held a press conference (left), during which F.D.R. tossed off the phrase "unconditional surrender" and thus began a debate that is still going on. It had been a productive conference, but when it was over and everyone was heading home again, there was still the problem of the man in far-off Russia. An invasion in the Mediterranean was not what Stalin was after, nor were proclamations, however strongly worded. He had had enough of those.

Present at Casablanca and excluded from every talk that mattered was Charles de Gaulle. No one seemed to know quite what to do with him. But before the conference was over, his differences with the Allies had been patched up somewhat, and his future role had been much clarified.

The Other Half of the Big Four

BELOW AND RIGHT: UPI

The other half of the Big Four was composed of two strongmen who ruled the two biggest countries in the world, Marshal Joseph Stalin of Russia (right), and Generalissimo Chiang Kai-shek of China (shown above with his wife, Madame Chiang). Both were fighting for their lives, but each with a different enemy; and both felt that they were being left out in the cold by Roosevelt and Churchill, who were fighting their two enemies at the same time. Chiang wanted the promise of more help in his war with the Japanese. At Cairo he got what he wanted. Stalin wanted a firm commitment for an Anglo-American assault on Nazi-occupied France. At Teheran he too got what he wanted.

At Teheran Stalin agreed to get into the fight with Japan once Hitler was out of the way. Here Tojo (right) stands with Constantin Smetanin, Stalin's ambassador in Tokyo until replaced in 1942. At left is Yosuke Matsuoka, the Japanese Foreign Minister.

While the Americans and British were conferring at Morocco, the Russians were putting an end to the Nazi Sixth Army at Stalingrad. The war had reached its great turning point. Now Russia, the country American military experts had once figured Hitler could crush in three months, was a gigantic world power; and it was right under the thumb of one man, Joseph Stalin. When Casablanca produced no sign of the kind of second front Stalin thought he had been promised, his attitude toward the West hit a new low. But by the end of November, 1943, the Big Three were finally pulling their chairs up to a conference table at Teheran. Stalin turned out to be not so hard to deal with after all, and at long last a date for the invasion of France was settled on. The conference was considered a rousing success, and it came on top of a Roosevelt and Churchill meeting with Chiang Kai-shek a few days before in Cairo. The Allies were still far from working in perfect harmony, but compared to the Axis partnership, theirs was a four-way marriage made in heaven.

The one good thing about Pierre Laval was that he looked like a traitor and so was easy to hate. When Hitler decided to grab the rest of France at the time of the Allied invasion of North Africa in 1942, Laval, then Vichy Premier, went along with the idea. Below, with General von Manstein, Hitler confers about his overriding preoccupation, the war against Russia.

The Axis Gang

The Tripartite Pact never was much of an alliance, and by the beginning of 1943, it was hardly more than words on paper. There was no coordination, no cooperation, just one Adolf Hitler, who busied himself as Supreme Commander of the *Wehrmacht* as well as absolute dictator of the Reich. Hitler had tried to get his old Fascist friend Franco to join the fight, telling him they would all be in the same boat should the Allies triumph. But Franco decided to sit this one out. Hitler had also tried to get the Japanese to attack the Russians, but he had no luck there either. About all he was left with were the Vichy Frenchman Laval and Mussolini. By then the *Duce* (at left with Hitler) was a sick man, living on a diet of milk and rice, whose political strength at home was growing more feeble by the day. In late 1942, he had tried to talk Hitler into making peace with the Russians. It was their only chance to avoid disaster, he argued. The *Führer*, of course, would have none of it. About all Mussolini was good for now, it seemed, was strutting about in one of his snappy getups. But then, at least he still looked like he amounted to something.

321

"...we naturally cannot accept questions of right and wrong"

WIDE WORLD

Joseph Goebbels

Lack of coordination was one problem besetting the enemy powers; another, far more debilitating, was the awful internal rot that ran through the Nazi regime from top to bottom. No document better illustrates the sort of mentality it took to be a high-ranking Nazi than the famous Goebbels Diaries. *The little minister of propaganda was one of history's biggest and most vicious liars, but at night, in his diary, he put down the truth as he saw it.*

MARCH 2, 1943

. . . We are now definitely pushing the Jews out of Berlin. They were suddenly rounded up last Saturday, and are to be carted off to the East as quickly as possible. Unfortunately our better circles, especially the intellectuals, once again have failed to understand our policy about the Jews and in some cases have even taken their part. As a result our plans were tipped off prematurely, so that a lot of Jews slipped through our hands. But we will catch them yet. . . .

At 4 P.M. I drove up to Goering's home. His home is high up on the mountain in almost wintry quiet. Goering received me most charmingly and is very open-hearted. His dress is somewhat baroque and would, if one did not know him, strike one as somewhat funny. But that's the way he is, and one must put up with his idiosyncrasies; they sometimes even have a charm about them. . . .

Goering evidenced the greatest concern about the Fuehrer. To him, too, the Fuehrer seems to have aged fifteen years during the three-and-a-half years of war. It is a tragic thing that the Fuehrer has become such a recluse and leads so unhealthy a life. He doesn't get out into the fresh air. He does not relax. He sits in his bunker, fusses and broods. If one could only transfer him to other surroundings! But he has made up his mind to conduct this war in his own Spartan manner, and I suppose nothing can be done about it.

But it is equally essential that we succeed somehow in making up for the lack of leadership in our domestic and foreign policy. One must not bother the Fuehrer with everything. The Fuehrer must be kept free for the military leadership. One can understand his present mood of sometimes being fed up with life and occasionally even saying that death holds no terrors for him; but for that very reason we must now become his strongest personal support. As was always the case during crises of the Party, the duty of the Fuehrer's closest friends in time of need consists in gathering about him and forming a solid phalanx around his person. . . .

Goering realizes perfectly what is in store for all of us if we show any weakness in this war. He has no illusions about that. On the Jewish question, especially, we have taken a position from which there is no escape. That is a good thing. Experience teaches that a movement and a people who have burned their bridges fight with much greater determination than those who are still able to retreat.

MARCH 7, 1943

. . . During the night Essen suffered an exceptionally severe raid. The city of the Krupps has been hard hit. The number of dead, too, is considerable. If the English continue their raids on this scale, they will make things exceedingly difficult for us. The dangerous thing about this matter, looking at it psychologically, is the fact that the population can see no way of doing anything about it. . . .

MARCH 9, 1943

. . . Naturally the Fuehrer will under no circumstances let air warfare continue in a slipshod way as hitherto. One need only to think six months ahead, then we would face ruin in many cities, sustain thousands of casualties, and find the morale of our people somewhat impaired. This must not be, come what may. The Fuehrer is going to see to it under all circumstances that British terror be answered by terror on our side. . . . Moreover, the Luftwaffe command staffs must be taken out of Paris; in fact, not only these, but also other command staffs. Paris is a dangerous place. No occupation force has ever stuck it out in this city without harm to its soul. . . .

The Fuehrer fully endorses my anti-Bolshevik propaganda. That is the best horse we now have in our stable. He also approves of my tactics in letting the Bolshevik reports of victories go out into the world unchallenged. Let Europe get the creeps; all the sooner will it become sensible. . . .

MARCH 20, 1943

It remains to be seen whether an invasion will actually be attempted or not. Should the English and the Americans actually prepare for it, they will most assuredly look for a point where we are not very strong. I don't believe that the invasion will take place in the west, but more likely in the south or southeast. But these are more conjectures without any basis of fact. . . .

I proposed to the Fuehrer in the future not to bombard slums but the residential sections of the plutocracy when making air raids on England. According to my experience this makes the deepest impression. The Fuehrer agrees with this. It doesn't pay to attack harbors or industrial cities. At present we haven't

sufficient means for such attacks. . . .

The Fuehrer is happy over my report that the Jews have for the most part been evacuated from Berlin. He is right in saying that the war has made possible for us the solution of a whole series of problems that could never have been solved in normal times. The Jews will certainly be the losers in this war, come what may. . . .

APRIL 9, 1943

. . . A report on interrogations of American prisoners is really gruesome. These American boys are human material that can in no way stand comparison with our people. One has the impression of dealing with a herd of savages. The Americans are coming to Europe with a spiritual emptiness that really makes you shake your head. They are uneducated and don't know anything. For instance, they ask whether Bavaria belongs to Germany and similar things. One can imagine what would happen to Europe if this dilettantism could spread unchallenged. But we, after all, will have something to say about that! . . .

APRIL 17, 1943

. . . A number of English papers and periodicals have been laid before me which give evidence of great respect for my person and my work. *News Chronicle* calls me the most dangerous member of the Nazi gang. I can be very proud of this praise. . . .

APRIL 26, 1943

It is reported that the churches in Moscow were overcrowded [on Easter day]. The Soviets, to a certain extent, have restored freedom of religion. That's very sharp and clever tactics. It would be a good thing if we also were somewhat more elastic in these matters. . . .

MAY 1, 1943

. . . The Soviets at the moment are extremely insolent and arrogant. They are quite conscious of the security of their position. They have no consideration whatever for their Anglo-Saxon allies. . . . The men in power in the Kremlin know exactly how far they can go. There is great bitterness in London and Washington about it which nobody seeks to disguise. The Anglo-Saxon camp is in a blue funk about the fact that our propaganda has succeeded in driving so deep a wedge into the enemy coalition.

MAY 8, 1943

. . . The Fuehrer argued that the anti-Semitism which formerly animated the Party and was advocated by it must again become the focal point of our spiritual struggle. . . .

The Fuehrer once more traced in detail the parallel between 1932 and today. It is truly amazing and most convincing. Everything that happened then is being repeated today, and just as in 1932 we attained victory only by a stubbornness that sometimes looked like veritable madness, so, too, we shall achieve it today. . . .

The Fuehrer gave expression to his unshakable conviction that the Reich will be the master of all Europe. We shall yet have to engage in many fights, but these will undoubtedly lead to most wonderful victories. From there on the way to world domination is practically certain. . . .

In this connection we naturally cannot accept questions of right and wrong even as a basis of discussion. The loss of this war would constitute the greatest wrong to the German people, victory would give us the greatest right. After all, only the victor will have the possibility of proving to the world the moral justification for his struggle. . . .

Politics and Physics

In 1933, the year Hitler and Franklin Roosevelt came to power, a shaggy physics professor named Albert Einstein (opposite page) left Germany to live in the United States. Six years later, and more than two years before Pearl Harbor, Einstein sent F.D.R. a letter warning that because of recent developments in atomic research, there was every likelihood that a terrible new kind of bomb could be made, and that some sort of American scientific action should be set in motion by the Government. Not quite a year later, on the day after Paris fell, Roosevelt made what would turn out to be one of the crucial decisions of the war. He set up the board of scientists that, working with the British, would develop the atomic bomb. Politics and physics had become irretrievably intertwined. And it was the same in the enemy camp. The Nazis were working on a variety of scientific projects, including an atomic bomb. But Hitler was never willing to give his bomb program the kind of budget it required. Rockets were to be more to his liking. One of the ironies of the war was that Hitler's V-2 rocket weapons would come out of work done years before by the American rocketry pioneer, Dr. Robert Goddard, while the atomic bomb would come out of the original theories of a German, Einstein, who had been driven from his homeland because he was a Jew.

WIDE WORLD

KLEE AND MERK, *Birth of a Missile*, GEO. G. HARRAP & CO., LONDON

To organize an "all-out" effort to make an atomic bomb, F.D.R. set up the Office of Scientific Research in 1941. Its members included, from left to right above, Dr. A. N. Richards, Dr. J. C. Hunsaker, Dr. Vannevar Bush, who headed the group, Harvey H. Bundy, and Dr. James B. Conant, then president of Harvard. The Germans, meanwhile, were making rapid advances in the field of rocketry under the direction of Colonel Walter Dornberger, shown at left with his top scientist, the brilliant Wernher von Braun.

Counterattack in the Pacific

In the summer of 1942, the eastern boundary of the Japanese Empire ran from the Aleutians in the North Pacific down past Wake Island in the Central Pacific to the Gilberts on the equator; its western boundary ran from the Manchurian-Soviet border through eastern China and Burma to India; on the south it took in Sumatra, Java, Timor, half of New Guinea, and all of the Solomons. But by the summer of 1942, Japan's time of swift and furious expansion was about over. The Japanese never felt strong enough to attack Russia; they could have pushed on into India without much trouble, but chose to hold off; and the Battle of Midway had already finished any hopes they had of destroying the American Pacific Fleet and driving farther east. There was, however, one front left for them where the prospects for conquest still looked promising. If they could drive across the Owen Stanley Mountains on New Guinea and take Port Moresby on that island's southern coast, and if they could set up airfields on the southern Solomons, they would have bases almost on top of Australia and the supply lines from the United States.

Australia was the one place where the Allies could organize for a counterattack, and the build-up there under MacArthur was moving fast. Australian units in the Middle East had been called home. New units in Australia and New Zealand were being raised. And the United States Navy was moving American planes, guns, and troops in impressive numbers across the Pacific. Germany may have been the priority target according to official American strategy, but in the first half of 1942, about four times as many men were being sent to the Pacific as to Europe.

So when it was discovered that the Japanese were constructing an air base on Guadalcanal, one of the southernmost of the Solomon Islands, and that the lifeline to Australia might soon be cut by land-based bombers, a major amphibious assault already agreed on in Washington was rushed into action. At dawn on the seventh of August, exactly eight months after Pearl Harbor, the first big Allied invasion armada of the war appeared off the coast of Guadalcanal and its steaming little satellites, Tulagi, Florida Island, and Gavutu. After an intensive three-hour bombardment, combat groups of the 1st Marines went ashore. Although there was sharp fighting on the offshore islets, the initial Guadalcanal landing was unopposed. The Marines, commanded by Major General Alexander A. Vandegrift, swiftly captured their main objective, the still unfinished airstrip, and renamed it Henderson Field. But the calm was deceptive. Before it had ended, the campaign would include six separate naval encounters and a bloody jungle fight that would drag on for nearly eight months.

Two days after the landings, a Japanese naval task force struck back fiercely against American ships off Guadalcanal. In what became known as the Battle of Savo Island, the Japanese sank one Australian and three American cruisers. But then, to the astonishment of the beleaguered Allies, the enemy commander called off the attack and disappeared without touching a cluster of defenseless transports loaded down with reinforcements.

Marines storm a heavily fortified Japanese bomb shelter on Tarawa.

Throughout August and September, the beachhead was built up until some seventeen thousand Marines occupied a seven-by-four-mile strip, including Henderson Field. The Japanese decided that Guadalcanal had to be cleared and sent shiploads of reinforcements from Rabaul down the waters between the adjacent islands, a passage the Americans called "the Slot." Japanese cruisers and destroyers hammered at the Marines on the island and at American and Australian convoys trying to supply them.

In mid-October the Japanese moved a task force that included four carriers north of Guadalcanal. On the night of the twenty-sixth, the Battle of the Santa Cruz Islands began, when two United States carrier forces, led by the *Hornet* and the *Enterprise* and commanded by Admiral Thomas Kinkaid, went to meet them. The battle cost the Japanese two destroyers sunk and several heavier units damaged, including two carriers and two battleships. But it also cost the United States the *Hornet*, which was sunk by Japanese destroyers after it had been badly damaged by dive bombers.

Finally, on the night of November 13, the Imperial Fleet staged a dramatic sortie. This, the most furious sea encounter of the Solomons, became known as the Naval Battle of Guadalcanal. Led by two battleships, a Japanese force came down "the Slot" to land more troops and delivered a heavy shelling attack on a much smaller American task force. All night there was a tremendous mix-up, with the smaller, more maneuverable American ships pressing the attack. Ships sometimes drew so close that they had trouble depressing their guns. The Americans lost two cruisers sunk and two damaged, which they could ill afford; but the Japanese lost a battleship. The following night, a second Japanese flotilla was located by planes from the *Enterprise* and was heavily punished. Bombers from Henderson Field took off in daylight and sank seven and damaged four of eleven Japanese transports ferrying reinforcements. On the night of November 14–15, the Japanese mustered their remaining naval strength, led by a battleship and four cruisers, in an effort to cut off the beachhead. At this moment an American flotilla commanded by Admiral Willis A. Lee roared up Ironbottom Sound, so named for the number of ships already rusting beneath its greasy surface. Lee sank another Imperial battleship and damaged two more cruisers, repelling Japanese efforts to build up their land forces. By dawn of the fifteenth, it was clear that the attempt had failed.

The land campaign, which lasted until February, was the first Marine experience in that particular kind of jungle warfare with which they were to become so intimately acquainted during the next three years. They had to learn how to hack their way through tangles of roots, always on the lookout for snipers lashed to tree branches or hidden in the underbrush. They became familiar with malarial mosquitoes, scorpions, and snakes, and accustomed to distinguishing the cries of animals from those of enemy sentries. They fought their way forward through intense heat and the foul slime of decomposing vegetation, blasting the Japanese from jungle strongpoints and hillside caves. Progress at first was painfully slow and nerve-racking. However, once it was clear that the Imperial Fleet had been driven off and that the flow of enemy reinforcements was dammed, the jungle advance gathered momentum. Finally, in the first week of February, the Japanese managed to bring destroyers in at night and evacuate about twelve thousand troops at Cape Esperance, on the island's northwestern tip. By the ninth, not a single living enemy was left on Guadalcanal. The Japanese had suffered their first land defeat of the war, and the first American offensive was a success.

When MacArthur arrived in Australia from Bataan in March, 1942, he found scant forces there for the defensive action needed if the Japanese were to be stopped in their surge southward. Even so, he decided that the best way to protect Australia was to throw as much strength as he could into New Guinea, in order to hold the Japanese on the far side of the Owen Stanley Mountains and secure the vital Australian base at Port Moresby. The first Japanese try at taking Port Moresby resulted in the inconclusive Battle of the Coral Sea in May, 1942.

Then, on July 21, the Japanese landed at Buna, on the north coast, and proceeded to do what no one among the Allied strategists had thought possible; they crossed the Owen Stanleys and drove on Port Moresby. By mid-September, at the time when the Allied campaign on Guadalcanal was looking very doubtful indeed, the Japanese were within thirty miles of Port Moresby. But MacArthur rushed in troops and planes, and in the next ten months the Allies battled the Japanese back over the mountains, took Buna, and began the long drive up the northern coast of New Guinea that was to be one side of a giant pincers movement that would eventually isolate Rabaul, Japan's Gibraltar of the South Pacific.

MacArthur had stopped the Japanese advance in New Guinea. The Japanese now tried to save their New Guinea forces by reinforcing the garrisons at Lae and Salamaua. On March 1, 1943, United States reconnaissance planes spotted a powerful Imperial convoy carrying seven thousand troops and trying, under cover of bad weather, to make from Rabaul through the Bismarck Sea to Lae, on New Guinea's northeastern coast. Two days later, on March 3, in the major action of the three-day Battle of the Bismarck Sea, Major General George C. Kenney's

Fifth Air Force, operating from Papua, smashed the convoy and Japanese plans for holding New Guinea. By the time they finished, they had sunk or damaged most of the ten warships and twelve transports in the formation, drowning all save a handful of the reinforcements. The Japanese lost one hundred and two aircraft. Kenney's B-17's and B-25's had given, as Churchill put it, "a striking testimony to the proper use of air power."

Thus, at last, Tokyo found its dynamism checked at its outermost fringes. Thrust back from Guadalcanal and New Guinea, it withdrew from the borders of India and the sea around Ceylon when those crucial areas lay open for the taking; and across the mainland Asian battlefront, Japan's energies continued to be drained in a brutal war with China that produced few, if any, definitive results.

By mid-summer of 1943, MacArthur had four American divisions and six Australian divisions supported by Admiral William F. Halsey's South Pacific Fleet. Nimitz had nine U.S. Army and Marine divisions in the Central Pacific. With these relatively small forces, they stepped up the counterattack against strong Japanese dispositions in heavily fortified bases. They moved up the Solomons and New Guinea and inward across the little-known, savage Gilberts, Marshalls, and Marianas. The two great American captains, MacArthur and Nimitz, who had spent a lifetime in services with wholly different traditional and tactical concepts, perfected a novel kind of island-hopping warfare, the goal of which was to outflank and bypass enemy strongpoints wherever it proved to be possible, leaving isolated garrisons far to the rear of the actual fighting front.

There was something fatefully repetitious about that twin advance by the forces of the arrogant, jauntily-capped MacArthur, and of the deeply honest Nimitz, with his clear blue eyes and modest, craggy face. Island after island, the story was nearly always the same: Japanese troops holed up in their elaborate bunkers, listening to distant radio broadcasts, dreaming of their dainty, pastel-kimonoed wives, waiting for the inevitable storm of fire and death from offshore. Outside, the clear Pacific and the endless rhythm of the surf. And all the while, lumbering through swells, the grey ships filled with sweating Marines; no smoking on the blacked-out decks; the dull thud of engines; the rattling of planes being readied by their mechanics; the creaking of davits and the hum of ammunition lifts in the quiet predawn. And then, the sudden and terrible explosion of light and sound, turning paradise to fury. When the last bomb and shell had fallen and the last machine-gun barrel cooled, swarms of Seabees came with their monstrous machinery to sweep away the mess and carve still another base for the inexorable advance. Or—sometimes—there was simply quiet again.

All the time that MacArthur's forces were pressing along the northern coast of New Guinea, the Marines and the Army started up the Solomon Islands "ladder": the Russell Islands (February, 1943), New Georgia (June), Vella Lavella (August), Choiseul and the Treasury Islands (October), and finally, Bougainville (in November), the biggest island of the chain. All the while, the Air Corps and carrier-based dive bombers pounded away at Rabaul.

Within little more than a year, MacArthur's effective and economical strategy had reached far up the Southwest Pacific archipelagoes and severed some one hundred and thirty-five thousand Japanese from all prospect of rescue. Simultaneously, Nimitz guided Spruance's Fifth Fleet westward, encompassing the Gilberts, the Marshalls, the Carolines, and the Marianas, ravaging enemy ships and garrisons with the power of their carrier planes, and asserting a freedom of maneuver that seemed unimaginable less than two years after Pearl Harbor had crippled the U.S. Navy.

Makin and Tarawa in the Gilberts, where the Central and South Pacific commands met, were now assailed by Nimitz. On November 20, his carriers started a heavy bombardment of Makin. A few days later, the island was overwhelmed in a short, sharp series of amphibious assaults marked by a fanatical defense by a garrison well-fortified with rice wine. Tarawa, an atoll of some two dozen islets linked by coral reefs, was a more difficult objective. Tokyo had boasted that it could not be taken by assault. The principal strongpoint at Betio, held by three thousand crack Imperial Marines, comprised hundreds of connected pillboxes made of concrete and coral work, reinforced with steel beams and coconut logs. These positions were intensely shelled and bombed by the Americans; nevertheless, when the Marines waded ashore, they were met by withering fire.

The battle was one of the bloodiest fights of the whole Pacific campaign. American ships maintained a steady artillery barrage as landing barges discharged troops and supplies and Marines stormed each bastion with flame throwers and grenades. Colonel David Shoup, commander of the 2nd Marine Regiment, reported to the flagship standing offshore: "Our casualties heavy. Enemy casualties unknown. Situation: we are winning." Four days later, his optimism proved warranted: the Americans had won. But they paid a price of eleven hundred lives.

Promptly the ingenious Seabee's set to work constructing a base for an attack on the Marshalls to the north. There the main target was Kwajalein, largest atoll in the world, 66 miles long and 18 miles wide. This time Nimitz took no chances before sending his men ashore; his ships and planes dropped fifteen thousand tons of explosives on Kwajalein before the first landing craft touched ground. The atoll was a mass of dust-covered rubble when the invasion began, but the Japanese, who were for the first time defending a piece of prewar Imperial territory, fought savagely from the debris. Again the American advance was initially painstakingly slow as each fortification had to be reduced, blasted, or burned out. But by early 1944, Nimitz's task forces had succeeded in mastering all the Gilberts and Marshalls, and his carrier raids had so shattered the great Carolines air base of Truk to the west that its garrison of fifty thousand could be easily bypassed. For the rest of the war, Truk lay useless.

While the new technique of amphibious fighting was proceeding in the tropical Pacific, an odd, militarily unimportant but politically and emotionally vital campaign took place along the northeastern edge of the Japanese empire, in the Aleutian sealing grounds. In 1942, when Yamamoto led his fleet to Midway, a small force was simultaneously sent to occupy the barren islands of Attu and Kiska. The move was, in fact, a strategic feint, but it was also a check to any designs the Allies might have for using the Aleutians as an invasion route to Tokyo. American public opinion saw it as just the opposite; Alaska and the Pacific northwest were now, it seemed, seriously threatened. The American high command wished to choke off any such possibilities and to clear the way for lend-lease shipments to the Soviet Pacific port of Vladivostok. It was decided to eject the Japanese.

On May 11, 1943, U.S. 7th Division troops began landings on mountainous, treeless Attu. They fought for eighteen days amid fog and rain, which hampered aerial and naval support and imprisoned armor in the cold, sucking mud. On May 29, the desperate Japanese defenders staged a suicide charge. From a ridge between Chichagof Harbor and Sarana Bay, Colonel Yasuyo Yamasaki led his surviving forces down on the Americans screaming: "Japanese drink blood like wine." Those who were not butchered along the slopes held hand grenades to their bellies and blew out their intestines. Among letters found in the pockets of the dead, one said: "I will become a deity with a smile in this heavy fog. I am only waiting for the day of death."

The liberation of Kiska three months later was a different story. A large force, including five thousand Canadians, nervously crept about the island for five days looking for the enemy, sometimes shooting at each other among exploding booby traps. At the end the astonishing discovery was made that, prior to the landings, shielded by the dank, boreal mist, the Japanese had quietly and quite brilliantly evacuated their entire garrison.

Though command arrangements for the war against Japan were often enormously complicated, the over-all idea was simply that the United States had the responsibility for the entire "Pacific area," while Britain took charge of South Asia and the Middle East. But even so, China had to be accorded a special position, as it was regarded as a region of special American interest. Chiang Kai-shek was recognized as supreme commander, but his chief of staff was an American general, Stilwell. Stilwell also commanded United States forces in what became the China-Burma-India theater and thus had the dubious distinction of being simultaneously responsible to Washington, to Chiang, and to the British commander in India. Stilwell was not ideally suited to the task. He was brave and aggressive but almost totally without tact. He quarreled with the British and denounced Chiang for his "stupid, gutless command."

Chiang on the other hand, thanks to circumstance, geography, and Roosevelt's personal prejudice, was accorded considerable influence and played his cards shrewdly. He gave more thought to his postwar problems and the inevitable power struggle with the Communists than to the war itself. He banked on the traditional sympathy of the American people, whose commercial and missionary interests in China dated back for generations, on the American vision of a postwar China that could act as a balance to Japan, and on the fact of China's vast geography and population.

Washington was as adamant in its support of Chiang in Asia as in its opposition to de Gaulle in Europe; and oddly enough, although Mao Tse-tung's Communist armies, based around Sian, were at times fighting Chiang as well as the Japanese, Stalin endorsed Roosevelt's backing of the Generalissimo. Churchill, however, later on reported: "I had found the extraordinary significance of China in American minds, even at the top, strangely out of proportion. I was conscious of a standard of values which accorded China almost an equal fighting power with the British Empire, and rated the Chinese armies as a factor to be mentioned in the same breath as the armies of Russia. I told the President how much I felt American opinion overestimated the contributions which China could make to the general war. He differed strongly. There were five hundred million people in China. What would happen if this enormous population developed in the same way as Japan had done in the last century and got ahold of modern weapons? I replied I was speaking of the present war, which was quite enough to go on with for the time being." The "enormous population" did indeed, subsequently get "hold of modern weapons," but it was not that China envisioned by Roosevelt.

During the war, Chiang reigned supreme in Allied calculations, and Chiang insisted that Burma should be the scene of the initial mainland offensive against the Japanese. He opposed operations in the north, where his own divisions would have to provide needed man power. Instead, he argued: "Burma is the key to the whole campaign in Asia. After the enemy has been cleared out of Burma, his next stand would be in North China and, finally, in Manchuria." Churchill was unenthusiastic, agreeing with the American admirals King and Nimitz, who wished to force an ultimate decision by sea power. But by appealing for an extension of the supply route across Burma in order to sustain Chinese morale, Chiang gained Roosevelt's backing.

A Southeast Asia Command was created under the English king's cousin, Lord Louis Mountbatten, and was charged with conducting a war of which Mountbatten's own government did not heartily approve. The command depended upon an American military system that sought different objectives, and upon a Chinese Government that was fighting almost a private war for purposes largely its own. The Casablanca Conference of January, 1943, nevertheless agreed on a Burma campaign that, from its very genesis, was marked by quarrels and discord. Churchill complained to his Chiefs of Staff: "Going into the swampy jungles to fight the Japanese is like going into the water to fight a shark." Mountbatten viewed Burma as a subsidiary objective. Stilwell favored a Burmese drive—but only in the north, where he wished Chiang would do some serious fighting. Major General Claire Chennault, by now commanding the U.S. Fourteenth Air Force in China, agreed with Chiang that divisions were less important than aircraft but wanted the Japanese to be bombed out of Burma. No one was satisfied. Stilwell and Chennault carried their acrimonious debate right to the Trident Conference in Washington in May, 1943. The irascible Stilwell shouted: "It's the ground soldier slogging through the mud and fighting in the trenches who will win the war." Chennault hollered back: "But God damn it, Stilwell, there aren't any men in the trenches."

The Allied carpenters, however, managed to fashion an operation one of whose goals was to increase to ten thousand tons a month the capacity of the Air Transport supply system over the Burmese Hump to China. Their new plan assigned to Mountbatten and Stilwell the task of investing northern and central Burma. A specially trained American infantry combat team known as the Galahad Force, commanded by Brigadier General Frank D. Merrill, was ordered to join the Chinese 22nd and 39th divisions coming down the Hukwang Valley.

Aware of Allied preparations, the Japanese initiated their own offensive during the 1943–44 winter. They attempted to capture the Indian province of Assam and to sever the link to China via the Hump and the Ledo Road, which was being built across north Burma from India to hook up with the old Burma Road into China. British and Indian air-borne troops were able to check and finally reverse this short-lived invasion. Then, with the British driving along the Bay of Bengal in the south and the Chinese and Merrill advancing on Myitkyina in the north, the Japanese were forced gradually backward. Major General Orde Wingate, the English disciplinarian who had already earned fame in Ethiopia, dropped on the Japanese rear with his long-range penetration groups.

Wingate's Chindits (a mispronunciation of Chinthe, the Burmese word for lion) and Merrill's Marauders fought remarkably well, outdoing the Japanese in a type of jungle combat the latter had originated. Throughout the end of 1943, when the Japanese tried again to move on India, Wingate's commandos kept the invaders off balance, severing their communications lines. They were supplied exclusively from the air and managed to build a landing strip far behind enemy lines. Merrill, for his part, persuaded a tribe of dark, belligerent north Burmese, called Kachins, to join him in fighting the Japanese. American OSS representatives formed a Kachin unit called Detachment 101 and managed to kill 5,447 Japanese, with a loss of only 15 Americans and 70 Kachins. Despite divergent national political ambitions and despite rivalries and jealousies among strategists and commanders at the top, Allied field action in Burma was remarkably effective. Wingate, unfortunately, was killed on March 24, 1944, in a plane crash. Churchill called him "a man of genius who might well have become also a man of destiny." He was only forty-one.

The campaign against Japan covered flabbergasting distances; its scope was enormous; and Allied interests were so disparate and contradictory that it was difficult to coordinate strategic plans. The critically important Soviet-Manchurian frontier remained quiescent until weeks after the Nazi surrender in Europe, as it was in the interests of both Russia and Japan to honor their non-aggression pact. Native nationalism in colonial Indochina, Malaya, Indonesia, Burma, and India initially favored the Japanese. Subsequently, however, the invaders' barbarity turned these populations against them, much as Ukrainian nationalists changed their attitude toward the Germans once they got acquainted with the facts of life under the Nazis. China's principal use to the Allies was as an enormous bog that sucked up Japanese armies. The real road to Tokyo would be by sea, and at the close of 1943, there was still plenty of road to travel.

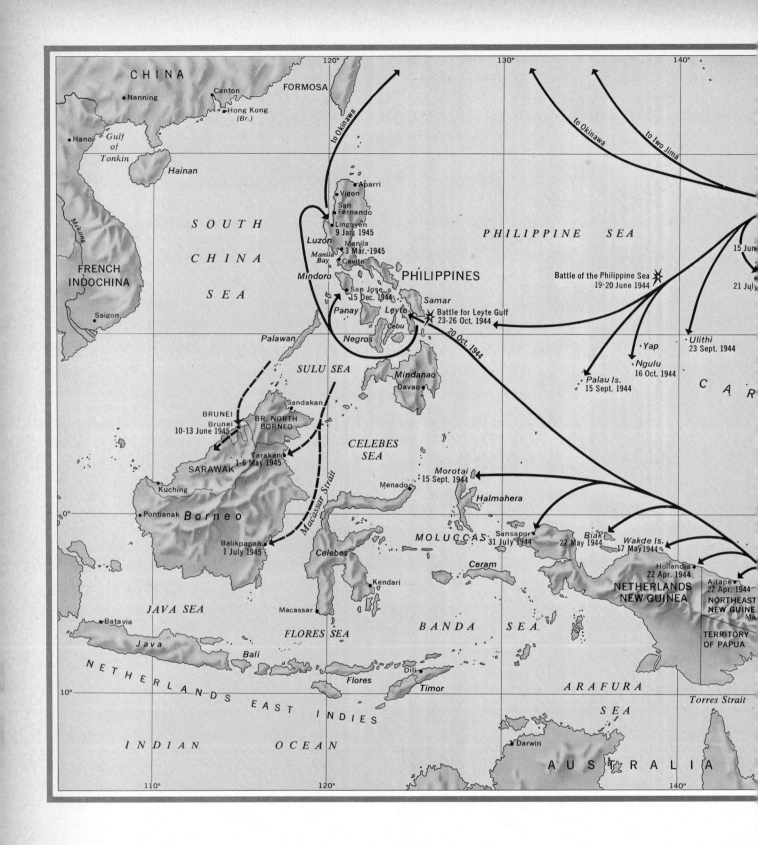

CHINA
• Nanning
• Canton
Hong Kong (Br.)
FORMOSA
• Hanoi
Gulf of Tonkin
Hainan
FRENCH INDOCHINA
Mekong
• Saigon

SOUTH CHINA SEA

to Okinawa

• Aparri
• Vigon
San Fernando
Lingayen
9 Jan. 1945
Luzon
Manila
3 Mar. 1945
Manila Bay
Cavite
Mindoro
San Jose
15 Dec. 1944
Panay
PHILIPPINES
Samar
Leyte
Battle for Leyte Gulf
23-26 Oct. 1944
Cebu
Negros
20 Oct. 1944
Palawan

PHILIPPINE SEA

to Okinawa
to Iwo Jima

15 Jun
21 July

Battle of the Philippine Sea
19-20 June 1944

• Yap
Ulithi
23 Sept. 1944

• Ngulu
16 Oct. 1944

Palau Is.
15 Sept. 1944

CAR

SULU SEA

BRUNEI
Brunei
10-13 June 1945
BR. NORTH BORNEO
Sandakan
Tarakan
1-6 May 1945
SARAWAK
Kuching
Pontianak
Borneo
Balikpapan
1 July 1945

Macassar Strait

CELEBES SEA

Mindanao
Davao

CELEBES

Menado

MOLUCCAS

Morotai
15 Sept. 1944

Halmahera

Sansapor
31 July 1944
Biak
27 May 1944
Wakde Is.
17 May 1944
Hollandia
22 Apr. 1944
Aitape
22 Apr. 1944
NETHERLANDS NEW GUINEA
NORTHEAST NEW GUINE
Ma

JAVA SEA
• Batavia
Java
Bali
FLORES SEA
Kendari
Macassar
Ceram
BANDA SEA
NETHERLANDS EAST INDIES
Flores
Dili
Timor
ARAFURA SEA
Torres Strait
TERRITORY OF PAPUA

INDIAN OCEAN
• Darwin
AUSTRALIA

Strategy of Island-Hopping

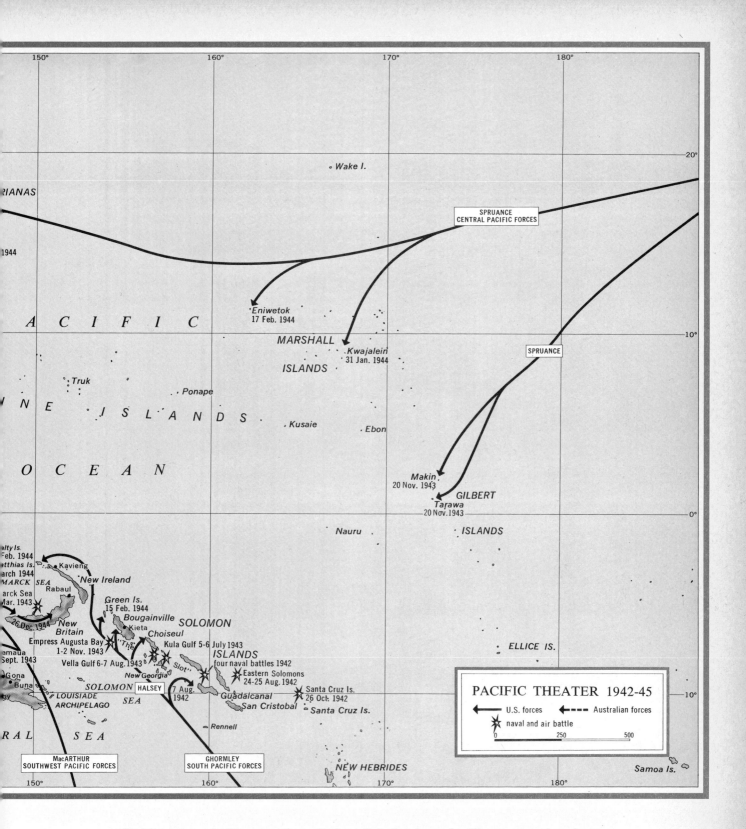

° Wake I.

20°

SPRUANCE
CENTRAL PACIFIC FORCES

1944

·Eniwetok
17 Feb. 1944

MARSHALL

SPRUANCE

·Kwajalein
·31 Jan. 1944

ISLANDS

10°

·Truk

· Ponape

ISLANDS

· Kusaie   · Ebon

OCEAN

Makin
20 Nov. 1943

GILBERT

Tarawa
20 Nov.1943

ISLANDS

0°

Nauru

· ISLANDS

lty Is.
Feb. 1944
tthias Is.
arch 1944
Kavieng
New Ireland
MARCK SEA
arck Sea
Rabaul
Mar. 1943

Green Is.
15 Feb. 1944
Bougainville
Kieta
Choiseul

SOLOMON

ELLICE IS.

26 Dec. 1944
New
Britain
Empress Augusta Bay
1-2 Nov. 1943
Kula Gulf 5-6 July 1943

ISLANDS

amaua
Sept. 1943
Vella Gulf 6-7 Aug. 1943
New Georgia
Slot"

four naval battles 1942
Eastern Solomons
24-25 Aug. 1942

Gona
Buna
y

SOLOMON

HALSEY

SEA

7 Aug.
1942

Guadalcanal
San Cristobal

Santa Cruz Is.
26 Oct. 1942
· Santa Cruz Is.

10°

RAL   SEA

· Rennell

PACIFIC THEATER 1942-45

⬅ U.S. forces   ⬅--- Australian forces

✴ naval and air battle

0   250   500

MacARTHUR
SOUTHWEST PACIFIC FORCES

GHORMLEY
SOUTH PACIFIC FORCES

NEW HEBRIDES

Samoa Is.

Unlike the war in Europe, where the lay of the land was familiar to most Americans, the war in the Pacific often seemed hard to follow. MacArthur's men fought at places with strange names that were a problem to find on the map. And the amount of ocean that had to be conquered was so vast that a lot of people never did quite get the picture. As this map shows, the scale of the Pacific war was enormous, the strategy essentially simple. Two great thrusts westward, one starting at Guadalcanal (lower right), the other at the Gilbert and Marshall Islands (center), would converge on the Philippines. Islands along the way would be taken one after the other, unless, as was the case with Rabaul and Truk, they could be merely bypassed.

The Admirals and the General

With his flamboyant headgear, his sunglasses and corn cob pipe, he looked like an actor playing the role of a great general. He also had the sort of press an actor likes; he arranged that, in part, by keeping his subordinates as anonymous as possible. But the truth also was that Douglas MacArthur, Supreme Commander of Allied Forces in the Southwest Pacific, was a great general. He had one of the most distinguished military careers on record (top of his class at West Point, a hero in the first war, Army Chief of Staff), and it is doubtful that anyone in any of the services knew more about the Pacific theater. Nonetheless, the war that would be waged to return him to the Philippines, as he had promised, would be a Navy war, and the three admirals below—Nimitz, King, and Halsey—would have every bit as much to do with the strategy and tactics of winning that war as he had.

Ernest J. King (center), Chief of Naval Operations, was a spare, no-nonsense officer with a strong distaste for publicity, some enemies among the Army and British brass, and one of the sharpest strategic minds in Washington. Chester Nimitz (left), Commander in Chief of the Pacific Fleet, was a mild-mannered Texan promoted past 28 officers to take over after Pearl Harbor. William F. Halsey (right) was Commander of the South Pacific Fleet and the war's most colorful admiral.

ABOVE: U.S. ARMY; BELOW: IMPERIAL WAR MUSEUM, LONDON

The Forgotten Sideshow

There was a way to get at the Japanese overland. Equip and train a Chinese army; put American officers in charge and strike across northern Burma into China's Yunnan Province; then head northeast across China, gathering strength from the Chinese people all the way. This, in essence, was one of two strategic ideas for that theater of the war that was on the bottom of almost everyone's priority list: China-Burma-India, or "C.B.I." The other idea was to use China as a base for air strikes against the Japanese Army in China and Burma, and against Japan itself. As it turned out, both ideas were tried; the result was some of the fiercest jungle fighting of the war, and some of the thorniest political infighting.

In command of the Chinese-American ground forces was hard-bitten, outspoken General Joseph W. ("Vinegar Joe") Stilwell, who had walked his men out of Burma to India in 1942, and who was convinced that the best way back was also by land. In October, 1943, he launched an attack on Burma from near Ledo, India. As his two Chinese divisions pushed forward, he hacked out the Ledo Road, which would eventually cut through jungle and over mountains to link up with the Burma Road, the main supply route into China. At the same time, British and American guerrilla units (Wingate's Raiders and Merrill's Marauders) began a vicious campaign behind Japanese lines. But most of the fighting in Burma was carried on by the British Fourteenth Army, which suffered heavy losses before driving the enemy out of Mandalay and Rangoon in the spring of 1945.

By the time the Burma Road was reopened, the war was about over, and F.D.R. had moved Stilwell out of his job at the request of Generalissimo Chiang Kai-shek. Stilwell had a low opinion of the Chinese dictator and made no effort to hide the fact. Chiang seemed reluctant to do much fighting; his Government was seething with corruption; and in the north, the Chinese Communists had set up their own hostile regime. The result was often a three-way war in which the Japanese benefited and Chiang called for more lend-lease while backing the other part of United States strategy—air power.

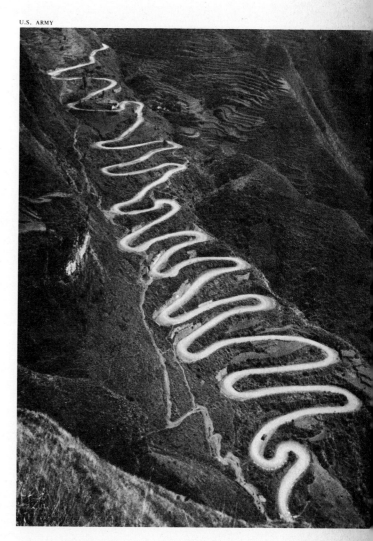

One of the main objectives of the struggle in Burma was the treacherous Burma Road (above). Sealed off by the Japanese in 1942, it was not reopened to Allied convoys until 1945.

Prime American proponent of the C.B.I. land offensive was "Vinegar Joe" Stilwell, who was Chiang Kai-shek's chief of staff. At left above he is shown in the foreground leading his battered army on a 20-day retreat out of Burma in May, 1942. At left, two riflemen of the British-Indian Fourteenth Army move past a Burmese pagoda. The Fourteenth suffered 40,000 casualties in the first half of 1942 alone, fighting malaria, typhus, and jungle weather, as well as three Japanese armies.

Heroes in the Sky

The man in command of the Allied air offensive over China was General Claire Chennault. Like Stilwell, Chennault was an old China hand and just as headstrong about beating the Japanese *his* way. Moreover, unlike Stilwell, he had Chiang on his side. Chennault had been an unofficial "adviser" to Chiang since 1937; in 1941, he had put together a group of volunteer American pilots, known as the "Flying Tigers," who were paid $600 a month for fighting for China, plus $500 a kill. Their kills were many. In the summer of 1942, Chennault's command became the Fourteenth Air Force and included heavy bombers. But perhaps the greatest success of the whole theater was the convoy of C-47 transports that flew "the Hump," the 20,000-foot-high Himalayas, which separated China from Allied supply bases in India. The Air Transport Command was a costly business in every way (eight hundred and fifty airmen would be killed before it was over), but it kept China alive and in the war.

Everything from trucks to hand grenades to K-rations "flew the Hump" in C-46's such as this one. By 1945, the Air Transport Command was delivering 45,000 tons a month to besieged China. General Claire Chennault (right) organized the daring and flamboyant "Flying Tigers" and was a heroic symbol to the Chinese through the entire war. They called him "Old Leather Face."

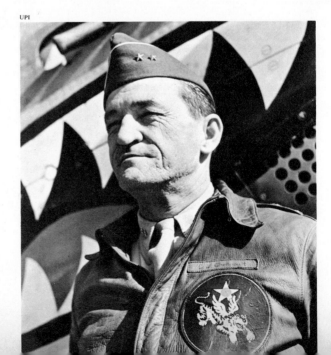

At right is a Chinese leaflet that says: "Happy New Year! This American pilot helped you to chase the Japanese out of Chinese sky. Help him. The ancient, tired god of gates is sleeping now. The terror of Japanese devil entered millions of Chinese families. The ancient god cannot stop them anymore. This strong young soldier, this American fighting pilot, with the help of the courageous Chinese army, they together will protect the old and the young in your family. But he and his Chinese colleagues need your help when they are hurt, lost, or hungry. They need your comfort and friendship. Help them! They are fighting the war for you. Friends of the occupied territory, attention. Please do not let anyone see this leaflet. If the Japanese should see this, they will torture you."

From remote mountain plateaus inside China, Chennault's giant B-29 bombers hit at mainland Japan and Japanese strongholds on th

Chinese coast. The modern bases were built in a way as old as China. Here swarms of coolies work on the huge Laowingping airfield in 1944.

U.S. MARINE CORPS

Guadalcanal

The road to Tokyo began on an island in the Pacific that few Americans had ever heard of and none of the military planners knew much about. But on Guadalcanal, one of the Solomons, the Japanese were building an air base from which to strike at American convoys to Australia. The island had to be taken, and quickly. The landing was America's first big amphibious assault. On August 7, 1942, some 10,000 Marines went ashore almost unopposed. By sundown the next day they had secured their major objective, which they renamed Henderson Field, as well as great quantities of gasoline, ammunition, tents, and rice. The Japanese, it seemed, had fled in panic. But on the night of August 8–9, the United States Navy took one of its worst whippings ever near Savo Island, just off Guadalcanal, and withdrew, leaving the Marines all alone. Then began the enemy counterattack. "The Tokyo Express," the name the Marines gave the fast Japanese ships that came down "the Slot" between the Solomon Islands, began pouring in fresh troops and supplies. The fighting was fierce and kept up for six months. For a long while there was doubt as to just which way it would go.

WIDE WORLD

The landing was a full surprise. Hardly a shot was fired as the Marines came ashore and the photographers took their pictures (left). In command of the operation was Major General Alexander Vandegrift (right), a soft-spoken professional fighting man. But the troops under him were young (the average age was nineteen) and green, and they had been told next to nothing about the 92-mile-long island. In the next six months they would learn very much indeed.

343

The Enemy is Met

U.S. ARMY

From offshore, Guadalcanal looked like the South Seas "Isle of Enchantment" in the color travelogues. Onshore, it was pure hell. The heat was terrible; there were drenching rains, rats, and bugs of every description; men were struck down by malaria and dysentery and their skin broke out in jungle rot. But worst of all was the enemy. He came screaming out of the jungle at night in wild suicide charges. He fought according to no code an American could understand; he was tricky and deadly. He seemed to live in the jungle like an animal and moved through it just as silently. The only way to beat him, the Marines quickly decided, was to kill him off like an animal. By the time the last enemy sniper was silenced, there were 24,000 dead Japanese. The dead Americans totaled 1,752. This was the first time the Japanese had been defeated on land since they went to war. It was also the first time the Americans fully realized what sort of foe they were up against and the kind of country they would have to fight him in. This was no clean, modern campaign decided by advanced technology, no recruiting poster sort of war. And in February, 1943, when the Japanese evacuated what was left of their forces (about 12,000 men), Tokyo was still 3,000 miles away.

Convinced the Americans would tire quickly of jungle war, the Japanese sent in some of their toughest, best-trained infantry and artillery units (above). For months the Marines fought a bloody defensive action. At Henderson Field, at Tenaru River and Matanikau River, the enemy dead piled up in mangled heaps after banzai attacks. Only now and then did the Marines get a look at a live prisoner such as this one; the Japanese soldier preferred to fight until he fell.

UPI

Offshore, fierce sea battles were waged, as shown in the map above. Both sides fought to stop reinforcements, and both suffered heavy losses. At the end of 1942, bolstered by the Army and by air cover, the Marines went on the attack and soon cleared the island. At right, members of the 1st Marine Division, their ranks riddled by malaria, await evacuation after their part of the fighting had ended. They would not see action again for another year.

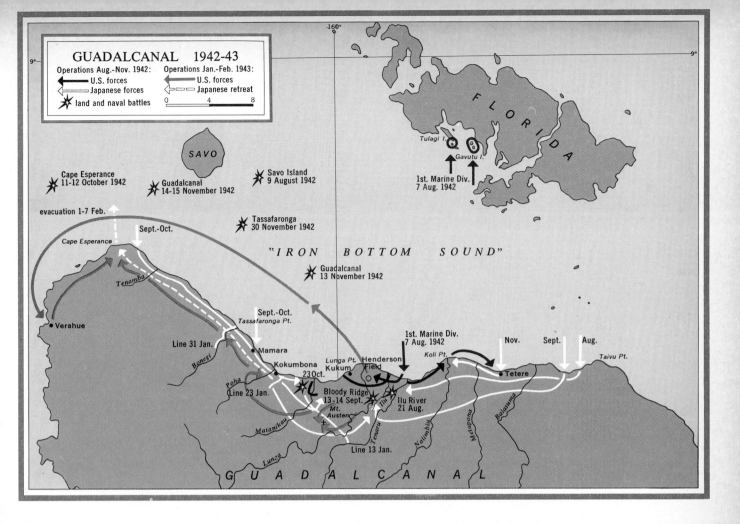

GUADALCANAL 1942-43

Operations Aug.-Nov. 1942:
- ← U.S. forces
- ⇐ Japanese forces
- ✦ land and naval battles

Operations Jan.-Feb. 1943:
- ← U.S. forces
- ⇐--- Japanese retreat

0   4   8

FLORIDA

Tulagi I.

Gavutu I.

1st. Marine Div.
7 Aug. 1942

SAVO

✦ Cape Esperance
11-12 October 1942

✦ Guadalcanal
14-15 November 1942

✦ Savo Island
9 August 1942

evacuation 1-7 Feb.

Sept.-Oct.

✦ Tassafaronga
30 November 1942

"IRON BOTTOM SOUND"

Cape Esperance

Tenamba

✦ Guadalcanal
13 November 1942

Verahue

Sept.-Oct.
Tassafaronga Pt.

Line 31 Jan.

Bonegi

Mamara

Kokumbona
23 Oct.

Poha

Line 23 Jan.

Matanikau

Lunga

Lunga Pt.

Kukum

Henderson
Field

Bloody Ridge
13-14 Sept.

Mt.
Austen

Ilu

Tenaru

Ilu River
21 Aug.

Line 13 Jan.

Nalimbiu

1st. Marine Div.
7 Aug. 1942

Koli Pt.

Metapona

Tetere

Balasuna

Nov.   Sept.   Aug.

Taivu Pt.

GUADALCANAL

The fighting over on Guadalcanal, the Marines set up housekeeping and established a rest and retraining center. Here, under huge

coconut trees, four men of the 3rd Marines stroll the main street of their division headquarters after a typical South Seas "shower."

"...what I'd give for a piece of blueberry pie"

John Hersey on Guadalcanal

In February, 1943, the same month the fighting stopped on Guadalcanal, a small book appeared in the United States titled Into the Valley. *The author was a young magazine journalist named John Hersey. For two weeks during the previous October, he had been with the Marines on Guadalcanal; he had marched with them, swatted mosquitoes and dodged enemy fire with them. His description of jungle combat had an immediate impact back home. But what left the most lasting impression was a little quote about blueberry pie.*

. . . these men looked like the sort you would pick for bodyguard on a dark night. This was especially true if you looked, not at their faces, but at their gear and physique.

The only element of uniformity was their battle dress. "Utilities," as they are called, are of tough green cloth, which will neither tear nor show in the jungle. The shirt has an open collar, loose sleeves, and, over the heart, a patch pocket with the Marine Corps insignia, a globe symbolizing the Marines' ubiquitousness (they are proud of it: *"From the halls of Montezuma to the shores of Tripoli . . ."*). The pants are generous, like overalls. Most of Company H had their pants tucked into their socks, or tied snug around their ankles; many had them tied, as I did, with pieces of captured Japanese straw rope.

But aside from their utilities, they were as various and vicious looking as a bunch of pirates. No two packs were of the same size. Each man brought just what he thought he would want and need. The minimum was a poncho, a canteen, rations and a spoon. More provident men had slipped in a few symbols, at least, of comfort: cigarets in little water-tight tins, salt tablets to com-

pensate for sweat, small first aid packages.

Every man had sneaked along something he thought no one else had—something he had wheedled from the quartermaster or swiped from a store-tent. Before our departure from camp a young captain had taken me into his tent and slipped me two extra bars of Ration D, the chocolate ration, which he said he had gotten never mind where. "In the Marines it's every man for himself as far as equipment goes," he said.

Captain Rigaud's men were certainly armed in this spirit. Each man was weaponed to his own taste and heart's content. Captain Rigaud himself carried one of the handiest of Marine weapons, a Browning automatic rifle. The company's proper weapons, heavy machine guns, were carried dismantled, one man carrying the barrel assembly, another the tripod, and a whole squad the ammunition, in heavy metal boxes. But even some of the men assigned to machine guns carried personal arms. Some of the company had old 1903 bolt-action Springfields. Almost all carried knives, slung from their belts, fastened to their packs, or strapped to their legs. Several had field shovels, which they knew how to swing nastily. Some carried .45-calibre automatic pistols. Pockets bulged with grenades. Some were not satisfied with one bayonet, but carried two. There were even a couple of Japanese bayonets. The greatest refinement was an ugly weapon I spotted in the tunic pocket of a corporal—a twelve-inch screwdriver.

I asked him how he happened to bring that along.

"Oh," he said, "just found it on my person."

"When do you expect to use it?"

"Never can tell, might lose my

bayonet with some Japs in the neighborhood."

But the faces of Captain Rigaud's men were not the faces of bullies. When you looked into the eyes of those boys, you did not feel sorry for the Japs: you felt sorry for the boys. The uniforms, the bravado, the air of wearing a knife in the teeth—these were just camouflage. The truth was all over those faces. . . .

The men stood in a tight little knot right in the trail, where they had discussed the runner's news. . . . Although the conversation might have taken place on any of several fronts, and any military men, from colonel to messboy, might have been the speakers, it would not be fair to identify specific men. . . .

Captain Rigaud started it, by whispering to me, in comment on the confusion: "It's the same as always. They never tell us enough."

"Not only about what we're doing," another said. "We never get anything but the damnedest scuttlebutt about what's going on in the world. We don't even know who's winning."

"Yeah," said a third. "Tell us what's going on." I was their most recent connection with the outside world, and they started pouring out questions.

"Are the Russians holding on?"

I said they had done much better than anyone had thought possible.

"Why the hell isn't Dugout Dug doing anything?"

I said that MacArthur had not been sent any supplies, except for the merest replacements, and no general could do anything with nothing—as he himself had said.

"Well why haven't they sent him anything?"

By this time I realized that they didn't really want answers to their questions. They just wanted to throw out their questions, as if they were merely waving their arms in angry gestures of protest.

"Are we going to be left holding the bag here, like those poor suckers in the Philippines?"

"Why the bejeezus hasn't the Navy had some PT boats in here sooner to stop that godawful shelling at night?"

"They always told us that marines were supposed to take some place, and then the Army would come along right away so as the marines could take something else. Where the hell's all the Army? . . ."

"Can't they do something about the divided command out here? You'd think we were two allies, instead of the most powerful single nation on earth."

"Where's all the power, anyhow? Where's that world-beating P-47 we've heard so much about? Where's that famous new Navy fighter, what is it, the F4U? Where's all that great production?"

The questions became formulas:

". . . strikes . . . ?"

". . . politics . . . ?"

". . . propaganda . . . ?"

This was my chance. Now was the time to ask these men what they were fighting for.

These men were not especial malcontents. I had heard questions like these asked by too many men to think this an outstanding group of complainants. But here they were, perhaps about to give their lives for their country, and yet exercising, until it nearly collapsed from being exercised, the right of free speech. How could men harboring such doubts and such protests fight with enthusiasm? What was there in it for them?

And so I said: "I wonder if I could ask you fellows one question. It's something I've been wondering about quite a bit here on this island.

What would you say you were fighting for? Today, here in this valley, what are you fighting for?"

The excited flush, which had come into their faces as they asked their questions, went out again. Their faces became pale. Their eyes wandered. They looked like men bothered by a memory. They did not answer for what seemed a very long time.

Then one of them spoke, but not to me. He spoke to the others, and for a second I thought he was changing the subject or making fun of me, but of course he was not. He was answering my question very specifically.

He whispered: "Jesus, what I'd give for a piece of blueberry pie."

Another whispered: "Personally I prefer mince."

A third whispered: "Make mine apple with a few raisins in it and lots of cinnamon: you know, Southern style."

Fighting for pie. Of course that is not exactly what they meant. Here, in a place where they had lived for several weeks mostly on captured Japanese rice, then finally had gone on to such delicacies as canned corned beef and Navy beans, where they were usually hungry and never given a treat—here pie was their symbol of home.

In other places there are other symbols. For some men, in places where there is plenty of good food but no liquor, it is a good bottle of scotch whiskey. In other places, where there's drink but no dames, they say they'd give their left arm for a blonde. For certain men, books are the thing; for others, music; for others, movies. But for all of them, these things are just badges of home. When they say they are fighting for these things, they mean that they are fighting for home—"to get the goddam thing over and get home."

349

Slaughter at Sea

From August to November, 1942, the Navy was being hard hit in a seesaw war off Guadalcanal. The enemy was having no easy time of it either. But the United States carrier *Enterprise* had been badly damaged; the carriers *Wasp* and *Hornet* had gone down; and at the Naval Battle of Guadalcanal (November 12–15, 1942), one of the most mixed-up sea fights in history, the United States lost four destroyers and two cruisers, one of which, *Juneau*, went to the bottom with 700 men, including five brothers named Sullivan. But then came the turning point, at the Battle of the Bismarck Sea. Under the cover of strong winds and rain, a Japanese flotilla loaded down with aviation fuel and 7,000 troops had set out from Rabaul to reinforce Japanese units on New Guinea. There were eight destroyers and eight transports. The Army Air Corps on New Guinea had been waiting (even rehearsing) for just such a move. On March 2 and 3, after the foul weather had blown out to sea, American and Australian planes set upon the Japanese ships. The planes were equipped with slow-fused bombs that enabled them to roar in masthead high, "skip" their bombs into the enemy, and pull out before the explosion. The technique was astonishingly effective. All eight transports were knocked out, and four of the destroyers. This was the last time the Japanese would try a major sea-borne troop movement.

At center above, the carrier Hornet burns after being hit by bombs, torpedoes, and suicide planes during the big, indecisive Battle of Santa Cruz, on October 26, 1942. At right, trailing a telltale oil slick, a crippled Japanese destroyer takes evasive action as bombs burst off her bow during the Battle of the Bismarck Sea, called by MacArthur one of the decisive battles of the war.

The Navy's Deadliest Weapon

From Midway until the Japanese surrender, the Navy fought another kind of war in the Pacific, about which the people back home heard very little. Keeping the operations of the "Silent Service" silent was important to its success. And its success was something fantastic: United States subs sank more Japanese tonnage than all other naval and air units combined. In the early part of the war, American torpedoes were faulty, kills few. But by the fall of 1943, the problem had been licked, and the year's tally would be 22 enemy warships sent under, and 296 merchant ships. Japanese defenses against underwater attack were scanty. For some reason or other, the Japanese high command had given a defensive war at sea little thought. About one American sub out of four never came back, but by the spring of 1945, the Japanese life line had been cut.

The "Silent Service" took volunteers only and was noted for its high esprit de corps. One out of every seven submariners lost his life.

United States subs were operating inside enemy home waters, close enough for a periscope view of Mt. Fuji (above), as early as 1943. Below, five American subs head for Pearl Harbor after a 7,000-mile mission. Other bases were in Fremantle and Brisbane, Australia.

Giant Step Around Rabaul

In the summer of 1943, the Allies decided to put off invading Rabaul—the great Japanese stronghold on New Britain—for that year at least, and to outflank it instead by moving up the Solomons to the west, New Guinea to the east. Clearing the Japanese out of the central Solomons took all summer. Then, on November 1, the Marines went ashore on Bougainville, top rung on the Solomons "ladder." Again the battleground was miserable jungle, like that depicted here by combat artist Kerr Eby. But this time the Marines took only enough to build an air strip for strikes against Rabaul, which was hit hard from the air but then bypassed entirely.

Rabaul, Japan's mighty overseas fortress, was almost flattened by continuous air assaults. This extraordinary photograph show

Japanese warships desperately maneuvering out of the harbor for open sea during a carrier-plane strike in November, 1943.

The Tough War in New Guinea

The distance across New Guinea's Papua Peninsula, from Port Moresby on the southern coast to Buna on the northern coast, is only 120 miles by air. But in between are the Owen Stanley Mountains, a jagged, jungle-covered range that rears up well over two miles high. In the summer of 1942, the Australians were concentrated on the southern side of the mountains; the Japanese, after a series of amphibious landings on the northern shore, were pushing inland from Buna. The mountains, the Australians, and the Coral Sea were the last barriers between the oncoming Japanese and Australia. The Australians considered the mountains impassable. But the experienced Japanese jungle fighters, under General Horii, paid no attention to that; despite sickness and heavy casualties, they crossed the Owen Stanleys over the narrow Kokoda Trail and by mid-September were within thirty-two miles of Port Moresby.

Then the Australians counterattacked, along with American reinforcements, and drove the Japanese back over the mountains again. The Japanese retreat turned into a rout. Japanese by the thousands died of starvation and disease; and General Horii was drowned in a river crossing. By November, however, the Allies bogged down at Buna; they too were hollow-eyed with jungle fever and hunger, and casualties had been severe. MacArthur airlifted in some 15,000 fresh troops to help turn the tide. Then, in December, he sent in a new general, Robert L. Eichelberger, telling him to take Buna or not to come back alive. By the end of January, 1943, Buna was in Allied hands.

The Buna campaign was an Army show and did not get as much notice as Guadalcanal, but the fighting was every bit as savage, and the cost in dead and wounded was even higher. The long push up the northern coast of New Guinea, the other side of the great encirclement of Rabaul, began next. New Guinea is the world's second biggest island; the drive would take two more years.

At right above, American tanks and "Aussies" attack enemy bunkers at Cape Endaiadere, near Buna. At right, Allied sick and wounded wait to be moved to the rear by local tribesmen. Allied casualties in the bitterly fought Buna campaign (dead, wounded, or felled by disease) came to a staggering 17,215.

ABOVE: AUSTRALIAN WAR MEMORIAL; BELOW: U.S. ARMY

"We never lost that beachhead"

UPI

General Robert L. Eichelberger

The very able General Eichelberger, though always in or near the thick of the fighting in the Buna campaign, came out of it without a scratch and, perhaps equally remarkable, without a dose of malaria. He had lost thirty pounds in thirty days, but he was fit and ready for new assignments, one of which turned out to be looking after Mrs. Roosevelt during her visit to Australia in August, 1943. The tall, gray-haired Eichelberger was a good judge of friend and foe alike. Of the Australians he said: "When the going is tough, in a brawl or battle, there is no better fighting partner than the man from Down Under." His professional admiration for the Japanese advance over the Owen Stanleys was considerable. "Fortitude is admirable under any flag," he later wrote, "and those Japanese soldiers had it." When Eichelberger first flew into New Guinea, there was some question about the fighting spirit of the American units. His account of the action follows.

I watched the advance from the forward regimental command post, which was about a hundred and twenty-five yards from Buna Village. The troops moved forward a few yards, heard the typewriter clatter of Jap machine guns, ducked down, and stayed down. My little group and I left the observation post and moved through one company that was bogged down.

I spoke to the troops as we walked along. "Lads, come along with us."

And they did. In the same fashion we were able to lead several units against the bunkers at Buna Village. There is an ancient military maxim that a commander must be seen by his troops in combat. When I arrived at Buna there was a rule against officers wearing insignia of rank at the front because this might draw enemy fire. I was glad on that particular day that there were three stars on my collar which glittered in the sun. How else would those sick and cast-down soldiers have known their commander was in there with them? They knew, being sensible men, that a bullet is no respecter of rank. As I wrote to General Sutherland that evening: "The number of our troops who tried to avoid combat today could be numbered on your fingers."

The snipers were there, all right. On one occasion all of us were pinned to the ground for fifteen minutes while tracer bullets cleared our backs with inches to spare. Fifteen minutes, with imminent death blowing coolly on your sweat-wet shirt, can seem like a long time! . . .

There had been one important success in that day's fighting. A platoon of G Company, 126th Infantry, had found a crevice in the Japanese defenses and had driven through to the sea on the narrow spit of land between Buna Village and Buna Mission. The commander of the platoon was Staff Sergeant Herman J. Bottcher, a fine combat soldier. The breakthrough was, possibly, lucky: the holding of the position was accomplished by intelligence and sheer guts.

Bottcher had only eighteen men with him, and he was sure that next morning his toehold on the sea would be attacked from both sides by infuriated Japs. He kept his men at work all night in the darkness. They dug themselves in. Before morning I managed to see to it that ammunition and a few additional men were sent in to the spot. Their one machine gun was emplaced in the sand. It seemed unlikely that this small force could hold off an attack from two sides. But Bottcher, in his calculations, accepted gambler's odds. It was a narrow beach, and he guessed that there would not be simultaneous attacks because of enemy lack of communications.

Bottcher was right. Japanese from Buna Village attacked about dawn, and the machine gun discouraged them. Japanese from Buna Mission attacked in force a while later, wading across the shallows from the other direction. With his hand on the hot machine gun, Bottcher was able to mow them down like wheat in a field. It was sharp and clear daylight when the last attack took place. For days after, the evidence of Sergeant Bottcher's victory rolled in and out with the tide—the evidence was the sea-carried and drifting bodies of Japanese soldiers. Because American newspaper and magazine photographers appeared some days later to snap grim, realistic pictures of the Japanese dead, that stretch of sand between Buna Village and Giropa Point is now identified in history as Maggot Beach, and, if I may say so, with reason.

We never lost that beachhead. On my recommendation the Allied commander commissioned Bottcher as a captain of infantry for bravery on the field of battle. He was one of the best Americans I have ever known. He had been born in Germany and still talked with a faint Germanic accent. A profound anti-Nazi, he came to this country early in the 1930's, took out his first papers, spent a year at the University of California, and then went to Spain to fight against Franco. His combat experience was extremely useful at Buna, and his patriotism as a new American was vigorous and determined. Two years later . . . he was killed in combat in the Philippines campaign.

Bottcher's platoon at Buna had absorbed some of his devil-may-care attitude. Byers, whom I had ap-pointed to succeed the wounded Waldron as commander of the forward elements of the 32nd Division, went forward on the morning of the 6th to confer with the troops who had achieved that heartening success. He chatted with the friendly, bear-like Bottcher, who said they could hold out. Then Byers talked with the thin group of doughboys. He was prepared to promise deliveries of—figuratively speaking—peacock tongues and garlic pickles and hot sausages and beef steaks and turkey, if they would just maintain their hard-won position on the sea.

"What do you need?" Byers demanded.

The American soldier is nonconformist and unpredictable. One member of Bottcher's platoon gave the answer. He turned a half-somersault on the sand and held the pose. Swamp water had rotted away the seat of his trousers and his naked buttocks were exposed. "Pants," said the GI. "For God's sake, General, pants!" . . .

On December 18 tanks and troops jumped off. It was a spectacular and dramatic assault, and a brave one. From the New Strip to the sea was about half a mile. American troops wheeled to the west in support, and other Americans were assigned to mopping up duties. But behind the tanks went the fresh and jaunty Aussie veterans, tall, mustached, erect, with their blazing tommy guns swinging before them. Concealed Japanese positions . . . burst into flame. There was the greasy smell of tracer fire from the snipers' seats in the trees, and heavy machine-gun fire from barricades and entrenchments.

Steadily tanks and infantrymen advanced through the spare, high coconut trees, seemingly impervious to the heavy opposition. There were a hundred and fifty Japanese bunkers on Cape Endaiadere. Three tanks were destroyed by Japanese pompom fire, and infantry casualties were extraordinarily high. . . . I'm sure that Aussie battalion lost nearly half its fighting force in killed and wounded. Nevertheless, the job was done. The sea was reached, and mopping-up began. . . .

Back in the swamp area, American troops were struggling still to cross Entrance Creek. Tanks would have been useless there. Even horse-drawn carts would have bogged down. . . .

Still, Entrance Creek had to be crossed, and I ordered the sore spot of The Triangle "contained" while the fresh troops of the 127th Infantry came forward. They were brisk and free of malaria; they were full of enthusiasm and full of fight. These troops took on the job of crossing Entrance Creek, and I still am proud of them. The job chosen for them in their first introduction to battle was the most difficult of all military maneuvers—a crossing of an unfordable stream under fire at night.

They made it. The first men crossed in small canvas boats and established a narrow bridgehead on the western border of Government Gardens. Then pontoons were laid down, and the anchored boats became stepping-stones. . . . Enemy resistance was stiff; every crossing of the deep stream drew heavy fire; every inch on the east bank was sorely contested. Yet by December 23 the bridgehead had been so enlarged that the Americans could take off from there in an all-out attack next morning.

Now five other companies were poised to make the projected breakthrough between Buna Mission and Giropa Point. For the first time in many days I felt a lightening of spirit and a surge of optimism. . . .

In this painting by Ogden Pleissner, American bombers return to Adak, in the Aleutians, after a raid. Fogs, mud, frost, and howling winds made the islands rough places to run an air war.

At the Northern End of the Pacific

At the start of the war the Japanese and the Americans both saw the cold, barren Aleutian Islands as an obvious way for the other side to invade their homeland. But the Japanese moved first, occupying Attu and Kiska as a diversionary tactic during the Battle of Midway. A year later, the United States sent a huge force to drive them out, bypassing Kiska and landing the Army's 7th Division on Attu on May 11, 1943. The Japanese put up a vicious defense and in final desperation launched a futile 1,000-man suicide assault against American lines. Kiska was next; 34,000 American and Canadian troops moved in on August 15, but much to their surprise found the place deserted. Under the cover of fog, a Japanese task force had slipped by the Navy blockade and had taken off more than 5,000 men in just fifty-five minutes. It was one of the most brilliant evacuations of the war. From then on, the Aleutians were used as American air bases.

With this sign, an English-speaking Japanese marked the grave of an American pilot downed over Kiska. It reads: "Sleeping here, a brave air-hero who lost youth and happiness for his mother land, July 25, Nippon Army." On July 28, the Nippon Army on Kiska pulled out to fight again another day.

U.S. NAVY

363

Above, amphibious LVT's full of Marines grind ashore at Betio, the largest of the tiny coral islets that make up Tarawa and scene of the bloody battle of November 20–23. Note the spray being kicked up by Japanese machine gun bullets. Machine gunners on the LVT's (at right in picture) were fully exposed to enemy fire. On the beach the cover was not much better. At left, loaded down with machine gun ammunition, his helmet on backward, a Marine moves forward on Betio, where the enemy hit back from huge bomb-proofs. Admiral Keiji Shibasaki, the Japanese commander on Betio, had boasted, "A million men cannot take Tarawa in a hundred years." As it was, some 5,600 Marines took it in three days, despite mistakes in planning. At right, dead Marines lie sprawled across the beach. Betio is only two and a half miles long, 600 yards wide. On a per-square-foot basis, few pieces of real estate were ever so dearly paid for. The newspapers called it "Terrible Tarawa"; investigations followed. But countless lives were saved during later assaults because of the lessons learned here.

Costly Lesson at Tarawa

Hydrographic experts had warned Admiral Kelly Turner about the tricky tides around the Gilbert Islands, the sixteen tiny atolls on the equator in the central Pacific. The American offensive for the fall of 1943 called for a strike at the biggest of the Gilberts, Tarawa, on November 20, in the morning. There was a chance the tides would be low then, and the landing craft might run aground on coral ledges offshore; no one could say for sure. Admiral Turner decided to take the risk, and he lost. The first waves of Marines went in on the amphibious tractors that Marines call LVT's or Amtracks (left), and they made it; but after that, the flat-bottomed Higgins boats began clanging onto the reefs, which were covered with only three feet of water. The Marines had to wade in hundreds of yards, under murderous fire. Only about half of them made it.

No one had expected such resistance. The island had been pounded for hours from the sea, and it had been bombed for a full week. But what no one knew before Tarawa was just how well 4,500 Japanese could hold out under bombardment, inside their sand-covered concrete bunkers. Nearly all of the killing had to be done by Marines. The cost was terrible: 991 Marines dead, 2,311 wounded. Of the Japanese force, only seventeen came through alive. But the Americans learned vital lessons about taking heavily fortified coral strongholds. In February, when they moved against Kwajalein to the northwest, they began with two months of bombing; and before any troops went ashore, the Navy lobbed in 15,000 tons of explosives. Moreover, the right sort of landing equipment was used. The American losses were a third of what they were at Tarawa, although Kwajalein was held by twice as many Japanese.

Enter the Seabees

U.S. NAVY

UPI

During an island assault, Seabees kept supplies coming in; the fighting over, they set up camp (right) and with their gigantic machines (above) set to work building a new base.

The Seabee was a professional man. He had been a steam-shovel operator or a carpenter, a plumber or a mining engineer before the war. He liked to describe himself as "a soldier in a sailor's uniform, with Marine training, doing civilian work at WPA wages." The Seabees (or CB's, from the Navy's Construction Battalions) were in on every landing in the Pacific. On Tarawa, on Makin (taken at the time of Tarawa), on Kwajalein and Enewitok in the Marshalls, the Seabees turned acres of smoldering ruins and shell-pocked coral into what looked like tropical boomtowns, and they did it almost overnight. They moved in with bulldozers and earth movers, and plenty of the wonder bug-killer DDT; they built air strips, harbor facilities, roads, bridges, hospitals, everything needed for a modern military base that was, as a sign on Tarawa pointed out, 9,137 miles from Naugatuck, Connecticut.

Italy

The Italian campaign of 1944–45 was a serious strategic error, in my opinion. It was of course both logical and necessary to eliminate Hitler's principal partner in the European war and to gain southern Italy's port facilities and air bases, from which every corner of *Festung Europa* could be bombed. But it was folly to keep on driving up the narrow, mountainous peninsula, where geography favored defense and greatly handicapped any heavily mechanized ground advance.

The argument that the painful Italian thrust pinned down German divisions that otherwise would have been free to fight elsewhere is, I believe, fallacious. Had the Allies been content to hold a river line from the Garigliano across to the Sangro, a line they had reached by mid-January, 1944, they could have mustered from Naples the expedition for their landing in southern France and would have retained the vital air bases at Foggia.

Such a strategy still would have required the Germans to maintain large troop concentrations in Italy, in order to prop up Mussolini's regime in the north and to guard against amphibious end-runs such as that at Anzio. Italy was wide open to naval assaults and landings, a possibility the Nazis were forced to guard against continually.

Churchill always wanted to cross the Adriatic and, with the help of Greek, Yugoslav, and Albanian guerrillas, march up the Balkans and into the Danube Valley. But the United States turned a deaf ear to his proposals, and one ultimate result of the decision to press the Italian campaign was Churchill's subsequent deal with Stalin, dividing the Balkan countries into wartime spheres of influence that lasted on into peace, with only Greece being accorded a dominant Western bias.

The basic decision to attack at Sicily was reached at the Casablanca Conference in January, 1943. That same month, General Mark Clark had activated the U.S. Fifth Army in northern Morocco, while General Alphonse Juin, French commander in North Africa, was forming an Expeditionary Corps of Moroccans, Algerians, and French nationals. (Clark was later to say of them, "A more gallant fighting organization never existed.")

The forces of Clark and Juin were held in reserve for the invasion of mainland Italy. But on July 5, the U.S. Seventh Army under Patton embarked from Oran, Algiers, and Bizerte for Sicily, in an armada commanded by Vice Admiral H. Kent Hewitt. Simultaneously, Montgomery's British Eighth Army sailed from Tripoli, Benghazi, Alexandria, Port Said, and distant Haifa and Beirut. There were nearly 3,000 landing craft and warships, 160,000 troops, 14,000 vehicles, 600 tanks, and 1,800 artillery pieces. Britain undertook to supply 80 per cent of the naval cover and 45 per cent of the air cover required; the rest was assumed by the United States.

For weeks, enemy defenses had been softened up by continued bombing on Sicily, south Italy, Sardinia, and the little cluster of offshore islands that included strongly fortified Pantelleria. Eisenhower had decided to invade Pantelleria as a first step, but on June 11, it had surrendered without a fight after heavy aerial bombardment.

Near Cassino, GIs take on that formidable Axis ally: Italian mud.

The only Allied casualty was a private bitten by a mule. Sicily itself was a far tougher nut: barren, mountainous, and held by three hundred thousand Italian and German soldiers under Field Marshal Alfred Kesselring. Kesselring thought that if Sicily would be Eisenhower's next target, the landing must come on the southwest coast, opposite Tunisia, or on the north coast, close to Messina, the escape route to the mainland.

Just to keep Kesselring confused, the Allies spread rumors of an impending attack on Greece or Sardinia. British intelligence dressed a corpse in a Royal Marines uniform, adorned it with false credentials and "secret" documents indicating that the real assault would come in Greece, and floated the body ashore in Spain. The Spanish authorities immediately handed the faked papers on to Nazi intelligence. This ingenious deception was accompanied by a publicized trip to the Middle East by an actor who looked astonishingly like Montgomery and was dressed in the General's uniform.

On the afternoon of July 9, the invasion armada converged south of Malta, in the midst of heavy seas and thirty-five-mile-an-hour winds. The gale kept blowing as night fell, and the landing faced disaster. But by dawn of the tenth, both gusts and waves subsided. The landing craft pitched through the breakers and began discharging men and machines, including an ingenious new amphibious load-carrier known as DUKW, on Sicily's south coast. Despite the fact that a large number of British airborne troops were drowned when their gliders were prematurely released into the sea, Eisenhower was able to report before noon: "The success of the landings is already assured." Thanks in part to foul weather, the initial lodgment had come as a tactical surprise. Although some German panzers struck back sharply, most of the Italian defenders offered only token resistance. They surrendered in droves or, wearing civilian clothes, vanished into the hills. The Sicilians themselves greeted the invaders joyfully, handing out fruit, flowers, and wine.

Montgomery's Eighth Army slashed up the east coast, swiftly taking ancient Syracuse, and entered the malaria-infested Catanian plain. There, meeting stiff German resistance, the British commander cautiously halted to bring up his main strength—a decision that inspired American complaints. Patton's Seventh Army landed at Gela and Licata in the south and proceeded, according to Patton's theory of war, to "go like Hell." Within two weeks he would drive all the way to Palermo on the northern coast of Sicily, slicing the island in half. On July 20, he was ordered to head for Messina. The Germans withdrew slowly toward the northeast, fighting a dogged defense until mid-August, when sixty thousand of them managed to escape to the toe of Italy across the narrow Strait of Messina. This was a considerable achievement; nevertheless, by the time the American forces took Messina on August 17, the Axis had lost 135,000 prisoners and 32,000 dead or wounded. Allied casualties came to a total of 31,158.

The Allies, whose intelligence from Italy was both accurate and extensive, had prepared the political and psychological machinery to benefit from the collapse of Sicily. On July 17, United States and British aircraft had begun dropping over Rome and other cities leaflets signed by Roosevelt and Churchill: "Mussolini carried you into this war as the satellite of a brutal destroyer of peoples and liberties. Mussolini plunged you into a war which he thought Hitler had already won. In spite of Italy's great vulnerability to attack by air and sea, your Fascist leaders sent your sons, your ships, your air forces, to distant battlefields to aid Germany in her attempt to conquer England, Russia, and the world. . . . The time has now come for you, the Italian people, to consult your own self-respect and your own interests and your own desire for a restoration of national dignity, security, and peace. The time has come for you to decide whether Italians shall die for Mussolini and Hitler—or live for Italy, and for civilization."

Mussolini's control had started to crumble long before the Sicilian landing. As Allied air power had smashed Italian cities and communications, national morale faded; the food situation worsened; strikes and riots broke out in industrial centers. Mussolini's secret police advised him that many ardent Fascists were now conspiring against him: Count Dino Grandi; Marshal Pietro Badoglio, the conqueror of Ethiopia; General Vittorio Ambrosio, Chief of the General Staff.

On July 19, as the British and Americans were smashing across Sicily, Mussolini conferred with Hitler at a villa near Rimini. The *Führer* counseled: "Sicily must be made into a Stalingrad. . . . We must hold out until winter, when new secret weapons will be ready for use against England." But he offered no further reinforcements for the collapsing Italian Army, and the dialogue was punctuated by the bleak news that seven hundred Allied aircraft had bombed Rome.

Five days later, the *Duce* summoned the Fascist Grand Council to the Palazzo Venezia for its first meeting since 1939. In a passionate two-hour speech, he sought to arouse his weary, black-shirted collaborators. But he failed. Grandi had the audacity to introduce a resolution demanding that Mussolini relinquish to King Victor Emmanuel the command of the armed forces. Nineteen of the Fascists supported this motion; seven opposed, and two abstained. Mussolini strode out of the room, aware that his game was up.

The council ended in the early morning hours of Sunday, July 25. Later that day, the angry *Duce* called on Victor Emmanuel, who informed him that he was no longer head of the Government. "The soldiers don't want to fight any more," said the hapless little king. "At this moment you are the most hated man in Italy." When he left the palace, Mussolini was arrested by *carabinièri*, shoved into an ambulance, and smuggled off to internment on the island of Ponza. The king took command of his dissolving military forces and instructed Badoglio to form a new cabinet. The Italian people demonstrated with ferocious joy.

The Allies, although their agents had established contact with anti-Fascist elements at various levels, proved inept and slow-moving at this critical moment. For five weeks they bickered over surrender negotiations. Then, on August 19, General Giuseppe Castellano met American and British military representatives in Lisbon. He made a rather startling offer to switch sides and join the Allies against Germany. Terms accepting this proposal were finally negotiated, approved by the king, and communicated to Eisenhower's headquarters on the first of September. It was planned that they should be announced by Badoglio over the radio on September 8, to coincide with the intended Allied landing that same night on the mainland at Salerno.

Eisenhower drafted an emergency plan for a daring parachute landing on Rome and, on September 7, sent General Maxwell Taylor on a secret visit to the Italian capital to estimate German military strength and how much support the Allies might expect from the Italians. But the venture was dropped. On September 8, at eight o'clock in the evening, Badoglio announced on the radio that the nation was giving up its fight.

Both the *Gestapo* and the *Abwehr* (the intelligence bureau of the German high command) had had advance information of the conspiracy to overthrow Mussolini and had kept abreast of Italy's dealings with the Allies. While the envoys of Eisenhower and Badoglio were negotiating, Hitler had rushed crack units to Kesselring's aid. When the mainland invasion finally came, it was heavily and effectively opposed.

The first lodgment on the Italian peninsula was made by Montgomery's Eighth Army, which on September 3 crossed the Strait of Messina under heavy artillery and air cover and raced northward through Calabria. Six days later, Mark Clark's U.S. Fifth Army disembarked on the sandy beaches along the Gulf of Salerno. Montgomery had a relatively easy time. As his veteran troops fanned northward and eastward, they were joined by six thousand men of the First British Airborne Division, which seized the naval base of Taranto on September 9 and then swept up to the Adriatic port of Bari.

Clark's forces, however, ran into difficulty from the start. They were landed by night without benefit of preliminary shelling, in the hope of achieving surprise. It was believed that by entering Italy as far north as Salerno, they could quickly take nearby Naples. But the German coastal defenses were inviolate. Furthermore, the GIs, having just heard the announcement of Italy's surrender, expected an easy landing. Instead they were met by heavy artillery and tank fire. They found themselves compressed into a small beachhead that extended less than five miles inland. Many assault boats were unable to reach their designated targets. Paratroopers sent to back them up suffered heavy losses en route. German loudspeakers meanwhile kept roaring in English: "Come on in and give up. You're covered." The invasion fleet suffered from confused communications and had trouble discharging heavy weapons. Four days after the landings, Kesselring staged a massive counterattack that almost split the Fifth Army in two. Berlin radio began hailing the prospect of "another Dunkirk."

At this crucial point, from bases in Sicily and North Africa, the U.S. Strategic Air Force began bombing the hills surrounding Salerno, and Montgomery was ordered to speed up his advance in order to relieve the pressure on his beleaguered allies. Clark organized everyone into fighting units: truck drivers, mechanics, and even a regimental band, which defended a hill thenceforth called Piccolo Peak. The Germans began to waver and finally, on September 15, to withdraw to Naples. Clark seized the initiative. Within a month he had unloaded 135,000 troops, 30,000 vehicles, and 100,000 tons of supplies to nourish a northward drive. At the same time, Fighting French troops, aided by local guerrillas, captured Corsica, and the Germans abandoned Sardinia. The bulk of the Italian fleet sailed into Malta for internment.

Italy had by now become a battleground in which the Italians themselves figured only as doleful victims. Badoglio and the king's scheme to switch sides and thus avoid disaster had backfired. In 1940 Mussolini had said: "If the Germans ever get here they will never go home." He was right. Hitler left Kesselring to fight the campaign in the south, sent Rommel to organize northern Italian defenses, and took ruthlessly effective control of all the area not already in Allied hands.

Badoglio and the royal family had fled Rome in a panic on September 9, and had reconstituted the semblance of a government in Brindisi, far to the south. A week later,

Badoglio, the old Fascist, summoned his countrymen "to fight the Germans in every way, everywhere, and all the time." On October 13, Victor Emmanuel formally declared war on Germany. Italy was recognized by the Allies as a "co-belligerent." She was promised that her punishment would be lessened according to the degree of success with which she worked her miserable passage.

The German answer to betrayal, facilitated by five weeks' delay in surrender parleys, was formidable. Nazi military headquarters ordered immediate disarming of all Italian troops. Within an hour of Badoglio's announcement of an armistice, Nazi patrols took over from Salerno to Nice and the Brenner Pass. Italy's Fourth Army on the French border was disbanded. Rommel seized Trieste and the routes to Yugoslavia, thus completing the isolation of thirty-two Italian divisions. Most of these capitulated. It has been estimated that Germany took 640,000 Italian prisoners on the peninsula and in the Balkans; the majority were shipped to Nazi internment camps, where some 30,000 died. Rome capitulated to a threat of *Luftwaffe* bombs, and on September 11, Kesselring proclaimed all Italy a war theater under German control. The Nazis seized Italy's gold reserves and began immediate persecution of those Jews who had managed to survive Mussolini's half-hearted strictions.

While the great mass of Italian soldiers deserted or yielded without a struggle, there were two divisions in southwest Yugoslavia that joined Tito as a "Garibaldi Partisan Division." In France, Albania, and Greece, many Italians linked up with local guerrillas. In northern Italy, partisans achieved a splended record fighting the Nazis. Nevertheless, such determination was rare. Only seven of Italy's sixty-one divisions became available to the Allies, and the morale of these troops was poor, although some forty-eight thousand did take part in the final 1945 drive against the Germans.

Mussolini himself had one more great adventure in store. From Ponza he was removed to a small mountain resort in the Abruzzi, from which Hitler swore to save him. In mid-September, 1943, Otto Skorzeny, the remarkable Nazi commando leader, overran the resort with glider troops and kidnapped the *Duce* in a light airplane. He was thenceforth set up as the puppet head of a Fascist Republic in the north, proclaiming: "I, Mussolini, resume supreme direction of Fascism in Italy." History has paid scant attention to the episode.

Meanwhile, the Fifth Army of General Clark, a tall, hawk-nosed, fearless, ambitious, and incredibly vain commander, had successfully passed its test at Salerno and now drove on Naples, the most important single prize in south Italy. The Germans, fighting a skilled defense, did not bother to defend the city but, taking vengeance for Italy's defection, smashed it and withdrew northward. When the Americans and British entered Naples early on the morning of October 1, they found that the port and everything within three hundred yards of it had been destroyed by the Nazis. The population was half-starved, frightened by looters, and bullied by criminals released from prison by the departing Germans. The grand old university had been deliberately wrecked; hospitals had been looted; and a number of hostages had been taken off. The citizens of Naples gave their Allied conquerors a wild welcome. American engineers set to work on the wreckage and soon had the harbor and neighboring airfields in operation.

To the northeast, Montgomery's Eighth Army had succeeded, against relatively slight opposition, in achieving its initial objectives. The extensive network of airfields at Foggia began furnishing fighter cover to advancing Allied troops as well as dispatching bombers over Austria and the Balkans. But Kesselring, with his fine eye for terrain, established a new position to frustrate Clark on the north bank of the Volturno River, where Garibaldi had won a significant victory in 1860. There began the slow hacking campaign in which, pushing between rock ridges and along muddy valleys through Italy's worst winter in decades, the Allies inched toward Rome and Tuscany.

To pursue this ill-conceived strategy, the Allies installed another team of commanders. Eisenhower had been recalled to England to prepare for the Normandy invasion. With him he took his most renowned generals: Montgomery, Bradley, and Patton. Sir Harold Alexander, who had, with minimal fanfare, supervised Montgomery's operations from the Nile to Tunisia, was left behind as commander in Italy. Under him were Clark and the calm, little-known Sir Oliver Leese, who headed the British Eighth Army on the Adriatic. General Ira Eaker, a tough, poker-faced American, took over the Allied Mediterranean air forces. General Sir Henry "Jumbo" Wilson, whose affable demeanor and swollen shape masked a far greater talent for generalship than history remembers, was given ultimate responsibility for the theater.

Hitler likewise reordered his command. He sent Rommel to France and left Italy to Kesselring, ordering him to hold "at all costs for the sake of the political consequences which would follow a completely successful defense. The *Führer* expects the bitterest struggle for every yard."

Kesselring did what he was told. Clark was slowed up on the Volturno and at successive hilltop villages, but the Allies hoped to outflank the Germans by amphibious tactics. On January 22, 1944, they swept by sea around the right flank of the Germans' Gustav Line and landed two divisions thirty-three miles south of Rome, at the pleasant resort towns of Anzio and Nettuno.

Anzio came close to being a disaster. The initial landing went well, but it was not exploited, and the surprised Germans had ample time to mass troops and artillery around the beachhead's perimeter. Their eventual counterattacks almost succeeded in wiping out the beachhead. The purpose of the landing—to relieve pressure from the main drive along the road to Rome—failed. Churchill, who had endorsed the project, admitted: "The story of Anzio was a story of high opportunity and shattered hopes, of skillful inception on our part and swift recovery by the enemy, of valor shared by both."

The failure at Anzio threw the main weight of the campaign back on the positions around the town of Cassino, hinge of Kesselring's Gustav Line. Apart from its magnificent position along the Liri and Rapido rivers, giving it domination of the narrow valley leading up toward Rome, Cassino was marked by a monastery built on the massif above it by St. Benedict in the sixth century. The historic Abbey of Monte Cassino had been successively ravaged by conquerors and an earthquake in the Middle Ages. It was now to be destroyed again.

From the heights around the abbey, German eighty-eights were picking off Allied armor, while mortars and *nebelwerfers*, dubbed "screaming meemies" by the Americans, were plastering the advancing infantry. The Allied command concluded that the advantages posed by monastery could no longer be ignored. There was a suspicion that Nazi outposts actually had been established within the abbey—although this was later disproved. At any rate, a conclave of generals resolved that the fortress sanctuary must be destroyed. Leaflets were dropped over enemy lines saying: "Against our will we are now obliged to direct our weapons against the Monastery itself. We warn you so that you may now save yourselves. Leave the Monastery at once." And on February 15, the vast abbey was bombed by two hundred and fifty-four planes. Only the cell and tomb of St. Benedict escaped damage.

The attack on this holy shrine achieved nothing but a world-wide wave of protest, which was carefully fanned by German propaganda. The Nazi defenders moved into the ruins and set up impregnable positions amid the shattered masonry. The town of Cassino itself was hit again and again by Allied guns and aircraft. One raid, in which I participated as an observer, involved more aircraft than had yet been used on any operation; the entire town was obliterated in a cloud of flame, smoke, and shattered stone. Yet despite the attacks, when Allied patrols sought to enter Cassino, they were promptly driven back by the expert German First Parachute Division.

That was a winter of deep discontent for Alexander's armies, which included Americans, British, Canadians, French, New Zealanders, South Africans, Poles, Indians, Brazilians, Greeks, Moroccans, Algerians, Senegalese, a brigade of Palestinian Jews, and a handful of royalist Italians. The mud was like glue at midday and like iron in the freezing nights. Cold winds and snow swept the jagged crags. Dead GIs lay in the cratered valley they called Purple Heart, their throats eaten out by scavenger dogs. Trench foot and frostbite were common. A brave battalion of Japanese Americans from Hawaii suffered heavily from the cold; few sights were more pathetic than their tiny cast-off shoes on the monastery slopes. A force of Nepalese Gurkha was cut off for days on an outpost below the abbey. Each day, in this battle in a bowl, American fighter-bombers dropped gaily-colored parachutes with canisters of ammunition, food, and water to the isolated hillmen, who scrambled to secure them amid withering machine-gun fire. Among the most disheartening sights of all was Vesuvius, far to the south of the battle line. The volcano exploded in a sudden eruption that cast an ashen cloud far exceeding anything the Allies, with all their aircraft and artillery, could produce at Cassino.

At last, on May 14, 1944, after a reordering of forces, the Allied command began a new offensive, moving the Fifth and Eighth Armies across the Garigliano and Rapido rivers and breaking Kesselring's Gustav Line after a week of difficult assault. The Polish troops of General Anders, reassembled from prisoner-of-war camps in Russia and allowed to join the British in the Middle East, were given the honor of capturing the abbey. Their role is still marked by a cemetery filled with Polish names.

Once again the Germans began a difficult but orderly withdrawal. The Fifth Army thrust out from its separated Cassino and Anzio positions, entering Rome at last on June 4, 1944, and marching through the Piazza Venezia. Clark, who rode into Rome with the vanguard on June 5, recalls: "There were gay crowds in the streets, many of them waving flags, as our infantry marched through the capital. Flowers were stuck in the muzzles of the soldiers' rifles and of guns on the tanks. Many Romans seemed to be on the verge of hysteria in their enthusiasm for the American troops. . . . It was on this day that a doughboy made the classic remark of the Italian campaign, when he took a long look at the ruins of the Colosseum, whistled softly, and said, 'Gee, I didn't know our bombers had done *that* much damage in Rome.'"

The fall of Rome marked the beginning of the last phase of the European war. Two days later, Eisenhower's forces landed in Normandy and burst through the front door of the *Führer's* Fortress Europe.

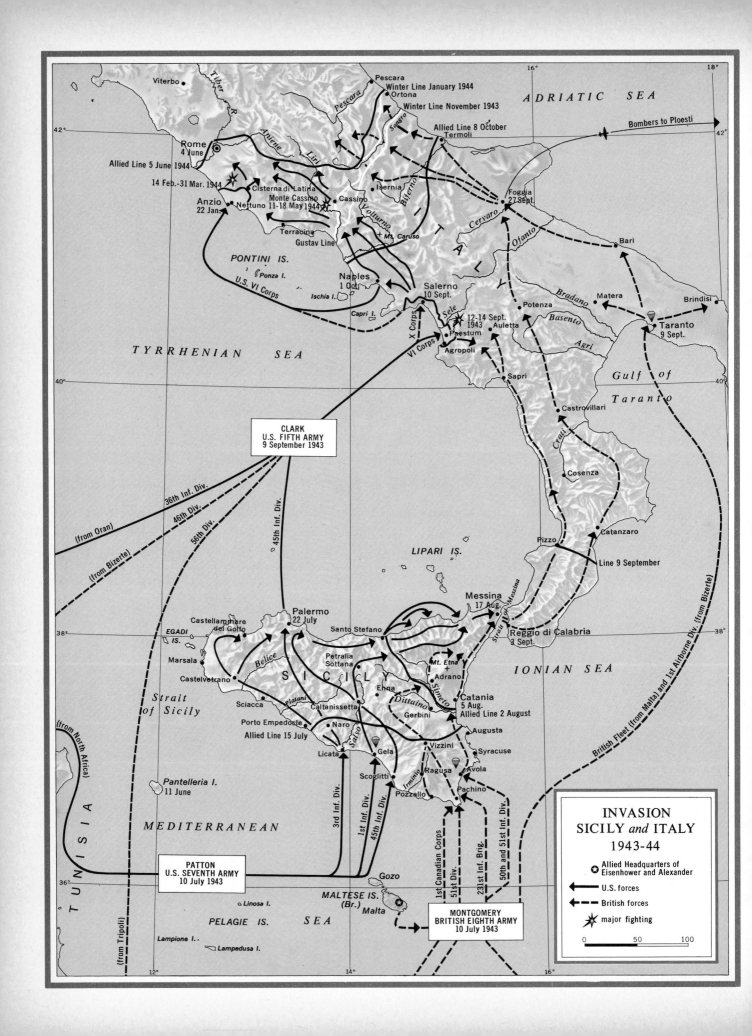

Viterbo •

Pescara
Winter Line January 1944
• Ortona
Winter Line November 1943
ADRIATIC   SEA

Rome
4 June
Allied Line 5 June 1944
Allied Line 8 October
Termoli
Bombers to Ploesti
42°
14 Feb.-31 Mar. 1944
Cisterna di Latina
Monte Cassino
Cassino
Foggia
27 Sept.
Anzio
22 Jan.
Neptuno 11-18 May 1944
Isernia
Cervaro
Ofanto
Bari
Terracina
+ Mt. Caruso
PONTINI IS.
Gustav Line
Naples
1 Oct
Salerno
10 Sept.
Bradano
Matera
Brindisi
Ponza I.
Ischia I.
Sele
12-14 Sept.
1943
Auletta
Basento
Taranto
9 Sept.
U.S. VI Corps
Capri I.
Paestum
Agropoli
Agri
40°
TYRRHENIAN   SEA
Sapri
Gulf   of
Taranto
CLARK
U.S. FIFTH ARMY
9 September 1943
Castrovillari
36th Inf. Div.
(from Oran)
46th Div.
56th Div.
Cosenza
(from Bizerte)
Pizzo
Catanzaro
Line 9 September
LIPARI IS.
Messina
17 Aug.
Reggio di Calabria
3 Sept.
IONIAN   SEA
Castellammare
del Golfo
Palermo
22 July
Santo Stefano
EGADI
IS.
Petralia
Sottana
Marsala
Castelvetrano
SICILY
Belice
Mt. Etna
+
Adrano
Ehna
Sciacca
Platani
Caltanissetta
Dittaino
Gerbini
Catania
5 Aug.
Allied Line 2 August
Strait
of Sicily
Porto Empedocle
Naro
Simeto
Augusta
(from North Africa)
Allied Line 15 July
Licata
Scalso
Gela
Vizzini
Syracuse
Pantelleria I.
11 June
Scoglitti
Irminio
Ragusa
Avola
Pachino
MEDITERRANEAN
3rd Inf. Div.
1st Inf. Div.
45th Inf. Div.
Pozzallo
PATTON
U.S. SEVENTH ARMY
10 July 1943
Gozo
36°
(from Tripoli)
Linosa I.
MALTESE IS.
(Br.)
Malta
1st Canadian Corps
51st Div.
231st Inf. Brig.
50th and 51st Inf. Div.
British Fleet (from Malta) and 1st Airborne Div. (from Bizerte)
PELAGIE IS.
SEA
MONTGOMERY
BRITISH EIGHTH ARMY
10 July 1943
Lampione I.
Lampedusa I.

INVASION
SICILY and ITALY
1943-44

⊕ Allied Headquarters of
Eisenhower and Alexander

━━► U.S. forces

┅┅► British forces

✷ major fighting

0   50   100

Soft Underbelly?

Authorized at Casablanca in January, 1943, the Allied invasion of Sicily in July was to be a campaign of limited objectives, aimed at freeing Mediterranean shipping from Axis harassment, diverting German strength from the Russian front, and increasing the pressure on Italy to desert Hitler. It was also hoped that Messina, on Sicily's northeast coast, could be seized fast enough to seal off the third of a million Axis troops on the island before they could escape across the two-mile-wide Straits to the mainland. Churchill, however, saw the invasion as a preliminary to an attack on Italy, the "soft underbelly" of Europe, and his view finally prevailed. But as Samuel Eliot Morison later wrote, "the underbelly proved to be boned with the Apennines, plated with the hard scales of Kesselring's armor, and shadowed by the wings of the Luftwaffe." From Salerno to Anzio to Cassino, "sunny Italy" would provide some of the hardest fighting of the war. Muddy plains, snow-choked mountains, and the freezing cold of an exceptionally severe Italian winter proved to be among the most effective collaborators that the soldiers of the Third Reich ever had.

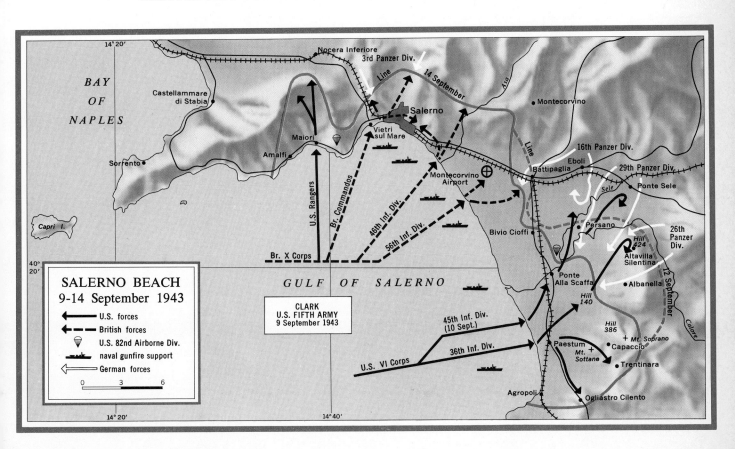

SALERNO BEACH
9–14 September 1943

← U.S. forces
← British forces
U.S. 82nd Airborne Div.
naval gunfire support
German forces

0   3   6

CLARK
U.S. FIFTH ARMY
9 September 1943

Operation Husky

At dawn on the tenth of July, the Allies disembarked a powerful invasion force on five beaches along the southern coast of Sicily. An attack had been expected by the enemy, but the locations and the timing of the landings (the morning after a strong mistral) took them by surprise. German tanks and planes were rushed in to bolster the Italian shore defenses, but deadly fire support from the offshore Allied armada, the perseverance of the sailors who manned the landing craft, the heroism of paratroopers and infantrymen, and the sheer size of the offensive made the success of Operation Husky inevitable. By the end of the next day, 80,000 troops and some 8,000 vehicles had been put ashore; on the twelfth, Kesselring flew to Rome to tell Mussolini that the island would soon be in Allied hands. It was not, however, to be an easy victory. Although Patton's Seventh Army speedily overran western Sicily, it did so only after a series of small but fierce engagements on rocky terrain that made even unopposed travel arduous. And Montgomery's Eighth Army, after capturing Syracuse on the east coast, was temporarily pinned down by strong Axis defense on the malarial plains south of Catania.

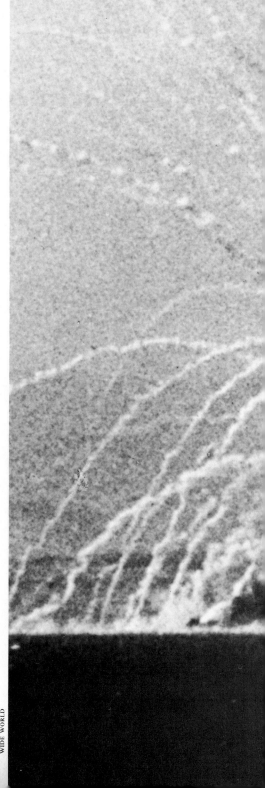

Above, landing craft bearing men of the 3rd Infantry Division approach the beach at Licata, Sicily. To the east, off Gela, German dive bombers blasted the invasion fleet and scored a direct hit on an American ammunitions ship (right). At left is Field Marshal Kesselring—nicknamed "Smiling Alfred" by the Allies—who commanded Axis troops on Sicily, including the highly-vaunted Hermann Göring Division.

On July 22, just twelve days after the initial Allied landings on Sicily, tanks of the Seventh Army rolled into Palermo. Patton's

...men were welcomed by the capital's jubilant residents, who waved flags and shouted "Long live America" and "Down with Mussolini."

Above left are General Maxwell Taylor and Marshal Badoglio, during the former's secret visit to Rome, September 7, 1943. Warned by the Italians that German strength around the capital was formidable, Taylor advised Eisenhower to cancel an air-borne assault planned for the eighth. Italy's king, Victor Emmanuel, is at top right. Below is Mussolini, with the German paratroopers who, on September 12, 1943, freed him from imprisonment in a resort hotel at Gran Sasso, and, at bottom, with Hitler, who welcomed him to Vienna after his liberation and set him up as a puppet dictator.

Il Duce Falls

As Allied troops moved across Sicily, Mussolini was at Rimini in northern Italy begging Hitler for more troops to resist the now-certain invasion of Italy. Hitler gave him only empty promises, and an exhausted and disheartened *Duce* returned to Rome and his downfall. On July 24, black-uniformed members of the Fascist Grand Council met to depose him and, they hoped, to save their own skins while there was still time. Formally stripped of power by King Victor Emmanuel, Mussolini was arrested on the twenty-fifth and spirited off to the first of a series of isolated prisons, while Marshal Pietro Badoglio, hero of the early Fascist victory in Ethiopia, became head of the Italian Government. Six days later, American and British forces on Sicily linked up south of Mount Etna and began the final and toughest phase of Operation Husky. Pursuing the elite German troops from crag to crag, they pushed toward Messina. Allied engineers performed miracles, throwing trestles over deep gaps after the retreating enemy had destroyed bridges. Masses of heavy equipment had to be moved over narrow, primitive roads. At Troina, more than a dozen desperate German counterattacks were thrown back. On August 17, the Allies took Messina, and the island was theirs, although naval and air forces failed to prevent the escape to Italy of some 60,000 German troops. Meanwhile, Badoglio was busy negotiating for a surrender that would allow Italy to declare war on Germany. The Allies, determined to avoid criticism such as had followed their dealings with the unsavory Darlan in Africa, demanded an unconditional armistice. Finally, on September 3, the same day that Montgomery's army crossed to the mainland and began marching north, the Italians formally agreed to the Allied terms. On September 8, Badoglio announced the surrender, an hour and a half after Eisenhower had broadcast the same news to the troops aboard ships bound for Salerno.

At right, an American private quaffs a drink given to him by a policeman in Troina, a town in north-central Sicily. The entire island was captured by the Allies by August 17, much to the relief of the German-hating Sicilians.

Salerno

To achieve surprise at Salerno, the Allies decided to go in without preliminary bombing; but the Germans were waiting for them with all the strength that Kesselring could muster. Salerno, however, was not, as the Nazis had hoped, another Dunkirk. The invasion began at 3:30 A.M. on September 9; with incredible courage, the Fifth Army fought its way up the beaches, around or over mines, barbed wire, machine-gun emplacements, tanks, and fallen bodies. Of crucial importance was the gunfire from American and British ships and, later, from the air forces. When a ferocious German attack, beginning on the thirteenth, failed to cut down the invaders, and when an advance group from the Eighth Army approached from the south, the Germans began their fighting retreat to the north bank of the Volturno River.

General Mark Clark, above with General Gerald Templer of the British 56th Infantry Division, led the Fifth Army at Salerno. At right is the American beachhead at Paestum. Despite Nazi tanks and mobile guns, soldiers of the VI Corps reached Monte Soprano, at top right, by nightfall on September 9. The ancient watchtower, built by the Greeks, is shown at lower right.

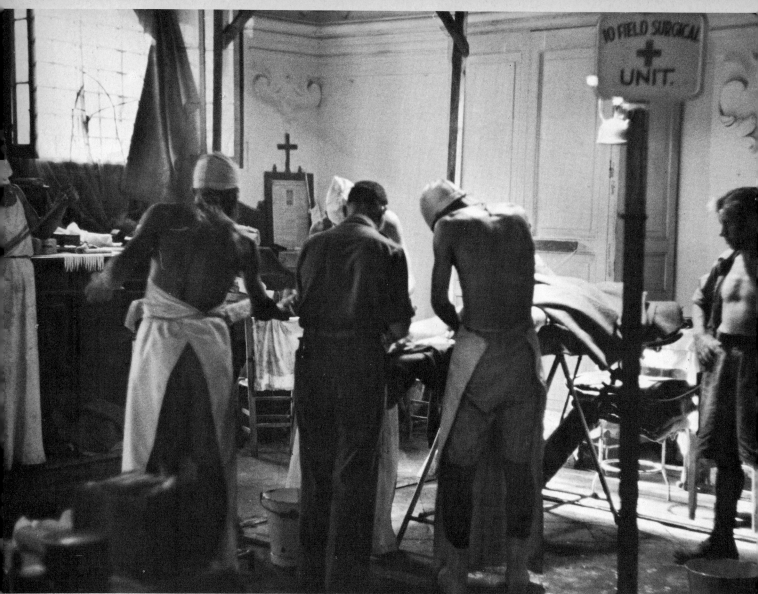

ROBERT CAPA, *Images of War,* ©1964

Modern War amid Ancient Reminders

This was a far different place to fight a war than North Africa had been. The people seemed "more civilized" one GI said. What he may have meant was that Italy showed signs almost everywhere of a heritage and a way of life that the Allied armies were fighting for. Few men, of course, had much time to think of it quite that way. A massive temple built by the Greeks several hundred years before Christ was some sight, to be sure, but it was also as good a spot as any to set up a field headquarters. A little church in a shell-gutted Italian village certainly stood for everything that the Nazi was not, but for the moment it made a first-rate place to bring the wounded—and in those last weeks of September, during the drive on Naples, the wounded were coming back from the front in alarming numbers. But by October, Naples and its deep-water port were in Allied hands, and the British Eighth Army had secured the air base at Foggia, on the other side of the Italian peninsula. Phase one of the Italian campaign was over. Now came the hard push to Rome.

At right, close by to the landing beaches at Paestum, the ancient Greek Temple of Neptune is put to use as an American Army field headquarters. (On page 383, the temple can be seen at right center.) Above, a Fifth Army surgeon operates on a wounded GI inside a church at Maiori, where bitter fighting took place as the Germans withdrew northward to Naples.

"Dead men had been coming down the mountain all evening"

Ernie Pyle

The Allies entered Naples on October 1; Rome was only 100 miles to the north, but it was to be eight more grueling months before the men of the Allied armies would reach the Eternal City. Of the correspondents who covered this phase of the war in Italy, the most famous and the best liked by the men he wrote about was Ernie Pyle. The following excerpt, from his book Brave Men, *was an attempt to explain why the progress of the war in Italy was so slow.*

Our troops were living in almost inconceivable misery. The fertile black valleys were knee-deep in mud. Thousands of the men had not been dry for weeks. Other thousands lay at night in the high mountains with the temperature below freezing and the thin snow sifting over them. They dug into the stones and slept in little chasms and behind rocks and in half-caves. They lived like men of prehistoric times, and a club would have become them more than a machine gun. How they survived the dreadful winter at all was beyond us who had the opportunity of drier beds in the warmer valleys. . . .

You've heard of trench mouth and athlete's foot, but still another occupational disease of warfare sprang up on both sides in the Italian war. It was called "trench foot," and was well known in the last war. . . .

Trench foot comes from a man's feet being wet and cold for long periods and from not taking off his shoes often enough. In the mountains the soldiers sometimes went for two weeks or longer without ever having their shoes off or being able to get their feet dry. The tissues gradually seem to go dead, and sores break out. It is almost the same as circulation stopping and the flesh dying. In extreme cases gangrene occurs. We had cases where amputation was necessary. And in others soldiers couldn't walk again for six months or more. . . .

Sometimes the men let trench foot go so long without complaining that they were finally unable to walk and had to be taken down the mountain in litters. Others got down under their own power, agonizingly. One boy was a day and a half getting down the mountain on what would normally be a two-hour descent. He arrived at the bottom barefooted, carrying his shoes in his hand, his feet bleeding. He was in a kind of a daze from the pain.

The fighting on the mountaintop almost reached the caveman stage sometimes. Americans and Germans were frequently so close that they actually threw rocks at each other. Many more hand grenades were used than in any other phase of the Mediterranean war. And you have to be pretty close when you throw hand grenades.

Rocks played a big part in the mountain war. Men hid behind rocks, threw rocks, slept in rock crevices, and even were killed by flying rocks.

When an artillery shell bursts on a loose rock surface, rock fragments are thrown for many yards. In one battalion fifteen per cent of the casualties were from flying rocks. Also, now and then an artillery burst from a steep hillside would loosen big boulders which went leaping and bounding down the mountainside for thousands of yards. The boys said such a rock sounded like a windstorm coming down the mountainside.

When soldiers came down the mountain out of battle they were dirty, grimy, unshaven and weary. They looked ten years older than they were. They didn't smile much. But the human body and mind recover rapidly. After a couple of days down below they began to pick up. It was a sight to see a bunch of combat soldiers after they had shaved and washed up. As one said, "We all look sick after we've cleaned up, we're so white."

It was funny to hear them talk. One night in our cowshed I heard one of them tell how he was going to keep his son out of the next war. "As soon as I get home I'm going to put ten-pound weights in his hands and make him jump off the garage roof, to break down his arches," he said. "I'm going to feed him a little ground glass to give him a bad stomach, and I'm going to make him read by candlelight all the time to ruin his eyes. When I get through with him he'll be double-4 double-F."

In this war I have known a lot of officers who were loved and respected by the soldiers under them. But never have I crossed the trail of any man as beloved as Captain Henry T. Waskow, of Belton, Texas.

Captain Waskow was a company commander in the Thirty-sixth Division. He had led his company since long before it left the States. He was very young, only in his middle twenties, but he carried in him a sincerity and a gentleness that made people want to be guided by him.

"After my father, he came next," a sergeant told me.

"He always looked after us," a soldier said. "He'd go to bat for us every time."

"I've never known him to do anything unfair," another said.

I was at the foot of the mule trail the night they brought Captain Waskow down. The moon was nearly full, and you could see far up the trail. . . .

Dead men had been coming down the mountain all evening, lashed onto the backs of mules. They came lying belly-down across the wooden packsaddles, their heads hanging down on one side, their stiffened legs sticking out awkwardly from the other, bobbing up and down as the mules walked. . . .

I don't know who the first one was. You feel small in the presence of dead men, and you don't ask silly questions.

They slid him down from the mule, and stood him on his feet for a moment. In the half-light he might have been merely a sick man standing there leaning on the others. Then they laid him on the ground in the shadow of the stone wall alongside the road. We left him there beside the road, that first one, and we all went back into the cowshed and sat on water cans or lay on the straw, waiting for the next batch of mules.

Somebody said the dead soldier had been dead for four days, and then nobody said anything more about it. We talked soldier talk for an hour or more; the dead man lay all alone, outside in the shadow of the wall.

Then a soldier came into the cowshed and said there were some more bodies outside. We went out into the road. Four mules stood there in the moonlight, in the road where the trail came down off the mountain. The soldiers who led them stood there waiting.

"This one is Captain Waskow," one of them said quietly.

Two men unlashed his body from the mule and lifted it off and laid it in the shadow beside the stone wall. Other men took the other bodies off. Finally, there were five lying end to end in a long row. You don't cover up dead men in the combat zones. They just lie there in the shadows until somebody comes after them.

The unburdened mules moved off to their olive grove. The men in the road seemed reluctant to leave. They stood around, and gradually I could sense them moving, one by one, close to Captain Waskow's body. Not so much to look, I think, as to say something in finality to him and to themselves. I stood close by and I could hear.

One soldier came and looked down, and he said out loud, "God damn it!"

That's all he said, and then he walked away.

Another one came, and he said, "God damn it to hell anyway!" He looked down for a few last moments and then turned and left.

Another man came. I think he was an officer. It was hard to tell officers from men in the dim light, for everybody was bearded and grimy. The man looked down into the dead captain's face and then spoke directly to him, as though he were alive, "I'm sorry, old man."

Then a soldier came and stood beside the officer and bent over, and he too spoke to his dead captain, not in a whisper but awfully tenderly, and he said, "I sure am sorry, sir."

Then the first man squatted down, and he reached down and took the captain's hand, and he sat there for a full five minutes holding the dead hand in his own and looking intently into the dead face. And he never uttered a sound all the time he sat there.

Finally he put the hand down. He reached over and gently straightened the points of the captain's shirt collar, and then he sort of rearranged the tattered edges of the uniform around the wound, and then he got up and walked away down the road in the moonlight, all alone.

The rest of us went back into the cowshed, leaving the five dead men lying in a line end to end in the shadow of the low stone wall. We lay down on the straw in the cowshed, and pretty soon we were all asleep.

Siege at Anzio

"I had hoped that we were hurling a wildcat onto the shore, but all we got was a stranded whale." Thus did Winston Churchill describe the Allied landings at Anzio and Nettuno on January 22, 1944. The invasion was designed to surprise the Germans by making an end run around the Gustav Line, followed by a fast breakout to the Alban Hills and the road to Rome. But the American VI Corps paused for ten days to consolidate the beachhead before pushing inland, and the Anzio forces soon found themselves pinned down. The *Luftwaffe* swept into action, and Nazi reserve forces were rushed in from quiet sectors on the Gustav Line, over roads and bridges that the Allies thought had been irreparably damaged by their air forces. For almost four months, the invaders remained trapped on the beachheads, every foot of which was vulnerable to the German artillery on the nearby hills. Foxholes, the usual refuge from bombardments, were often completely filled by rain water; surface shelters built of sandbags and the few buildings that had not been smashed to rubble were the only protection. Not until May 11, when a massive assault was launched by both the Fifth and Eighth armies along the Gustav Line, were the men at Anzio able to break out. All told, they suffered some 59,000 casualties, more than half of which were caused by disease, exhaustion, and the strain of waiting to see where the next shell would explode.

Lieutenant General Lucian Truscott (left) was the stern but admired leader of the 3rd Division at the Anzio landing. On February 23, he replaced the commander of the VI Corps, Major General John P. Lucas (above), who was criticized for not moving rapidly from the beach after the invasion. His decision to consolidate has been defended, however, by those who feel he had too few men for any other move. At right, LST's unload men on the shell-blasted streets of Anzio, which had been a popular Italian resort.

Winter Stalemate

Above, while a friend covers him, a Scottish soldier kicks open the door of a house in the mountain town of Colle, Italy. At left, men of the 141st Infantry Regiment fire an 81-mm. mortar while the Allied forces cross the Rapido River on May 12.

Moving troops freely between Anzio and the Gustav Line, General Kesselring held off the Allies through the hard winter of 1943–44. From well-fortified positions in the mountains, the Germans poured their fire down on the attackers day after day. For all the modern weapons used by both sides, it was a strange, old-fashioned kind of war: trucks and tanks were rendered virtually useless by mud, snow, and mountains; supplies were moved by mules, and men lived not unlike they did in World War I. For both sides, it was a bloody, nerve-racking, and seemingly endless business. But with the approach of spring, the Allies moved to break the stalemate. In April, the Strategic Air Forces flew 21,000 sorties against bridges, railroads, and other German supply lines. The British Eighth Army, commanded by Sir Oliver Leese since Montgomery had been called to England, relieved Clark's Fifth Army at positions along the Gustav Line, so that the Americans were free to move up the Tyrrhenian coast toward Anzio. The big offensive started on May 11; the next day the Allies crossed the Garigliano and Rapido rivers, and the German line began to crumble. Then, on May 18, came word that Cassino had fallen.

Above: the abbot of Monte Cassino with German soldiers. The abbot and a few priests remained in a subterranean chapel throughout the bombing.

Cassino

Guarding the inland road to Rome were the town of Cassino and the heavily-fortified mountains behind it. From the peaks, especially the one on which the famed monastery at Monte Cassino sat, the Germans had a clear view of everything below. For four months, in the worst of weather, the Allies suffered tremendous casualties in vain efforts to overwhelm the defenders; even the bombing of the abbey was futile. Finally, in May, Polish and British troops captured what had become a symbol of Nazi invulnerability.

Rebuilt in the fourteenth century on the site of the monastery founded in 529, Monte Cassino was pulverized by 500 tons of Allied bombs on February 14, 1944 (above). The tomb and cell of St. Benedict, the abbey's founder, remained intact amidst the ruins (below).

On May 23, as the Eighth Army continued its push up the Italian boot, the Fifth Army forces at Anzio smashed through the German defenses. Two days later, Truscott's men captured Cisterna and joined up with the rest of the Fifth, and on the fourth of June, General Mark Clark led the American forces into Rome. (At left, U.S. tanks pass the Colosseum; at right, an American private receives a grateful welcome.) But glorious as the day was, the war in Italy would go on for almost a year.

"Th' hell this ain't th' most important hole in th' world. I'm in it."

Over Here

When American troops went into action in North Africa and Italy, their abilities were assayed with considerable curiosity by their more experienced allies and enemies. Britain's Chief of Staff, Sir Alan Brooke, decided: "The Americans had a lot to learn. . . . But in the art of war . . . when they once got down to it they were determined to make a success of it." Field Marshal Rommel reflected afterward: "What was really amazing was the speed with which the Americans adapted themselves to modern warfare. They were assisted in this by their tremendous practical and material sense and by their lack of all understanding for tradition and useless theories." He concluded: "Starting from scratch an army has been created in the very minimum of time, which, in equipment, armament and organization of all arms, surpasses anything the world has yet seen."

The fact was that U.S. Armed Forces were built, to use Rommel's phrase, "in a minimum of time," out of whatever the draft boards were able to send along. Those whom Alan Brooke saw as "determined to make a success of it" were the standard U.S. Government Issues, the very nonmilitary male civilian Americans, the GIs. In the early years of the war, the Navy and the Marine Corps were fleshed out with volunteers only. But the American soldier was in uniform because he had no other choice. He had to be taught how to fight, and once taught, he had no great desire to fight; but, at the same time he had no doubt that he would win.

This average American soldier of World War II was taller and heavier than his father who had fought in World War I. When he went off to serve his country, he had had some high school education; he knew how to drive a car, how to swim, how to do the jitterbug or the Big Apple or the Lindy. He usually came from a city or big town. Chances were he had never fired a rifle; he spoke no other language than his own; and as yet he had not learned how to shoot craps. Once in the hands of the Army, he was given a remarkably fast haircut at no charge, then punctured with innoculations, garbed in a floppy olive-drab outfit called "fatigues," and put under the tutelage of a hard-cussing buck sergeant who barked weird commands and soon had him throwing out his chest and talking in a jargon that he would remember for the rest of his life.

One of the best descriptions of this process was written by a draftee from North Carolina named Marion Hargrove. In his best-selling book on life at Fort Bragg, *See Here, Private Hargrove*, he included an anonymous letter that was going the rounds of his company:

"Dear, unfortunate civilian friend: I am very enthusiastic about Army life. We lie around in bed every morning until at least six o'clock. This, of course, gives us plenty of time to get washed and dressed and make the bunks, etc., by 6:10. At 6:15 we stand outside and shiver while some (deleted) blows a bugle. After we are reasonably chilled, we grope our way through the darkness to the mess hall. Here we have a hearty breakfast consisting of

SPAM

an unidentified liquid and a choice of white or rye crusts.

"After gorging ourselves with this delicious repast, we waddle our way back to the barracks. We have nothing to do until 7:30 so we just sit around and scrub toilets, mop the floors, wash windows and pick up all the match sticks and cigarette butts within a radius of 2,000 feet of the barracks.

"Soon the sergeant comes in and says, 'Come out in the sunshine, kiddies!' So we go out and bask in the wonderful North Carolina sunshine—of course, we stand knee-deep in the wonderful North Carolina sand. To limber up, we do a few simple calisthenics, such as touching your toes with both feet off the ground and grabbing yourself by the hair and holding yourself at arm's length.

"At eight o'clock we put on our light packs and go for a tramp in the hills. The light pack includes gun, bayonet, canteen, fork, knife, spoon, meat cans, cup, shaving kit, pup tent, raincoat, cartridge belt, first aid kit, fire extinguisher, tent pins, rope, tent pole, hand ax, small spade, and a few other negligible items. Carrying my light pack, I weigh 217¼ pounds. I weighed 131 pounds when I left home, so you can see how easy it is to gain weight in the Army."

As Hargrove himself pointed out, the only weak spot in the letter was the part about breakfast. As a matter of fact, U.S. Army meals, even at the front, were, for the most part, pretty good. "A" rations, served in areas where food could be preserved under refrigeration, were excellent. The combat rations "C" and "K," though still recalled with horror by millions of American men, were superior to those provided by other armies. The "C" ration included ten different meat compounds (the most celebrated of them being the ubiquitous Spam), stews, spaghetti, vegetables, dehydrated eggs and potatoes. The "K" comprised ingenious compounds that, if nothing else, were nourishing. Also among the combat food was the famous "D" bar, which was hard as a rock and took about half an hour to gnaw through. The main trouble with the diet was that it was monotonous. Men wrote home desperately for anything spicy, anything that had flavor. The greatest gifts for "the boys overseas" were fruitcakes, jam, and salami.

As the immense machinery for turning civilians into soldiers picked up speed and units became ready to head for the Pacific, Africa, and England, the War and Navy Departments thoughtfully issued them pocket guidebooks with tips on how to get along overseas. Those who were bound for Britain were advised: "The British don't know how to make a good cup of coffee. You don't know how to make a good cup of tea—It's an even swap"; and a special glossary explained that in England, dust bin means ash can, lift is elevator, first floor is second floor, flicks are movies, and a dickey is a rumble seat. Soldiers embarking for North Africa were cautioned that Muhammadans are not "heathens," and that when indulging in a local meal, "it is advisable not to drink much liquid after eating *kuskus* as the grain is only partly cooked and bloating will result." They were also admonished: "If you enter a bakery, leave your shoes at the door. . . . Never try to remove the veil [from a Moslem woman]. This is most important. Serious injury if not death at the hands of Moslem men may result. . . ."

Once overseas, the GI was kept in touch with relatives and friends at home by V-mail—little letters that could reach even the most outlandish destination in about ten days—and by miniature overseas editions of magazines and books. He was looked after by the Red Cross, which, along with collecting blood plasma, making bandages, and recruiting nurses, set up "clubmobiles" where girls served coffee and doughnuts. The U.S.O. put on dances and stage shows for him, and sent such Hollywood celebrities as Joe E. Brown, Bing Crosby, Bob Hope, Jo Stafford, and Frances Langford to far-flung desert and jungle

SGT. GEORGE BAKER

sites and to the Aleutian Islands. They gave the lonely GI a laugh or the rare chance to let fly with a wolf call. Bob Hope endeared himself to hundreds of wounded men by coming up to their beds and saying: "Hi. Did you see my show tonight or were you already sick?"

To keep the American soldier fit and fighting, an array of new drugs and preventive medicines was developed. Special clothing—jackets, boots, headgear—were devised to protect him against extremes of temperature and terrain. To keep him out of trouble, especially when he went on leave, a police force was set up; its white belts, gloves, leggings, helmet liners and "MP" armbands became well-known symbols around the world. And to advise "the folks back home" on his latest doings, a force of some seven hundred correspondents was mustered by American newspapers, magazines, and radio stations. During 1944 alone, they sent back some two hundred million words from the battlefronts. (The Normandy landings alone were reported by some four hundred and fifty correspondents.) They traveled by landing craft, tank, truck, jeep, mule, and foot through Italy, France, Germany, and, island by island, across the Pacific. They wrote about the men who were making the decisions that affected the GI's life—Eisenhower, Bradley, Patton, Arnold, and Spaatz in Europe; MacArthur, Nimitz, Halsey, Smith, Vandegrift in the Pacific. For millions of mothers and fathers, wives and sweethearts, knowing just who these commanders were was vitally important.

But the man about whom the most was written was, inevitably, the man who was himself commanded, who did the bulk of the fighting even in an age of mechanized war: the nearly always uncomfortable, unromantic, anonymous infantryman, the GI. Various correspondents evaluated his professional skills. A *New York Times* reporter, for example, wrote:

"The Americans were not as good campaigners—as differentiated as fighters—as the British. Nor would they adopt the attitude that war is a natural part of life, held by the French soldiers. . . . They were unhappy in defensive fighting, at their best in a big push forward. The only emotion they would show was a deep pride in their combat team or division, a burning desire to see that it 'did the job.'

"In action the American attacked silently, not singing as did the British or shouting as did the French. . . . There were German prisoners who testified to the fear of these silent soldiers moving remorselessly forward that grew in the ranks of the German divisions."

Other correspondents described the terror of war, its filth, fear, and loneliness, its comradeship, heroism, and humor; the hours and hours of boredom, and the moments of indescribable exhilaration. There was John Hersey on Guadalcanal, Joe Liebling in North Africa; there were John Dos Passos, Ernest Hemingway, John Steinbeck, Ed Murrow, and others less famous. Some were killed. Of these, perhaps the best, and certainly the GI's own personal favorite, was a middle-aged newspaperman named Ernie Pyle, who wrote with compassion and distinction and who followed the "mud-rain-frost-and-wind-boys," as he called them, right up until the day that he was shot and killed by a sniper's bullet on the Pacific island of Ie Shima.

Pyle wrote: "I believe that I have a new patience with humanity that I've never had before. . . . I don't see how any survivor of war can ever be cruel to anything, ever again." When he was buried, the following inscription was put on his grave marker: "At This Spot the 77th Infantry Division Lost a Buddy. Ernie Pyle. 18 April 1945."

Among the hardiest of those who sought to describe the war were the photographers, many of whom were in the heart of the action, and who, often as not, remained anonymous. Perhaps the best of them was Hungarian-

born Robert Capa—who survived the war, despite the risks he took, only to be killed in Indochina in 1954. Capa was determined to immortalize "the little man whose future was at stake in a world he could not change."

Sergeant George Baker was another who set out to accomplish the same thing, but in quite a different fashion. He created the indestructible "Sad Sack," whose comic-strip adventures appeared in the Army magazine *Yank*. But the man who did more than anyone to immortalize the American infantryman was Bill Mauldin, a boyish-looking GI who drew cartoons for the Army newspaper, *Stars and Stripes*. Mauldin was only twenty when he went overseas and rapidly became the best-known American war cartoonist, a kind of reincarnated Bruce Bairnsfather, the British cartoonist of the First War. He captured the grim wit of the foxhole in a way loved by the enlisted men themselves, detested by some of their officers. The secret of his humor and of its impact among the men was that it was caste-conscious; it said to the enlisted man, "I'm with you, and only we together know what it's all about." His two cartoon characters, Willie and Joe, became the heartbreaking and hilariously funny heroes of an army that was fighting as hard as it could, with little fanfare and a lot of griping, to get the job over with and get home, *alive*.

After the war Mauldin wrote a book, *Up Front*, which included the pick of his cartoons and his own comments on the war. What he had to say, like his drawing, put the "glories" of life at the front on their proper level. For example: "It's a little better when you can lie down, even in the mud. Rocks are better than mud because you can curl yourself around the big rocks, even if you wake up with sore bruises where the little rocks dug into you. When you wake up in the mud your cigarettes are all wet and you have an ache in your joints and a rattle in your chest."

There were only three punctuations to the dreary life of a front-line infantryman: relief, wounds, or death. A Marine's grave marker on Guadalcanal summarized the period in between:

And when he gets to Heaven,
To Saint Peter he will tell:
One more marine reporting, sir—
I've served my time in Hell.

As the first shiploads of coffins began coming back to the United States, they brought home to America the hard truth of war as nothing else could—not even those letters and telegrams being delivered to so many front doors: "We regret to inform you. . . ." As the death toll steadily mounted, little-known villages that were tucked away in obscure corners of the country suddenly felt as if they had suffered from some Biblical plague. Salinas, California, with a population of 11,586 and Harrodsburg, Kentucky, with 4,673, respectively contributed 150 and 76 men to the tragedy of Bataan.

There was a determined effort by the American command and its Graves Registration Service to keep track of all those who died, even when their remains were unidentifiable. Nevertheless, there were places in Europe and on islands in the Pacific where trenches were dug, the bodies dumped in after identification had been removed, a row of crosses put up, and a dog tag hung on each cross. And the sailor's grave, as always in war, was the sea. Before it was all over, 201,367 Americans were killed, more than the battle dead of the Union and Confederate Armies in the Civil War.

Those who lived, simply stumbled back from the edge of the canyon, psychologically neither dead nor alive. Ernie Pyle wrote: "In their eyes as they pass is not hatred, not excitement, not despair, not the tonic of their victory. There is just the simple expression of being there as if they had been doing that forever, and nothing else." Pyle also said: "A soldier who has been a long time in the line does have a 'look' in his eyes that anyone

The Sad Sack, © 1944

who knows about it can discern . . . it is a look that is a display room for what lies behind it—exhaustion, lack of sleep, tension for too long, weariness that is too great, fear beyond fear, misery to the point of numbness, a look of surpassing indifference to anything anybody can do." (It was a "look" that the GIs called "combat fatigue" or "nervous in the service" and that, by 1945, had translated itself into mental collapse for some five hundred thousand men.)

The incredible psychological pressures of war produced a strange form of spiritual bends in a good many men, who, when granted a momentary release from duty, sought to express their very joy in survival, sometimes in the age-old ways of the soldier, other times in fashions that seemed almost inexplicable. The GIs celebrated their triumph over death or masked their fears or fought their boredom in wild ecstasies of gambling, often playing for stakes they never would have believed possible in their civilian days. After all, what was three or four thousand dollars, when they were used to putting up their lives? And along with the dice and poker went the glossy photographs of American glamour girls—the "pin-up"—or the snapshots of sweetheart or wife that decorated barracks walls and bulkheads from Fort Dix to Bizerte to Ulithi. As a sentimental reminder, if all this was not enough, the names of girl friends, dogs, home towns, and cartoon characters and a lively variety of pet slogans were inscribed on the sides of tanks and airplanes.

Wherever they went in a bewildering and foreign world, the Americans often befriended ragged, big-eyed children, giving them candy bars and chewing gum. Also, wherever they went, they sought strong drink and feminine companionship. In North Africa they bought huge quantities of terrible home brew from Arab traders. In Italy they purchased all the grappa in sight, naming it Kickapoo Joy Juice after a concoction served in a well-known comic strip. The Canadians, for their part, dis-

tilled a wicked drink called "Steam," and an Iroquois sergeant among them was widely known as "C.P.R." (Canadian Pacific Railway) because he always "had steam up." Out in the Pacific, marines and sailors improvised every imaginable means of producing a potation with a kick in it. One technique was to filter hair tonic through bread and then mix it with grape juice. Like virtually every other drink devised in the Pacific, it was known as "Jungle Juice."

In England and, after their liberation started, in Italy and France, the juxtaposition of GIs and old, hitherto stable societies produced jealousies and conflict, heightened by emotional strains and contrasting economic levels. Quarrels over women erupted as normal peacetime sexual morality lapsed into confusion, and as different army pay scales gave the Americans an advantage in entertaining that they were quick to use. One sour complaint among Britons was: "The trouble with you Yanks is that you're over-paid, over-sexed and over here." The GIs quipped back: "You're sore because you're under-paid, under-sexed and under Eisenhower."

Still, it is doubtful whether any army of such numbers or such power ever behaved better or, for that matter, was so well received, even among conquered enemies. The GI came and went, in Europe and the Pacific. He took home new notions about the earth, about people who were not American, not rich, not powerful, who represented a different race or faith. He left behind some of his own ideas and a great many dead comrades. He also left behind a curious marking that was chalked on rocks, on city walls, on lavatories: "Kilroy was here." No one ever found out for sure who Kilroy was, where he came from, or why anyone would care enough about him to scrawl his name across half the globe. But that Kilroy was there was absolutely certain; and if he had not made the world safe for democracy, he had at least helped to rid it of an inhuman despotism.

Moments like this were the best part of it: the shooting had stopped (for the time being); the enemy had been whipped again; the

nd was that much closer. These triumphant-looking Americans are posing with a captured Japanese gun at Hollandia, New Guinea.

At least half the business of soldiering with the United States Army meant standing in line, or so it seemed. The other half was being shipped, bussed, trucked, or trained here and there for days on end. "Hurry up and wait," was a standard gripe, and very often the places where the waiting was done did not offer exactly the comforts of home. These pictures could have been taken on any of a dozen fronts or seas. As it was, they were taken in Sicily and somewhere en route from England to Africa.

LEFT AND RIGHT: U.S. ARMY

Even the smallest pleasures became memorable events, whether it was clowning it up in Italy for a snapshot to send back home, or watching an after-dinner movie in the rain on Guadalcanal. There was the first taste of fresh vegetables after months at sea, or a cold beer. Just seeing a woman, almost any woman, was something, and so were dog-eared magazines full of advertisements for soap and whiskey and white shirts. Almost anything civilian was wonderful to look at. But best of all was mail from home; there was never quite enough of that.

Sleep came easy, anywhere, anytime, sitting, standing, lying down. Distractions never mattered much either, as is indicated by the

man at left. The scene is inside a Quonset hut at the air base on Adak, in the Aleutians. The game: poker. The decor: early GI.

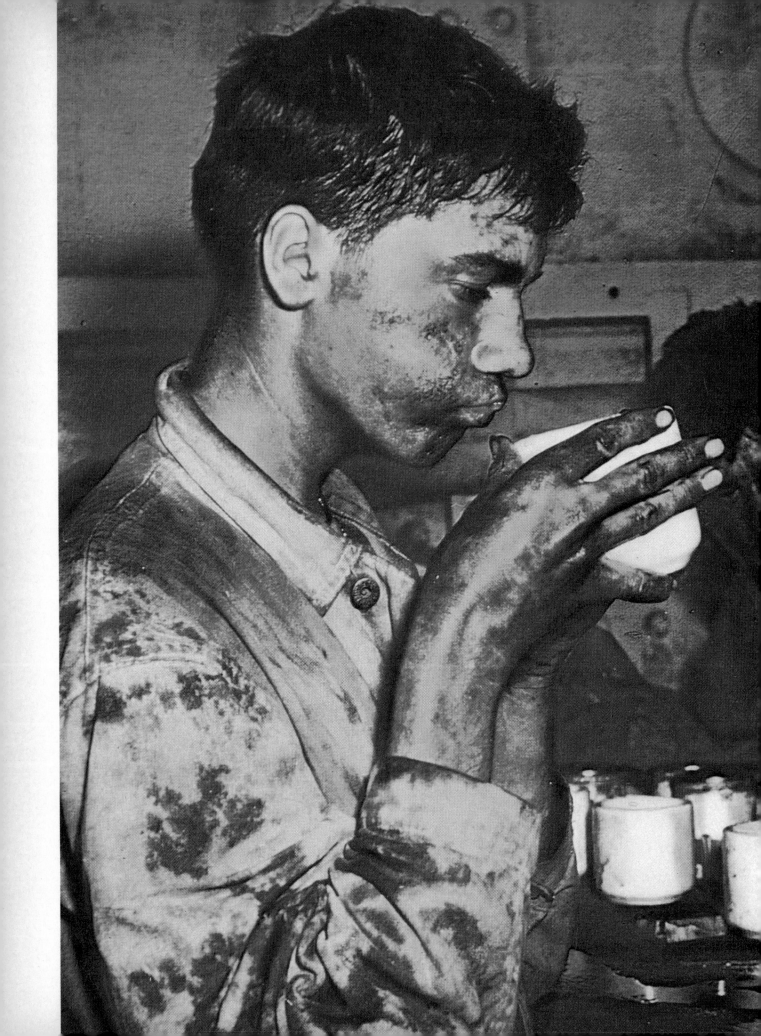

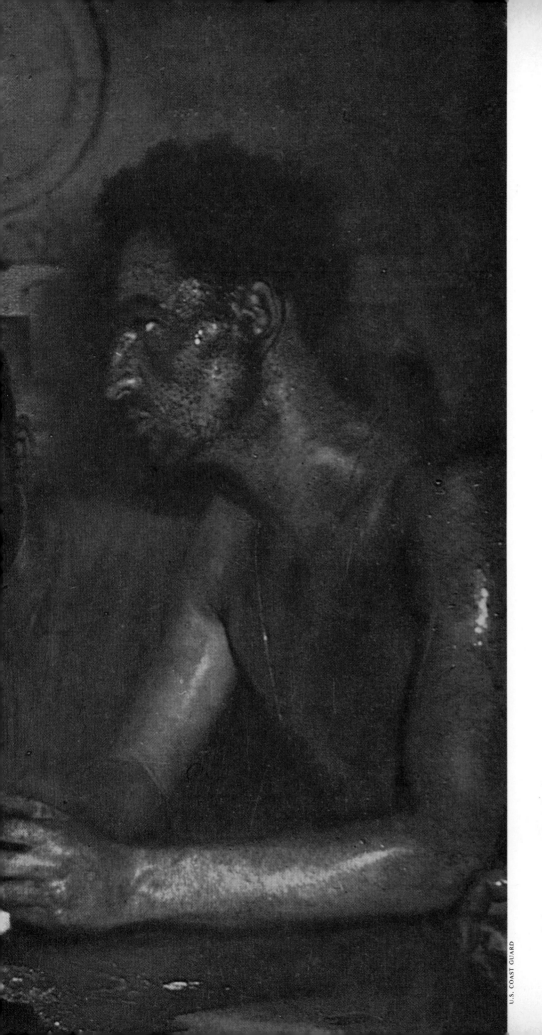

There was generally plenty of talk about combat, but nearly always by men who had not as yet experienced it. After they had, they preferred to talk about other things. The men in this photograph have just been through two days and two nights of fighting on Eniwetok Island in the Marshalls, in February, 1944. They are members of the 22nd Marine Regiment, and the battle was their first combat.

411

Men wrote letters home telling about places they passed through, friends they made, things that happened along the way. A show put on by some of the men in the outfit would be described as though it had been just about the most hilarious performance of all time, which was the way it had seemed. Or a man might choose to write about the sounds and smells of the jungle, or about seeing the wounded brought in for the first time. It was, in any case, war seen in the off-hours, without gloss or panorama. These sketches, drawn by combat artists who were with American units in both theaters, capture some of that same feeling.

A street scene in Luxembourg, by Aaron Bohrod.

Wreckage at Clark Field in the Philippines, by Frede Vidar.

SP Gun
Weiswampach, Lux.

A GI stage show on Ascension Island, by Peter Hurd.

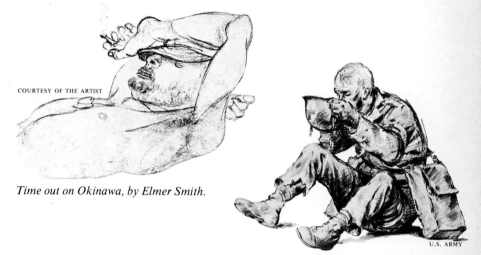

Time out on Okinawa, by Elmer Smith.

Medical corpsman in Italy, by Joseph Hirsch.

Portrait of a Marine, by Donald Dickson.

Wounded bomber crewman in England, by Lawrence Beall Smith.

There were some faces that would stick in a man's mind the rest of his life. It might be that of the first buck sergeant he ran up against in basic training, or the grime-covered "dogface" he shared a foxhole with at Anzio for five hours under fire and then never saw again. But there were at least two faces every man who ever served would never forget: "the Old Man" (in this case, Admiral Marc Mitscher, left), and the one everybody called "the Kid."

The Air War

Like nearly every part of the Nazi war machine, Adolf Hitler's much-publicized *Luftwaffe* was built for a short conflict, a blitzkrieg. The *Führer* was confident of quick triumph. Not until 1942 did he make any plans to modernize his aircraft; and by then it was too late. In 1940, an official directive of the Berlin Air Ministry ordered the postponement of work on all planes that would not be operational within two years. The directive explained: "Such types will not be wanted after the war."

From 1939 until 1941, the *Luftwaffe* controlled the skies on each front. But in 1942 things began to change. Germany found itself engaged in a four-front aerial war: over England, over North Africa, over the Soviet Union, and over the Reich itself. In 1939, Göring had pompously boasted: "If bombs drop on Germany, my name is Meyer." By 1942, sardonic Germans were calling him "Herr Meyer" night after night.

As the British and, later, the Americans intruded ever more deeply and persistently—even to Berlin—Göring moved his fighter squadrons into occupied nations facing Britain and established a primitive early warning system. When the Allied bombers headed east for German targets, they were hit first by these "outer" squadrons and then met by successive fighter wings.

But the *Luftwaffe* was extensively overcommitted by 1942, and the size and scope of Allied raids, smashing railway yards, factories, and cities from Cologne to Berlin, brought the war bitterly home to the German nation, making a mockery of all the Nazi regime's grandiose promises of security. There were public calls for retaliatory strikes on Britain, just as the British had demanded similar strikes on Germany during their arduous year 1940–1941, but the *Luftwaffe* no longer had enough planes and pilots to satisfy any such craving for revenge. In October, 1942, Göring was forced to confess in a speech broadcast from Munich: "There are those who ask why we do not go in for reprisals. The answer is simple: it is because most of our bombers are needed more urgently at Stalingrad and in the Caucasus. . . . The winner in this war will be the side which knows how to concentrate its strength at the critical point in the battle. Our cities in the West and North-west have to stand up to hard blows, but I have come away from my many visits to them with the firm conviction that their morale is equal to the trial."

An initial hint of what lay in store for Germany occurred on the night of August 24, 1940, when a small number of R.A.F. planes for the first time fought their way to Berlin. The damage caused was negligible; but the wail of sirens, the groping fingers of searchlights, and the grunt of antiaircraft guns made the heady Germans think. By November 13, 1940, the British had mastered the art of piercing the distant German capital's defenses. On that night, Molotov had been bargaining with Ribbentrop for spheres of influence in a conquered world. The two ministers and their staffs were forced to take shelter, but Ribbentrop assured his guest that Britain was finished. Molotov shrewdly inquired: "If that is so, why are we in

The waiting hours: ground crews of the 96th Bomb Group watch for the return of bombers at Snetherton Heath, an American airbase in England.

417

this shelter, and whose are these bombs which fall?" Those were the last significant Nazi-Soviet talks. They failed, and the world, as it turned out, was not to be conquered. Churchill remarked with relish: "We had heard about the conference beforehand and, though not invited to join in the discussion, did not wish to be entirely left out of the proceedings."

The R.A.F.'s harassing raids increased in 1941 as the *Luftwaffe* was drawn into Russia, and by 1942, enough British planes and pilots had been prepared for broad-scale strategic bombing. On May 30, 1942, came the first of the war's vast saturation raids: a thousand English planes attacked Cologne and left the Rhineland city blazing. Soon afterward came a succession of hammer blows that devastated Berlin, Hamburg, Dortmund, Leipzig, Essen. The R.A.F.'s Sir Arthur Harris reported that his planes were destroying two and a half German cities a month and warned the Germans that they had but two alternatives, annihilation or surrender. The nation suffered thousands upon thousands of killed and wounded, but German morale and Nazi discipline held firm.

But the British did not limit themselves to city-smashing. They struck power plants, radar stations, railroads. In one sensational raid, carefully prepared and using specially tested projectiles, the R.A.F. on May 16, 1943, blew up the Möhne dam, on which four million Germans and the Ruhr industrial complex depended for water and energy. This daring operation was led by Wing Commander Guy Penrose Gibson, who received the Victoria Cross, and who was shot down and killed in a later action. As Gibson flew his Lancaster up and down the dam, he saw the water of the dammed lake rising "like stirred porridge in the moonlight, rushing through a great breach." A few minutes later, he reported: "The valley was beginning to fill with fog and . . . we saw cars speeding along the roads in front of this great wave of water which was chasing them. . . . I saw their headlights burning and I saw water overtake them, wave by wave, and then the color of the headlights underneath the water changing from light blue to green, from green to dark purple until there was no longer anything except the water bouncing down."

The Germans had to stand up to an Allied strategy in which the British bombed by night and the Americans by day. This pattern was the result of a compromise to an argument between the Royal Air Force and the U.S. Army Air Forces.

The original argument was propounded by two resolute advocates of air power, the R.A.F.'s Sir Arthur ("Bomber") Harris, and Carl ("Tooey") Spaatz, who led the American bomber force based in Britain. Harris believed that if German cities were pulverized, German morale would crack. Furthermore, he argued, it would be foolish to accomplish the job by day bombing, which cost too heavily in planes and trained crews. Spaatz, on the other hand, refused to limit himself to the night-bombing methods of Harris or to broad metropolitan targets. He claimed it was unrealistic to assume that the Germans would knuckle under once their cities were smashed, just as it had been unrealistic for the Germans to assume that Britain would quit when it was being hammered by the *Luftwaffe*. He insisted on pin-point bombing in long-ranging day raids that would knock out vital industrial and transportation centers.

When the United States entered World War II, determined to concentrate on destroying Germany before Japan, the initial burden fell upon the U.S. Army Air Corps. Its first effective unit in Europe was the Eighth Air Force, organized on January 28, 1942, and in May placed under the command of Spaatz, who established a series of bases in Britain with headquarters at Bushy Park, near London.

From the start, the Americans were given wholehearted cooperation by the battle-tested R.A.F., but there was no letup to the British argument against daytime raids. They had seen the *Luftwaffe* defeated over Britain in 1940 when it had employed such tactics, and they themselves had suffered heavy losses from daytime raids on Germany. But Spaatz was eager to use his planes, particularly the B-17, for the pinpoint work they had been built for.

Nowadays the B-17 "Flying Fortress" seems almost as diminutive and archaic—in comparison with the swept-wing, swing-wing, and delta-wing bombers that have survived into the missile age—as the strut-and-piano-wire biplanes of World War I. Yet it was a remarkable weapon for its time, built to fly high and fast, its hydraulic turrets fitted with pairs of .50-caliber Browning machine guns that swung simultaneously against attacking planes, permitting the tight echelons of bombers to spit out a storm of concentrated fire. Furthermore, the B-17 was equipped with the precise Norden bombsight, which, its admirers claimed, could "drop a bomb in a pickle barrel." Spaatz proved that, by formation flying and with added protection from long-range fighters, his planes could force their way through to chosen targets. On September 8, 1942, the Washington and London high commands agreed to go ahead with American day bombing, coordinated with Britain's night raids. Still, as late as the Casablanca conference in early 1943, Churchill expressed his conviction that the results of day assaults were too meager to justify their heavy cost.

But Churchill finally agreed to try United States strategy. As a consequence, the Allies worked out a program of "around the clock bombing." Germany was pounded night and day. When the sun went down over Hitler's *Festung Europa*, Royal Air Force Stirlings and Lancasters rumbled through the Rhineland mists and on to Saxony and Brandenburg. And when, through the swirling smoke, the sun arose in the East again, American Liberators and Flying Fortresses came roaring down the aerial avenues. A complicated timetable was devised to avoid congestion of the narrow air space above the British isles. But despite the tremendous accomplishments of strategic bombing, its effectiveness versus cost has continued to be a matter of debate among military experts.

By 1943, the Eighth Air Force could concentrate on weakening the *Luftwaffe* and gradually softening up German defenses for the ultimate land invasion. That August 17—one year after twelve United States planes first struck Germany—three hundred and seventy-six Eighth Air Force bombers hammered Regensburg and Schweinfurt, where Nazi fighters and the ball bearings for their engines were manufactured. Casualties were very heavy, and sixty of the planes on the missions did not come back. After the war Adolf Galland, the famous *Luftwaffe* fighter ace, wrote that the first raid on Schweinfurt came as a great shock to the German high command. "If the German ball-bearing industry, their Achilles' heel, were to be destroyed or paralyzed, then the armament production of the whole Reich would suffer heavily. Speer [Albert Speer, who ran Hitler's armament program], in a postwar report, pointed out that with a continuation of the raids the German armament industry would have been essentially weakened within two months, and in four months would have come to a complete standstill. But luckily the first raid on Schweinfurt and Messerschmitt-Regensburg proved a disaster for the enemy. . . ."

Initially it seemed that the offensive could not be maintained. As it turned out, within four months, a fuel container known as the drop-tank became available to extend the range of American fighters. Thereafter, U.S. Thunderbolts and Mustangs could travel half again as far beside the lumbering B-17's and B-24's. The speedy Mustang, World War II's longest-range fighter, became known to bomber crews as "little friend."

The British likewise improved the deadliness of their nocturnal armadas. They developed the Beaufighter, which could accompany night bombers for six hours without refueling, and whose sophisticated radar equipment spotted Nazi planes in the foggy dark. Thereafter, without cease, the two air forces roared over Germany. During "Big Week," February 19–25, 1944, the R.A.F. put 2,300 bombers over Germany at night, and the American Air Force, 3,800 during daytime. Desperately seeking to fend off this particular series of assaults, the *Luftwaffe* lost 450 planes—a rate it could not long sustain. By that same summer, Göring's air fleet had been crippled. Eisenhower was able to reassure his D-Day troops in early June, "If you see fighting aircraft over you, they will be ours."

Typical of the combined Anglo-American air strategies were the attacks on Hamburg, Germany's principal seaport, which housed some of the Reich's biggest oil refineries, and on Ploesti, the Rumanian oil-producing center on which Hitler drew heavily for fuel. Hamburg was easily identifiable to bombers coming in across the North Sea's open water or groping up the Elbe. During daylight hours, American bombers battered its refineries and U-boat pens; at night its docks, refineries, and dwellings were savagely hammered by British heavy bombers flying in close formation and employing for the first time a very simple but highly effective method of fouling the enemy's radar. The planes dumped huge batches of tinfoil of the right length and width to float slowly down over the target as a shield against radar waves. German fighter defenses and flak directed by radar were thus knocked totally out of whack. The R.A.F. alone, in four raids between July 24 and August 3, 1943, killed an estimated forty-three thousand people in the grand old Hanseatic city. This terrible event became known to Germans as "*Die Katastrophe.*" Countless lives were snuffed out by lack of oxygen in the fire storm produced in Hamburg. After *Die Katastrophe*, one Hamburg woman watched rescue workers stack corpses in trucks, then shivered and said: "If there were a God He would have shown some mercy to them." An elderly man replied: "Leave God out of this. Men make war, not God."

The decision to risk heavy losses by bombing Ploesti was made at the Trident Conference in Washington, May, 1943, and the attack was launched that August 1 by a force of one hundred and seventy-eight American B-24 bombers taking off from Libya. A small raid had already been staged by thirteen Liberators (B-24's) on June 11, 1942, but it did little damage. Indeed, it had the adverse effect of encouraging the Nazis to strengthen Rumania's antiaircraft defenses.

The 1943 raiders took off from Benghazi for a fifteen-hundred-mile flight across the Mediterranean and the German-occupied Balkans and met successive fighter attacks long before they approached their target. Nevertheless, they fought their way through, and soon the refineries and oil tanks were covered with brilliant orange flame and billowing black smoke. The damage wreaked was substantial, but losses were severe. Four hundred and forty-six of the 1,733 men on the mission were killed, and only 33 of the original 178 planes came through fit to fly again. Many planes were shot down over Rumania (where 108 men were imprisoned) and Bulgaria, while others gradually collapsed into the Aegean as they struggled to make their way back toward Africa. Still others found haven in neutral Turkey, where the crews were well received and interned in comfort.

Although Hitler's defeats in Russia and the Mediterranean meant that the perimeter of air space that he had to defend was contracted, he was able to muster fewer and fewer fighters. And although the largely obsolescent Soviet Air Force of some twelve thousand combat planes had been eviscerated by the Nazis in 1941, new designs were created. Modern types began to emerge from Siberian factories: the highly maneuverable MIG and all-weather YAK fighters; the clumsy but invincible Stormovik. Little by little, a resurgent Soviet Air Force took its toll of the *Luftwaffe*, and "General Winter," Russia's oldest and most vicious ally, froze it into immobility. During the cold months of 1942–43, *Luftwaffe* operations on the Soviet front were cut to 25 per cent. By 1943, furthermore, the Russians began to receive substantial reinforcements of American P-39's, P-40's, A-20's, and B-25's, and British Hurricanes.

After V-E Day, *Luftwaffe* officers agreed with one of their number: "There is no doubt that the Americans harmed us most. The Russians were negligible as far as the home front was concerned, and we could have stood the British attacks on our cities. But the American devastation of our airfields, factories and oil depots made it impossible for us to keep going."

What really brought the *Luftwaffe* down was the application of a successful Allied strategy. Like determined dogs hounding a dying stag, American, British, and Russian fighters slashed away at their victim while American and British bombers prevented him from regaining sustenance. Had the Germans been able to shake free and concentrate on one single front for sufficient time, they might have achieved a major aerial victory. But the combination of losses to the West, South, and East and the destruction of replacement centers gradually whittled the mighty *Luftwaffe*. By the war's last year, it was almost helpless to defend Germany. In two British and one American raids on Dresden, February 13–14, 1945, one hundred and thirty-five thousand people lost their lives.

German scientists sought to recapture the upper hand by ingenuity. They developed and actually produced impressive numbers of the Messerschmitt 262 jet, which could easily kill normal propeller-driven fighters, thanks to its astounding speed—540 miles an hour. But production was hampered by Hitler's insistence on giving priority to the manufacture of bombers and *Vergeltungswaffen*, or revenge weapons—the V-1 and V-2, with which he wanted above all to punish Britain's civilian population.

The *Führer* became obsessed with this idea. When *Luftwaffe* generals and Göring explained the immense value of the ME-262 in staving off Allied attacks, Hitler became furious. "I want bombers, bombers, bombers," he shouted. "Your fighters are no damned good!" He refused for almost half a year even to look at a test flight; then he promptly commanded that the new jet be converted into a bomber, for which it had neither the range nor the load capacity.

His view of the V-1 and V-2 was equally illogical. At first he remained convinced that the war could be won without bothering to give priority to experimental weapons. When the first doubts of victory finally began to bother him, he ordered sudden mass production of the V-2. Walter Dornberger, a scientist involved in the project, complained that he himself had not envisioned the rocket as an annihilation weapon. Hitler replied: "No, I realize that *you* didn't think of it! But I did."

Both V-1 and V-2 originated at the experimental center of Peenemünde, on the Baltic. The V-1, dubbed "Buzz Bomb" by the British, was a pilotless plane loaded with explosives, of which more than eight thousand were aimed at London in Hitler's frenzy for vengeance. However, many went astray (one even hit Hitler's bunker) or were shot down, and only 2,420 reached their target. These did extensive but far from crippling damage.

The V-2 was more frightening, a rocket forerunner of the long-range ballistic missile. It carried a tank of liquid oxygen that allowed it to fly above the earth's atmosphere, and it was aimed from fixed positions, like long-range artillery. Fortunately, Hitler, by according priority of materials and labor to conventional arms, deferred assembly-line production of this terrible instrument until it was too late for it to have a material effect on the war's outcome. By then, Allied reconnaissance and espionage had learned of the Peenemünde experiments and located many rocket sites under construction. As a result, bomber raids concentrated on these targets in 1943 and 1944, killing many leading scientists and reducing the power of the V-weapons counteroffensive. Only about eleven hundred V-2's were successfully exploded in England. They destroyed hundreds of buildings, caused thousands of casualties, but did not materially alter the war's course.

Preparations for American involvement in the Asian air war were going on before the United States actually became a belligerent. A retired Air Corps officer named Claire L. Chennault had formed a flying Foreign Legion for Chiang Kai-shek in his struggle against Japan. This formation was soon destroyed, but with Washington's permission, Chennault recruited new American volunteers for an organization with the cover name of Central Aircraft Manufacturing Company (CAMCO). Washington loaned Chiang the money to buy one hundred Curtiss P-40 Tomahawks and to hire pilots. This force, called the American Volunteer Group (AVG), was shipped in small batches to Burma, under assumed identities, and began training in September, 1941. The pilots had scarcely completed their course when Pearl Harbor came, and they went into action as the Flying Tigers, so called for their winged tiger insigne devised by the Walt Disney Studios. These Flying Tigers became romantic heroes, and they were an important morale factor back home. It was somehow comforting to know in December, 1941, that a group of American fliers were shooting down Zeros. The AVG subsequently became the Fourteenth U.S. Air Force. It was the first Pacific air formation to employ rockets, and it also introduced an internationally integrated unit, the Chinese-American Combat Wing.

The air war in Asia was from the start a paramount factor both over sea and over land. Its importance can be summed up simply by two terminal events—Pearl Harbor and Hiroshima-Nagasaki. They signify the enormous change that occurred so rapidly in control of the skies.

When the Pacific conflict started in 1941, Japan held a perceptible lead in numbers of planes and crews who were veterans of the China campaign. The Japanese Army and Navy together had some three thousand operational aircraft and twice that number of pilots with at least five hundred hours flying experience. (These original pilots were far more skilled than the Americans had imagined; but the quality of their replacements declined.) Japan was already producing 425 planes and 225 pilots each month. The United States possessed fewer than nine hundred planes in the Pacific area. A heavy proportion of these were destroyed in Honolulu and the Philippines during Japan's initial surprise attacks. Furthermore, although the early American fighters were sturdier and more heavily armored, none of them could rival the maneuverability of the famous Japanese Zero.

Nevertheless, as the immense United States production facilities began turning out ever vaster numbers and ever better plane types, the balance began immutably to shift. Japanese aircraft strength attained an approximate top level of four thousand, but by the end of 1944, the United States had about ten thousand war planes plus eight thousand transports at its disposal in the Pacific. These included the fastest propeller fighter ever built, the Mustang, and, in the end, the B-29 Superfortress, which carried out the A-bomb raids. From a steadily constricting circle of land bases on the Pacific islands, from China, from India, and eventually from Burma, the U.S. Army Air Corps moved in ever more menacingly, while Admiral Nimitz's immense carrier task forces sailed closer and closer to Tokyo itself.

The B-29 was the ultimate air weapon of World War II, even more important than Germany's V-2 because the latter, although it served as forerunner for ballistic missiles, came too late and did too little damage. The B-29 developed from General "Hap" Arnold's insistence on a superbomber that could fly farther and with a bigger load than any other aircraft. It was blueprinted in 1940, before the United States was in the war. By the time it was in production, it had become a sixty-ton machine, capable when loaded of flying sixteen hours without stop. The first of these monsters was sent to India in April, 1944, and enormous airfields were built for them both in eastern India and western China. The first actual Superfortress raid was on June 5, 1944, from India to the railroad marshaling yards of Bangkok. Ten days later, another raid took off from the Chinese base network against Yawata, the Japanese steel center on Kyushu Island. But it was only after Major General Curtis E. LeMay, only thirty-eight years old, took over the XX Bomber Command and began to use it for close-formation daylight raids, a tactic he had mastered while serving with the Eighth Air Force in England, that the B-29's began to do their most terrible and insistent damage.

The monster planes were shifted from the China-Burma-India theater to the XXI Bomber Command in Saipan, Tinian, and Guam as soon as Aviation Engineers, hard on the heels of the conquering Marines, had managed to carve sufficiently large airdromes out of the jungles and atolls of the Marianas. At last, by November 24, they began their final campaign in earnest with a raid on the aircraft plants outside Tokyo. From then on, relentlessly, they were employed with increasing force against plane factories and harbors of Japan's home islands, hammering the main cities one by one.

In 1945, tons of explosives made of jellied gasoline and magnesium began to whistle down on Tokyo, Kobe, Nagoya. Indeed, on August 2, just four days before Hiroshima disappeared beneath the first insidious mushroom cloud, eight hundred and fifty-five Superfortresses wiped out six Japanese cities in one single massive operation. It was thus entirely plain before the first nuclear bomb was dropped that the so-called conventional plane using the so-called conventional explosive was, all by itself, a weapon of staggering destructive capacity. The bomber, so long considered the ultimate in strategic might, had reached its moment of total and awful triumph.

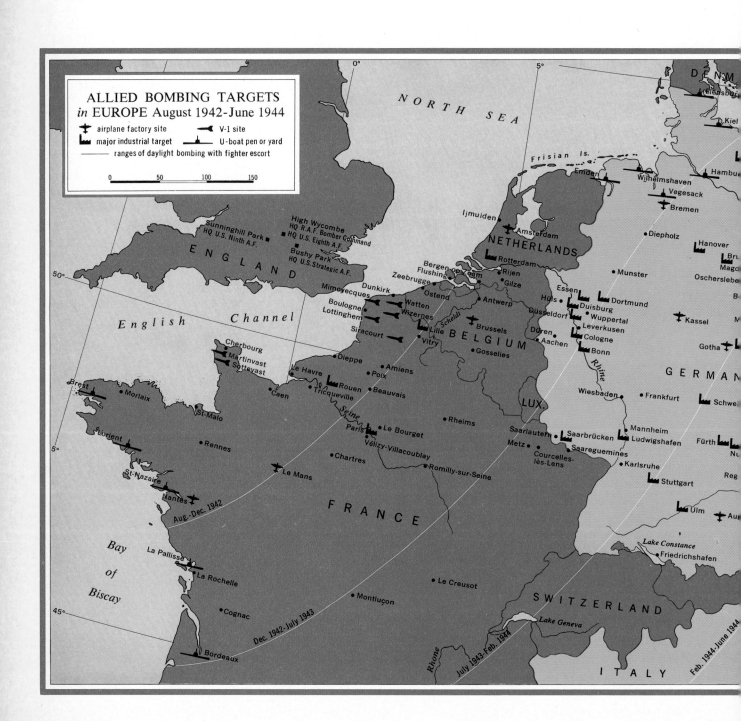

ALLIED BOMBING TARGETS
in EUROPE August 1942 - June 1944

- ✈ airplane factory site
- 🏭 major industrial target
- ◄ V-1 site
- ⚓ U-boat pen or yard
- ── ranges of daylight bombing with fighter escort

0   50   100   150

NORTH SEA

DENM.

Flensburg
Kiel
Frisian Is.
Emden
Wilhelmshaven
Vegesack
Bremen
Ijmuiden
Amsterdam
Hamburg
NETHERLANDS
Diepholz
Hanover
Bru
Rotterdam
Munster
Magd
Oscherslebe
Rijen
Gilze
Essen
Dortmund
Bergen-op-Zoom
Flushing
Hüls
Duisburg
B
Zeebrugge
Wuppertal
Kassel
Dunkirk
Antwerp
Düsseldorf
Leverkusen
Gotha
Ostend
Cologne
Boulogne
Watten
Brussels
Düren
Aachen
Lottinghem
Wizernes
Lille
BELGIUM
Bonn
GERMAN
Siracourt
Vitry
Scheldt
Gosselies
Wiesbaden
Frankfurt
Schwe

High Wycombe
HQ R.A.F. Bomber Command
Sunninghill Park
HQ U.S. Ninth A.F.
HQ U.S. Eighth A.F.
Bushy Park
HQ U.S. Strategic A.F.

ENGLAND

Mimoyecques

English   Channel

Cherbourg
Martinvast
Sotteveast
Dieppe
Amiens
Poix
LUX.
Le Havre
Rouen
Beauvais
Rhine
Brest
Morlaix
Tricqueville
Caen
Mannheim
Ludwigshafen
St-Malo
Saarlautern
Saarbrücken
Fürth
Nu
Lorient
Rennes
Seine
Rheims
Metz
Courcelles-lès-Lens
Saareguemines
Karlsruhe
Reg
St-Nazaire
Chartres
Le Mans
Paris
Le Bourget
Stuttgart
Nantes
Vélizy-Villacoublay
Aug.-Dec. 1942
FRANCE
Romilly-sur-Seine
Ulm
Au

Bay
of
Biscay

La Pallisse
La Rochelle
Lake Constance
Friedrichshafen

Cognac
Montluçon
Le Creusot
SWITZERLAND

Dec. 1942-July 1943

Bordeaux
Rhone
Lake Geneva
July 1943-Feb. 1944
ITALY
Feb. 1944-June 1944

0°   5°

50°

5°

45°

By Night and by Day

Great Britain and the United States agreed completely on the need for a massive, sustained air offensive to cripple the German war machine, but the two allies were not in accord on the best strategy for such an offensive. The Royal Air Force had been hitting targets in Germany since 1940, bombing at night, when most *Luftwaffe* fighters were grounded. But the same darkness that protected the bombers also obscured the target and made it necessary to blanket an area with explosives to be sure the target was hit. This British saturation bombing was indiscriminate; it killed civilians in large numbers while it was destroying factories and railroad yards. The U.S. Army Air Corps, on the other hand, entered the war committed to a strategy of high-altitude daylight precision bombing. It was expected that the massed guns of the formations of heavily armed bombers would be able to repel Nazi fighters.

The first American heavy bombers began operating out of England in August, 1942. The build-up was slow, but by the spring of 1943, the R.A.F. and the A.A.F. between them were pounding Germany night and day. The *Luftwaffe* reacted vigorously, causing heavy losses to the American forces despite the strong defensive fire of the bomber fleets. Fighter escorts were sent with the bombers but because of limited range could fly only part way to the target. By the fall of 1943, bomber losses were exorbitant; in one week in October, 153 aircraft were lost. The defeat was so overwhelming that bombing of German targets beyond fighter-escort range was discontinued. But this range was soon greatly extended (see map) by a simple invention called the drop tank, an auxiliary gas tank hung under the wing, that could be jettisoned when empty. Then, in December, 1943, the P-51 Mustang appeared, a remarkable fighter whose combat radius from its base—with drop tanks—was 850 miles. It could thus escort a bomber almost anywhere in Germany. With this advantage, the air war turned in the Allies' favor. By D-Day the *Luftwaffe* was shattered, German production crippled, and communications wrecked. Even so, the air offensive against Germany would be only well begun by that time. Three times as great a weight of explosives would be dropped on Hitler's Reich after D-Day as before.

Bomber Command

While British fighter pilots were making their grim stand in the Battle of Britain, the R.A.F. Bomber Command was fighting its own little war. Each night the big planes rumbled off to hit German ports and industrial cities—and to bomb Berlin, a profound shock to the victory-drunk German people. The R.A.F. made its decision in favor of night bombing after taking heavy losses in day operations, and especially after observing the havoc its own fighters caused among Göring's daytime bombers over England. But night bombing had its weaknesses and hazards. Late in 1940, an investigation of the accuracy of R.A.F. bombing revealed that two thirds of the crews had not hit within five miles of the target. Scientists corrected this intolerable situation with a device, called "Oboe," by which planes could be sent precisely over the target with a directional beam from England. Later, air-borne radar was devised that gave bomber crews a picture of the earth beneath them, regardless of darkness or clouds. Losses due to *Luftwaffe* night fighters were greatly cut with the discovery that the enemy radar could be confused by the dropping of clouds of small tinfoil strips. Night bombing never became a sinecure, but it was possible for a crew to return from a nine-hour flight over enemy territory still able to smile (right). In May, 1942, the R.A.F. made its first thousand-plane raid (actually 1,130 planes) when it attacked Cologne. From then on, city after city was devastated. There were some protests in Great Britain about the killing of civilians in nighttime saturation bombing that made it impossible to limit destruction to military objectives. But most Britons, after going through the Blitz, felt that the Germans were getting just what they had asked for.

424

They Flew by Day

The Eighth Air Force flew its first combat mission from England in August of 1942. Its build-up was slow, and the British, on the basis of their own experience, were skeptical of American ideas on daylight bombing and did their best to persuade the A.A.F. to change to night bombing. American confidence was based on two things. One was the top quality of its heavy bombers, principally the B-17 Flying Fortress, able to fly high and fast and heavily armed to repel enemy fighters. The other was the extremely accurate Norden bombsight. As it developed, the British were largely right and the Americans wrong, for the heavy bombers could not defend themselves against determined fighter opposition by day. It was not until they received long-range fighter escorts that the daytime precision-bombing Americans truly complemented the night-flying Britons.

The ground crew of the B-24 Liberator "Shoot Luke" check over their plane (left) following its return from its twenty-seventh mission. Above, British Air Marshal Sir Arthur Tedder, at left, and American Major General Carl Spaatz, the commander of the Eighth Air Force, strike an allied-unity pose.

427

The October 14, 1943, daylight raid on the ball bearing factory at Schweinfurt (far right) was an attempt to destroy an industry vital to every aspect of modern mechanized war. But the raid proved to be so costly—62 B-17's lost—that missions deep inside Germany without escort were suspended. At near right, American bombs fall on the Focke-Wulf aircraft factory at Bremen in December of 1943. Sustained day and night attacks crippled the German aircraft industry beyond any hope of recovery by the spring of 1944.

"The fighters queued up like a bread line and let us have it"

Lt. Col. Beirne Lay, Jr.

One of the costliest of the 1943 American daylight missions was the Regensburg raid of August 17. Of the 146 B-17's that took off from England that morning, 24 were lost. The target was a factory where Messerschmitt (ME-109) fighters were assembled. The reason the Allied strategists (and the bomber crews) were so anxious to destroy it is made vividly clear in this account by Lieutenant Colonel Beirne Lay, a copilot on the raid, who ten days earlier had requested that he be switched from a desk job to combat duty.

. . . The fear was unpleasant, but it was bearable. I knew that I was going to die, and so were a lot of others. . . .

A few minutes later we absorbed the first wave of a hailstorm of individual fighter attacks that were to engulf us clear to the target in such a blizzard of bullets and shells that a chronological account is difficult. It was at 10:41, over Eupen, that I looked out the window after a minute's lull, and saw two whole squadrons, twelve Me-109's and eleven FW-190's climbing parallel to us as though they were on a steep escalator. The first squadron had reached our level and was pulling ahead to turn into us. The second was not far behind. Several thousand feet below us were many more fighters, their noses cocked up in a maximum climb. Over the interphone came reports of an equal number of enemy aircraft deploying on the other side of the formation.

For the first time I noticed an ME-110 sitting out of range on our level out to the right. He was to stay with us all the way to the target, apparently radioing our position and weak spots to fresh *Staffeln* waiting farther down the road.

At the sight of all these fighters,

I had the distinct feeling of being trapped—that the Hun had been tipped off or at least had guessed our destination and was set for us. We were already through the German fighter belt. Obviously, they had moved a lot of squadrons back in a fluid defense in depth, and they must have been saving up some outfits for the inner defense that we didn't know about. The life expectancy of our group seemed definitely limited, since it had already appeared that the fighters, instead of wasting fuel trying to overhaul the preceding groups, were glad to take a cut at us.

Swinging their yellow noses around in a wide U turn, the twelve-ship squadron of Me-109's came in from twelve to two o'clock in pairs. The main event was on. I fought an impulse to close my eyes, and overcame it.

A shining silver rectangle of metal sailed past over our right wing. I recognized it as a main-exit door. Seconds later, a black lump came hurtling through the formation, barely missing several propellers. It was a man, clasping his knees to his head, revolving like a diver in a triple somersault, shooting by us so close that I saw a piece of paper blow out of his leather jacket. He was evidently making a delayed jump, for I didn't see his parachute open.

A B-17 turned gradually out of the formation to the right, maintaining altitude. In a split second it completely vanished in a brilliant explosion, from which the only remains were four balls of fire, the fuel tanks, which were quickly consumed as they fell earthward.

I saw blue, red, yellow and aluminum-colored fighters. Their tactics were running fairly true to form, with frontal attacks hitting the low squadron and rear attackers going for the lead and high squadrons. Some of the jerries shot at us with rockets, and an attempt at air-to-air bombing was made with little black time-fuse sticks, dropped from above, which exploded in small gray puffs off to one side of the formation. Several of the FW's did some nice deflection shooting on side attacks from 500 yards at the high group, then raked the low group on the breakaway at closer range with their noses cocked in a side slip, to keep the formation in their sights longer in the turn. External fuel tanks were visible under the bellies or wings of at least two squadrons, shedding uncomfortable light on the mystery of their ability to tail us so far from their bases.

The manner of the assaults indicated that the pilots knew where we were going and were inspired with a fanatical determination to stop us before we got there. Many pressed attacks home to 250 yards or less, or bolted right through the formation wide out, firing long twenty-second bursts, often presenting point-blank targets on the breakaway. Some committed the fatal error of pulling up instead of going down and out. More experienced pilots came in on frontal attacks with a noticeably slower rate of closure, apparently throttled back, obtaining greater accuracy. But no tactics could halt the close-knit juggernauts of our Fortresses, nor save the single-seaters from paying a terrible price.

Our airplane was endangered by various debris. Emergency hatches, exit doors, prematurely opened parachutes, bodies and assorted fragments of B-17's and Hun fighters breezed past us in the slip stream.

I watched two fighters explode not far beneath, disappear in sheets of orange flame; B-17's dropping out in every stage of distress, from engines on fire to controls shot away; friendly and enemy parachutes floating down, and, on the green carpet far below us, funeral pyres of smoke from fallen fighters, marking our trail.

On we flew through the cluttered wake of a desperate air battle, where disintegrating aircraft were commonplace and the white dots of sixty parachutes in the air at one time were hardly worth a second look. . . .

I took the controls for a while. The first thing I saw when Murphy resumed flying was a B-17 turning slowly out to the right, its cockpit a mass of flames. The copilot crawled out of his window, held on with one hand, reached back for his parachute, buckled it on, let go and was whisked back into the horizontal stabilizer of the tail. I believe the impact killed him. His parachute didn't open.

I looked forward and almost ducked as I watched the tail gunner of a B-17 ahead of us take a bead right on our windshield and cut loose with a stream of tracers that missed us by a few feet as he fired on a fighter attacking us from six o'clock low. I almost ducked again when our own top-turret gunner's twin muzzles pounded away a foot above my head in the full forward position, giving a realistic imitation of cannon shells exploding in the cockpit, while I gave an even better imitation of a man jumping six inches out of his seat.

Still no letup. The fighters queued up like a bread line and let us have it. Each second of time had a cannon shell in it. The strain of being a clay duck in the wrong end of that aerial shooting gallery became almost intolerable. Our Piccadilly Lily shook steadily with the fire of its .50's, and the air inside was wispy with smoke. I checked the engine instruments for the thousandth time. Normal. No injured crew members yet. . . .

Near the initial point, at 11:50, one hour and a half after the first of at least 200 individual fighter attacks, the pressure eased off, although hostiles were still in the vicinity. . . . Almost idly, I watched a crippled B-17 pull over to the curb and drop its wheels and open its bomb bay, jettisoning its bombs. Three Me-109's circled it closely, but held their fire while the crew bailed out. I remembered now that a little while back I had seen other Hun fighters hold their fire, even when being shot at by a B-17 from which the crew were bailing. But I doubt if sportsmanship had anything to do with it. They hoped to get a B-17 down fairly intact.

And then our weary, battered column, short twenty-four bombers, but still holding the close formation that had brought the remainder through by sheer air discipline and gunnery, turned in to the target. I knew that our bombardiers were grim as death while they synchronized their sights on the great Me-109 shops lying below us in a curve of the winding blue Danube, close to the outskirts of Regensburg. Our B-17 gave a slight lift and a red light went out on the instrument panel. Our bombs were away. We turned from the target toward the snow-capped Alps. I looked back and saw a beautiful sight—a rectangular pillar of smoke rising from the Me-109 plant. Only one burst was over and into the town. Even from this great height I could see that we had smeared the objective . . .

The Glamorous Service

"Uncle Willie!"

To the public, the airman was a dashing, romantic figure, and he usually obliged by playing the part. He removed the stiffening band from his cap and let the crown flop down in devil-may-care fashion, he sang about going off into the wild blue yonder, and he had a strong *esprit de corps* and pride in his trade. It seemed natural that when motion picture idols like Clark Gable and James Stewart went into service, they should go into the Eighth Air Force. The flying officers—pilot, copilot, bombardier, and navigator—as well as crew members of the heavy bombers were not as individualistic as the fighter pilots, because their job demanded teamwork; but they, too, took on the distinctive aura of men who fought their war in the sky. But the A.A.F. required seven unromantic figures on the ground for every one in the air. Maintenance was an enormous task; during the latter half of 1943, about 30 per cent of the bombers on each mission were battle damaged. Men had to be trained as mechanics, weather experts, in many specialties. The ground crews did not share the glamour, but neither did they face the jeopardy of the airman. There was scant glamour for Jesse D. Franks, Jr. (opposite), the first man to die in the ill-fated Ploesti raid. He jumped from his burning B-24 at treetop level and his chute did not open. "One never knows what tomorrow may bring," he had written his father the night before.

The youthfulness and rapid promotion of fliers were well known, and no fighting man could miss the point of Bill Mauldin's cartoon (above) with battle-weary GI Willie being greeted by a boyish nephew with pilot's wings and a colonel's eagles. At right, a crewman of the B-17 "Grin 'n Bare It" wears his plane's insigne and a tally of her 36 missions on his jacket. Below, Major James Stewart receives the Air Medal on completing ten missions. The actor became full colonel and flew 20 missions over Germany.

LEFT AND ABOVE: U.S. AIR FORCE

Lost in Action

ALL THIS PAGE: U.S. AIR FORCE

Flying a B-17 or B-24 was hard work for all aboard, and there was always the dread certainty that many would not be coming back. During 1943, losses were sometimes appalling—53 out of 178 planes at Ploesti, 60 of 376 in twin raids on Schweinfurt and Regensburg, 65 of 291 in the Schweinfurt bombing—and one out of every ten planes was common. The chances of the crew of a plane hit hard five miles up were shaved very slim. Bombers died in many ways, sometimes in an instant as their bomb loads were hit, sometimes in flames, sometimes spiraling down with a wing or tail blown off. German fighters moved in to cut to bits any crippled bomber that fell behind. Many planes returned home damaged, some so badly that it was a miracle they remained in the air, and there were always dead and wounded for the waiting ambulances. Not until the "Big Week" in February, 1944, was the Nazi fighter opposition battered into near impotence and bombing made somewhat less perilous.

A B-17 over Berlin (above), one wing afire, holds formation to complete its bombing run. Below, a B-24 in Italy, wing torn by flak and on fire, begins its plunge to the earth. At right, a low-level A-20 Havoc goes down under enemy fire in France.

A flier who parachuted safely onto German soil was still not certain of surviving, for civilians were encouraged to lynch downed airmen, and prisoners of war were executed on flimsy pretexts. The Nazis recorded, at right, their sadistic murder of American, Dutch, and British airmen at Mauthausen concentration camp in Austria in September, 1944. They were forced to carry 60-pound rocks, barefoot, up a steep quarry slope. When they collapsed, they were stoned and beaten. By the next morning, the last man was dead.

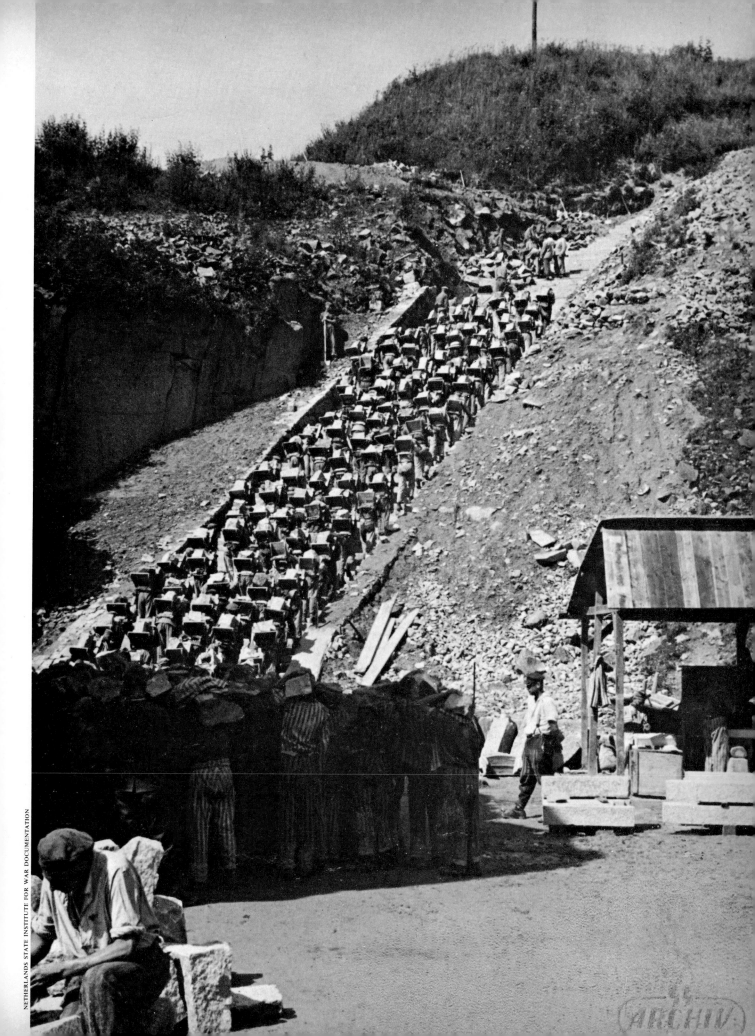

The heavy bombers kept coming by the hundreds, British and American, night and day, flying in precise formations and filling th

air with their drone. After the spring of 1944, they were seldom challenged; most Luftwaffe *planes were destroyed and their pilots dead.*

Where the Bombs Failed

The bomber offensive against Germany led to seeming contradictions. Despite the tremendous weight of explosives dropped on the Third Reich during 1943, the over-all level of armaments production did not fall. This, however, did not mean that factories were not being destroyed, but rather that the Nazis were stepping up output in occupied countries. And, contrary to what might be expected, it was not a shortage of planes but a lack of pilots that finally stopped the *Luftwaffe*. In their all-out assault the last part of February, 1944—the so-called "Big Week"—the Allies pounded German air industry with some 6,100 bombers, while fighters flew more than 3,600 sorties. Plane production was badly disrupted, but the irreparable loss was the pilots killed when 450 German planes went down during the week; the *Luftwaffe* could not train new pilots that fast. Hindsight seems to show that British night area bombing was not a soundly conceived idea. Its defenders claimed that if civilians as well as factories were hit, German morale would crack. But the Germans underwent far worse bombings than the British had without giving way.

American heavy bombers were sometimes called on for tactical instead of strategic bombing, as in attempts to destroy the U-boat shelters along the coast from Norway to France. The submarine pens at Plougastel-Daoulas in France (above) were among the ones attacked. However, reinforced concrete roofs, a dozen or more feet thick, made it very difficult to do serious damage. At right, a German family in a state of shock is helped by a home guard after a bombing of Mannheim. Few German cities escaped the bombs.

The Flying Fortress

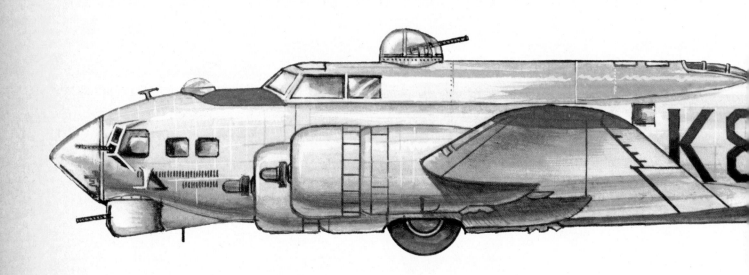

The Boeing B-17 Flying Fortress was probably the best-known plane of a war that saw many famous planes (a number of which are shown in the special portfolios that follow). This may have been in part because it did so much of its work in the well-publicized bombing of Germany, while the much more numerous B-24 Liberator flew most of its missions in the Mediterranean and the lonely reaches of the Pacific. Nevertheless, the Fortress was a great plane, heavily armed and armored, high flying, and able to take an amazing amount of punishment and still get home. The Fortress pictured above is officially designated the B-17G, the "G" meaning that it is the seventh modification of the original B-17. America went to war with B-17D's, a version with a tall, narrow rudder, no tail or nose guns, no ball turret below—in fact, the casual observer would not consider it and the B-17G the same plane. The B-17G went into production in July, 1943, and was the last and most numerous of the models. In outward appearance it differed from the preceding version only in the "chin" turret with two .50-caliber machine guns beneath the nose of the plane. This was added because the Flying Fortress was most vulnerable to

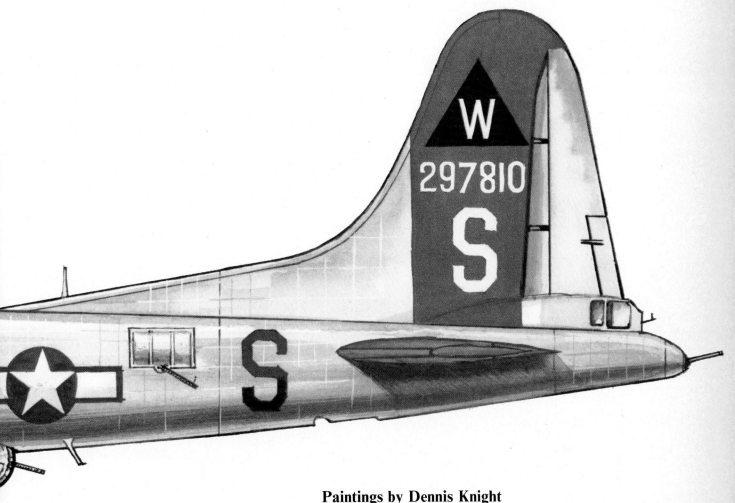

Paintings by Dennis Knight

fighter attacks from straight ahead. In all, the plane carried thirteen .50-caliber machine guns—an awesome array of firepower for an enemy aircraft to face, especially since Fortresses flew in tight formations of about eighteen planes to mass their gunfire, with two or three such formations stacked vertically to further increase the deadliness. To break up these bullet-spewing formations and pick off isolated cripples, Nazi pilots first fired rockets and even dropped bombs among the B-17's. The Fortress thus never lived up to planners' expectations that it would be able to take care of itself on long-range daylight missions, and deep penetrations of Germany had to await the development of escort fighters able to accompany them all the way. But the Fortress's capabilities as a high-altitude bomber disappointed no one. With the Norden bombsight, its ten-man crew performed marvels of precision bombing from 25,000 feet. While the B-17 could carry a maximum bomb load of 17,600 pounds for a very short distance, this dropped rapidly as range increased, and a 4,000–5,000-pound bomb load was typical on a German mission. The plane's top speed was about 300 miles per hour, its cruising speed only about 160.

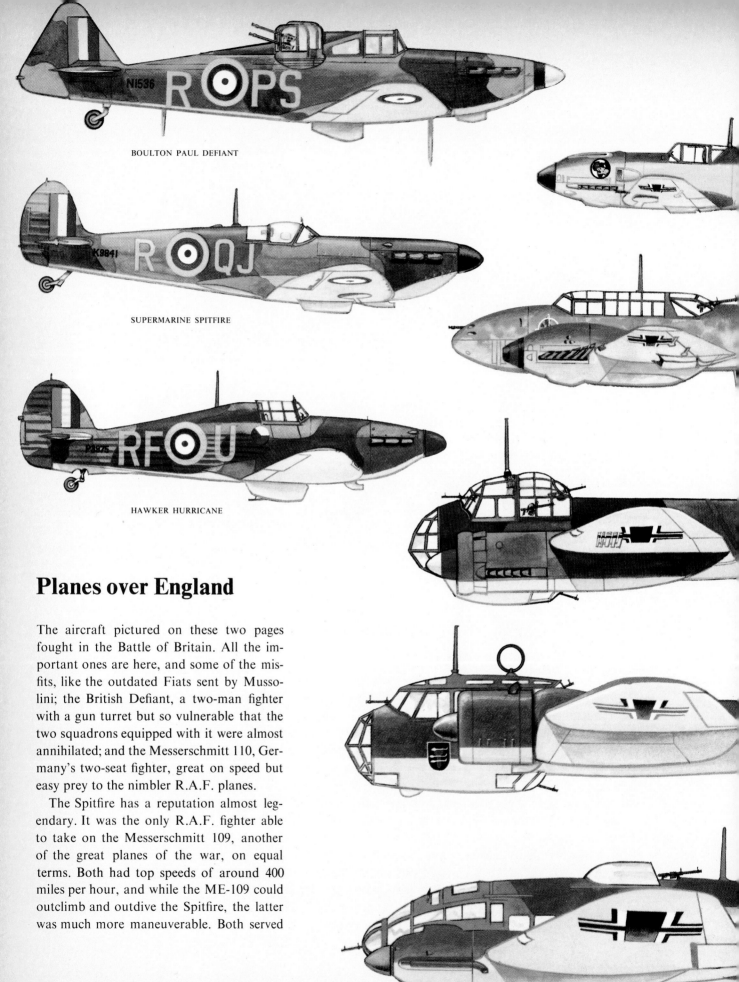

BOULTON PAUL DEFIANT

SUPERMARINE SPITFIRE

HAWKER HURRICANE

Planes over England

The aircraft pictured on these two pages fought in the Battle of Britain. All the important ones are here, and some of the misfits, like the outdated Fiats sent by Mussolini; the British Defiant, a two-man fighter with a gun turret but so vulnerable that the two squadrons equipped with it were almost annihilated; and the Messerschmitt 110, Germany's two-seat fighter, great on speed but easy prey to the nimbler R.A.F. planes.

The Spitfire has a reputation almost legendary. It was the only R.A.F. fighter able to take on the Messerschmitt 109, another of the great planes of the war, on equal terms. Both had top speeds of around 400 miles per hour, and while the ME-109 could outclimb and outdive the Spitfire, the latter was much more maneuverable. Both served

MESSERSCHMITT ME-109E

JUNKERS JU-87

MESSERSCHMITT ME-110

FIAT CR-42

JUNKERS JU-88

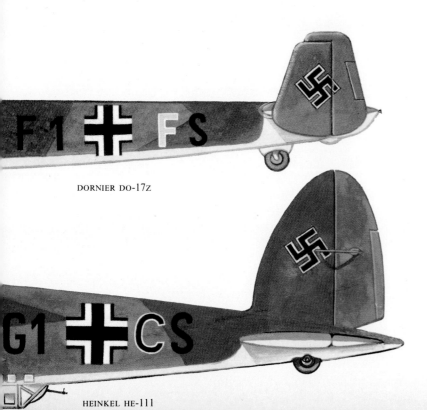

DORNIER DO-17Z

HEINKEL HE-111

throughout the war on every fighting front. A sea-going version of the Spitfire, called the Seafire, was used on carriers. The Hurricane was the other R.A.F. plane that won the Battle of Britain. Since it was slower than the ME-109, it usually attacked Nazi bombers while the Spitfires went after enemy fighters. Nevertheless, it proved maneuverable enough to take care of itself in combat with the speedy ME-109.

The four Nazi bombers here had one thing in common: they were shot down in large numbers. One merits a special word: the Junkers 87 was the notorious Stuka dive bomber that terrorized troops and civilians from Poland to France. But it was very slow, and when it met opposition for the first time over England, it was easily destroyed.

443

Planes over Europe

The European war produced so many notable aircraft that the ten pictured here cannot begin to complete the list. However, if to these are added the Flying Fortress and the important planes of the Battle of Britain, shown on previous pages, then at least the majority of the best-known ones are included. America's other heavy bomber, the B-24 Liberator, saw more action over the Mediterranean than Germany because it had less armament and armor than the B-17 and was prone to catch fire when hit. The Lancaster and Halifax were mainstays of the British night fleets, but the darling of the R.A.F. Bomber Command was the two-engine Mosquito, built of wood and fast enough to outrun enemy fighters and bomb by day. It specialized in daring exploits; one squadron planned its attack on Berlin to break up a parade being reviewed by Göring.

The Focke-Wulf 190, which appeared late in 1941, shifted fighter superiority to the *Luftwaffe* until an improved version of the Spitfire appeared. The great American fighters were the distinctive, twin-boomed P-38 Lightning, the big, versatile P-47 Thunderbolt, and the P-51 Mustang. The Mustang was probably the best of all fighters to appear during the war. The Russian YAK-3, light and maneuverable, was simply built because of the limitations of the Soviet aircraft industry. And the Messerschmitt 262 was the first jet plane of the war. It might have changed the course of the conflict, but Hitler ordered it redesigned as a bomber, then reversed himself so late that only a few appeared in the closing months of the war.

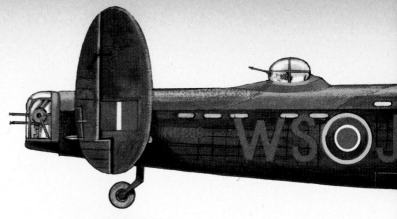

AVRO LANCASTER

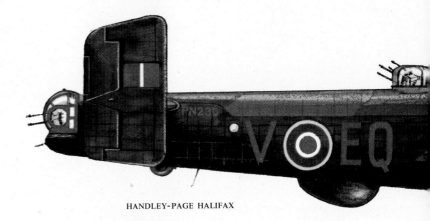

HANDLEY-PAGE HALIFAX

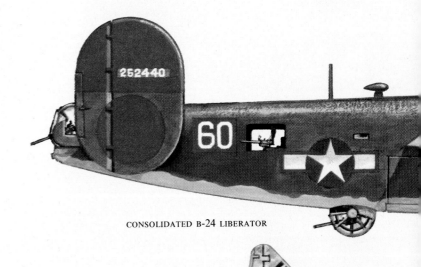

CONSOLIDATED B-24 LIBERATOR

MESSERSCHMITT ME-262

FOCKE-WULF FW-190

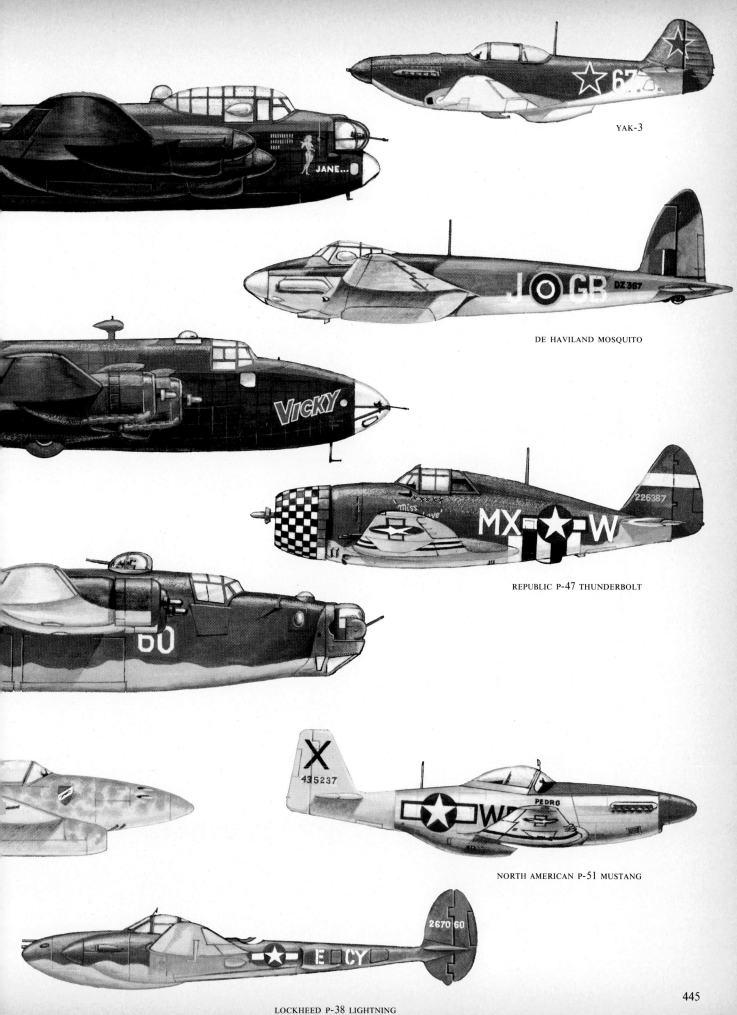

YAK-3

DE HAVILAND MOSQUITO

REPUBLIC P-47 THUNDERBOLT

NORTH AMERICAN P-51 MUSTANG

LOCKHEED P-38 LIGHTNING

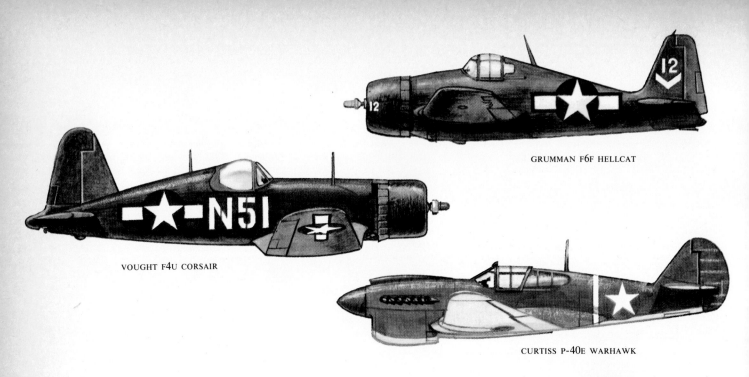

GRUMMAN F6F HELLCAT

VOUGHT F4U CORSAIR

CURTISS P-40E WARHAWK

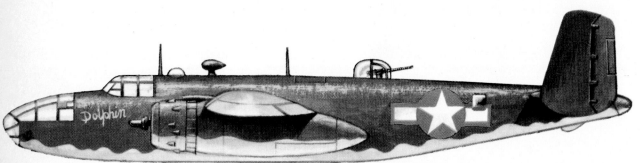

NORTH AMERICAN B-25D MITCHELL

GRUMMAN TBF-1 AVENGER

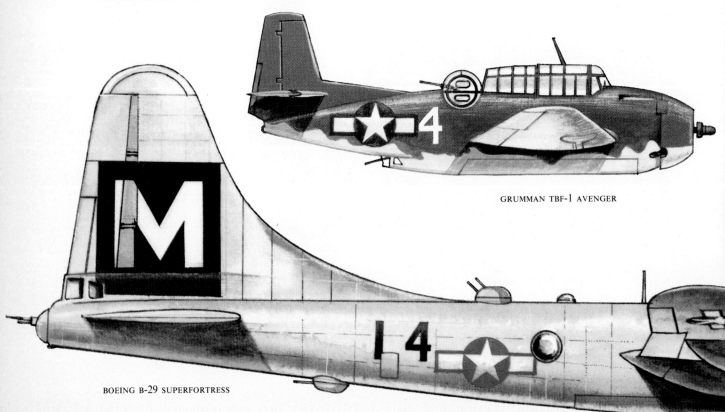

BOEING B-29 SUPERFORTRESS

Planes of the Pacific

Virtually all the American planes that saw service in Europe were also used in the Pacific, but the reverse was not always the case. The outstanding example was the huge B-29 Superfortress, which bombed only Japanese targets. American carrier planes also did most of their work in the Pacific: the Hellcat, the Corsair (flown by Marine squadrons), and the Avenger torpedo-bomber. The Japanese carrier-based Nakajima B5N1 ("Kate" in the American code-name system) played a leading part in the Pearl Harbor attack. The Zero-sen, though a good plane, had an early reputation out of all proportion to its abilities. The "Tony," a formidable high-altitude fighter, caused much worry when it began attacking B-29's over Japan in the last months of the war. The Japanese Navy's two-engine land-based bomber was the "Betty"; its lack of armor made it very vulnerable. Although the B-25 Mitchell served around the world, its most spectacular role was in the Pacific, when these normally land-based bombers took off from a carrier with the Doolittle raiders to attack Tokyo. And the P-40 Warhawk was best known, with a shark's mouth painted under its nose, as the plane of the Flying Tigers in Burma and China.

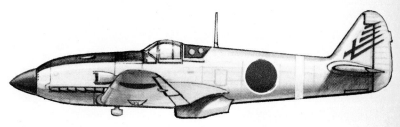

KAWASAKI HIEN "TONY"

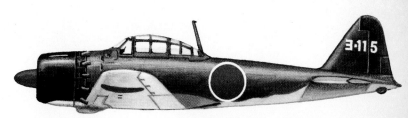

MITSUBISHI ZERO-SEN "ZEKE"

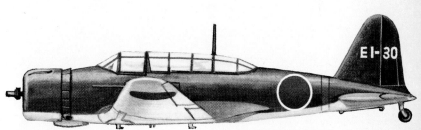

NAKAJIMA B5N1 "KATE"

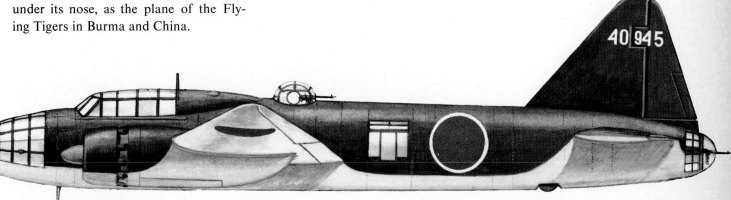

MITSUBISHI G4M1 "BETTY"

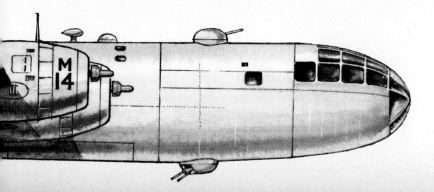

Hasten the Homecoming

FROM THE SATURDAY EVENING POST COVER PAINTING
BY NORMAN ROCKWELL

BUY VICTORY BONDS

The Home Fronts

Adolf Hitler's early successes on the battlefields of Europe and Russia brought with them a wave of support in Germany, even from those who hitherto had been reluctant to accept his brutal Nazi system. And as Hitler set about remaking Europe for Germany's benefit, life on the German home front seemed to be picking up, to the benefit of all. In fact, at first, with the help of loot from conquered areas, redirected Continental factory and farm output, the planning of an efficient and highly centralized Berlin Government, and the use of enslaved laborers from subject territories, the *Führer's* Third Reich flourished, and no one seemed displeased about that. Moreover, inherent German patriotism, martial spirit, and a habit of obedience were gradually shaped by *Gestapo* rigor and diabolically effective propaganda into a national instrument that brooked no opposition to the regime or whatever it was up to, including its most heinous offenses against human decency: extirpation of Jews, enserfment of foreign civilians, mockery of a free press, and a growing intolerance of religion. Although a small German underground existed inside the Reich and was in touch with such distinguished *émigrés* as Ernst Reuter, future mayor of West Berlin, and although this underground included certain brave and renowned individuals, such as Carl Goerdeler, ex-mayor of Leipzig, and Pastor Dietrich Bonhoeffer, it was ineffectual. The terror mounted. Indeed, in 1944, one out of every twelve hundred German adults was arrested for political or religious "offenses"—the latter being equivalent to the former.

D'Olier's *U.S. Strategic Bombing Survey* carefully analyzed this dictatorial system. It pointed out: "This elaborate machinery of control and compulsion was surrounded by a fringe of terror, symbolized by Gestapo, Elite Guards and the concentration camp. Although only very few actually knew much about the conditions in concentration camps, rumors and half-knowledge provided a powerful deterrent. . . . A stark fear of the unknown or partly known, increased by the observable severity of official punishment meted out to political offenders, enhanced and perhaps even exaggerated the demonstrable power of the control groups, and tended to cover up real gaps in their control. . . . The propaganda machine managed to persuade the man in the street for a long time that, for better or for worse, he was 'in for it,' because the world was bent on destroying Germany and the Germans. . . . Once the war was well under way, the Germans who enjoyed any advantage of position or economic status had a vested interest in German victory."

The German people accustomed themselves, without seeming aware of the fact, to living in a spiritual hell long before Allied air power turned it into a physical hell. The appalling deeds of their masters at home and their soldiers abroad escaped the majority or were viewed with a deliberately blind eye. If the Germans ate less well, if they dressed in ersatz materials, if they relinquished the last vestiges of freedom, they were fed, clothed, and excited by dreams of triumph and a thousand-year Reich.

As a consequence of both their courage and their ig-

A Norman Rockwell poster shows what America was working hardest for.

norance, the morale of the Germans withstood the ardors of Allied air raids, even though, as these increased, disillusion and doubt were privately nourished. Slowly a condiment of bitter humor was added to the diet of destruction. By the time Berlin was becoming a shambles, its citizens were caustically reminding each other of the *Führer's* architectural forecast: "Give me four years and I promise you you won't recognize your towns." Outside one leveled warehouse, a sign was prominently posted: "Open day and night now."

In his desperate effort to regain the initiative after the tide began to turn, Hitler filled Germany with forced labor to replace drafted workers. By early autumn, 1944, some 7,500,000 foreigners had been rounded up in occupied Europe and shipped to the Reich in boxcars, to a brutal half-life of endless toil, semistarvation, illness, and, in the end, often death. To these were added about two million prisoners of war, many of whom, in violation of the Hague and Geneva conventions, were made to work in ordnance plants.

One military memorandum, dated June 12, 1944, brusquely ordered: "Army Group Center intends to apprehend forty to fifty thousand youths from the age of 10 to 14 . . . and transport them to the Reich. . . . It is intended to allot these juveniles primarily to the German trades as apprentices. . . . This action is not only aimed at preventing a direct reinforcement of the enemy's strength but also as a reduction of his biological potentialities."

It was not until after the war, during the war criminal trials, that the full horror was exposed. A doctor assigned to inspect foreign laborers in a Krupp factory reported at Nuremberg: "Upon my first visit I found these females suffering from open festering wounds and other diseases. . . . They had no shoes and went about in their bare feet. . . . Their hair was shorn. The camp was surrounded by barbed wire and closely guarded by S.S. guards."

There was deliberate official encouragement to maltreat war prisoners—above all the unfortunate Russians, of whom more than two million died after capture. But Nazi bosses did not want the German people to become too exercised by public brutality. Heinrich Mueller, then *Gestapo* chief, warned his subordinates: "It was particularly noted that when marching, for example, from the railroad station to the camp, a rather large number of prisoners collapsed on the way from exhaustion, either dead or half dead, and had to be picked up by a truck following the convoy. It cannot be prevented that the German people take notice of these occurrences."

The captive hordes, both military and civilian, sought desperately and frequently to escape. But this was especially difficult because of close police supervision, added to constant exhaustion from sickness and hunger. Western prisoners were far better treated than those from Slavic nations. Through the Red Cross they had more care and closer contact with home. Not only did they organize effective means of spreading true war news, but there were many famous escapes. The Germans took ruthlessly repressive measures. Fifty British fliers caught in 1944 after fleeing their camp at Sagan were murdered at Hitler's personal order. The *Führer* commanded: "All enemies on so-called commando missions in Europe or Africa challenged by German troops, even if they are in uniform, whether armed or unarmed, in battle or in flight, are to be slaughtered to the last man." General Jodl prudently added these underlined words: "*This order is intended for commanders only and must not under any circumstances fall into enemy hands.*"

Despite this horror, the moral rot, the suffering and the constant bombing, the Reich's formidable war machine rolled on. During the first four years of war, ammunition production multiplied 2.6 times, artillery 4.8 times, armor 8.7 times, and aircraft 2.7 times. Albert Speer, youthful Nazi Minister of Arms and Munitions, saw to it that whatever happened in the totalitarian state, ordnance production increased. D'Olier's *Survey* found that despite intensification of Allied bombing and huge *Wehrmacht* losses, "the German army [as distinct from the *Luftwaffe*] was better equipped with weapons at the beginning of 1944 than at the start of the Russian War." The only serious shortage was in steel, although the *Luftwaffe* also was hampered by inadequate aircraft types, a result of Hitler's original conviction that the conflict would not be a long one.

The Germans were politically and intellectually benumbed by the time the war ended. Interrogated prisoners later conceded their folly. Elite Guard General Petrie said: "Propaganda was everything. We had to depend on it, and we took it as fact when we saw it printed." Franz Hofer, regional Nazi leader in Austria's Tyrol, acknowledged: "We believed in what the propaganda told us. It worked on us rather than on you." And Lieutenant General Huebner admitted: "We believed they [the Propaganda Ministry] must have known something, else they wouldn't have made such statements."

When Japan entered the war, its masses, also reared in a heritage that emphasized their superior qualities, were likewise easily subject to propaganda. After their first startling successes, there seemed to be little anxiety about the nation's future. The first shocking awareness of potential trouble came on April 18, 1942, when Doolittle's bombers suddenly pecked at Tokyo. One capital resident later said: "We finally began to realize that all we were told was not true—that the Government had lied when it said we were invulnerable. We then started to doubt that we were also invincible."

After Midway, after Guadalcanal, after successive German setbacks in the West, these doubts grew, but it was only on June 15, 1944, when sixty-eight Superfortresses struck Kyushu, that the Japanese people saw what lay in store. Tokyo was forced to tell them that "since the outbreak of the East Asian War everyone has recognized the difficulty of avoiding air attacks." The press began to talk of "a front behind the lines" and to exhort each civilian to remember he was "a warrior defending his country." Tokyo radio often broadcast an inane chant:

Why should we be afraid of air raids?
The big sky is protected with iron defenses.
For young and old it is time to stand up;
We are loaded with the honor of defending
   the homeland.
Come on, enemy planes! Come on many times!

And the planes came, more of them and more often. Air raid drills were frequent, even at night. Women were made to practice running uphill, bearing buckets of water; sandbags and pails were placed outside homes; enormous instruments resembling fly swatters were distributed to beat out flames.

By 1943 life was distinctly more austere. The rice reserve disappeared. Food became perilously scarce; the hungry were everywhere. Rations of electricity and gas became more strict. Women were asked to do without their colorful kimonos, and civilian consumption of cloth fell 95 per cent. Black market profiteering spread. Foreign Minister Shigemitsu wrote in his memoirs: "To live at all, the people reverted to a primitive existence. . . . They had never quite understood what the war was all about. To them the war was not theirs but a military war. . . . discipline suffered, while public resentment against the Army and Navy grew apace. As these social disturbances grew, the gendarmerie and police went ruthlessly about their task of enforcing the powers of the Army in order to whip the people on to further exertions."

Until 1944, Tojo's officer-dominated dictatorship remained politically secure. Backed by the powerful Imperial Rule Assistance Association, it had gained 80 per cent of the seats in the Diet early in the war and later had persuaded Japan's skeptical industrial barons, the *zaibatsu*, that the glorious economic program for subduing East Asia was bound to succeed. The Japanese stock market continued to boom. But Tojo made the same mistake as Hitler, failing to expand war production at a time when he had opportunity to do so. By 1944, when Japanese industry had achieved maximum efficiency, Allied successes were amputating Japan's access to raw materials. The air offensive against the home islands had cut output by 60 per cent before the war ended.

In its initially successful attempt to achieve economic self-sufficiency, Japan had sought to stress its "liberating" role and to loosen East Asia from the grip of the colonial Westerner, who was depicted as a racial enemy in much the same sense as the Nazis depicted the Slavs. Tokyo's propaganda stressed American immigration restrictions and anti-Negro prejudice, British arrogance in India and Malaya, Dutch brutality in Indonesia. One result of this was to encourage cruelty to white war prisoners. The Japanese military code disapproved of the practice of surrender, and Tokyo had never signed the Geneva convention. Thus it did not feel bound to Western conventions of humane warfare. Massacre, hunger, torture, and sheer callousness often marked treatment of Allied captives.

Japan's racist tenets at first succeeded in attracting the support of anti-imperialist Asians. They gained initial lip service from nationalist leaders such as Indonesia's Sukarno and Hatta, India's Subhas Chandra Bose, the Burmese revolutionists, and the bewildered followers of Premier Chang Ching-hui in Manchukuo (Chinese Manchuria) and Wang Ching-wei, puppet prime minister of occupied China. But this racist appeal dwindled together with the legend of Tokyo's invincibility. Japanese brutality, tactlessness, and indifference and a determination to "Nipponize" conquered areas soon antagonized the new revolutionary movements. They began to react against Tokyo's secret police, the *Kempeitai*, quite as strongly as they had opposed their previous white masters; only now, thanks to war, they had arms with which to express political opinions. When Japan, isolated and smashed, went down amid a sea of enemies, included among them were millions of Asian peoples who, for a short period of time, had been subjects of the Greater East Asia Co-Prosperity Sphere.

On the Allied side, morale in Russia was at first severely shaken during the war's early months, although it remained constantly high in Britain and never faltered in the United States. The war in the Soviet Union came after Stalin had spent seven years repressing his subjects, murdering thousands, sending millions to prison camps, and spreading fear through a muted nation.

However, any initial hopes there may have been for a better life under the Nazis were short-lived, and Stalin focused his propaganda on national rather than ideological themes. The monolithic Soviet state harnessed everyone to the war effort. Women were mobilized to run tractors on collective farms. Those not fit for military service, the wounded, and the very old were conscripted into the labor force and were called upon to fight in emergencies like the battles for Leningrad and Moscow.

Most Soviet citizens, even those who bitterly resented Stalin, dug in with grim determination, living on the edge of starvation, often cut off from news of soldier relatives. In blacked-out Moscow during December, 1941, I was once arrested for "smoking ostentatiously" in the darkened, snow-filled streets. When a woman approached me, begging for food, I gave her the ruble equivalent of two dollars. She spat and said: "What can I do with that? Give me bread." During the 1941–42 winter, the foreign press was billeted in Moscow's Metropole Hotel and given privileged meals. Among items regularly served was a fruit dish so filled with worms that we dubbed it "motorized compote." At official Government banquets for visiting statesmen, the sallow waiters customarily stole scraps. We used to save bread and sugar for our secretaries; nevertheless, mine, originally a hefty woman, lost forty pounds during the war's first two years.

The Soviet home front was resolute, bitter, and marked by a wild hatred of the Germans that exceeded anything in Britain or America. I visited a hospital most of whose patients were members of tank crews who had suffered terrible face wounds and were being restored by plastic surgery. Except for those completely blinded, all of these men, some without jaws, some without noses, some without ears, expressed but one aspiration: to get back to the front and kill more Nazis. And as the Red Army regathered and surged forward on the attack, a new aura of confidence started to spread through the ravaged, suffering nation. At night, batteries around the Kremlin began to boom salutes to victories, and the country's war songs assumed a note of savage joy.

The British, an inherently less emotional people than the Russians, showed a comparably less frantic reaction both in adversity and success. Under Churchill's incandescent leadership, they managed to meet the challenge of 1940 alone and virtually unarmed, yet with a striking national calm. They simply refused, for the most part, even to contemplate the thought that they might lose the Battle of Britain, even though, for quite some time, logic argued against victory.

Britain adopted a system of tightly rationing food, shoes, and household goods. Gasoline and textiles were rigidly restricted, newspapers and magazines thin. The B.B.C. assumed an immense new importance as the essential organ for both informing and entertaining the English people and their restless allies in occupied Europe.

The British survived two aerial ordeals—the Blitz and The V-1, V-2 terror—with courage and endurance. Good-naturedly they went into shelters or helped local police forces as air-raid wardens and fire-fighting patrols. Somehow they managed to get to work despite scrambled transportation systems. Beside the ruins of their dwellings, they cheered Churchill as he visited his home front, cigar between clenched teeth, giving his victory signal.

As early as 1940, life had become appallingly thin and threadbare, and it was to remain so until long after the war ended. Shipping on which the island lived was almost wholly devoted to essential cargoes, and the treasury was bare. Housing was strained as buildings in cities were destroyed by bombing, families were evacuated to the country to be billeted with others, and the United Kingdom filled with troops mustered by the Americans, Canadians, Poles, and Free French for the final invasion.

Women played a far greater role than ever before, taking jobs as chauffeurs, laborers, ferry pilots, wardens, and farmers, and asserting a new and energetic independence of their own. Most important, the old social structures and traditions of personal diffidence were broken down as rich and poor rubbed shoulders in air raid shelters. The atmosphere of the English pub, with all its cozy intimacy, managed somehow to grip the nation in its time of most arduous difficulty. "Roll Out the Barrel" and "Kiss Me Goodnight Sergeant Major" were sung in dire moments with as much fervor as "God Save the King" when theater curtains rolled down early to allow the audience time to get home before the *Luftwaffe* arrived.

Unlike its Allies and its enemies, the United States lived a comparatively paradisiacal existence during World War II, the sole important island of unabated security in a total conflict. As such, its function was not only to furnish vigorous new man power but to serve as an unassailable arsenal. President Roosevelt made this clear in his famous January, 1942, address to Congress, in which he promised that the United States would produce, by 1943, an annual 125,000 airplanes, 75,000 tanks and 8,000,000 dead-weight tons of shipping. He called in a Sears Roebuck executive, the shrewd, flat-voiced Midwesterner Donald Nelson, asked him how he liked the title "War Production Board," and, when Nelson approved it, said: "*You* are the chairman."

Soon the clatter of hammers, the clash of gears, and the sputtering of foundries encompassed the country. Locomotives, planes, trucks, steel landing mats, telephones, aluminum sheets, radar, and above all guns and ammunition poured out in measureless quantities. On October 27, 1944, Roosevelt proudly told his fellow citizens: "The production which has flowed from this country to all the battlefronts of the world has been due to the efforts of American business, American labor and American farmers, working together as a patriotic team." It was a fine statement, even if not entirely accurate, as, inevitably, there had been friction along the way between labor and management and government. (At the start of the war, the AFL and the CIO had agreed to a no-strike pledge, and union officials, if not all unions, lived up to it. The one major exception was John L. Lewis, who took his coal miners out on strike four times during the course of the war.) And if the size of the output was staggering, so also was its cost: between 1941 and 1945, the national debt rose from forty-eight billion to two hundred and forty-seven billion dollars.

To help foot the bill, Americans at home paid higher taxes and bought some six billion dollars worth of war bonds. They also put up with the few deprivations the war put upon them: ration stamps and shortages of butter, gasoline, textiles, meat, cigarettes, automobiles and automobile tires, apartments, refrigerators—the list went on and on. The Government's Office of Price Administration fixed the cost of certain consumer goods, and all too often shoppers were wearily reminded: "Don't ya know there's a war on!"

Newspapers, magazines, radio, and cinema joined to remind the nation of bleaker realities beyond our fortunate continent. Documentary films like *The Fighting Lady* and *The Battle of the Beaches* and Hollywood films like *Hitler's Children* and *Mrs. Miniver* recalled the ruthlessness of battlefronts and the suffering of foreign friends. There were even appallingly crude propaganda movies designed to stir up sympathy for the unhappy Russians. One of these, *Mission to Moscow*, was taken to the Soviet capital by its "hero," former ambassador Joseph Davies, an innocent admirer of Stalin, and shown in the Kremlin, to the Politburo's amusement.

Once it really got into the fight, the United States went at it with a violent, aggressive, uninhibited vigor that astonished both friends and enemies. It was not only the extent of this effort that was impressive, but also its ingenuity. One observer remarked: "The Seabees could probably have erected the Pyramids on any of our beachheads had such construction been adjudged militarily desirable." The whole nation pitched in. The undrafted population floated from city to city and factory to factory as new enterprises sucked up energy. Washington's broad avenues, which had not yet managed to dispose of World War I's temporary buildings, were packed with mushrooming clusters of new offices. Almost overnight, the inrush of a new bureaucracy swelled the Capital from an overgrown village to an underdeveloped metropolis. Servants, nursemaids, clerks, cooks, doormen, messengers abandoned nonessential jobs and flocked off to war plants, where girls and old men hammered, riveted, and operated cranes. The impact on American habits was profound and permanent. Women who had known little except how to run a home became familiar with the time clock and fat pay checks. (Though fifteen million men were in uniform, the total labor force was greatly expanded, thanks in good part to the addition of some six million women.) When the war ended, families who had been accustomed to servants often found that they no longer had them, and that they could do without them.

There was also a minor revival of the speakeasy philosophy of prohibition days as some citizens preferred not to honor certain laws or adhere to certain patterns of patriotic behavior urged by the Government. Hoarding went on in a good many communities; ration stamps and tokens were bargained off. Novel black markets sprang up in everything from beef to tires. The same taxi driver who had once guided fares to illicit booze joints now took them to illicit gas stations. Bellboys managed to produce cigarettes, and butchers found fat steaks—for a price. And with the nation busily at work and wages higher than ever before, there was plenty of money around.

A tremendous exuberance gripped the population, which showed in pride over the achievements of its soldiery, confidence in its ability to surmount unexpected problems, eagerness to tackle unfamiliar enterprises, and an absolute lack of inhibition. It was also true that the thirties had been lean years indeed; it was wonderful to be back at work again in full force. In his last Navy Day speech before his death, Roosevelt mirrored some of this spirit. He proudly pointed out that, apart from its battlefield successes and its large industrial production, the country's achievement "has meant establishing for our Army and Navy supply lines extending over 56,000 miles —more than twice the circumference of this earth. It has meant establishing the lines of the Air Transport Command—one hundred and fifty thousand miles of air supply system running regularly."

In distributing favors among World War II belligerents, fortune was generous to the United States. The American Dream of isolation was to a large measure preserved throughout the conflict, in the sense that we were never occupied like so much of Europe and Asia and never pounded by aerial attacks. We experienced victory without having pondered defeat. And we emerged ebullient, confident in our global position and in the belief that at last this earth had become politically habitable. For a few brief years, we felt assured that if again a malefactor disturbed this pleasant horizon, we alone possessed in our atomic treasury the power that could squash him.

Inside Hitler's Germany

The first two years of the war were a heady time on the German home front. How very much had been accomplished! All Europe (or all of it that was really needed) was under German control; Germany, just as Hitler had promised, was again a world power. There was, to be sure, a good deal of unpleasantness to contend with: air raids, shortages of almost everything, and perhaps most disturbing of all, the thought of what might be in store for Germany should its fortunes take a sharp turn for the worse. Sons and husbands, home on leave, were talking behind closed doors about what they had seen the *S.S.* doing on the Russian front; and at home, the *Gestapo* and its activities were all too apparent to anyone with eyes to see and a little imagination. Then, in 1942, came El Alamein and Stalingrad. The air raids grew steadily worse. Sirens screamed like clockwork; city people scarcely ever had a full night's sleep. By 1943, the destruction and suffering in places like Hamburg, Frankfurt, even Berlin itself, were beyond belief. But faith in the *Führer* flagged very little through all this, nor did the German people's allegiance to duty, obedience, and hard, hard work.

Life at the top of the Nazi social order went along with only minor discomforts right up until the end, while demands on the German people grew increasingly harsh. At right top: a moment of high Nazi gaiety at a wedding reception in 1944 for Gretl Braun, sister of Hitler's mistress, Eva Braun. (Eva is seen at rear center.) At bottom right, German women give clothing to a van marked, "The Führer *expects your sacrifice, for the army and the homeguard. So that your pride, your home guardsman can show himself in uniform, clean out your closets now and your chests and please bring everything to us." At left: Heinrich Himmler, head of the ubiquitous, dreaded* Gestapo.

454

The Final Solution

All through the war, stories kept coming out of Germany and the occupied countries about the terrible things being done to the Jews. But they were not widely believed; no society could be that rotten, no regime, not even the Nazis, could be that vile. Besides, people said, there had been German atrocity stories during the first war, and they had turned out to be a lot of propaganda. It was only when the Allies broke into Germany in 1945 that the world came to the awful realization that scenes such as these, and far worse, had been taking place throughout the Nazi empire since the very first weeks of war in 1939. The sickness had been there from the start, of course, in *Mein Kampf* and Hitler's speeches in the 1930's. The evils of life, the Nazis had ranted, were the doings of the Jew; get rid of him, and the world would be right again. The idea was essential to Nazi ideology, and when Hitler took power, he set up camps for Jews and other "enemies of the state" and put through laws denying them certain rights. He staged violent demonstrations against them, and no one did anything to stop him. Furthermore, in several speeches he warned that if the Jews dared touch off another world war, then they deserved to be destroyed. When war came, it mattered not at all who had started it; for the Nazis, the time had come for what their official memorandum termed "the final solution of the Jewish question." Every Jew they could lay hands on would be murdered.

The photographs at right, taken in Poland and Holland, show the various stages in the Nazi campaign against the Jews. Throughout Germany and the countries conquered by Hitler, the pattern was much the same: Jews were hunted down, humiliated in public (at top left, Nazi soldiers shave an orthodox Polish Jew), beaten, and pressed into labor gangs. Sometimes whole neighborhoods were lined up against a wall and shot. More often, Jews were rounded up and shipped in boxcars to a death by starvation, disease, torture, machine gun, or gas chamber.

456

The end of the line for perhaps as many as six million Jewish men, women, and children was one of thirty-odd death camps that were set up by the Nazis in Germany and the occupied countries. The scene at right is from a German film found after the war. The location is not known, but it may have been at Belsen, Ravensbrück, or Buchenwald, where Jewish women were imprisoned in great numbers.

"And all because they are Jews!"

Anne Frank

Since July of 1942, fifteen-year-old Anne Frank had been cooped up with her family and four others inside a few small rooms concealed in her father's former office building in Amsterdam. Then, on August 4, 1944, Dutch Nazi police discovered the door that led to their hiding place. Seven months later, in March, 1945, Anne Frank died of typhus in the Bergen-Belsen concentration camp. But during the two years she had been in hiding, Anne had kept a diary, which was left behind in a heap of rubbish. Published shortly after the end of the war under the title The Diary of a Young Girl, *it quickly became one of the best-known books of all time.*

SATURDAY, 20 JUNE, 1942

. . . My father was thirty-six when he married my mother, who was then twenty-five. My sister Margot was born in 1926 in Frankfort-on-Main, I followed on June 12, 1929, and, as we are Jewish, we emigrated to Holland in 1933, where my father was appointed Managing Director of Travies N.V. This firm is in close relationship with the firm of Kolen & Co. in the same building, of which my father is a partner.

The rest of our family, however, felt the full impact of Hitler's anti-Jewish laws, so life was filled with anxiety. In 1938 after the pogroms, my two uncles (my mother's brothers) escaped to the U.S.A. My old grandmother came to us, she was then seventy-three. After May 1940 good times rapidly fled: first the war, then the capitulation, followed by the arrival of the Germans, which is when the sufferings of us Jews really began. Anti-Jewish decrees followed each other in quick succession. Jews must wear a yellow star, Jews must hand in their bicycles, Jews are banned from trams and are forbidden to drive. Jews are only allowed to do their shopping between three and five o'clock and then only in shops which bear the placard "Jewish shop." Jews must be indoors by eight o'clock and cannot even sit in their own gardens after that hour. Jews are forbidden to visit theaters, cinemas, and other places of entertainment. Jews may not take part in public sports. Swimming baths, tennis courts, hockey fields, and other sports grounds are all prohibited to them. Jews may not visit Christians. Jews must go to Jewish schools, and many more restrictions of a similar kind.

SATURDAY, 11 JULY, 1942

Daddy, Mummy, and Margot can't get used to the sound of the Westertoren clock yet, which tells us the time every quarter of an hour. I can. I loved it from the start, and especially in the night it's like a faithful friend.

MONDAY, 21 SEPTEMBER, 1942

. . . I'm busy with Daddy working out his family tree: as we go along he tells me little bits about everyone —it's terribly interesting. Mr. Koophuis brings a few special books for me every other week. I'm thrilled with the *Joop ter Heul* series. I've enjoyed the whole of Cissy van Marxveldt very much. And I've read *Een Zomerzotheid* four times and I still laugh about some of the ludicrous situations that arise.

Term time has begun again, I'm working hard at my French and manage to pump in five irregular verbs per day. Peter sighs and groans over his English. A few schoolbooks have just arrived; we have a good stock of exercise books, pencils, rubbers, and labels, as I brought these with me. I sometimes listen to the Dutch news from London, heard Prince Bernhard recently. He said that Princess Juliana is expecting a baby about next January. I think it is lovely: it surprises the others that I should be so keen on the Royal Family.

SATURDAY, 7 NOVEMBER, 1942

. . . Sometimes I believe that God wants to try me, both now and later on; I must become good through my own efforts, without examples and without good advice. Then later on I shall be all the stronger. Who besides me will ever read these letters? From whom but myself shall I get comfort? As I need comforting often, I frequently feel weak, and dissatisfied with myself; my shortcomings are too great. I know this, and every day I try to improve myself, again and again. . . .

THURSDAY, 19 NOVEMBER, 1942

. . . Apart from that, all goes well. Dussell has told us a lot about the outside world, which we have missed for so long now. He had very sad news. Countless friends and acquaintances have gone to a terrible fate. Evening after evening the green and gray army lorries trundle past. The Germans ring at every front door to inquire if there are any Jews living in the house. If there are, then the whole family has to go at once. If they don't find any, they go on to the next house. No one has a chance of evading them unless one goes into hiding. Often they go around with lists, and only ring when they know they can get a good haul. Sometimes they let them off for cash—so much per head. It seems like the slave hunts of olden times. But it's certainly no joke; it's much too tragic for that. In the evenings when it's dark, I often see rows of good, innocent people accompanied by crying children, walking on and on, in charge of a couple of these chaps, bullied and knocked about until they al-

most drop. No one is spared—old people, babies, expectant mothers, the sick. . . .

How fortunate we are here, so well cared for and undisturbed. . . .

I feel wicked sleeping in a warm bed, while my dearest friends have been knocked down or have fallen into a gutter somewhere out in the cold night. I get frightened when I think of close friends who have now been delivered into the hands of the cruelest brutes that walk the earth. And all because they are Jews!

SATURDAY, 28 NOVEMBER, 1942

We have used too much electricity, more than our ration. Result: the utmost economy and the prospect of having it cut off. No light for a fortnight; a pleasant thought, that, but who knows, perhaps it won't happen after all! It's too dark to read in the afternoons after four or half past. We pass the time in all sorts of crazy ways: asking riddles, physical training in the dark, talking English and French, criticizing books. But it all begins to pall in the end. Yesterday evening I discovered something new: to peer through a powerful pair of field glasses into the lighted rooms of the houses at the back. In the daytime we can't allow even as much as a centimeter's chink to appear between our curtains, but it can't do any harm after dark. I never knew before that neighbors could be such interesting people. At any rate, ours are. I found one couple having a meal, one family was in the act of taking a home movie; and the dentist opposite was just attending to an old lady, who was awfully scared. . . .

WEDNESDAY, 13 JANUARY, 1943

Everything has upset me again this morning, so I wasn't able to

finish a single thing properly.

It is terrible outside. Day and night more of those poor miserable people are being dragged off, with nothing but a rucksack and a little money. On the way they are deprived even of these possessions. Families are torn apart, the men, women, and children all being separated. Children coming home from school find that their parents have disappeared. Women return from shopping to find their homes shut up and their families gone. . . .

TUESDAY, 11 APRIL, 1944

. . . Who has inflicted this upon us? Who has made us Jews different from all other people? Who has allowed us to suffer so terribly up till now? It is God that has made us as we are, but it will be God, too, who will raise us up again. If we bear all this suffering and if there are still Jews left, when it is over, then Jews, instead of being doomed, will be held up as an example. Who knows, it might even be our religion from which the world and all peoples learn good, and for that reason and that reason only do we have to suffer now. We can never become just Netherlanders, or just English, or representatives of any country for that matter, we will always remain Jews, but we want it, too.

Be brave! Let us remain aware of our task and not grumble, a solution will come, God has never deserted our people. Right through the ages there have been Jews, through all the ages they have had to suffer, but it has made them strong too; the weak fall, but the strong will remain and never go under!

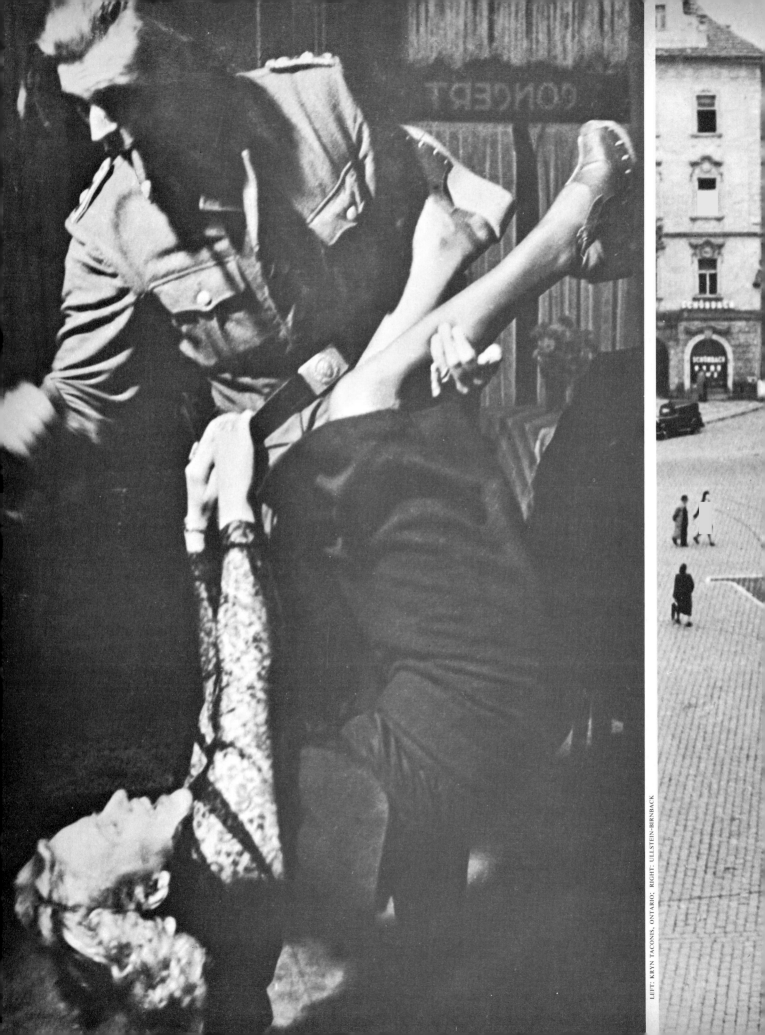

EDVARD SCHMOLKA

In the fifteen European countries Hitler took over, there was never any escaping the German presence. Life was dominated by them. In the remarkable photograph at far left, a Dutch collaborator is caught in the middle of a wild dance with a Nazi officer in an Amsterdam cafe. (The picture was taken by a photographer who carried his camera concealed in a briefcase.) The huge "V" in the middle of a central square in Prague was the German answer to the "V-for-Victory" signs being scribbled everywhere by the Czech underground. Rather than try to fight the symbol, German propagandists simply said that the "V" was for a Germano-Latin "Viktoria" and painted their own in prominent places. It was a clever ploy, but made no difference really. Throughout occupied Europe, the "V" continued to stand, as Churchill said, for "the unconquerable will of the occupied territories, and a portent of the fate awaiting the Nazi tyranny."

463

La Résistance

After the French surrender at Compiègne in 1940, "correct" behavior was the order of the day for the army of occupation. The demoralized, politically decadent French would be shown that the pride of the Nazi state, the soldier, was courteous, forthright, even cultured. But when the technique failed to vitiate French hatred, and when the French became troublesome about Nazi looting and the rounding up of Jews, other measures were taken. The Nazis reverted to type, and the resistance began to grow. At first there were very few involved, maybe only a thousand a year after Compiègne. The French Communists joined the fight when Hitler struck Russia, and proved themselves highly expert at it; and many more joined in late 1942, after Hitler took over southern France. But still it was only a relative handful of brave men and women who were sabotaging Nazi-run munitions factories, tying up German troops, cutting communications lines, and supplying the Allies with quantities of information on the enemy. That most Frenchmen (and, for that matter, most Dutchmen, Poles, Greeks, and all the rest who came under the Nazi boot) chose to mind their own business as much as possible is not surprising, considering the efficiency and savage brutality of the *Gestapo.* What counts is that thousands did go underground and join the fight, despite the terrible risks, causing Hitler no end of trouble and unquestionably hastening the day of Allied victory.

Above, in the early days of the occupation, Parisians watch as a German soldier takes advantage of life in Hitler's army. At right is Jean Moulin, who ran the resistance for de Gaulle until June, 1943, when he was captured by the Gestapo *and tortured to death. Known as "Max," he wore a scarf to hide the scar left by an unsuccessful attempt to cut his own throat when the Nazis had tortured him earlier, in 1940.*

Forging papers for crossing the border into Vichy France (a checkpoint is shown at top right) was a major activity of the resistance at the start. Later the movement became more violent. Bridges were blown, patrols ambushed, trains derailed (center). For the resistance fighter, there was little glory and certain death by torture or firing squad if ever he was taken prisoner.

Austerity in Japan

The Japanese people were told that Roosevelt and Churchill were power-mad men completely to blame for the war, and Allied fighting men were called beasts, cannibals, and gangsters and were accused of all manner of inhuman acts, including bombing hospital ships. Life in Japan became increasingly bleak as American planes and submarines methodically wiped out Japanese shipping. Electricity, gas, oil, and other items were rationed, and food became so scarce that by the end of the war, cases of malnutrition were common. Each home was required to have an air-raid shelter in its garden, but these were merely deep holes and proved useless when B-29's fire-bombed the tindery cities. As the man-power shortage grew, boys of ten or twelve did heavy work such as loading freight on trains, and children were taken from their schools by their teachers to work in factories. Yet even though the people saw defeat around them, the radio broadcast news only of victories to the end.

Japanese walk across an American flag painted on the sidewalk (above). By defiling the flag in such a manner, they supposedly whip up their hatred for the United States. At right, the parents of a dead soldier carry a scroll with their son's picture to a shrine honoring the war dead.

Total war killed impartially. Here Japanese school children, wearing protective gauze masks, head for an air-raid shelter. Although

MAINICHI GRAPHIC–BIRNBACK

shelters gave some protection when American planes dropped high explosives, they were useless during the terrible fire-bomb raids.

The Mood
of America

The United States, unlike her allies Britain and Russia (whose home-front experiences were pictured earlier), never had her continental territory violated, cities bombed, or civilians slain. But Americans knew what war meant, and unlike 1917, they went to war without much cheering. At home, taking up arms brought inconveniences but little pain; actually, millions were earning more money than ever before in their lives. But it was not a prosperity many rejoiced in. So many millions of men were going into uniform—over 15,000,000 by war's end—that scarcely a home in the country was not affected. And there were countless irritating and bewildering changes. There was rationing and shortages. New automobiles or refrigerators were not to be had. Women put on coveralls and went to work in factories, or joined the armed forces and put on uniforms. The mood of the nation was "let's get it over with"; it was significant that there were no rousing songs to compare with "Over There" of 1917. For a time, people sang "Praise the Lord and Pass the Ammunition," but the song probably owed its popularity more to its bounce than to its patriotic sentiments.

Millions of women were brought out of their homes and into war production work of many types. At left, seamstresses work on flags and banners in the Philadelphia Quartermaster Depot. At right, radio songstress Kate Smith opens a war-bond sales drive in New York. Motion picture stars and other celebrities took part in giant bond rallies; the campaign urging the public to purchase war bonds was constant, and it made use of every medium. During the war, the total of $36,000,000,000 worth of Series "E" bonds was sold.

471

The Way It Was at Home

Göring, Mussolini, and Premier Tojo, with good friend, were caricatured by artist Arthur Szyk.

What was life like in America during the war? It was a time of saying good-by and of waiting. It was also a time of moving about. Trains shuttled across the country night and day, hauling servicemen and civilians on a multitude of war missions. And young women who in normal times would still be under parental eyes moved far from home, some in the WAVES or WAACs or Coast Guard SPARs or Women Marines, others to work in war plants. Store shelves went empty as goods ranging from facial tissues and hairpins to cameras and alarm clocks disappeared. Cigarettes were scarce, and many people learned to roll their own. The ration stamp was a necessity of life, for among items on the rationed list were meats, butter, sugar, coffee, almost all canned and frozen foods, gasoline, and shoes. Men's trousers went cuffless to save cloth, and an old toothpaste tube had to be turned in when buying a new one. There were tin can collections, waste paper collections, aluminum drives, and housewives salvaged grease from cooking. Manufacturers with nothing to sell told in their ads how they were helping win the war: auto makers boasted of their tanks, a typewriter manufacturer talked about its armor-piercing shells. Some brags were farfetched, and a radio producer was so irritated by the line "Lucky Strike Green has gone to war" (referring to a color change in a cigarette package) that he cancelled the company's sponsorship of his program. But without dissent, Americans hated the Japanese, loathed all that the Nazi system stood for, and felt contempt for Mussolini.

Ration stamps issued in 1943.

Women workers load turret guns of a completed bomber.

Familiar sight in gas-scarce times.

LUCKY STRIKE GREEN HAS GONE TO WAR!

So here's the smart new uniform for fine tobacco

Lucky Strike reiterated its slogan through magazines, billboards, and radio, rather overstating its contribution toward victory.

The U.S. Army made use of posters with a pun (above) in its campaign to recruit women ordnance workers. At left, children in New York bring in a cart loaded with pots and pans that they have collected during an aluminum drive.

Almost every city had recreational facilities, and a great many well-known
personalities gave both their time and
talents to entertain servicemen. At
left, Vice-President Truman plays and
actress Lauren Bacall lolls atop the
piano at Washington's National Press
Club Canteen. Below, a hostess at the
Stage Door Canteen in New York
serves birthday cake. Theater people
manned the canteen completely, from
entertaining to making sandwiches and
sweeping up. Women Marines (right),
at chow at Cherry Point Air Station,
typify the high status of women in
this war. Each of the four services had
its women's auxiliary, and a total of
200,000 women enlisted. Many served
in specialized jobs, such as in airfield
control-tower operations, as aviation
mechanics, and as code-room clerks.

The Great Dictator (1940)
Charlie Chaplin, Jack Oakie

A Yank in the RAF (1941)
Tyrone Power, Betty Grable

Hollywood Under Arms

Hollywood was stirred by the same currents that swept the rest of the nation. At least a quarter of the motion picture industry's male employees, from stars to grips, went into uniform. Other stars appeared at hundreds of bond rallies and gave thousands of free performances to servicemen in hospitals and in every war area around the world. But in the business of making movies, the industry too often avoided the realities of war and stuck to innocuous—and safe—escape-type films. After all, the argument went, the fighting man overseas who made up a big part of the audience was sick of war and wanted movies with lots of girls and lots of laughs.

However, excellent war—not necessarily combat—pictures were produced, films of the caliber of *Thirty Seconds Over Tokyo, Mrs. Miniver,* and *Casablanca.* There were also mediocre ones, like *Mission to Moscow,* which wrapped Stalin in white robes, or *For Whom the Bell Tolls,* made pointless because it carefully expunged the Spanish Civil War background. And there were horrors, like *Keep Your Powder Dry,* a concoction about three glamour-girl WAACs, and *Four Jills in a Jeep,* which showed that war can be great fun for four actresses touring the fronts. (At right is a gallery of stills from war-year movies, with some of their stars.) The industry also worked with the services to produce documentaries of actual combat. The first of these was *The Battle of Midway;* by far the best was the feature-length *Fighting Lady,* about life on an aircraft carrier.

Desperate Journey (1942)
Raymond Massey

Road to Morocco (1942)
Bob Hope, Dorothy Lamour, Bing Crosby

This is the Army (1943)
George Murphy

The North Star (1943)
Erich von Stroheim

Guadalcanal Diary (1943)
Anthony Quinn

Mission to Moscow (1943)
Walter Huston, Ann Harding

Meet Me in St. Louis (1944)
Margaret O'Brien, Judy Garland

The Purple Heart (1944)
Dana Andrews, Richard Loo

That Night in Rio (1941)
Carmen Miranda

Man Hunt (1941)
George Sanders, Walter Pidgeon

Buck Privates (1941)
Bud Abbott, Lou Costello

Casablanca (1942)
Claude Rains, Humphrey Bogart

Underground (1942)
Martin Kosleck

Mrs. Miniver (1942)
Greer Garson, Helmut Dantine

The Pied Piper (1942)
Otto Preminger, Monty Woolley

Bataan (1943)
George Murphy, Robert Taylor

Bombardier (1943)
Randolph Scott, Barton MacLane

Edge of Darkness (1943)
Helmut Dantine

Song of Russia (1943)
Robert Taylor, Susan Peters

Five Graves to Cairo (1943)
Erich von Stroheim

See Here, Private Hargrove (1944)
Robert Walker

White Cliffs of Dover (1944)
Irene Dunne, Alan Marshall

30 Seconds over Tokyo (1944)
Spencer Tracy

Cover Girl (1944)
Rita Hayworth

Since You Went Away (1944)
Joseph Cotten, Claudette Colbert

The Sullivans (1944)

The Keys of the Kingdom (1944)
Gregory Peck

Back to Bataan (1945)
John Wayne

Our Men and Machines

The American home front suffered little during the war. Food was rationed, but no one went hungry; gasoline was rationed, but chiefly for those who had no pressing reason to drive. Nevertheless, it was from this secure American homeland that there came a flood of guns, planes, tanks, ships, bandages, telephone wire, dried beans, and all the multitudinous other items that not only equipped the huge American fighting machine but were copious enough to be shared with our allies as well. And from the training camps in America came the citizen army to fight a two-front war, and not a cheap one, for our costs in blood were comparable with those of any anti-Axis nation except Russia and China. The home front was not as far from the war front as it seemed.

ALFRED EISENSTAEDT, © TIME, INC.

THE BOEING COMPANY

The Boeing Company's Seattle plant marked the end of an era on April 9, 1945, when it turned out its final B-17 Flying Fortress (right). A B-29 Superfortress stands in the background. Above, the most-repeated of tableaus throughout the war years: a soldier and his girl say good-by.

478

TOKYO

BERLIN

The 6981ᴴᴴ SEATTLE BUILT Boeing FLYING FORTRESS

Assault on Fortress Europe

By the spring of 1944, Hitler's chain of fortifications around Europe, from the Channel on the west to the Apennines and Aegean Islands on the south and the Vistula on the east, was formidable but uneven. Behind these strategic positions, the firmness of Nazi control was corrupted as internal forces of liberation organized with ever-mounting effect. All through France, the Maquis and saboteurs and spies of the resistance prepared for the final struggle. Similar if smaller undergrounds seethed inside Holland and Norway. Armed units, largely Communist-led, sprang up in Nazi-controlled northern Italy. In the Balkans, despite quarrels between Communists and anti-Communists, vigorous bands were active in Greece, Albania, and Yugoslavia, where Tito's partisans had created history's most effective guerrilla army. Even Poland, barely accessible to Western help, had a notable military underground. Finally, added to occupied Europe's fevered restlessness, Hitler's satellites, Hungary and Rumania, had already begun secret negotiations with Allied agents in the hope of buying back respectability.

These widely scattered freedom forces had developed apace since 1942, when Stalin first began to clamor for a second front. He suspected that the West was secretly delaying a cross-Channel invasion in the hope that Germany and Russia would batter each other to death—the reverse of what he himself had once hoped to promote between Germany and France. In the spring of 1942, Britain and the United States, in fact, were wholly in favor of such a second front and had been working on various plans for many months. But it became increasingly evident that neither the troops nor the technical equipment yet existed for any operation sufficiently large to stand a chance of success. Churchill had no intention of sacrificing another generation of young Englishmen on any enterprise as barren as those of World War I, and Roosevelt soon discovered that America, heavily engaged in the Pacific, was short on warships and landing craft.

Therefore, although Allied planners continued to contemplate a future landing in France, in the end they settled on a large commando sortie against Dieppe, on the coast of France, in August, 1942. A raiding force of five thousand men, primarily Canadian, attacked Dieppe, and more than half were killed, wounded, or captured.

That France should be the target of a later and larger assault was agreed on by both Washington and London. Planning was started on what would be known as Operation Overlord. In late 1943, at Cairo, Roosevelt and Churchill agreed that Eisenhower should command the operation. A few days earlier, at Teheran, they had informed Stalin that the cross-channel invasion would take place in the spring of 1944.

Fresh from victories in Africa and Italy, Eisenhower set up headquarters in England in March. On February 12, 1944, he was ordered: "You will enter the continent of Europe and, in conjunction with the other United Nations, undertake operations aimed at the heart of Germany and the destruction of her armed forces."

On January 17, 1944, he took command of Supreme

D-Day: Americans head across the Channel to the Normandy beaches.

Headquarters, Allied Expeditionary Force—henceforth known as SHAEF—which replaced a planning group under Britain's Lieutenant General Sir Frederick Morgan that had been working on invasion blueprints for a year. Eisenhower expanded the scope of their provisional plan and, after long consultation with logistical and meteorological experts, decided to invade in June. Some sixty miles of beaches along Normandy's Cotentin Peninsula were chosen as the assault area, even though they were relatively distant, subject to heavy surf, and short on port facilities. The latter problem, it was hoped, could be solved by towing two prefabricated, concrete harbors, known as "Mulberries," to the scene.

The Dieppe raid had incited the Germans to expand their Atlantic Wall, but it also gave the Allies a more accurate idea of the kind of tactics needed to break through the Nazi defense shell. As a consequence, not only was the unprecedented idea of an invading force bringing along its own seaports adopted, but new kinds of landing craft to disembark heavy vehicles as well as troops close to the shore, amphibious vehicles, including the awkward DUKW, and flail tanks to beat out mines with whirling chains were developed by inventive technicians, as well as a trans-Channel fuel pipeline called PLUTO (Pipe-Line Under the Ocean). Allied ingenuity seemed limitless. For a time the British even considered constructing enormous aircraft landing platforms of frozen sea water and sawdust.

The invasion build-up was enormous, and all southern England gradually became one huge military encampment. Ports filled up with transport ships; airfields became packed with fighters and bombers; the pleasant English countryside was cluttered with parked tanks, trucks, jeeps; and urban areas were jammed with billeted troops. By early June, nearly three million Allied soldiers, sailors, and airmen were ready for the assault. The actual attack was to be accomplished by 176,475 men, 20,111 vehicles, 1,500 tanks, and 12,000 planes. Eisenhower subsequently recalled: "The mighty host was tense as a coiled spring, and indeed that is exactly what it was—a great human spring, coiled for the moment when its energy should be released and it would vault the English Channel in the greatest amphibious assault ever attempted." It was Eisenhower's plan to drop three airborne divisions in Normandy to cut up German communications and block reinforcements, then to land his first five divisions on the Normandy shore between Caen and the Cherbourg Peninsula.

Such monumental preparations could not, of course, be kept from German intelligence. Everyone knew the invasion was coming. But the vital factors of exactly when and where were unknown to the enemy, and these secrets remained essential to success. The Allies worked out several careful deception plans. An actor who resembled Montgomery was sent to North Africa to attract Nazi attention to the Mediterranean. A skeleton American First Army Group was set up along England's southeastern coast, dummy tanks were deployed to fool *Luftwaffe* reconnaissance, and fake messages were radioed for the benefit of German interceptors. Rumors and Allied bombing raids strongly hinted at attacks against the Pas de Calais, Holland, and even Norway. The Germans were confused enough to withhold vital reserves until certain that the Normandy landings indeed represented the main Allied offensive.

Field Marshal Gerd von Rundstedt, who had been called out of retirement to command the German forces in the West, had no use for Hitler's Atlantic Wall of concrete fortifications as an effective way to stop the Allies. His idea was to hold his strength well back from the beaches and to fight decisive battles at places of his own choosing. Hitler, however, in the fall of 1943 had put the daring Rommel under Rundstedt to act as the principal chief of operations. Rommel inspected the Atlantic defenses, found them sadly lacking, and went to work. For six months, half a million men labored constructing giant pillboxes and murderous hazards of every variety. Rommel placed little reliance on static defense alone. The only way to defeat an Allied landing, he argued, was to meet it head on and destroy it. "The war will be won or lost on the beaches," he told his aide. "The first twenty-four hours of the invasion will be decisive." He erected advance barriers at beaches where he thought a debarkation likely. He booby-trapped and flooded rear areas where air-borne landings might come. He gathered available armor, guns, rockets, and mortars, then positioned reserves to strike either at the mouth of the Somme, where he expected the principal landing, or at Normandy, where he looked for a subsidiary thrust.

Hitler guessed more shrewdly. Over a month before D-Day, he reckoned that Eisenhower would seek his main lodgment on the Cotentin Peninsula. His intelligence service even gained advance knowledge of the two lines from Paul Verlaine's poem, "Chanson d'Automne," that would alert the French underground to imminent assault. But Allied deception measures and the weakness of *Luftwaffe* reconnaissance (there were only one hundred and nineteen German fighters along the Channel, against about five thousand for the Allies) left the *Wehrmacht* command bewildered when the signal came.

The weather had turned unfavorable. Rommel decided that the invasion could not come immediately and drove back to Germany on June 4 to join his wife on her birthday on June 6, and to see Hitler. As a result, he would be twenty-four hours late in getting back to the front. His strategy of immediate riposte was thus to begin a day late. As for Hitler, on the morning of D-Day he was fast asleep at his headquarters, doped with barbiturates; no one thought it wise to awaken him.

Eisenhower had decided, after intensive consultation, that because of the tide schedule, the most feasible days for landing were June 5, 6, or 7. Sunday, June 4, a gale blew up, but his forecasters predicted clear weather Tuesday morning, to be followed by more bad weather. Faced with the choice between a possible critical delay or a gamble with the elements, he decided to go. Early June 6, the largest amphibious force ever seen, including four thousand ships and covered by eleven thousand planes, hurled itself against the Atlantic Wall of which Hitler had boasted: "No power on earth can drive us out of this region against our will."

It was 3:32 A.M. New York time when a radio flash announced the invasion and Eisenhower's Order of the Day: "The tide has turned. The free men of the world are marching together to victory." A few hours later, President Roosevelt led the American people in prayer: "Almighty God: Our sons, pride of our Nation, this day have set out upon a mighty endeavor, a struggle to preserve our Republic, our religion, and our civilization and to set free a suffering humanity. . . ."

As the invasion armada headed toward France on the evening of June 5, American and British paratroopers and glider units landed in pell-mell confusion behind the German lines and scattered through the darkness. When Major General Maxwell Taylor dropped with his staff and found only a handful of enlisted men, he commented wryly: "Never have so few been commanded by so many."

Before daylight on the sixth, despite the tangle, an initial lodgment had been successfully achieved. Then, as they peered from their pillboxes, the Germans suddenly saw a galaxy of ships of different sizes and shapes sliding out of the early morning mist. By 5:30 A.M., the assault units were headed for shore. They pushed across the beaches and fought inland to the isolated paratroopers.

Gradually, swarming with men, tanks, and amphibious supply carriers, the beachheads expanded: the Americans at Utah and Omaha beaches, the British at Gold, Juno, and Sword. Tanks flailed through mine fields, and infantry scrambled over underwater and shore obstacles to burst through to the *bocage*, Normandy's stiff hedgerows. Unbelieving peasants greeted their liberators: "*Ah, mon Dieu, ne nous quittez pas maintenant*" ("My God, don't leave us now").

By nightfall nearly one hundred and fifty-five thousand Allied troops were ashore and had taken some eighty square miles of France. The invasion had achieved complete surprise, and within a few days, it was evident that the Allies were in France to stay. Lieutenant General Hans Speidel, Rommel's chief of staff, subsequently acknowledged: "The first phase of the invasion ended with an obvious military, political and psychological success for the Allies. . . . From June 9 on, the initiative lay with the Allies." When Rommel and Rundstedt warned Hitler that the position was critical, the *Führer* shut them up. He repeated his familiar instruction: hold at all costs.

A week after D-Day, the Nazis produced their last trump, something entirely new in warfare, the V-weapons. London was once again battered from the air, but this time by little jet-engined V-1 "buzz bombs" that by the end of the summer had killed more than six thousand people and destroyed some seventy-five thousand buildings. But Hitler's passion for revenge obscured his military logic. While London lived through the V-1 terror, the great embarkation ports of Southampton and Portsmouth were spared. By September, when the *Führer* unleashed the big, long-range V-2 rocket bombs, it was too late to alter the war's outcome.

A few days after the first V-1 hit England, an event took place inside Germany that, had it succeeded, might have ended the war in Europe that year. The rather disorganized anti-Nazi conspirators who had been intermittently plotting against Hitler recruited a resolute professional Army officer, Lieutenant Colonel Count Klaus von Stauffenberg, a brave soldier who had lost an eye, a hand, and two additional fingers fighting for his fatherland, and who loathed the *Führer*. Together with General Friedrich Olbricht, Deputy Commander of the German Home Army, Stauffenberg planned a coup d'état. He personally would undertake to murder Hitler, and once word of his deed had been flashed by the code word "Walkyrie," Olbricht and other commanders in the conspiracy would quickly seize control of the Reich.

The landings in France and the rapid Soviet advance prompted Stauffenberg to move swiftly, before the Allied position became so powerful that a post-Hitler government could not hope for compromise. Therefore, when summoned to a meeting at Hitler's East Prussian headquarters, he took a briefcase containing a time bomb. He intended to leave this inside the concrete bunker where such conferences were normally held, and then to leave. Although the place of the meeting was changed to a wooden guesthouse, Stauffenberg followed his plan, placed his briefcase underneath the oaken conference table, just six feet from Hitler's legs, then left the room.

At 12:37 P.M., July 20, there was a tremendous explosion. Four men were killed, twenty wounded. That there were no more casualties was due to someone's accidentally having shifted the briefcase. Hitler, although partly protected by the table, was temporarily paralyzed in one arm, and also burned and deafened. Heusinger, not a member of the conspiracy, told me years afterward: "When I came to I did not immediately know what had happened. I was lying on my back with a weight on my chest. I pushed myself upward and realized I was using someone's head as a support. My hand was full of hair. When I looked down I saw it was Hitler's."

Stauffenberg had confidently flown back to Berlin, but Olbricht received a telephone message telling him the *Führer* was alive. As the conspirators issued and countermanded confused orders, loyal Nazi units moved to round them up. Some, including Olbricht and Stauffenberg, were immediately shot. Others committed suicide. Rommel, who was suspected of being directly involved in the plot (which he was not), was offered the chance to take poison and thus save his family from retribution. It was announced that he had died of wounds suffered in an automobile accident, and he was given a hero's funeral. A huge *Gestapo* roundup took place; almost fifteen thousand suspects were arrested, and perhaps as many as five thousand were put to death. Some of the more distinguished plotters were tried in a specially constituted "People's Court," humiliated, and then slowly strangled on meathooks. Their agony was filmed on Hitler's order, and the film was then shown to selected military audiences as a warning.

While the Nazis crushed their opponents at home, Eisenhower moved as rapidly as his logistical difficulties permitted into the second phase of his plan. This phase had two objectives: the capture of Cherbourg, and the build-up of sufficient forces and matériel to break out toward Germany. By June 27, when General "Lightning Joe" Collins's U.S. VII Corps took Cherbourg, there were a million Allied troops in Normandy. Ordering Montgomery's British and Canadian forces to hold a "hinge" at Caen, in the first week of August Eisenhower sent his blitzkrieg expert, Patton, swinging southward, eastward, and around to envelop the main German army. As his command car moved through fields of burning rubble and blackened German corpses, Patton shouted above the roar of his artillery: "Compared to war, all other forms of human endeavor shrink to insignificance. God, how I love it." He wrote to his wife: "Peace is going to be hell on me."

Then, before dawn on August 7, the enemy counterattacked from the town of Mortain, striking toward Avranches on the sea. With Patton completing his end run and Montgomery ready to push in from Caen, it seemed that the Germans were about to be caught in a mammoth envelopment. But Montgomery was slow to close the German escape corridor in the Falaise gap. He was sharply criticized for this caution. Eisenhower and Omar Bradley both felt that he had let far too many enemy troops break out of the trap. Bradley wrote in his memoirs: "If Monty's tactics mystified me, they dismayed Eisenhower even more." The arrogant Patton proposed to Bradley: "Let me go on to Falaise and we'll drive the British back into the sea for another Dunkirk." Even so, eight infantry and two panzer divisions were obliterated. The liberation was off and rolling well.

On August 15, the Nazis were struck another blow, a landing in southern France known as Dragoon. Churchill, who had argued against this invasion, considered it at least well named, "because I was dragooned into it." A fleet of over fifteen hundred ships, including nine aircraft carriers, arrived off the Riviera between Toulon and Cannes. The landing took place with minimal resistance. Helped by French Maquis and resistance agents, the American Seventh Army, under Lieutenant General Alexander Patch, and General Jean de Lattre de Tassigny's French First Army rolled up the Rhone Valley and, within a month, joined Patton's forces north of Switzerland at Épinal, giving the Allies a continuous line from Switzerland to the Atlantic.

As the Germans retreated toward the Rhine, the fate of Paris became a matter of acute military concern. Eisenhower, who was primarily interested in destroying the German armies, had no desire to become involved in any subsidiary operation, no matter how important sentimentally or politically, or to assume the logistical burden of feeding four million Parisians. He sent precise orders to General Pierre Koenig, commander of the French Forces of the Interior (F.F.I.), that "no armed movements were to go off in Paris or anywhere else" until he had given a specific command. However, without Eisenhower's knowledge, de Gaulle secretly instructed Koenig to seize the capital as soon as he could and told General Jacques Leclerc, whose armored division was under Eisenhower, to ignore SHAEF discipline if necessary and march on the capital.

The combination of French chauvinism outside and inside Paris precipitated an attack. The Paris police went on strike, and three thousand armed gendarmes seized the prefecture on August 19. The following day, although ordered by Hitler to devastate the city, its commander, General Dietrich von Choltitz, negotiated a surrender that permitted him to withdraw the occupying garrison while leaving Paris undestroyed. Eisenhower was forced to accept human and political reality. On August 25, Leclerc, followed by the U.S. 4th Infantry Division, entered the City of Light and formally accepted Choltitz's surrender. The next day Patton sent a message to Eisenhower: "Dear Ike: Today I spat in the Seine." And de Gaulle, amid loud acclaim, marched down the Champs-Élysées and established his hold on France.

Liberation of Paris involved many troops and much fuel, and it undoubtedly delayed the rush toward Hitler's Rhine defenses. Bradley later wrote: "We needed just two more weeks of gasoline [to reach the Rhine]. . . . Those were my thoughts about Paris. I didn't want to lose those two weeks there, and perhaps we did."

As summer ended, German territory was being terribly constricted. The Russians drove in hard from the East, and Tito's Yugoslav partisans were carving up *Wehrmacht* units in the Balkans. The Fifth and Eighth armies in Italy, although weakened by Dragoon, nibbled through Tuscany toward the Po. And Eisenhower's steadily growing forces pushed into Belgium and, from Switzerland northwestward, established themselves near the Rhine.

Eisenhower's plan to approach Germany along an extensive front was hotly disputed by Montgomery, who wanted a narrow, concentrated thrust at Berlin. Montgomery recounts: "I was unable to persuade the Americans to take the risk—which, in any case, was practically nil. So it was *not* done, and the war went on into 1945 —thus increasing our post-war political problems, and tragically wasting a great many valuable young lives." In any event, his idea was dismissed by SHAEF, primarily for reasons of logistics. The Allied armies were outrunning their supply system. Eisenhower preferred prudence, and to shore up his line for the final penetration of the Reich, he decided to consolidate his position along the Rhine. By September he resolved on the capture of that great river's Dutch debouchment by an extensive air-borne operation aimed at the Dutch towns of Eindhoven, Nijmegen, and Arnhem, while obliterating Walcheren Island, where a tough German force was preventing the use of Antwerp, Belgium's main port.

The air drop on the Low Countries was only a partial success and ended inconclusively. Although some twenty thousand men took part, Arnhem, the British objective, was fiercely defended by the Germans, and Britain's First Airborne Division lost three fourths of its roster.

By October the Americans had captured their first German city, Aachen, ancient citadel of Charlemagne. They moved on into the Hürtgen Forest, where they battled through snow-covered mine fields, taking heavy losses. It was at this stage that Hitler decided on a bold counterthrust, which he called "Watch on the Rhine," to pierce the Allied lines where they joined in the Ardennes Forest. His objective was to break through to Antwerp, severing Eisenhower's supply lines and perhaps sufficiently demoralizing the West to prepare the way for a negotiated peace. In mid-September a group of high-ranking commanders, including Field Marshal Model and Colonel General Jodl, began work on highly secret and comprehensive plans. Then, on December 11 and 12, at his Eagle's Nest headquarters near Frankfurt, the *Führer* received the division commanders who would be involved in the crucial operation.

An important aspect of the Ardennes campaign was called "Greif," which, under the famous *S.S.* adventurer, Otto Skorzeny, would befuddle the Allies with specially trained, English-speaking troops wearing American uniforms. This scheme was largely frustrated, despite the fact that, when a Nazi officer was captured with operational orders for "Greif" in his possession, a wave of suspicion swept the American lines that anyone might be a German agent. Rundstedt scraped up twenty-four divisions, and masses of armor moved to the take-off line under cover of heavy forest and a continuing fog. On the morning of December 16, eight panzer divisions broke through weak Allied defenses on a seventy-mile front.

The attack was a total surprise and at first achieved astonishing success. However, the Americans around the crossroads town of Bastogne created a bristling hedge-hog position, and the offensive slowly began to lose steam. Eisenhower sent Patton to relieve Bastogne, whose commander, Brigadier General Anthony McAuliffe, had answered a German surrender demand with the now-famous laconic reply: "Nuts." What became known as the Battle of the Bulge, because of its initial dent in the Allied line, petered out in a succession of sharp counterattacks. The Germans, faced with no alternative to disaster, drew back inside the Reich in January, 1945.

Through 1944, Hitler had fought back with increasing frenzy. In the spring he had occupied Hungary to curb Danubian collapse. When the Atlantic Wall fell, he had ordered the destruction of London by V-weapons, and of Paris by *S.S.* demolitions. He had sought to terrify internal opposition by appalling cruelty. He even had managed to launch one final military offensive. Yet when the year ended, it was clear that he was doomed. That last December, General Hasso von Manteuffel was impressed by the *Führer*'s "stooped figure with a pale and puffy face, hunched in his chair, his hands trembling, his left arm subject to a violent twitching which he did his best to conceal, a sick man apparently borne down by the burden of his responsibility."

The Drive to the Rhine

More than two years had been put into the build-up for the Allied assault on Hitler's Fortress Europe, and when it came, on June 6, 1944, everything went much according to plan. Within five days, sixteen divisions had landed in Normandy. By the end of the month, more than a million men were ashore; the beachhead was firm. But fighting through the tough *bocage* country of Normandy took much longer than had been expected. The breakout did not come until late July, from St. Lô, when American armor and infantry swept southward, isolating the ports of Brittany as they had already sealed off Cherbourg on the Cotentin Peninsula. Then they swung to the east, pivoting on the British forces under Montgomery, who shoved steadily against the Germans in the area northwest of Paris. In mid-August the effect of the *Führer's* enraged refusal to authorize retreats began to show on a large scale when nearly 100,000 German soldiers were surrounded and captured near Falaise. Meanwhile, on August 15, a combined French and American army commanded by General Alexander Patch landed on the Mediterranean coast of France and, bolstered by some 50,000 troops of the French Maquis, rapidly pushed northward. Ten days later, Paris was liberated, and the Allies pushed on with hardly a break in stride. By mid-September Hitler had withdrawn to the West Wall, along the German border. There was talk among the Allies of the war ending before Christmas, but the *Führer* already had plans under way for a massive counterattack in the Ardennes that would come just a few days before Christmas.

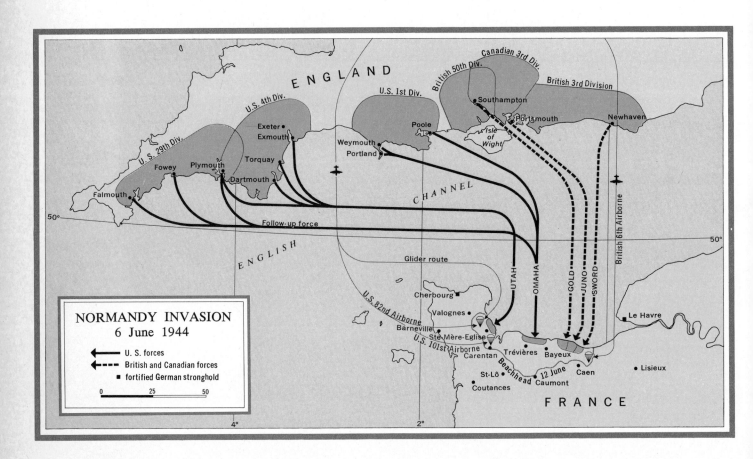

NORMANDY INVASION
6 June 1944

← U. S. forces
◄--- British and Canadian forces
■ fortified German stronghold

0   25   50

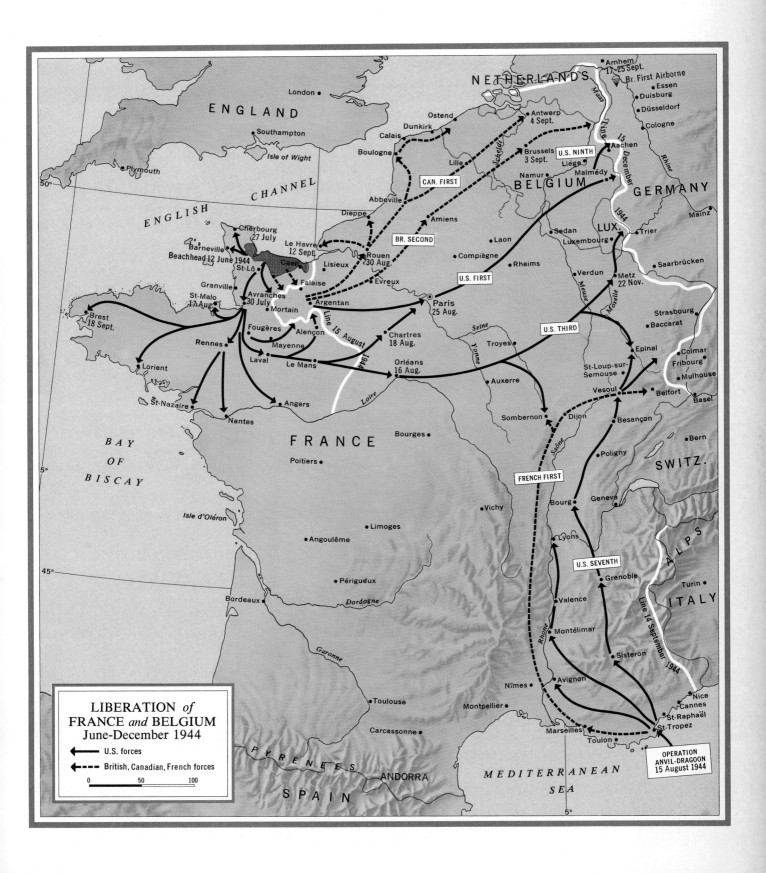

ENGLAND

London
Southampton
Isle of Wight
Plymouth

NETHERLANDS

Arnhem
17-25 Sept.
Br. First Airborne
Essen
Duisburg
Düsseldorf
Cologne

Ostend
Dunkirk
Antwerp
4 Sept.

Calais
Boulogne
Lille

Brussels
3 Sept.
Namur
Malmédy
Aachen
15 December

CAN. FIRST
BELGIUM
Liège
U.S. NINTH
Malmédy
GERMANY

Abbeville
BR. SECOND
Amiens
Sedan
Luxembourg
LUX.
Trier
Mainz

ENGLISH CHANNEL

Dieppe
Rouen
30 Aug.
Laon
Compiègne
Rheims
Verdun
Saarbrücken

Cherbourg
27 July
Le Havre
12 Sept.
Barneville
Beachhead 12 June 1944
Caen
Lisieux
Evreux
U.S. FIRST
Metz
22 Nov.
Strasbourg
Baccarat

St-Lô
Falaise
Paris
25 Aug.
Seine
Troyes
U.S. THIRD
Epinal
Colmar
Fribourg
Mulhouse

Granville
Avranches
30 July
Argentan
Yonne
Auxerre
St-Loup-sur-Semouse
Basel

St-Malo
17 Aug.
Mortain
Line 15 August
Chartres
18 Aug.
Vesoul
Belfort

Brest
18 Sept.
Fougères
Alençon
Mayenne
Orléans
16 Aug.
Sombernon
Dijon
Besançon
Bern

Rennes
Laval
Le Mans
Loire
FRENCH FIRST
Poligny
SWITZ.

Lorient
Angers
Bourges
Bourg
Geneva

St-Nazaire
Nantes
Poitiers
BAY OF BISCAY

Isle d'Oléron
Limoges
Angoulême
Vichy
Lyons
U.S. SEVENTH
Grenoble
ALPS
Turin
ITALY

Périgueux
Valence
Line 14 September 1944

Bordeaux
Dordogne
Montélimar
Sisteron

Garonne
Avignon
Nice
Cannes
St-Raphaël
St-Tropez

Toulouse
Nîmes
Marseilles
Toulon
OPERATION ANVIL-DRAGOON
15 August 1944

Carcassonne
Montpellier

PYRÉNÉES
ANDORRA
SPAIN
MEDITERRANEAN SEA

LIBERATION of
FRANCE and BELGIUM
June-December 1944

⟵ U.S. forces
⟵ British, Canadian, French forces

0   50   100

487

COMMAND RECONNAISSANCE TRUCK ("JEEP")

TWO-AND-ONE-HALF-TON TRUCK ("DEUCE AND A HALF")

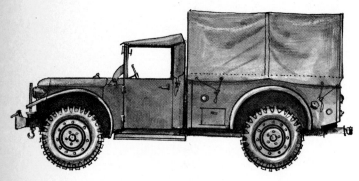

THREE-QUARTER-TON TRUCK

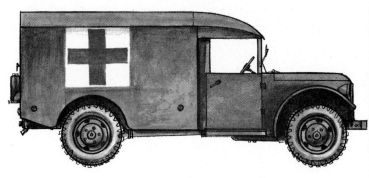

AMBULANCE ("MEAT WAGON")

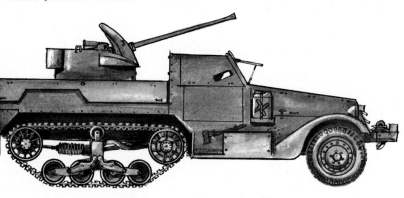

TWIN 40-MM. AA GUNS ("FLAK WAGON")

AMPHIBIOUS TRUCK (DUKW, "DUCK")

Hell on Wheels

If, as General Sherman said, war is hell, then World War II, from the point of view of the ground forces, was hell on wheels. Hundreds of thousands of motor vehicles had been streaming from German, Russian, British, and, above all, American assembly lines for several years, but it was not until the Allied armies crossed over to France that mechanized warfare reached its great crescendo. Not only in quantity, but in quality and ingenuity, World War II vehicles were astonishing, from the "Truck, Command Reconnaissance, ¼-Ton 4 x 4"—the tough little jeep—through the amphibious DUKW to the terrifying German 62-ton Tiger tank with its 88-mm. gun. The fourteen vehicles shown here are some of the best known of the many that became a major part of nearly every soldier's life in Europe and were a major reason why it would be a far different kind of fight in France than it had been the last time the American Army had fought there.

DRAWINGS BY DENNIS KNIGHT

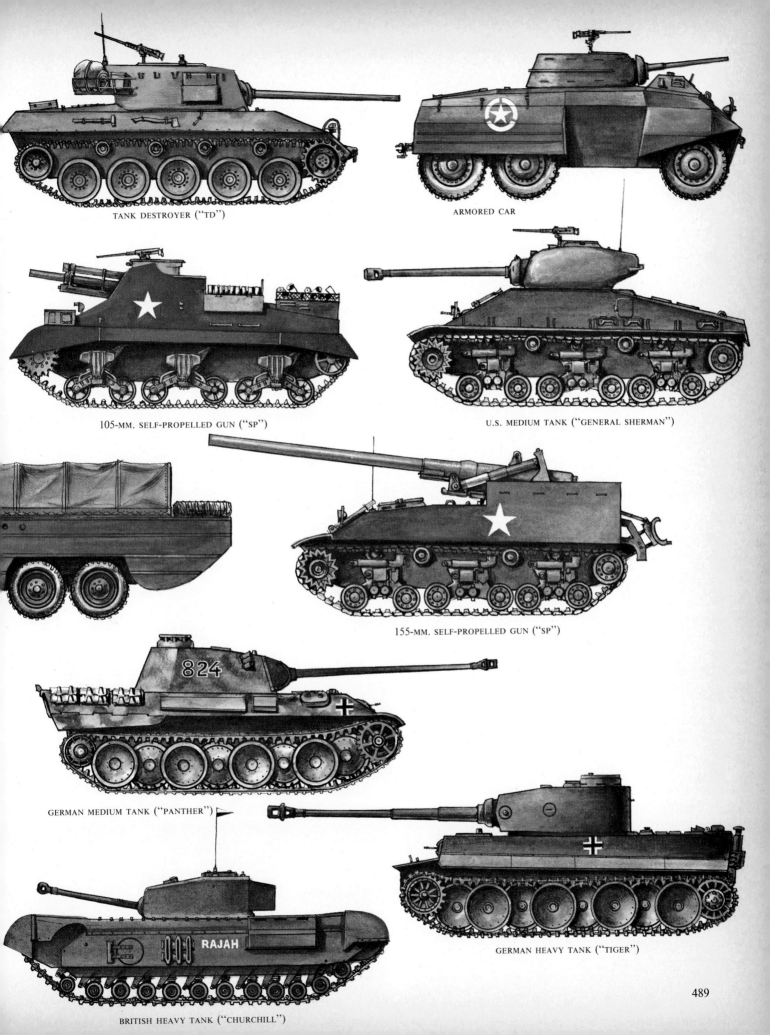

TANK DESTROYER ("TD")

ARMORED CAR

105-MM. SELF-PROPELLED GUN ("SP")

U.S. MEDIUM TANK ("GENERAL SHERMAN")

155-MM. SELF-PROPELLED GUN ("SP")

GERMAN MEDIUM TANK ("PANTHER")

824

GERMAN HEAVY TANK ("TIGER")

RAJAH

BRITISH HEAVY TANK ("CHURCHILL")

The Like of Ike

"He looks sort of like the guys you know at home," one American soldier said after seeing Eisenhower during an inspection tour early in 1944. The Germans said, "The American General has an athletic appearance, full health and strength, a well-formed head and jaw showing great will, and is a man whom his countrymen would call a heman." He was all that, without doubt, and his kind of midwestern glamour was important; but Dwight D. Eisenhower, the fifty-three-year-old, four-star Supreme Commander of the Allied Expeditionary Forces, also had an uncommon ability to work with the Englishmen, Scots, Irishmen, Canadians, Poles, Belgians, Dutchmen, Czechs, Frenchmen, and Americans who made up the force of some two million men massed in England for the strike at Europe. Eisenhower had an intuitive restraint and moderation that made him a superb arbitrator between the sometimes bitterly competitive Allies; and it was this above all that had lead Roosevelt and General Marshall to give him the job.

Not the least of Ike's troubles was the keen little British field commander who is seen peering over his shoulder in the photograph at right. Montgomery struck many American generals as eternally trying to elbow them aside and take more credit than was due both for himself and for his troops. Eisenhower understood the problem very well, but he also accurately appraised Montgomery's great military talents and fully appreciated how very much the man meant to the British people. With much thought and patience, Ike managed to prevent an open break that might have seriously damaged the campaign against Germany.

490

As D-Day drew near, the biggest stockpile of military equipment and supplies in history stacked up in England—nearly six million tons.

"It was the rich man's recipe," wrote an apologist for Germany's defeat after the war, with some truth. Above: an ordnance depot.

Awaiting the Onslaught

The Dieppe Raid in August, 1942, had been a terrible failure for the Allies. The British and Canadians had found that Hitler's "Fortress Europe" was no hollow propaganda phrase. But the attack had put quite a scare into the German high command. In the fall of 1943, on Hitler's orders, Field Marshal Rommel began looking over the Atlantic defenses and found them far from adequate. An impregnable line from Holland to Spain was obviously impossible, even if there were plenty of time, and Rommel, like everyone else, knew that time was running out fast. "The war will be won or lost on the beaches," he said, and set to work to do everything possible to make the beaches if not impregnable, very uninviting indeed. By the end of 1943, he had more than half a million men at work. Most of the effort was concentrated in the Pas de Calais area, which the Germans figured the likeliest place for an Allied landing, as the Channel is narrowest there. But miles and miles of other beaches were well strewn with the obstacles and mines that the field marshal was so partial to and even designed himself. By the end of May, 1944, work seemed to be progressing well enough for him to feel free to plan a short leave back in Germany with his wife, whose birthday was coming up on the sixth of June.

Above: Field Marshal Rommel, profiled against a French beach thoroughly planted with mined obstacles (see close-up below), looks out to where the invasion fleet will appear later—or sooner. At right: several of Germany's most lethally efficient panzer divisions were ready to move up and destroy any Allied beachhead. But they were not under Rommel's direct control: Would they be deployed quickly enough?

SUPREME HEADQUARTERS
ALLIED EXPEDITIONARY FORCE

Soldiers, Sailors and Airmen of the Allied Expeditionary Force!

You are about to embark upon the Great Crusade, toward which we have striven these many months. The eyes of the world are upon you. The hopes and prayers of liberty-loving people everywhere march with you. In company with our brave Allies and brothers-in-arms on other Fronts, you will bring about the destruction of the German war machine, the elimination of Nazi tyranny over the oppressed peoples of Europe, and security for ourselves in a free world.

Your task will not be an easy one. Your enemy is well trained, well equipped and battle-hardened. He will fight savagely.

But this is the year 1944! Much has happened since the Nazi triumphs of 1940-41. The United Nations have inflicted upon the Germans great defeats, in open battle, man-to-man. Our air offensive has seriously reduced their strength in the air and their capacity to wage war on the ground. Our Home Fronts have given us an overwhelming superiority in weapons and munitions of war, and placed at our disposal great reserves of trained fighting men. The tide has turned! The free men of the world are marching together to Victory!

I have full confidence in your courage, devotion to duty and skill in battle. We will accept nothing less than full Victory!

Good Luck! And let us all beseech the blessing of Almighty God upon this great and noble undertaking.

Dwight Eisenhower

Ike had no way of addressing his assault forces personally, as Shakespeare's Henry V did in his famous Normandy invasion speech ("Once more unto the breach, dear friends . . ."), but he did issue a confident hortatory message (left), which was distributed to every man just before the Allied armada got under way. (Ike also wrote out another statement that he fervently hoped never to release, announcing a withdrawal from the French shore because of invincible enemy resistance.) On the morning of June 6, General Alfred Jodl's personal situation map (right) showed everything normal. The Allied units based in England were identified with considerable accuracy, though there was some doubt about the exact location of a few units, noted with question marks. But there was no indication that some 176,000 men were then en route to the Normandy coast.

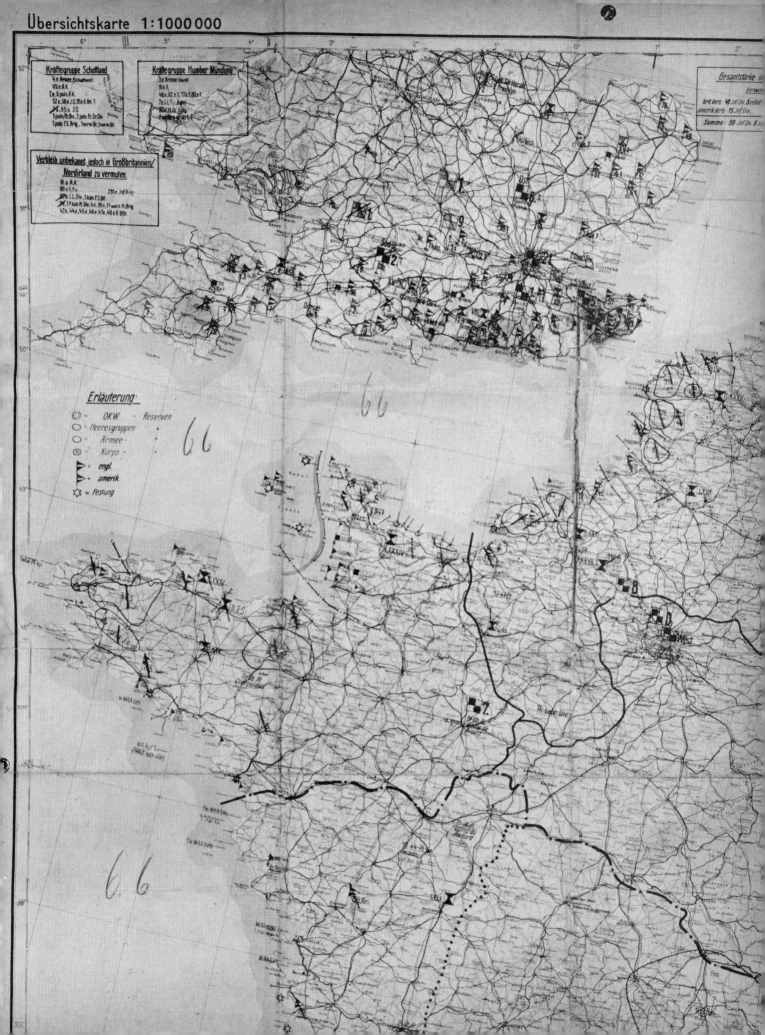

Übersichtskarte 1:1000000

Hitting the Beaches

The first assault wave hit the Normandy beaches at 6:30 A.M. on June 6. Planning had been as complete as possible, and the men had been thoroughly briefed; but in the vast confusion of invasion under enemy fire, the best-laid plans often came unglued. No one had expected that so many men would become seasick in the choppy Channel. Men died uselessly when they left their landing craft too soon and stepped into water over their heads; others fell into underwater shell craters and drowned. Many tanks equipped with the flotation devices that had worked so well in practice foundered as they tried to come in through the surf. The Allied air bombing that was to have knocked out German beach defense guns had not been accurate, especially at Omaha Beach, where the bombs had been laid down too far inland to do much good. As a result, the gunfire that met American troops there was more murderous than anything they had been prepared for. (However, magnificent Navy gunfire gradually put many of the German guns out of action.) At Utah Beach the defenders, as had been predicted, were second-rate troops who soon surrendered; but behind Omaha, a crack German infantry division was stationed. It had been moved into the defenses weeks before, without having been detected by Allied intelligence. On the other hand, the beaten *Luftwaffe* put in even less of an appearance than intelligence had predicted. Thousands of Allied planes ruled the sky, providing constant air cover and bombing bridges, roads, and railways to prevent enemy reinforcements from being brought up from the interior.

LEFT: IMPERIAL WAR MUSEUM, LONDON; RIGHT: U.S. COAST GUARD

D-Day, H-Hour: British and American soldiers confront a moment none will forget as their landing craft chug inexorably toward the Nor-

LEFT: ROBERT CAPA, *Images of War*, © 1964

LEFT AND RIGHT: IMPERIAL WAR MUSEUM, LONDON

Some struck it rough—a deadly storm of enemy fire sweeping the landing obstacles and the beaches themselves, with little letup as the

LEFT: U.S. ARMY; RIGHT: U.S. NAVY

RIGHT: U.S. AIR FORCE

In the afternoon of D-Day, there were the badly wounded and the shocked; the curious, amused by German ingenuity that had misfired

RIGHT: IMPERIAL WAR MUSEUM, LONDON

...mandy beaches. Some came ashore easily, like these second-wave Canadian bicycle troops at Juno, looking almost as if on a holiday.

RIGHT: U.S. ARMY

RIGHT: U.S. COAST GUARD

...first assault waves moved inland. Hundreds of men were hit while they were still in the water and had to be dragged up onto the shore.

RIGHT: IMPERIAL WAR MUSEUM, LONDON

RIGHT: ROBERT CAPA, Images of War, © 1964

...the crumpled Allied gliders, whose air-borne troops never saw France after all; terrified Nazi prisoners; and the jetsam of the dead.

"I remember thinking how peaceful the land looked"

General Matthew B. Ridgway

Volumes have been written about what was to become known as "the longest day." The following are from accounts written by men who were there, beginning with General Ridgway, who led the 82nd Airborne Division, which, along with the 101st Airborne and the British 6th Airborne, was dropped behind the Normandy beaches on the night of June 5–6.

. . . Wing to wing, the big planes snuggled close in their tight formation, we crossed to the coast of France. I was sitting straight across the aisle from the doorless exit. Even at fifteen hundred feet I could tell the Channel was rough, for we passed over a small patrol craft—one of the check points for our navigators—and the light it displayed for us was bobbing like a cork in a millrace. No light showed on the land, but in the pale glow of a rising moon, I could clearly see each farm and field below. And I remember thinking how peaceful the land looked, each house and hedgerow, path and little stream bathed in the silver of the moonlight. And I felt that if it were not for the noise of the engines we could hear the farm dogs baying, and the sound of the barnyard roosters crowing for midnight. . . . Beside the door, a red light glowed. Four minutes left. Down the line of bucket seats, the No. 4 man in the stick stood up. It was Captain Schouvaloff, brother-in-law of Fëdor Chaliapin, the opera singer. He was a get-rich-quick paratrooper, as I was, a man who had had no formal jump training. I was taking him along as a language officer, for he spoke both German and Russian, and we knew that in the Cotentin Peninsula, which we were to seize, the Germans were using captured Russians as combat troops.

A brilliant linguist, he was also something of a clown. Standing up, wearing a look of mock bewilderment on his face, he held up the hook on his static line—the life line of the parachutist which jerks his canopy from its pack as he dives clear of the plane.

"Pray tell me," said Schouvaloff, in his thick accent, "what does one do with this strange device?" . . .

A bell rang loudly, a green light glowed. The jumpmaster, crouched in the door, went out with a yell— "Let's go!" With a paratrooper, still laughing, breathing hard on my neck, I leaped out after him.

—General Matthew B. Ridgway

Our preinvasion breakfast was served at 3:00 A.M. The mess boys of the U.S.S. *Chase* wore immaculate white jackets and served hot cakes, sausages, eggs, and coffee with unusual zest and politeness. But the preinvasion stomachs were preoccupied, and most of the noble effort was left on the plates.

At 4:00 A.M. we were assembled on the open deck. The invasion barges were swinging on the cranes, ready to be lowered. Waiting for the first ray of light, the two thousand men stood in perfect silence; whatever they were thinking, it was some kind of prayer. . . . None of us was at all impatient, and we wouldn't have minded standing in the darkness for a very long time. But the sun had no way of knowing that this day was different from all others, and rose on its usual schedule. The first-wavers stumbled into their barges, and—as if on slow-moving elevators—we descended onto the sea. The sea was rough and we were wet before our barge pushed away from the mother ship. It was already clear that General Eisenhower would not lead his people across the Channel with dry feet or dry else.

In no time, the men started to

puke. But this was a polite as well as a carefully prepared invasion, and little paper bags had been provided for the purpose. . . .

—Robert Capa

At 5:30 A.M., all of a sudden, the bombardment of the Calvados coast by hundreds of ships' guns began. The previously prepared automatic defense measures were put into operation. The prearranged orders for "Operation Normandy" were issued.

The Chief of Staff of Army Group B reported by telephone to his Commander in Chief at Herrlingen between 6:00 and 6:30 A.M. on the events and on the first steps taken. Marshal Rommel gave his approval. He at once canceled his trip to Berchtesgaden and was back at his battle headquarters at La Roche Guyon between 4:00 and 5:00 P.M.

It was impossible to issue strategic orders in the early hours of the invasion, before reconnaissance reports had produced a clear picture of enemy movements. We could do nothing but wait patiently. . . .

—Lieutenant General Hans Speidel

. . . The flat bottom of our barge hit the earth of France. The boatswain lowered the steel-covered barge front, and there, between the grotesque designs of steel obstacles sticking out of the water, was a thin line of land covered with smoke— our Europe, the "Easy Red" beach.

My beautiful France looked sordid and uninviting, and a German machine gun, spitting bullets around the barge, fully spoiled my return. The men from my barge waded in the water. Waist-deep, with rifles ready to shoot, with the invasion obstacles and the smoking beach in the background—this was good enough for the photographer. I paused for a moment on the gangplank to take my first real picture of the invasion. The boatswain who was in an understandable hurry to get the hell out of there, mistook my picture-taking attitude for explicable hesitation, and helped me make up my mind with a well-aimed kick in the rear. The water was cold, and the beach still more than a hundred yards away. The bullets tore holes in the water around me, and I made for the nearest steel obstacle. A soldier got there at the same time, and for a few minutes we shared its cover. He took the waterproofing off his rifle and began to shoot without much aiming at the smoke-hidden beach. The sound of his rifle gave him enough courage to move forward and he left the obstacle to me. It was a foot larger now, and I felt safe enough to take pictures of the other guys hiding just like I was.

—Robert Capa

Two kinds of people are staying on this beach, the dead and those who are going to die—now let's get the hell out of here.

—Colonel George A. Taylor

They're murdering us here. Let's move inland and get murdered.

—Colonel Charles Canham

The wreckage was vast and startling. The awful waste and destruction of war, even aside from the loss of human life, has always been one of its outstanding features to those who are in it. Anything and everything is expendable. And we did expend on our beachhead in Normandy during those first few hours.

For a mile out from the beach there were scores of tanks and trucks and boats that were not visible, for they were at the bottom of the water —swamped by overloading, or hit by shells, or sunk by mines. Most of their crews were lost.

There were trucks tipped half over and swamped, partly sunken barges, and the angled-up corners of jeeps, and small landing craft half submerged. . . .

On the beach itself, high and dry, were all kinds of wrecked vehicles. There were tanks that had only just made the beach before being knocked out. There were jeeps that had burned to a dull gray. There were big derricks on caterpillar treads that didn't quite make it. There were half-tracks carrying office equipment that had been made into a shambles by a single shell hit, their interiors still holding the useless equipage of smashed typewriters, telephones, office files. . . .

In this shore-line museum of carnage there were abandoned rolls of barbed wire and smashed bulldozers and big stacks of thrown-away life belts and piles of shells still waiting to be moved. In the water floated empty life rafts and soldiers' packs and ration boxes, and mysterious oranges. On the beach lay snarled rolls of telephone wire and big rolls of steel matting and stacks of broken, rusting rifles.

On the beach lay, expended, sufficient men and mechanism for a small war. They were gone forever now. And yet we could afford it.

We could afford it because we were on, we had our toe hold, and behind us there were such enormous replacements for this wreckage on the beach that you could hardly conceive of the sum total. Men and equipment were flowing from England in such a gigantic stream that it made the waste on the beachhead seem like nothing at all, really nothing at all.

—Ernie Pyle

Outside Carentan, France, ten miles inland from the invasion beaches, a French peasant prays over the body of a young American soldier killed in front of the man's home. Allied casualties continued to mount as armies pressed into the Norman countryside. But by June 17, the day this picture was taken, both Rommel and Rundstedt recognized the futility of trying to contain the Allies and urged a withdrawal. But Hitler refused.

LEFT: IMPERIAL WAR MUSEUM, LONDON; RIGHT: BLACK STAR

The V-1 (above, one is being pushed to its launching ramp) was an ungainly creation, half airplane and half bomb. Far more aesthetic in its design, and apparently highly evocative of admiration and awe among the Germans who worked with it, was the V-2, a specimen of which is seen poised (left) for blast-off. The beauty disappeared with a fearful bang when the rocket hit, however. The devastation in the London street shown below was a typical result.

Nazi Vengeance

It was fortunate for the free world that the invasion of northern Europe came no later than it did. For Hitler's promises of secret weapons were not simply more propaganda. His scientists and engineers had made astonishing progress in weapons development. In underground workshops at Peenemünde, a number of rockets and jet-propelled flying bombs were on the drawing boards or in advanced stages of construction. By the spring of 1944, two were operational, and Hitler ordered them used as his *Vergeltungswaffen* (vengeance weapons) shortly after it became clear that the Allies had indeed landed in force in Normandy. Typically, the *Führer* decided to use these new weapons against England's civilian population rather than Allied troops or supply concentrations, and on the night of June 13–14, 1944, the first V-1, or buzz-bomb, came down on London. During that summer, 2,000 V-1's, launched from Belgium and northern France, killed some 6,000 Londoners and wounded some 40,000 others. The flight of the buzz-bomb, at about 400 miles per hour, was perfectly visible as well as audible, and the Royal Air Force became adept at intercepting and destroying them before they reached their targets. Much more menacing, because there was no defense against it, was the giant V-2, a forty-six-foot, fourteen-ton rocket, of which about a ton was a high-explosive warhead. Coming down from a parabola whose peak was sixty miles up, it struck at a speed over four times that of sound. Hundreds hit London late in the summer and on into the fall; only the capture of the launching sites by Allied armies finally put an end to them. The Germans were also first into the skies with jet-propelled military aircraft, a few of which would get into action against the Allies before V-E Day.

German aerial innovations (top to bottom): Messerschmitt "New York" long-range bomber, designed especially for bombing New York (only two were built); Messerschmitt Storm Bird, a fighter-bomber and the first operational jet; Dornier Arrow, with front and rear propellers, capable of well over 400 m.p.h.; Junkers 287, which would have been the first big jet bomber but was still on assembly lines at war's end; Arado Lightning, a jet bomber that saw some action in 1944–45; Heinkel Salamander, which was slated to be a mass-produced jet fighter (it never made it).

The Plot That Failed

Above: Hitler's conference room after the bomb explosion. Right: a shaken Führer, *having put on clean clothes, discusses the event with such cronies as Bormann (behind Hitler's right shoulder) and General Jodl (with head bandaged).*

While the British and Americans struggled to break out of the Normandy beachhead, a clique of highly placed German officers who saw that Hitler was dragging Germany to total destruction made a desperate effort to get rid of him. On July 20, 1944, Count Klaus von Stauffenberg was summoned to a conference at Hitler's so-called "Wolf's Lair" in East Prussia. He carried into the room a briefcase concealing a time bomb. Leaving it under the conference table near Hitler, he slipped out on a pretext, waited until the tremendous explosion occurred, and then coolly bluffed his way past *S.S.* guards and took a plane for Berlin, confident that he had accomplished his mission. As it happened, while four others died from the bomb, Hitler was injured only slightly. In Berlin, Stauffenberg's collaborators moved with uncertainty, and their elaborate scheme for taking over the capital fizzled. By midnight it was over; the immediate leaders (including Stauffenberg) had been shot. In the following months, the *Gestapo* rounded up suspects by the hundred: nearly 5,000 of them suffered death, often after the cruelest torture.

Breakout in Normandy

One obstacle badly underestimated by the Allies was the patchwork of hedgerows covering most of Normandy. For centuries, Norman farmers have fenced each small field with solid ramparts of earth, often four feet high, surmounted by hedges whose tangled roots bind each row into a natural fortification. Until an inventive American sergeant named Culin came up with the idea of mounting steel "tusks" on the front of each tank, American armored units found the hedgerows impenetrable. The struggle to move deeper into France was one small skirmish after another (above), fought field by field, town by town, from June 6 until July 18, when St. Lô finally fell. After that came the breakout and the Battle of France, as the Americans advanced as much as 40 miles a day under a general who had not been heard from since Sicily, George Patton.

Counterpoint in Generals

It was with strong misgivings that General Omar Bradley (left), commander of the U.S. Twelfth Army Group, heard that Eisenhower had named General George S. Patton (right) to lead the new Third Army, which was scheduled to join the Allied breakout from the beachhead. In Africa and Sicily, the modest and conscientious Bradley had served under Patton and had found him to be a superb combat general, but hotheaded, profane, unpredictable. (There had been a notorious incident in Sicily: Patton, touring an evacuation hospital, had slapped a shell-shocked soldier twice and called him "yellow.") Other American generals of the Normandy invasion—the air-borne Ridgway, Gavin, and Taylor, for instance—would later become well known, but this pair was already famous. And now Patton was serving under Bradley, commander of the newly formed Twelfth Army Group. It was soon apparent that the two made a superb team; Patton's dash and drive in the field was a perfect complement to Bradley's careful planning. Within days after the breakout began on July 25, Patton's armored divisions had swept westward through Brittany; others had swung south and east to partially close the neck of a trap around the German Seventh Army of Field Marshal von Kluge. Artillery and aircraft pounded the almost encircled men ceaselessly in what became a bloody slaughter; but Montgomery, coming down from the north to meet Patton and finish closing the neck of the trap, moved too slowly. Much of the German army escaped through the gap remaining at the town of Falaise. By late August, the Germans were in retreat across the whole of France, for on the fifteenth, Allied forces had landed on the Riviera coast and were advancing rapidly northward.

In mid-August, the skies of the French Riviera blossomed with Allied parachutes, part of the Seventh Army's amphibious assault from

U.S. AIR FORCE

the Mediterranean. Less than a month later, these troops met Patton's near the Swiss border, putting most of France in Allied hands.

After four years of German occupation, the people of France
had much frustration and hatred
to get rid of. Death was the fate
of many genuine collaborators;
for women who had fraternized
with the Nazis, there were shaven
heads and the contemptuous
hoots of their countrymen as
they were forced to parade
around town. Some of them were
harlots, but others were just
girls who unfortunately had
fallen in love with German soldiers and had acted accordingly.

516

When the steady Allied advance made it clear that Paris would soon be free, the French underground began coming out into the open. There was street fighting in the city and its suburbs; in some places, German outposts were forced to surrender—usually with little regard for the rules of war. To scream, jeer, and kick at members of "the master race" who had been their captors for so long was a rare pleasure for French civilians.

The Liberation of Paris

Ike and Bradley had hoped that Paris would be temporarily by-passed as the Allies rushed toward the Seine; they were perfectly willing to let the Germans go on feeding the city's 4,000,000 inhabitants for a while longer. But they had not reckoned on the explosive mood of the French Forces of the Interior —the resistance organization—in Paris. By August 19, these partisans were openly shooting at German soldiers, and the German commandant was threatening to carry out Hitler's orders to destroy the city before the Allies arrived. Into this dangerous situation stepped the Swedish Consul General, Raoul Nordling, with a plan that he hoped would save the city, as well as many French and German lives. With the commandant's full cooperation, Nordling sent several representatives through the German and American lines to Bradley's headquarters, asking for an immediate Allied advance on Paris so that the German staff could surrender to regular enemy troops rather than to the F.F.I. Bradley, thoughtfully taking French national pride into consideration, ordered the French 2nd Armored Division, under Major General Jacques Leclerc, to move in, followed by an American division. On the morning of August 25, the German garrison surrendered after very light resistance, and once more Paris was a free city.

YANK MAGAZINE

U.S. ARMY

UPI

General Dietrich von Choltitz (left), German commandant in Paris, became a kind of hero by default: he avoided demolishing the city. There was as much truth as humor in the "Sad Sack" cartoon above; few American combat soldiers did more than march quickly through Paris, and they were lucky if they got a quick kiss. On the opposite page: Charles de Gaulle's moment of triumph, his return to Paris on August 26, amid screams and weeping and cries of "Vive de Gaulle!" He told the French, "These are moments which surpass every one of our poor lives."

Costly Setback in Holland

As Allied armies all along the front headed for the Rhine early in September, Field Marshal Montgomery decided that a bold airborne stroke could open a "carpet" for an end-run through Holland, around the northern terminus of the Siegfried Line. Bradley had deep misgivings, but Eisenhower gave his approval, since in any event he was anxious to overrun the V-1 and V-2 launching sites and open up the ports of the Low Countries. On September 17, in an operation cheerfully code-named Market-Garden, one British and two American airborne divisions parachuted into Holland to capture crucial bridges across canals and rivers. The Americans had relatively good luck, but the British 1st Airborne's 9,000 troopers, who dropped near Arnhem, just north of the Lower Rhine, ran into aggressive German defenders who captured the Allied battle plan and used it for directing their counterattack. The British tanks that were supposed to cut through to join the 1st Airborne were unable to make it, and by the end of September, the division had lost more than two thirds of its men. Meanwhile, the shores of the Scheldt estuary, leading from the North Sea to Antwerp's great port facilities, remained honeycombed with German troops, and it was not until mid-November that they were cleaned out after arduous fighting. The long delay in opening Antwerp to Allied shipping, in Bradley's view, meant "an irrevocable logistical loss to the Allies."

Most of Holland's towns had been spared the war's devastations, but Allied efforts in the fall of 1944, and the German resistance that they engendered, changed all that in many places. Above right: a Dutch father attempts to rush his children to safety as British tanks roll into town. Right: to impede the British route through Antwerp, the Germans launched increasing numbers of flying bombs at the city. One has just exploded near this intersection. Left: the face of this soldier of the Royal Scots reflects the stubbornness with which the German troops resisted being expelled from the Scheldt estuary.

By November, few of Hitler's troops were left in France, and panic spread among those that were. Here some of them are frantically

trying to escape into Switzerland and are being fired on by the S.S.—a scene no one would have believed five months earlier.

Above: in the first swift momentum of the Nazi counteroffensive, German infantry-men move westward past stalled and burning American vehicles. Below: Brigadier General Anthony McAuliffe, in command of the surrounded American troops at Bastogne, Belgium, refused a German surrender demand with a single word: "Nuts."

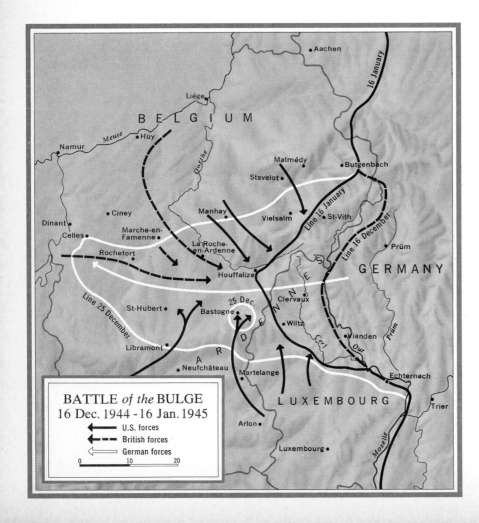

BATTLE of the BULGE
16 Dec. 1944 - 16 Jan. 1945

⬅ U.S. forces
⬅ British forces
⬅ German forces

0   10   20

The Last Blitzkrieg

The Bulge was the biggest, the most stunning, and the most confused battle fought on the Western Front in World War II. The *Führer* had conceived the massive German counterattack himself and had it executed against the advice of most of his top generals. It was to be a surprise thrust of great power, sending panzer divisions and infantry bursting through Belgium's Ardennes Forest to cut the Allied forces in two at the most weakly held part of their front. The sudden onslaught began at five in the morning on December 16, 1944. Before it was over, more than a million soldiers were involved. Surrounded Americans made a heroic stand at Bastogne, refusing to surrender in the face of what looked like impossible odds; not far away, more Americans surrendered at one time and place—over 8,000 of them—than in any other episode of the entire war except Bataan. The front line broke up into an unsolved jigsaw puzzle, and there were days when nobody, including the local townspeople, was sure which side held a given town. Some of the greenest troops in the American Army fought against some of Hitler's most battle-hardened veterans. Prisoners on both sides were captured, liberated, and recaptured; on both sides, captives were killed by infuriated captors after they had surrendered. The weather turned bitter cold, and wounded men froze to death in foxholes. When the month-long battle was over, not much apparently had changed except that thousands of men had died. For after the Germans' initial, shocking success between December 16 and 19, Montgomery's armies on the north and Bradley's on the south squeezed hard, and the Germans withdrew. By January 16, 1945, the Ardennes front had been re-established to about where it had been a month before.

After the Bulge

Despite the fact that the Battle of the Bulge ended close to where it started, its effect on the last stages of the war in Europe was great. Hitler had bet too much, and he had lost heavily in men and matériel at a time when he could ill afford to lose anything. German casualties in the Bulge were estimated at over 120,000 in dead, wounded, and captured. Hundreds of ruined tanks and artillery pieces were left behind. And now, on the Eastern Front, the Red avalanche was moving fast. "Those bottom-of-the-barrel reserves that might have slowed the Russian onslaught," wrote Bradley, "had been squandered instead against us in the Ardennes." At the same time, the Allies in the West had been shaken out of all complacency by the viciousness with which the Nazi could strike in his death struggle. Clearly there were still many weeks of savage fighting ahead, but the last hundred days of the "thousand-year" Third Reich had begun.

Right: an endless line of American supply trucks moves eastward through Bastogne on January 22, 1945. Hitler had envisaged such a scene—only with German trucks carrying captured Allied supplies back to his crumbling Reich. Above: American war prisoners, shot at Malmédy after surrendering, are numbered for identification.

Closing In on Japan

At the start of 1944, the Western powers, having forged an iron ring around the Japanese Empire, were beginning to screw it tight like some immense garrote. All the outer island bastions had been reconquered, from the Solomons to the Aleutians. The Allies were pushing slowly forward in the Burmese jungles; Japan's huge land army was still bogged down in China, robbed of any clear victory; and Tokyo was forced to remain ever more on guard in the north, where the Soviet Union, having repulsed Germany in distant Europe, once again became a menace along the Manchurian frontier and opposite the northern Japanese islands.

Of all these widespread fronts, by far the most important was that on the ocean itself. In the two years since Pearl Harbor, much to Japan's astonishment, United States industrial energy had produced an incomparable new fleet and new air forces, and the American high command had developed a technique of island-hopping amphibious advances, moving westward over the Pacific. The Third, Fifth, and Seventh Fleets, reorganized in March, 1943, by Admiral Ernest J. King, Chief of Naval Operations, were assigned special carrier task forces bearing F6F Grumman Hellcat planes that were at last able to outfight the Japanese Zeros. There were also new torpedo planes and dive bombers. A generation of air-minded commanders had assumed direction of this new kind of naval war: Admirals Halsey and Spruance; Vice-Admirals Marc A. Mitscher and John H. Towers; Rear Admirals Arthur W. Radford, Frederick C. Sherman,

Alfred Montgomery, and Charles Pownall. Together with the Marine Corps and MacArthur's army, they had devised the famous leap-frog method of circumventing enemy strongholds, harrying them with bombing attacks and landing far behind them on islands that could provide airfields and ports from which to stage further advances. By 1944, thousands of square miles of contested waters had been reconquered. American naval strength had become paramount on the world's seas: some forty-seven hundred vessels, including six hundred and thirteen warships, and more than eighteen thousand aircraft. By late summer of 1944, almost one hundred U.S. fleet and escort carriers were roaming the Pacific.

From the start, as they planned their offensive, the Joint Chiefs of Staff foresaw that Japan itself would have to be bombed mercilessly prior to any climactic invasion, in order to wear down the defending army and disrupt communications and the ability to move reserves against a landing. At first it was hoped that such an aerial assault could be mounted from eastern China, and blueprints were drawn up for the eventual capture of a South Chinese port to supply such an operation. In 1943, the high command had hoped to work toward this by occupying Luzon, in the Philippines, and Formosa. And though Admiral King originally had wished to save time by bypassing the Philippines, it was decided in March, 1944, to take those islands where we had suffered such a humiliating defeat. MacArthur was ordered to prepare a Luzon invasion for February, 1945, while Nimitz would simultaneously attack Formosa. In the end, the Formosan project was dropped and the date for the Philippine invasion advanced. But first it was necessary to secure more advanced bases in the western Pacific from which to counter Japanese air and naval attacks.

Therefore, on June 15, 1944, just as Eisenhower was consolidating his Normandy beachhead, Nimitz's forces hit Saipan in the Marianas, some thirteen hundred miles east of the Philippines and more than three thousand miles west of Hawaii. Saipan was defended by thirty-two thousand Japanese under the elderly Lieutenant General Yoshitsugu Saito. An armada of 535 ships, commanded by Admiral Spruance, carried 127,000 men, of whom two thirds were Marines. Four days after the landing, the Japanese fleet steamed into the area, and in a hot, cloudless sky with optimum visibility, the most intensive carrier battle of the war took place, an event the Americans promptly called the Great Marianas Turkey Shoot. During two days of fighting in the air above Saipan and at sea, the United States forces lost one hundred and thirty aircraft, against almost five hundred Japanese land- and ship-based planes. The Imperial Fleet limped back in the direction of the Philippines and, with scarcely any remaining fighter protection, lost three carriers on the way. The air was cleared, and the path to the Marianas at last lay unhindered.

The fighting on Saipan itself was ferocious. The Japanese staged successive banzai attacks, particularly against the U.S. 27th Division. But the defenders fought with more ardor than skill and in three weeks' time were overwhelmed. Saito himself had no wish to outlive his troops. On July 7, as the end neared, he knelt on the floor of his cave command post and, shouting "Hurrah for the Emperor," stabbed himself with his ceremonial sword. His principal officers followed suit. Admiral Nagumo, who had commanded the carrier strikes at Pearl Harbor and at Midway and was at this time in command of a small-craft fleet at Saipan, shot himself.

The American forces started mopping up isolated pockets of resistance, and when they had finished, they counted 23,811 Japanese dead. Among the casualties were hundreds of Japanese civilians who had taken refuge along the pitted line of escarpments on Saipan's northern shore. When they saw that all was lost, they disregarded the surrender appeals of the Americans and set about the ghastly business of mass suicide. In one of the war's most dreadful episodes, they hurled babies down from cliffs and jumped after them, or blew themselves up with grenades. United States losses on Saipan were also heavy: more than sixteen thousand casualties, including 3,426 deaths.

On July 23, Marine Lieutenant General Holland M. ("Howling Mad") Smith continued the Marianas offensive by seizing Tinian. He lost only 195 dead against almost thirty times that number of Japanese. On August 10, Rear Admiral W. L. Ainsworth reoccupied Guam, the last of the Marianas, after almost three weeks of combat.

Here again there was a tough, swirling struggle. Even cooks and clerks were at times thrown into action when Japanese counterattacks pierced the American lines. Bulldozers sealed hundreds of snipers in caves, while ferocious night banzai charges were cut down by Marine riflemen and machine-gunners. When the Marines finally entered Agana, the island capital, a combat correspondent reported that they "found nothing there." But there was more than a little joy among the victors when they discovered that Guam had been Japan's main liquor dump for the central Pacific and was rich in Scotch, rye, bourbon, beer, and sake.

Thus by August the Marianas as well as the Gilberts and strategic airfields along the northern coast of New Guinea were in American possession. The British general Orde Wingate's famous raiding forces had chopped deep into northern Burma. Merrill's Marauders, the comparable U.S. force, were working with Chinese troops to safeguard the new Ledo Road, designed to connect South China and Allied bases in India.

But although the Japanese were being slowly driven westward and northward in the waters of the Pacific, on the Asian mainland their strength was largely intact. These mainland forces blocked further advances in Burma. And, fearing the long-range B-29's that the Air Corps was just bringing into action from India and China, the Japanese overran seven Chinese airfields where Chennault's Fourteenth Air Force had been established to support Chiang Kai-shek. This China offensive was, in fact, the most serious Tokyo managed to launch during the final two years of the war. Driving southward from Hunan Province and westward from Canton, battle-hardened divisions expelled Chiang from much strategically valuable territory and delayed the opening of overland communications between China and Calcutta, India.

One result of Japan's 1944 land campaign in Burma and China was a change in the Allied command structure for Southeast Asia. When it was agreed that an American would command the invasion of Europe, the British, who had hoped for Sir Alan Brooke, were somewhat disappointed. As a result, they were given the consolation prize of Southeast Asia, and Lord Louis (later Earl) Mountbatten was placed in charge of that difficult theater. He established headquarters first at Delhi and subsequently at Kandy in Ceylon and resolved to be as diplomatic as possible with his independent-minded American subordinates, above all the headstrong "Vinegar Joe" Stilwell.

This was no easy undertaking. Stilwell's own posthumous diaries confirm that he felt scant loyalty either to the dashing royal admiral, whom he somewhat scornfully called "Loooie," or to his plans. Nor, for that matter, did Stilwell's successor, Major General Albert C. Wedemeyer, improve relations much, despite his more agreeable manners. Stilwell was recalled in late 1944, and to improve operational control after the Japanese drive, his former command was divided between Wedemeyer, in charge of the China theater under Chiang, and Lieutenant General Daniel I. Sultan, another American, in charge of the Burma-India theater.

Despite their resurgence in China and their relative success in holding the Burma front, the Japanese saw quite plainly that their fate hung upon the outcome of the Pacific Ocean campaign. Following the loss of Saipan and the obvious harbinger of disaster in the first B-29 raids on Japan, the Tojo Government fell. It was replaced by a cabinet, under the venerable General Kuniaki Koiso, that was clearly lacking in confidence of final victory, if not yet ready to seek peace. The new Navy minister, Admiral Mitsumasa Yonai, asked his fleet commander, Admiral Soemu Toyoda: "Can we hold out till the end of the year?" Toyoda replied: "It will probably be extremely difficult to do so."

At this juncture the United States amphibious giant leapt forward once again in a huge stride, ignoring the isolated Japanese strongholds of Truk and Rabaul far to the east and striking the Palau Islands in the direction of the Philippines. This offensive opened at Peleliu in mid-September, 1944. Some forty-five thousand Marines and soldiers hit the tiny island and were immediately faced with stiff resistance. The brutal, difficult battle lasted a month. A particularly tough defense was put up by the island garrison along a cave-pocked massif dubbed Bloody Nose Ridge by the Americans, who lost almost eighteen hundred dead and another eight thousand wounded. More than eleven thousand Japanese were killed.

Slowly the gateway to the Philippines was opening. That sprawling cluster of islands, once Spanish and later under American suzerainty, held the strategic key to Southeast Asia, the South China coast, and Japanese Formosa. In an effort to gain Filipino cooperation, Tokyo had established a puppet government in October, 1943, under José Laurel, a rich nationalistic and anti-American politician. However, his regime failed to gain any substantial popularity. With the assistance of American agents, armed resistance movements sprang up in the mountains, in hinterland villages, and, underground, in some cities. As early as March, 1944, Imperial General Headquarters acknowledged that "even after their independence, there remains among all classes in the Philippines a strong undercurrent of pro-American sentiment. . . . something steadfast, which cannot be destroyed. . . . Guerrilla activities are gradually increasing."

Defense of the archipelago was in the hands of Field Marshal Hisaichi Terauchi, whose main combat strength was the Fourteenth Army under General Tomoyuki Yamashita, Japan's most celebrated general. Yamashita, who had conquered Singapore, bragged that he would issue to MacArthur the same ultimatum he had presented to the British General Percival: "All I want to know from you is yes or no." The Japanese had established numerous strongpoints, airfields, and naval bases throughout the islands, but their primary concern was to hold Luzon at all costs.

Tokyo very properly assumed that MacArthur had meant what he said in 1942 when he had promised to return. Imperial Headquarters had drawn up the plan—called *Sho-Go* ("Victory Operation")—for a "general decisive battle" that was to smash any American assault along the vast island chain starting at the Philippines in the south and ending at the Kuriles in the north. The operation was to start just as soon as the intentions of the Allies became clear.

On October 6, 1944, the Japanese ambassador in Moscow learned from the Soviet Foreign Office that the U.S. Fourteenth and Twentieth Air Forces were about to start heavy bombing offensives designed to cut off the Philippines. After studying American fleet movements and spotting a large assemblage of transports near Hollandia and Wakde, off the north coast of New Guinea, Imperial Headquarters calculated that the invasion would aim at Leyte and begin during the final ten days of October.

Tokyo was right. However, for fear of committing his main fleet too soon, before being certain of MacArthur's precise target, Admiral Toyoda, the cautious Japanese naval commander, did not begin to move his forces until American warships were discerned approaching Leyte Gulf, north of Mindanao. It took four days before the Imperial Fleet was in position to make its final challenge against the U.S. Third and Seventh Fleets.

American preparation for the landing had been careful and extensive. All through mid-October, air strikes hammered up and down the Philippines, more or less as had been predicted by the astonishingly indiscreet Soviets. Admiral Mitscher's Task Force 38 attacked Japanese airfields as far to the north as Formosa, destroying or crippling an estimated three thousand Japanese aircraft.

But only after the first large elements of MacArthur's liberating army had landed on Leyte did the Imperial Navy begin its desperate riposte. In the last days of October, some 70 Japanese warships and 716 planes, split into three separate commands, opposed 166 American warships and 1,280 planes in the greatest naval battle of all time, the Battle for Leyte Gulf.

Toyoda, following the Japanese *Sho-Go* plan, split his fleet into three separate forces. A small Northern Force under Vice-Admiral Jisaburo Ozawa, made up mostly of carriers without planes, was used as a decoy to lure Halsey's Third Fleet northward and away from the Leyte Gulf beachhead and its supporting Seventh Fleet under Vice-Admiral Thomas C. Kinkaid. Meanwhile, Vice-Admiral Takeo Kurita, whose Singapore fleet then constituted 60 per cent of Tokyo's major naval units, was to take his Central Force through San Bernardino Strait between Luzon and Samar and come down into Leyte Gulf from the north. At the same time, a smaller Southern Force under Vice-Admiral Shoji Nishimura was to come through Surigao Strait and enter Leyte Gulf from the south. The beachhead with its unloading ships, caught between the two of them, would be wiped out, and so would Kinkaid's Seventh Fleet. Then when Halsey returned, they would fall on him and destroy him.

So went the plan. Under some circumstances it might have succeeded. Without Japanese air power, it was doomed. The Americans struck first. Kurita, steaming in from the west, was detected by two U.S. submarines, which sank two of his cruisers and disabled a third. The next day, in the Battle of the Sibuyan Sea, one of the Japanese Navy's great battleships, *Musashi*, was sunk by American carrier planes.

But now Halsey fell for Ozawa's decoy trick and ran off north in pursuit, leaving San Bernardino Strait unguarded. And Kinkaid steamed south, rightly guessing that another Japanese force might try to come through Surigao Strait. There, on the night of October 24–25, his Seventh Fleet destroyed Admiral Nishimura's Southern Force. Nishimura had come under attack by American destroyers and PT boats as he steamed through the straits and had already lost three destroyers before he came up to the Seventh Fleet. As he approached, Rear Admiral Jesse Oldendorf, who was in tactical command, performed the classical maneuver of capping the T: as each Japanese vessel came up, the guns of the entire Seventh Fleet concentrated on it. The entire Japanese force, except for one destroyer, was wiped out.

The next day, Admiral Kurita brought his Central Force, still powerful and consisting of four battleships,

six cruisers, and numerous destroyers, through San Bernardino Strait and found himself near a force of sixteen escort carriers with their destroyer escorts. The carriers were divided into three tactical units; one, called Taffy 3 and commanded by Rear Admiral Clifton Sprague, almost immediately came under fire from the guns of the Japanese force. After a heroic battle, in which the planes of all sixteen carriers as well as the destroyers of Taffy 3 took part, Kurita finally broke off the action. One American carrier and three destroyers had been sunk and other ships badly hurt, but three enemy cruisers had also gone down. Kurita could have gone in and shelled the defenseless beaches, but instead he turned and retired west. Later he explained that intercepted messages had led him to believe a large American force was on its way to cut him off.

The Battle for Leyte Gulf marked the first appearance of kamikaze, or suicide, planes. On October 19, Vice-Admiral Takijiro Ohnishi had met with senior commanders at Mabalacat fighter base in the Philippines and announced: "With so few planes we can assure success only through suicide attack. Each fighter must be armed with a 550-pound bomb and crash land on a carrier deck." This was the origin of the technique of kamikaze, which in Japanese means "divine wind." The word refers to a typhoon that blew away a Mongol fleet which had sailed to invade Japan in the Middle Ages.

Even while Admiral Clifton Sprague's carriers of Taffy 3 were fighting with Kurita's force, the escort carrier *Santee* of Rear Admiral Thomas Sprague's Taffy 1, a few miles away, was hit by a suicide plane. It thus became the first ship to be crashed by a kamikaze. The time was 7:40 A.M. Soon after, another kamikaze hit the *Suwannee* in the same force. Then, just before 11:00, when Kurita had turned away and Taffy 3 was counting her wounds, she came under attack. Five kamikazes either did minor damage to carriers or were shot down, but a sixth crashed through the flight deck of the *St. Lo*, set off bomb and torpedo explosions, and sent her to the bottom. Thus Japan first tested what was to become one of her most terrible weapons.

The kamikaze pilots pressed home their attack with great persistence and resolve. From that moment until the war was actually ending, it was considered a great privilege among young Japanese airmen to volunteer for these one-way missions. Farewell letters written by these pilots to their families have since been collected. One said: "Think kindly of me and consider it my good fortune to have done something praiseworthy." Another sadly reflected: "Every man is doomed to go his own way in time." Still another pilot concluded the last page of his diary: "Like cherry blossoms/In the spring/Let us fall/Clean and radiant." All were in their early twenties.

Although they could not turn the tide of war and although they were shot down in droves by the concerted antiaircraft fire of the vessels that they attacked, the kamikazes did great damage, above all later on at Iwo Jima and Okinawa. Before the conflict ended the following August, the kamikaze special attack corps had sunk or damaged more than three hundred U.S. ships and had exacted some fifteen thousand casualties. On the eve of the final surrender, when he committed hara-kiri, Ohnishi, who had first conceived of the idea of a flying suicide corps, wrote: "They fought well and died valiantly with faith in our ultimate victory. In death I wish to atone for my part in the failure to achieve that victory. I apologize to the souls of those dead fliers and to their bereaved families."

Halsey to the north meanwhile had discovered Ozawa's decoy force and exacted swift revenge. He sank four carriers, a cruiser, and two destroyers. Thus, in the entire series of battles off Leyte, Japan suffered immense naval losses, which it could ill afford. Unfortunately, despite the magnitude of this great victory, it soon became a matter of acid argument among the admirals. Just the way Bradley and Patton blamed Montgomery for allowing the encircled Germans in Normandy to flee through the Falaise gap, Kinkaid blamed Halsey for falling for the Japanese trick and not blocking the San Bernardino Strait. Through that strait, the badly mauled Kurita was able to escape with four capital ships, about all Tokyo had left. Halsey in turn resented that he could not finish off Ozawa's force but had to return urgently southward to help out Kinkaid. In any case, the strategic results of the combined victory were enormous. The naval power that Japan had first established in 1905 by sinking a mighty Russian fleet was finally and irreparably crushed.

Even more immediately important, however, was the fact that the Imperial Navy had wholly failed to interrupt the American landings on Leyte by sinking the assembled transports and supply ships. The liberation of the Philippines was now well begun. Carrying out the pledge he had made at Corregidor, MacArthur had returned and planted the Stars and Stripes on Filipino soil, nine hundred and forty-eight days after he had been ordered to leave by President Roosevelt.

On October 20, the charismatic old general waded ashore on the Leyte beach of Palo, and shortly afterward, in a sudden monsoon rain, he stood by a truck-mounted microphone and broadcast: "This is the Voice of Freedom, General MacArthur speaking. People of the Philippines: I have returned! . . . At my side is your President,

Sergio Osmeña, worthy successor of that great patriot Manuel Quezon, with members of his Cabinet. The seat of your Government is now, therefore, firmly reestablished on Philippine soil."

Yamashita managed to reinforce his garrison, and the last grim phase of the Asian campaign started.

On October 21, MacArthur occupied Tacloban airport. By early November, he had expelled his enemies from the island's southern and northeastern sectors. By now the guerrilla movement was producing aid on Leyte and becoming increasingly active on the other islands. The Japanese sought desperately to contain and reverse MacArthur's surge and, despite their loss of control over the sea passages, attempted to bring up reinforcements. However, on the night of December 6–7, almost exactly three years after their first raids on the Philippines, they lost six warships crammed with soldiers and supplies. The following week, an additional three transports were sunk, and Yamashita's position became hopeless. By December 16, the Americans had taken Ormoc, and by the end of the month, organized resistance had ceased on Leyte. MacArthur had already moved on to Mindoro and was starting his preparations for the final assault on Luzon and the capital, Manila.

By the time the Leyte struggle ended, the Japanese had lost 56,263 dead against only 2,888 Americans, an impressively disproportionate victory. Only 389 Japanese had, however, surrendered. Marshal Terauchi, lacking the necessary naval support to move his troops from one island pocket to another and hammered by constant aerial attacks, withdrew to the Asian mainland and established headquarters in Saigon.

In his report on the war, General Marshall recalled that at the end of the Leyte battle, men of the U.S. 32nd Division found a letter written by an unknown Japanese soldier. It read: "I am exhausted. We have no food. The enemy are now within 500 meters of us. Mother, my dear wife and son, I am writing this letter to you by dim candle light. Our end is near. What will be the future of Japan if this island should fall into enemy hands? Our air force has not arrived. . . . Hundreds of pale soldiers of Japan are awaiting our glorious end and nothing else. This is a repetition of what occurred in the Solomons, New Georgia and other islands. How well are the people of Japan prepared to fight the decisive battle with the will to win . . . ?"

By the time the fighting in Leyte Gulf and on Leyte Island was over, not only did the Philippines lie open; Japan itself was naked, unprotected by its customary shield of naval power, exposed to assault from almost anywhere. The answer to the Japanese soldier's question would come soon—and terribly.

Leapfrog Campaign

General MacArthur's long, tough leap-frogging campaign along the northern coast of New Guinea had only one purpose: to bring him closer to the Philippines. As mid-1944 neared, the pace of the campaign quickened. On May 27, landings were made on Biak, a Japanese base off the New Guinea coast, an island honeycombed with caves from which the defenders had to be blasted. Troops went ashore on Noemfoor Island, west of Biak, on July 2 (the paratroops at left are landing on Noemfoor's Japanese-built airstrip). And on July 30 the final landing began on Vogelkop Peninsula, the western tip of New Guinea. As soon as the enemy was cleared from each site, airfield construction commenced, to support the advance toward the Philippines. Fighting in New Guinea's steamy jungles had been misery, but duty even on the established bases was no soft snap. It was hot and rainy, insects swarmed, disease flourished. The supply situation was snafued; of 600,000 C-rations received at Biak, two thirds were corned beef. However, the war was soon to leave New Guinea behind. Plans called for MacArthur to take the island of Morotai to the northwest in mid-September, while Admiral Nimitz, coming through the central Pacific, was seizing the Palaus. Then, using those islands as advance bases, the next move would be against the Philippines.

535

The Marianas—Another Long Step

While MacArthur was advancing along the New Guinea coast, Admiral Nimitz moved against the southern Marianas—Guam, Saipan, and Tinian—to the north. The Navy wanted the islands as a supply and submarine base; the Army Air Force needed airfields from which the new B-29's could operate against Japan. The Saipan landings, which involved one Army and two Marine divisions, began on June 15, 1944. The island was rocky, with hills and many caves, so that bombardment did little damage to the defenders. The American advance was slow and costly, and the island was not declared under American control until July 9, though Japanese were being hunted out of caves and brush for months after that. Tinian, smaller, flatter, and only three and a half miles away, was assaulted by landing forces on July 24 and secured in a little more than a week. The Guam landings began on July 21. The Japanese fought vigorously from caves and hills, but organized resistance had ended by August 10. On November 24, the first force of B-29's, 111 strong, took off from Saipan to bomb Japan.

Marines of the first wave on the Saipan beachhead (above) take cover behind sand dunes while organizing to move on against heavy enemy fire. At right, a Marine on Saipan is caught by the photographer in the moment he sags after being struck by a Japanese mortar-shell fragment. The picture is blurred because the concussion from the shell explosion jarred the camera.

An Army-Marine force that invaded the Palaus in mid-September ran into fierce resistance, a water shortage, and temperatures as

high as 115 degrees. The bitterest fighting was on Peleliu Island, where the Marines pictured above are pinned down by enemy fire.

"...they charge toward the Marine foxholes, throwing grenades and howling: *'Ban-zai-ai!'*"

Sergeant Alvin M. Josephy, Jr.

Guam, the biggest and southernmost of the Marianas, was the last to be taken. A Guam assault by the 3rd Marine Division had been scheduled for mid-June, 1944, but when enemy resistance on Saipan turned out to be a lot stiffer than had been expected, the 3rd Division was held in reserve and the Guam D-Day put off until July 21. As a result, the Marines sat it out on board their ships for more than 50 days. The landing on Guam was brought off with expert smoothness, nonetheless. But on the night of July 25, the Japanese struck back with a wild, drunken suicide rush, described here by Sergeant Alvin M. Josephy, Jr., a Marine Corps combat correspondent on Guam.

At about three A.M. a rifleman named Martinez heard a swishing of grass out ahead of him, like men moving about. Then he noticed the *pang* of pieces of metal hitting each other and a busy stirring in the darkness that made him uneasy. He peered into the mist but was unable to see anything. Then, as he listened, other things happened. A barrage of hand grenades flew through the darkness and exploded behind him. They kept coming, and he noticed mortar shells beginning to crash more frequently on the ridge.

He woke the other two men in his foxhole. They had been curled in their ponchos, and they got to their feet uncertainly. At the same moment an orange signal flare shot up from the Japanese lines. A singsong voice shouted into the night, and an avalanche of screaming forms bounded suddenly into view. With their bayonets gleaming in the light of sudden flares, they charged toward the Marine foxholes, throwing grenades and howling: "*Ban-zai-ai!*" like a pack of animals.

The Marines awoke with a start.

Along the ridge, wet, groggy men bolted to their feet and grabbed their weapons. Grenades exploded like a crashing curtain against the onrushing Japs. A man on a telephone yelled for uninterrupted flares, and flickering lights began to hang in the air like giant overhead fires.

All along the line the enemy attack was on. Red tracer bullets flashed through the blackness. Japanese orange signal flares and American white illumination shells lit up the night like the Fourth of July, silhouetting the running forms of the enemy. On the right and the left the attack was stopped cold. As fast as the Japs came, they were mowed down by automatic rifles and machine guns. The enemy assault gradually focused on a draw where some American tanks were parked. The tanks fired their 75s at the charging masses. At first the Japs attacked the steel monsters like swarms of ants, firing their rifles at the metal sides and clambering up and over the tanks in a vain attempt to get at the crews inside. They screamed and pounded drunkenly on the turrets and locked hatches, but in their excitement they failed to damage a single tank. Finally, as if engaged in a wild game of follow-the-leader, many of them streamed past the tanks, down the draw toward the beach.

The rest, cringing before the tank fire, moved to the left, hoping to break through our lines and get to the draw farther down the slope of the ridge, behind the tanks. The front they now charged was that of B Company. Here, against the 75 men, the full force of the Japanese attack broke.

In their three-man foxhole, the rifleman Martinez and his two companions had maintained steady fire directly ahead, diverting the first rush of Japs to other sections of the line. During a pause in the fighting, one man left the hole to go back for more hand grenades. Martinez and a Marine named Wimmer were left alone. Around them they saw some of the other Marines withdrawing.

Trying to decide whether to withdraw themselves, Martinez and Wimmer were confronted suddenly by the first wave of Japs. With bayonets fixed, the enemy came more slowly, throwing grenades and then falling to the ground to wait for the bursts. The first grenades exploded around the Marines without harming them. Then one shattered Wimmer's rifle, and the two men decided it was time to withdraw.

As they crawled out of their foxhole and ran and slid down the slope of the ridge, they noticed a group of screaming figures pour over the crest farther to the right and run headlong down the hill. It was the first indication that the enemy were breaking through. Now Japs would be in our rear, and it would no longer be easy to tell friend from foe.

Martinez and Wimmer reached their platoon command post—an old shellhole ten yards from the top of the ridge, held by Second Lieutenant Edward W. Mulcahy. When the two Marines reached him, Mulcahy was trying desperately to make his field telephone work; but the wires to the rear had already been cut by mortar shells.

Wimmer slid into the hole beside the Lieutenant, and Martinez lay on the forward lip of earth as protection with his rifle. The night was hideous with explosions, lights, screaming enemy, and the odor of *sake*. Against the skyline a handful of Japs appeared. Martinez fired at them, and they backed out of sight. A moment later a string of hand grenades rolled down toward the Marines. Though most of them bounced harmlessly by to explode behind them, one blew up in front of Wimmer's face. Fragments shattered Mulcahy's carbine and struck him on the left side of the head and body. It felt as if he had been slammed with a two-by-four plank.

When he regained his breath, he saw Wimmer holding out his pistol.

"You take it, Lieutenant," Wimmer said in a strange voice.

The Lieutenant protested. The enlisted man would need the weapon for himself.

Wimmer raised his head and smiled. "That's all right, sir," he breathed. "I can't see any more."

The shocked Lieutenant tried to bandage Wimmer's splintered face. The noise from the top of the ridge showed that Marines were still up there, fighting back. It gave the three men hope. The Lieutenant began to shout in the night, like a football coach "Hold that line, men! You can do it!"

The Marine line on the crest, however, had by now disintegrated into a handful of desperate knots of men, fighting together with the fury of human beings trying not to be killed.

Action around two heavy machine guns was typical of what was occurring. A Jap grenade hit one gun, temporarily putting it out of action. The crew members fixed it quickly and started firing again. A second grenade hit the gun's jacket and exploded, knocking off the cover and putting it completely out of the fight. The same blast wounded one of the men. His three companions moved him to a foxhole ten yards behind the shattered gun. One man jumped in beside him, and the other two ran back to the machine-gun foxholes with their carbines. Heaving grenades like wild men, they managed to stall any Jap frontal charge for the moment.

Meanwhile, the other gun was also silenced. Riflemen in foxholes near by heard a sudden unearthly screaming from the gun position. By the wavering light of flares, they saw one of the crew members trying to pull a Japanese bayonet out of another Marine's body. The same instant a wave of Japs appeared from nowhere and swept over both men. Three of the enemy, stopping at the silent machine gun, tried to turn it around to fire at the Marines. In their hysteria, one of them pulled the trigger before the gun was turned, and the bullets sprayed a group of Japs racing across the top of the ridge. Finally the Japs tried to lift the entire gun on its mount and turn the whole thing. A Marine automatic rifleman blasted them with his BAR, and the Japs dropped the gun. Two of them fell over the bodies of the Marine crew. The third pulled out a grenade and, holding it to his head, blew himself up. A moment later another band of Japs appeared. Again, several paused at the gun and tried to swing the heavy weapon around. They had almost succeeded, when from the darkness a lone, drunken Jap raced headlong at them, tripped several feet away over a body, and flew through the air. There was a blinding flash as he literally blew apart. He had been a human bomb, carrying a land mine and a blast charge on his waist. . . .

At about 0600, three hours after the enemy attack had begun, a last wave of Japs charged over the top of the hill. It was the wildest, most drunken group of all, bunched together, howling, stumbling and waving swords, bayonets, and long poles. Some were already wounded and were swathed in gory bandages. The Marines yelled back at them and chopped them down in their mad rush. In a moment it was over. The last wave of the three-hour attack died to a man.

Marianas Turkey Shoot

By the spring of 1944, the Japanese fleet had assembled planes and had trained pilots (though poorly, by American standards) to replace its disastrous losses in the fighting around Rabaul. The competent Vice-Admiral Jisaburo Ozawa was given the assignment of bringing to battle and destroying the U.S. Pacific Fleet (at left, fleet carriers, led by the *Essex*, steam somewhere in the Pacific). The Japanese believed their opportunity had come when Americans began invading Saipan on June 15. Ozawa headed there, certain the American fleet would be in the area. Although outnumbered fifteen to nine in carriers and in every other type of ship except heavy cruisers, Ozawa's planes outranged the Americans, and he would have the help of some 100 land-based planes on Guam. The Japanese fleet was the first to locate its foe and began sending out air strikes the morning of June 19. But the American radar gave sufficient warning to let fighter planes swarm up, while bombers flew in to attack the Guam airfields. The battle was so one-sided that it has been dubbed "the Great Marianas Turkey Shoot"; in a few hours, Ozawa lost 346 planes, while only 30 American aircraft were downed. Damage to American ships was negligible—one battleship was hit by a single bomb—but while the Turkey Shoot was going on, American submarines sank two Japanese carriers. The fleeing enemy fleet was struck again the next afternoon, at a cost to Ozawa of another carrier, two oilers, and almost all his remaining planes. When American fliers returned in the darkness, almost out of gas, Vice-Admiral Marc Mitscher, on board his flagship, the *Lexington*, ordered all ships to turn on their lights in defiance of submarine danger. Eighty planes, out of gas, ditched in the water, but almost all the pilots were rescued. Meanwhile, Ozawa returned to base with only 35 planes left. This, the Battle of the Philippine Sea, had been the greatest carrier battle of the war. Never again would Japanese carrier forces be a threat.

A fleet aircraft carrier was a huge and complex creation, an intricately organized floating community of almost 3,000 men who were needed to keep it functioning. Everything about it was in superlatives, from its huge engines to the dial telephone system that connected all rooms and spaces to the amount of bread baked every day. And these ships existed for one single purpose: to get planes into the air and down again. The photographs on these two pages, all made on the second Lexington, catch small glimpses of life on and around the flight deck. As often as not, that life consisted of waiting and killing time.

All hands take setting-up exercises on the flight deck.

Mechanics overhaul a dive bomber.

Plane handlers relax waiting return of a strike.

Walking art gallery.

A damaged plane is moved—fast!

"Boardman" queries incoming pilots.

Wounded pilot is taken to sick bay.

Crew wipes up oil after a crack-up in a bad landing.

Air-crewmen unwind over a game of "Red Dog."

Torpedo bomber pilots wait in the ready room.

A flak-damaged Hellcat crashes into the cable barrier.

Fighter ace indicates six "kills."

The Battle of Leyte Gulf

The two Pacific offensives—MacArthur up from New Guinea and Nimitz through the central Pacific—finally joined in the invasion of Leyte in the Philippines. The landings were not difficult, but they brought out the Japanese Navy in its last big bid for victory. The action, lasting from October 23–27, 1944, was complex, but basic Japanese strategy was to lure the U.S. Third Fleet away with a Northern Force made up largely of empty carriers; then a Central and a Southern Force from the west would converge on Leyte Gulf and annihilate the unprotected forces at the beachhead.

On October 23, the Central Force had two cruisers sunk and a third damaged by American submarines. The next day, planes of Halsey's Third Fleet attacked the Central Force, sinking a battleship and sending a damaged cruiser home, while Japanese land-based planes mortally wounded the light carrier *Princeton*. But now Halsey discovered the decoy Northern Force and set off in full cry, forgetting all else. At the same time, Admiral Kinkaid of the U.S. Seventh Fleet, guessing correctly that another enemy force would approach from the south, steamed to Surigao Strait, where his battleships and cruisers blew the Southern Force to bits as it came in range.

On October 25, the Central Force entered Leyte Gulf. It had suffered damage but was still very strong, and the two American fleets that could have protected the invasion beaches were now far away. But the Japanese had charged almost into the middle of a force of escort aircraft carriers. The battle should have been completely one-sided, but the Americans, though badly hurt —a carrier and three destroyers sunk—were able to sink three enemy cruisers and so confused the Japanese that they withdrew without shelling the invasion beaches. Meanwhile, Halsey was chasing the decoy force far to the north. His planes sank four carriers, a cruiser, and two destroyers, but he finally had to answer urgent pleas for help from the escort carriers. He arrived too late either to help or to intercept any ships of the retiring Central Force.

Vice-Admiral Ozawa (above) commanded the decoy Northern Force. Though he expected total destruction, he saved most of his ships. Vice-Admiral Kurita of the Central Force (below) missed his big chance to wipe out the beachhead.

It required a message directly from Admiral Nimitz in Pearl Harbor to make Admiral William F. Halsey, Jr. (left) return to protect the landing forces at Leyte. Halsey always insisted that his pursuit to the north had been the appropriate action.

Return to Manila

U.S. COAST GUARD

General MacArthur (above) tours the beachhead at Lingayen Gulf in a jeep. At right, Philippine guerrillas bring in a trussed-up Japanese for questioning. These forces were experts at harassing the Japanese.

After Leyte, the next big move was into Luzon, Manila's island. But first, as a steppingstone, to provide airfields to protect the long, exposed route to the invasion area, landings were made on Mindoro on December 15. The Luzon landings began January 9, 1945, in Lingayen Gulf. Opposition was light, but the voyage there had been a nightmare, because for the first time, kamikaze suicide planes appeared in large numbers and as a definite tactical weapon. On February 3, American troops reached the suburbs of Manila and freed some 5,000 Allied prisoners, but it took until March 4 to clear the city, for the 20,000 Japanese fought almost to the last man. In the house-to-house struggle, Manila was almost destroyed. Corregidor fell on February 26, after holding out ten days against paratroops who dropped on the island while destroyers just offshore blew up pillboxes and fired directly into caves full of Japanese. After that, it was a matter of flushing out scattered Japanese from mountain and jungle. There were, however, still 50,500 left to surrender at the end of the war.

OCMH, U.S. ARMY

No rows of white crosses mark the graves of men who pay the price of victory at sea. Those who die on the deep lie in the deep. Wrapped in their canvas shrouds, the bodies of Coastguardsmen from the crew of the troop transport Callaway await commitment to the ocean. They were some of the hundreds of men of the Navy killed by kamikaze attacks during the invasion at Luzon's Lingayen Gulf.

Smashing the Third Reich

By early 1945, the military situation required the principal Allied leaders to meet and settle three terminal problems. They had to arrange how to wind up the war in Europe without any ugly incidents when their armies came together in the Continent's heart. They had to decide on the division of the spoils of victory. And they had to coordinate a final offensive against Japan.

The site chosen for this biggest and most fateful meeting of World War II was Yalta, on the Black Sea shore, in Russia's recently liberated Crimea. On February 4, Roosevelt, Churchill, and Stalin gathered with their staffs in palaces that once were tenanted by vacationing Czars, but which by then were in a sorry state, thanks to the Nazi occupation. The palaces themselves were still standing, but the rest of Yalta had been destroyed. (Roosevelt was outraged by this "reckless, senseless fury" of the Nazis, as he was later to report to Congress.) Indeed, the Soviet Government had to requisition furniture, chambermaids, and waiters from Moscow's principal hotels and hastily dispatch them to the Crimea in order to make its guests comfortable.

Much has been written about what was decided at Yalta, and earnest men still argue whether its decisions were wise or necessary. De Gaulle was not represented and resented the fact ever after. Supporters of Chiang Kai-shek hold that, to insure Russia's attack on Japan, China's sovereignty was fatally impaired. And above all, it is contended that Yalta gave Moscow too much and thus helped produce the Cold War.

At the time, a foolproof understanding was not all that neat and easy to arrange. Germany was still very much alive and fighting desperately with its V-weapons. The advancing Western armies were hampered by supply problems; they had been hit hard at the Battle of the Bulge and had still to cross the Rhine. The Red Army, which had borne the brunt of Hitler's fury, was now in control of Bulgaria, Rumania, Poland, and East Prussia. Perhaps most important of all, Roosevelt did not yet know whether secret nuclear experiments going on at home would produce a workable atomic warhead in time to guarantee Japan's collapse without direct invasion and enormous American casualties. Nonetheless, certain facts now can be seen with clarity.

Churchill's last efforts to induce Roosevelt to push eastward and save much of the Balkans and Germany from Soviet occupation had failed, for reasons previously described. Roosevelt himself was a tired, frail man. When he later addressed Congress, this proud, brave cripple for the first time publicly referred to "the ten pounds of steel on the bottom of my legs."

Stalin, on the other hand, was calm, confident, and wholly assured that his unilateral aims were at last on the verge of success. He felt that he could insist on Anglo-American acceptance of these aims. That spring, before the conflict ended, he was to tell Marshal Tito: "This war is unlike all past wars. Whoever occupies a territory imposes his own social system. Everyone imposes his system as far as his army can advance." And, westward into Europe, eastward into Asia, he was resolved to impose the Communist system.

Churchill could do little in the contest between the weary, idealistic Roosevelt and the laconic, resolute Stalin. Roosevelt was a dreamer; in some respects, he had never learned the hard reality of international bargaining. Anthony Eden, who had his own prejudices, subsequently complained that Roosevelt displayed a certain frivolity when dealing with the fate of nations.

A redoubtable effort has been made by Roosevelt's admirers to demonstrate that Stalin made more concessions at Yalta than did the West. Among the concessions they enumerate are final arrangements for the United Nations, closer military coordination, and French participation in the occupation of Germany. Edward Stettinius, the Secretary of State, claimed that the Yalta agreements "were, on the whole, a diplomatic triumph for the United States and Great Britain. . . . The real difficulties with the Soviet Union came after Yalta when the agreements were not respected." Perhaps; but Harry S. Truman, when he succeeded Roosevelt, did his utmost at Potsdam to revise what he felt were Yalta's overgenerous concessions to Russia.

The Americans sought at Yalta to insure Russia's promised aid against Japan, after a German surrender, while keeping Moscow's voice muted on the fundamental problems of China's political future and the division of the Japanese Empire.

The Big Three exchanged briefings on their offensives against Germany and agreed to synchronize them. They decided that the defeated Reich would be divided into four occupation zones (France's to come from Anglo-American territory), and that reparations should include "the use of German labor." They endorsed a new Provisional Government for Poland that would include both Soviet-sponsored Communists and *émigré* representation from London. They accepted an eastern Polish border along the Curzon Line, with unspecified accessions in the west at Germany's expense. Free elections were pledged for eastern Europe. And in Asia, Russia was promised the return of all lands and concessions lost in the disastrous 1904–5 Japanese war.

Appended to these accords were three secret understandings. The Anglo-Americans and the Russians agreed to exchange each other's liberated prisoners and—more cynically—to repatriate each other's civilians as they were rounded up in Germany. This, of course, meant a Western obligation to send back to the U.S.S.R. many thousands of deserters and political refugees, who were to suffer on their return. The second secret understanding—secret until France could be informed—arranged a

voting formula with a veto for permanent members in the Security Council of the proposed United Nations. In the third secret understanding, Russia formally promised to enter the war with Japan "in two or three months after Germany has surrendered."

Even before Yalta, the grand coalition had begun to coordinate its final military assault on Germany, closing the vise from west and east. On January 6, 1945, Churchill had asked Stalin in a special message to renew the Red Army offensive and thus relieve pressure on the Western Front. When Stalin promised a new thrust along the Vistula, Churchill wired: "May all good fortune rest upon your noble venture." As for the poor Poles, over 200,000 of them had been allowed to die futilely in Warsaw in the fall of 1944, when an uprising of their underground Home Army, first encouraged by Moscow, was then denied desperately needed Soviet aid. The Home Army leadership would undoubtedly prove troublesome when it came to establishing a Communist-controlled government in Poland; so Stalin dismissed their brave efforts as an "adventuristic affair" and did nothing to help. The Red Army made no attempt to cross the Vistula and enter the capital until the Nazis had crushed the rebellion early in October. One desperate Polish patriot wrote:

We are waiting for thee, red pest,
To deliver us from black death.

On January 12, the Russian drive began on a huge front between the Danube and the Baltic. The most famous Russian commanders were engaged: Zhukov, Rokossovski, Vassilevski, Konev. The target was Berlin.

According to the official Soviet history, the Russians had now mustered an overwhelming superiority over the Germans: "5.5 times more men . . . 7.8 times more guns, 5.7 times more tanks, and 17.6 times more planes." They ground on across Poland and into the Prussian province of Brandenburg.

Hungary, which since 1943 had sought intermittently to sign an armistice with the West in secret negotiations at Istanbul, surrendered to Moscow January 20, 1945. Nazi units, however, held on in Budapest until February 13, ruining that splendid city in the process. The Yugoslav partisans and a few regiments of Bulgarians, who had now turned against Hitler, joined the Red Army as it smashed up into Austria. Subservient governments were established by Russian henchmen in Sofia, Bucharest, Budapest. Coalitions clearly dominated by Communists took over in Poland, Yugoslavia, and the Slovakian portion of Czechoslovakia.

Although Patton's American tanks had reached western Czechoslovakia, they were halted by a decision from

Washington, which wished at all costs to avoid any accidental collision between the U.S. and Soviet forces as they advanced toward each other.

By April 13, the Soviet juggernaut had taken Vienna. Three days later, far to the north, it began to storm in force across the Oder River. By April 21, Zhukov reached the outskirts of Berlin, and the European war's last great battle started. Marshal Ivan Konev in his memoirs recalls that he and Zhukov had been summoned to the Kremlin on April 1 and told that "the Anglo-American command was preparing an operation aimed at capturing Berlin and with the object of capturing it before the Soviet Army." (Possibly this referred to the Montgomery plan already long since rejected by Eisenhower.) Stalin then turned to his two greatest marshals and asked: "So who's going to take Berlin then, we or the Allies?"

Stalin suspected the German generals of preferring to surrender to the West, in search of a deal to contain the Soviet advance. Furthermore, the Allies, after destroying the Ardennes counteroffensive, had started smashing forward again at a fast clip, driving down the Moselle and Roer rivers into the Rhine Valley. In February, Montgomery's tanks had managed to squash through the flooded delta country around Nijmegen as the U.S. First Army pushed steadily toward Cologne. The Germans retreated to the eastern bank of their most famous river, the Rhine, and waited for the first attempts to cross.

On March 7, 1945, Eisenhower benefited from a remarkable bit of luck. While the U.S. 9th Armored Division was rumbling toward the town of Remagen, a German prisoner warned his captors that in forty-five minutes, at precisely 4:00 P.M., the great bridge spanning the swollen Rhine there would be blown up. The Americans raced to seize it. Although two demolition charges exploded with minor damage, they captured the span intact, crossed it, and established a strongpoint on the other side of Hitler's last natural defense in the west. Hitler was furious. He set up a special court-martial to try the officers in charge of the bridge, and four of them were executed. He then fired Rundstedt and replaced him with Kesselring, who later said: "Never was there more concentrated bad luck at one place than at Remagen."

From then on, the German collapse accelerated on all fronts. In northern Italy, the U.S. Fifth and British Eighth Armies launched a new spring offensive against the twenty-six Nazi divisions that were holding a line along the Po and the passes leading northward into German Austria. One by one, the famous cities that still were being held by the Nazis in the name of Mussolini's rump Fascist Republic fell: Bologna, Ferrara, Modena, Mantua, Verona, and finally, Genoa and Milan.

Collapse of the Italian front had been hastened by a fascinating secret negotiation. Since late summer, 1944, the Nazis had made various efforts to sound out their different enemies on a possible separate peace. Ribbentrop, apparently with Hitler's blessing, had explored the chance of compromise with Moscow. Himmler, perhaps hoping to save his own skin, sent the S.S. General Karl Wolff to northern Italy to try to make an arrangement with the Italian partisans. When this failed, Himmler's principal Italian representative, Colonel Friedrich Dollmann, together with Wolff's adjutant, contacted an American O.S.S. agent in the Swiss border city of Lugano. Wolff himself was smuggled to Switzerland, where, on March 8, he was received in Zurich by Allen Dulles, head of O.S.S. operations for Europe. On March 19, still in Switzerland, Wolff met two Allied generals wearing mufti, one of whom, Lyman Lemnitzer, was to become chairman of the U.S. Joint Chiefs of Staff and after that NATO commander. By the end of April, terms of capitulation had been substantially agreed upon. They were finally implemented May 2.

Meanwhile, from their Rhineland bridgehead, the Allies swept northward to encircle and reduce the Ruhr, where so much of Hitler's arsenal had been made. Eisenhower methodically enveloped one German army after another, thus preventing any final Nazi withdrawal to a northern or southern redoubt. Just as he would earlier have preferred to bypass Paris, he now preferred to avoid a race for Berlin, despite all its political and symbolic importance. His aide, Captain Harry C. Butcher, wrote that for Eisenhower, "the taking of Berlin would be a mere show; what he wanted to do was to end the war as quickly and economically in lives as possible."

Concentrating on this desire for speed and low casualties, the Supreme Allied Commander set and sprang a series of swift traps. His Ninth and First Armies joined east of the Ruhr and captured that sprawling complex of factories and four hundred thousand German troops. His Sixth Army Group swung southward toward Switzerland and on to the Austrian border. The Twelfth Army Group ground eastward to the Elbe, the final juncture for a meeting with the Russians.

As the Americans, British, and Free French broke through the walls of Hitler's Third Reich, they discovered to their horror that even the most ghastly tales about Nazi atrocities were understatements. One after another they penetrated the unbelievable hells of Buchenwald, Dachau, and Bergen-Belsen, while the Russians, approaching from the east, entered the death mills of Lublin-Maidanek and Auschwitz.

In these and numerous other concentration camps, the

Nazis incarcerated, starved, and murdered more than ten million human beings, including at least 5,700,000 of Europe's Jews, for the crime of being what Hitler considered "inferior" by blood or for having opposed his rule. All of Germany's renowned efficiency was employed to perfect operation of these abattoirs. Men, women, and children were forced against their will to work for the slave empire, were tortured in its name, were finally killed by it. Often, most appalling of all, their corpses were boiled for soap, their hair was used for mattresses and the fillings in their teeth for the system's gold hoard. Sometimes, their tattooed skins were used to decorate lamp shades. Never had there been so immense a crime.

After he had seen his first concentration camp near the aristocratic town of Gotha, Eisenhower cabled Washington and London to send journalists and members of Congress and Parliament to Germany as soon as possible. "I felt," he later wrote, "that the evidence should be immediately placed before the American and British publics in a fashion that would leave no room for cynical doubt."

As these diabolisms were uncovered, an event occurred that tended to enhance bitter emotions among the conquering armies. On April 12, 1945, a tired and prematurely old Franklin Roosevelt was resting at Warm Springs, Georgia, when suddenly he complained: "I have a terrific headache." Two hours later, he was dead of a cerebral hemorrhage. His death was succinctly announced in the regular Army-Navy casualty lists: "Roosevelt, Franklin D., Commander in Chief, wife, Mrs. Anna Eleanor Roosevelt, the White House."

Churchill called this "a loss of the British nation and of the cause of freedom in every land." Chiang Kai-shek began a fast and meditation. The streets of Moscow were filled with weeping men and women. Goebbels telephoned Hitler with delight: "My *Führer*, I congratulate you! Roosevelt is dead! It is written in the stars that the second half of April will be a turning point for us." Hitler himself issued an Order of the Day describing Roosevelt as "the greatest war criminal of all times." And Harry Truman, a modest but decisive man, moved into the American seat of power to usher the world into the atomic age.

Roosevelt died at Warm Springs in what for him was a tranquil haven and knowing that his cause had won. Such was not to be the fate of the Axis dictators.

Mussolini was the first to go. By the end of April, as the Allies were approaching Milan, last big city of his puppet Republic, and as partisans were swarming up to the Swiss border, the *Duce* sought the mediation of the archbishop of Milan, Ildefonso Cardinal Schuster. At the archbishop's palace he discovered that the Germans were already in the process of surrendering. He then tele-

phoned his wife to say farewell, gathered money and some of his secret files, and took off northward with a few followers and his young mistress, Clara Petacci. On April 27, his little caravan joined a German antiaircraft battery retiring toward the Tyrol. They were soon stopped by a partisan roadblock. Mussolini disguised himself in a German helmet and military overcoat, but at the village of Dongo he was recognized and seized. On April 28, near lovely Lake Como, the *Duce* and his mistress were stood against a wall, read the death sentence by Colonel Valerio (Walter Audisio), the partisan commander, and shot. The bodies were trucked to Milan, kicked, beaten, and strung up by the feet in front of a gasoline station.

When Hitler received the news, he knew that his turn had come. The Battle of Berlin was raging all around him, though his Chancellery was still defended against the Russians. On April 29, he dictated his personal will and his political testament. He named Martin Bormann, the number two Nazi, as his executor and expelled Göring and Himmler from the party because of their disloyalty to his frenzied last-minute commands. He appointed Grand Admiral Karl Doenitz President of the Reich and Supreme Commander of the Armed Forces. He made a last appeal against "international Jewry" and then concluded: "I myself and my wife—in order to escape the shame of overthrow or capitulation—choose death." His wife was the plump Eva Braun, whom he married the day before his suicide.

Hitler ordered that his favorite Alsatian dog be poisoned, and poison was distributed to his secretaries. Then, early in the morning of April 30, he shook hands with remaining members of his entourage and retired with Eva Braun. Goebbels, Bormann, and a few other Nazi bosses were left behind to send the final telegrams. About 3:15 that afternoon, Eva Braun, sprawled on a sofa, took poison. At 3:30, Hitler, seated at a table near her, shot himself in the mouth with a pistol. The corpses were taken into the Chancellery garden by Bormann, Hitler's valet, and a surgeon, placed in a Russian shellhole, doused in gasoline, and burned. Goebbels had an *S.S.* orderly shoot him and his wife after she had poisoned their six children. Bormann disappeared without a trace.

By the time of Hitler's death, thousands of Berliners were scurrying from their besieged capital in a hysterical effort to avoid Soviet retribution, as, block by block, floor by floor, the troops of Zhukov and Konev bored through the burning city.

An officer with a German tank unit at Tempelhof airfield kept a diary which gives some faint idea of that last terrible fight: "We retreat again, under heavy Russian air attacks. Inscriptions on the house walls: 'The hour before sunrise is the darkest,' and 'We retreat, but we are winning.'. . . The night is fiery red. Heavy shelling. Otherwise a terrible silence. . . . Women and children huddling in niches and corners and listening for the sounds of battle. . . . Nervous breakdowns. The wounded that are not simply torn apart are hardly taken in anywhere. The civilians in their cellars are afraid of them. Too many of them have been hanged as deserters."

On May 2, Berlin at last fell.

For a few more days, disconnected fragments of the *Wehrmacht* thrashed about in isolated sectors between the Austrian Tyrol and Scandinavia. Bormann had sent Doenitz Hitler's last message saying: "Grand Admiral Doenitz: In place of the former Reich Marshal Göring the Führer appoints you as his successor. Written authority is on its way. You will immediately take all such measures as the situation requires." Doenitz, whom nobody bothered to tell that Hitler was dead, wired back: "My Führer! My loyalty to you will be unconditional."

Hitler's Thousand-Year Reich lasted a bit more than twelve years. The Doenitz Reich survived Hitler by a week. The German radio announced that the *Führer* had died "fighting to his last breath against Bolshevism." It said nothing of suicide. Doenitz went on the air to regret the "hero's death" of Hitler. He publicly hinted at a desire to arrange accommodation with the Western Allies against "the advancing Bolshevik enemy." On May 5, Admiral Hans von Friedeburg even sought an eleventh-hour deal at Eisenhower's headquarters in Rheims while all German forces in northwest Germany, Holland, and Denmark were already capitulating.

Friedeburg hoped to stall negotiations long enough to bring the maximum number of troops and refugees westward, eluding Russia's grasp before the fighting ceased. Eisenhower, however, threatened to close the entire Allied front against such refugees unless there was an immediate, total cease-fire. On May 5, Army Group G, comprising all German forces in Austria, yielded to the Sixth Army Group. The actual surrender came at 2:41 A.M., May 7, 1945, in a modest schoolhouse at Rheims.

Friedeburg, Field Marshal Alfred Gustav Jodl, and his aide, Major General Wilhelm Oxenius, signed the terms. Eisenhower refused to attend in person. Instead he sent British, French, Soviet, and American emissaries to accept unconditional surrender of all German forces to both the Western Allies and the Soviet Union, together and simultaneously. When the brief ceremony ended, Jodl said with much difficulty: "With this signature, the German people and armed forces are, for better or worse, delivered into the victor's hands." The Allied representatives made no comment. The Germans were then conducted to Eisenhower's office and asked if they understood what they had signed. "Ja," said Jodl. Next day, to symbolize unity among the victors, the ceremony was repeated in Berlin, where Zhukov signed for the Soviet Union. May 8 thus became the historical V-E Day.

London, Paris, New York, Moscow, the entire world, save for Japan, rejoiced at the news. Eisenhower told his troops in a Victory Order of the Day: "Let us have no part in the profitless quarrels in which other men will inevitably engage as to what country, what service, won the European war. Every man, every woman, of every nation here represented has served according to his or her ability, and the efforts of each have contributed to the outcome." President Truman said to the American people in a radio address: "We must work to bind up the wounds of a suffering world—to build an abiding peace, a peace rooted in justice and in law. We can build such a peace only by hard, toilsome, painstaking work—by understanding and working with our Allies in peace as we have in war."

In Moscow, crowds, which had been expecting the great news almost hourly since Berlin's fall, swarmed into the Red Square, brushing aside enormous police reinforcements. A thousand guns fired thirty rounds each to signalize "complete and total victory."

The announcement came long before dawn, and thousands of people poured into the streets wearing everything from pajamas to fur coats. The crowd stayed on and on and grew ever larger. There had been no such demonstration in Moscow since the Revolution's earliest wild days. Hordes gathered in front of the British and American embassies, and whenever a foreigner was spotted, he was gently plucked up by a hundred hands and passed along with cheers. George Kennan, U.S. chargé d'affaires, made a speech from the embassy balcony, where the Red banner hung beside the Stars and Stripes. Roars went up: "Long live Truman!" "Long live Roosevelt's memory!" "Long live the great Americans!"

Far away, on America's Pacific Coast, a conference was meeting at San Francisco to create the United Nations. From April 25, not long after Roosevelt's death, until June 26, shortly before the first nuclear device was exploded in secret, the world's new leaders argued about the structure of the organization they were building. They debated the "fundamental human rights" to which they would henceforth dedicate themselves, rights including "social progress and better standards of life" and "the equal rights of men and women." At the insistence of a Republican member of the United States delegation, Senator Arthur H. Vandenberg of Michigan, one word was added to the list—"justice."

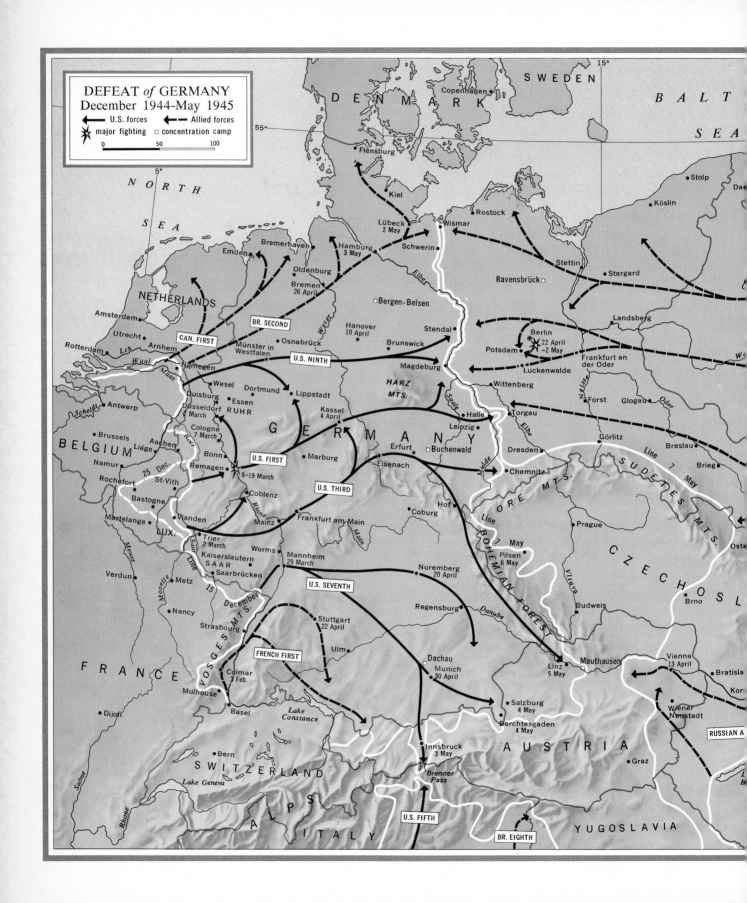

DEFEAT of GERMANY
December 1944–May 1945

← U.S. forces   ⇐ Allied forces
✳ major fighting   ☐ concentration camp

0   50   100

On German Soil

After the Battle of the Bulge had been concluded in January, 1945, the *Wehrmacht* was never again a serious threat on the Western Front, and its bolt was soon shot in the east as well. There was fight still left in it, but with the forces arrayed against it, defeat was inevitable. German man-power reserves were exhausted, armor was scarce, motor fuel supplies were drying up, the *Luftwaffe* was virtually gone. On January 12, the Russians, already in Poland and East Prussia, opened a massive offensive and within two weeks were inside Germany itself. The Allied armies began their own offensive in the west on February 23. They were then approximately on the German border over most of its length, and General Eisenhower's next objective was to force the enemy across the Rhine River. From this strong defensive position, the Allies would then prepare for a break-through. But the situation changed with the capture of a railroad bridge across the Rhine at Remagen; the Allies had a bridgehead, and the advance continued. In the meantime, strategic bombing continued, with the German oil industry having top priority in order to halt the Nazi mechanisms of war. Large cities received second priority, and transportation came third. On April 16, strategic bombing was ended because so few targets remained. By March 23, the Saar with its important industries had been captured; in April, the great industrial Ruhr was captured, and with it an entire German army group of 400,000 men. At this time Eisenhower made the decision not to race the Russians to Berlin but to stop at the Elbe River, which had been agreed upon at Yalta as the dividing line between Soviet and Western zones of postwar occupation. The British protested strongly, but the General had based his decision on military rather than political considerations. After the Ruhr pocket was gone, the Allied armies met no major organized opposition, while in the east the Russians fought their last great battle in Berlin. Russians and Allies met. German forces in Italy surrendered on April 29. The Nazi Government for what was left of Germany capitulated, and it was all over on May 8.

WALTER HAHN, DRESDEN

Three Men at Yalta

President Roosevelt had a little more than two months to live when he met with Stalin and Churchill in early February, 1945, at Yalta, in Russia. Germany was in flames, and there were many problems to be discussed. Some of the agreements reached had long-lasting repercussions. Roosevelt agreed to pay a high price, some of it at China's expense, for Russia's brief and unnecessary part in the war against Japan—but at the time there was no way of knowing how soon Japan would collapse. Germany was divided into occupation zones—but the Allies did not expect Stalin to make the division permanent. Allied failure to get guaranteed access to their zones in Berlin, deep inside Russian-occupied Germany, still plagues them. Another cause of future friction was Stalin's promise of free elections in Poland, which he broke within weeks. Roosevelt had gone to Yalta optimistic about the future and confident that his personal charm could win Stalin. He was already disillusioned before his death.

Two days after the Yalta meeting ended, Dresden was bombed and almost obliterated (above) by the resulting fires. Estimates of the dead ran well over 100,-000. In the picture, bodies are being cremated on five separate pyres. At right, Churchill, Roosevelt, and Stalin pose at Yalta. Standing immediately behind them, from left: Foreign Minister Anthony Eden, Secretary of State Edward R. Stettinius, British Undersecretary Sir Alexander Cadogan, Foreign Commissar Vyacheslav Molotov, and Ambassador Averell Harriman.

U.S. First Army tanks and infantry (upper left) cross the Rhine bridge at Remagen, Germany, under fire to establish a bridgehead. The Remagen bridge was seized before it could be destroyed and was the only one remaining across the Rhine. It stood for ten crucial days in March, 1945, before collapsing from damage done by the Nazis; by that time, the east bank was secure, and pontoon bridges were operating. Farther south, Third Army assault troops (bottom left) crouch behind the sides of an amphibious truck as they cross the Rhine. And at right, soldiers of the Seventh Army move through Waldenburg, deep in Germany, which was taken in mid-April.

A picture symbolic of Germany's military might brought low: American soldiers of the Seventh Army pose along the barrel of a giant

captured 274-mm. railroad gun. When the photograph was made on April 10, 1945, Hitler's Third Reich had not quite a month left.

They Had Not Known

In stacks, the dead at Gusen concentration camp in Austria await burial (above). At right, German civilians are forced to view the bodies of Jewish women who starved during a 300-mile march.

As the Allied forces drove deep into Germany, they came on the first concentration camps and revealed the full depravity of Hitler's Third Reich. American Third Army troops were battle-hardened, but they were aghast at what they found at Buchenwald: the bodies piled in heaps, the living who were little more than skin drawn over skeletons, the gas chambers, the crematories that had burned day and night. Buchenwald was only four or five miles from Weimar, the cultural center of an older and better Germany, but when residents of Weimar were forced to tour Buchenwald, they protested that they had not the slightest idea these horrors existed. On April 14, the British freed Belsen and found some 55,000 still alive, and dead by the thousands everywhere: in open mass graves, scattered about the grounds, even sharing bunks with the sick living. As camp after camp was liberated, a cold anger filled the Allied troops, while everywhere the German civilians insisted that they had not known of these enormities, although it was said that the stench of the camps and the odor of the crematories had carried far over the countryside.

To Make Murder Pay

Concentration camps had a single purpose: to facilitate mass murder. They were staffed with *S.S.* thugs and sadists (the glum *S.S.* women at right, British prisoners, were experts in brutality at Belsen) who used a variety of means to accomplish their ends: the machine gun, the gas chamber, starvation, poison, brutality, disease, overwork. But the Nazi regime profited even from murder. While the aged, the very young, and the infirm were killed on arrival, the strong were usually hired out as laborers in mines or factories until they, too, became useless from hunger, neglect, and overwork. At Auschwitz, the most horrible of all the camps, where an estimated 3,000,000 perished, the great I.G. Farben chemical trust built a plant to take advantage of the cheap slave labor. With Germanic efficiency, the *S.S.* worked out the average profit to be expected from a slave laborer (below), down to the residual yield from the gold in his teeth. Nothing was wasted. Americans found all neatly sorted in Buchenwald warehouses: bales of women's hair, spectacles, dentures, clothing. A sight that especially infuriated them was a bin with thousands of pairs of babies' shoes.

Macht ohne Moral, RÖDERBERG-VERLAG, FRANKFURT/MAIN

**Rentabilitätsberechnung der SS über Ausnützung
der Häftlinge in den Konzentrationslagern**

Rentabilitätsberechnung

Täglicher Verleihlohn durchschnittlich RM 6,—

abzüglich Ernährung   RM —,60

durchschnittl. Lebensdauer 9 Mt. = 270 x RM 5,30 = RM 1431,—

abzüglich Bekl. Amort. RM —,10 _____

Erlös aus rationeller Verwertung der Leiche:

1. Zahngold	3. Wertsachen
2. Kleidung	4. Geld

abzüglich Verbrennungskosten   RM 2,—

durchschnittlicher Nettogewinn   RM   200,—

Gesamtgewinn nach 9 Monaten   RM 1631,—

zuzüglich Erlös aus Knochen und Aschenverwertung.

**Table of profits (or yield) per prisoner in
concentration camps (established by SS)**

Rental accounting

Average income from rental of prisoner, per day   RM [Reichsmark] 6.00

Deduction for nourishment, per day   RM 0.60

Average life expectancy: 9 months: 270 [days] by RM 5.30 = RM 1431.00

Minus amortization on clothing   RM 0.10 _____

Profits from rational utilization of corpse:

1. Gold teeth	3. Articles of value
2. Clothing	4. Money

Minus costs of cremation   RM 2.00

Average net profit   RM 200.00

Total profit after 9 months   RM 1631.00

This estimate does not include profits from [sale of] bones and ashes.

IMPERIAL WAR MUSEUM, LONDON

President Roosevelt Dies

At left, President Roosevelt's funeral cortege passes along a Washington avenue. Above, Harry Truman is sworn in, at 7:09 P.M. by the mantle clock. A score of officials and members of Congress saw the brief ceremony. Those in the picture, from left: Secretary of Agriculture Claude Wickard; unidentified; Attorney General Francis Biddle; Truman; Secretary of State Edward Stettinius, Jr.; Mrs. Truman; Secretary of the Interior Harold Ickes; Chief Justice Harlan F. Stone; and House Speaker Sam Rayburn.

Franklin Delano Roosevelt, thirty-second President of the United States, died on April 12, 1945. American forces in the Pacific were then methodically clearing Okinawa against Japanese resistance. In Europe, the U.S. Army made its first crossing of the Elbe on the day of the President's death and was about fifty miles from Berlin. Joseph Goebbels in Berlin, on hearing the news, called Hitler to congratulate him; the propaganda minister was ecstatic, for some astrological hocus-pocus assured him that this was the turning point of the war. But American military momentum did not falter as the new Commander in Chief, Harry Truman, took over. President Truman would not have an easy time. In immemorial tradition, he had been limited as Vice-President to presiding over the Senate and attending ceremonial functions. This man who shortly would have to decide whether to use the atomic bomb did not even know on April 12 that such a device existed. ". . . last night the whole weight of the moon and stars fell on me," he told the press. "Please pray for me."

Americans and Russians fraternize at Torgau on the Elbe. It was here, some 75 miles south of Berlin, that advance patrols of the American and Soviet armies met for the first time on April 25 and cut Germany in two. The young ladies are also in the Red Army, serving as staff secretaries and clerks. A black-bordered photograph of Roosevelt hangs beside the picture of Stalin; very probably none of the new President Truman could be found anywhere.

572

The Guns Fall Silent

From his bunker deep under the Reichschancellery garden in Berlin, Hitler fought out his war to its mad end. Long after the situation was hopeless, he was confident of a victory that would smash the enemy. But this fantasy faded as massive, irresistible Soviet forces broke into the city, and he was shattered by news of the treason of Himmler and Göring and of the death of Mussolini. Meanwhile, the American armies stood fast on the Elbe River. General Eisenhower had decided against a costly drive on Berlin, since, by the Yalta agreement, all country east of the Elbe would only have to be turned over to the Russians. By April 25, Berlin was besieged. With Russian shells exploding in the chancellery garden, Hitler and Eva Braun, his bride of only a day, ended their lives on April 30. Two days later, the German forces in the city asked for a cease fire. Only a fragment of the Third Reich remained.

On his birthday, April 20, Hitler awards the Iron Cross to Hitler Youth members for bravery against the Russians. Children like these were put in uniform in the war's last desperate days. At right is Marshal Ivan Konev, commander of the First Ukrainian Front in the final offensive.

" 'That must be the Russians,' I said in the calmest voice I could manage"

WENDEL, *Hausfrau at War*

Else Wendel

"Two eyes for an eye," was the Russian motto as they drove on Berlin, and the Russian soldiers lived up to it with such incredible fury that even the Russian high command began taking measures to hold back on the senseless bloodshed, the rape and plunder. The Russian sweep through East Prussia came in early April; they took Vienna on the thirteenth, and three days later they launched their final big push to Berlin, which was then just thirty-five miles to the west. For the Germans it was a last agonizing nightmare, worse than all the other nightmares they had been living with for so long. In short, it was the same anguish Germany had inflicted on millions of others.

. . . In Poland a few regrettable things happened from time to time, but, on the whole, a fairly strict discipline was maintained as regards 'rape.' The most common offence in Poland was *'dai chasy'*—'give me your wrist-watch.' There was an awful lot of petty thieving and robbery. Our fellows were just crazy about wrist-watches—there's no getting away from it. But the looting and raping in a big way did not start until our soldiers got to Germany. Our fellows were so sex-starved that they often raped old women of sixty, or seventy or even eighty—much to these grandmothers' surprise, if not downright delight. But I admit it was a nasty business, and the record of the Kazakhs and other Asiatic troops was particularly bad.
—A Russian Major,
As Told to Alexander Werth

Dawn is just breaking; our operating room is packed with people. A small candle-end serves us as illumination. We have got through the night somehow or other. Only a few Russians still haunt our basement.

A dead woman is lying on the operating table and is always attended to as soon as a Russian appears. Lying on the floor and dozing, I can hear Doktora's voice in the next room, comforting some one. It is a miracle that she has come through this hellish night unharmed.

Just as we had feared, the Russians had found some alcohol. Right next to us in the Menthal liqueur factory some thousands of gallons, carefully hidden, were still lying, saved up by the irony of fate for just this moment. Now something like a tide of rats flowed over us, worse than all the plagues of Egypt together. Not a moment went by but the barrel of an automatic was rammed against my back or my belly, and a grimacing mask yelled at me for sulfa. Apparently most of these devils have got venereal disease. Our dispensaries were burned out long ago, and the huge supply of drugs was lying trampled to bits in the corridors. With a certain malicious glee I could point again and again to the devastation caused by their buddies. They burst in here from the factory in crowds—officers, soldiers, riflewomen, all drunk. And not a chance of hiding anybody from them, because the whole neighborhood was lit up as bright as day by the burning buildings.

We kept close together waiting for the end to come in some form or other. The fear of death which had hardly figured in our thoughts since the days of the last air raids was now completely dispelled by something infinitely worse. On all sides we heard the desperate screams of women: "Shoot me then! Shoot me!" But the tormentors preferred a wrestling match to any actual use of their guns.

Soon none of the women had any strength left to resist. In a few hours a change came over them; their spirit died, you heard hysterical laughter which made the Russians even more excited. . . .

—Hans Count von Lehndorff,
An East Prussian Surgeon

Panic had reached its peak in the city. Hordes of soldiers stationed in Berlin deserted and were shot on the spot or hanged from the nearest tree. A few clad only in underclothes were dangling on a tree quite near our house. On their chests they had placards reading: "We betrayed the Führer." . . .

The S.S. went into underground stations, picked out among the sheltering crowds a few men whose faces they did not like, and shot them then and there.

The scourge of our district was a small one-legged *Hauptscharführer* of the S.S. who stumped through the street on crutches, a machine-pistol at the ready, followed by his men. Anyone he didn't like the look of he instantly shot. The gang went down cellars at random and dragged all the men outside, giving them rifles and ordering them straight to the front. Anyone who hesitated was shot.

The front was a few streets away. . . .

—Claus Fuhrmann,
Clerk

. . . When the second morning came we heard loud, hoarse shouting from the Russian troops and there was the sound of rifles and machine guns.

Heiner and I stood in the lounge and looked out. The Russians were swarming into our street, running, shooting and shouting. I nearly screamed aloud in terror, then I remembered Heiner.

"Quick," I said to him, "upstairs."

He turned round, his face ghastly pale. He flung his arms round me, and held me close for a second, then he rushed up the stairs towards his hole in the roof, and I snatched up a book from the bookcase and went down to the cellars. I was too agitated to look at the boys, but merely opened the book and began to read aloud to them. It was a fairy story book. I had grabbed it at random from the children's bookshelves in my panic.

The fairy story was about a princess who was born blind. Wolfgang and Klaus became fascinated. It wasn't often I had time to read to them nowadays. There I sat in the cellar just saying the words and trying to keep my voice steady, with one ear listening for the Russians and the other trying to hear whether all was well with Heiner.

The poor shepherd in the story had just seen the beautiful blind princess and decided to give his life so that she might see, when we were interrupted by a sharp banging on the door which I had locked and bolted.

"That must be the Russians," I said in the calmest voice I could manage. I went upstairs, telling the boys to stay absolutely silent in the cellar. Two Russian soldiers stood at the door with their rifles and guns loaded and pointing at me. I stood and stared and so did they for a second. Never shall I forget that moment.

Then, in broken German, one of them said: "Arms up!" I held my arms up. The Russian stepped forward and searched me thoroughly for weapons. He took nothing from me, not even my wrist watch.

When they were satisfied that I was unarmed, one of them spoke again. "Where is the man?" he asked.

"There isn't a man," I replied.

"Yes there is."

"No."

"We'll find him. Show your house!"

They indicated that I was to go through the house with them. I had to go ahead, and they followed with the rifle and gun behind me. While we went through the rooms I kept wondering if someone had betrayed Heiner. Why had they said: "Yes, there *is* a man." Suddenly I noticed Heiner's hat hanging from a peg by the front entrance door. Had they noticed it? I was seized with cold fear.

Now they wished to see the cellar. The staircase was dark as the electricity was cut off. I could sense the Russian behind me becoming nervous. Then I felt the gun pressed against my neck. It was a clear warning that if I was leading them into a trap, I should fall first!

I opened the door into the cellar. A candle was burning there, and the two small boys were standing with their mouths wide open and staring at me and the soldiers. They looked so thin and pale and frightened they might have been carved out of stone. Immediately the Russian saw them, he took the gun off my neck and broke into loud laughter. "Oh, children!" he shouted. The other Russian smiled and let his rifle drop to his side. Then he turned to me and indicated that the search was off, and I was to return upstairs with them. Actually I was more nervous on the way upstairs than on the way down. In reaction my legs shook so much I nearly fell twice on the steps. They took me outside the house and stood me up against the door post, aimed and shot . . . not *at* me, but to each side of me. Then they turned and left me standing there, turned to stone now, in relief and astonishment.

—Else Wendel,
Berlin Housewife

Nuremberg had been the city of the great Nazi Party Rallies and of Hitler's frenetic speeches; it was soon to be the scene of the war

crime trials. When American forces reached the city, they found that even its medieval heart had been devastated by Allied bombs.

The rapidly advancing Allied armies opened many prison gates; these jubilant men are some of the 6,000 Allied prisoners, 3,300 of

them Americans, liberated by the U.S. Seventh Army at Bad Orb, Germany. German treatment of prisoners was almost universally bad.

Armed resistance continued in Germany for several days after the fall of Berlin, but it was disorganized and hopeless. On May 7, the remnants of the Third Reich surrendered unconditionally. The reaction to the news was much the same in all the Allied countries: an outpouring of unrestrained happiness. At left, joyous Russians jam Moscow's Red Square. Below, Londoners acclaim Churchill as he rides to Parliament to make his victory-day speech. At right, celebrators in New York's Wall Street cheer victory in Europe.

Aftermath in Germany

In most defeated nations, some government remains to pick up the pieces and go forward. In Germany there was none at all, and the victorious powers governed even the smallest villages. "Give me ten years and you will not be able to recognize Germany," Hitler had said in 1933. It was certainly not recognizable in 1945, twelve years later. Some 3,250,000 Germans had been killed in Hitler's battles, a like number had died from other causes, 1,300,000 were missing, the maimed were everywhere. The nation was in chaos: cities smashed, bridges wrecked, railroads cut to bits. The Allies applied themselves to the minimum tasks of keeping the Germans from starving and beginning the rehabilitation of the nations Hitler had enslaved. But the big job was still the unfinished business in the western Pacific.

Some American soldiers got occupation duty, some were sent to the Pacific, but for most, the end of the war in Europe meant going home. The Queen Mary (above) carries homeward-bound troops. Coming home is not so joyful for the German veteran of Stalingrad at right; he does not know whether home and family still exist.

The End of the Rising Sun

Even before the mopping-up had ended on Leyte in the Philippines, MacArthur sent Lieutenant General Walter Krueger's Sixth Army on a long, hooking loop through Surigao Strait, the Mindanao Sea, and on to Lingayen Gulf and Luzon, key to the whole Philippines archipelago. On January 9, 1945, some sixty-eight thousand Americans began clambering ashore on the vulnerable Lingayen beaches in what became the largest United States land campaign of the Pacific War. (More American forces were engaged on Luzon than in either Africa or Italy.)

Krueger's objective was Manila, the national capital and a magnificent port. But Krueger was opposed by an impressive army under General Yamashita, comprising 250,000 men divided into three groups: Shobu Group of 140,000 men in the North Central sector, defending Lingayen Gulf; Kembu Group of 30,000 men, defending the network of airbases around Clark Field; and Shimbu Group of 80,000 men in southern Luzon.

Despite their size and dispositions, Yamashita's troops had already been weakened by harassing guerrilla attacks and steady United States air bombardment, and they were unable to stop Krueger. By January 31, the Americans had moved deep into the Central Plain and had expelled the Japanese to the mountainous north and east. They prepared for the final drive on Manila, timed to coincide with an Eighth Army drive across the base of the famous Bataan Peninsula, which had begun with landings at San Antonio Bay on the twenty-ninth.

On February 3, the U.S. 1st Cavalry Division reached the outskirts of the capital, but it took twenty-nine days to complete the occupation against desperate house-to-house resistance. When the rubble of Manila finally was freed on March 4, several Japanese units on Luzon remained in effective condition, and Yamashita continued fighting from stronghold pockets until the very end of the war. But MacArthur had achieved his principal goal, and he set about establishing on Luzon a great base from which to invade Japan itself.

Two weeks after returning to the capital where he had spent so many years, MacArthur was back on Corregidor. He issued an order: "Hoist the colors and let no enemy ever haul them down." At last, on July 5, he was able to announce that the campaign was over. In the Philippines the Americans had annihilated 450,000 of the Emperor's best remaining troops.

It was Admiral Spruance, a quiet, philosophical, but resolute sailor, later a highly successful diplomat, who had helped dissuade Nimitz and Washington from the original plan of moving directly to Formosa instead of to the Philippines. So when Iwo Jima and Okinawa were chosen for invasion right after Luzon, it was fitting that Spruance's Fifth Fleet should land the V Marine Corps, which was under Major General Harry Schmidt, on Iwo. D-day was February 19.

Only 775 miles from Honshu, a main island of Japan, the barren, volcanic island of Iwo Jima was of particular importance to the B-29 offensive. It was being used by the Japanese as a radar warning station and as a base

Tokyo in March, 1945: one section after the terrible fire-bomb raid.

for fighter interceptors. But even more important, once captured, its three airfields could be employed by P-51 Mustangs to provide fighter escort for the huge B-29's as they flew the thousand-mile return trip to their bases in the Marianas to the south. The eight square miles of Iwo were defended by more than twenty thousand valiant Japanese under Lieutenant General Tadamichi Kuribayashi. The island had been well prepared with extensive mine fields, lengthy underground tunnels, and communications systems protected by artillery fortified with concrete made from the island's black volcanic ash.

Initially, there was virtually no Allied cover on the exposed beaches, and the conquest of the ugly little island presented the Marine Corps with the largest bill of its brave and bloody history. The Marines took Iwo inch by inch, crawling forward on their stomachs or behind tanks that bogged down in the volcanic ash. Men with rifles and flame throwers fought their way from pillbox to foxhole, climbing the dominant defensive feature, rocky Mount Suribachi, where on February 23, after three days of furious combat, the Marines hoisted the Stars and Stripes and photographer Joe Rosenthal of the Associated Press took one of the war's most famous pictures. To secure the island took a total of twenty-six days and 20,965 American casualties, including 6,821 dead. Lieutenant General Holland M. "Howling Mad" Smith commented succinctly: "The fighting was the toughest the Marines ran across in 168 years." The price of Iwo came high, but by the war's end, 24,761 B-29 crewmen had used its airfields for emergency landings.

By now the Pacific offensive was working like a one-two punch. On March 26, 1945, Lieutenant General Simon Bolivar Buckner's Tenth Army landed its 77th Division in the Kerama Islands, west of Okinawa, principal center of the Ryukyu chain. The small islands were quickly subdued and became a seaplane base and anchorage for supply ships during the operation. At the same time, Marines took the nearby Keise Islands, artillery was emplaced, and Okinawa, just eight miles away, came under direct attack.

Okinawa was a rather poor chunk of land comprising some 700 square miles, but its strategic value was immense. It was only 350 miles from Japan proper, and it had good harbor facilities and plenty of room to stage troops. It would provide an ideal jumping-off place for any invasion of Japan. This island was the stake of the war's last and biggest amphibious assault. Vice-Admiral Richmond Turner had elaborated the actual operations plan for its capture on February 9, ten days before the Iwo Jima landing. He arranged concentric invasions by forces under himself, Spruance, Mitscher, and Buckner (who commanded seven Marine and Army divisions).

The mere fact that Japan's defenses had been constricted by a tightening ring and that the Japanese therefore could no longer pretend feints and diversions worried the invaders. They were aware that Lieutenant General Mitsuru Ushijima, Okinawa's commander, had more than one hundred thousand men and three thousand aircraft at his disposal, and that the kamikaze menace, originated at Leyte and embellished at Iwo Jima, would now, surely, reach a ferocious peak.

The Okinawa landing began at 8:30 A.M., April 1, Easter Sunday. By the time the battle ended, eighty-two days later, over 300,000 troops were on the island. During the first hours of the invasion, the American commanders, who were expecting immediate resistance as at Iwo Jima, were surprised to find almost no opposition on the beaches. In fact, there seemed to be little opposition anywhere. Five hours after the first Marines were ashore, they had captured one vital air strip and not a shot had been fired.

If everything seemed to be going much too easily, it was because Ushijima had pulled back to the southern part of the island. He had decided on a defense in depth designed to attract the main assault forces and then cut them off, instead of risking piecemeal losses to heavier American naval artillery and air power. Five days elapsed while the Marines muttered that Okinawa was "the screwiest damned place in the Pacific." Then the Japanese struck. On April 6 and 7, nearly 700 enemy aircraft, including some 350 kamikazes, pounded the American beachheads and the task forces assembled offshore.

The first five hours of the battle that was designed to smash the American invaders of Okinawa took a toll of six American ships and 135 kamikaze pilots. The Japanese committed their largest battleship, the 72,908 ton *Yamato*, without air cover and with fuel enough only for a one-way trip. On April 7, despite its screen of eight destroyers and the light cruiser *Yahagi*, it was sunk in less than two hours—along with four destroyers and the *Yahagi*. The Imperial Fleet was gone.

From then on, the land conquest of Okinawa proceeded in a bloody series of pushes. The Americans first reduced the northern defenses and then turned southward. The ultimate and most fiercely defended position was in the ancient city of Shuri, a center of pre-Chinese, pre-Japanese culture. There Marine flamethrowers burned their way through dugouts in immemorial cemeteries. When the last strongpoint on Kiiyama Peninsula fell, 110,071 Japanese were dead, nine for every American. Buckner was among the Americans killed. Before dawn on June 22, Ushijima and his principal subordinate,

Lieutenant General Cho, knelt in full dress uniform before their headquarters cave and cut out their entrails.

The persistent thrust of American sea power, whose destruction had been calculated at Pearl Harbor, closed in upon Japan's Pacific fringes, backed up by an ever-encroaching land power and a formidable air power. What was left of an Asian front simply fell apart. While B-29 bombers continued their pulverizing operations from the Marianas, the stalemate in Burma and, ultimately, China had turned into a Japanese retreat.

Along the Manchurian-Soviet border, where a truce of mutual convenience had been arranged between Moscow and Tokyo, a day of reckoning was due. As disaster loomed over Germany, it became increasingly necessary for Japan to keep ground forces opposite the border.

As early as the spring of 1944, the Japanese General Staff had begun plans for defense against a Russian attack. At Yalta, Stalin had been promised—as booty for joining in the Pacific war—the Kurile Islands and southern Sakhalin (which had been lost to Japan in 1905), as well as Russian privileges in Chinese ports and railways. On April 5, 1945, Molotov informed the Japanese embassy in Moscow that the U.S.S.R. was denouncing its Neutrality Pact because the situation had "radically changed." On May 15, Tokyo annulled its alliance with a German state that had ceased to exist. But the gesture was meaningless; it was quite apparent that a new front soon would open, at a most disastrous moment for the Emperor. The Japanese sought to stave off the reckoning by sending out peace feelers, but to no avail. When the Big Three victors met at Potsdam in July, Stalin told the British and Americans of these overtures. Truman then confided to Stalin the secret that the United States possessed a "new" bomb that could have a decisive effect on the war. But he avoided disclosing the weapon's full import.

While Tokyo alerted its Manchurian army, it was facing accumulating difficulty in China itself. A 1944 offensive there had not succeeded in altering the strategic balance. Despite mutual recriminations, both Mao's Communists and Chiang's Kuomintang armies continued to nibble at areas occupied by a Japan that no longer had troops to spare. By early 1945, Mountbatten's forces had managed to open land communications between Burma and China. Mountbatten flew to Manila, where MacArthur promised to help prevent the Japanese from reinforcing their Singapore and Malayan garrisons. At Potsdam, Marshall authorized Mountbatten to assume over neutral Siam (Thailand) whatever control he required and to plan for eventual operations in formerly Dutch Sumatra and in French Indochina, whose territory was thereby withdrawn from MacArthur's supervision.

By this time, Japan's most dreadful tribulations had begun. General Curtis LeMay had made of the Marianas a massive Superfortress base. Once he had assembled there three wings of long-range B-29's, he began a devastating series of raids against Japan's helpless main island cities. Starting in February, 1945, employing a new bomb containing magnesium and jellied gasoline, bombers burned out factories, docks, urban areas, and Tokyo itself. Japan, with jerry-built houses and overconcentrated industrial centers, was peculiarly vulnerable to incendiary attack. LeMay made the most of the situation, reducing the armament and crews of his planes so they could carry a maximum weight of fire bombs.

In mid-March he dispatched 334 B-29's from Guam, Saipan, and Tinian on the most destructive single bombing mission ever recorded. It did more damage than even the dreadful atomic explosions that were to wipe out Hiroshima and Nagasaki.

On the night of March 9–10, just after midnight, the pounding of Tokyo started amid a high wind. Within half an hour, the resulting fires had flamed wholly out of control. A factory worker who took refuge in a school compound later described his experience: "The fires were incredible by now, with flames leaping hundreds of feet into the air. There seemed to be a solid wall of fire rolling toward the building. All the windows were closed to prevent sparks from pouring into the rooms and setting the school ablaze. . . . Many people were already gasping for breath. With every passing minute the air became more foul. . . . the noise was a continuing, crashing roar. The great bombers were still coming over Tokyo in an endless stream. . . . Fire-winds filled with burning particles rushed up and down the streets. I watched people —adults and children—running for their lives, dashing madly about like rats. The flames raced after them like living things, striking them down. They died by the hundreds right in front of me. Wherever I turned my eyes, I saw people running away from the school grounds seeking air to breathe. They raced away from the school into a devil's cauldron of twisting, seething fire. The whole spectacle with its blinding lights and thundering noise reminded me of the paintings of Purgatory." A Japanese newspaperman wrote: "The city was as bright as at sunrise; clouds of smoke, soot, even sparks driven by the storm, flew over it. That night we thought the whole of Tokyo was reduced to ashes." The fire department estimated that the raid killed 97,000 people, wounded 125,000, and left 1,200,000 homeless.

One by one Japan's cities were reduced: Tokyo, then Nagoya, Kobe, Osaka. Each devastation was so terrible that currents of heat were flung upward into the sky, tossing the vengeful airplanes and tearing helmets from the heads of their crews. In one ten-day blitz, the Superfortresses wholly flattened 32 square miles of Japan's four most important centers.

By April 6, MacArthur was given command of all U.S. Army forces in the Pacific and was directed, with Nimitz, the Naval commander, to prepare for the war's final operations. This task was rendered far easier than the Joint Chiefs of Staff could foresee by the accomplishment of a scientific miracle.

At 5:30 A.M., July 16, in a remote New Mexican desert, the first atomic device was placed upon a steel tower near Alamogordo Air Base and detonated. Under the direction of Dr. J. Robert Oppenheimer, a theoretical physicist from the University of California, the July 16 test was successfully staged, producing what an official War Department release later described as "a revolutionary weapon destined to change war as we know it, or which may even be the instrumentality to end all wars."

Tentative manufacture of the bomb had been begun by General Groves's Manhattan Engineer District in 1942. American, British, and French scientists had pooled their knowledge, and following Fermi's 1942 chain-reaction experiment, the United States had built two gigantic plants at Oak Ridge, Tennessee, and Hanford, Washington, to separate a uranium derivative known as U-235 and to make plutonium. At Los Alamos, New Mexico, Oppenheimer established a laboratory to work on producing a warhead. However, until its actual testing in July, no one, not even its sponsors, could be certain that it would work. So secret was the project that only a handful of persons were even aware of its existence, and they did not include Harry Truman, then Vice-President. The day after Roosevelt died, Secretary of State James F. Byrnes told Truman of the coming experiment, but his first thorough briefing did not come until twelve days later, from Secretary of War Henry L. Stimson.

Pandora's terrible box opened—never again to be slammed shut—just as dawn unfolded July 16. As the countdown ended, Oppenheimer, standing with Groves in a distant control station, shouted, "Now!" The assembled officers and scientists peered through their dark glasses at the auroral burst of flame, and Oppenheimer thought of two passages from the Hindu epic, *Bhagavad-Gita*. One went: "If the radiance of a thousand suns were to burst into the sky, that would be the splendor of the Mighty One." The other: "I am become Death, the shatterer of worlds." A tremendous blast rushed out across the desert, and above it rose the first of those awful mushroom-shaped clouds.

It remained for Truman to decide if, how, where, and when this fantastic weapon should be employed. Twelve days before the test, Churchill had given the President British consent in principle to drop the bomb on Japan. Truman himself was to write in his *Memoirs*: "Let there be no mistake about it, I regarded the bomb as a military weapon and never had any doubt that it should be used." When he told Stalin about the bomb at Potsdam, Stalin replied that he hoped the United States "would make good use" of it.

There was some discussion among American leaders on what preliminary warning should be addressed to Tokyo prior to employment of the two bombs already being assembled on Tinian. Undersecretary of State Joseph C. Grew urged that Japan be alerted to its danger with a message indicating no insistence on the Emperor's abdication. Stimson echoed this view, but Byrnes opposed it. On July 26, the Potsdam Declaration was issued, with an ultimatum demanding that Japan surrender unconditionally or face complete destruction. Two days later, Premier Suzuki announced that his Government would ignore it. Lieutenant General Spaatz, by now Commanding General of the U.S. Army Strategic Air Forces in the Pacific, had been instructed to prepare to utilize the first of the two fabricated bombs after August 3, weather permitting, against one of four cities: Hiroshima, Kokura, Niigata, or Nagasaki. Following Suzuki's action, this order was confirmed. A B-29 from the 509th Composite Group, with a specially trained crew commanded by Colonel Paul W. Tibbets, Jr., was chosen for the first mission.

At 8:15 A.M., August 6, Tibbets released over Hiroshima a uranium bomb of the type called "Little Boy." He reported later: "As far as I was concerned it was a perfect operation." On August 9, a plutonium bomb known as "Fat Boy" was dropped on Nagasaki. The destruction in each case exceeded the most careful extrapolations of scientists, and it was hours before the mushroom clouds, smoke, and flames had sufficiently blown away to permit adequate photo-reconnaissance.

It is impossible to convey the full meaning of these twin events. The casualty toll was staggering and, of course, fails to suggest the indescribable suffering incurred, but estimates claim—no one knows for certain—that from seventy to eighty thousand people were killed at Hiroshima and an equal number were injured, and that some forty thousand died at Nagasaki and about sixty thousand were injured.

Militarily, the denouement was swift. Truman announced: "We are now prepared to obliterate rapidly and completely every productive enterprise the Japanese have above ground in any city." On August 8, Molotov summoned in Ambassador Sato and informed him that the Soviet Union was declaring war. The very next day, three Russian army groups rolled over Japan's Kwantung Army and within a few days had penetrated deep into Manchuria. On August 10, Tokyo sued for peace on the basis of the Allies' Potsdam Declaration, but requested that Hirohito be retained as Emperor. (Truman, acting on advice from Grew, Stimson, and Leahy, came to the decision that this stipulation was in the best interests of the United States.)

The actual surrender was decided at a final meeting of the Supreme War Council, in the presence of the Emperor. Hirohito said: "I cannot bear to see my innocent people suffer any longer." Following a lengthy discussion, Suzuki rose and quietly remarked: "Gentlemen, we have spent hours in deliberation without coming to a decision and yet agreement is not in sight. You are fully aware that we cannot afford to waste even a minute at this juncture. I propose, therefore, to seek the imperial guidance and substitute it for the decision of this conference." He then advanced sadly to the throne. The diminutive Hirohito, by avocation a marine biologist, who kept a portrait of Abraham Lincoln in his study, said he felt compelled to accept the Allies' terms.

These terms stipulated that "from the moment of surrender the authority of the Emperor and the Japanese Government to rule the state shall be subject to the Supreme Commander of the Allied Powers." On August 15, in a taped radio message, his first direct voice communication with his people, the Emperor informed them that the war was over and it was time to "pave the way for a grand peace for all generations to come."

The Russians spurned the announcement as "only a general statement on Japan's capitulation." They continued their brief but fierce offensive. The Kwantung Army surrendered August 22, but Soviet air-borne troops and the Red Fleet moved on to Dairen and Port Arthur in Manchuria and seized southern Sakhalin and the Kuriles. The Japanese fought sporadically until September 12. The Russians captured 594,000 Japanese and killed some 80,000, against their own losses of 8,000 dead and 22,000 wounded. On August 26, Sir Frederick Browning, on behalf of Mountbatten, accepted the Japanese surrender of Southeast Asia in Rangoon. And, starting August 28, American troops began a mass and unopposed landing on Japan's home islands, occupying all strategic centers.

Although there were several separate Japanese capitulations on widely separated fronts—with China regaining sovereignty over Inner Mongolia, Manchuria, Formosa, and Hainan, and with Britain reoccupying Hong Kong and accepting a formal Japanese surrender in Singapore on September 12—the crucial and historical act confirming Imperial Japan's defeat took place aboard the 45,000-ton battleship, U.S.S. *Missouri*, on September 2, 1945, in Tokyo Bay.

The event was staged with a high sense of drama. Suzuki had resigned August 15. The new Premier, Prince Higashikuni, was able to avoid the capitulation ceremony for protocol reasons—he was the Emperor's uncle. Instead, the one-legged Foreign Minister, Mamoru Shigemitsu, wearing striped pants and top hat, limped aboard the *Missouri* from a gig that flew the Stars and Stripes, accompanied by General Yoshijiro Umezu, representative of the General Staff.

The *Missouri*, flagship of the U.S. Pacific Fleet, was flying the same flag that had waved over the Capitol in Washington the day Pearl Harbor was attacked. Jammed together on the deck was a mass of correspondents and Allied officers: British and Australians with scarlet bands on their caps and collars; Gaullist French with vivid decorations; Dutch with gold-looped emblems; Chinese in olive drab; Russians in stiff shoulder-boards, headed by the obscure Lieutenant General Derevyanko; and the Americans, simply garbed in plain suntans.

After MacArthur had opened the ceremony with a brief and generous address, Shigemitsu, with great dignity, signed two copies of the surrender document in Japanese and English. Umezu followed. Then MacArthur strode forward, bringing with him two high officers who had been rescued from Japanese prisoner-of-war camps: Lieutenant General Jonathan M. Wainwright, whom he had been forced to leave behind at Corregidor, and Lieutenant General Sir Arthur Percival, the loser of Singapore. MacArthur then signed, followed by Nimitz and the Allied delegates.

The handsome general, looking a generation younger than his years, said: "We are gathered here, representatives of the major warring powers, to conclude a solemn agreement whereby peace may be restored. The issues, involving divergent ideals and ideologies, have been determined on the battlefields of the world and hence are not for our discussion or debate. Nor is it for us here to meet, representing as we do a majority of the people of the earth, in a spirit of distrust, malice, or hatred. But rather it is for us, both victors and vanquished, to serve, committing all our peoples unreservedly to faithful compliance with the understandings they are here formally to assume. It is my earnest hope . . . that from this solemn occasion a better world shall emerge . . . a world dedicated to the dignity of man. . . . Let us pray that peace be now restored to the world, and that God will preserve it always. These proceedings are closed."

Next Objective: Iwo Jima

Iwo Jima, halfway between the Marianas and Japan, was a small island, but it was not one that could be bypassed. From its airfields, Japanese planes intercepted B-29's raiding Japan and attacked the big bombers at their bases in the Marianas. Besides needing to end these problems, the Americans wanted Iwo for an emergency landing field for B-29's in trouble, and as a base from which fighters could fly cover to Japan for the Superfortresses. The invasion was set for February 19, 1945; bombing began the August before and soon became daily, the longest, most sustained preassault bombardment of any spot in the Pacific. For three days before the landings, warships also pounded the island with their big guns. But the Japanese had pierced the volcanic rock with miles of tunnels, and a network of concealed gun positions permitted weapons of every caliber to sweep the entire island and the water offshore. The bombardment did little good, and many men would die as a result.

Lt. Gen. Holland M. Smith of the U.S. Marines (left) was in command of troops of the Iwo Jima expedition—three Marine divisions. Above, some 5th Division Marines engage in light housekeeping on their landing craft on their way to Iwo Jima.

593

Marines rush ashore as their landing craft hits the Iwo Jima beach. A heavy preassault bombardment temporarily knocked out enemy

GEORGE BURNS

gunfire, and the first wave landed without trouble; but later arrivals were heavily shelled, and wrecks soon littered the beach.

Costly Chunk of Rock and Black Sand

Japanese gunfire had been silenced for the moment when the Iwo Jima landings began on February 19, but an unforeseen difficulty appeared. Men coming ashore sank to their calves in volcanic ash, and the armored amtracks were unable to climb from the beach up a high terrace of the loose black stuff. Japanese gunfire soon resumed. The Marines moving inland were pinned down by an enemy they could not see; low hummocks of sand were the tops of pillboxes, with their gun slits only a few inches above ground. When tanks came ashore, they were blasted by hidden antitank guns. Battleships and smaller warships offshore did magnificent work destroying enemy positions, but in most cases they had to be rooted out by men in yard-by-yard advances with flame throwers and demolition charges. Mount Suribachi, the island's one peak, from which the enemy had been raining shells into the congested landing beach with devastating effect, was finally scaled on February 23. Fighting among the gullies and caves of the rocky northeast end of the island continued until a final Japanese counterattack on March 26. It was the costliest operation in Marine history.

LEFT: LOUIS R. LOWERY; RIGHT: U.S. MARINE CORPS

RIGHT: WIDE WORLD

Marines hug the Iwo Jima beach (left) after landing. At right, rocket launchers, employed later in the campaign, fire at enemy positions.

LEFT: U.S. NAVY; RIGHT: U.S. ARMY

At left, two marines use flame throwers to kill holed-up Japanese. At right, three of the few Japanese to surrender come out of hiding.

The first assault wave heads for the beach on D-Day. Mount Suribachi, bristling with deeply dug-in artillery, is in the background.

These two dead Marines (left) were among the very first of 6,821 Americans to die at Iwo Jima. Right, supplies are unloaded under fire.

The first flag is raised on Mount Suribachi (left). A larger flag goes up several hours later (center). At right, the banner triumphant.

A chaplain celebrating mass on Iwo Jima gives the communion wafer to a Marine. His church is the top of Mount Suribachi; his altar

is a makeshift. The fighting was still going on in full intensity when this picture was made, and these men returned to battle.

ABOVE: MAINICHI GRAPHIC–BIRNBACK; BELOW: KODANSHA INTERNATIONAL–BIRNBACK

ABOVE: MAINICHI GRAPHIC–BIRNBACK; BELOW: U.S. NAVAL INSTITUTE

The Divine Wind

The kamikaze attack had become an integral part of Japanese tactics after its successful tryout at Leyte Gulf, where it sank an escort carrier and damaged others. From then on, Allied seamen came to know suicide pilots well. Kamikaze—"divine wind" in English—attacks during the Lingayen Gulf operation were very effective, sinking four Allied vessels and damaging forty-three. At Iwo Jima, suicide planes sank an escort carrier and hurt five other ships, including two carriers. Kamikaze tactics were well suited to the Japanese character and to the Empire's desperate military situation. Almost all of Japan's top pilots were dead, and most of her first-line planes had been destroyed. But an obsolete plane was just as effective when loaded with explosives, and a young man could quickly be taught enough flying to get a plane to the Allied fleet and then dive it into a ship. American and British seamen underwent their most fearsome trial by suicide planes during the Okinawa campaign. They were within close range of the airfields on the Japanese home islands, and both the invasion fleet and the fast carrier force were hit again and again. Thirty ships were sunk, and though none was larger than a destroyer, 368 were damaged, including carriers and battleships, some put out of action for months. Almost 5,000 Navy men were killed. As the campaign progressed, tactics to cope with the suicide planes were developed, while at the same time the Japanese were having difficulty finding young men willing to kill themselves. Many returned saying they had been unable to find the Allied fleet.

The pictures at left show supposedly typical moments in the brief lives of the kamikaze pilots. From the top they are, according to the Japanese description: the last toast before the take-off; pilots smile at young girls gathered to bid them farewell; suicide pilot Sergeant Omura writes a last letter home to his mother; and at bottom, the final take-off. At right, antiaircraft gun crews try to identify planes as friend or enemy during the Mindoro invasion in December of 1944.

The photographs on these and the next two pages are typical of hundreds of episodes during the kamikaze attacks in the western Pacific. At upper left, a 40-mm. battery in an unidentified carrier fires at a suicide plane during a strike at Tokyo. Upper right, a kamikaze plane attacks the battleship Missouri. Bottom left, explosions follow a hit on the Franklin. Bomb and gasoline blasts wracked the carrier for hours, but although she was grievously hurt, with 724 dead, her crew brought her back to the United States under her own power. And at bottom right, the carrier Bunker Hill transfers her wounded onto the cruiser Wilkes Barre after being hit by a kamikaze plane.

The crew of the Bunker Hill fights a flight-deck fire after a suicide plane dove into the ship on May 11, 1945, off Okinawa. Almost

400 officers and men died, and with the carrier put out of action, Admiral Marc Mitscher, aboard, transferred his flag to the Enterprise.

"It was a fight to the finish"

Seaman First Class James J. Fahey

Among the following accounts of the kamikaze campaign is an excerpt from one of the war's most remarkable documents, a diary kept against regulations by a sailor named James J. Fahey, of Waltham, Massachusetts. Day after day he described life aboard the cruiser Montpelier, *providing a rare and vivid account of the war in the Pacific as seen from the fighting man's point of view.*

. . . It is absolutely out of the question for you to return alive. Your mission involves certain death. Your bodies will be dead, but not your spirits. The death of a single one of you will be the birth of a million others. Neglect nothing that may affect your training or your health. You must not leave behind you any cause for regret, which would follow you into eternity. And, lastly: do not be in too much of a hurry to die. If you cannot find your target, turn back; next time you may find a more favorable opportunity. Choose a death which brings about a maximum result.

—From the First Order to the Kamikazes

Contrary to my usual habit, I woke early, at five o'clock. I did my exercises stripped to the waist. I felt extremely well.

Now one has only to place a sheet of paper into the little box which usually contains the ashes of the dead. I wonder if that is true? I wanted to send you parings of my nails and a few locks of my hair, but I had my hair cut yesterday and my nails are already too short. I am sorry, but unfortunately it is too late. Neither my nails nor my hair will grow again in one night.

I do not want a grave. I would feel oppressed if they were to put me into a narrow vault. A vaga-bond, such as I, has no need of it. Will you tell my parents that?

Do not weep because I am about to die. If I were to live and one of my dear ones to die, I would do all in my power to cheer those who remain behind. I would try to be brave.

11:30 a.m.—the last morning. I shall now have breakfast and then go to the aerodrome. I am busy with my final briefing and have no time to write any more. So I bid you farewell.

Excuse this illegible letter and the jerky sentences.

Keep in good health.

I believe in the victory of Greater Asia.

I pray for the happiness of you all, and I beg your forgiveness for my lack of piety.

I leave for the attack with a smile on my face. The moon will be full to-night. As I fly over the open sea off Okinawa I will choose the enemy ship that is to be my target.

I will show you that I know how to die bravely.

With all my respectful affection,

—Akio Otsuka, A Kamikaze Pilot

There was one maintenance man who made a point of meticulously scouring and polishing the cockpit of each kamikaze plane he tended. It was his theory that the cockpit was the pilot's coffin and as such it should be spotless. One recipient of this service was so pleasantly surprised that he summoned and thanked his benefactor, saying that the neatness of the plane meant a great deal to him. The maintenance man's eyes dimmed with tears, and, unable to speak, he ran along with one hand on the wing tip of the plane as it taxied for its final take-off.

—Commander Tadashi Nakajima

Jap planes and bombs were hitting all around us. Some of our ships were being hit by suicide planes, bombs and machine gun fire. It was a fight to the finish. While all this was taking place our ship had its hands full with Jap planes. We knocked our share of planes down but we also got hit by 3 suicide planes, but lucky for us they dropped their bombs before they crashed into us. In the meantime exploding planes overhead were showering us with their parts. It looked like it was raining plane parts. They were falling all over the ship. Quite a few of the men were hit by big pieces of Jap planes. We were supposed to have air coverage but all we had was 4 P-38 fighters, and when we opened up on the Jap planes they got out of the range of our exploding shells. They must have had a ring side seat of the show. The men on my mount were also showered with parts of Jap planes. One suicide dive bomber was heading right for us while we were firing at other attacking planes and if the 40 mm. mount behind us on the port side did not blow the Jap wing off it would have killed all of us. When the wing was blown off it, the plane turned some and bounced off into the water and the bombs blew part of the plane onto our ship. Another suicide plane crashed into one of the 5 inch mounts, pushing the side of the mount in and injuring some of the men inside. A lot of 5 inch shells were damaged. It was a miracle they did not explode. If that happened the powder and shells would have blown up the ship. Our 40 mm. mount is not too far away The men threw the 5 inch shells over the side. They expected them to go off at any time. A Jap dive bomber crashed into one of the 40 mm. mounts but lucky for them it dropped its bombs on another ship before crashing. Parts of the plane flew everywhere when it crashed into the mount. Part of the motor hit Tomlinson, he had chunks of it all over him, his stomach, back, legs etc. The rest of the crew were wounded, most of them were sprayed with gasoline from the plane. Tomlinson was thrown a great distance and at first they thought he was knocked over the side. They finally found him in a corner in bad shape. One of the mt. Captains had the wires cut on his phones and kept talking into the phone, because he did not know they were cut by shrapnel until one of the fellows told him. The explosions were terrific as the suicide planes exploded in the water not too far away from our ship. The water was covered with black smoke that rose high into the air. The water looked like it was on fire. It would have been curtains for us if they had crashed into us.

Another suicide plane just overshot us. It grazed the 6 inch turret. . . . There was a terrific explosion as the bombs exploded, about 20 ft. away. If we were going a little faster we would have been hit. The Jap planes that were not destroyed with our shells crashed into the water close by or hit our ships. It is a tough job to hold back this tidal wave of suicide planes. They come at you from all directions and also straight down at us at a very fast pace but some of the men have time for a few fast jokes, "This would be a great time to run out of ammunition." "This is mass suicide at its best." Another suicide plane came down at us in a very steep dive. It was a near miss, it just missed the 5 inch mount. The starboard side of the ship was showered with water and fragments. How long will our luck hold out? The Good Lord is really watching over us. This was very close to my 40 mm. mount and we were showered with debris. If the suicide plane exploded on the 5 inch mount, the ammunition would have gone up. . . .

. . . During a little lull in the action the men would look around for Jap souvenirs and what souvenirs they were. I got part of the plane. The deck near my mount was covered with blood, guts, brains, tongues, scalps, hearts, arms etc. from the Jap pilots. One of the Marines cut the ring off the finger of one of the dead pilots. They had to put the hose on to wash the blood off the deck. The deck ran red with blood. The Japs were spattered all over the place. . . . I cannot think of everything that happened because too many things were happening at the same time.

These suicide or kamikaze pilots wanted to destroy us, our ships and themselves. This gives you an idea what kind of an enemy we are fighting. . . . You do not discourage the Japs, they never give up, you have to kill them. It is an honor to die for the Emperor. . . .

—James J. Fahey

Among those of us who were there, in the Philippines and at Okinawa, I doubt if there is anyone who can depict with complete clarity our mixed emotions as we watched a man about to die—a man *determined* to die in order that he might destroy us in the process. There was a hypnotic fascination to a sight so alien to our Western philosophy. We watched each plunging kamikaze with the detached horror of one witnessing a terrible spectacle rather than as the intended victim. We forgot self for the moment as we groped hopelessly for the thoughts of that other man up there. . . .

—Vice-Admiral C. R. Brown

U.S. MARINE CORPS

Last Stop Before Japan

The last and the largest amphibious operation of the Pacific war was the invasion of Okinawa, a prime strategic objective only 325 miles south of the Japanese island of Kyushu. On April 1, a joint Army-Marine assault force began landing on Okinawa's west coast; Admiral Raymond Spruance had command of the amphibious operation, but once ashore, the force, as the Tenth Army, came under the command of Lieutenant General Simon B. Buckner, Jr. American forces cleared the northern part of the long island with little trouble, but the Japanese had concentrated in the south and fought desperately. Meanwhile, the Navy offshore was suffering heavily—including almost 5,000 killed—from kamikaze attacks. Not until June 22 did resistance on the island finally cease. About 11,000 Japanese surrendered; the rest, some 110,000, died. General Buckner was among the approximately 7,600 Americans lost in the land fighting.

A wounded civilian on Okinawa is flushed out of his hiding place by Marines (above). The Okinawans had been convinced that the Americans meant to harm them. At right: Harmon Field on Guam, one of the three big B-29 bases in the Marianas that continued their air attacks against Japan all through the Okinawa campaign. A similar base built on Okinawa launched only one raid before the end of the war.

Futility at Potsdam

President Truman met with Churchill and Stalin at Potsdam, near war-ravaged Berlin, during the last half of July, 1945. (British elections were held during early July, and Churchill was defeated and replaced for the later Potsdam sessions by the new Prime Minister, Clement Attlee.) It was the last of the wartime conferences, and it accomplished little. Stalin was urged to make good on his promise to declare war on Japan, although some American military men were now cooling to the idea. It was decided to settle the question of Poland's western boundaries later—an empty gesture, for the Poles had already moved into eastern Germany after evicting the Germans there and plainly meant to stay. At one point the Americans threatened to leave the conference because of Stalin's insistence on reparations so huge that they would have left Germany without enough to subsist on. But the most important event during the conference occurred elsewhere: President Truman received word that the first atomic test explosion at Alamogordo, New Mexico, had been successful. The President at once joined Britain and China in the Potsdam Declaration, a surrender ultimatum to Japan.

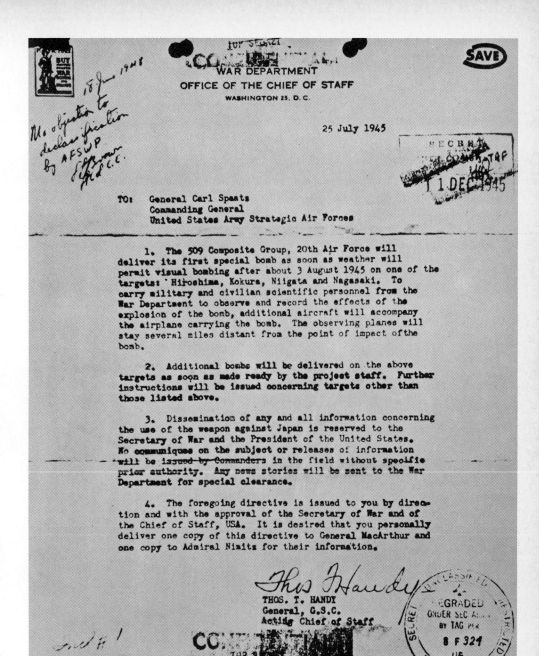

Churchill, Truman, and Stalin link hands at Potsdam (left) in a show of harmony greater than actually existed. At the right is the directive that ordered General Carl Spaatz, in command of U.S. Strategic Air Forces, to drop the first "special bomb" on any one of four designated cities. Two of the cities named were Hiroshima and Nagasaki. And below is an early atomic bomb of the type called "Little Boy" and dropped on Hiroshima. It was 28 inches in diameter and 120 inches long. Weighing 9,000 pounds, its explosive power was the same as that of 20,000 tons of TNT.

TOP SECRET

WAR DEPARTMENT
OFFICE OF THE CHIEF OF STAFF
WASHINGTON 25, D. C.

25 July 1945

TO: General Carl Spaatz
       Commanding General
       United States Army Strategic Air Forces

1. The 509 Composite Group, 20th Air Force will deliver its first special bomb as soon as weather will permit visual bombing after about 3 August 1945 on one of the targets: Hiroshima, Kokura, Niigata and Nagasaki. To carry military and civilian scientific personnel from the War Department to observe and record the effects of the explosion of the bomb, additional aircraft will accompany the airplane carrying the bomb. The observing planes will stay several miles distant from the point of impact of the bomb.

2. Additional bombs will be delivered on the above targets as soon as made ready by the project staff. Further instructions will be issued concerning targets other than those listed above.

3. Dissemination of any and all information concerning the use of the weapon against Japan is reserved to the Secretary of War and the President of the United States. No communiques on the subject or releases of information will be issued by Commanders in the field without specific prior authority. Any news stories will be sent to the War Department for special clearance.

4. The foregoing directive is issued to you by direction and with the approval of the Secretary of War and of the Chief of Staff, USA. It is desired that you personally deliver one copy of this directive to General MacArthur and one copy to Admiral Nimitz for their information.

THOS. T. HANDY
General, G.S.C.
Acting Chief of Staff

Death of Hiroshima

At 9:15 on the morning of August 6, 1945, more than half the city of Hiroshima was obliterated. The first atomic bomb to be used against a city had exploded two thousand feet above the center of Hiroshima, and an area of more than four square miles, or 60 per cent of the city's area, was absolutely erased. Beyond the zone of utter death and destruction, lightly built houses were knocked flat as far as three miles from ground zero, so that 80 per cent of all buildings were destroyed and almost all the rest badly damaged. No one knows how many died, for thousands disappeared, seared to ashes, without leaving a trace, but the figure was between 70,000 and 80,000, and about the same number were injured, many of them horribly burned. The picture at right was taken by a Japanese news photographer when the horrors of the event were at their height. The picture, blurred by smoke and ash from the fires that followed the blast, is of victims waiting to receive first aid on the outer edge of the city. On August 9, three days later, Nagasaki became the victim of the second atomic bomb. Again the effects were awesome and fearful. The Japanese Supreme War Council gave in to the inevitable and on the fourteenth decided to capitulate. The next day, Emperor Hirohito broadcast to his people—the first time he had ever talked to them —to say that the years of fighting were ended.

612

Nagasaki lies shattered and scorched after its nuclear attack. Because the city is on uneven ground, sections were shielded from

the blast, and casualties and destruction, although terrible, were less than at Hiroshima. Damage to industry, though, was greater.

"We accept their Joint Declaration"

Emperor Hirohito

The following tell something of the events that took place during the first weeks of August, 1945, five years and a little more than eleven months after Adolf Hitler invaded Poland.

. . . we made our turn, and as we leveled out of our turn the flash occurred. The man in the tail gunner's position said, "I can see it coming," meaning the shock wave. . . . Well, by the time he said that, the first one hit us. It was a real wallop—a real bang. It made a lot of noise and it really shook the airplane. . . .

There was the mushroom cloud growing up, and we watched it blossom. And down below it the thing reminded me more of a boiling pot of tar than any other description I can give it. It was black and boiling underneath with a steam haze on top of it. And, of course, we had seen the city when we went in, and there was nothing to see when we came back. It was covered by this boiling, black-looking mess.

—Colonel Paul W. Tibbets, Jr.,
Pilot of the "Enola Gay"

The crew said "My God" and couldn't believe what had happened.
—Navy Captain William S. Parsons,
Ordnance Expert on the "Enola Gay"

On August 6th there wasn't a cloud in the sky above Hiroshima, and a mild, hardly perceptible wind blew from the south. . . .

At nine minutes past seven in the morning an air-raid warning sounded and four American B-29 planes appeared. To the north of the town two of them turned and made off to the south and disappeared in the direction of the Shoho Sea. The other two, after having circled the neighborhood of Shukai, flew off at a high speed southward in the direction of the Bingo Sea.

At seven thirty-one the all clear was given. Feeling themselves safe, people came out of their shelters and went about their affairs and the work of the day began.

Suddenly a glaring whitish-pink light appeared in the sky accompanied by an unnatural tremor that was followed almost immediately by a wave of suffocating heat and a wind that swept away everything in its path.

Within a few seconds the thousands of people in the streets and the gardens in the center of the town were scorched by a wave of searing heat. Many were killed instantly, others lay writhing on the ground, screaming in agony from the intolerable pain of their burns. Everything standing upright in the way of the blast, walls, houses, factories, and other buildings, was annihilated; and the débris spun round in a whirlwind and was carried up into the air. Trams were picked up and tossed aside as though they had neither weight nor solidity. Trains were flung off the rails as though they were toys. Horses, dogs, and cattle suffered the same fate as human beings. Every living thing was petrified in an attitude of indescribable suffering. Even the vegetation did not escape. Trees went up in flames, the rice plants lost their greenness, the grass burned on the ground. . . .

Beyond the zone of utter death in which nothing remained alive, houses collapsed in a whirl of beams, bricks, and girders. Up to about three miles from the center of the explosion, lightly built houses were flattened as though they had been built of cardboard. Those who were inside were either killed or wounded. Those who managed to extricate themselves by some miracle found themselves surrounded by a ring of fire. And the few who succeeded in making their way to safety generally died twenty or thirty days later from the delayed effects of the deadly gamma rays. . . .

About half an hour after the explosion, while the sky all around Hiroshima was still cloudless, a fine rain began to fall on the town and continued for about five minutes. It was caused by the sudden rise of overheated air to a great height, where it condensed and fell back as rain. Then the violent wind rose, and the fires extended with terrible rapidity because most Japanese houses are built only of timber and straw.

—*A Japanese Journalist*

On August 15th, for the first time in history, the Emperor of Japan addressed his people by radio. The moment the emperor began to speak, our amah knelt down before the loudspeaker and then stretched herself out at full length, her forehead touching the floor.

—Marcel Junod

Most of the twenty or so people . . . were women and children; there were only two or three elderly men there and Terry. . . . One woman, her right leg bandaged to the hip, had fled the heavily bombed Kanda district of Tokyo with her grandchildren and her daughter-in-law; another woman in her forties had brought her five children to our mountains from the city. A few farm people from the region surrounding Tateshina were there. The children were afraid, awed and quiet; they kept close, huddling around their parents.

All were grave and solemn with unspoken wonder at two things: How would the Emperor's voice, which they had never in their lives heard, sound? What was their final destiny which the voice of the *tennō* would reveal?

They sat and listened intently when the high-pitched and quavering voice began. Leaning forward with brows furrowed and heads cocked to one side, they concentrated upon the sound. There was an eeriness about it, the way the people strained as if they were deaf, for the voice was loud enough and distinct; they heard the words easily as their future life or death was announced—but they could not understand. The Emperor spoke in Court Japanese and only Terry could comprehend.

As Terry translated and they grasped the sense of what was being said, that it meant surrender, the bandaged woman began to weep— not loudly or hysterically but with deep sobs that racked her body. The children started crying and before the Emperor had finished, all his people there were weeping audibly. The voice stopped. Silently the old men, the women, and their children, rose and bowed to each other and without any sound each went along the path leading to his own house.

—Gwen Terasaki

We, the Emperor, have ordered the Imperial Government to notify the four countries, the United States, Great Britain, China and the Soviet Union, that We accept their Joint Declaration. To ensure the tranquillity of the subjects of the Empire and share with all the countries of the world the joys of co-prosperity, such is the rule that was left to Us by the Founder of the Empire of Our Illustrious Ancestors, which We have endeavoured to follow. Today, however, the military situation can no longer take a favourable turn, and the general tendencies of the world are not to our advantage either.

What is worse, the enemy, who has recently made use of an in-human bomb, is incessantly subjecting innocent people to grievous wounds and massacre. The devastation is taking on incalculable proportions. To continue the war under these conditions would not only lead to the annihilation of Our Nation, but the destruction of human civilization as well. . . .

—Emperor Hirohito

At 7 P.M. the White House correspondents gathered in my office. . . .

When everybody was in, I stood by my desk and read this statement:

"I have received this afternoon a message from the Japanese Government in reply to the message forwarded to that Government by the Secretary of State on August eleventh. I deem this reply a full acceptance of the Potsdam Declaration which specifies the unconditional surrender of Japan. . . ."

The correspondents shouted congratulations as they rushed out the doors to flash the word to their papers. Mrs. Truman and I went out to the fountain on the north lawn. A vast crowd had assembled outside the gates, and when I made a V sign in the manner of Churchill, a great cheer went up. I remained outside only a few minutes and then went back into the White House and called my mother at her home in Grandview, Missouri.

Around eight o'clock the crowds outside were still growing, and I went out on the north portico and spoke a few words through a loudspeaker that had been set up there. This was a most significant and dramatic moment, and I felt deeply moved by the excitement, perhaps as much as were the crowds that were celebrating in cities and towns all over the nation. . . .

The guns were silenced. The war was over. . . .

—President Truman

KODANSHA INTERNATIONAL–BIRNBACK

The Day the War Ended

There had been wild celebrating on V-E Day, but under it had been the sobering realization that another war remained to be fought out. There was no such inhibiting fact on V-J Day, August 15, 1945. Whistles blew, church bells rang, crowds filled the streets, bars overflowed, workers left their jobs, strangers embraced, and in San Francisco two young ladies were so transported by patriotic emotion that they bathed naked in a public fountain. Less exuberant citizens went to church to pray, and to give thanks for victory and peace. Others seriously discussed the conflict just ended, and many were certain that this, at last, had been the war to end wars, for after this experience no nation could ever repeat the insanity of taking up arms against a neighbor. But the flush of excitement subsided, and both the boisterous and the philosophical began to think about serious future concerns, such as how long it might be before they could expect to be able to buy a brand-new automobile.

The end of the war was not a cause for universal rejoicing. Above, weeping Japanese kneel before a radio in the street of their bomb-shattered neighborhood on August 15 to hear their Emperor tell them that the war is over for Japan. At right, and in entirely different mood, a sailor in New York's Times Square on V-J Day helps celebrate the historic occasion in one of a sailor's favorite ways.

Japan had surrendered on August 14, but such things have to be done formally, and it required some time to assemble the full cast of necessary participants. Then, on September 2, on the deck of the battleship Missouri, at anchor in Tokyo Bay, the surrender document was signed by the two unhappy Japanese representatives, and by generals and admirals of the United States, Great Britain, China, Russia, the Netherlands, New Zealand, Canada, France, and Australia. General MacArthur made a conciliatory address, and the ceremony was history. Soon after, MacArthur took up his duties in Tokyo as occupation director.

U.S. ARMY

Ludwig
Haider
Lokführer.
Vergast 23. 4. 43

The Legacy

On August 7, 1945, the day after Hiroshima, Stalin convened five leading Soviet physicists and, putting them under the charge of his secret police boss, Lavrenti Beria, ordered them to catch up with American atomic achievements. On July 10, 1949—from three to six years before Washington believed it possible—Russia exploded its first A-bomb. The United States reacted by testing an infinitely deadlier hydrogen bomb on November 1, 1952. Then, on August 20, 1953, Georgi Malenkov, the first post-Stalin premier, announced a similar Soviet test. The nuclear race was on and has yet to be halted.

Like its predecessor, World War II bequeathed to its survivors more problems than it settled—except this time there was a quantum jump. Even before the hot war ended, a cold war had started among the victors, and against this background loomed the stark fact that man had at last invented weapons able to destroy mankind. This had an immediate impact upon the power relationships of a perplexed and deeply wounded earth.

As early as the spring of 1945, President Truman, coached by Byrnes and Stimson on the diplomatic import of the nuclear secret, had decided that we were "in a position to dictate our own terms at the end of the war." On April 23, the new President received Molotov and addressed him sharply on the rapid and grave deterioration in eastern Europe. The Soviet foreign minister complained: "I have never been talked to like that in my life." Truman answered: "Carry out your agreements and you won't get talked to like that."

So, in an uneasy atmosphere of mutual mistrust, and with Yalta pledges violated by one side and atomic strength possessed by the other, the victorious armies started their military occupation of Germany. This moment had originally been foreseen with savage relish. The British harbored few generous thoughts toward any Germans; hatred burned in Russia; and in America, there was a bitterness unusual in our national character. Henry Morgenthau, Jr., Roosevelt's Secretary of the Treasury, wanted to turn Germany into a pasture. Roosevelt told his Cabinet that as far as he was concerned, the Germans "could live happily . . . on soup from soup kitchens."

Truman, however, discharged Morgenthau and, relying increasingly on the advice of Byrnes and Stimson, began at least a logical policy toward the Germans. The Russians, meanwhile, allowed their troops to take vengeance in rape and pillage before they settled down to looting everything that could be moved. There was a race by both victors, eastern and western, to capture equipment. In the Harz Mountains, the Americans located a cache of V–2 documents and also rounded up dozens of intact rockets. These, with the aid of some of Hitler's principal experts, eventually were developed into a United States missile system.

After much diplomatic bargaining, the American and British armies withdrew from advanced positions to their prearranged occupation lines. The zones both of Berlin and of Germany itself were taken over by the victors along frontiers that still exist today. But the wreckage of

In memoriam: inside Mauthausen gas chamber, where thousands died.

the Third Reich—what was left after Russia took East Prussia, and Poland moved to the Oder-Neisse border—remained partitioned. No formal peace was made. Byrnes was later to write: "We should recognize that the Soviet Union, alone of all the major powers, was not eager to obtain an early peace settlement." Thus, although settlements were arranged with Italy and the Axis satellites, the greatest nation in Europe's heart remained split in two. And as time went on, both Germanies tended to forget Hitler with what the Swiss theologian, Karl Barth, had called "the remarkable German quality of living down in the grand manner all unpleasant memories."

Those Nazi chiefs who had not already, like Hitler, Goebbels, and Himmler, committed suicide, were tried in a four-power court at Nuremberg under a new and ex post facto body of law dealing with aggressive warfare and "crimes against humanity."

On October 18, 1945, the prosecutors issued indictments against twenty-one Nazis, who were given thirty days to prepare their defense. On November 20, the accused were assembled in a mud-colored building—one of the few Nuremberg structures to survive the bombs—and the trial got under way. It lasted ten months. The details of what the Nazis had accomplished in their death camps, the so-called medical experiments they had conducted, their slave labor program, the horrors they had inflicted wherever they went, were, day by day, exposed in thousands upon thousands of words of testimony, motion pictures, and grisly exhibits. A war-weary world soon became all too familiar with the overwhelming and, alas, virtually incomprehensible statistics of the Nazi nightmare, and with the expressionless faces of the inconsequential-looking men in the prisoners' dock.

That vindictiveness was not the purpose of the trial was shown by the difference in sentences handed down. Some, like Hans Fritsche, an editor and propagandist, Franz von Papen, former chancellor and diplomat, and the financial genius Hjalmar Horace Greeley Schacht, were acquitted. The most odious were sentenced to death, including the *S.A.* boss, Martin Bormann, *in absentia*, and Göring, who managed to poison himself an hour before he was to have been executed. Ribbentrop, Kaltenbrunner, Rosenberg, Frank, Streicher, Frick, Sauckel, Seyss-Inquart, Keitel, and Jodl were hanged.

Prominent Japanese war leaders were similarly tried. Two committed suicide: General Shigeru Honjo and Prince Fumimaro Konoye, who had been premier three times. Seven were sentenced to hanging, including General Hideki Tojo. Tojo sought, unsuccessfully, to kill himself. Before he finally mounted the scaffold he wrote a farewell poem: "It is good-by./Over the mountains I

go today/To the bosom of Buddha./So, happy am I." The Japanese said to each other: "Pity. Pity."

Both Germany and Japan were placed under military rule, although Truman's new tough policy kept Russian troops from participating in the Japanese occupation. Germany was truncated in the east and temporarily lost the Saar. Japan yielded all its mainland empire, the Kuriles, and southern Sakhalin Island, while Okinawa became to all intents an American strategic colony.

Immediately after the war ended, the Americans and British started a pell-mell demobilization. Despite the brief interlude in which Truman successfully reversed the policy of conciliating Stalin, the Yalta formula, as interpreted by Moscow and enforced by its military presence, became a pattern for the postwar map. Succeeding years demonstrated that there exists an inherent incompatibility between the Western demand at Yalta for "free and unfettered" elections in eastern Europe, and the concession that eastern European governments should be "friendly to the Soviet Union."

Fortunately, the United Nations, already born before the end of World War II, helped prevent the cold war from turning into holocaust. Stimulated largely by the State Department under Secretary Hull, ardently embraced by Roosevelt, endorsed by Churchill and accepted by Stalin, this organization grew out of a set of international conferences at a Washington, D.C., estate, Dumbarton Oaks, in 1944.

The United Nations was designed to include all peace-loving states but to leave with the great powers the authority to enforce peace. Although it failed to attain its dreams, it provided a valuable sounding board for world opinion and a center for secret crisis negotiations. And the mere existence of the U.N. in the stormy years since World War II has sometimes helped ease otherwise unendurable pressures.

These pressures have become increasingly complex. The strategic emphasis placed by the Allies on winning a hot-war victory in Europe before tackling Asia was continued into the cold war. Europe, with all its intellectual and industrial power, was from the start an area of primordial concern. Russia has always expanded more easily into Asia, where it could introduce a higher standard of living. But American policy forced it to concentrate on European problems, thus permitting in Asia the rise of Russia's most dangerous ultimate rival, China.

The United States wisely saw that it could not successfully survive the immediate postwar years as an isolated power, and that it required Europe's support. Therefore a series of diplomatically unprecedented commitments was made: the Truman Doctrine, to defend Greece and

Turkey; the Marshall Plan, to reinvigorate Europe's latent strength; the North Atlantic Treaty Organization, to conserve that strength. Within a remarkably short time, Europe began again to speak with a proud and authoritative voice. Indeed, within another decade, the Continent was prepared to contemplate a different future, founded upon neither nationalistic rivalries, dissolved empires, nor American sustenance.

Meanwhile, Moscow pursued three fundamental policy tenets. The first was to regain all eastern European territory once held by the Czars. Stalin took back Rumania's Bessarabian and north Bucovina provinces, eastern Poland, and the Baltic States. He also seized East Prussia, but left most of Finland intact, although it had been a Russian duchy. The second tenet was to insure friendship of eastern European lands by installing Communist regimes. The third tenet was to bind its ideological empire into an economic and military bloc.

Soviet attempts to expand were deliberately countered by an American doctrine of containment. Although within ten months of Germany's collapse the United States had reduced its forces in Europe from 3,500,000 to 400,000 men, a communist guerrilla uprising in Greece was put down with American aid. Likewise, Soviet efforts to bully Iran and Turkey failed. Not until some years later—under Khrushchev, not Stalin—did Moscow discover how to gain a position in the Middle East by the simple device of exporting surplus arms.

It was in the East, not the West, that the major postwar problems ultimately assumed shape. Japan fell rapidly under American domination, which Russia was never able to challenge. General MacArthur, in charge of the Allied occupation, put through a remarkable democratization program, including a constitution insuring political freedom and outlawing war. The Emperor, probably to his intense delight, was stripped of all but symbolic status and allowed to go back to his passion of marine biology. Hirohito issued an Imperial Rescript saying that his ties with his subjects were "not predicated on the false conception that the Emperor is divine and that the Japanese people are superior to other races and fated to rule the world."

Although Russia could not meet the United States's Oriental challenge in Japan, it could in China. Stalin did not really formulate a consistent Chinese policy until after his troops had defeated the Japanese in Manchuria. Originally, indeed, he seemed to prefer Chiang Kai-shek to Mao Tse-tung, and the Chinese Communists complained about Moscow's "erroneous tendencies." But, from the moment that Mao's armies finally smashed the Kuomintang, the Russians sought to make China into communism's Asiatic counterpoise to United States island bastions from Japan to the Philippines.

Washington tried without success to frustrate the communization of China. A mission by General Patrick Hurley failed to compose differences between Chiang and Mao. When General Marshall was dispatched on a similar enterprise, he announced a truce between the rival ideologists in early 1946; but this truce collapsed. By the end of 1949, the huge country was in Mao's hands.

Initially, Moscow seemed to be succeeding. But just at a time when Stalin's successors, aware of Russia's responsibilities as a nuclear power, were discarding both Stalinism and the belief in war's inevitability, China was accepting both theories. This contradiction produced an ideological schism more profound than any since Catholicism split between Rome and Constantinople.

What was originally, in the cold war's first phase, a protracted conflict between the United States and the U.S.S.R., now seems, in retrospect, a relatively simple problem. Both sides recognized a balance of terror and managed to hold the essentials of what had become a postwar status quo. This was above all true for Europe, where armistice, if not peace, came before it came to Asia—in both the hot and cold wars.

Now there are other players in the game. The paramount pair of powers are paramount only in terms of ultimate implications, not in the application of their strength. Both America and Russia had, a decade ago, become accustomed to certain illusions. They each believed in their ability to shape the world. Both are coming to realize that this is beyond their means. The quantum jump into perplexity achieved by World War II remains a blazing fact. All nations, giants and midgets, are caught up in destiny's whirlwind. New members knock at the door of the atomic club, and scientific genius races ahead far more rapidly than the political wisdom that must guide it.

Left: a watch from Hiroshima points forever to the moment when tens of thousands died and the coming of the nuclear age was revealed to mankind.

Overleaf: Symbol of today's divided world, the Wall in Berlin. The wall was erected to prevent East Germans from escaping to the western zone.
JUDITH HARKISON

625

LISL STEINER, PHOTO RESEARCHERS

"Today we are faced with the
pre-eminent fact that,
if civilization is to survive,
we must cultivate the
science of human relationships—
the ability of all peoples,
of all kinds, to live together
and work together
in the same world, at peace...."

—From an undelivered speech
by Franklin D. Roosevelt,
written shortly before his death

United Nations General Assembly

Acknowledgments

The Editors are grateful to the following individuals and institutions for their assistance and counsel in the preparation of this book, and for their cooperation in making available documentary and pictorial material in their collections:

Bundesarchiv, Coblenz: Prof. Dr. W. Gley
CBS News: Barbara Sapinsley
Documentation Française, Paris
Embassy of the Polish People's Republic, Washington, D.C.: Dr. Marian Spalinski
Family of Jesse D. Franks, Jr.
Pierce G. Fredericks, New York
Commander Fred Freeman, USNR, Washington, D.C.
Eric L. P. Greweldinger, Bad Homburg
Lieutenant Colonel Gene Gurney, USAF, Prince Frederick, Md.
Imperial War Museum, London: J. F. Golding, W. P. Mayes, Mrs. M. Davis, M. Brennan
Library of Congress: Prints and Photographs Division, Virginia Daiker, Milton Kaplan; Publications Reading Room, William Kilroy
Museum of the History of Leningrad: Mrs. Belova
National Archives: Audio Visual Branch, Joe Thomas, Jean Coleman, Paul White; Office of Military Archives, Robert Wolfe, Richard Bauer; World War II Reference Branch, Wilbur J. Nigh
National Maritime Museum, Greenwich, England: Edward H. H. Archibald
Netherlands State Institute for War Documentation: Dr. A. H. Paape
Osterreichische Nationalbibliothek, Vienna: Bild-Archiv und Porträt-sammlung, Hofrat Dr. Hans Pauer
George Perry, London
Franklin D. Roosevelt Library, Hyde Park, N.Y.: Elizabeth Drewry, Edgar B. Nixon, Raymond Corry
Sotamuseo, Helsinki: Paavo Talvio
U.S. Air Force: ACIC Services, Virginia Fincik; Art and Museum Branch, Major Lloyd M. Peterson
U.S. Army: Office of the Chief of Military History, George Hobart, Marian McNaughton, Ruth Phillips, Norma Sherris; Signal Corps Photo Library, Donna Traxler, Annie L. Sely
U.S. Coast Guard: Elizabeth A. Segedi
U.S. Department of Defense, Magazine and Book Branch, Directorate for Information Services: Colonel C. V. Glines, USAF (Chief); Lieutenant Colonel C. W. Burtyk, USA (Deputy Chief); Helen Burnard; Lieutenant Commander Dan Dagle, USN; Yeoman Second Class William Henry, USN; Major Barbara J. Smith, WAC
U.S. Marine Corps: Colonel D. G. Derryberry
U.S. Naval Institute: Joan B. Machinchick
U.S. Naval Photographic Center, Motion Picture Library: Greg Kennedy
U.S. Navy, Combat Art Section: Charles Lawrence
YIVO (Institute for Jewish Research), New York
Special research and photography: Victor Amato, Washington; Susanne Puddefoot, Mary Jenkins, London; Victor Louis, Moscow; Bianca Spantigatti, Rome; Art Miyazawa, Tokyo

The Editors also make grateful acknowledgment for permission to quote from the following works:

Barbarossa by Alan Clark. Copyright © 1965 by Alan Clark. The quotation by a Nazi lieutenant on pages 252–53 reprinted by permission of William Morrow and Company, Inc.

Berlin: Story of a Battle by Andrew Tully. Copyright © 1963 by Andrew Tully. The excerpt from a German officer's diary on pages 556–57 reprinted by permission of Simon and Schuster, Inc.

Berlin Diary by William L. Shirer. Copyright 1940, 1941 by William L. Shirer. The excerpt on pages 36–37 reprinted by permission of Alfred A. Knopf, Inc.

Bomber Offensive by Sir Arthur Harris. Copyright 1947 by Wm. Collins Sons & Co. Ltd. The excerpt on page 230 reprinted by permission of David Higham Associates, Ltd.

Brave Men by Ernie Pyle. Copyright 1943, 1944 by Scripps-Howard Newspaper Alliance; copyright 1944 by Holt, Rinehart and Winston, Inc. The excerpts on pages 386–87, 400–401, and 503 reprinted by permission of Holt, Rinehart and Winston, Inc.

Bridge to the Sun by Gwen Terasaki. Copyright 1957 by University of North Carolina Press. The excerpt on page 617 reprinted by permission of University of North Carolina Press.

Calculated Risk by General Mark Clark. Copyright 1950 by Mark Clark. The quotation on page 373 reprinted by permission of Harper & Row, Publishers, Inc.

Closing the Ring by Winston S. Churchill. Copyright 1951 by Houghton Mifflin Company. The quotations on pages 373 and 388 reprinted by permission of Houghton Mifflin Company

Crusade in Europe by Dwight D. Eisenhower. Copyright 1948 by Doubleday and Company, Inc. The quotations on pages 220, 482, and 556 reprinted by permission of Doubleday and Company, Inc.

Defeat in the West by Milton Shulman. Copyright 1948 by E. P. Dutton & Company. The quotation by Von Rundstedt on page 60 reprinted by permission of Secker & Warburg Ltd.

The Divine Wind by Captain Rikihei Inoguchi and Commander Tadashi Nakajima. The excerpts by Commander Tadashi Nakajima on page 606 and Vice-Admiral C. R. Brown on page 607 reprinted by permission of United States Naval Institute

Dunkirk by A. D. Divine. Copyright 1948 by A. D. Divine. The excerpt on pages 86–87 reprinted by permission of A. Watkins, Inc.

The Dyess Story by Lt. Col. William E. Dyess. Copyright 1944 by Marajen Stevick Dyess. The excerpt on pages 172–73 reprinted by permission of G. P. Putnam's Sons.

The Fatal Decisions edited by Seymour Freiden and William Richardson. Copyright © 1956 by William Sloane Associates, Inc. The excerpt by General Günther Blumentritt on page 272 reprinted by permission of William Morrow and Company, Inc.

The First and the Last by Adolf Galland, translated by Mervyn Savill. Copyright 1954 by Henry Holt and Company, Inc. The excerpt on page 419 reprinted by permission of Holt, Rinehart and Winston, Inc.

Flight to Arras by Antoine de Saint-Exupéry, translated by Lewis Galantiere. Copyright 1942 by Harcourt, Brace & World, Inc. The excerpt on pages 92–93 reprinted by permission of Harcourt, Brace & World, Inc.

Follow My Leader by Louis Hagen. The excerpt on page 577 by Claus Fuhrmann reproduced by permission of Paul Hamlyn, Publishers

The Gathering Storm by Winston S. Churchill. Copyright 1948 by Houghton Mifflin Company. The quotations on page 59 reprinted by permission of Houghton Mifflin Company

The Goebbels Diaries edited by Louis P. Lochner. Copyright 1948 by The Fireside Press, Inc. The excerpt on pages 322–23 reprinted by permission of Doubleday & Company, Inc.

The Grand Alliance by Winston S. Churchill. Copyright· 1950 by Houghton Mifflin Company. The quotations on pages 100, 218, and 306 reprinted by permission of Houghton Mifflin

Hausfrau at War by Else Wendel. Copyright 1957 by Odhams Books Ltd. The excerpts on pages 576–77 reprinted by permission of Winant, Towers Ltd

The Hinge of Fate by Winston S. Churchill. Copyright 1950 by Houghton Mifflin Company. The quotations on pages 307, 330, and 331 reprinted by permission of Houghton Mifflin

"I Saw Regensburg Destroyed" by Lt. Col. Beirne Lay, Jr. Copyright 1943 by The Curtis Publishing Company. The excerpt on pages 430–31 reprinted by permission of Harold Ober Associates, Inc., New York

Images of War by Robert Capa. Copyright © 1964 by Cornell Capa. The excerpts on pages 502–3 reprinted by permission of Grossman Publishers, Inc.

Into the Valley by John Hersey. Copyright 1942, 1943 by John Hersey. The excerpt on pages 348–49 reprinted by permission of Alfred A. Knopf, Inc.

Invasion 1944 by Hans Speidel. Copyright 1950 by Henry Regnery Company. The excerpt on page 503 reprinted by permission of Henry Regnery Company

Japan and Her Destiny by Mamoru Shigemitsu, translated by Oswald White, edited by Maj. Gen. F. S. G. Piggott. Copyright 1958 by E. P. Dutton & Co., Inc. The quotation on page 451 reprinted by permission of E. P. Dutton & Co., Inc.

The Labyrinth: Memoirs of Walter Schellenberg translated by Louis Hagen. Copyright 1956 by Harper & Brothers. The quotation on page 58 reprinted by permission of Harper & Row, Publishers

Last Letters from Stalingrad edited and translated by Franz Schneider and Charles Gullans. Copyright © 1961 by The Hudson Review, Inc. The excerpts on pages 298–99 reprinted by permission of William Morrow and Company, Inc.

The Long and the Short and the Tall by Alvin M. Josephy, Jr. Copyright 1946 by Alfred A. Knopf, Inc. The excerpt on pages 540–41 reprinted by permission of Alfred A. Knopf, Inc.

The Memoirs of General Lord Ismay. Copyright © 1960 by The Viking Press, Inc. The quotations on pages 306 and 307 reprinted by permission of The Viking Press, Inc.

Men at War edited by Ernest Hemingway. Copyright 1942 by Crown Publishers, Inc. The quotations on pages 17 and 146 reprinted by permission of Crown Publishers, Inc.

Moscow Dateline by Henry C. Cassidy. Copyright © 1943 by Henry C. Cassidy. The excerpt on page 272 reprinted by permission of Henry C. Cassidy

Moscow Tram Stop by Heinrich Haape. Copyright 1957 by Wm. Collins Sons & Co. Ltd. The excerpt on pages 272–73 reprinted by permission of Wm. Collins Sons & Co. Ltd.

Our Jungle Road to Tokyo by Robert L. Eichelberger. Copyright 1949, 1950 by Robert L. Eichelberger. The excerpt on pages 360–61 reprinted by permission of The Viking Press, Inc.

Pacific War Diary by James J. Fahey. Copyright © 1963 by James J. Fahey. The excerpt on page 607 reprinted by permission of Houghton Mifflin Company

Panzer Battles by Maj. Gen. F. W. von Mellenthin. Copyright 1956 by the University of Oklahoma Press. The excerpt on page 231 reprinted by permission of the University of Oklahoma Press.

Panzer Leader by Heinz Guderian, translated by Constantine Fitzgibbon. Published by E. P. Dutton & Co. The excerpt on pages 68–69 reprinted by permission of E. P. Dutton & Co.

The Rommel Papers edited by B. H. Liddell Hart. Copyright 1953 by Harcourt, Brace and Company. The quotations on pages 221, 230, 231, and 397 reprinted by permission of Harcourt, Brace & World, Inc.

Roosevelt and Hopkins by Robert E. Sherwood. Copyright 1948 by Robert E. Sherwood. The excerpts on pages 132 and 138–39 reprinted by permission of Harper & Row, Publishers

Royal Air Force, 1939–1945 (Vol. II) by Denis Richards and Hilary St. George Saunders. The quotation by Guy Penrose Gibson on page 418 reprinted by permission of H. M. Stationery Office, London

Russia at War by Alexander Werth. Copyright © 1964 by Alexander Werth. The excerpts on pages 273 and 576 reprinted by permission of E. P. Dutton & Co., Inc.

See Here, Private Hargrove by Marion Hargrove. Copyright 1943 by Marion Hargrove. The excerpt on pages 397–98 reprinted by permission of Marion Hargrove

Soldier: The Memoirs of Matthew B. Ridgway, As Told to Harold H. Martin. Copyright © 1956 by Matthew B. Ridgway and Harold H. Martin; copyright © 1956 by the Curtis Publishing Company. The excerpt on page 502 reprinted by permission of Harper & Row

A Soldier's Story by Omar N. Bradley. Copyright 1951 by Henry Holt and Company. The quotations on pages 484 and 526 reprinted by permission of Holt, Rinehart and Winston

Their Finest Hour by Winston S. Churchill. Copyright 1949 by Houghton Mifflin Company. The quotation on page 182 reprinted by permission of Houghton Mifflin Company

This Is London by Edward R. Murrow. The excerpt on pages 114–15 to be included in a comprehensive volume of broadcasts and speeches by Edward R. Murrow, edited by Edward Bliss, Jr., published in 1967 by Alfred A. Knopf, Inc.

Tobruk by Anthony Heckstall-Smith. Copyright © 1959 by Anthony Heckstall-Smith. The leaflet on page 230 and the letters on pages 230–31 reprinted by permission of W. W. Norton & Company, Inc.

Tobruk 1941 by Chester Wilmot. The excerpts by Corporal McLeish, Lt. Schorm, and an Australian gunner on pages 230–31 reprinted by permission of Angus & Robertson, Ltd.

Token of a Covenant by Hans Graf von Lehndorff. Copyright © 1964 by Henry Regnery Company. The excerpt on pages 576–77 reprinted by permission of Henry Regnery Company

A Torch to the Enemy by Martin Caidin. Copyright © 1960 by Martin Caidin. The account by a factory worker on page 589 reprinted by permission of Ballantine Books

Up Front by Bill Mauldin. Copyright 1945 by Bill Mauldin and Henry Holt and Company, Inc. The cartoons on pages 396 and 433 reproduced by permission of Bill Mauldin. The quotation on page 400 reprinted by permission of Holt, Rinehart and Winston, Inc.

The War by Louis L. Snyder. Copyright © 1960 by Louis L. Snyder

Warrior Without Weapons by Marcel Junod. Copyright 1951 by The Macmillan Co. The excerpt by a Japanese journalist on pages 616–17 reprinted by permission of Jonathan Cape, Ltd.

The Works of Anne Frank. Copyright © 1959 by Otto H. Frank. The excerpt on pages 460–61 reprinted by permission of Doubleday & Company, Inc.

Year of Decisions by Harry S. Truman (Vol. 1 of *Memoirs*). Copyright © 1955 by Time, Inc. The excerpt on page 617 reprinted by permission of Harry S. Truman.

The Year of Stalingrad by Alexander Werth. Copyright 1946 by Alexander Werth. The excerpt on pages 202–3 reprinted by permission of Alfred A. Knopf, Inc., New York

The lines from "The Sinking of the Reuben James" by Woody Guthrie are reprinted by permission of the copyright owners, MCA Music. © Copyright MCMXLI by MCA Music, a division of MCA Inc., New York; Leeds Music Company, New York, New York. Used by permission. All rights reserved.

The lines from "(We're Gonna Hang Out) the Washing on the Siegfried Line" are reprinted by permission of the copyright owners, The Peter Maurice Music Co., Ltd., London

Index

"A" Rations, 398
Aachen, 485
Abbeville, 59
ABC–1, 146
Abruzzi, 372
Abwehr, 308, 371
Achilles, 182, 188
Acropolis, 123
Adak, 362–63, 408–9
Adriatic Sea, 369, 371
Advisory Committee on Uranium, 309
Aegean Islands, 481
Aegean Sea, 420
Africa, 17, 20, 301, 311, 380, 398, 404. *See also* North Africa; Army, British; Army, German
Afrika Korps. *See* Army, German
Ainsworth, Rear Adm. W. L., 530
Air Force, Australian, 350
Air Force, British (R.A.F.): 59, 88, 98, 100, 131, 142, 147, 182, 331, 371, 419, 436–37, 502, 507; against Afrika Korps, 219, 241; at Arnhem air-borne attack, 485, 520; in Battle of Britain, 97, 98–99, 105, 106, 109, 110–11, 114–15, 442–43; at Dunkirk, 84; bombing of Germany, 228, 417, 418, 419, 420, 423, 424, 438, 444; defense of Malta, 101, 233
Air Force, French: defeat of, 88, 90–91
Air Force, German (*Luftwaffe*): 21, 40, 42, 49, 53, 59, 98, 181, 251, 417, 434, 441, 444, 450; destroys Belgrade, 100; in Battle of Britain, 98–99, 105, 109, 112–13, 114–15, 117, 191, 424, 442–43, 452; in Crete, 124; destruction by Allies, 419, 420, 423, 436–37, 438, 559; in Greece, 123; in Italy, 372, 373, 376, 388; in Low Countries and France, 59, 60, 76, 84; bombs Malta, 233; in Mediterranean, 183; during Normandy invasion, 376–77, 482, 499; in North Africa, 218; in Poland, 58, 64; in Russia, 21, 250, 291, 418, 420
Air Force, Italian, 38–39, 100, 218
Air Force, Japanese: 164, 206, 593; kamikaze tactics, 532, 548, 550, 588, 600–601, 603–5, 608. *See also* Army, Japanese and Navy, Japanese
Air Force, Russian, 21, 58, 250, 420
Air Forces, Allied, 372, 376, 417, 418–19, 420, 482
Air Forces, U.S., in Europe: 433, 434, 444; daylight bombing, 418, 423, 427; bombing of Germany, 417, 418, 419, 420, 421, 423, 427, 428, 430, 433, 434, 438, 446–47; in Italy, 371, 391; bombing of Ploesti, 419–20

Air Forces, U.S., in Pacific: 421, 446–47, 536, 587; in Aleutians, 363; in China-Burma-India Theater, 331, 337, 339; Doolittle raid on Tokyo, 149, 178; bombing of Japan, 331, 338, 421, 451, 530, 531, 587–90, 593; at Midway, 213–14; in southwest Pacific, 328–29, 344, 350–51, 355, 356–57; Pearl Harbor losses, 147
Air Transport Command, U.S., 337
Aircraft, British: Beaufighter, 419; Catalina, 194–95; Defiant, 442; Gladiator, 101; Halifax, 444; Hurricane, 97, 98, 420, 442; Lancaster, 419, 444; Liberator, 235; Mosquito, 444, 445; Spitfire, 98, 442; Stirling, 419
Aircraft, German: 18, 417, 420, 450; DO-172, 443; FW-190, 444; HE-111, 443; JU-87 (Stuka), 18, 58, 59, 64, 65, 443; JU-88, 443; ME-109, 107, 430, 442, 443; ME-110, 442, 443; ME-262 (jet), 420, 444; robot, 309; late experimental types, 507. *See also* V-1 and V-2
Aircraft, Italian: Fiat, 443
Aircraft, Japanese: production, 421; "Betty," 447; "Kate," 447; "Tony," 447; "Zeke" or Zero, 154, 421, 447
Aircraft, Russian: development of, 253; MIG, 420; Stormovik, 420; YAK, 420, 444, 445
Aircraft, U.S.: 134, 149, 421; A-20 Havoc, 420, 434; B-17 Flying Fortress, 43, 147, 148, 163, 329, 418, 419, 427, 428, 434, 440–41, 444, 478; B-24 Liberator, 419–20, 427, 433, 436, 440, 444; B-25 Mitchell, 149, 178, 329, 420, 446, 447; B-29 Superfortress, 340–41, 421, 446–47, 451, 466, 478, 530, 531, 536, 587–88, 589–90, 593; C-46 (transport), 338; F4U Corsair, 446, 447; F6F Hellcat, 446, 447, 529; PBY Catalina, 132; P-38 Lightning, 213, 444, 445; P-39 Airacobra, 420; P-40 Warhawk, 420, 446, 447; P-47 Thunderbolt, 419, 444, 445; P-51 Mustang, 419, 421, 423, 444, 445, 588; TBF Avenger, 446, 447; XB-15, 43
Aisne River, 60, 88
Ajax, 182, 188
Akagi, 213
Alabama, 26
Alamogordo, 590, 610
Alaska, 149, 185, 330
Alban Hills, 388
Albania: 99, 100, 123, 183; Italian invasion of, 21, 217, 218; resistance movements in, 308, 369, 372, 481
Aleutian Islands: 146, 150, 399, 408–9; Japanese advance in, 185, 213, 327; U.S. recapture of, 330, 362–63. *See also* Attu and Kiska

Alexander, Field Marshal Sir Harold, 218, 234, 235, 372
Alexandria, 182, 183, 218, 222, 233, 369
Algeria, 182, 220, 222
Algiers, 220, 243, 369
All Quiet on the Western Front, 43
Allies, 130, 134, 146, 242–43, 305, 306, 620. *See also* individual countries
Ambrosio, Gen. Vittorio, 370
America First Committee, 130, 140. *See also* Isolationism, U.S.
American Federation of Labor (AF of L), 453
American Volunteer Group (AVG), 421. *See also* Flying Tigers
Amphibious warfare: development of, 184, 327, 329, 330, 342–43, 358, 363, 364–65, 376; operations, 147, 148, 242, 370, 372–73, 482 ff., 514–15, 608. *See also* specific campaigns
Amsterdam, 79
Amtracks (LVT's), 365, 596
Andalsnes, 59
Andaman Islands, 148
Anders, Gen., 373
Ankara, 309
Anschluss, 49, 50
Anti-Semitism: German, 19, 32; U.S., 130, 140. *See also* Jews
Antwerp: 82, 309, 485; German occupation and Allied capture of, 485, 520
Anzio: Allied landings at, 369, 373, 375, 388, 395; map of, 374
Apennines, 481
Apsheron Peninsula, 308
Aramco, 308
Arc de Triomphe, 94, 95
Archangel, 184
Ardennes campaigns, 59, 82, 485–86, 525, 555
Argentia Bay, 142. *See also* Roosevelt and Churchill
Argentina: 182; *Graf Spee* crew interned at, 188
Arizona, 147, 154, 156–57
Armament, Russian, 251
Army, Allied: coordination problems, 246; in Germany, 555; in Sicily and Italy, 370, 373, 376, 380
Army, Anglo-French: in blitzkrieg, 60, 82, 95
Army, Australian, 327, 329, 358–59, 360–61
Army, Belgian, 60, 82
Army, British: in Burma, 337; in Crete, 124, 183; in Desert War, 183, 217–19, 221, 222, 224, 227, 228, 230, 233, 235, 236, 241, 244; at Dunkirk, 60, 97, 103; in invasion of France and advance to Rhine, 486, 525, 555, 566; in Germany, 555, 559, 623; in Greece, 100, 123; in Italy, 371, 372, 373, 380, 382, 384, 388, 391, 392, 395, 485, 555; in North Africa invasion, 220, 221, 222, 246; in Norway, 59; in Sic-

ily, 369, 370, 376; at Singapore, 160–61; compared to U.S., 399, 401
Army, Bulgarian, 99, 100
Army, Canadian: Dieppe raid, 481; on Kiska, 330, 363
Army, Chinese, 46, 330, 331, 337, 589
Army, Dutch, 76
Army, Ethiopian, 20
Army, Finnish, 58, 72–73, 254
Army, French: in Battle of France (1940), 59, 60, 61, 63, 66, 70, 84, 88–89, 90, 92–93, 95; return to France, 484, 486, 518; in Italy, 371; in North Africa, 220, 246, 369; compared to U.S., 399
Army, German: Ardennes offensive, 485, 525, 526, 559; blitzkrieg in West, 58, 59, 60, 63, 66, 76, 82, 84, 88, 90–91, 94, 95; defeated in France, 481, 482, 484, 486, 504, 512, 518, 520, 522–23, 524; in Germany, and defeat of, 555–57, 559; Hitler takes command, 321; in Italy, 369, 371, 372, 373, 375, 382, 388, 392, 555, 556, 559; besieges Leningrad, 252, 267, 280; 1939–40 strength, 28–29; in North Africa (Afrika Korps), 183, 218, 219–20, 221, 222, 227, 228, 230–31, 233, 236, 242, 244, 246; invades Norway and Denmark, 59; attacks Poland, 57, 58, 63, 64; prewar activities, 18, 19, 27, 28–29, 32, 49, 50, 53, 57; reduction proposed by Hitler, 265; invades Russia, 101, 121, 126, 249, 250, 254, 256, 258–59, 265, 269, 274; losses in Russia, 251, 286, 301; 1942 Russian offensive, 252, 286, 289; 1943 Russian offensive, 253, 301, 303, 375; treatment of Russians, 260, 262–63, 450; in Russian winter, 251–52, 270, 272–73, 276; in Sicily, 370, 371, 376, 380; S.S. units in, 450, 454, 508, 568; at Stalingrad, 252, 253, 254, 282, 289, 291, 293, 294, 296, 298–99, 301–2, 319; in Yugoslavia, 100, 485
Army, Greek, 99–100, 183, 217
Army, Hungarian, 99, 100, 254, 286
Army, Italian: in Albania, 183; invades Ethiopia, 20; attacks Greece, 100, 123; in North Africa, 183, 217–18, 219–20, 221, 222, 224, 228, 241; units in Russia, 286; in Sicily, 370; after surrender of Italy, 372
Army, Japanese: early aggressions, 20, 131; on Attu and Kiska, 330, 363; aviation, 421; in China-Burma-India Theater, 331, 529, 530, 589, 591; on Guadalcanal, 328, 344; on Iwo Jima, 588, 593–97; in Malayan campaign, 147; on Marianas, 530, 536, 540–41; on New Guinea, 184, 328–29, 358–59, 360–61; on Okinawa, 588–89,

608; invades Philippines, 148, 162–63, 164, 169; in Philippines (1944–45), 531, 533, 548, 587; surrender to U.S.S.R., 591
Army, New Zealand, 327
Army, Norwegian, 74
Army, Philippine, 147
Army, Polish, 58, 64, 373, 392
Army, Russian: 250–51, 253, 267, 276, 277–78, 294, 573; occupies eastern European territories, 58, 61; against Japanese, 591; at Leningrad, 280; in 1941–42 fighting, 249, 250, 251–52, 265, 267, 269, 274, 286, 289; in 1943 offensive, 253, 254, 301, 303; in 1944–45 offensives into Germany, 485, 553, 554, 555, 556, 559, 573, 574, 576–77, 623; pre-war development, 18, 21, 27, 58; Russo-Finnish War, 58, 59, 72–73; at Stalingrad, 252, 253, 291, 293, 296, 319
Army, Rumanian, 254, 286, 296
Army, U.S.: 43, 130, 149, 384, 397–400, 404, 407, 408–9, 412–13, 453, 472, 478, 584; in Aleutions, 330, 363; in Burma, 147–48; invades southern France, 484, 486, 514–15, 555; in Germany, 554–55, 559, 563, 564–65, 567, 573, 623, 625; in Italy, 369, 371, 372, 373, 382, 384, 386–87, 388, 391, 395, 485, 555; in Japan, 591; invades Normandy, 482, 483, 484, 486, 499, 511, 512; in North Africa, 220, 221, 222, 241, 243, 246; invades Okinawa, 588–89, 608; central Pacific campaign, 329, 333, 529, 530, 536, 538–39; in southwest Pacific, 327, 329, 344, 358; at Pearl Harbor, 154; defends Philippines, 147; liberation of Philippines, 532, 548, 587; advances to Rhine, 485, 518, 525; in Sicily, 369, 370, 376, 378–79, 380
Army, Yugoslav, 100, 121
Arnhem, 485, 520
Arnim, Gen. Jürgen von, 221
Arnold, Gen. Henry H., 149, 312, 399, 421
Assam, 331
Athenia, 188
Athens, 100, 123
Atlantic, Battle of: 142, 183–84, 186, 191, 193, 317; map, 186–87
Atlantic Charter, 133, 142
Atlantic Wall, 482, 483, 494
Atomic age, 556, 624–25
Atomic bomb: development of, 130, 309, 324, 453, 553, 557, 589, 590, 610–11; use of, 421, 590, 612, 614–15, 616
Attlee, Clement: 610; quoted, 97
Attu, 330, 363
Auchinleck, Gen. Sir Claude, 218, 228, 233, 234, 235
Augusta, 132
Auschwitz, 555–56, 568
Australia: Allied defense of, 147, 148, 167, 184–85, 220, 327, 328, 353

Austria: 17, 19, 22, 79, 372, 555, 557; Anschluss, 19, 21, 49, 50, 63; Russian Army in, 554
Avranches, 484
Axis, 130, 146, 305, 306, 321. See also individual countries
Axis Sally (Mildred Gillars), 308

Bacall, Lauren, 474
Bad Orb, 581
Badoglio, Marshal Pietro, 370, 371–72, 380
Baker, Sgt. George, 400
Baltic Sea, 59, 250
Baltic States, 21, 57, 58, 99, 101, 121, 217, 305, 306, 307, 369, 372, 419, 485, 554
Bangkok, 421
Barbarossa, Operation. See Operations, German
Bari, 371
Bastogne, 485, 524–25, 526. See also Bulge, Battle of the
Bataan, 328, 525, 587; defense of and surrender, 147–49, 166–67; Death March, 149, 168–69, 170–71; map of, 166
Battle of the Beaches, the, 453
Battle of Midway, the, 476
Bazna, Elyesa (Cicero), 309
B.B.C. See Radio: British
Beaverbrook, Lord William, 132
Beirut, 369
Belgium: 88, 99, 129, 309; 1940 German invasion of, 59, 60, 76–77, 82–83; 1944–45 Allied advance through, 485, 507, 520–21, 524–27; map of, 487
Belgorod, 301
Belgrade, 100, 121, 249
Beneš, Eduard, 21
Bengal, Bay of, 148, 331
Benghazi, 224, 369, 419
Berezina River, 250
Bergen, 182
Bergen-Belsen, 458–59, 460, 461, 555, 566–67, 568–69
Berlin, Germany: 21, 101, 249, 293, 454, 485, 508, 555, 571, 610; bombing of, 110, 417–18, 424, 444; Soviet advance on, 554–57, 559, 574–77; surrender of, 557, 583; occupation of, 560, 623–24
Bessarabia: U.S.S.R. gains control of, 21, 57, 61, 99, 625
Betio, 329, 364
Biak, 535
Bialystok, 58
Biddle, Francis, 571
Bielaja Smert ("White Death"), 72
Big Four, 306, 317–18
Big Three, 306–7, 319, 554, 589
"Big Week," 419, 434, 438
Bismarck, 182–83, 195, 206
Bismarck Sea, Battle of the, 328–29, 350–51
Bizerte: 369, 401; falls to Allies, 221, 244, 246
Black markets: in Japan, 451; in U.S., 453
Black Sea, 61, 101, 249, 560

Black Shirts, 25, 370
Blitz, 99, 112, 452. See also London
Blitzkrieg: 57 ff.; German tactics, 63, 64, 76, 82, 95, 121, 124, 218, 250, 254, 265, 286, 294, 417
Bloody Nose Ridge, 531
Blumentritt, Gen. Günther (eye-witness), 272
Bock, Field Marshal Fedor von: in invasion of France, 58, 59; in invasion of U.S.S.R., 249–51, 254, 265
Boeing Aircraft Company, 478
Bologna, 555
Bon, Cape, 221
Bonhoeffer, Pastor Dietrich, 449
Borah, Sen. William E., 129
Bordeaux, 61, 95
Borneo, 148
Bormann, Martin, 508, 556, 557
Bose, Subhas Chandra, 148, 451
Bougainville, 329, 354–55
Bradley, Gen. Omar: 399, 533; in North Africa, 221; in Allied invasion of Europe, 372, 512, 518, 520; compared with Patton, 512; quoted, 484, 485, 526
Brandenburg, 554
Brauchitsch, Field Marshal Walther von, 66, 249–50
Braun, Eva, 454, 556, 574
Braun, Gretl, 454
Braun, Wernher von, 324
Bremen, 191, 428
Brenner Pass, 372
Brest-Litovsk, 250
Brindisi, 371
Brisbane, 353
Britain, Battle of: 98–99, 105–21, 130, 137, 418, 424, 444, 452; planes in, pictured, 442–43. See also Air Force, British, and Air Force, German
Brittany, 486, 512
Brooke, Sir Alan: 530; quoted, 397
Brooklyn Navy Yard, 174–75
Brown House (Munich), 30
Brown Shirts, 34–35
Browning, Sir Frederick, 591
Browning .50-caliber machine guns, 418
Broz, Josip. See Tito
Bryansk, 269
Bucharest, 100
Buchenwald, 458, 555–56, 566
Buckner, Lt. Gen. Simon B., Jr., 588, 608
Bucovina, 61, 625
Budënny, Marshal Semën, 250–52, 265, 267, 270
Budapest, 554
Bulgaria, 17, 99–101, 121, 420, 553
Bulge, Battle of the: 485, 524–27, 553, 559; map of, 524. See also Ardennes campaign; Army, British; Army, German; and Army, U.S.
Bulldozers, 366
Buna, 328, 358, 360–61
Bund. See German-American Bund

Bundy, Harvey H., 324
Bunker Hill, 603, 604–5
Burma, 145–48, 327, 331, 336–37, 421, 447, 451, 529, 530, 531. See also China-Burma-India Theater
Burma Road, 331, 337
Bush, Dr. Vannevar, 130, 309, 324
Bushido, 146
Bushy Park, 418
Butcher, Capt. Henry C.: quoted, 555
Byrnes, James F.: 590, 623; quoted, 624

"C" Rations, 398
Cadogan, Sir Alexander, 560
Caen, 484
Cairo, 100, 217–18, 221, 235
Cairo Conference. See Conferences: Cairo
Calabria, 371
Calcutta, 530
California, 176–77
California, 147
California Arabian Standard Oil Company, 308
Camp O'Donnell, 169
Camp Shelby, 311
Canada, 130
Canaris, Adm. Wilhelm, 308
Canham, Col. Charles, 503
Cannes, 484
Canton, 530
Capa, Robert, 400, 502–3 (eye-witness)
Caribbean Sea, 131, 134, 184
Carol, King of Rumania, 99
Caroline Islands, 329–30
Casablanca, 220–21
Casablanca, 476
Casablanca Conference. See Conferences: Casablanca
Case White. See Operations, German
Case Yellow. See Operations, German
Cassidy, Henry C. (eyewitness), 272
Cassino, 149, 373–75, 391–92
Castellano, Gen. Giuseppe, 371
Casualties: Allied, 148, 358, 370, 388, 392, 504; Axis, 221, 370; British and Empire, 60, 98–99, 100, 124, 186, 188, 233, 331, 337, 358, 420, 481, 485, 507, 520; Chinese, 478; Dutch, 76; French, 182; German, 58, 60, 100, 124, 186, 220, 222, 251, 269, 276, 286, 296, 301, 419, 420, 423, 424, 526, 560, 584; Japanese, 328, 329, 331, 344, 358, 363, 365, 421, 530, 531, 533, 587, 588, 589, 590, 591, 608, 612; Polish, 58, 554; Russian, 250, 252, 262–63, 265, 282, 478; U.S., 149, 154, 169, 183, 188, 329, 331, 344, 358, 365, 384, 400, 419–20, 423, 433, 478, 525, 530, 531, 533, 603, 604–5, 608; Yugoslav, 121
Catanian Plain, 370, 376

Caucasus Mountains, 251–52, 254, 286
Cavite Naval Base, 164
Central Aircraft Manufacturing Company (CAMCO), 42
Central Plain, 587
Ceylon, 148, 329
Chad Territory, 221
Chamberlain, Neville, 21, 50–52, 55, 70, 97–98
Champs-Élysées, 60
Chang Ching-hui, Premier, 451
"Chanson d'Automne," 482
Chelyabinsk, 251
Chennault, Maj. Gen. Claire, 331, 338, 340–41, 420–21, 530
Cherbourg, 484, 486
Chiang Kai-shek, 46, 147, 252, 305–6, 330–31, 337, 420–21, 530, 553, 556, 589, 625; at Cairo Conference, 307, 318–19; quoted, 331
Chiang Kai-shek, Madame, 307, 318
Chicago, 309
Chichagof Harbor, 330
China: 18, 46, 149, 153, 178, 306, 331, 421, 447, 451, 591; Japanese invasion of, 20, 44–47, 131, 145, 147–48, 153, 327, 329, 531; in Allied strategy, 133, 318, 330–31, 338–41, 420–21, 529, 530; postwar, 560, 589, 610, 624–25
China-Burma-India Theater (C.B.I.), 330–31, 336–41, 421
Cho, Lt. Gen., 589
Choiseul, 329
Choltitz, Gen. Dietrich von, 484–85, 518
Christian X, King of Denmark, 59
Chuikov, Marshal Vasili, 252–53, 293
Churchill, Winston: 126, 148, 149, 238–39, 305, 311, 313, 318, 370, 466; described and characterized, 97–98, 118, 306, 307, 308, 452, 583, 590, 624; becomes Prime Minister, 59, 95, 98; conferences, 132–34, 142, 218, 306–7, 319, 553–54, 560–61, 610–11; drafts Atlantic Charter, 133; foreign policy, 61, 98, 100, 132, 134, 148, 305–8; military decisions, 99, 101, 184, 233, 235, 313, 331, 369, 375, 418, 481, 484, 553; Roosevelt, relations with, 98, 130, 306, 313; voted out of office, 610; quoted, 21, 59, 61, 99, 100, 110, 131, 133, 147, 182, 184, 198, 218, 220, 234, 272, 306, 307, 329, 330, 331, 373, 375, 388, 418, 463, 554, 556
Ciano, Count Galeazzo, 20, 60–61, 99
Cicero. See Bazna, Elyesa
Cisterna, 395
Citadel, Operation. See Operations, German
Clark, Gen. Mark W.: in Italy, 19, 369, 371–73, 382, 391, 395; in North Africa, 220–21; quoted, 373

Clark Field, 147, 163
Clemenceau, Georges, 17, 22
"Climb Mount Niitaka," 146
Codes, Japanese, 146, 185, 213
Cold war, 553
Colle, 391
Collins, Gen. "Lightning Joe," 484
Cologne, 417–18, 424, 555
Colonialism, 17, 130, 145, 147–48, 305–6, 331, 451
Colosseum, 394–95
Combined Chiefs of Staff, 305
Comintern, 20
Commando raids, 308, 481
Commissar Order, 249
Committee to Defend America by Aiding the Allies, 130, 140, 141
Communism: 19–20, 32, 41, 130, 140, 149, 305, 307, 330, 337, 464, 481, 554; in China, 589, 625; in U.S.S.R., 20, 25, 57, 97, 101, 250–51, 260, 267, 270, 305, 625
Compiègne, 61, 95, 464
Compton, Dr. Arthur, 309
Conant, Dr. James B., 309, 324
Concentration camps, 57, 79, 148, 434, 449, 456–61, 555–56, 566–69, 622–24
Conferences: Argentia Bay, 132–33, 142; Cairo, 307–8, 318–19, 481; Casablanca, 306–8, 314–17, 319, 331, 418; Dumbarton Oaks, 624; Potsdam, 554, 589, 610–11; San Francisco, 557; Teheran, 306–8, 318–19, 481; Washington (Trident), 331, 419; Yalta, 306, 553–54, 559, 560–61, 574, 589, 623, 624
Congress, U.S., 25, 134, 147
Congress of Industrial Organizations (CIO), 453
Construction Battalions (Seabees), 329, 366–67
Convoys: Allied, 98, 131, 142, 183–84, 186, 191, 196–203, 232–33, 253, 328, 337; Axis, 218, 228, 233, 328
Coolidge, Calvin, 26, 27
Coral Sea, 358
Coral Sea, Battle of the, 184–85, 208–9, 210, 213, 328
Corregidor, 148–49, 172–73, 533, 548, 587, 591; map, 166
Corsica, 371
Cotentin Peninsula, 482, 486
Coughlin, Father Charles E., 129–30, 140, 141
Coventry, 99, 116–17
Cracow, 58
Crete, 100–101, 124–25, 183, 217, 308
Crimea, 252, 553
Cripps, Sir Stafford, 99, 101, 148, 251
Croatia, 100, 101
Crusader (British tank), 241
Cunningham, Gen. Sir Alan, 218
Cunningham, Adm. Sir Andrew, 124, 183
Curzon Line, 306, 554
Cyprus, 101, 183
Cyrenaica, 218

Czechoslovakia, 21, 49–50, 52–53, 57, 463, 554

"D" Bar, 398
D-Day (France). See Operations, Allied: Overlord
Dachau, 555–56
Dairen, 591
Daladier, Édouard, 21, 50
Danube River, 100, 554
Danube Valley, 369
Danzig, 188
Dardanelles, 99
Darlan, Adm. Jean Louis: 61, 220–21, 242, 243, 305, 380; assassinated, 220
Davies, Joseph, 453
Dawes, Charles G., 18
DDT, 366
"Death March." See Bataan
Declaration of the United Nations, 133
De Gaulle, Gen. Charles: 95, 242, 305, 330, 464, 553; broadcast to France (June 18, 1940), 61; in North Africa (1943), 220–21, 306–7, 317; orders liberation of Paris and return to Paris, 484, 518; quoted, 253, 306–7
Degtyarev (Russian machine gun), 251
Delhi, 148, 530
Democratic party (U.S.), 130, 137, 313
Denmark: German invasion of, 59, 74, 76; surrender of German forces in, 557
Denver, Colo., 184
Depression, 18–19, 27, 42
Derevyanko, Lt. Gen., 591
Derna, 224, 233
Desert Rats, 218. See also Army, British: in Desert War
Desert War. See North Africa; Army, British; and Army, German
"Destroyers for Bases," 130, 134, 181, 193
Detachment 101, 331
Deutschland, 188
"Die Katastrophe." See Hamburg, bombing of
Dieppe: commando raid at, 481–82; failure of raid, 494
Dill, Gen. Sir John, 100
Dimitrov, Georgi, 21
Divine, A. D. (eyewitness), 86
Dnieper River, 252
Dobruja, 99
Doenitz, Adm. Karl: 191; as president of the Reich, 556–57; quoted, 184, 557
Dollmann, Col. Friedrich, 555
Donets River, 252
Doolittle, Lt. Col. James, 149, 178, 447, 450–51
"Dora" (German gun), 252
Dornberger, Col. Walter, 324, 420
Dortmund, 418
Draft, U.S., 130, 134, 149, 175
Dragoon, Operation. See Operations, Allied

Dresden, 420
Drop-tank, 419, 423
Duce, Il. See Mussolini, Benito
DUKW, 370, 482
Dulles, Allen, 308
Dumbarton Oaks Conference. See Conferences
Dunkirk: 8–9, 86–87, 88, 101, 103, 123, 124, 134, 185, 382; evacuation of Allied army at, 60, 82, 84–85, 97, 105
Dutch East Indies, 131, 145, 147, 148, 150
Dyess, Col. William E. (eyewitness), 170–71

Eagle's Nest, 485
Eaker, Gen. Ira, 372
East Prussia, 57, 254, 553, 559, 624
Eben Emael, Fort, 59–60, 82
Eden, Sir Anthony: 314; sent by Churchill to Greece, 100; at Yalta Conference, 554, 560–61
Egypt: 98, 100, 220, 228; British and German fighting in, 217–18, 220, 233, 236, 238; Italian invasion of, 222, 224
Eichelberger, Lt. Gen. Robert L., 358, 360–61 (eyewitness)
Eighteenth Party Congress (U.S.S.R.), 57
Eindhoven, 485
Einstein, Albert, 309, 324, 325
Eisenhower, Gen. Dwight D: 246, 380, 399, 530; characterized, 43, 219–21, 485, 490–91; Operation Torch and North Africa, 220, 221, 242, 244; Operation Husky and Sicily and Italy, 370, 371; Operation Overlord and invasion of France, 372–73, 481–85, 490–91, 512, 518; defeat of Germany, 520, 555, 557, 559, 574; quoted, 220, 370, 380, 419, 482, 483, 496, 556, 557
El Agheila, 228
El Alamein, Battle of, 97, 185, 219, 221, 222, 233, 236, 239, 241, 253, 301, 454
El Guettar, 221
Elbe River: 419; crossing of, 571; U.S. and Russian troops meet at, 555, 559, 573–74
Emigrés (Polish), 306
Endaiadere, Cape, 358–59
Enewitok, 366, 411
England. See Great Britain
English Channel: 58, 82, 86, 98, 481; strategic importance of, 59, 63, 181, 317
"Enola Gay," 590, 616
Enterprise, 213–14, 328, 605
Épinal, 484
Eritrea, 20, 217
Esperance, Cape, 328
Espionage and sabotage: Allied, 308, 309, 420; British, 99, 100, 309; French, 464, 481; German, 308–9; Russian, 250, 253
Essen, 418
Essex, 543

Estonia, 61, 99
Ethiopia: 146, 217, 331, 370–80; 1935 Italian invasion of, 20, 38–39
Exeter, 182, 188

Falaise, 512
Falaise gap, 219, 484, 486, 533
Fascism: 19; Italian, 25, 38–39, 370; Spanish, 20, 41, 321; U.S., 130, 141
Fascist Grand Council, 370–71, 380
Fascist Republic, 372, 555, 556
"Fat Boy," 590
Federal Bureau of Investigation (FBI), 309
Felix, Operation. *See* Operations, German
Fermi, Enrico, 309
Fermor, Patrick Leigh, 308
Festung Europa, 369
Fighting Lady, The, 453, 476
Finland: 21; in Russo-Finnish War, 58–59, 61, 72–73; German troops in, 100–101
Fleming, Capt. Richard, 214
Fletcher, Rear Adm. Frank, 185, 213
Florida Island, 327
"Flying Tigers" (American Volunteer Group), 338, 421, 447
Foch, Marshal Ferdinand, 61
Foggia: importance of air bases at, 369, 372, 384
For Whom the Bell Tolls, 476
"Former Naval Person," 98
Formosa, 307, 529, 531, 587, 591
Forrestal, James V., 312
Forts. *See* individual names
"Four Freedoms," 131
Four Jills in a Jeep, 476
France: 63, 100, 129, 134, 220, 305–9, 314, 318, 399, 434, 438, 443, 481; as British ally before German invasion, 17–19, 21, 41, 49–50, 53, 55, 57–59, 61, 66, 70, 73, 76, 82; German invasion and fall of, 59, 60, 61, 84–95, 98, 103, 130, 191; Vichy, 61, 101, 131, 153, 220–21, 242–43, 305, 320–21; Nazi occupation, 99, 308, 372, 464, 481–82, 507, 516–17; Allied invasion of and advance in, 307, 309, 317, 319, 369, 481–87, 498–505, 510–11, 512, 514–15, 518–19, 524–27, 554; maps of, 486, 487. *See also* Resistance movements: French, and Army, French
Franco, Francisco, 20, 40–41, 183, 321
Franco-British Union, 61
Frank, Anne, 79, 460–61 (eyewitness)
Frank, Hans, 624
Frankfurt, 454
Franklin, 603
Franks, Hans, 79
Franks, Jesse D., Jr., 432, 433
Free French, 61, 95, 220–21, 242, 305, 555
Freemantle, 353

French Forces of the Interior (F.F.I.). *See* Resistance movements: French
Frick, Wilhelm, 624
Friedeburg, Adm. Hans von, 557
Fritsche, Hans, 624
Führer. *See* Hitler, Adolf

Gable, Clark, 433
Galahad Force, 331
Galland, Adolf: quoted, 419
Gamelin, Gen. Maurice, 60
Gandhi, Mahatma: quoted, 148
"Garibaldi Partisan Division," 372
Gariboldi, Gen. Italo, 227
Garigliano River, 369, 373, 391
Garigliano-Sangro River Line, 369
Gasoline: 153; rationing of, in U.S., 472, 473
Gavin, Gen. James, 512
Gavutu, 327
Gazala-Bir Hacheim Line, 233
Gela, 370, 376
"General Winter," 251, 420
Geneva Disarmament Conference, 49
Genoa, 555
Georgia (Georgian Soviet Socialist Republic), 307
German-American Bund, 141, 149
German Americans, 129, 137
German Intelligence Bureau. *See Abwehr*
German Workers' party, 30
Germany: 63, 70, 95, 101, 124, 126, 145, 146, 148, 184, 243, 308, 370, 399, 449, 481; post-World-War-I conditions and rise of Hitler's Third Reich (to 1939), 17–20, 22, 25, 27, 30, 32–37, 41, 49, 61, 129; relations with U.S.S.R. and invasion of, 21, 57, 97, 100, 101, 126, 249 ff., 256, 265, 305; territorial expansion, (1938–39), 49, 50, 53; invasion of Poland, and war in west, 55, 57–61, 66, 88, 95, 191; expansion in eastern Europe, 99, 100–101, 121, 123, 485; Axis partners, relations with, 131, 153, 218, 372; relations with U.S. and declaration of war on, 130–31, 147, 149, 159; wartime home front, described, 253, 322–23, 449–50, 454, 458, 484, 508; scientific development in (V-1 and V-2, etc.), 309, 324, 420, 507; Allied bombing of, 417–20, 423–24, 427–28, 430–31, 434, 438, 440, 441, 444, 446–47, 450, 454, 578–79; concentration camps in, 449, 566, 568; Allied assault on and defeat of, 485–86, 526, 552–85, 589; surrender of, 557, 559; occupation of, 559, 560, 610, 623–24. *See also* Army, German; Navy, German; Air Force, German; and Hitler
Gestapo: 249, 371, 449, 450, 454; brutality of, in occupied countries, 464; conducts roundup after 1944 bomb attempt on Hitler, 484, 508
GI: characterized, 397–400
Gibraltar, 101, 183
Gibraltar, Strait of, 183
Gibson, Guy Penrose: quoted, 418
Gilbert Islands: 327, 530; U.S. advances in, 329–30, 333, 364–65
Ginza, 152–53
Giraud, Gen. Henri Honoré: in North Africa, 220, 221, 305, 306, 307
Goddard, Dr. Robert, 324
Godesberg, 50–51
Goebbels, Dr. Joseph, 126, 322–23 (eyewitness), 571, 624; death of, 556; quoted, 556
Goerdeler, Carl, 449
Gold Beach, 483
Good Hope, Cape of, 183, 233
Göring, Hermann: 43, 54–55, 59, 60, 61, 420, 472, 574; leads *Luftwaffe* in Battle of Britain, 98, 105–6, 109, 110; expelled from Nazi party, 556; suicide of, 624; quoted, 219, 417
Goriunov (Russian machine gun), 251
Gott, W. H. E., 218
Götterdämmerung, 97
"Government Issue," 397
Graf Spee: pursuit and scuttling of, 182, 188
Grand Hotel (Kuibyshev), 146
Grandi, Count Dino, 370
Graves Registration Service, 400
Graziani, Marshal Rodolfo, 217–18, 222
Great Britain, 61, 101, 129, 130, 134, 181, 191, 193, 256, 305, 306, 308, 314, 330, 331, 370, 398, 404, 417, 481; foreign policy (1920–39), 17–19, 21, 41, 49–50, 53, 55, 57–58; declaration of war on Germany, 58, 66, 188; Churchill becomes Prime Minister, 59, 98; aid to Norway, 59; aid to Finland and actions in the "Phony War," 58–59, 70, 73; reactions to German invasion of France and the Low Countries, 61, 76, 82; home front described, 66, 221, 451–52; wartime strategy of, 74, 84, 100, 217, 305, 423; conduct of the war (1939–42), 97–127; German plans for invasion of, 98, 100, 109; Battle of Britain and Blitz, 98–99, 105–21, 130; espionage and intelligence plans of, 100, 370; Hess flight to, 101, 126; importance of Mediterranean and North Africa in strategy of, 100–101, 123, 181, 183, 217, 233, 242; U.S. aid to and alliances with, 130–31, 133–34, 142, 145–46, 186, 305, 324, 590; losses to Japan in Asia, 147, 160–61; defense of Burma and India, 147–48; Allied build-up in, for European offensive, 423, 427, 430, 452, 482, 490, 492–93;
effect of revenge weapons (V-1 and V-2) on, 420, 424, 452, 483, 506–7; postwar, 610, 624
"Great Debate," 140
Great Marianas Turkey Shoot. *See* Marianas Turkey Shoot
Greater East Asia Co-Prosperity Sphere, 145, 451
Greece: 21, 22, 100, 124, 183, 217, 305, 370, 384; invades Turkey (1920's), 20, 22; Italian invasion of, 99–100; German invasion of, 100, 123, 183, 249; British aid to, 100, 227, 308; guerrilla war in, 369, 372, 481
Greer, 193
Greif. *See* Operations, German
Grew, Joseph C.: 154, 313, 590, 591; quoted, 146
Grey, Sir Edward: quoted, 22
Gronzy, 308
Groves, Maj. Gen. Leslie R., 309
Guadalcanal: 150, 220, 327–28, 399, 400, 407, 451; in U.S. Pacific strategy, 327, 333; Naval Battle of, 328, 342–44, 350; invasion of, by U.S. Marines, 342–43, 344–45, 346–47, 348–49
Guam: 149, 589; Japanese control of, 162–63, 543; U.S. recapture of, 530, 536; air bases on, 421, 608; Japanese banzai attack on, described, 540–41
Guderian, Heinz: 58, 68–69 (eyewitness); quoted, 250–51
"Guernica," 21, 40–41
Guerrilla warfare: 21, 253, 308; in Greece, 369, 372, 481, 625; in Philippines, 531, 533, 548, 587; in Yugoslavia, 369, 481. *See also* Resistance movements
Gusen, 566
Gustav Line, 372–73, 388
Guthrie, Woody, 193

Haakon VII, King of Norway, 59
Haape, Heinrich (eyewitness), 272–73
Hague, The, 76
Hahn, Otto, 309
Haifa, 369
Haile Selassie, Emperor of Ethiopia, 20, 39, 217
Hainan, 591
Halban, Hans von, 309
Halder, Col. Gen. Franz: 249; quoted, 251, 252
Halsey, Adm. William F.: 213, 335, 399, 529; South Pacific Fleet commander (1943), 329; in Battle for Leyte Gulf, 532, 533, 547; at Japanese surrender ceremonies, 591
Hamburg: bombing of, 418–19, 454
Hamilton, Duke of, 101, 126
"Happy Time, The," 191. *See also* Navy, German; Submarines, German; and Navy, British
Harmon Field, 608

Harriman, Averell, 132, 314
Harris, Sir Arthur, 418, 230 (eyewitness)
Harz Mountains, 623
Haw Haw, Lord (William Joyce), 308
Hawaiian Islands, 146, 149, 154, 185, 220, 373
Heavy water, 309
Hebrides, 188
Heeresleitung Office, 18
Heisenberg, Werner, 309
Helsinki, 58
Hemingway, Ernest: 21, 399; quoted, 17, 146
Henderson Field, 327, 343, 344
Henlein, Konrad, 21
Herblock, 72
Herkules, Operation. *See* Operations, German
Hersey, John, 348–49 (eyewitness), 399
Hess, Rudolf: 61, 126; flight to England, 101, 126
Hewitt, Vice-Adm. H. Kent, 369
Hickam Field, 147
Higashikuni, Prince, 591
Higgins, Andrew, 184
Higgins boats, 365
Hill 609, 221
Hillary, Richard: quoted, 99
Himalayas, the, 338
Himmler, Heinrich, 249, 454, 555, 556, 574, 624
Hindenburg, Paul von, 32
Hirohito, Emperor: 210–11, 590, 625; broadcast on surrender, 591, 612, 617, 618
Hiroshima: 14–15, 421, 589, 624–25; atomic attack on, 590, 611–12, 615–17, 623
Hiryu, 213
Hitler, Adolf: 28–29, 54–55, 84, 97, 98, 99, 101, 126, 149, 153, 181, 191, 236, 243, 249, 252, 265, 305, 308, 319–21, 324, 444, 450, 472, 556, 565, 566, 624; early years (to 1933), 19–20, 25, 30, 32, 49; building the Reich (to 1939), 19–21, 34–37, 41, 49–51, 53, 454; blitzkrieg (1939–40), 55, 57–61, 63–64, 74, 76, 84, 95, 98–99, 103, 109, 186, 193; war in Russia and the Balkans, 57, 100–101, 121, 249, 252–54, 256, 260, 269, 272, 274, 280, 289, 301, 308; war in North Africa and the Mediterranean, 183, 218–19, 221–22, 227, 233, 241; conspiracy against, 308, 483–84, 508; Mussolini and Italy, relations with, 370–72, 380; war in the west (1944–45), 417, 449–50, 482–86, 494, 504, 518, 525; last days and death of, 555–57, 571, 574; strategy, 21, 58–59, 63, 74, 97–101, 181, 183, 220, 227, 249, 251–54, 256, 269, 286, 301, 305, 308, 321, 372, 482, 485, 486; V-weapons program, 309, 420, 483, 485, 507; quoted, 57, 99, 101, 256, 296, 370, 420, 483, 556, 557, 584

Hitler Youth, 33
Hitler's Children, 453
Hofer, Franz: quoted, 450
Holland. *See* Netherlands
Hollandia, 402–3, 531
Hollywood, 453, 476–77
Homma, Gen. Masaharu: leads attack on Philippines, 147, 148–49, 164, 165, 169, 173
Hong Kong, 147, 306
Honjo, Gen. Shigeru, 624
Honolulu, 146, 154, 185, 421
Hood, 182
Hoover, Herbert, 42
Hoovervilles, 19
Hopkins, Harry: 132, 138–39, 142, 193, 313; quoted, 132
Hornet, 149, 213–14, 328; in Doolittle raid, 178; lost at Battle of Santa Cruz Islands, 350–51
"Horst Wessel Lied," 61
Horthy, Adm. Miklós, 99
Horü, General, 358
House of Commons, 97
Howitzer, 152-mm. (Russian), 286
HR-1776 (Lend-Lease Bill), 131
Huebner, Lt. Gen.: quoted, 450
Hukwang Valley, 331
Hull, Cordell: 153, 312, 313, 624; in talks with Japanese at time of Pearl Harbor, 146, 158; quoted, 146
"Hump, the," 331, 338
Hunan Province, 530
Hundred Days, 19
Hungary, 17, 99, 101, 121, 481, 485, 554
Hunsaker, Dr. J. C., 324
Hurley, Gen. Patrick, 625
Hürtgen Forest, 12–13, 485
Hutchins, Robert M., 131

Ibn Saud, King of Saudi Arabia, 308
Iceland: U.S. air bases in, 184; strategic value of (1941), 192–93
Ickes, Harold, 308, 571
Ie Shima, 399
I.G. Farben Chemical Trust, 568
Ilyushin, Sergei, 253
Imperial Rule Assistance Association, 451
India: 218, 327, 329, 331, 421, 451; Japanese offensives in, 147–48, 331, 337; Allied bases in, 338, 530. *See also* China-Burma-India Theater
Indian Ocean, 148
Indochina, 131, 147, 153, 331, 400, 589
Indonesia, 331, 451
Inouye, Vice-Adm. Shigeyoshi, 184–85
Iran, 148, 217, 253, 308, 625
Iraq, 101, 217
Irish Americans, 129, 137
Irish Sea, 183
Iron and steel: strategic value of, 59, 450; U.S. embargo on ex-

port to Japan, 134, 153
Ironbottom Sound, 328
Ismay, Gen. Sir Hastings: 306–7; quoted, 306
Isolationism, U.S.: from 1920 to 1940, 20, 21, 27, 42, 129–30, 131, 134, 137; in "Great Debate," 140–41; end of, 149, 159, 175, 453
Italian Somaliland, 217
Italy: 126, 145, 183, 307, 397, 399, 401, 407, 434, 587, 624; in 1920's and 1930's, 19–20, 21, 22, 25, 38–39, 41; declares war on France, 60, 95; claims in eastern Europe, 99–100, 101, 123, 217; in Tripartite Pact, 131, 153; declares war on U.S., 147, 159; invasion of Egypt, 224; Allied invasion of and nature of war in (1943–45), 221, 369–95, 485, 555; ouster of Mussolini Government and surrender to Allies, 305, 370–71, 380; declares war on Germany, 372; resistance movements, 308, 370, 372, 481, 555, 556; maps, 374, 375. *See also* Army, Italian
Iwo Jima: 533; U.S. invasion of, 587–88, 592–99; kamikaze attacks on, 600

Japan, 98, 131, 137, 142, 147, 184, 185, 278, 308, 319, 321, 330, 533, 554, 593, 608; in 1920's and 1930's, 20, 44–47, 145, 148, 181; invasion of China, 20, 44–47, 131, 145, 153, 329, 589; diplomatic relations with U.S. (1920–41), 131, 134, 145, 146, 153, 158, 472; Tojo Government, 145, 531; colonialism, 133, 145, 307, 327, 451; joins Axis, 131, 152–53, 305, 589; attack on Pearl Harbor, 131–32, 144, 146, 147, 150, 154–59; advance in Asia, 131, 148, 150; advance in the Pacific, 147, 148, 160–73; Doolittle raid on, 149, 178–79, 450–51; war in the Pacific, 327–67, 528–51, 586–609; U.S. bombing of, 340–41, 421, 447, 466, 468–69, 531, 586–90, 611, 612, 616–17; wartime conditions in, 421, 450–51, 466–69; war with U.S.S.R., 560, 589–91, 610; surrender and occupation of, 590–91, 610, 612, 617–18, 620–21, 624–25. *See also* Army, Japanese and Navy, Japanese
Japanese Americans (nisei), 149
Java, 148, 327
Java Sea, Battle of the, 148
Jet aircraft, 420, 444, 507
Jews: German treatment of, 19, 32, 79, 372, 449, 456, 458–59, 460–61, 464, 556, 566
Jodl, Col. Gen. Alfred Gustav, 101, 249, 450, 485, 496, 508, 624; quoted, 557
Joint Chiefs of Staff, U.S., 307, 555, 590
Joliot-Curie, Frédéric, 309

Josephy, Sergeant Alvin M., Jr. (eyewitness), 540–41
Juin, Gen. Alphonse, 369
Juneau, 350
Jungle tactics, 328, 331, 337, 344–49, 358
Juno Beach, 483
Junod, Marcel (eyewitness), 617

"K" Rations, 338, 398
Kaga, 213
Kaiser, Henry J., 205
Kaiser Wilhelm II, 61
Kaiser Wilhelm Institute, 309
Kaltenbach, Fred, 308
Kamikaze. *See* Air Force, Japanese
Kano, Lt., 173
Karelian Isthmus, 58, 72
Kasserine Pass, Battle of: 221–22, 244, 246; map of, 223
Katyn Forest, 58
Katyusha rockets, 251, 253
Kearny, 192–93
Keep Your Powder Dry, 476
Keise Islands, 588
Keitel, Field Marshal Wilhelm, 61, 624
Kempeitai, 451
Kennan, George, 557
Kenny, Maj. Gen. George C., 328–29
Kerama Islands, 588
Kesselring, Field Marshal Alfred: 370–72, 376, 382, 391; quoted, 555
Khandrov, 251
Kharkov, 251, 252, 253
Khrushchev, Nikita, 252, 625
Kiev, 249, 252, 253
Kiiyama Peninsula, 588
"Kilroy," 401
Kimmel, Adm. Husband E., 154
King, Fleet Adm. Ernest J., 312, 313, 331, 335, 529
Kinkaid, Adm. Thomas: at Battle of the Santa Cruz Islands, 328; at Battle for Leyte Gulf, 532–33, 547
Kiska, 330, 363
Kleist, Paul Ludwig von, 60
Kluge, Field Marshal Gunther von, 58, 512
Knatchbull-Hugessen, Sir Hughe, 309
Knox, Frank, 312, 313
Kobe, 421, 589–90
Koch, Erich, 260
Koenig, Gen. Pierre, 484
Koischwitz, Otto, 308
Koiso, Gen. Kuniaki, 531
Kokoda Trail, 358
Kokura, 590
Konev, Marshal Ivan, 253, 554, 555, 556, 574, 575
Konoye, Prince Fumimaro, 145, 624
Korea, 307
Kremlin, 250, 251, 274
Krueger, Gen. Walter, 587
Krupp Works, 450
Kuhn, Fritz, 140, 141
Kuibyshev, 146, 251, 269

Kuribayashi, Lt. Gen. Tadamichi, 588
Kurile Islands, 153, 589, 591, 624
Kurita, Vice-Adm. Takeo, 532–33, 547
Kursk salient, 253, 301, 303
Kurusu, Saburo, 146, 153, 158
Kusaka, Vice-Adm. Jinichi, 185
KV-2 (Russian tank), 253
Kwajalein, 329–30, 365, 366
Kyushu Island, 421, 608

Labor, U.S., 137, 149, 453
Ladoga, Lake, 282
"Ladoga Lifeline," 282
Lae, 328
Langsdorff, Capt. Hans: scuttling of *Graf Spee* and suicide of, 182, 188
Laowingping, 340–41
Latin America, 130, 146
Latvia, 61, 99
Laurel, José, 531
Laval, Pierre: 61; Vichy Premier of France, 320–21
Lavochkin, Semyon, 253
Lay, Lt. Col. Beirne, Jr. (eyewitness), 430–31
League of Nations, 17, 20, 26, 27, 38–39, 44, 49, 58, 145
Leahy, Fleet Adm. William D., 313, 591
Lebanon, 217
Lebensraum, 21, 256
Leclerc, Maj. Gen. Jacques, 484–85, 518
Leclerc, Jean, 221
Ledo Road, 331, 337, 530
Lee, Adm. Willis A., 328
Leeb, Field Marshal Wilhelm von: in invasion of Russia, 249, 250, 252, 254, 265, 280
Leese, Sir Oliver, 372, 391
Leipzig, 418, 449
Le May, Maj. Gen. Curtis E., 421, 589
Lemnitzer, Lyman, 555
Lend-Lease: 105, 131–33, 142, 193, 198–99, 204, 253, 330, 337; chart of, 132–33
Lenin, Nikolai, 17–18, 20, 25
Leningrad: 452; German siege of, 249, 250, 252, 254, 265, 267, 280, 282, 283–84, 286
Leopold III, King of Belgium: 58; capitulates, 60, 82, 83
Lewis, John L., 137, 140, 453
Lexington (first): sunk in Battle of Coral Sea, 185, 208–9
Lexington (second): 529; at Marianas Turkey Shoot, 543; life on, described, 544–45
Leyte, 531–33, 547, 587
Leyte Gulf, Battle for, 531–33, 546–47, 600
Liberty Ships, 204–5
Libya, 183, 217–18, 221, 222, 224, 227, 228, 230, 233, 419
Licata, 370, 376
Liège, 59
"Lightning War." *See* Blitzkrieg
Lightoller, Commander C. H., (eyewitness), 86–87

Lindbergh, Col. Charles A., 43, 130, 141, 149
Lingayen Gulf, 548, 587, 600
Liri River, 373
List, Gen. Siegmund Wilhelm, 58
Lithuania, 22, 61, 99
"Little Boy," 590, 611
Lloyd George, David, 17, 22, 98
London: 21, 22, 58, 59, 132, 238, 314, 418, 557, 583; Blitz, 98–99, 110, 112–13, 114–15; V-1's and V-2's used against, 309, 420, 483, 485, 506–7
Longstop Hill, 221
Los Alamos, 590
Low, Capt. Francis S., 149
Low Countries, 95, 98, 130, 485, 520. *See also* Belgium, Netherlands, Luxembourg
LST's, 388
Lublin, 58
Lublin-Maidanek, 555–56
Lucas, Maj. Gen. John P., 388
Lucky Strike Cigarettes, 472, 473
Ludendorff, Gen. Erich, 19
Luftwaffe. See Air Force, German
Lugano, 555
Luitpold Arena, 34–35
Luxembourg, 59, 76
Luzon: 147; Japanese landings on, 147; Allied invasion of, 529–32, 548, 587
Lvov, 58

Maas (Meuse) River, 76, 82
MacArthur, Gen. Douglas: 43, 333, 399, 531, 589; characterized, 329, 335; defense of Philippines (1941–42), 146–48, 164–65, 167; defense of Australia, and New Guinea campaign, 184–85, 327, 328, 329, 358, 535, 547; return to Philippines, 529, 532, 533, 548, 587; in surrender and occupation of Japan, 587, 590–91, 620, 625; quoted, 148, 350, 533, 587, 591
McAuliffe, Brig. Gen. Anthony: 524; quoted, 485
McCormick, Col. Robert, 130
McKinley, Fort, 164
McLeish, Corp. R. (eyewitness), 230–31
Madagascar, 217
Maginot Line: 21, 59, 66; smashed by German panzers, 60
Magnitogorsk, 251
Maiori, 384
Maisky, Ivan, 314
Makin, 329, 366
Malaya, 145, 147, 331
Malenkov, Georgi, 252, 623
Malinta Hill, 172–73
Malmédy massacre, 526
Malta: 183, 220, 236, 370, 371; British defense of, 98, 101, 183, 218, 233; in German strategy, 183, 218, 232–33; Battle of, 232–33
Manchukuo. *See* Manchuria
Manchuria: 145, 307, 331, 451, 529, 589, 591, 625; Japanese invasion of and establishment

of puppet state (Manchukuo), 20, 44, 46, 131, 145, 327; Russian campaign in, 591
Mandalay, 337
Manhattan Engineer District, 309, 509
Manila: Japanese capture of, 147, 164–65; U.S. capture of, 548, 587, 589
Mannerheim, Field Marshal Carl von, 72, 252
Mannerheim Line, 72
Mannheim, 438
Manstein, Field Marshal Erich von, 253, 296, 320
Manteuffel, Gen. Hasso von, 485
Mao Tse-tung, 46, 305, 330, 589, 625
Maps (in order of appearance):
World War II in Europe, Sept. 1939–June 1941, 62–63
Pacific Theatre of War, 7 Dec. 1941–6 Aug. 1942, 150–51
Attack on Pearl Harbor, 7 Dec. 1941, 150
Bataan and Corregidor, 29 Dec. 1941–6 May 1942, 166
Battle of the Atlantic, 1939–43, 186–87
Campaigns in North Africa, Oct. 1942–May 1943, 222–23
Kasserine Pass, 14–22 Feb. 1943, 223
German Offensive in Russia, 1941–42, 254–55
Battle of Stalingrad, 18–23 Nov. 1942, 254
Pacific Theatre, 1942–45, 332–33
Guadalcanal, 1942–43, 345
Invasion of Sicily and Italy, 1943–44, 374
Salerno Beach, 9–14 Sept. 1943, 375
Allied Bombing Targets in Europe, Aug. 1942–June 1944, 422–23
Normandy Invasion, 6 June 1944, 486
Liberation of France and Belgium, June–Dec. 1944, 487
Battle of the Bulge, 16 Dec. 1944–16 Jan. 1945, 524
Defeat of Germany, Dec. 1944–May 1945, 558–59
Maquis. *See* Resistance movements: French
Mare Island Naval Shipyard, 184
Mareth Line, 221
Mariana Islands: 10–11, 329, 593; U.S. air bases in, 421, 588, 589, 608; U.S. advance in, 530, 536, 540–41, 543
Marianas Turkey Shoot, 530, 543
Marines, U.S.: 184, 329, 397, 400, 421, 529 ff., 588; at Bougainville, 355; on Guadalcanal, 327, 328, 342–43, 344–45, 346–47, 348–49; invade Iwo Jima, 587–88, 593–99; invade Marianas, 530, 536, 540–41; invade Okinawa, 588–89, 608; at Pearl Harbor, 154; invade Peleliu,

531, 538–39; take Tarawa, 326–27, 329, 364–65; on Wake Island, 163; women in, 472, 474
Mariupol, 251
Mark II (German tank), 259
Market-Garden, Operation. *See* Operations, Allied
Marshall, Gen. George C.: 312, 313, 589, 625; selects Eisenhower to lead Torch and Overlord, 220, 490; Marshall Plan, 625; quoted, 181, 218, 533
Marshall Islands: U.S. advance in, 329, 330, 333, 365, 411
Matanikan River, 344
Matilda (British tank), 241
Matsuoka, Yosuke, 319
Mauldin, Bill, 400, 433
Mauthausen, 434, 622–23
"Max." *See* Moulin, Jean
Mediterranean Sea: 95, 220, 419, 440, 482; strategic importance of, 98, 101, 182, 183, 228, 233, 306, 317, 375
Mein Kampf, 19, 30, 49, 126, 256, 456
Mellenthin, Gen. F. W. von (eyewitness), 231
Merrill, Brig. Gen. Frank D., 331
Merrill's Marauders (Galahad Force), 331, 337, 530
Mers-el-Kebir, 182
Messe, Field Marshal Alessandro, 221
Messerschmitt, Willi, 101
Messina: Allied invasion of, 370, 375, 380
Messina, Strait of, 370, 371, 375
Meuse (Maas) River, 76, 82
Middle East, 100, 101, 308, 330, 370, 625
Midway: 149, 163, 220, 330, 451, 530; Battle of, 150, 185, 213–14, 327
Mikuma, 214
Milan, 555, 556
Mindanao, 148, 531
Mindanao Sea, 587
Mindoro, 548, 600–01
Minsk, 250, 260
Mission to Moscow, 453, 476
Missouri, 591, 603, 620–21
Mitchell, Brig. Gen. William, 26, 27
Mitkyina, 331
Mitscher, Vice-Adm. Marc A., 414–15, 529, 531, 543, 588, 605
Model, Field Marshal Walther, 485
Modena, 555
Modlin, 58
Mogami, 214
Möhne dam, 418
Molotov, Vyacheslav, 21, 58, 132, 249–50, 417–18, 589–91; quoted, 623
Monastir Gap, 100
Monnet, Jean, 61
Monte Cassino: Allied bombing and capture of, 373, 392–93
Monte Cassino, Abbot of, 392
Montevideo, 182, 188
Montgomery, Rear Adm. Alfred, 529

Montgomery, Field Marshal Sir Bernard: 234, 235, 238–39, 244, 391, 533; described and characterized, 218–19; in France (1939–40), 70; leads British Eighth Army in North Africa, 218–19, 221, 222, 236, 241, 246; in invasion of Sicily and Italy, 369, 370, 371, 372, 376; in invasion of Europe (1944–45), 372, 484–85, 486, 512, 520; dispute with Eisenhower, 485, 490; quoted, 219, 221, 485
"Montgomery's double" (deception plan), 370, 482
Montreal, 188
Morgan, Lt. Gen. Sir Frederick, 482
Morgenthau, Henry, 623
Morison, Samuel Eliot; quoted, 375
Morocco: 221, 306, 369; Allied landings in (Torch), 220, 222, 242; Roosevelt-Churchill meeting (Jan., 1943), 314, 319
Morotai, 535
Morshead, Gen. Leslie (eyewitness), 230
Mortain, 484
Moscow: 21, 25, 46, 101, 121, 253, 303, 452, 557, 583; Battle of, 101, 249–52, 254, 265, 269, 270–74, 277–78; Allied conferences in, 132, 142, 306, 314
Moselle River, 555
Motion pictures (U.S.). See Hollywood
Moulin, Jean ("Max"), 464
Mount Etna, 380
Mount Suribachi, 588, 596–97, 598–99
Mountbatten, Adm. Lord Louis, 99, 331, 530–31, 589, 591
Mozdok, 301
Mrs. Miniver, 453, 476
Mueller, Heinrich, 450
Mukden Incident, 20
Munich Agreement, 19, 21, 30, 50–51, 53, 57, 63
Munich Putsch, 19, 30
Murmansk Run, 184, 202–3
Murphy, Robert, 19, 220
Murrow, Edward R., 112, 114–15 (eyewitness), 399
Musashi, 181, 210–11, 532
Mussolini, Benito: 95, 98, 305, 308, 372, 442, 472, 574; rise to power (1920–40), 19–20, 21, 25, 38–39, 41, 60–61; Greek campaign, 99–100, 101, 123, 249; plans for conquest in North Africa and the Mediterranean, 218–19, 221–22, 227, 233; meeting with Hitler at Rimini (1943), 370, 380; fall and death of, 321, 370–71, 372, 376, 380, 555, 556; quoted, 371, 372
Mussolini, Vittorio, 20

Nagasaki: 421, 589, 590–91; atomic attack on, 611–12, 614–15

Nagato, 146
Nagoya, 421, 589–90
Nagumo, Vice-Adm. Chuichi: 213; in Battle of Midway, 185; suicide of, on Saipan, 530
Namsos, 59
Naples: 183, 386; Allied advance on, 369, 371–72, 384; German destruction of, 372
Narvik, 59, 74
National Defense Research Committee, 130
National Press Club Canteen (Washington, D.C.), 474
Navies, Allied, 376, 483
Navy, Australian, 148, 185, 327
Navy, British: 98, 181, 191; in Atlantic, 182–83, 183–84, 186, 188, 193; at Dunkirk, 60; defeated off Malaya, 147, 206–7; in Mediterranean, 124, 182, 183, 218, 219, 220, 228, 230–31, 233, 242, 382; off Norway, 59, 74. See also Convoys: Allied, and individual ships
Navy, Dutch, 148
Navy, French, 61, 98, 182, 183, 242, 243
Navy, German, 59, 74, 98, 181, 182–83, 183–84, 186, 188, 191, 196–97
Navy, Italian, 181–82, 183, 232–33, 371
Navy, Japanese: 181, 210–11, 352–53, 421, 447; early actions against British, 147, 148; at Battle of Java Sea, 148; at Kiska, 363; at Battle for Leyte Gulf, 531, 532, 533, 547; at Battle of Midway, 185, 213; attack on Pearl Harbor, 146; at Battle of Philippine Sea, 530, 543; and southwest Pacific actions, 184–85, 327, 328–29, 350–51, 356–57
Navy, U.S.: 98, 130, 159, 181, 184–85, 329, 335, 352–53, 421, 472, 529, 536, 544–45; in Battle of Atlantic, 131, 142, 183–84, 192–93; Construction Battalions (Seabees), 329, 366–67; in Battle of Coral Sea, 184–85, 208–9; on D-Day, 483, 499; at Guadalcanal campaign, 327, 328, 343, 350–51; kamikaze attacks on, 532, 533, 550, 600–607; at Kiska, 363; in Battle for Leyte Gulf, 531 ff., 547; in Mediterranean, 183, 220, 382; at Battle of Midway, 185, 213; Pearl Harbor and effects, 144, 145, 146–47, 148, 154, 156–57, 184; at Battle of Philippine Sea, 530, 543; supports island advances, 329–30, 350–51, 356–57, 364–65, 529 ff., 543, 587–88, 593–96, 600, 608
Nazi party: growth and development of, in Germany, 19, 25, 30, 32, 34–35, 36–37, 49, 53; brutality of policies, 121, 250, 556, 568, 624; philosophy of, 260, 305, 456–57, 556
Nazi-Soviet Pact, 21, 55, 249, 256

Nelson, Donald, 452
Netherlands: 61, 148, 482; German invasion and occupation of, 59, 76, 79, 80–81, 460–61, 494, 520; resistance in, 79, 99, 481; Allied invasion of, 520, 557. See also Resistance movements: Dutch
Nettuno, 373, 388
Neutrality, U.S., 42, 130, 131, 134, 142
Neutrality Acts, U.S.: (1794), 129; (1935), 129; (1936), 129; (1937), 134; (1939), 129, 134
Nevada, 147
New Britain, 355, 356–57
New Deal, 19
New Georgia, 329
New Guinea: 145, 328, 329, 402–3, 530, 531; Japanese invasion and offensives in, 148, 184–85, 208, 327–29, 358–59; Allied campaign and advances in, 350, 360–61, 535–36, 547
New York City, N.Y., 21, 55, 184, 474, 557, 583, 618–19
Newfoundland, 130, 183, 184
Nice, 372
Nielson Field, 164
Niigata, 590
Nijmegen, 485, 555
Nile River, 181, 235
Nile Valley, 219, 222
Nimitz, Fleet Adm. Chester W.: 331, 335, 399, 421, 529–30, 591; commands central Pacific, 213, 329–30, 535, 536, 547, 587, 590; described and compared to MacArthur, 329; quoted, 185
Nisei, 149
Nishimura, Vice-Adm. Shoji, 532
Noemfoor Island, 535
Nomura, Kichisaburo, 146, 153, 158
Norden bombsight, 418, 427, 441
Nordling, Raoul, 518
Normandy: Allied invasion of and advances in, 307, 481, 482, 483, 486, 496, 499, 502, 504, 511, 529; map of, 486. See also Operations, Allied: Overlord
Norris, Kathleen, 141
North Africa: 61, 101, 125, 148, 181, 217 ff., 220, 222, 224, 233, 241, 246, 384, 397, 399, 401, 417, 482, 512, 587; Axis offensive in, 101, 183, 218, 227; Allied landings and advance in, 220–21, 242, 306, 320; map of campaigns in, 222–23. See also Army, British; Army, German; Army, Italian; and Army, U.S.
North Atlantic, 182, 198–99
North Sea, 419, 520
Norway: 73, 76, 98, 184, 438, 482; German invasion of, 59, 74; resistance movement in, 59, 99, 481
Nuremberg: Nazi party rallies at, 34–35, 36–37, 49; bombing of, 578–79; war crime trials at, 450, 578–79, 624
Nye, Sen. Gerald P., 141
Nye committee, 42

Oahu, 154
Oak Ridge, 590
O'Connor, Lt. Gen. Richard, 224
Oder River, 555
Office of Price Administration, 453
Office of Production Management, 130
Office of Scientific Research and Development, 309, 324
Office of Strategic Services (OSS), 308, 331, 555
Office of War Information (OWI), 308
Ohnishi, Vice-Adm. Takijiro, 532, 533
Oil, 131, 145, 148, 308
Okinawa: 571, 624; U.S. invasion of, 533, 587–89, 600, 608–9; kamikaze attacks on, 533, 600, 608–9
Oklahoma, 147, 154
Olbricht, Gen. Friedrich: in anti-Hitler conspiracy (1944), 483–84
Oldendorf, Rear Adm. Jesse, 532
Omaha Beach, 483, 499
Operations, Allied: Dragoon, 484, 485; Husky, 376, 380; Market-Garden, 520; Overlord, 307, 372, 481, 482, 483, 486, 490, 492–93, 496, 499, 500–501, 502–3; Roundup, 306; Sledgehammer, 220; Torch, 220, 222, 242, 244
Operations, German: Barbarossa, 100, 101, 249 ff., 254, 256, 308; Case White, 57; Case Yellow, 59; Citadel, 253; Eagle, 109; Felix, 183; Greif, 485; Herkules, 218; Punishment, 121; Sea Lion, 98, 99, 109; Typhoon, 269; Watch on the Rhine, 485
Operations, Japanese: Operational Order No. 1 (Pearl Harbor), 146; Sho-Go, 531, 532
Oppenheimer, Dr. J. Robert: quoted, 590
Oran: 369; British attack French fleet at, 182, 183, 242; Allied landing at (Torch), 220
Orel, 250, 253, 269, 301
Orlando, Vittorio Emanuele, 22
Ormoc, 533
Osaka, 589
OSS. See Office of Strategic Services
Overlord, Operation. See Operations, Allied
Owen Stanley Mountains: Japanese attempt to cross, 327, 328, 358, 360–61
Oxenius, Maj. Gen. Wilhelm, 557
Ozawa, Vice-Adm. Jisaburo: 148; leads Northern Force in Battle for Leyte Gulf, 532–33; leads Japanese Navy in Marianas offensive, 543

Pacelli, Eugenio. See Pius XII
Pacific Ocean, 329, 398, 399, 440
Pacific Theater: Allied strategy in, 145–46, 149, 185, 220, 307, 319, 327, 328, 329, 331, 333,

335, 481, 529, 531, 535, 547, 608; Japanese gains and strategy in, 150, 160–61, 162–63, 181, 327; maps of (1941–42), 150–51, (1942–45), 332–33

Pacifism (U.S.), 130, 140, 149

Paestum, 382, 384

Palaus Islands: U.S. invasion of, 531, 535, 538–39

Palermo, 370, 378–79

Palo, 533

Panama, 149

Pantelleria, 369

Panther (German tank), 301

Panzers: *See* Army, German, and Tanks and mechanized vehicles, Axis

Papen, Franz von, 624

Papua, 58, 146, 329, 358–59

Paris: 58, 94, 95, 324, 486, 557; declared an open city (1940), 60, 88; liberated, 484–85, 486, 518

Parsons, Capt. William S., 616

Pas de Calais, 482, 494

Patch, Lt. Gen. Alexander: commands U.S. Seventh Army in invasion of southern France, 484, 486

Patterson, Robert P., 313

Patton, Gen. George S., Jr.: 244, 399, 533; at Kasserine Pass, 221; commands U.S. Seventh Army in Sicily, 369, 370, 376, 378–79; leads U.S. Third Army in invasion of Europe, 372, 484–85, 511–12, 554–55; strategy and tactics, 370, 484, 511; quoted, 484, 485

Paul, Prince of Yugoslavia, 100

Paulus, Field Marshal Friedrich: 219, 301; commands German Sixth Army at Stalingrad, 252–53, 289, 296

Pearl Harbor: 98, 140, 213, 305, 311, 324, 327, 329, 353, 421, 447, 530, 589, 591; Japanese attack on, 131–32, 145–48, 150, 153–59, 181; map of, 150

Peenemünde, 309, 420, 507

Peleliu Island, 531, 539

Percival, Gen. Sir Arthur, 147, 161, 531, 591

Persian Gulf, 308

Persian Gulf Service Command, 253

Petacci, Clara, 556

Pétain, Marshal Henri Philippe, 61, 88, 95, 220

Peter, King of Yugoslavia, 100

Petlyakov, Vladimir, 253

Philippine Islands: Japanese capture of, 145–49, 163–73, 185; U.S. advance on and liberation of, 333, 335, 421, 529, 531, 533, 535, 547–48, 587; resistance movement in, 531, 533, 587

Philippine Sea, Battle of the, 543. *See also* Marianas Turkey Shoot

Phillips, Adm. Sir Tom, 147, 208

"Phony War," 59

Picasso, Pablo, 21, 40–41

Piccolo Peak, 371

Pipe-Line Under the Ocean. *See* PLUTO

Pius XII, Pope: 58; quoted, 19

Ploesti: U.S. bombing raid on, 419–20, 433–34

Plougastel-Daoulas, 438

PLUTO (Pipe-Line Under the Ocean), 482

Po River, 485

Poland: 21, 22, 79, 100, 101, 182, 254, 305, 306, 443, 553, 610, 625; partition of (German and Russian), 20, 21, 55, 57, 58, 61, 132, 307; German invasion of, 57–58, 63–69, 256; resistance movement in, 99, 481; Russian advance and communist takeover in, 554, 559–60, 624

Political Warfare Executive (PWE), 308

Ponza, 371, 372

Port Arthur, 591

Port Moresby: Japanese advance on, 184–85, 209, 327–28, 358

Port Said, 218, 369

Potsdam Conference. *See* Conferences: Potsdam

Potsdam Declaration, 590, 591, 610

Pownall, Rear Adm. Charles, 529

Prague, 21, 52–53

Prince of Wales: 132, 182; sinking of, 147, 206–7

Princeton, 547

Prinz Eugen, 182

Prisoners of war: British, 147, 148, 434, 450, 548, 580–81; German, 246, 251, 253, 303, 486, 525; Japanese, 533, 591, 608; Russian, 250, 252, 253, 269, 276, 278, 450; U.S., 149, 169, 170–71, 222, 434, 450, 525, 526, 548, 580–81; other, 100, 218, 224

Propaganda: Allied, 129, 308; British, 42, 99, 101, 130–31, 182; German, 60, 182, 260, 308, 322–23, 373, 449, 450, 456, 463; Japanese, 147, 148, 450–51, 466; U.S., 453, 472

PT boats, 148

Purple Heart, 373

Pyle, Ernie: 386–87 (eyewitness), 503; quoted, 399, 400–401

Qattara Depression, 219, 236

Queen Mary, 584

Quisling, Vidkun, 59, 74

Quonset hut, 408–9

Rabaul, 213, 328, 329, 333, 354–55, 356–57, 531, 543

Radar: British, 98–99, 106, 424; German, 419; U.S., 184, 543

Radek, Karl, 18, 20

Radford, Rear Adm. Arthur W., 529

Radio: 308; British, 99, 452; Japanese, 148, 466; U.S., 129–30

Raeder, Grand Adm. Erich, 181, 191

Railroad gun, 274-mm., 564–65

Rangoon, 337, 591

Rankin, Jeannette, 147

Rapallo, Treaty of, 18, 21, 27

Rapido River, 373, 391

Rastenburg, 483

Rationing: Great Britain, 452; Japan, 451, 466; U.S., 453, 471, 472, 473, 478

Ravensbrück, 458

Rayburn, Rep. Sam, 571

Red Cross, 175, 398, 450

Red Sea, 217

Red Square, 25, 557

Regensburg: bombing of, 419, 430–31, 434

Reichenau, Field Marshal Walther von, 58, 252

Reichstag, 19, 32, 103

Remagen, 555, 559, 563

"Remember Pearl Harbor," 175

Rentenmark, 18, 19

Reparations (German), 18

Republican party (U.S.), 130, 137, 313

Repulse, 147, 206–7

Resistance movements: Dutch, 79, 463, 481; French, 464, 481, 482, 484, 486, 518; Yugoslav, 481, 485, 554; other, 99, 260, 449, 463, 481, 531, 555, 587

Reuben James, 183, 193

Revenge weapons. *See* V-1, V-2

Reynaud, Paul, 61

Rheims, 557

Rhine River and Valley, 484, 485, 520, 553, 555, 559, 563

Rhineland, 19, 49, 418

Rhône Valley, 484

Ribbentrop, Joachim von: 21, 55, 58, 61, 95, 99, 417–18, 555; executed, 624

Richards, Dr. A. N., 324

Ridgway, Lt. Gen. Matthew B., 502, 512

Rimini, 370, 380

River Plate, Battle of the, 182

Rjukan, 309

Rocket development. *See* V-2

Rockwell, Norman, 448, 449

Roebling, Donald, 184

Roer River, 555

Röhm, Ernst, 34–35

Rokossovski, Marshal Konstantin, 253, 554

Rome: 25, 370, 372, 376, 380, 388; Allied advance in and capture of, 370, 371, 372, 373, 384, 386–87, 394–95

Rome-Berlin Axis, 20, 38, 41

Rommel, Field Marshal Erwin: 60, 101, 181, 230, 233–35, 242; leads Afrika Korps in North Africa; 183, 218–19, 221–22, 227, 228–29, 230, 231, 233–34, 236, 241, 244, 246; in Italy (1943–44), 371, 372; in defense of Europe (1944), 482–83, 494; death of, 484; quoted, 219, 221, 230, 231, 397, 482, 494

Roosevelt, Eleanor (Mrs. Franklin D.), 42, 360–61, 556

Roosevelt, Franklin Delano: 130, 146, 306, 318, 370, 466, 533, 573, 623, 624; described and characterized, 134, 307–8, 310–11, 553; elections and domestic measures, 19, 42, 130, 137, 305; foreign policy (1933–41), 58–59, 132, 145, 153, 193; Churchill, relations with, 98, 130, 132–33, 314; lend-lease program, 131, 138–39, 184; conferences, 132–33, 142, 305, 306–7, 319, 330, 553–54, 560–61; wartime decisions, 148–49, 158, 167, 176, 184, 307, 313, 337, 452, 452–53, 481, 490; atomic bomb, development of, 309, 324; death of, 556, 557, 570–71, 590; quoted, 60–61, 130, 131, 132–33, 134, 137, 147, 178, 306, 307, 452–53, 453, 483, 556

Rosenberg, Alfred, 624

Rosenthal, Joe, 588

Rostov, 252

Rotterdam, 76, 80–81, 100

Royal Air Force. *See* Air Force, British

Royal Oak, 188

Ruhr, 418, 555, 559

Rumania, 21, 58, 61, 99, 100, 101, 419–20, 481, 553, 625

Rundstedt, Field Marshal Gerd von: 251, 504; in invasion of France, 59, 60, 83–84; in invasion of Russia, 249, 250, 252, 254, 265; defense of France (1944), 482, 483, 555; quoted, 60, 109

Rupel, Fort, 100

Russell Islands, 329

Russia. *See* Union of Soviet Socialist Republics

Russo-Finnish War, 72–73. *See also* Union of Soviet Socialist Republics and Finland

Rykov, Aleksei, 25

Ryukyu Islands, 588

Saarland, 19, 559, 624

Sabotage. *See* Espionage and sabotage

"Sad Sack," 400, 518

St. Benedict's Tomb: escapes destruction in bombing of Monte Cassino, 373, 392–93

Saint-Exupéry, Antoine de (eyewitness), 90–91

Saint Lô: Allied breakout at (July, 1944), 486, 511

St. Lo, 532

Saint-Nazaire, 182

Saipan: 185, 421, 531, 540, 589; U.S. invasion of, 530, 536, 543

Saito, Lt. Gen. Yoshitsugu, 530

Sakhalin Island, 589, 591, 624

Salamaua, 328

Salerno: Allied landings at, 371–72, 375, 380, 382–83; maps of Allied landings at, 374, 375

Salinas, Calif.: 400; nisei internment camp at, 176–77

Samar, 532

Samurai, 44–45, 145

San Antonio Bay, 587

San Bernardino Strait, 532, 533

San Francisco Conference. *See*

Conferences: San Francisco
Sangro River, 369
Santa Cruz Islands, Battle of the, 328, 350–51
Santee, 532
Sarana Bay, 330
Sardinia, 369, 370, 371
Sato, Ambassador, 591
Sauckel, Fritz, 624
Saudi Arabia, 308
Sava River, 100
Savo Island, Battle of, 327, 343
Scapa Flow, 188
Schacht, Hjalmar, 18, 19, 624
Scheldt Estuary, 520
Schellenberg, Walter: quoted, 58
Schleswig-Holstein, 188
Schmidt, Maj. Gen. Harry, 587–88
Schorm, Lt. (eyewitness), 231
Schulenburg, Count Werner von der, 249–50
Schuschnigg, Kurt von, 49
Schweinfurt: U.S. raids on, 419, 428, 434
Scotland, 101, 126, 184, 188
Sea Lion, Operation. *See* Operations, German
Seabees. *See* Construction Battalions
Second Front: in Allied strategy, 242, 305, 306, 311, 314, 481
Security Council, United Nations, 554
See Here, Private Hargrove, 397–98
Seeckt, Gen. Hans von: builds German Army in 1920's, 18–21, 27, 28, 61, 101; quoted, 18
Seine River, 60, 518
Senate, U.S., 17, 27
Serbia, 101
Sevastopol, 252
Seyss-Inquart, Artur von, 79, 624
Shaka, 46–47
Shanghai Incident, 44
Shangri-la, 149, 278
Sheffield, 198–99
Shepheard's Hotel, 217
Sherman, Rear Adm. Frederick C., 529
Sherwood, Robert E., 130, 138–39 (eyewitness), 193
Shibasaki, Adm. Keiji: quoted, 364
Shigemitsu, Mamoru, 591; quoted, 451
Shipbuilding (U.S.), 27, 204–5
Shirer, William L., 36–37 (eyewitness), 68
Sho-Go. *See* Operations, Japanese
Shoho, 20, 185
Short, Lt. Gen. Walter C., 154
Shoup, Col. David: quoted, 329
Shpagin machine pistols, 251
Shuri, 588
Siam, Gulf of, 206
Sian, 330
Siberia, 253, 278
Sibuyan Sea, Battle of the, 532
Sicily: 218, 233, 404, 511, 512; Allied invasion of, 221, 306, 317, 369, 370, 375, 376, 378–

79, 380; Allied strategy in, 370, 375, 376; map of Allied invasion, 374
Sidi Barrani, 217, 224
Siegfried Line, 66, 520
Simović, Gen. Dušan, 100
Singapore: 145, 148, 531, 591; falls to Japanese, 147, 148, 160–61
Sino-Soviet Nonaggression Pact, 331
Sino-Soviet relations, 131, 305
Sitzkrieg (Phony War), 70
Skoplje, 100
Skorzeny, Otto: rescues Mussolini, 372; leads Operation Greif, 485
Sledgehammer, Operation. *See* Operations, Allied
"Slot, the," 328, 343
Smetanin, Constantin, 319
Smigly-Rydz, Marshal Edward, 58
Smith, Lt. Gen. Holland M.: 399, 530, 593; quoted, 588
Smith, Kate, 471
Smolensk: 101; falls to Germans, 250; Russians retake, 253, 265
Solomon Islands: 184, 327–28, 329; Guadalcanal campaign in, 150, 327, 342–43, 344–45, 346–47, 348–49; Japanese control of, 327; in Pacific strategy (1943), 355
Somme-Aisne line, 88
Somme River, 60, 88
Soryu, 213
Southeast Asia Command, Allied, 331
Southern Pacific Command, Allied, 329
Soviet-Finnish Nonaggression Pact, 58
Soviet-Polish Nonaggression Pact, 58
Spaatz, Gen. Carl: 399, 590; upholds concept of daylight bombing, 418; commands U.S. Eighth Air Force, 427; quoted, 611
Spain: 220; civil war in, 20–21, 40–41; neutrality of, 183, 321, 494; in "Man Who Never Was" plan, 370. *See also* Operations, German: Felix
SPARS, 472
Spatha, Cape, 183
Special Operations Executive. *See* Espionage and sabotage: British
Speer, Albert, 419, 450
Speidel, Lt. Gen. Hans: 219, 503; quoted, 483
Spies. *See* Espionage and sabotage
Sprague, Rear Adm. Clifton, 532
Sprague, Rear Adm. Thomas, 532
Spruance, Adm. Raymond: in Battle of Midway, 185, 213–14; commands Fifth Fleet, 329; leads attack on Saipan, 529, 530; commands invasion of Okinawa, 588, 608; invasion of Iwo Jima, 587
S.S. See Army, German

Stage Door Canteen, 474
Stalin, Marshal Joseph: 73, 99, 132, 142, 146, 218, 251, 260, 277, 308, 318, 453, 573, 623, 624; described and characterized, 19–21, 25, 54–55, 267, 305, 307, 308, 313, 451, 476; Hitler, diplomatic relations with, 54–55, 57, 61, 249; reaction to German invasion of Russia, 250, 256; strategy against Germans, 251, 252, 269; refuses to attend Casablanca Conference, 306, 317; policy in Asia, 305, 306, 330; Churchill and Roosevelt, relations with, 306, 314; at Teheran Conference, 306, 307, 319, 481; demands second front, 311, 481; at Yalta Conference, 553–54, 589, 560–61; at Potsdam Conference, 589, 610–611; quoted, 20, 57, 250, 270, 271, 305, 307–8, 553
Stalin-JS (Russian tank), 253
Stalin Line, 250
Stalingrad: 101, 185, 219, 220, 286, 454; Battle of, 97, 252–54, 288–89, 291, 293, 296, 298–99, 301; map of Nov., 1942, battle, 254
Stauffenberg, Col. Count Klaus von: in conspiracy against Hitler, 483–84, 508; death of, 484, 508
Steinhardt, Laurence, 251
Stettinius, Edward R., Jr.: 312, 313, 554, 560–61, 571; quoted, 554
Stilwell, Gen. Joseph: in China-Burma-India Theater, 147–48, 331, 337, 531; differences with Chiang Kai-shek, 307, 330; quoted, 148
Stimson, Henry L., 20, 131, 134–35, 312, 313, 590, 591, 623
Storm troopers, 34–35
Strategic bombing, 418, 559
Streicher, Julius, 624
Stumme, Gen. Georg von, 219
Submarines, German (U-boats): 98, 134, 181, 182, 184, 188, 196–97; in Battle of Atlantic, 131, 183–84, 186, 191, 196–97, 198–99
Submarines, U.S., 352–53
Sudetenland, 21, 50, 53
Suez, 218, 228
Suez Canal, 183, 235
Sukarno, 451
Sultan, Gen. Daniel I., 531
Sumatra, 327, 589
Supreme Headquarters, Allied Expeditionary Force, 481
Supreme War Council (Japanese), 145
Surigao Strait, Battle of, 532, 547, 587
Suwannee, 532
Suzuki, Adm. Kantaro: 590; quoted, 591
Sverdlovsk, 251
Sweden, 59, 73, 308
Switzerland, 555
Sword Beach, 483

Syracuse, 370, 376
Syria, 101, 217
Szyk, Arthur, 472

T-34 (Russian tank), 250, 265, 269, 286, 301
Tanaka Memorial, 145
Tanks and mechanized vehicles, Allied: pictured, 488–89; British, 233, 236, 241; French, 60; Russian, 250, 253, 265, 269, 286, 301; U.S., 482; tactics, 484, 511
Tanks and mechanized vehicles, Axis: 60, 253, 259, 265, 294, 301; pictured, 488–89; tactics, 64, 253, 265, 525. *See also* Blitzkrieg
Taranto, 183, 371
Tarawa: U.S. invasion of, 326–27, 329, 364–65; Seabees at, 366
Tassigny, Gen. Jean de Lattre de, 484
Taylor, Col. George A., 503
Taylor, Maj. Gen. Maxwell: 380, 512; special mission to Rome on Italian surrender, 371; in D-Day invasion, 483; quoted, 483
Tedder, Air Chief Marshal Sir Arthur, 427
Teheran Conference. *See* Conferences: Teheran
Tempelhof Airfield, 556
Templer, Gen. Gerald, 382
Tenaru River, 344
Tennessee, 147, 156–57
Terasaki, Gwen (eyewitness), 617
Terauchi, Field Marshal Hisaichi, 531, 533
Thailand, 145, 147, 589
Thermopylae, 100
Third Reich. *See* Germany
Thirty Seconds over Tokyo, 476
Thoma, Gen. Ritter von, 219
Thomas, Norman, 140
Thrace, 100
Tibbets, Col. Paul W., Jr.: 590; quoted, 590, 616 (eyewitness)
Tiger (German tank), 253, 301
Times Square, 618–19
Timor, 327
Timoshenko, Marshal Semën, 250, 251, 252, 267, 270
Tinian, 421, 530, 536, 589, 590
Tito, Marshal: in Spanish Civil War, 21; leads Yugoslav Communists, 305, 307, 372, 481, 485, 553
Tizard, Sir Henry, 98, 99
Tobruk: British defense of, 218, 227–28, 230–31; German capture of, 233
Tojo, Gen. Hideki: 146, 319, 472; becomes Premier of Japan, 131, 145, 153; fall of, 531; death of, 624; quoted, 624
Tokyo: 153, 319, 421; Doolittle raid on, 149, 178, 447, 450–51; bombing of, 586, 587, 589–90
Tokyo Bay, 591, 620
"Tokyo Express, The," 343
Tokyo Rose (Iva d'Aquino), 308

Torch, Operation. *See* Operations, Allied

Torgau, 573

Toulon: 484; French fleet at, 182; seized by Germans, 243

Tours, 95

Towers, Adm. John H., 529

Toyoda, Adm. Soemu: in Leyte defense (1944), 531–32; quoted, 531

Transylvania, 99

Treasury Islands, 329

Trident Conference. *See* Conferences: Washington (Trident)

Trieste, 372

Tripartite Pact: 131, 145, 153; failure of, 321

Tripoli: Rommel arrives in (Feb., 1941), 227; embarkation point for invasion of Sicily, 369

Tripolitania, 217, 218, 224

Troina, 380

Trondheim, 59

Trotsky, Leon, 18, 101

Truk: in Pacific war strategy, 330, 333, 531

Truman, Harry S., 474, 554, 573, 624; becomes President of U.S., 556, 571, 590; at Potsdam Conference, 589, 610–11; quoted, 557, 571, 590, 617 (eyewitness), 623

Truman, Mrs. Harry (Bess), 571

Truman Doctrine, 624–25

Truscott, Lt. Gen. Lucian, 388, 395

Tukhachevski, Marshal Mikhail, 18, 20

Tula, 18, 251

Tulagi, 327

Tunis: 221, 244, 246; falls to Allies, 221, 246

Tunisia: 233, 241, 246, 370; German and Italian occupation of, 221; Allied advance on, 244

Turkey, 17, 20, 22, 101, 307, 308, 420, 625

Turner, Vice-Adm. Richmond Kelly, 365, 588

Tuscany, 372, 485

Tyorkin, Vasili, 301

Typhoon, Operation. *See* Operations, German

Tyrrhenian Coast, 391

U-boats. *See* Submarines, German

U-47 (German submarine), 188

U-158 (German submarine), 191

U-235 (uranium derivative), 590

Udet, Lt. Gen. Ernst, 105

Ukraine: 270, 331; German advance in, 249–54

Umezu, Gen. Yoshijiro, 591

"Unconditional Surrender," 307

Underground. *See* Resistance movements

Union of Soviet Socialist Republics: 61, 98, 131, 132, 133, 142, 148, 149, 178, 184, 242, 282, 305, 306, 307, 314, 318, 321, 327, 330, 331, 449, 451–52, 453, 481, 529, 531, 553–54, 556, 560–61, 623; in the 1920's and 1930's, 17–18, 19, 20, 21, 22, 25, 27, 41, 46, 50, 97; partition of Poland and advance in eastern Europe, 55, 57–58, 61, 66, 99, 256; war with Finland, 58–59, 72–73, 100; German invasion of, and war in, 97, 100, 101, 121, 126, 181, 249 ff., 265, 270, 272–303, 308, 317, 319, 320, 375, 417, 451–52, 454, 555; wartime conditions in, 250–51, 253, 260, 262–63, 269, 272–73, 282, 451–52; declares war on Japan, 560, 589, 590–91, 610; in postwar period, 557, 624, 625; map of, 254–55. *See* Army, Russian

United Nations, 305, 554, 557, 624

United Service Organization (U.S.O.), 398–99

United States: 98, 129 ff., 148, 184, 185, 242, 305, 308, 327, 330, 337, 370, 420, 421, 423, 471, 481, 531, 620, 623; in 1920's and 1930's, 17–21, 25, 27, 42, 49; economy of, 18–19, 27, 149, 308; isolationism in, 42, 55, 129–30, 134, 137, 140–41; neutrality of, 41, 42, 129–31, 134, 142, 305; foreign policy, (1939–41), 59, 101, 129, 132, 133; 1940 election, 130, 137; diplomatic relations with Japan, 131, 134, 145, 146, 153, 158; aid to and cooperation with Great Britain, 130, 131, 132, 133, 134, 142, 145–46, 181, 186, 191, 193, 235; preparation for war and defenses of (1939–41), 130–31, 134, 146, 184, 192–93, 421; declaration of and mobilization for war, 131–32, 146–47, 149, 150, 159; home front, described, 149, 174–78, 306, 330, 451–53, 470–78; wartime production, 184, 204–5, 421, 452–53, 478, 529; rationing in, 471, 472, 478; women, war contribution of, 471–72, 474; relations with U.S.S.R., 554, 610; development and use of atomic bomb, 130, 309, 324, 553, 589, 590, 610–11, 614–15; in postwar period, 618, 623–25

U.S. Strategic Bombing Survey, 449, 450

Ural Mountains, 251, 269

Uruguay, 182, 188

Ushijima, Lt. Gen. Mitsuru, 588, 589

Utah Beach, 483, 499

V-E Day, 420, 557, 582–83, 618

"V-for-Victory," 99, 463

V-J Day, 618

V-Mail, 398

V-1 (buzz bomb), 420, 452, 483, 506, 507, 520

V-2 (rocket weapon), 324, 420–21, 452, 483, 506–7, 520

Valerio, Col. (Walter Audisio), 556

Vandegrift, Lt. Gen. Alexander A., 327, 343, 399

Vandenberg, Sen. Arthur H., 557

Vassilevski, Marshal, 554

Vella Lavella, 329

Verona, 555

Versailles Treaty, 17, 22, 27, 32, 49, 182

Vichy, 95

Vichy France. *See* France: Vichy

Victor Emmanuel, King of Italy, 370, 371, 372, 380

Vienna: 48–49, 380; Soviets take, 555, 576

Vienna Agreement, 99, 100

Viipuri, 58

Vistula River, 481, 554

Vladivostok, 149, 330

Vlasov, Col. Gen. Andrei, 251–52

Vogelkop Peninsula, 535

Volga River, 251, 269, 291, 293, 296, 301

Volksdeutsch, 21, 100

Volturno River, 372, 382

Voroshilov, Marshal Kliment, 250, 267

Vyazma, 251, 269

WAAC, 472, 476

Wainwright, Lt. Gen. Jonathan: defense of Bataan, 148, 167; surrender of Corregidor, 148, 172–73; at surrender ceremony, 591

Wakde, 531

Wake Island, 148–49, 163, 327

Walcheren Island, 485

Waldenburg, 563

Wallace, Henry A., 311

Wang Ching-wei, 451

War bonds, U.S., 471

War Department, U.S., 134, 398

War Production Board, 149, 452

Warm Springs, 556

Warren, Earl, 176

Warsaw: German siege and capture of, 58, 66; uprising in, 554

Washington, D.C., 43, 331, 453, 591

Washington Arms Conference, 27

Wasp, 183

Watch on the Rhine. *See* Operations, German

Watson-Watt, Sir Robert, 98–99

Wavell, Field Marshal Sir Archibald: commands British Army in Egypt, 217–18, 222, 224, 230

WAVES, 472

Wedemeyer, Gen. Albert C., 531

Wehrmacht. *See* Army, German

Welles, Sumner, 312, 313

Wendel, Else (eyewitness), 576–77

"We're Gonna Hang Out the Washing on the Siegfried Line," 70

Werth, Alexander, 202–3 (eyewitness), 273

West Virginia, 147, 156–57

West Wall: German retreat to, 486

Western Desert: British campaign in, 217

Weygand, Gen. Maxime, 60, 88

Weygand Line, 88

Wheeler, Sen. Burton K.: 130; quoted, 149

White, Case. *See* Operations, German

White, William Allen: 130, 141; quoted, 130

Wickard, Claude, 571

Wilhelmina, Queen of the Netherlands, 76

Wilkes Barre, 603

"Willie and Joe" (cartoon), 396–97, 400

Willkie, Wendell L., 130, 136–37

Wilson, Sir Henry, 372

Wilson, Woodrow, 17, 22, 25, 27, 129, 130

Wingate, Brig. Gen. Orde: in Ethiopia, 217; in China-Burma-India, 331, 530; death of, 331

Wingate's Chindits, 331, 337

Wolf packs, 196–97

Wolf's Lair, 508

Wolff, Gen. Karl, 555

Women: Great Britain, 452; Japan, 451; U.S.S.R., 451–52, 573; U.S., 149, 453, 471–72, 474–75

Women Marines, 472, 474

World War I, 17–18, 19, 22, 27, 42, 43, 74, 98, 129, 391, 481

Yahagi, 588

Yalta Conference. *See* Conferences: Yalta

Yamamoto, Adm. Isoroku: 330; plans Pearl Harbor attack, 146; plans Battle of Midway, 185, 212–13; death of, 212–13

Yamasaki, Col. Yasuyo, 330

Yamashita, Gen. Tomoyuki: 161; defense of Philippines (1944–45), 531, 533, 587; quoted, 531

Yamato, 181, 588

Yawata, 421

Yellow, Case. *See* Operations, German

Yelnya, 250, 253

Yonai, Adm. Mitsumasa, 531

Yorktown: in Battle of the Coral Sea, 185, 208; in Battle of Midway, 185, 213

Yugoslavia: 123, 249, 305; German invasion, and surrender of, 100–101, 121, 183, 372; resistance movements in, 308, 369, 481; Communist take-over of, 554. *See also* Resistance movements: Yugoslav

Zaibatsu, 451

Zhukov, Marshal George: 267; commands Moscow front, 251, 252, 270, 274; commands Stalingrad front, 252, 253; leads Russian offensive (1943), 253, 301; organizes Leningrad defense, 280; reaches Berlin, 554–57; tactics, 250, 252, 253; quoted, 555

Zog, King, 21